T0180400

Lecture Notes in Computer Science 14064

Founding Editors

Gerhard Goos
Juris Hartmanis

The series Lecture Notes in Computer Science (LNCS), including its subseries Lecture Notes in Artificial Intelligence (LNAI) and Lecture Notes in Bioinformatics (LNBI), has established itself as a medium for the publication of new developments in computer science and information technology research, teaching, and education.

LNCS enjoys close cooperation with the computer science R & D community, the series counts many renowned academics among its volume editors and paper authors, and collaborates with prestigious societies. Its mission is to serve this international community by providing an invaluable service, mainly focused on the publication of conference and workshop proceedings and postproceedings. LNCS commenced publication in 1973.

Nadia El Mrabet · Luca De Feo ·
Sylvain Duquesne
Editors

Progress in Cryptology - AFRICACRYPT 2023

14th International Conference
on Cryptology in Africa, Sousse, Tunisia, July 19–21, 2023
Proceedings

 Springer

Editors
Nadia El Mrabet ⓘ
EMSE
Saint-Étienne, France

Luca De Feo ⓘ
IBM Research Europe
Rüschlikon, Switzerland

Sylvain Duquesne ⓘ
Université de Rennes 1
Rennes Cedex, France

ISSN 0302-9743   ISSN 1611-3349 (electronic)
Lecture Notes in Computer Science
ISBN 978-3-031-37678-8   ISBN 978-3-031-37679-5 (eBook)
https://doi.org/10.1007/978-3-031-37679-5

This Springer imprint is published by the registered company Springer Nature Switzerland AG
The registered company address is: Gewerbestrasse 11, 6330 Cham, Switzerland

Preface

This volume contains the papers accepted for presentation at Africacrypt 2023, the 14th International Conference on the Theory and Application of Cryptographic Techniques in Africa. The aim of this series of conferences is to provide an international forum for practitioners and researchers from industry, academia, and government agencies for a discussion of all forms of cryptography and its applications. The initiative of organizing Africacrypt started in 2008 and it was first held in Morocco. Subsequent yearly events were held in Tunisia, South Africa, Senegal, Morocco, Egypt and Tunisia. This year, Africacrypt 2023 is organized by the University of Monastir and the Tunisian Mathematical Society in cooperation with the International Association for Cryptologic Research (IACR). It was held in Sousse, during July 19–21, under the high patronage of the Tunisian minister of communication technologies.

We received 59 submissions authored by researchers from countries from all over the world. After a double-blind reviewing process that included online discussion and involved 47 Program Committee members and 23 external reviewers, we decided to accept 21 papers resulting in an acceptance rate of around 35%. All submitted papers received at least three reviews. We thank the Program Committee and the external reviewers for their diligent work and fruitful discussions and we thank the authors of all submitted papers for supporting the conference.

The conference program featured three keynote speakers, Ward Beullens from IBM Research Europe, Switzerland, Anne Canteaut from INRIA Paris, France and Koray Karabina from the National Research Council of Canada. We were happy that they agreed to attend and deliver their keynotes physically. The technical program was also enriched by a poster session organized by Abderrahmane Nitaj and Hoda Alkhzaimi. We thank them for taking this part of the program fully out of our hands and taking care of submissions, final versions, and chairing the poster session. A Capture the Flag (CTF) competition was introduced in the conference this year and was organized by Souheib Youssfi, Alyssa Berriche and Ahmed Belkahla.

The General Chairs, Leila Ben Abdelghani from the University of Monastir, Tunisia and Loubna Ghammam from ITK Engineering GmbH (Bosch), Germany, were a pleasure to work with. We thank the staff at Springer for their help with the proceedings production. Without our sponsors, in particular the Technology Innovation Institute from Abu Dhabi as a platinum sponsor, not all of the support for speakers and local organization facilities would have been possible and we thank them for that.

Acting as program chairs for Africacrypt 2023 was a privilege and a great experience, thanks go to all those people who helped us make this conference a big success.

May 2023

Luca De Feo
Sylvain Duquesne
Nadia El Mrabet

Organization

General Chairs

Leila Ben Abdelghani   University of Monastir, Tunisia
Loubna Ghammam   ITK Engineering GmbH (Bosch), Germany

Program Chairs

Nadia El Mrabet   École des Mines de Saint-Étienne, France
Luca De Feo   IBM Research Europe, Switzerland
Sylvain Duquesne   University of Rennes, France

Invited Speakers

Ward Beullens   IBM Research Europe, Switzerland
Anne Canteaut   INRIA Paris, France
Koray Karabina   National Research Council, Canada

Steering Committee

Souheib Yousfi (Chair)   University of Carthage, Tunisia
Nizar Kerkeni   University of Monastir, Tunisia
Lina Mortajine   ITK Engineering GmbH (Bosch), Germany
Abderrahmane Nitaj   University of Caen Normandie, France
Sami Omar   University of Bahrain, Bahrain
Amal Samti   University of Monastir, Tunisia

Program Committee

Riham AlTawy   University of Victoria, Canada
Laila El Aimani   University of Caddi Ayyad, Morocco
Hoda Alkhzaimi   NYU Abu Dhabi, United Arab Emirates

Greg Alpar	Open University, The Netherlands
Kevin Atighechi	University of Clermont-Ferrand, France
Hatem M. Bahig	Ain Shams University, Egypt
Hussain Benazza	UMI, ENSAM Meknes, Morocco
Shivam Bhasin	Temasek Lab, Nanyang Technological University, Singapore
Sebastien Canard	Orange Labs, France
Suvradip Chakraborty	ETH, Switzerland
Chitchanok Chuengsatiansup	University of Melbourne, Australia
Tingting Cui	HangZhou DianZi University, China
Joan Daemen	Radboud University, The Netherlands
Youssef El Housni	ConsenSys R&D, France
Georgios Fotiadis	University of Luxembourg
Emmanuel Fouotsa	University of Bamenda, Cameroon
Gina Gallegos-Garcia	Instituto Politécnico Nacional, Mexico
Romain Gay	IBM Research, Switzerland
Loubna Ghammam	ITK Engineering Gmbh (Bosch), Germany
Satrajit Ghosh	IIT Kharagpur, India
Lorenzo Grassi	Radboud University, The Netherlands
Javier Herranz	Universitat Politécnica de Catalunya, Spain
Akinori Hosoyamada	NTT, Japan
Sorina Ionica	University of Picardie, France
Juliane Kramer	TU Darmstadt, Germany
Fabien Laguillaumie	University of Montpellier, France
Patrick Longa	Microsoft Research, Redmond, US
Marc Manzano	SandboxAQ, Spain
Sarah McCarthy	University of Waterloo, Canada
Marine Minier	Université de Lorraine, France
Mainack Mondal	Indian Institute of Technology (IIT), India
Abderrahmane Nitaj	University of Caen Normandie, France
Sami Omar	University of Bahrain, Bahrain
Yanbin Pan	Chinese Academy of Science, China
Sikhar Patranabis	IBM Research, India
Christophe Petit	University of Birmingham, UK
Elizabeth A. Quaglia	Royal Holloway, University of London, UK
Divya Ravi	Aarhus University, Denmark
Joost Renes	NXP, The Netherlands
Yann Rotella	Université Paris-Saclay, France
Simona Samardjiska	Radboud University, The Netherlands
Ali Aydin Selcuk	TOBB University of Economics and Technology, Turkey
Dave Singelee	KU Leuven, Belgium

Djiby Sow   University of Dakar, Senegal
Pontelimon Stanica   Naval Postgraduate School, Monterey, USA
Vanessa Vitse   University of Grenoble, France
Souheib Yousfi   University of Carthage, Tunisia

Additional Reviewers

Khalid Abdelmoumen   Jodie Knapp
Ismail Afia   Matthieu Lequesne
Barbara Jiabao Benedikt   Soundes Marzougui
Harishma Boyapally   Lina Mortajine
Guilhem Castagnos   Georgio Nicolas
Marwa Chaieb   Jean-Baptiste Orfila
Alfonso Francisco De Abiega L'Eglisse   Aurel Page
Kevin Andrae Delgado Vargas   Santanu Sarkar
Siemen Dhooghe   Ugur Sen
Sayon Duttagupta   Ferdinand Sibleyras
Samed Düzlü   Marloes Venema
Paul Frixons   Yanhong Xu
Koustabh Ghosh   Trevor Yap
Tchoffo Saha Gustave   Steven Yue
Çağdaş Gül   Murat Burhan İlter

Contents

Theory

Post-quantum Cryptography

MinRank in the Head
Short Signatures from Zero-Knowledge Proofs

Gora Adj⬤, Luis Rivera-Zamarripa$^{(\boxtimes)}$⬤, and Javier Verbel⬤

Technology Innovation Institute, Abu Dhabi, UAE
{gora.adj,luis.zamarripa,javier.verbel}@tii.ae

Abstract. In recent years, many digital signature scheme proposals have been built from the so-called MPC-in-the-head paradigm. This has shown to be an outstanding way to design efficient signatures with security based on hard problems.

MinRank is an NP-complete problem extensively studied due to its applications to cryptanalysis since its introduction in 1999. However, only a few schemes base their security on its intractability, and their signature size is large compared with other proposals based on NP problems. This paper introduces the first MinRank-based digital signature scheme that uses the MPC-in-the-head paradigm, allowing to achieve small signature sizes and running times. For NIST's category I parameter set, we obtain signatures of 6.5KB, which is competitive with the shortest proposals in the literature that are based on non-structured problems.

Keywords: MinRank · zero-knowledge · proof of knowledge · MPC-in-the-Hea

1 Introduction

Signature schemes form an essential part of almost every secure digital communication protocol, allowing the receiver of a message to verify its authenticity (the identity of the sender) and integrity (no unauthorized modifications of the message). One way to design signature schemes is via *zero-knowledge proofs of knowledge*, which consists of executing an interactive *identification protocol* between a prover and a verifier. In this, the prover tries to convince the verifier that she knows a witness of a public statement without revealing any information beyond the fact that the statement is true. An essential property of zero-knowledge proofs is the *soundness error*, defined as the probability that an adversary successfully convinces the verifier about the truth of the public statement without knowing a witness.

In 2007, Ishai, Kushilevitz, Ostrovsky, and Sahai [22] introduced the MPC-in-the-head paradigm to build zero-knowledge proofs of knowledge from *multiparty computation* (MPC) protocols. In an MPC protocol, a set of N parties jointly compute the image of a function on their local and private inputs without revealing any information beyond the computed image. In principle, one can use

ⓒ The Author(s), under exclusive license to Springer Nature Switzerland AG 2023
N. El Mrabet et al. (Eds.): AFRICACRYPT 2023, LNCS 14064, pp. 3–27, 2023.
https://doi.org/10.1007/978-3-031-37679-5_1

the MPC-in-the-head paradigm to prove, in zero-knowledge, the knowledge of a solution to any problem that is verifiable using a logical circuit. However, due to the potentially large size of the resulting verification circuit, such a generic approach is not always the optimal one, and more efficient options might be found by exploiting the specific structure of the problem.

The MinRank problem is an NP-complete problem introduced by Buss, Frandsen, and Shallit in [9]. It is defined by an integer r and a set of matrices $M_0, M_1, \ldots, M_k$ over a finite field $\mathbb{F}_q$. In its decisional version, the goal is to decide whether or not there exists a combination $M_0 + \sum_{i=1}^{k} \alpha_i M_i$ of the matrices having rank at most r, where the $\alpha_i \in \mathbb{F}_q$.

The MinRank problem appeared first in cryptology in the cryptanalysis of the HFE cryptosystem [24]. There, Kipnis and Shamir proposed the so-called *Kipnis-Shamir modeling*, where an instance of the MinRank problem is modeled as a system of bilinear equations. The hardness of MinRank seems to be a reasonable assumption to make when designing secure *post-quantum schemes*. First, due to its relevance in cryptanalysis [7,8,20,27], several classical algorithms solving this problem have been extensively studied [1–3,12,15,16,24,28]. Second, random instances of the MinRank problem are expected to be hard [1, Sec. 5.6]. Finally, it is known no quantum algorithm that improves over classical algorithms that solve the MinRank problem.

Despite the believed hardness of MinRank, only three cryptographic schemes based on this problem have been proposed in the literature, and all of them are signature schemes built from zero-knowledge proofs: Courtois' scheme [12], MR-DSS [11], and the scheme by Santoso, Ikematsu, Nakamura and Yasuda [26].

Our Contributions. We propose a provable secure signature scheme based on the hardness of the MinRank problem by introducing the first MPC protocol specifically designed to prove knowledge of a solution of an instance of the MinRank problem. Our scheme is highly inspired by the work of Feneuil, Joux, and Rivain [17] by following their MPC-in-the-head paradigm, then obtaining an honest-verifier zero-knowledge 5-pass identification scheme, and finally using the generalized Fiat-Shamir transformation to turn the identification scheme into a digital signature scheme. To make our adaption from [17] work, we needed to bring the following novelties.

- Generalize the simultaneous verification of two scalar multiplication triples of [4]to matrix multiplication triples.
- Employ the Kipnis-Shamir modeling to translate MinRank instances for the verification of matrix multiplication triples. This considerably improves the communication cost of our signature scheme over the usual rank decomposition modeling.
- Sample the second challenge in our 5-pass identification scheme and signature scheme from the so-called *exceptional sets of matrices* to ease the soundness and unforgeabilty analysis.

We obtain a soundness error of $\frac{1}{N} + \frac{N-1}{q^n N}$ for our MinRank-based identification scheme, where N is the number of parties in the MPC protocol, n the number of columns of every M_i $(0 \leq i \leq k)$, and q the size of the base field.

Assuming the hardness of MinRank, we prove that our scheme is *existentially unforgeable under chosen messages attack* (EUF-CMA). We propose several parameter sets for the new scheme. Each of them targets security levels above either 143, 207, or 273 bits.

In terms of signature size, our scheme is smaller than MR-DSS by a factor greater than 3.75 for the parameters suggested in [5] while achieving public keys of similar sizes. We stress that our work extends naturally to ring signatures in the same way as MR-DSS, see [5, Section 5] for more details.

Related Works. MinRank-based signature schemes built on zero-knowledge proofs started with Courtois' scheme in 2001 [12], where the identification scheme has a soundness error of 2/3. More than 20 years later, Bellini, Esser, Sanna, and Verbel introduced MR-DSS [5], improving the soundness error of Courtois' protocol to 1/2. Santoso, Ikematsu, Nakamura, and Yasuda [26] also proposed a MinRank-based signature scheme with proofs of soundness error 1/2, but with larger signatures than Courtois and MR-DSS for comparable parameter sets (see [5, Appendix C]).

MPC protocols to verify multiplication triples of shares of elements in a finite field have been proposed by Baum and Nof in [4] (see also [25]). To design a new signature scheme based on the syndrome decoding problem, Feneuil, Joux, and Rivain used in [17] the Baum-Nof MPC protocol to verify multiplication triples of shares of univariate polynomials. As mentioned above, our work in this paper has been mostly inspired by the ideas in [17].

Organization of the Paper. The remainder of the paper is organized as follows. In Sect. 2, we provide the relevant background on zero-knowledge proofs of knowledge, the MPC-in-the-head paradigm, the MinRank problem, and digital signatures. In Sect. 4, we adapt the verification of multiplication triples from [4] to the case of matrix multiplications. Our zero-knowledge protocol for the MinRank problem is presented in Sect. 5, and the subsequent signature scheme in Sect. 6. In Sect. 7, we compare our signature scheme with some relevant ones in the literature. We draw our conclusions in Sect. 8.

2   Preliminaries

This section presents the preliminary concepts and notations that are used throughout the paper.

Notation. All over this paper, we use λ to denote the security parameter, $\mathbb{F}_q$ denotes a finite field of q elements. For any positive integer n, we denote $[n] = \{1, 2, \ldots, n\}$. For positive integers m, n, the notation $\mathbb{F}_q^{m \times n}$ refers to the set of matrices over $\mathbb{F}_q$ of m rows and n columns. For $k > 0$, we use $\boldsymbol{M}$ to denote a tuple of $k + 1$ matrices $(M_0, M_1, \ldots, M_k) \in (\mathbb{F}_q^{m \times n})^{k+1}$. For a given vector $\boldsymbol{\alpha} = (\alpha_1, \ldots, \alpha_k)^T \in \mathbb{F}_q^k$, we define $\boldsymbol{M}_{\boldsymbol{\alpha}} = \sum_{i=1}^{k} \alpha_i M_i$.

The notation $a \leftarrow \mathcal{A}(x)$ indicates that a is the output of an algorithm $\mathcal{A}$ on input x, and $a \xleftarrow{\$} \mathcal{S}$ means that a is sampled uniformly at random from a set $\mathcal{S}$.

Definition 1 (Collision-Resistant Hash Functions). *We say that a function* $h : \{0,1\}^* \to \{0,1\}^{p(\lambda)}$, *with* $p(\cdot)$ *a polynomial, is a collision-resistant hash function if it can be computed in polynomial time and for any probabilistic polynomial algorithm* $\mathcal{A}$, *there exists a negligible function* ε *such that*

$$\Pr[(x_1, x_2) \leftarrow \mathcal{A}(1^\lambda, h) \mid x_1 \neq x_2, h(x_1) = h(x_2)] < \varepsilon(\lambda).$$

We consider in this paper hash functions $\mathsf{Hash}_0, \mathsf{Hash}_1$ and $\mathsf{Hash}_2 : \{0,1\}^* \to \{0,1\}^{2\lambda}$ that we assume to be collision resistant.

Definition 2 (Indistinguishability). *Two distributions* $\{D_\lambda\}_\lambda$ *and* $\{E_\lambda\}_\lambda$ *are said to be* $(t(\lambda), \varepsilon(\lambda))$-*indistinguishable for functions* t *and* ε, *if for any probabilistic algorithm* $\mathcal{A}$ *running in time at most* $t(\lambda)$, *we have*

$$\left| \Pr\left[1 \leftarrow \mathcal{A}(x) \mid x \leftarrow D_\lambda\right] - \Pr\left[1 \leftarrow \mathcal{A}(x) \mid x \leftarrow E_\lambda\right] \right| \leq \varepsilon(\lambda).$$

When ε *is negligible for any* t *polynomial in* λ, *we just say that the two distributions are indistinguishable.*

Definition 3 (Pseudorandom Generator (PRG)). *Let* $G : \{0,1\}^* \to \{0,1\}^*$ *be a function such that for any* $s \in \{0,1\}^\lambda$ *we have* $G(s) \in \{0,1\}^{p(\lambda)}$, *where* $p(\cdot)$ *is a polynomial. We say that* G *is a* (t, ε)-*secure pseudorandom generator if* $p(\lambda) > \lambda$ *and the distributions* $\{G(s) \mid s \xleftarrow{\$} \{0,1\}^\lambda\}$ *and* $\{r \mid r \xleftarrow{\$} \{0,1\}^{p(\lambda)}\}$ *are* (t, ε)-*indistinguishable.*

In the description of our signing algorithm (Fig. 4), we make call of a function TreePRG, which, on input of a root seed in $\{0,1\}^\lambda$ and a positive integer N, generates a binary tree of N leaves using a PRG : $\{0,1\}^\lambda \to \{0,1\}^{2\lambda}$, such that each nodes has seed value in $\{0,1\}^\lambda$ (we refer to [6, Section 2.6]).

2.1 Commitment Schemes

In our *identification scheme*, which is presented in Sect. 5, we use a commitment function Com : $\{0,1\}^* \times \{0,1\}^\lambda \to \{0,1\}^{2\lambda}$ that is assumed *computationally hiding* and *computationally binding*. We formally define these concepts.

Definition 4 (Computational hiding). *A commitment scheme* Com *is said to be* (t, ε)-*hiding if for every pair of messages* (m, m'), *the distributions* $\{c \mid c \leftarrow \mathsf{Com}(m, \rho), \rho \xleftarrow{\$} \{0,1\}^\lambda)\}$ *and* $\{c \mid c \leftarrow \mathsf{Com}(m', \rho), \rho \xleftarrow{\$} \{0,1\}^\lambda)\}$ *are* (t, ε)-*indistinguishable.* Com *is said computationally hiding if the two distributions are indistinguishable.*

Definition 5 (Computational binding). *We say that* Com *is computationally binding if for all algorithms* $\mathcal{A}$ *running in time polynomial in* λ, *the probability that* $\mathcal{A}$ *outputs two different messages committing to the same value is negligible, i.e., for a negligible* $\varepsilon(\lambda)$, *we have*

$$\Pr\left[\mathsf{Com}(m, \rho) = \mathsf{Com}(m', \rho') \mid (m, \rho, m', \rho') \leftarrow \mathcal{A}(1^\lambda)\right] \leq \varepsilon(\lambda).$$

2.2   Digital Signature Schemes

Definition 6 (Signature scheme). *A digital signature scheme is a tuple of three probabilistic polynomial-time algorithms* (KeyGen, Sign, Verf) *verifying:*

1. *The key-generation algorithm* KeyGen *takes as input a security parameter* 1^λ *and outputs a pair of public/private keys* (pk, sk).
2. *The signing algorithm* Sign *takes a message* msg $\in \{0,1\}^*$ *and a private key* sk, *and outputs a signature* σ.
3. *The verification algorithm* Verf *is deterministic. It takes as input a message* msg $\in \{0,1\}^*$, *a signature* σ, *and a public key* pk. *It outputs 1 to mean that it* **accepts** σ *as a valid signature for* msg, *otherwise it* **rejects** *outputting 0.*

A signature scheme is defined to be secure if it has the following properties.

Correctness: if for every security parameter λ, every (pk, sk) $\leftarrow$ KeyGen(1^λ), and every message msg $\in \{0,1\}^*$ it holds that $1 \leftarrow$ Verf$\big(\text{pk}, \text{msg}, \text{Sign}(\text{sk}, \text{msg})\big)$

Existential unforgeability under adaptive chosen-message attacks (EUF-CMA): if for all probabilistic polynomial-time adversaries $\mathcal{A}$, the probability

$$\Pr\left[1 \leftarrow \text{Verf}(\text{pk}, \text{msg}^*, \sigma^*) \,\middle|\, \begin{array}{l} (\text{pk}, \text{sk}) \leftarrow \text{KeyGen}(1^\lambda) \\ (\text{msg}^*, \sigma^*) \leftarrow \mathcal{A}^{\mathcal{O}_{\text{Sign}(\text{sk}, \cdot)}(\text{pk})} \end{array}\right]$$

is a negligible function in λ, where $\mathcal{A}$ is given access to a signing oracle $\mathcal{O}_{\text{Sign}(\text{sk}, \cdot)}$, and msg* has not been queried to $\mathcal{O}_{\text{Sign}(\text{sk}, \cdot)}$.

2.3   5-Pass Identification Schemes

An identification scheme (IDS) is an interactive protocol between a *prover* P and a *verifier* V, where P wants to prove its knowledge of a secret value sk to V, with (pk, sk) satisfying a given relation, for a public value pk.

Definition 7 (5-pass identification scheme). *A 5-pass IDS is a tuple of three probabilistic polynomial-time algorithms* (KeyGen, P, V) *such that*

1. (pk, sk) $\leftarrow$ *KeyGen*(1^λ).
2. P *and* V *follow the protocol in Fig. 1, and at the end of this,* V *outputs 1, if it* **accepts** *that* P *knows* sk, *otherwise it* **rejects** *outputting 0.*

A *transcript* of a 5-pass IDS is a tuple $(\text{com}, \text{ch}_1, \text{rsp}_1, \text{ch}_2, \text{rsp}_2)$ (as in Fig. 1) referring to all the messages exchanged between P and V in one execution of the IDS. We require an IDS to fulfill the following security properties.

Correctness: if for any $\lambda \in \mathbb{N}$ and (pk, sk) $\leftarrow$ KeyGen(1^λ) it holds, where $(\text{com}, \text{ch}_1, \text{rsp}_1, \text{ch}_2, \text{rsp}_2)$ is the transcript of an execution of the protocol between P(pk, sk) and V(pk).

Soundness (with soundness error ε): if, given a key pair (pk, sk), for every polynomial-time adversary $\tilde{\mathcal{P}}$ such that

$$\tilde{\varepsilon} = \Pr\left[1 \leftarrow \text{V}(\text{pk}, \text{com}_{\tilde{\mathcal{P}}}, \text{ch}_1, \text{rsp}_{1,\tilde{\mathcal{P}}}, \text{ch}_2, \text{rsp}_{2,\tilde{\mathcal{P}}})\right] > \varepsilon,$$

where $(\text{com}_{\tilde{P}}, \text{ch}_1, \text{rsp}_{1,\tilde{P}}, \text{ch}_2, \text{rsp}_{2,\tilde{P}})$ is the transcript of an execution of the protocol between $\tilde{P}(\text{pk})$ and $V(\text{pk})$, then there exists an *extractor* $\mathcal{E}$ which, given rewindable black-box access to $\tilde{P}$, outputs in time polynomial in $(\lambda, \tilde{\varepsilon} - \varepsilon)$ a *witness* $\tilde{\text{sk}}$ such that $(\text{pk}, \tilde{\text{sk}})$ verifies the same relation as (pk, sk).

Honest-verifier zero-knowledge: if there exists a probabilistic polynomial-time *simulator* $\mathcal{S}(\text{pk})$ that outputs a transcript $(\text{com}, \text{ch}_1, \text{rsp}_1, \text{ch}_2, \text{rsp}_2)$ from a distribution that is computationally indistinguishable from the distribution of transcripts of an honest execution of the protocol between $P(\text{pk}, \text{sk})$ and $V(\text{pk})$.

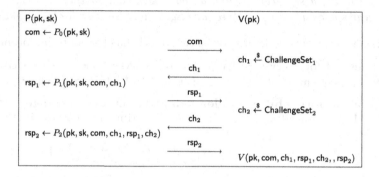

Fig. 1. Canonical 5-pass IDS.

2.4 The MinRank Problem

This section details the underlying hard problem of our signature scheme.

Problem 1 (The MinRank problem). Let $\mathbb{F}_q$ be a finite field with q elements, and m, n, k, r be positive integers. The MinRank problem with parameters (q, m, n, k, r) is defined as: given a $(k+1)$-tuple $\boldsymbol{M} = (M_0, M_1, \ldots, M_k) \in (\mathbb{F}_q^{m \times n})^{k+1}$, find $\boldsymbol{\alpha} = (\alpha_1, \ldots, \alpha_k)^T \in \mathbb{F}_q^k$ such that $\mathsf{Rank}(M_0 + \sum_{i=1}^{k} \alpha_i M_i) \leq r$.

The Kipnis-Shamir modeling [24] states that if a vector $\boldsymbol{\alpha} = (\alpha_1, \ldots, \alpha_k)^T \in \mathbb{F}_q^k$ and a matrix $K \in \mathbb{F}_q^{r \times (n-r)}$ are such that

$$\left(M_0 + \sum_{i=1}^{k} \alpha_i M_i\right) \cdot \begin{bmatrix} I \\ K \end{bmatrix} = O, \tag{1}$$

where $O \in \mathbb{F}_q^{n \times (n-r)}$ is the zero matrix, and $I \in \mathbb{F}_q^{(n-r) \times (n-r)}$ is non-singular, then $\boldsymbol{\alpha}$ is a solution of the MinRank problem with matrices $(M_0, M_1, \ldots, M_k)$.

To solve an instance of the MinRank problem, Kipnis and Shamir proposed to solve the bilinear system where the equations are given by the entries of the left-hand side matrix of Eq. (1). The sets of variables in such a system are the $\alpha_1, \ldots, \alpha_k$ and the entries of K.

2.5   Multi-party Computation

An MPC protocol enables N parties to collaboratively compute the image $z = f(x_1, \ldots, x_N)$ for a given function f, where each secret value x_i is only known by the i-th party. An MPC protocol is considered secure and correct if, upon completion, every party i knows z, while at the same time, preserving the confidentiality of the input values x_i.

A core concept in MPC protocols is that of *sharing*. We say that a tuple $\llbracket A \rrbracket := (\llbracket A \rrbracket_1, \llbracket A \rrbracket_2, \ldots, \llbracket A \rrbracket_N)$, where each $\llbracket A \rrbracket_i$ is called a *share* of A, is a sharing of a value A with *threshold* $t < N$ if A can be efficiently recovered from any t'-sized subset of elements in $\llbracket A \rrbracket$ with $t' > t$. When A is an element in a ring, we say that $\llbracket A \rrbracket$ is an additive sharing of A if $A = \sum_{i=1}^{N} \llbracket A \rrbracket_i$. In this paper we only deal with additive sharings, which have threshold $t = N - 1$.

The operations $\llbracket A + B \rrbracket$, $\llbracket A \rrbracket \cdot C$ and $C \cdot \llbracket A \rrbracket$, for shared values A, B and non-shared C, mean that every party $i \in [N]$ computes $\llbracket A \rrbracket_i + \llbracket B \rrbracket_i$, $\llbracket A \rrbracket_i \cdot C$ and $C \cdot \llbracket A \rrbracket_i$, respectively. However, the operations $\llbracket A \rrbracket + C$, for a shared value A and non-shared C, means that only the party $i = 1$ computes $\llbracket A \rrbracket_1 + C$.

3   Exceptional Sets of Matrices over a Finite Fields

In our zero-knowledge protocol, Sect. 5, the first challenge space consists of an *exceptional set* of square matrices. Following an approach similar to [14, Prop. 3], we build such sets of matrices over finite fields.

Proposition 1 (Exceptional set of non-singular matrices). *Let* $\mathbb{F}_q$ *be a finite field with q elements, f an irreducible polynomial of degree $n \geq 1$. Let C_f be the companion matrix of f. Then,*

$$\mathcal{E}_f := \left\{ \sum_{i=0}^{n-1} c_i \cdot C_f^i \mid (c_0, c_1, \ldots, c_{n-1}) \in \mathbb{F}_q^n \right\} \subset \mathbb{F}_q^{n \times n}$$

is an exceptional set of q^n matrices, i.e., for all $R, R' \in \mathcal{E}_f$ with $R \neq R'$, we have that $(R - R')$ is invertible.

Proof. Since $\mathbb{E} := \mathbb{F}_q[x]/\langle f \rangle$ is a field, any non-zero $g := \sum_{i=0}^{n-1} c_i x \in \mathbb{E}$ defines an invertible $\mathbb{F}_q$-linear map $L_g(a) = a \cdot g$ from $\mathbb{E}$ to $\mathbb{E}$. Hence, the matrix representation $G \in \mathbb{F}_q^{n \times n}$ of L_g in the ordered basis $\{1, x, x^2, \ldots, x^{n-1}\}$ is an invertible matrix. Finally, we note that $G = \sum_{i=0}^{n-1} c_i \cdot C_f^i$. $\square$

4   Matrix-Multiplication Triple Verification

In this section, we present a generalization of the protocol by Baum and Nof [4] that verifies multiplication triples of matrices, i.e., a triple of matrix sharings $(\llbracket X \rrbracket, \llbracket Y \rrbracket, \llbracket Z \rrbracket)$ such that $Z = X \cdot Y$.

Similarly to the protocol in [4], to verify a matrix-multiplication triple $(\llbracket X \rrbracket, \llbracket Y \rrbracket, \llbracket Z \rrbracket)$ we use a *random* triple $(\llbracket A \rrbracket, \llbracket B \rrbracket, \llbracket C \rrbracket)$. Assuming that all the matrix products are well defined, the following MPC protocol verifies the correctness of both triples, $(\llbracket X \rrbracket, \llbracket Y \rrbracket, \llbracket Z \rrbracket)$ and $(\llbracket A \rrbracket, \llbracket B \rrbracket, \llbracket C \rrbracket)$ in an MPC manner.

1. The parties sample a matrix $R \overset{\$}{\leftarrow} \mathcal{E}_f$, where $\mathcal{E}_f$ is defined as in Proposition 1.
2. Each party computes $[\![S_1]\!] = R [\![X]\!] + [\![A]\!]$ and $[\![S_2]\!] = [\![Y]\!] + [\![B]\!]$.
3. The parties publish $[\![S_1]\!]$ and $[\![S_2]\!]$ so that all of them can obtain S_1 and S_2.
4. The first party computes $[\![V]\!] = R [\![Z]\!] - [\![C]\!] + S_1 \cdot [\![B]\!] + [\![A]\!] \cdot S_2 - S_1 \cdot S_2$,
   and each other party computes $[\![V]\!] = R [\![Z]\!] - [\![C]\!] + S_1 \cdot [\![B]\!] + [\![A]\!] \cdot S_2$.
5. The parties reveal $[\![V]\!]$ to have V. They **accept** if $V = 0$, or **reject** otherwise.

Proposition 2. *If* $([\![X]\!], [\![Y]\!], [\![Z]\!])$ *or* $([\![A]\!], [\![B]\!], [\![C]\!])$ *is an incorrect multiplication triple, then the parties output* **accept** *in the above protocol with probability at most* $\frac{1}{|\mathcal{E}_f|} = \frac{1}{q^n}$.

Proof. Let $\Delta_Z = Z - X \cdot Y$ and $\Delta_C = C - A \cdot B$. If the parties output **accept**, this means that $V = 0$, i.e., $R \cdot \Delta_Z - \Delta_C = 0$, and we have the following cases.

- If $\Delta_Z = 0$ and $\Delta_C \neq 0$, then $V \neq 0$, which is in contradiction with the **accept** assumption.
- In the case $\Delta_Z \neq 0$, the equality $R \cdot \Delta_Z = \Delta_C$ happens for at most one $R \in \mathcal{E}_f$, since $\mathcal{E}_f$ is an exceptional set, whence the bound probability $\frac{1}{q^n}$. □

5 A Zero-Knowledge Protocol on the MinRank Problem

We present in this section a zero-knowledge protocol based the MinRank problem, using the Kipnis-Shamir modeling. For simplicity, we describe the protocol for square matrices, but it can be generalized to non-square matrices.

We let $\boldsymbol{M} = (M_0, M_1, \ldots, M_k) \subset (\mathbb{F}_q^{n \times n})^{k+1}$ be an instance of the MinRank problem with parameters (q, n, k, r). Notice that in Eq. (1) of the Kipnis-Shamir modeling, if we fix I as the identity matrix of size $n - r$, then it holds

$$M_0^L + \sum_{i=1}^k \alpha_i M_i^L = - \left(M_0^R + \sum_{i=1}^k \alpha_i M_i^R \right) \cdot K, \qquad (2)$$

denoted $\boldsymbol{M}_\alpha^L = \boldsymbol{M}_\alpha^R K$, where $M_i^L \in \mathbb{F}_q^{n \times (n-r)}$, $M_i^R \in \mathbb{F}_q^{n \times r}$ satisfy $M_i = [M_i^L | M_i^R]$, for all $i \in [0, k]$. The pair $(\boldsymbol{\alpha}, K)$ is called a witness of $\boldsymbol{M}$.

5.1 Description of the Protocol

Our proposed zero-knowledge protocol is described in Fig. 2, where $\mathcal{E}_f$ is as in Proposition 1. It follows the MPC-in-the-head paradigm over the MPC protocol depicted below to verify solutions of instances of the MinRank problem.

An MPC Protocol for the MinRank Problem. In this protocol, we assume that all the parties know the set of input matrices $\boldsymbol{M}$. Also, each party holds a pair of additive shares $([\![\boldsymbol{\alpha}]\!], [\![K]\!])$ (with $\boldsymbol{\alpha}, K$ satisfying Eq. (2)) and a triple of shares $([\![A]\!], [\![B]\!], [\![C]\!])$ of a random matrix-multiplication triple. The protocol proceeds as follows:

1. The parties locally compute $[\![\boldsymbol{M}_\alpha^L]\!]$ and $[\![\boldsymbol{M}_\alpha^R]\!]$.

ZKProof(Prover(M, α, K), Verifier(M))

Round 1: Prover sets up the inputs for the MPC protocol

1 : seed $\xleftarrow{\$} \{0,1\}^{\lambda}$, $(\text{seed}_i, \rho_i)_{i \in [N]} \leftarrow \text{TreePRG}(\text{seed})$

2 : For each party $i \in [N-1]$

$\quad [\![A]\!]_i, [\![B]\!]_i, [\![\alpha]\!]_i, [\![C]\!]_i, [\![K]\!]_i \leftarrow \text{PRG}(\text{seed}_i)$

$\quad \text{state}_i \leftarrow \text{seed}_i$

3 : $[\![A]\!]_N, [\![B]\!]_N \leftarrow \text{PRG}(\text{seed}_N)$, $[\![\alpha]\!]_N \leftarrow \alpha - \sum_{i \neq N}[\![\alpha]\!]_i$

4 : $[\![K]\!]_N \leftarrow K - \sum_{i \neq N}[\![K]\!]_i$, $[\![C]\!]_N \leftarrow A \cdot B - \sum_{i \neq N}[\![C]\!]_i$

5 : $\text{aux} \leftarrow ([\![\alpha]\!]_N, [\![K]\!]_N, [\![C]\!]_N)$, $\text{state}_N \leftarrow \text{seed}_N \parallel \text{aux}$

6 : Commit to each party's state: $\text{com}_i \leftarrow \text{Com}(\text{state}_i, \rho_i)$, for all $i \in [N]$

7 : Prover computes $h \leftarrow \text{Hash}_1(\text{com}_1, \ldots, \text{com}_N)$ and sends it to Verifier

Round 2: Verifier samples $R \xleftarrow{\$} \mathbb{F}_q^{n \times n}$ and sends it to Prover

Round 3: Prover simulates the MPC protocol:

8 : The parties locally compute $[\![M_\alpha^L]\!]$ and $[\![M_\alpha^R]\!]$ using $[\![\alpha]\!]$

9 : They locally set $[\![S_1]\!] = R \cdot [\![M_\alpha^R]\!] + [\![A]\!]$, and $[\![S_2]\!] = [\![K]\!] + [\![B]\!]$

10 : The parties open $[\![S_1]\!]$ and $[\![S_2]\!]$ to obtain S_1 and S_2

11 : The parties locally set

$\quad [\![V]\!] = R \cdot [\![M_\alpha^L]\!] - [\![C]\!] + S_1 \cdot [\![B]\!] + [\![A]\!] \cdot S_2 - S_1 \cdot S_2$

12 : Prover sets $h' = \text{Hash}_2([\![S_1]\!]_1, [\![S_2]\!]_1, [\![V]\!]_1, \ldots, [\![S_1]\!]_N, [\![S_2]\!]_N, [\![V]\!]_N)$

13 : Prover sends h' to Verifier

Round 4: Verifier uniformly samples $i^* \xleftarrow{\$} [N]$ and sends it to Prover

Round 5: Prover sends $\text{rsp} = \{(\text{state}_i, \rho_i)_{i \neq i^*}, \text{com}_{i^*}, [\![S_1]\!]_{i^*}, [\![S_2]\!]_{i^*}\}$ to Verifier

Verification: Verifier accepts if and only if the following checks succeed:

14 : $\text{com}_i \leftarrow \text{Com}(\text{state}_i, \rho_i)$, for each $i \neq i^*$

15 : Check that $h = \text{Hash}_1(\text{com}_1, \ldots, \text{com}_N)$

16 : Compute $\{[\![S_1]\!]_i, [\![S_2]\!]_i\}_{i \neq i^*}$ from $\{\text{state}_i\}_{i \neq i^*}$, and $\{[\![V]\!]_i\}_{i \neq i^*}$

17 : $[\![V]\!]_{i^*} \leftarrow -\sum_{i \neq i^*}[\![V]\!]_i$

18 : Check that $h' = \text{Hash}_2([\![S_1]\!]_1, [\![S_2]\!]_1, [\![V]\!]_1, \ldots, [\![S_1]\!]_N, [\![S_2]\!]_N, [\![V]\!]_N)$

Fig. 2. Zero-knowledge proof for MinRank.

2. The parties follow the MPC protocol described in Sect. 4 to verify the multiplication triple ($[\![K]\!], [\![M_\alpha^R]\!], [\![M_\alpha^L]\!]$) by using the random triple.

Clearly, this MPC protocol proves the knowledge of a vector $\alpha \in \mathbb{F}_q^k$ and a matrix $K \in \mathbb{F}_q^{r \times (n-r)}$ satisfying $M_\alpha^L = M_\alpha^R K$, i.e., α is a solution of the MinRank instance given by M.

5.2 Security Proofs

The security properties of the zero-knowledge protocol are stated in the following theorems. Since the proofs of Theorem 2 and Theorem 3 are similar to the corresponding ones from [17], we provide them in Appendix A and Appendix B.

Theorem 1 (Correctness). *The protocol in Fig. 2 is perfectly correct, i.e., a prover with a witness of the underlying MinRank instance always succeeds in convincing a verifier.*

Proof. The correctness of the protocol shown in Fig. 2 follows from the correctness of the protocol to verify matrix-multiplication triples shown in Sect. 4. It is easy to see that when the prover appropriately executes all the steps in the protocol, all the checks by the verifier pass.   □

Theorem 2 (Soundness). *Assume the commitment scheme* Com *is binding and the hash function* Hash_1 *is collision-resistant. Suppose there exists an efficient prover* $\tilde{\mathcal{P}}$ *that, on input* $\boldsymbol{M}$*, convinces the honest verifier* V *on input* $\boldsymbol{M}$ *to accept with probability*

$$\tilde{\varepsilon} = \Pr[V(\boldsymbol{M}, h_{\tilde{\mathcal{P}}}, R, h'_{\tilde{\mathcal{P}}}, i^*, \mathsf{rsp}_{\tilde{\mathcal{P}}}) \to 1] > \varepsilon,$$

where $\varepsilon = \frac{1}{q^n} + (1 - \frac{1}{q^n}) \cdot \frac{1}{N}$*, then there exists an efficient probabilistic extraction algorithm* $\mathcal{E}$ *that, given rewindable black-box access to* $\tilde{\mathcal{P}}$*, produces a witness* $(\boldsymbol{\alpha}, K)$ *verifying* $\boldsymbol{M}_{\boldsymbol{\alpha}}^L = \boldsymbol{M}_{\boldsymbol{\alpha}}^R K$ *by making an average number of calls to* $\tilde{\mathcal{P}}$ *upper bounded by*

$$\frac{4}{\tilde{\varepsilon} - \varepsilon} \left(1 + \tilde{\varepsilon} \cdot \frac{2 \cdot \ln(2)}{\tilde{\varepsilon} - \varepsilon}\right).$$

Theorem 3 (Honest-Verifier Zero-Knowledge). *In the protocol in Fig. 2, if the PRG is* $(t, \varepsilon_{\mathrm{PRG}})$*-secure and the commitment scheme* $(t, \varepsilon_{\mathsf{com}})$*-hiding, then there exists an efficient simulator that outputs transcripts* $(t, \varepsilon_{\mathrm{PRG}} + \varepsilon_{\mathsf{com}})$*-indistinguishable from real transcripts of the protocol.*

5.3 Complexity of the MinRank Problem

This section shows our choices of parameters for the underlying MinRank problem of the signature scheme presented in this paper. We let $\boldsymbol{M} \in \left(\mathbb{F}_q^{n \times n}\right)^{k+1}$ be the MinRank instance, r be the target rank, and denote by E the rank-r matrix in the vector space generated by the matrices in $\boldsymbol{M}$.

Table 1 shows our bit security estimates for the proposed parameter sets. We suggest a pair of parameter sets for each of the NIST's security categories I, III, and V, targeting 143, 207, and 273 bits of security, respectively.

This is done by first estimating the complexity, in terms of multiplications in $\mathbb{F}_q$, of the most efficient algorithms to solve the MinRank problem. Then, we assume that every multiplication over $\mathbb{F}_q$ costs $(\log_2 q)^2$ bit operations, and we set $w = 2$ in the estimates below.

To directly solve instances of the MinRank problem, one uses the kernel-search algorithm and the support-minors modeling:

Kernel-Search. This algorithm was introduced in [21], and consists of guessing $\lceil k/n \rceil$ linearly independent vectors in the kernel of the unknown rank r matrix E. The expected number of $\mathbb{F}_q$ multiplications of this algorithm is

$$\mathcal{O}\left(q^{r \cdot \lceil k/n \rceil} \cdot k^\omega\right), \text{ where } 2 \leq \omega \leq 3 \text{ is a constant.}$$

Support-Minors Modelling (SM). This is an algebraic method to solve the MinRank problem, by Bardet et al. [1]. It models an instance as a bilinear system of equations that are then solved with an XL-like algorithm.

For $q > 2$, the complexity of solving the SM equations is computed as

$$\min \left\{ 3 \cdot k(r+1) \cdot A(b,n')^2, 7 \cdot A(b,n')^\omega \ \middle| \ \begin{array}{c} 1 \le b \le r+1, \\ r+b \le n' \le n, \\ A(b,n')-1 \le B(b,n') \end{array} \right\},$$

where $A(b,n') := \binom{n'}{r} \binom{k+b-1}{b},$

$$B(b,n') := \sum_{j=1}^{b} \sum_{i=1}^{j} \left\{ (-1)^{i+1} \binom{n'}{r+i} \binom{m+i-1}{i} \binom{k}{j-i} \right\}.$$

In [3], it is shown that a guess-and-solve (or hybrid) approach for the Min-Rank is more efficient than directly solving the problem.

Hybrid Approaches. We consider two hybridization approaches to estimate the number of multiplications in $\mathbb{F}_q$ required to solve a given MinRank instance. The first approach guesses l_v coefficients of the solution vector $\boldsymbol{\alpha}$. The second approach [3], guesses a vectors (with a specific structure) in the right-kernel of the secret E. When both approaches are combined, one derives MinRank instances $\tilde{M}$ with parameters $(q, m \times (n-a), k - am - l_v, r)$. The complexity of this hybrid approach is given by

$$q^{a \cdot r + l_v} \left(\mathsf{MR\_Complexity}(q, n \times (n-a), k - an - l_v, r) + \left(\min\{k, an\} \right)^\omega \right), \quad (3)$$

where $\mathsf{MR\_Complexity}(\cdot)$ returns the complexity to solve a random instance of the MinRank problem defined by the input parameters.

For every parameter set in Table 1, the minimum bit complexity was found for $l_v = 0$. The kernel-search algorithm for $a = 8$ minimizes the complexity for Ib, and IIIb. The SM modeling gives the optimal complexity for the remaining parameters sets; $a = 5$ for Ia, $a = 6$ for IIIa, $a = 9$ for Va and $a = 11$ for Vb.

6 The Signature Scheme

This section presents our signature scheme. We let $\mathsf{Hash}_0, \mathsf{Hash}_1, \mathsf{Hash}_2$ be collision-resistant hash functions, and PRG a secure pseudorandom generator.

6.1 Non-interactive Zero-Knowledge Proofs

We start by describing how to turn our interactive honest-verifier zero-knowledge protocol for the MinRank problem in Sect. 5, Fig. 2, into a multi-round non-interactive protocol. Specifically, we use a standard generalization of the Fiat-Shamir transformation [19] for canonical 5-pass IDS protocols. In the non-interactive protocol, the prover simulates τ executions (or rounds) of the canonical 5-pass IDS, which results in a transcript of the form $(h, \{R^{[\ell]}\}_{\ell \in [\tau]}, h', \{i^{*,[\ell]}\}_{\ell \in [\tau]}, \{\mathsf{rsp}^{[\ell]}\}_{\ell \in [\tau]})$, where $\mathsf{rsp}^{[\ell]}$, from the ℓ-th execution, corresponds to the response of the prover in Round 5 of Fig. 2.

More precisely, for a given random value $\mathsf{salt} \xleftarrow{\$} \{0, 1\}^{2\lambda}$ and a message $\mathsf{msg} \in \{0, 1\}^*$, the prover simulates τ executions of the protocol as follows. She starts by computing $\mathsf{com}^{[\ell]} := (\mathsf{com}_1^{[\ell]}, \ldots, \mathsf{com}_N^{[\ell]})$ just as in Fig. 2. Next, she calculates $h = \mathsf{Hash}_0(\mathsf{msg}, \mathsf{salt}, \mathsf{com}^{[1]}, \ldots, \mathsf{com}^{[\tau]})$ and produces $R^{[1]}, \ldots, R^{[\tau]} \leftarrow \mathrm{PRG}(h)$. Then, the prover follows τ runs of Round 3 of Fig. 2 to compute

$$\mathsf{rsp}_{1,\ell} := \left(\left[\!\left[S_1^{[\ell]} \right]\!\right]_1, \left[\!\left[S_2^{[\ell]} \right]\!\right]_1, \left[\!\left[V^{[\ell]} \right]\!\right]_1, \ldots, \left[\!\left[S_1^{[\ell]} \right]\!\right]_N, \left[\!\left[S_2^{[\ell]} \right]\!\right]_N, \left[\!\left[V^{[\ell]} \right]\!\right]_N \right).$$

The set of second challenges is computed as $i^{*,1}, \ldots, i^{*,\tau} \leftarrow \mathrm{PRG}(h')$, where $h' = \mathsf{Hash}_0 \left(\mathsf{msg}, \mathsf{salt}, h, \mathsf{rsp}_{1,1}, \ldots, \mathsf{rsp}_{1,\tau} \right)$. Finally, the prover uses the challenges $(i^{*,\ell})_{\ell \in [\tau]}$ to compute the responses $(\mathsf{rsp}^{[\ell]})_{\ell \in [\tau]}$ corresponding to the responses generated in Round 5 of Fig. 2.

We point out that applying the Fiat-Shamir transformation to the interactive proof of knowledge slightly harms the soundness of the protocol. Indeed, the Kales-Zaverucha [23] forgery attack on 5-pass Fiat-Shamir has a cost lower than that of the interactive protocol for the same number τ of repetitions. Thus, the forgery cost, in terms of the number of hashes, that has to be considered in our signature scheme is the following:

$$C(\tau, q, n, N) = \min_{0 \le k \le \tau} \left\{ \frac{1}{\sum_{i=k}^{\tau} \left(\frac{1}{q^n} \right)^i \left(1 - \frac{1}{q^n} \right)^{\tau-i} \binom{\tau}{i}} + N^{\tau-k} \right\}. \tag{4}$$

6.2   Description of the Signature Scheme

Figure 3 proposes a KeyGen algorithm generating a public key and a secret key that decompress into a MinRank instance M and a witness $(\boldsymbol{\alpha}, K)$ satisfying Eq. (1). Another variant providing smaller public keys is proposed by Di Scala and Sanna [13].

The signing algorithm Sign is detailed in Fig. 4. It receives as inputs the secret $(\boldsymbol{\alpha}, K)$, the corresponding public key M, and a message $\mathsf{msg} \in \{0, 1\}^*$. Then, it outputs a signature σ for the message msg.

The verification algorithm Verf, Fig. 4, takes as input the public key M, a message $\mathsf{msg} \in \{0, 1\}^*$ and a signature σ. Verf outputs **accept** if σ is considered as a valid signature of the message msg. Otherwise, it outputs **reject**.

6.3   EUF-CMA Security of the Signature Scheme

Theorem 4 provides the security guarantees of our signature scheme in the random oracle model. Its proof, presented in Appendix C, closely follows the one of [17, Theorem 5], which in turn is highly inspired by that of [10, Theorem 6.2].

KeyGen(1^λ)

$1:$ seed $\xleftarrow{\$} \{0,1\}^\lambda$, seed$_{\mathsf{pk}}$, seed$_{\mathsf{sk}} \leftarrow$ PRG(seed)

$2:$ $(\boldsymbol{\alpha}, K, E^R) \leftarrow$ PRG(seed$_{\mathsf{sk}}$), where $\boldsymbol{\alpha} \in \mathbb{F}_q^k$, $K \in \mathbb{F}_q^{r \times (n-r)}$, and $E^R \in \mathbb{F}_q^{m \times r}$

$3:$ $E \leftarrow [E^R \cdot K \mid E^R]$

$4:$ $(M_1, \ldots, M_k) \leftarrow$ PRG(seed$_{\mathsf{sk}}$), $\quad M_0 \leftarrow E - \sum_{i=1}^{k} \alpha_i M_i$

$5:$ **Output** (pk, sk) : pk $\leftarrow (M_0, \text{seed}_{\mathsf{pk}})$ and sk $\leftarrow$ seed$_{\mathsf{sk}}$

Fig. 3. Key generation algorithm for our MinRank-based signature scheme.

Theorem 4. *Suppose that PRG is $(t, \varepsilon_{\mathrm{PRG}})$-secure and any adversary running in time t has at most an advantage $\varepsilon_{\mathrm{MR}}$ against the underlying MinRank problem in Sect. 6.2. Then modelling* Hash$_0$, Hash$_1$ *and* Hash$_2$ *as random oracles, any adaptive chosen-message adversary against the signature scheme running in time t, making q_s signing queries, q_0 queries to* Hash$_0$*, q_1 to* Hash$_1$*, and q_2 to* Hash$_2$ *succeeds in outputting a valid forgery with probability at most*

$$\Pr\left[\text{Forge}\right] \leq \frac{(q_0 + \tau N q_s)^2}{2 \cdot 2^{2\lambda}} + \frac{q_s(q_s + q_0 + q_1 + q_2)}{2^{2\lambda}} + \tau q_s \varepsilon_{\mathrm{PRG}} + \varepsilon_{\mathrm{MR}} + \max_{s \in [\tau]} P(s),$$

where $P(s) = \left(1 - \left[1 - \left(\frac{1}{q^n}\right)^s \left(1 - \frac{1}{q^n}\right)^{\tau-s} \binom{\tau}{s}\right]^{q_1}\right)\left(1 - [1 - \frac{1}{N^{\tau-s}}]^{q_2}\right)$.

6.4   Parameters and Signature Size

The maximum bit size of our signature scheme is given as

$$6\lambda + \tau \left(\underbrace{(k + n(n-r) + 2r(n-r) + nr) \cdot \log_2 q}_{[\![\boldsymbol{\alpha}]\!]_N, [\![C]\!]_N, [\![K]\!]_N, [\![S_1]\!]_{i*}, [\![S_2]\!]_{i*}} + \underbrace{\lambda \cdot \log_2 N}_{\{\text{seed}_i\}_{i \neq i*}} + \underbrace{2\lambda}_{\text{com}_{i*}} \right).$$

Table 1 shows the proposed parameter sets and corresponding signature sizes. The values of N and τ denote the number of parties in the MPC protocol and the number of repetitions in the IDS, respectively. These two values are set to achieve a soundness error, in the non-interactive protocol, smaller than $2^{-\lambda}$.

7   Comparisons with Other Signatures Schemes

In this section, we compare our signature scheme with some proposals in the literature. Table 2 shows the signature and public key sizes of Courtois's scheme [12], MR-DSS [5], and our scheme for the sets of parameters proposed in [5]. For those parameter sets, minimizing the signature size of MR-DSS, our signature size is at least 3.75 (*resp.* 8.76) times smaller than MR-DSS (*resp.* Courtois' scheme). In terms of security, our scheme is comparable with these schemes

---

Sign$(M, \alpha, K, \text{msg})$

salt $\xleftarrow{\$} \{0,1\}^{2\lambda}$

Phase 1: Set up the views for the MPC protocols

for $\ell \in [\tau]$ do

1:   $\text{seed}^{[\ell]} \xleftarrow{\$} \{0,1\}^{\lambda}$, $(\text{seed}_i^{[\ell]})_{i \in [N]} \leftarrow \text{TreePRG}(\text{salt}, \text{seed}^{[\ell]})$

2:   for $i \in [N-1]$ do

     $[\![A^{[\ell]}]\!]_i, [\![B^{[\ell]}]\!]_i, [\![\alpha^{[\ell]}]\!]_i, [\![C^{[\ell]}]\!]_i, [\![K^{[\ell]}]\!]_i \leftarrow \text{PRG}(\text{salt}, \text{seed}_i^{[\ell]})$

     $\text{state}_i^{[\ell]} \leftarrow \text{seed}_i^{[\ell]}$

3:   $[\![A^{[\ell]}]\!]_N, [\![B^{[\ell]}]\!]_N \leftarrow \text{PRG}(\text{salt}, \text{seed}_N^{[\ell]})$, $[\![\alpha^{[\ell]}]\!]_N \leftarrow \alpha - \sum_{i \neq N} [\![\alpha^{[\ell]}]\!]_i$

4:   $[\![K^{[\ell]}]\!]_N \leftarrow K - \sum_{i \neq N} [\![K^{[\ell]}]\!]_i$, $[\![C^{[\ell]}]\!]_N \leftarrow A^{[\ell]} \cdot B^{[\ell]} - \sum_{i \neq N} [\![C^{[\ell]}]\!]_i$

5:   $\text{aux}^{[\ell]} \leftarrow ([\![\alpha^{[\ell]}]\!]_N, [\![K^{[\ell]}]\!]_N, [\![C^{[\ell]}]\!]_N)$, $\text{state}_N^{[\ell]} \leftarrow \text{seed}_N^{[\ell]} \parallel \text{aux}^{[\ell]}$

6:   $\text{com}_i^{[\ell]} \leftarrow \text{Hash}_0(\text{salt}, \ell, i, \text{state}_i^{[\ell]})$, for all $i \in [N]$

Phase 2: First challenges

7:   $h_1 \leftarrow \text{Hash}_1(\text{msg}, \text{salt}, \text{com}_1^{[1]}, \dots, \text{com}_N^{[1]}, \text{com}_1^{[2]}, \dots, \text{com}_N^{[\tau]})$

8:   $R^{[1]}, \dots, R^{[\tau]} \leftarrow \text{PRG}(h_1)$

Phase 3: Simulation of the MPC protocols

for $\ell \in [\tau]$ do

9:   Compute $[\![M_\alpha^{L,[\ell]}]\!], [\![M_\alpha^{R,[\ell]}]\!]$ from $[\![\alpha^{[\ell]}]\!]$

10:   $[\![S_1^{[\ell]}]\!] \leftarrow R^{[\ell]} \cdot [\![M_\alpha^{R,[\ell]}]\!] + [\![A^{[\ell]}]\!]$, $[\![S_2^{[\ell]}]\!] \leftarrow [\![K^{[\ell]}]\!] + [\![B^{[\ell]}]\!]$

11:   $S_1^{[\ell]} \leftarrow \sum_i [\![S_1^{[\ell]}]\!]_i$, $S_2^{[\ell]} \leftarrow \sum_i [\![S_2^{[\ell]}]\!]_i$

12:   $[\![V^{[\ell]}]\!] \leftarrow R^{[\ell]} \cdot [\![M_\alpha^{L,[\ell]}]\!] - [\![C^{[\ell]}]\!] + S_1^{[\ell]} \cdot [\![B^{[\ell]}]\!] + [\![A^{[\ell]}]\!] \cdot S_2^{[\ell]} - S_1^{[\ell]} \cdot S_2^{[\ell]}$

Phase 4: Second challenges

13:   $h_2 \leftarrow \text{Hash}_2(\text{msg}, \text{salt}, h_1, ([\![S_1^{[\ell]}]\!]_i, [\![S_2^{[\ell]}]\!]_i, [\![V_1^{[\ell]}]\!]_i)_{i \in [N], \ell \in [\tau]})$

14:   $i^{*,[1]}, \dots, i^{*,[\tau]} \leftarrow \text{PRG}(h_2)$

Phase 5: Assembling the signature σ

15:   $\sigma \leftarrow \text{salt} \mid h_1 \mid h_2 \mid \left((\text{state}_i^{[\ell]})_{i \neq i^{*,[\ell]}} \mid \text{com}_{i^{*,[\ell]}}^{[\ell]} \mid [\![S_1^{[\ell]}]\!]_{i^{*,[\ell]}} \mid [\![S_2^{[\ell]}]\!]_{i^{*,[\ell]}} \right)_{\ell \in [\tau]}$

Verf(M, msg, σ)

1:   $R^{[1]}, \dots, R^{[\tau]} \leftarrow \text{PRG}(h_1)$, $i^{*,[1]}, \dots, i^{*,[\tau]} \leftarrow \text{PRG}(h_2)$

2:   for all $\ell \in [\tau]$, all $i \in [N] \setminus i^{*,[\ell]}$ do

     $\text{com}_i^{[\ell]} \leftarrow \text{Hash}_0(\text{salt}, \ell, i, \text{state}_i^{[\ell]})$,

     Compute $[\![V^{[\ell]}]\!]_i$ as in Sign() using $(\text{state}_i^{[\ell]})_{i \neq i^{*,[\ell]}}, [\![S_1^{[\ell]}]\!]_{i^{*,[\ell]}}, [\![S_2^{[\ell]}]\!]_{i^{*,[\ell]}}$

3:   $[\![V^{[\ell]}]\!]_{i^{*,[\ell]}} \leftarrow -\sum_{i \neq i^{*,[\ell]}} [\![V^{[\ell]}]\!]_i$

4:   $h_1' \leftarrow \text{Hash}_1(\text{msg}, \text{salt}, \text{com}_1^{[1]}, \dots, \text{com}_N^{[1]}, \text{com}_1^{[2]}, \dots, \text{com}_{N-1}^{[\tau]}, \text{com}_N^{[\tau]})$

5:   $h_2' \leftarrow \text{Hash}_2(\text{msg}, \text{salt}, h_1, ([\![S_1^{[\ell]}]\!]_i, [\![S_2^{[\ell]}]\!]_i, [\![V_1^{[\ell]}]\!]_i)_{i \in [N], \ell \in [\tau]})$

6:   Output **accept** if $h_1' = h_1$ and $h_2' = h_2$, otherwise output **reject**

Fig. 4. Signing and verification algorithms for our MinRank-based signature scheme.

since they all rely on the hardness of random instances of the MinRank problem. Finally, our public keys are as short as MR-DSS.

Our signature scheme remains competitive when compared with schemes selected by NIST for standardization as shown in Table 3.

The optimal performance anylysis for each proposed variant is left for future work. However, given the similarity between our scheme and the one in [17], we

Table 1. Parameter sets and signature sizes of the proposed signature scheme.

Set	Variant	λ (bits)	q	n	k	r	N	τ	Bit security	Maximum signature size
Ia	Fast	128	16	15	79	6	16	34	144	10364
	Short						256	18		6695
Ib	Fast	128	16	16	142	4	16	34	155	11758
	Short						256	18		7422
IIIa	Fast	192	16	19	115	8	16	51	207	24114
	Short						256	27		14832
IIIb	Fast	192	16	19	167	6	16	51	229	24930
	Short						256	27		15858
Va	Fast	256	16	21	192	7	16	67	273	40827
	Short						256	35		25934
Vb	Fast	256	16	22	254	6	16	67	295	44211
	Short						256	35		27667

Table 2. Size comparison with other MinRank-based schemes.

Set	Signature (KB)			Public key (B)		
	Courtois	MR-DSS	This work	Courtois	MR-DSS	This work
Ib	65	27	7.2	144	73	73
IIIb	135	60	15.4	205	121	121
Vb	248	106	27	274	147	147

Table 3. Comparison with SPHINCS$^+$ and Dilithium schemes.

	This work		SPHINCS$^+$		Dilithium
	Fast	Short	Fast	Short	
Security level	1	1	1	1	2
Bit security	155	155	128	133	192
Public key size (bytes)	73	73	32	32	1,312
Signature size (bytes)	11,758	7,422	17,088	7,856	2,420

made estimates of the computational cost for our category I parameters based on their performance. It results then that the signing time for Ia-short and Ib-short in our scheme could be ≤ 30 ms, while the signing time for SPHINCS-SHA2-128s-simple is approximately 207 ms. On the other hand, our scheme offers signatures 1.45 times shorter than SPHINCS$^+$, but 4.8 times larger than Dilithium. However, in terms of security, Dilithium is based on a structured problem from lattices, while our scheme is based on random instances of a well-known NP-complete problem that is hard in the average case. Thus, we demonstrated that our scheme is highly competitive in terms of size and computational cost compared to similar schemes.

8   Conclusions and Future Work

In this work, we proposed a digital signature scheme that is EUF-CMA secure based on the hardness of random instances of the MinRank problem. The scheme follows the MPC-in-the-Head paradigm with an underlying MPC protocol that verifies a shared solution. Our proposal provides signatures significantly smaller than the previous MinRank-based signature schemes. Moreover, our scheme improves over SPHINCS+ in terms of signature size and over Dilithium on hardn sess assumption.

Future efforts will be considered to provide an efficient implementation of our scheme. This will help to assess the concrete efficiency of it in terms of signing and verification time. Additionally, it would be interesting to investigate in the future new techniques to further reduce the signature size. For instance, it is worthwhile investigating if using a *threshold linear secret sharing scheme* (as considered in [18]) yields more compact signatures. Finally, from the cryptanalytic side, it would be interesting to know how efficient the implementations of algorithms for solving the MinRank problem scale in practice; this shall help to understand the security of the here-proposed signature scheme in practice.

Acknowledgements. We thank the anonymous referees for their comments, and Mukul Kulkarni for responding to our questions about the security proofs. We also thank Carlo Sanna, Andre Esser, Stefano Barbero and Emanuele Bellini for their valuable comments on the paper.

A   Proof of Theorem 2 (Soundness)

Proof. We follow the soundness proof by Feneuil, Joux and Rivain in [17]. For simplicity, we assume that the commitment scheme is perfectly binding, since otherwise, if is was computationally binding, we would have to deal with cases of commitment collisions. For any set of successful transcripts corresponding to the same commitment, with at least two different challenges i^*:

– either the revealed shares of $[\![\alpha]\!], [\![K]\!]$ are not consistent, and then a hash collision is found, since the commitment scheme is assumed perfectly binding;
– or the openings are unique, and then $([\![\alpha]\!], [\![K]\!])$ is uniquely defined.

In the second case, this witness can be recovered from any two successful transcripts T_1 and T_2 corresponding to the same commitment and for which $i_1^* \neq i_2^*$. Let us call a witness $([\![\alpha]\!], [\![K]\!])$ a *good witness* whenever $M_\alpha^L = M_\alpha^R K$, i.e., α is a solution of the underlying MinRank problem.

Let $\tilde{\mathcal{P}}$, $\tilde{\varepsilon}$ and ε be as in Theorem 2. In figure Fig. 5, we describe an extractor $\mathcal{E}$ to find two valid transcripts T_1 and T_2 with a different second challenge. In

1. Repeat $+\infty$ times
2.   Run $\tilde{\mathcal{P}}$ with the honest verifier V to obtain a transcript T_1
3.   If T_1 is not a successful transcript, go to step 2
4.   Do Z times:
5.   Run $\tilde{\mathcal{P}}$ with V to obtain a transcript T_2
6.   If T_2 is a successful transcript, $i_2^* \neq i_1^*$ and (T_1, T_2) reveals a good witness,
7.   Return (T_1, T_2)

Fig. 5. Extractor $\mathcal{E}$.

what follows, we consider that $\mathcal{E}$ only receives transcripts with consistent shares since otherwise the extractor would find a hash collision.

Now, we want to estimate the number of calls $\mathcal{E}$ makes to $\tilde{\mathcal{P}}$ before returning (T_1, T_2) at step 7. We denote $\mathsf{succ}_{\tilde{\mathcal{P}}}$ the event that $\tilde{\mathcal{P}}$ succeeds in convincing a honest verifier V. By hypothesis, we have $\Pr[\mathsf{succ}_{\tilde{\mathcal{P}}}] = \tilde{\varepsilon} > \varepsilon$.

Let $\alpha \in (0, 1)$ be an arbitrary value such that $(1 - \alpha)\tilde{\varepsilon} > \varepsilon$. Also, let X_h be the random variable that samples the randomness used by $\tilde{\mathcal{P}}$ in the generation of the initial commitment h. We say that an x_h in the sample space of X_h is *good* if

$$\Pr[\mathsf{succ}_{\tilde{\mathcal{P}}} \mid X_h = x_h] \geq (1 - \alpha) \cdot \tilde{\varepsilon}.$$

By the Splitting Lemma [17, Lemma 5], we have for all realization x_h of X_h,

$$\Pr[x_h \text{ good} \mid \mathsf{succ}_{\tilde{\mathcal{P}}}] \geq \alpha.$$

Assume $\mathcal{E}$ obtains a successful transcript T_1 in Step 2 of Fig. 5, and let x_h be the underlying realization of X_h. Assume x_h is good. By definition, we have

$$\Pr[\mathsf{succ}_{\tilde{\mathcal{P}}} \mid X_h = x_h] \geq (1 - \alpha) \cdot \tilde{\varepsilon} > \varepsilon > \frac{1}{N},$$

implying that there must exist a successful transcript T_2 with $i_2^* \neq i_1^*$. As explained above, this implies that there exists a unique and well-defined witness corresponding to these transcripts. Let $([\![\alpha]\!], [\![K]\!])$ be that witness. Now, we show that $([\![\alpha]\!], [\![K]\!])$ is a good witness. Assume $([\![\alpha]\!], [\![K]\!])$ is bad (i.e., $M_\alpha^L \neq M_\alpha^R K$.). By contradiction, we will show that then we have $\Pr[\mathsf{succ}_{\tilde{\mathcal{P}}} | X_h = x_h] \leq \varepsilon$, meaning that x_h is not good.

Denote FP the event that a genuine execution of the MPC protocol outputs a false positive, i.e. a zero matrix V. Then from Proposition 2, we have $\Pr[\mathsf{FP}] \leq \frac{1}{q^n}$. We now upper bound the probability that the inner loop of Fig. 5 succeeds:

$$\Pr[\mathsf{succ}_{\tilde{\mathcal{P}}} \mid X_h = x_h] = \Pr[\mathsf{succ}_{\tilde{\mathcal{P}}}, \mathsf{FP} \mid X_h = x_h] + \Pr[\mathsf{succ}_{\tilde{\mathcal{P}}}, \overline{\mathsf{FP}} \mid X_h = x_h].$$

$$\leq \frac{1}{q^n} + (1 - \frac{1}{q^n}) \cdot \Pr[\mathsf{succ}_{\tilde{\mathcal{P}}} \mid X_h = x_h, \overline{\mathsf{FP}}].$$

Having a successful transcript means that the sharing $[\![V]\!]$ in the first response of the prover must encode the zero matrix. But, the event $\overline{\mathsf{FP}}$, when we have a bad witness, implies that a genuine execution outputs a non-zero matrix V. So, to have a successful transcript, the prover must cheat for the simulation of at least one party. If the prover cheats for several parties, there is no way it can produce a successful transcript, while if the prover cheats for exactly one party (among the N parties), the probability to be successful is at most $1/N$. Thus, $\Pr[\mathsf{succ}_{\tilde{p}}|X_h = x_h, \overline{\mathsf{FP}}] \leq 1/N$ and we have

$$\Pr[\mathsf{succ}_{\tilde{p}}|X_h = x_h] \leq \frac{1}{q^n} + (1 - \frac{1}{q^n}) \cdot \frac{1}{N} = \varepsilon,$$

meaning that x_h is not good. Thus, if x_h is good, then $(\llbracket \alpha \rrbracket, \llbracket K \rrbracket)$ is good.

Now, we lower bound the probability that the i-th iteration of the inner loop of Fig. 5 finds a successful transcript T_2 with $i^*_{T_1} \neq i^*_{T_2}$ with a good x_h. We have

$$\Pr[\mathsf{succ}_{\tilde{p}}^{T_2} \cap (i^*_{T_1} \neq i^*_{T_2}) \mid x_h \text{ good }]$$

$$= \Pr[\mathsf{succ}_{\tilde{p}}^{T_2} \mid x_h \text{ good }] - \Pr[\mathsf{succ}_{\tilde{p}}^{T_2} \cap (i^*_{T_1} = i^*_{T_2}) \mid x_h \text{ good }]$$

$$\geq (1 - \alpha)\tilde{\varepsilon} - \Pr[i^*_{T_1} = i^*_{T_2} \mid x_h \text{ good }] \geq (1 - \alpha)\tilde{\varepsilon} - \Pr[i^*_{T_1} = i^*_{T_2}]$$

$$= (1 - \alpha)\tilde{\varepsilon} - 1/N \geq (1 - \alpha)\tilde{\varepsilon} - \varepsilon.$$

Define $p_0 := (1 - \alpha) \cdot \tilde{\varepsilon} - \varepsilon$. By running $\tilde{\mathcal{P}}$ with the same x_h as for the good transcript Z times, we hence obtain a second non-colliding transcript T_2 with probability at least $1/2$ when

$$Z \approx \frac{\ln(2)}{\ln\left(\frac{1}{1-p_0}\right)} \leq \frac{\ln(2)}{p_0}.$$

Now, we upper bounded the average number of calls of $\mathcal{E}$ to $\tilde{\mathcal{P}}$ before finishing.

1. $\mathcal{E}$ makes an average number of calls $1/\tilde{\varepsilon}$ to obtain T_1
2. Then $\mathcal{E}$ makes at most Z calls to $\tilde{\mathcal{P}}$ using the same x_h as for T_1 to obtain a successful transcript T_2 such that $i^*_{T_1} \neq i^*_{T_2}$. The probability that such a T_2 is found is at least $\alpha/2$, since the probability that x_h is good is at least α, and whenever x_h is good the probability of finding T_2 is at least $1/2$.

Hence, the average number of calls of the extractor $\mathcal{E}$ to $\tilde{\mathcal{P}}$ is upper bounded by

$$\left(\frac{1}{\tilde{\varepsilon}} + Z\right) \cdot \frac{2}{\alpha} = \left(\frac{1}{\tilde{\varepsilon}} + \frac{\ln(2)}{(1 - \alpha) \cdot \tilde{\varepsilon} - \varepsilon}\right) \cdot \frac{2}{\alpha}$$

To obtain an α-free formula, we take α such that $(1 - \alpha) \cdot \tilde{\varepsilon} = \frac{1}{2}(\tilde{\varepsilon} + \varepsilon)$, implying $\alpha = \frac{1}{2}(1 - \frac{\varepsilon}{\tilde{\varepsilon}})$. Hence, the average number of calls to $\tilde{\mathcal{P}}$ is at most

$$\frac{4}{\tilde{\varepsilon} - \varepsilon}\left(1 + \tilde{\varepsilon} \cdot \frac{2 \cdot \ln(2)}{\tilde{\varepsilon} - \varepsilon}\right).$$

B   Proof of Theorem 3 (Zero-Knowledge)

Proof. As in the proof of the soundness, we follow the approach by Feneuil, Joux and Rivain in [17]. First, we describe in Fig. 6 an internal HVZK simulator $\mathcal{S}$ and show that its responses are $(t, \varepsilon_{\mathrm{PRG}})$-indistinguishable from the responses of an honest prover for the same challenge i^*. Then we describe a global HVZK simulator that uses $\mathcal{S}$ to output transcripts $(t, \varepsilon_{\mathrm{PRG}} + \varepsilon_{\mathrm{com}})$-indistinguishable from real transcripts of the protocol.

1. $\mathsf{seed} \overset{\$}{\leftarrow} \{0,1\}^\lambda$, $(\mathsf{seed}_i, \rho_i)_{i \in [N]} \leftarrow \mathsf{TreePRG}(\mathsf{seed})$
2. For each party $i \in [N] \setminus \{i^*\}$,
    - $[\![A]\!]_i, [\![B]\!]_i \leftarrow \mathrm{PRG}(\mathsf{seed}_i)$
    - If $i \neq N$,
        - $[\![\alpha]\!]_i, [\![C]\!]_i, [\![K]\!]_i \leftarrow \mathrm{PRG}(\mathsf{seed}_i)$, $\mathsf{state}_i = \mathsf{seed}_i$
    - Else,
        - $[\![\alpha]\!]_N \overset{\$}{\leftarrow} \mathbb{F}_q^k$, $[\![K]\!]_N \overset{\$}{\leftarrow} \mathbb{F}_q^{r \times (n-r)}$, $[\![C]\!]_N \overset{\$}{\leftarrow} \mathbb{F}_q^{n \times (n-r)}$
        - $\mathsf{aux} = ([\![\alpha]\!]_N, [\![K]\!]_N, [\![C]\!]_N)$, $\mathsf{state}_N = \mathsf{seed}_N \,\|\, \mathsf{aux}$
3. For party i^*,
    - $\mathsf{com}_{i^*} \leftarrow \mathrm{Com}(\mathsf{state}_{i^*}, \rho_{i^*})$
    - $[\![S_1]\!]_{i^*} \overset{\$}{\leftarrow} \mathbb{F}_q^{n \times r}$, $[\![S_2]\!]_{i^*} \overset{\$}{\leftarrow} \mathbb{F}_q^{r \times n - r}$, $[\![V]\!]_{i^*} = -\sum_{i \neq i^*} [\![V]\!]_i$
4. Run Phase 3 of Fig. 2 on each party $i \in [N] \setminus \{i^*\}$ to obtain $\{[\![S_1]\!]_i, [\![S_2]\!]_i, [\![V]\!]_i\}$.
5. Output the responses
    - $\mathsf{rsp}_1 = \mathrm{Hash}\big([\![S_1]\!]_1, [\![S_2]\!]_1, [\![V]\!]_1, \ldots, [\![S_1]\!]_N, [\![S_2]\!]_N, [\![V]\!]_N\big)$.
    - $\mathsf{rsp}_2 = \big((\mathsf{state}_i, \rho_i)_{i \neq i^*}, [\![S_1]\!]_{i^*}, [\![S_2]\!]_{i^*}\big)$

Fig. 6. Internal HVZK simulator $\mathcal{S}$ on input of challenges (R, i^*).

1. $\mathsf{seed} \overset{\$}{\leftarrow} \{0,1\}^\lambda$, $(\mathsf{seed}_i, \rho_i)_{i \in [N]} \leftarrow \mathsf{TreePRG}(\mathsf{seed})$
2. For each party $i \in [N]$,
    - $[\![A]\!]_i, [\![B]\!]_i \leftarrow \mathrm{PRG}(\mathsf{seed}_i)$
    - If $i \neq N$,
        - $[\![\alpha]\!]_i, [\![C]\!]_i, [\![K]\!]_i \leftarrow \mathrm{PRG}(\mathsf{seed}_i)$, $\mathsf{state}_i = \mathsf{seed}_i$
    - Else,
        - $[\![\alpha]\!]_N \leftarrow \alpha - \sum_{i \neq N} [\![\alpha]\!]_i$, $[\![K]\!]_N \leftarrow K - \sum_{i \neq N} [\![K]\!]_i$, $[\![C]\!]_N \leftarrow A \cdot B - \sum_{i \neq N} [\![C]\!]_i$
        - $\mathsf{aux} = ([\![\alpha]\!]_N, [\![K]\!]_N, [\![C]\!]_N)$, $\mathsf{state}_N = \mathsf{seed}_N \,\|\, \mathsf{aux}$
3. Run Phase 3 of Fig. 2 on all the parties to obtain $\{[\![S_1]\!]_i, [\![S_2]\!]_i, [\![V]\!]_i\}_{i \in [N]}$.
4. Output the responses
    - $\mathsf{rsp}_1 = \mathrm{Hash}\big([\![S_1]\!]_1, [\![S_2]\!]_1, [\![V]\!]_1, \ldots, [\![S_1]\!]_N, [\![S_2]\!]_N, [\![V]\!]_N\big)$.
    - $\mathsf{rsp}_2 = \big((\mathsf{state}_i, \rho_i)_{i \neq i^*}, [\![S_1]\!]_{i^*}, [\![S_2]\!]_{i^*}\big)$

Fig. 7. Simulator 0 on input of challenges (R, i^*).

To show the indistinguishability of outputs of simulator $\mathcal{S}$ from outputs of the protocol, we describe the following sequence of simulators.

Simulator 0 (Actual protocol). This simulator, described in Fig. 7, outputs $(\mathsf{rsp}_1, \mathsf{rsp}_2)$ from the transcript of a genuine execution of the protocol with a prover that knowns a witness (α, K) and receives challenges (R, i^*).

Simulator 1. Same as Simulator 0, but uses true randomness instead of seed-derived randomness for party i^*. If $i^* = N$, the values $[\![\alpha]\!]_N$, $[\![K]\!]_N$ and $[\![C]\!]_N$ are computed as described in the protocol (only $[\![A]\!]_N$ and $[\![B]\!]_N$ are generated from true randomness). It is easy to see that the probability of distinguishing Simulator 1 and Simulator 0 in running time t is no more than $\varepsilon_{\mathrm{PRG}}$.

Simulator 2. Replace $[\![\alpha]\!]_N$, $[\![K]\!]_N$ and $[\![C]\!]_N$ in Simulator 1 by uniformly random elements of the same type and compute $[\![V]\!]_{i^*} = -\sum_{i \neq i^*} [\![V]\!]_i$. We note that the obtained simulator is independent of the witness $(\boldsymbol{\alpha}, K)$ and solely takes the challenges (R, i^*) as input. Now we show that the output distributions of Simulator 1 and Simulator 2 are identical for $i^* = N$ or $i^* \neq N$.

If $i^* = N$, the changes only impact the shares $[\![S_1]\!]_N$, $[\![S_2]\!]_N$, $[\![V]\!]_N$ in the simulated responses. We can see that the distributions of those shares are identical in Simulator 2 as in Simulator 1. Indeed, in both cases, the shares $[\![S_1]\!]_N$ and $[\![S_2]\!]_N$ are uniformly distributed because of the uniformly sampled (in Simulator 1) additive terms $[\![A]\!]_N$ and $[\![B]\!]_N$, respectively, and independent of the rest. The share $[\![V]\!]_N$, as in Simulation 1, verifies $[\![V]\!]_N = -\sum_{i \neq N} [\![V]\!]_i$.

If $i^* \neq N$, the changes only impact $[\![S_1]\!]_N$, $[\![S_2]\!]_N$, $[\![V]\!]_N$, derived from $\mathsf{aux} = ([\![\boldsymbol{\alpha}]\!]_N, [\![K]\!]_N, [\![C]\!]_N)$, in the simulated response. But aux was already uniformly random in Simulator 1. Indeed, the shares in aux are computed by adding share values from parties $i \neq N$, including party i^* (which is uniformly random in Simulator 1). Therefore, the output distributions of Simulator 1 and Simulator 2 are identical.

Simulator 3 (Internal HVZK simulator). The only difference between Simulator 2 and the internal HVZK simulator $\mathcal{S}$ in Fig. 6 is that the latter directly draws $[\![S_1]\!]_{i^*}$ and $[\![S_2]\!]_{i^*}$ uniformly at random. As explained above, this does not impact the output distribution.

To sum up, we have shown that the internal simulator $\mathcal{S}$ outputs responses $(\mathsf{rsp}_1, \mathsf{rsp}_2)$ which are $(t, \varepsilon_{\mathrm{PRG}})$-indistinguishable from the responses of the real protocol on same challenges of an honest verifier. To obtain a global HVZK simulator, we proceed as in Fig. 8:

---

1. $R \xleftarrow{\$} \mathcal{E}_f$, $i^* \xleftarrow{\$} [N]$ (as an honest verifier).
2. Run the simulator $\mathcal{S}(R, i^*)$ to obtain
   - $\mathsf{rsp}_1 = \mathrm{Hash}\left([\![S_1]\!]_1, [\![S_2]\!]_1, [\![V]\!]_1, \ldots, [\![S_1]\!]_N, [\![S_2]\!]_N, [\![V]\!]_N\right)$.
   - $\mathsf{rsp}_2 = \left((\mathsf{state}_i, \rho_i)_{i \neq i^*}, [\![S_1]\!]_{i^*}, [\![S_2]\!]_{i^*}\right)$
3. Compute the initial commitment Com as follows
   - For each party $i \neq i^*$, compute the commitment $\mathsf{com}_i = \mathsf{Com}(\mathsf{state}_i, \rho_i)$
   - For party i^*, sample a random commitment $\mathsf{com}_{i^*} \xleftarrow{\$} \{0, 1\}^{2\lambda}$
   - Set $h = \mathrm{Hash}(\mathsf{com}_1, \ldots, \mathsf{com}_N)$
   - Update $\mathsf{rsp}_2 = \left((\mathsf{state}_i, \rho_i)_{i \neq i^*}, \mathsf{com}_{i^*}, [\![S_1]\!]_{i^*}, [\![S_2]\!]_{i^*}\right)$
4. Output the transcript $T = (h, R, \mathsf{rsp}_1, i^*, \mathsf{rsp}_2)$

Fig. 8. The global HVZK simulator.

Applying the hiding property of the commitment scheme on com_{i^*}, we then have that the global HVZK simulator outputs a transcript which is $(t, \varepsilon_{\mathrm{PRG}} + \varepsilon_{\mathsf{com}})$-indistinguishable from a real transcript of the protocol. $\qquad\square$

C   Proof of Theorem 4 (EUF-CMA)

Proof. Let $\mathcal{A}$ be an adversary making q_s signing queries, and q_0, q_1, q_2 queries to Hash_0, Hash_1 and Hash_2, respectively. To prove the theorem, we define in the following a sequence of experiments involving $\mathcal{A}$. We let $\Pr_i[\cdot]$ refer to the probability of an event in experiment i, and t denote the running time of the entire experiment, i.e., including $\mathcal{A}$'s running time, the time required to answer signing queries and to verify $\mathcal{A}$'s output.

Note that since Hash_0, Hash_1, and Hash_2 are modeled as random oracles, $\mathcal{A}$ can know the output of one of these on a prepared input only if it queries the oracle. Hence, if $\mathcal{A}$ outputs a forgery (msg, σ) at the end of an experiment, with

$$\sigma = \mathsf{salt} \mid h_1 \mid h_2 \mid \left(\left(\mathsf{state}_i^{[\ell]} \right)_{i \neq i^{*,[\ell]}} \mid \mathsf{com}_{i^{*,[\ell]}}^{[\ell]} \mid \left[\!\left[S_1^{[\ell]} \right]\!\right]_{i^{*,[\ell]}} \mid \left[\!\left[S_2^{[\ell]} \right]\!\right]_{i^{*,[\ell]}} \right)_{\ell \in [\tau]},$$

then there necessarily exists, at a given moment during the experiment, a query to Hash_2 made by $\mathcal{A}$ itself with output h_2 input, and an input of the form

$$\left(\mathsf{msg}, \mathsf{salt}, h_1, \left(\left[\!\left[S_1^{[\ell]} \right]\!\right]_i, \left[\!\left[S_2^{[\ell]} \right]\!\right]_i, \left[\!\left[V_1^{[\ell]} \right]\!\right]_i \right)_{i \in [N],\ \ell \in [\tau]} \right).$$

Experiment 1. This is the interaction of $\mathcal{A}$ with the real signature scheme. In more detail: first KeyGen is run to obtain M, α, K, and $\mathcal{A}$ is given the public key M. At the end of this experiment, $\mathcal{A}$ outputs a message/signature pair. We let Forge denote the event that the message was not previously queried by $\mathcal{A}$ to its signing oracle, and the signature is valid. Our goal is to upper-bound $\Pr_1[\mathsf{Forge}]$.

Experiment 2. This is the previous experiment with the difference that we abort if, during the course of the experiment, a collision in Hash_0 is found. Note that the number of queries to Hash_0 throughout the experiment (by either the adversary or the signing algorithm) is $q_0 + \tau N q_s$. Thus,

$$|\Pr_1[\mathsf{Forge}] - \Pr_2[\mathsf{Forge}]| \leq \frac{(q_0 + \tau N q_s)^2}{2 \cdot 2^{2\lambda}}.$$

Experiment 3. The difference with the previous experiment is that, when signing a message m, we begin by choosing h_1 and h_2 uniformly and then expand them as the challenges $\{R^{[1]}, \ldots, R^{[\tau]}\}$ and $\{i^{*,[1]}, \ldots, i^{*,[\tau]}\}$. Phases 1, 3 and 5 of Fig. 4 remain unchanged, but in phases 2 and 4 we simply set the output of Hash_1 to h_1 and the output of Hash_2 to h_2.

A difference in the outcome of this experiment compared to the previous one occurs only when, in the course of answering a signing query, the query to Hash_1 or the query to Hash_2 was ever made before by $\mathcal{A}$. The probability of each of these two events is upper bounded by that of having the same salt in the current signing query and in the relevant previous query, which is $\frac{1}{2^{2\lambda}}$. Therefore, we have

$$|\Pr_2[\mathsf{Forge}] - \Pr_3[\mathsf{Forge}]| \leq \frac{q_s \cdot (q_1 + q_2)}{2^{2\lambda}}.$$

Experiment 4. The difference with the previous experiment is that, for each $\ell \in [\tau]$, we sample $\mathsf{com}_{i^{*,[\ell]}}^{[\ell]}$ uniformly at random (i.e., without making the corresponding query to Hash_0).

A difference between this experiment and the previous one occurs only when, in the course of answering a signing query, Hash_0 receives an input that it was previously queried. However, such a collision cannot occur within the same signing query (since the indices i and ℓ are part of the input to Hash_0), and it occurs from a previous query (signing query or Hash_0 query made by the $\mathcal{A}$) with probability $\frac{1}{2^{2\lambda}}$ since there would be the same salt in the current signing query as in that previous query. Thus,

$$|\mathrm{Pr}_3[\mathsf{Forge}] - \mathrm{Pr}_4[\mathsf{Forge}]| \leq \frac{q_s \cdot (q_s + q_0)}{2^{2\lambda}}.$$

Experiment 5. We again modify the experiment. Now, for $\ell \in [\tau]$, the signer uses the internal HVZK simulator in Fig. 6 to generate the parties' views in one execution of Phases 1 and 3. We denote $\mathcal{S}_{\mathsf{salt}}(\cdot)$ a call to this simulator which appends salt to the sampled seed in input to TreePRG. Thus, signature queries are now answered as depicted in Fig. 9.

Observe that the secret $(\boldsymbol{\alpha}, K)$ is no longer used for generating signatures. Recall that an adversary against the internal HVZK simulator has a distinguishing advantage $\varepsilon_{\mathsf{PRG}}$ (corresponding to execution time t) since commitments are built outside of the simulator. It results in $|\mathrm{Pr}_4[\mathsf{Forge}] - \mathrm{Pr}_5[\mathsf{Forge}]| \leq \tau \cdot q_s \cdot \varepsilon_{\mathsf{PRG}}$.

Phase 0. salt $\xleftarrow{\$} \{0,1\}^{2\lambda}$.

1. Sample $h_1 \xleftarrow{\$} \{0,1\}^{2\lambda}$, compute $R^{[1]}, \ldots, R^{[\tau]} \leftarrow \mathrm{PRG}(h_1)$, where $R^{[\ell]} \in \mathcal{E}_f$.
2. Sample $h_2 \xleftarrow{\$} \{0,1\}^{2\lambda}$, compute $i^{*,[1]}, \ldots, i^{*,[\tau]} \leftarrow \mathrm{PRG}(h_2)$, where $i^{*,[\ell]} \in [N]$.

Phase 1 and 3. For each $\ell \in [\tau]$:

1. $(\mathrm{state}_i^{[\ell]})_{i \neq i^{*,[\ell]}}, \left(\llbracket S_1^{[\ell]} \rrbracket_i, \llbracket S_2^{[\ell]} \rrbracket_i, \llbracket V_1^{[\ell]} \rrbracket_i \right)_{i \in [N]} \leftarrow \mathcal{S}_{\mathsf{salt}}(R^{[\ell]}, i^{*,[\ell]})$.
2. Sample $\mathrm{com}_{i^*} \xleftarrow{\$} \{0,1\}^{2\lambda}$ and for $i \neq i^*$, compute $\mathrm{com}_i = \mathrm{Com}(\mathrm{state}_i, \rho_i)$

Phase 2 and 4.

1. Set $\mathsf{Hash}_1 \left(\mathsf{msg}, \mathsf{salt}, \mathrm{com}_1^{[1]}, \mathrm{com}_2^{[1]}, \ldots, \mathrm{com}_{N-1}^{[\tau]}, \mathrm{com}_N^{[\tau]} \right)$ equal to h_1.
2. Set $\mathsf{Hash}_2 \left(\mathsf{msg}, \mathsf{salt}, h_1, \left(\llbracket S_1^{[\ell]} \rrbracket_i, \llbracket S_2^{[\ell]} \rrbracket_i, \llbracket V_1^{[\ell]} \rrbracket_i \right)_{i \in [N], \ell \in [\tau]} \right)$ equal to h_2.

Phase 5: Assembling the signature. Output σ defined as

$$\sigma \leftarrow \mathsf{salt} \mid h_1 \mid h_2 \mid \left((\mathrm{state}_i^{[\ell]})_{i \neq i^{*,[\ell]}} \mid \mathrm{com}_{i^{*,[\ell]}}^{[\ell]} \mid \llbracket S_1^{[\ell]} \rrbracket_{i^{*,[\ell]}} \mid \llbracket S_2^{[\ell]} \rrbracket_{i^{*,[\ell]}} \right)_{\ell \in [\tau]}$$

Fig. 9. Experiment 5: Response to a signature query for a message msg.

Experiment 6. At any point during this experiment, we say that we have a correct execution ℓ^* if, in a query to Hash_2 with input

$$\left(\mathsf{msg}, \mathsf{salt}, h_1, \left(\llbracket S_1^{[\ell]} \rrbracket_i, \llbracket S_2^{[\ell]} \rrbracket_i, \llbracket V_1^{[\ell]} \rrbracket_i \right)_{i \in [N], \ell \in [\tau],} \right):$$

1. there is a previous query $h_1 \leftarrow \mathsf{Hash}_1 \left(\mathsf{msg}, \mathsf{salt}, \mathrm{com}_1^{[1]}, \ldots, \mathrm{com}_N^{[\tau]} \right)$,
2. and each $\mathrm{com}_i^{[\ell^*]}$ was output by a previous query (by either $\mathcal{A}$ or the signing oracle) to Hash_0 with input $(\mathsf{salt}, \ell, i, \mathrm{state}_i^{[\ell^*]})$,

3. and a good witness $(\boldsymbol{\alpha}, K)$ can be extracted from $\{\mathsf{state}_i^{[\ell^*]}\}_{i \in [N]}$.

In this experiment, it is checked in each query made by $\mathcal{A}$ to Hash_2 (where msg was not previously queried) if there is a correct execution. We call this event Solve. Note that if Solve occurs then the $\{\mathsf{state}_i^{[\ell]}\}_{i \in [N]}$ (which can be determined from the oracle queries of $\mathcal{A}$) allow to easily recover a solution $(\boldsymbol{\alpha}, K)$ of the MinRank instance given by $\boldsymbol{M}$. Thus, $\Pr_6[\mathsf{Solve}] \leq \varepsilon_{\mathrm{MR}}$. Hence,

$$\Pr_6[\mathsf{Forge}] = \Pr_6[\mathsf{Forge \ and \ Solve}] + \Pr_6[\mathsf{Forge \ and \ not \ Solve}]$$
$$\leq \varepsilon_{\mathrm{MR}} + \Pr_6[\mathsf{Forge \ and \ not \ Solve}].$$

Now, suppose we have a forgery (msg, σ) and Solve does not occur. Then for every $\ell \in [\tau]$, exactly one of the three following cases must occur:

a) $\mathsf{com}_{i^*, \ell}^{[\ell]}$ was not output by Hash_0.

b) • for all $i \in [N]$, $\mathsf{com}_i^{[\ell]}$ was output by a query to Hash_0 with input $\left(\mathsf{salt}, \ell, i, \mathsf{state}_i^{[\ell]}\right)$,

 • $\left[\!\left[S_2^{[\ell]}\right]\!\right]_{i^*}$ is obtained from $\mathsf{state}_{i^*}^{[\ell]}$, $\left[\!\left[S_1^{[\ell]}\right]\!\right]_{i^*}$ is obtained from $\mathsf{state}_{i^*}^{[\ell]}$ and h_1, and $\sum_{i \neq i^*, [\ell]} \left[\!\left[V^{[\ell]}\right]\!\right]_i$ is obtained from $\mathsf{state}_{i^*}^{[\ell]}$, h_1, $S_1^{[\ell]}$, $S_2^{[\ell]}$.

 • the witness $(\boldsymbol{\alpha}, K)$ extracted from $\{\mathsf{state}_i^{[\ell]}\}_{i \in [N]}$ is a bad witness.

b') • for all $i \in [N]$, $\mathsf{com}_i^{[\ell]}$ was output by a query to Hash_0 with input $\left(\mathsf{salt}, \ell, i, \mathsf{state}_i^{[\ell]}\right)$,

 • $\left[\!\left[S_2^{[\ell]}\right]\!\right]_{i^*}$ is not obtained from $\mathsf{state}_{i^*}^{[\ell]}$, or $\left[\!\left[S_1^{[\ell]}\right]\!\right]_{i^*}$ is not from $\mathsf{state}_{i^*}^{[\ell]}$ and h_1, or $\sum_{i \neq i^*, [\ell]} \left[\!\left[V^{[\ell]}\right]\!\right]_i$ is not from $\mathsf{state}_{i^*}^{[\ell]}$, h_1, $S_1^{[\ell]}$, $S_2^{[\ell]}$.

 • the witness $(\boldsymbol{\alpha}, K)$ extracted from $\{\mathsf{state}_i^{[\ell]}\}_{i \in [N]}$ is a bad witness.

Clearly, if b) occurs for a round $\ell \in [\tau]$, this means that the MPC protocol in Sect. 4 to verify matrix-multiplication triple is honestly followed by every party $i \in [N]$. Hence, from Proposition 2, we have that the adversary had probability $1/q^n$ to have b) satisfied for this round ℓ. This probability is in fact given by obtaining from h_1 one precise first challenge $R^{[\ell]}$ out of the q^n possibilities. Therefore, the probability of having exactly $s \in [\tau]$ rounds satisfying b) is at most

$$P_b(s) = \left(\frac{1}{q^n}\right)^s \left(1 - \frac{1}{q^n}\right)^{\tau - s} \binom{\tau}{s}.$$

If b) does not occur for a round $\ell \in [\tau]$, this clearly means that any other second challenge obtained from h_2 different from $i^{*, \ell}$ would make the forgery fail. Hence, the probability of having this round ℓ not leading to rejection is at most $1/N$. Therefore, the probability of having exactly $\tau - s \in [\tau]$ rounds satisfying a) or b') is at most

$$P_{a,b'}(s) = \frac{1}{N^{\tau - s}}.$$

In view of the above, the probability of having Forge and not Solve with exactly s rounds satisfying b) after q_1 queries to Hash_1 and q_2 queries to Hash_2 is at most

$$P(s) = \left(1 - (1 - P_b(s))^{q_1}\right)\left(1 - (1 - P_{a,b'}(s))^{q_2}\right).$$

Thus, we have
$$\Pr_6[\textsf{Forge and not Solve}] \leq \max_{0 \leq s \leq \tau} P(s).$$

References

1. Bardet, M., et al.: Improvements of algebraic attacks for solving the rank decoding and MinRank problems. In: Moriai, S., Wang, H. (eds.) ASIACRYPT 2020. LNCS, vol. 12491, pp. 507–536. Springer, Cham (2020). https://doi.org/10.1007/978-3-030-64837-4_17

2. Bardet, M., Bertin, M.: Improvement of algebraic attacks for solving superdetermined MinRank instances. CoRR abs/2208.01442 (2022). https://doi.org/10.48550/arXiv.2208.01442

3. Bardet, M., Briaud, P., Bros, M., Gaborit, P., Tillich, J.P.: Revisiting algebraic attacks on MinRank and on the rank decoding problem. Cryptology ePrint Archive, Paper 2022/1031 (2022). https://eprint.iacr.org/2022/1031

4. Baum, C., Nof, A.: Concretely-efficient zero-knowledge arguments for arithmetic circuits and their application to lattice-based cryptography. In: Kiayias, A., Kohlweiss, M., Wallden, P., Zikas, V. (eds.) PKC 2020. LNCS, vol. 12110, pp. 495–526. Springer, Cham (2020). https://doi.org/10.1007/978-3-030-45374-9_17

5. Bellini, E., Esser, A., Sanna, C., Verbel, J.: MR-DSS – smaller MinRank-based (ring-)signatures. Cryptology ePrint Archive, Paper 2022/973 (2022). https://eprint.iacr.org/2022/973

6. Beullens, W., Katsumata, S., Pintore, F.: Calamari and Falafl: logarithmic (linkable) ring signatures from isogenies and lattices. In: Moriai, S., Wang, H. (eds.) ASIACRYPT 2020. LNCS, vol. 12492, pp. 464–492. Springer, Cham (2020). https://doi.org/10.1007/978-3-030-64834-3_16

7. Beullens, W.: Improved cryptanalysis of UOV and rainbow. In: Canteaut, A., Standaert, F.-X. (eds.) EUROCRYPT 2021. LNCS, vol. 12696, pp. 348–373. Springer, Cham (2021). https://doi.org/10.1007/978-3-030-77870-5_13

8. Beullens, W.: Breaking rainbow takes a weekend on a laptop. Cryptology ePrint Archive, p. 214 (2022). https://eprint.iacr.org/2022/214

9. Buss, J.F., Frandsen, G.S., Shallit, J.O.: The computational complexity of some problems of linear algebra. J. Comput. Syst. Sci. **58**(3), 572 – 596 (1999). http://www.sciencedirect.com/science/article/pii/S0022000098916087

10. Chase, M., et al.: The picnic signature scheme. Design Document. Version 3.0 (2020). https://github.com/microsoft/Picnic/blob/master/spec/spec-v3.0.pdf

11. Chen, M.-S., Hülsing, A., Rijneveld, J., Samardjiska, S., Schwabe, P.: From 5-pass $\mathcal{MQ}$-based identification to $\mathcal{MQ}$-based signatures. In: Cheon, J.H., Takagi, T. (eds.) ASIACRYPT 2016. LNCS, vol. 10032, pp. 135–165. Springer, Heidelberg (2016). https://doi.org/10.1007/978-3-662-53890-6_5

12. Courtois, N.T.: Efficient zero-knowledge authentication based on a linear algebra problem MinRank. In: Boyd, C. (ed.) ASIACRYPT 2001. LNCS, vol. 2248, pp. 402–421. Springer, Heidelberg (2001). https://doi.org/10.1007/3-540-45682-1_24

13. Di Scala, A.J., Sanna, C.: Smaller public keys for MinRank-based schemes. arXiv preprint (2023). https://arxiv.org/abs/2302.12447

14. Escudero, D., Soria-Vazquez, E.: Efficient information-theoretic multi-party computation over non-commutative rings. In: Malkin, T., Peikert, C. (eds.) CRYPTO 2021. LNCS, vol. 12826, pp. 335–364. Springer, Cham (2021). https://doi.org/10.1007/978-3-030-84245-1_12

15. Faugère, J., Din, M.S.E., Spaenlehauer, P.: Computing loci of rank defects of linear matrices using Gröbner bases and applications to cryptology. In: Symbolic and Algebraic Computation, International Symposium, ISSAC, pp. 257–264 (2010). http://doi.acm.org/10.1145/1837934.1837984
16. Faugère, J.-C., Levy-dit-Vehel, F., Perret, L.: Cryptanalysis of MinRank. In: Wagner, D. (ed.) CRYPTO 2008. LNCS, vol. 5157, pp. 280–296. Springer, Heidelberg (2008). https://doi.org/10.1007/978-3-540-85174-5_16
17. Feneuil, T., Joux, A., Rivain, M.: Syndrome decoding in the head: shorter signatures from zero-knowledge proofs. Cryptology ePrint Archive, Paper 2022/188 (2022). https://eprint.iacr.org/2022/188
18. Feneuil, T., Rivain, M.: Threshold linear secret sharing to the rescue of MPC-in-the-head. Cryptology ePrint Archive, Paper 2022/1407 (2022). https://eprint.iacr.org/2022/1407
19. Fiat, A., Shamir, A.: How to prove yourself: practical solutions to identification and signature problems. In: Odlyzko, A.M. (ed.) CRYPTO 1986. LNCS, vol. 263, pp. 186–194. Springer, Heidelberg (1987). https://doi.org/10.1007/3-540-47721-7_12
20. Gaborit, P., Ruatta, O., Schrek, J.: On the complexity of the rank syndrome decoding problem. IEEE Trans. Inf. Theory 62(2), 1006–1019 (2016)
21. Goubin, L., Courtois, N.T.: Cryptanalysis of the TTM cryptosystem. In: Okamoto, T. (ed.) ASIACRYPT 2000. LNCS, vol. 1976, pp. 44–57. Springer, Heidelberg (2000). https://doi.org/10.1007/3-540-44448-3_4
22. Ishai, Y., Kushilevitz, E., Ostrovsky, R., Sahai, A.: Zero-knowledge from secure multiparty computation. In: STOC 2007, pp. 21–30. Association for Computing Machinery, New York (2007). https://doi.org/10.1145/1250790.1250794
23. Kales, D., Zaverucha, G.: An attack on some signature schemes constructed from five-pass identification schemes. In: Krenn, S., Shulman, H., Vaudenay, S. (eds.) CANS 2020. LNCS, vol. 12579, pp. 3–22. Springer, Cham (2020). https://doi.org/10.1007/978-3-030-65411-5_1
24. Kipnis, A., Shamir, A.: Cryptanalysis of the HFE public key cryptosystem by relinearization. In: Wiener, M. (ed.) CRYPTO 1999. LNCS, vol. 1666, pp. 19–30. Springer, Heidelberg (1999). https://doi.org/10.1007/3-540-48405-1_2
25. Lindell, Y., Nof, A.: A framework for constructing fast MPC over arithmetic circuits with malicious adversaries and an honest-majority. Association for Computing Machinery, New York (2017). https://doi.org/10.1145/3133956.3133999
26. Santoso, B., Ikematsu, Y., Nakamura, S., Yasuda, T.: Three-pass identification scheme based on MinRank problem with half cheating probability. CoRR abs/2205.03255 (2022). https://doi.org/10.48550/arXiv.2205.03255
27. Tao, C., Petzoldt, A., Ding, J.: Efficient key recovery for All HFE signature variants. In: Malkin, T., Peikert, C. (eds.) CRYPTO 2021. LNCS, vol. 12825, pp. 70–93. Springer, Cham (2021). https://doi.org/10.1007/978-3-030-84242-0_4
28. Verbel, J., Baena, J., Cabarcas, D., Perlner, R., Smith-Tone, D.: On the complexity of "superdetermined" minrank instances. In: Ding, J., Steinwandt, R. (eds.) PQCrypto 2019. LNCS, vol. 11505, pp. 167–186. Springer, Cham (2019). https://doi.org/10.1007/978-3-030-25510-7_10

Take Your MEDS: Digital Signatures from Matrix Code Equivalence

Tung Chou[1]([✉]), Ruben Niederhagen[1,2]([✉]), Edoardo Persichetti[3,4]([✉]),
Tovohery Hajatiana Randrianarisoa[5]([✉]), Krijn Reijnders[6]([✉]),
Simona Samardjiska[6]([✉]), and Monika Trimoska[6]([✉])

[1] Academia Sinica, Taipei, Taiwan
blueprint@crypto.tw, ruben@polycephaly.org
[2] University of Southern Denmark, Odense, Denmark
[3] Florida Atlantic University, Boca Raton, USA
epersichetti@fau.edu
[4] Sapienza University, Rome, Italy
[5] Umea University, Umea, Sweden
tovo@aims.ac.za
[6] Radboud Universiteit, Nijmegen, The Netherlands
{krijn,simonas,mtrimoska}@cs.ru.nl

Abstract. In this paper, we show how to use the Matrix Code Equivalence (MCE) problem as a new basis to construct signature schemes. This extends previous work on using isomorphism problems for signature schemes, a trend that has recently emerged in post-quantum cryptography. Our new formulation leverages a more general problem and allows for smaller data sizes, achieving competitive performance and great flexibility. Using MCE, we construct a zero-knowledge protocol which we turn into a signature scheme named Matrix Equivalence Digital Signature (MEDS). We provide an initial choice of parameters for MEDS, tailored to NIST's Category 1 security level, yielding public keys as small as 2.8 kB and signatures ranging from 18 kB to just around 6.5 kB, along with a reference implementation in C.

Keywords: group action · signature scheme · code-based cryptography · post-quantum cryptography · matrix codes

1 Introduction

Post-Quantum Cryptography (PQC) comprises all the primitives that are believed to be resistant against attackers equipped with a considerable quantum

An extended and correctly typeset version of this paper can be found at https://eprint.iacr.org/2022/1559.

Tung Chou is supported by Taiwan National Science and Technology Council (NSTC, previously Ministry of Science and Technology) grant 109-2222-E-001-001-MY3. Edoardo Persichetti is supported by NSF grant 1906360 and NSA grant H98230-22-1-0328. Monika Trimoska is supported by the ERC Starting Grant 805031 (EPOQUE).

N. El Mrabet et al. (Eds.): AFRICACRYPT 2023, LNCS 14064, pp. 28–52, 2023.
https://doi.org/10.1007/978-3-031-37679-5_2

computing power. Several such schemes have been around for a long time [39,44], some being in fact almost as old as RSA [36]; however, the area itself was not formalized as a whole until the early 2000s, for instance with the first edition of the PQCrypto conference [37]. The area has seen a dramatic increase in importance and volume of research over the past few years, partially thanks to NIST's interest and the launch of the PQC Standardization process in 2017 [38]. After 4 years and 3 rounds of evaluation, the process has crystallized certain mathematical tools as standard building blocks (e.g. lattices, linear codes, multivariate equations, isogenies etc.). Some algorithms [31,35,42] have now been selected for standardization, with an additional one or two to be selected among a restricted set of alternates [1,4,5] after another round of evaluation. While having a range of candidates ready for standardization may seem satisfactory, research is still active in designing PQC primitives. In particular, NIST has expressed the desire for a greater diversity among the hardness assumptions behind signature schemes, and announced a partial re-opening of the standardization process for precisely the purpose of collecting non-lattice-based protocols.

Cryptographic group actions are a popular and powerful instrument for constructing secure and efficient cryptographic protocols. The most well-known is, without a doubt, the action of finite groups on the integers modulo a prime, or the set of points on an elliptic curve, which give rise to the *Discrete Logarithm Problem (DLP)*, i.e. the backbone of public-key cryptography. Recently, proposals for post-quantum cryptographic group actions started to emerge, based on the tools identified above: for instance, isogenies [18], linear codes [14], trilinear forms [47] and even lattices [30]. All of these group actions provide very promising solutions for cryptographic schemes, for example signatures [8,23,47] and many others; at the same time, they are very different in nature, with unique positive and negative aspects.

Our Contribution. In this work, we formalize a new cryptographic group action based on the notion of *Matrix Code Equivalence*. This is similar in nature to the *code equivalence* notion at the basis of LESS [8,14], and in fact belongs to a larger class of isomorphism problems that include, for example, the lattice isomorphism problem, and the well-known isomorphism of polynomials [39]. The hardness of the MCE problem was studied in [22,45], from which it is possible to conclude that this is a suitable problem for post-quantum cryptography. Indeed, we show that it is possible to use MCE to build a zero-knowledge protocol, and hence a signature scheme, which we name *Matrix Equivalence Digital Signature*, or simply MEDS. For our security analysis, we first study in detail the collision attacks from [45] and then we develop two new attacks. The first attack that we propose uses a nontrivial algebraic modeling inspired from the minors modellings of MinRank in [7,26]. The second one is an adaptation of Leon's algorithm [34] for matrix codes. Based on this analysis, we provide an initial parameter choice, together with several computational optimizations, resulting in a scheme with great flexibility and very competitive data sizes. This group action allows for the construction of (linkable) ring signatures, with performance results that improve on the existing state of the art [9]. Due to limitations in space, the construction of ring signatures is included in an extended version of this work.

2   Preliminaries

Let $\mathbb{F}_q$ be the finite field of q elements. $\mathrm{GL}_n(q)$ and $\mathrm{AGL}_n(q)$ denote respectively the general linear group and the general affine group of degree n over $\mathbb{F}_q$. We use bold letters to denote vectors $\mathbf{a}, \mathbf{c}, \mathbf{x}, \ldots$, and matrices $\mathbf{A}, \mathbf{B}, \ldots$. The entries of a vector $\mathbf{a}$ are denoted by a_i, and we write $\mathbf{a} = (a_1, \ldots, a_n)$ for a (row) vector of dimension n over some field. Similarly, the entries of a matrix $\mathbf{A}$ are denoted by a_{ij}. Random sampling from a set S is denoted by $a \xleftarrow{\$} S$. For two matrices $\mathbf{A}$ and $\mathbf{B}$, we denote the Kronecker product by $\mathbf{A} \otimes \mathbf{B}$. Finally, we denote the set of all $m \times n$ matrices over $\mathbb{F}_q$ by $\mathcal{M}_{m,n}(\mathbb{F}_q)$.

2.1   Cryptographic Group Actions

Definition 1. Let X be a set and $(G, \cdot)$ be a group. A group action is a mapping

$$\star : G \times X \to X$$
$$(g, x) \mapsto g \star x$$

such that the following conditions hold for all $x \in X$:

- $e \star x = x$, where e is the identity element of G.
- $g_2 \star (g_1 \star x) = (g_2 \cdot g_1) \star x$, for all $g_1, g_2 \in G$.

A group action can have a number of mathematically desirable properties. For example, we say that a group action is:

- *Commutative*: for any $g_1, g_2 \in G$, we have $g_2 \star (g_1 \star x) = g_1 \star (g_2 \star x)$.
- *Transitive*: given $x_1, x_2 \in X$, there is some $g \in G$ such that $g \star x_1 = x_2$.
- *Free*: if $g \star x = x$, then g is the identity.

In particular, a *cryptographic* group action is a group action with some additional properties that are useful for cryptographic applications. To begin with, there are some desirable properties of computational nature. Namely, the following procedures should be efficient:

- *Evaluation*: given x and g, compute $g \star x$.
- *Sampling*: sample uniformly at random from G.
- *Membership testing*: verify that $x \in X$.

Finally, cryptographic group actions should come with security guarantees; for instance, the *vectorization problem* should be hard:

Problem 1 (Group Action Vectorization).
Given: The pair $x_1, x_2 \in X$.
Goal: Find, if any, $g \in G$ such that $g \star x_1 = x_2$.

Early constructions using this paradigm are based on the action of finite groups of prime order, for which the vectorization problem is the discrete logarithm problem. Lately, multiple isogeny-based constructions have appeared: see, for instance, the work of Couveignes in [21] and later by Rostovtsev and Stolbunov [46]. A general framework based on group actions was explored in more detail by [3], allowing for the design of several primitives. The holy grail are those cryptographic group actions that possess both the mathematical and cryptographic properties listed above. Currently, CSIDH [18] is the only post-quantum commutative cryptographic group action, although there is an ongoing debate about the efficiency and quantum hardness of its vectorization problem [15]. In Sect. 3, we introduce the group action that is relevant to our work.

2.2 Protocols

We give here an explicit characterization of the protocols we will build. The corresponding security definitions are presented only in an informal manner; formal definitions will are included in the full version of this work.[1]

Definition 2. A *Sigma protocol* is a three-pass interactive protocol between two parties: a prover $P = (P_1, P_2)$ and a verifier $V = (V_1, V_2)$. The protocol is composed of the following procedures:

I. Keygen: on input some public data (including system parameters), output a public key pk (the instance) and the corresponding secret key sk (the witness). Give sk to the prover; pk is distributed publicly and is available to all parties. For simplicity, we assume that the public data is available as input in all the remaining procedures.
II. Commit: on input the public key pk, P_1 outputs a public commitment cmt and sends it to the verifier.
III. Challenge: on input the public key pk and the commitment cmt, V_1 samples uniformly at random a challenge ch from the challenge space C and sends it to the prover.
IV. Response: on input the secret key sk, the public key pk, the commitment cmt and the challenge ch, P_2 outputs a response rsp and sends it to the verifier.
V. Verify: on input a public key pk, the commitment cmt, the challenge ch, and the response rsp, V_2 outputs either 1 (accept) if the *transcript* (cmt, ch, rsp) is valid, or 0 (reject) otherwise.

A Sigma protocol is usually required to satisfy the following properties. First, if the statement is true, an honest prover is always able to convince an honest verifier. This property is called *Completeness*. Secondly, a dishonest prover cannot convince an honest verifier other than with a small probability. This is captured by the *Soundness* property, which also bounds such probability, usually known as *soundness error* or, informally, *cheating probability*. Finally, the protocol has to be *Zero-Knowledge*, i.e. anyone observing the transcript (including the verifier) learns nothing other than the fact that the statement is true.

---

[1] https://eprint.iacr.org/2022/1559.pdf.

Definition 3. A *Digital Signature scheme* is a protocol between 2 parties: a signer S and a verifier V. The protocol is composed of the following procedures:

I. Keygen: on input the public data (including system parameters), output a secret signing key sk for S and the corresponding public verification key pk.
II. Sign: on input a secret key sk and a message msg, output a signature σ.
III. Verify: on input a public key pk, a message msg and a signature σ, V outputs either 1 (accept) if the signature is valid, or 0 (reject) otherwise.

Correctness means that an honest signer is always able to get verified. The usual desired security notion for signature schemes is *Unforgeability*, which guarantees computationally infeasible to forge a valid signature without knowing the secret signing key. Again, we leave formal definitions to the full version of this work.

3 The Matrix Code Equivalence Problem

A $[m \times n, k]$ *matrix code* is a subspace $\mathcal{C}$ of $\mathcal{M}_{m,n}(\mathbb{F}_q)$. These objects are usually measured with the rank metric, where the *distance* between two matrices $\mathbf{A}, \mathbf{B} \in \mathcal{M}_{m,n}(\mathbb{F}_q)$ is defined as $d(\mathbf{A}, \mathbf{B}) = \text{Rank}(\mathbf{A} - \mathbf{B})$. We denote the basis of the subspace by $\langle \mathbf{C_1}, \ldots, \mathbf{C_k} \rangle$, where the $\mathbf{C_i}$'s are linearly independent elements of $\mathcal{M}_{m,n}(\mathbb{F}_q)$. Due to symmetry, without loss of generality, in the rest of the text we will assume $m \leqslant n$.

For a matrix $\mathbf{A} \in \mathcal{M}_{m,n}(\mathbb{F}_q)$, let vec be a mapping that sends a matrix $\mathbf{A}$ to the vector $\text{vec}(\mathbf{A}) \in \mathbb{F}_q^{mn}$ obtained by 'flattening' $\mathbf{A}$, i.e.:

$$\text{vec} : \mathbf{A} = \begin{pmatrix} a_{1,1} & \cdots & a_{1,n} \\ \vdots & \ddots & \vdots \\ a_{m,1} & \cdots & a_{m,n} \end{pmatrix} \mapsto \text{vec}(\mathbf{A}) = (a_{1,1}, \ldots, a_{1,n}, \ldots, a_{m,1}, \ldots, a_{m,n}).$$

The inverse operation is denoted by mat, i.e. $\text{mat}(\text{vec}(\mathbf{A})) = \mathbf{A}$. Using the map vec, an $[m \times n, k]$ matrix code can be thought of as an $\mathbb{F}_q$-subspace of $\mathbb{F}_q^{mn}$, and thus we can represent it with a generator matrix $\mathbf{G} \in \mathbb{F}_q^{k \times mn}$, in a manner similar to the common representation for linear codes. Indeed, if $\mathcal{C}$ is an $[m \times n, k]$ matrix code over $\mathbb{F}_q$, we denote by $\text{vec}(\mathcal{C})$ the vectorization of $\mathcal{C}$ i.e.:

$$\text{vec}(\mathcal{C}) := \{\text{vec}(\mathbf{A}) : \mathbf{A} \in \mathcal{C}\}.$$

In this case, $\text{vec}(\mathcal{C})$ is a k-dimensional $\mathbb{F}_q$-subspace of $\mathbb{F}_q^{mn}$.

Definition 4. Let $\mathcal{C}$ and $\mathcal{D}$ be two $[m \times n, k]$ matrix codes over $\mathbb{F}_q$. We say that $\mathcal{C}$ and $\mathcal{D}$ are *equivalent* if there exist two matrices $\mathbf{A} \in \text{GL}_m(q)$ and $\mathbf{B} \in \text{GL}_n(q)$ such that $\mathcal{D} = \mathbf{A}\mathcal{C}\mathbf{B}$, i.e. for all $\mathbf{C} \in \mathcal{C}$, $\mathbf{A}\mathbf{C}\mathbf{B} \in \mathcal{D}$.

The equivalence between two matrix codes can be expressed using the Kronecker product of $\mathbf{A}^\top$ and $\mathbf{B}$, which we denote by $\mathbf{A}^\top \otimes \mathbf{B}$.

Lemma 1. *Let $\mathcal{C}$ and $\mathcal{D}$ be two $[m \times n, k]$ matrix codes over $\mathbb{F}_q$. Suppose that $\mathcal{C}$ and $\mathcal{D}$ are equivalent with $\mathcal{D} = \mathbf{A}\mathcal{C}\mathbf{B}$, with $\mathbf{A} \in \mathrm{GL}_m(q)$ and $\mathbf{B} \in \mathrm{GL}_n(q)$. If $\mathbf{G}$ and $\mathbf{G}'$ are generator matrices for $\mathcal{C}$ and $\mathcal{D}$ respectively, then there exists a $\mathbf{T} \in \mathrm{GL}_k(q)$ such that $\mathbf{G}' = \mathbf{T}\mathbf{G}(\mathbf{A}^\top \otimes \mathbf{B})$.*

It is common to write the generator matrices in systematic form (i.e., as a matrix of the shape $(I|M)$); we denote this operation by SF. Following Lemma 1, this gives us that $\mathcal{D} = \mathbf{A}\mathcal{C}\mathbf{B}$ if and only if $\mathsf{SF}(\mathbf{G}') = \mathsf{SF}(\mathbf{G}(\mathbf{A}^\top \otimes \mathbf{B}))$.
To simplify notation, we introduce the following operator:

$$\pi_{\mathbf{A},\mathbf{B}}(\mathbf{G}) := \mathbf{G}(\mathbf{A}^\top \otimes \mathbf{B}).$$

We are now ready to describe some hard problems connected to the objects we just introduced. The Matrix Code Equivalence (MCE) problem is formally defined as follows:

Problem 2 (Matrix Code Equivalence).
$\mathsf{MCE}(k, n, m, \mathcal{C}, \mathcal{D})$:
Given: Two k-dimensional matrix codes $\mathcal{C}, \mathcal{D} \subset \mathcal{M}_{m,n}(q)$.
Goal: Determine if there exist $\mathbf{A} \in \mathrm{GL}_m(q), \mathbf{B} \in \mathrm{GL}_n(q)$ such that $\mathcal{D} = \mathbf{A}\mathcal{C}\mathbf{B}$.

The map $(\mathbf{A}, \mathbf{B}) : \mathbf{C} \mapsto \mathbf{A}\mathbf{C}\mathbf{B}$ is an *isometry* between $\mathcal{C}$ and $\mathcal{D}$, in the sense that it preserves the rank i.e. $\mathrm{Rank}\,\mathbf{C} = \mathrm{Rank}(\mathbf{A}\mathbf{C}\mathbf{B})$. When $n = m$, such isometries can also be extended by transpositions of codewords, however, we choose to work with this smaller set of isometries for simplicity, at no cost to cryptographic security. Note that, although we defined MCE as a decisional problem, our signature construction relies on the computational version of it.

Remark 1. We thank Giuseppe D'Alconzo for the following sharp observation: An MCE instance of dimension k with $m \times n$ matrices over $\mathbb{F}_q$ can be viewed as a 3-tensor problem, which is symmetrical in its arguments k, m and n. This means that it is equivalent to an MCE instance of dimension m with $k \times n$ matrices and to an MCE instance of dimension n with $k \times m$ matrices. Switching to equivalent instances is a matter of changing perspective on the $k \times m \times n$ object over $\mathbb{F}_q$ defined by $A_{ijl} = A_{ij}^{(l)}$. In other words, each basis matrix $m \times n$ defines a slice of a cube, and one can take different slices for equivalent instances.

Finally, we present a *multiple-instance* version of MCE, which is at the base of one of the optimizations, using *multiple public keys*, which we will describe in Sect. 5. It is easy to see that this new problem reduces to MCE, as done for instance in [8] for the Hamming case.

Problem 3 (Multiple Matrix Code Equivalence).
$\mathsf{MMCE}(k, n, m, r, \mathcal{C}, \mathcal{D}_1, \dots, \mathcal{D}_r)$:
Given: $(r + 1)$ k-dimensional matrix codes $\mathcal{C}, \mathcal{D}_1, \dots, \mathcal{D}_r \subset \mathcal{M}_{m,n}(\mathbb{F}_q)$.
Goal: Find – if any – $\mathbf{A} \in \mathrm{GL}_m(q), \mathbf{B} \in \mathrm{GL}_n(q)$ such that $\mathcal{D}_i = \mathbf{A}\mathcal{C}\mathbf{B}$ for some $i \in \{1, \dots, r\}$.

The MCE problem has been shown to be at least as hard as the Code Equivalence problem in the Hamming metric [22]. Furthermore, under moderate assumptions, MCE is equivalent to the homogeneous version of the Quadratic Maps Linear Equivalence problem (QMLE) [45], which is considered the hardest among polynomial equivalence problems. An extensive security evaluation will be given in Sect. 6, encompassing an overview of the best attack techniques and concrete security estimates. From this, we infer a choice of parameters in Sect. 7.1.

To conclude, we now lay out the details of the MCE-based group action, given by the action of isometries on k-dimensional matrix codes. That is, the set X is formed by the k-dimensional matrix codes of size $m \times n$ over some base field $\mathbb{F}_q$, and the group $G = \mathrm{GL}_m(q) \times \mathrm{GL}_n(q)$ acts on this set via isometries as follows:

$$\star : \quad G \times X \quad \to \quad X$$
$$((\mathbf{A}, \mathbf{B}), \mathcal{C}) \mapsto \mathbf{A}\mathcal{C}\mathbf{B}$$

We write $\mathcal{G}_{m,n}(q)$ to denote this group of isometries and $\mathcal{M}_{k,m,n}(q)$ for the set of k-dimensional matrix codes; to simplify notation, we drop the indices k, m, n and q when clear from context. Then, for this MCE-based group action the Vectorization Problem is precisely Problem 2. This action is not commutative and in general neither transitive nor free. We can restrict the set $\mathcal{M}$ to a single well-chosen orbit to make the group action both transitive and free. In fact, picking any orbit generated from some starting code $\mathcal{C}$ ensures transitivity, and the group action is free if the chosen code $\mathcal{C}$ has trivial automorphism group $\mathrm{Aut}_{\mathcal{G}}(\mathcal{C}) := \{\varphi \in \mathcal{G} : \varphi(\mathcal{C}) = \mathcal{C}\}$, where trivial means up to scalars in $\mathbb{F}_q{}^2$. The non-commutativity is both positive and negative: although it limits the cryptographical design possibilities, e.g. key exchange becomes hard, it prevents quantum attacks to which commutative cryptographic group actions are vulnerable, such as Kuperberg's algorithm for the dihedral hidden subgroup problem [33].

With regards to efficiency, it is immediate to notice that our group action is very promising, given that the entirety of the operations in the proposed protocols is simple linear algebra; this is in contrast with code-based literature (where complex decoding algorithms are usually required) and other group actions (e.g. isogeny-based) which are burdened by computationally heavy operations. Further details about performance are given in details about performance are given Sect. 7.

4   Protocols from Matrix Code Equivalence

The efficient non-commutative cryptographic group action provided by MCE from Sect. 3 yields a promising building block for post-quantum cryptographic schemes. In this section, we obtain a digital signature scheme by

---

[2] More accurately, as the action of an isometry (A, B) is only interesting up to scalars $\lambda, \mu \in \mathbb{F}_q$, the group that is acting *freely* is $\mathrm{PGL}_m(q) \times \mathrm{PGL}_n(q)$.

Public Data	**I. Keygen()**

Public Data

$q, m, n, k, \lambda \in \mathbb{N}$.
hash : $\{0,1\}^* \to \{0,1\}^{2\lambda}$.

II. Commit(pk)

1. $\tilde{\mathbf{A}}, \tilde{\mathbf{B}} \xleftarrow{\$} \mathrm{GL}_m(q) \times \mathrm{GL}_n(q)$.
2. Compute $\tilde{\mathbf{G}} = \mathsf{SF}(\pi_{\tilde{\mathbf{A}}, \tilde{\mathbf{B}}}(\mathbf{G}_0))$.
3. Compute $h = \mathsf{hash}(\tilde{\mathbf{G}})$.
4. Set cmt $= h$.
5. Send cmt to verifier.

IV. Response(sk, pk, cmt, ch)

1. If ch $= 0$ set $(\mu, \nu) = (\tilde{\mathbf{A}}, \tilde{\mathbf{B}})$.
2. If ch $= 1$ set $(\mu, \nu) = (\tilde{\mathbf{A}} \mathbf{A}^{-1}, \mathbf{B}^{-1} \tilde{\mathbf{B}})$.
3. Set rsp $= (\mu, \nu)$.
4. Send rsp to verifier.

I. Keygen()

1. $\mathbf{G}_0 \xleftarrow{\$} \mathbb{F}_q^{k \times mn}$ in standard form
2. $(\mathbf{A}, \mathbf{B}) \xleftarrow{\$} \mathrm{GL}_m(q) \times \mathrm{GL}_n(q)$.
3. Compute $\mathbf{G}_1 = \mathsf{SF}(\pi_{\mathbf{A}, \mathbf{B}}(\mathbf{G}_0))$.
4. Set sk $= (\mathbf{A}, \mathbf{B})$ and pk $= (\mathbf{G}_0, \mathbf{G}_1)$.

III. Challenge()

1. $c \xleftarrow{\$} \{0, 1\}$.
2. Set ch $= c$.
3. Send ch to prover.

V. Verify(pk, cmt, ch, rsp)

1. If ch $= 0$ compute
   $h' = \mathsf{hash}(\mathsf{SF}(\pi_{\mu, \nu}(\mathbf{G}_0)))$.
2. If ch $= 1$ compute
   $h' = \mathsf{hash}(\mathsf{SF}(\pi_{\mu, \nu}(\mathbf{G}_1)))$.
3. Accept if $h' = $ cmt or reject otherwise.

Fig. 1. MCE Sigma Protocol

first designing a Sigma protocol and then applying the Fiat-Shamir transformation [28].

The first building block in our work is the Sigma protocol in Fig. 1, in which a Prover proves the knowledge of an isometry $(\mathbf{A}, \mathbf{B})$ between two equivalent matrix codes. The security result is given in Theorem 1. The proof is considered standard in the literature (similar to the one given in [14], for instance) and is therefore omitted in the interest of space.

Theorem 1. *The Sigma protocol described above is complete, 2-special sound and honest-verifier zero-knowledge assuming the hardness of the* MCE *problem.*

Applying the Fiat-Shamir transformation gives the signature scheme in Fig. 2.

Public Key and Signature Size. We begin by calculating the communication costs for the Sigma protocol of Fig. 1. Note that, for the case $c = 0$, the response (μ, ν) consists entirely of randomly-generated objects, and is efficiently represented by a single seed (that can be used to generate both matrices). This yields the following cost per round, in bits:

$$\begin{cases} 3\lambda + 1 & \text{if } c = 0 \\ 2\lambda + 1 + (m^2 + n^2)\lceil \log_2(q) \rceil & \text{if } c = 1 \end{cases}$$

remembering that seeds are λ bits and hash digests 2λ to avoid collision attacks.

For the signature scheme we calculate the sizes as follows. First, since the matrix $\mathbf{G}_0$ is random, it can also be represented via a short seed, and therefore

Public Data

$q, m, n, k, t = \lambda \in \mathbb{N}$.
hash $: \{0,1\}^* \rightarrow \{0,1\}^t$.

II. Sign(sk)

1. For all $i = 0, \ldots, t-1$:
   i. $\tilde{\mathbf{A}}_i, \tilde{\mathbf{B}}_i \xleftarrow{\$} \mathrm{GL}_m(q) \times \mathrm{GL}_n(q)$.
   ii. Compute $\tilde{\mathbf{G}}_i = \mathsf{SF}(\pi_{\tilde{\mathbf{A}}_i, \tilde{\mathbf{B}}_i}(\mathbf{G}_0))$.
2. Compute
   $h = \mathsf{hash}(\tilde{\mathbf{G}}_0, \ldots, \tilde{\mathbf{G}}_{t-1}, \mathsf{msg})$.
3. Parse $h = [h_0| \ldots |h_{t-1}]$, $h_i \in \{0,1\}$.
4. For all $i = 0, \ldots, t-1$:
   i. Set $(\mu_i, \nu_i) = (\tilde{\mathbf{A}}_i \mathbf{A}_{h_i}^{-1}, \mathbf{B}_{h_i}^{-1} \tilde{\mathbf{B}}_i)$.
5. Set $\sigma = (h, \mu_0, \ldots, \mu_{t-1}, \nu_0, \ldots, \nu_{t-1})$.
6. Send σ to verifier.

I. Keygen()

1. $\mathbf{G}_0 \xleftarrow{\$} \mathbb{F}_q^{k \times mn}$ in standard form
2. Set $\mathbf{A}_0 = \mathbf{I}_m$, $\mathbf{B}_0 = \mathbf{I}_n$.
3. $\mathbf{A}_1, \mathbf{B}_1 \xleftarrow{\$} \mathrm{GL}_m(q) \times \mathrm{GL}_n(q)$.
4. Compute $\mathbf{G}_1 = \mathsf{SF}(\pi_{\mathbf{A}_1, \mathbf{B}_1}(\mathbf{G}_0))$.
5. Set $\mathsf{sk} = (\mathbf{A}_1, \mathbf{B}_1)$ and $\mathsf{pk} = (\mathbf{G}_0, \mathbf{G}_1)$.

III. Verify(pk, msg, σ)

1. Parse $h = [h_0| \ldots |h_{t-1}]$, $h_i \in \{0,1\}$.
2. For all $i = 0, \ldots, t-1$:
   i. Set $\hat{\mathbf{G}}_i = \mathsf{SF}(\pi_{\mu_i, \nu_i}(\mathbf{G}_{h_i}))$.
3. Compute
   $h' = \mathsf{hash}(\hat{\mathbf{G}}_0, \ldots, \hat{\mathbf{G}}_{t-1}, \mathsf{msg})$.
4. Accept if $h' = h$ or reject otherwise.

Fig. 2. The basic signature scheme

can be included in the public key at negligible cost (see Algorithm I. of Fig. 2). Keeping in mind that the number of rounds t is equal to the value of the desired security level λ, the protocol above yields the following sizes (in bits):

– Public key size: $\lambda + k(mn - k)\lceil \log_2(q) \rceil$
– Average signature size: $t\left(1 + \dfrac{\lambda + (m^2 + n^2)\lceil \log_2(q) \rceil}{2}\right)$.

5   Matrix Equivalence Digital Signature—MEDS

We apply the following optimizations from the literature to the basic Fiat-Shamir-based signature scheme described in Sect. 4, to obtain our Matrix Equivalence Digital Signature (MEDS).

Multiple Keys. The first optimization is a popular one in literature [8,13,23], and it consists of utilizing multiple public keys, i.e. multiple equivalent codes $\mathbf{G}_0, \ldots, \mathbf{G}_{s-1}$, each defined as $\mathbf{G}_i = \mathsf{SF}(\pi_{\mathbf{A}_i, \mathbf{B}_i}(\mathbf{G}_0))$ for uniformly chosen secret keys[3] $(\mathbf{A}_i, \mathbf{B}_i)$. This allows to reduce the soundness error from $1/2$ to $1/2^\ell$, where $\ell = \lceil \log_2 s \rceil$. The optimization works by grouping the challenge bits into strings of ℓ bits, which can then be interpreted as binary representations of the indices $\{0, \ldots, s-1\}$, thus dictating which public key will be used in the protocol. Security is preserved since the proof of unforgeability can be easily modified to rely on a multi-instance version of the underlying problem: in our case, MMCE (Problem 3). Note that, although in the literature s is chosen to be a power of 2, this does not have to be the case. In this work, we will instead select the value of s based on the best outcome in terms of performance and signature size.

---

[3] Again, for convenience, we choose $\mathbf{A}_0 = \mathbf{I}_m$, $\mathbf{B}_0 = \mathbf{I}_n$.

Remark 2. This optimization comes at the cost of an s-fold increase in public-key size. As shown for instance in [23], it would be possible to reduce this impact by using Merkle trees to a hash of the tree commitment of all the public keys. This, however, would add some significant overhead to the signature size, because it would be necessary to include the paths for all openings. Considering the sizes of the objects involved, such an optimization is not advantageous in our case.

Partially Seeding the Public Key. The previous optimization comes at significant cost to the public key, so we propose a new optimization that trades public key size for private key size. This optimization is inspired by the trade-off in the key generation of Rainbow [24] and UOV [11]. It has not been previously used in Fiat-Shamir signatures, but we expect it can be used successfully in any scheme coming from equivalence problems especially the ones using the previous optimization, such as [8,13,23]. With this optimization, instead of generating the secret $(\mathbf{A}_i, \mathbf{B}_i)$ from a secret seed and then deriving the public $\mathbf{G}_i$, we generate $\mathbf{G}_i$ partially from a public seed and then use it to find $(\mathbf{A}_i, \mathbf{B}_i)$ and the rest of the public key $\mathbf{G}_i$. In more detail, in order to generate the public $\mathbf{G}_i$ and the corresponding secret $(\mathbf{A}_i, \mathbf{B}_i)$ we perform the following:

- We perform a secret change of basis of $\mathbf{G}_0$ by multiplying it by a secret matrix $\mathbf{T} \in \mathrm{GL}_k(q)$ to obtain $\mathbf{G}_0'$. Assume the codewords from $\mathbf{G}_0'$ are $\mathbf{P}_1^0, \mathbf{P}_2^0, \ldots, \mathbf{P}_k^0$.
- For each $i \in \{1, \ldots, s-1\}$, we generate from a public seed a complete $m \times n$ codeword $\mathbf{P}_1^i$ and the top $m-1$ rows of codeword $\mathbf{P}_2^i$ (depending on the parameters m, n one can get slightly more rows when $m \neq n$).
- Find $\mathbf{A}_i$ and $\mathbf{B}_i$ from the linear relations:

$$\mathbf{P}_1^i \mathbf{B}_i^{-1} = \mathbf{A}_i \mathbf{P}_1^0$$
$$\mathbf{P}_2^i \mathbf{B}_i^{-1} = \mathbf{A}_i \mathbf{P}_2^0$$

by fixing the first (top left) value of $\mathbf{A}_i$.
- Find $\mathbf{P}_j^i = \mathbf{A}_i \mathbf{P}_j^0 \mathbf{B}_i$ for all $j \in \{3, \ldots, k\}$.
- Construct the public $\mathbf{G}_i$ from $\mathbf{P}_1^i, \mathbf{P}_2^i, \ldots, \mathbf{P}_k^i$.

The public key then is the public seed together with $\mathbf{P}_3^i, \ldots, \mathbf{P}_k^i$. For verification, the complete $\mathbf{G}_i$ are reconstructed using the seed.

Fixed-Weight Challenges. Another common optimization is the use of fixed-weight challenges. The idea is to generate the challenge string h with a fixed number of 1s and 0s, i.e. Hamming weight, rather than uniformly at random. This is because, when $h_i = 0$, the response (μ_i, ν_i) consists entirely of randomly-generated objects, and so one can just transmit the seed used for generating them. This creates a noticeable imbalance between the two types of responses, and hence it makes sense to minimize the number of 1 values. To this end, one can utilize a so-called *weight-restricted hash function*, that outputs values in $\mathbb{Z}_{2,w}^t$, by which we denote the set of vectors with elements in $\{0, 1\}$ of length t and weight w. In this way, although the length of the challenge strings increases,

---

Public Data

$q, m, n, k, \lambda, t, s, w \in \mathbb{N}$.
hash : $\{0,1\}^* \to \{0,1\}^\lambda$.

I. Keygen()

1. $\mathbf{G}_0 \xleftarrow{\$} \mathbb{F}_q^{k \times mn}$ in standard form.
2. Set $\mathbf{A}_0 = \mathbf{I}_m$, $\mathbf{B}_0 = \mathbf{I}_n$.
3. $\mathbf{T} \xleftarrow{\$} \mathrm{GL}_k(q)$
4. Compute $\mathbf{G}_0' = \mathbf{T}\mathbf{G}_0$.
5. Parse the first two rows of $\mathbf{G}_0'$ into $\mathbf{P}_1^0, \mathbf{P}_2^0 \in \mathbb{F}_q^{m \times n}$
6. For all $j = 1, \ldots, s - 1$:
   i. $\mathbf{P}_1^j, \mathbf{P}_2^j \xleftarrow{\$} \mathbb{F}_q^{m \times n}$
   ii. Find $\mathbf{A}_j$ and $\mathbf{B}_j$ from:
   $$\mathbf{P}_1^j \mathbf{B}_j^{-1} = \mathbf{A}_j \mathbf{P}_1^0$$
   $$\mathbf{P}_2^j \mathbf{B}_j^{-1} = \mathbf{A}_j \mathbf{P}_2^0$$
   iii. Compute $\mathbf{G}_j = \mathrm{SF}(\pi_{\mathbf{A}_j, \mathbf{B}_j}(\mathbf{G}_0'))$.
7. Set $\mathsf{sk} = (\mathbf{A}_1^{-1}, \mathbf{B}_1^{-1}, \ldots, \mathbf{A}_{s-1}^{-1}, \mathbf{B}_{s-1}^{-1})$.
8. Set $\mathsf{pk} = (\mathbf{G}_0, \mathbf{G}_1, \ldots, \mathbf{G}_{s-1})$.

II. Sign(sk)

1. For all $i = 0, \ldots, t - 1$:
   i. $\tilde{\mathbf{A}}_i, \tilde{\mathbf{B}}_i \xleftarrow{\$} \mathrm{GL}_m(q) \times \mathrm{GL}_n(q)$.
   ii. Compute $\tilde{\mathbf{G}}_i = \mathrm{SF}(\pi_{\tilde{\mathbf{A}}_i, \tilde{\mathbf{B}}_i}(\mathbf{G}_0))$.
2. Compute
   $h = \mathsf{hash}(\tilde{\mathbf{G}}_0, \ldots, \tilde{\mathbf{G}}_{t-1}, \mathsf{msg})$.
3. Expand h to $(h_0, \ldots, h_{t-1})$, $0 \le h_i < s$.
4. For all $i = 0, \ldots, t - 1$:
   i. Set $(\mu_i, \nu_i) = (\tilde{\mathbf{A}}_i \mathbf{A}_{h_i}^{-1}, \mathbf{B}_{h_i}^{-1} \tilde{\mathbf{B}}_i)$.
5. Set $\sigma = (\mu_0, \ldots, \mu_{t-1}, \nu_0, \ldots, \nu_{t-1}, h)$.
6. Send σ to verifier.

III. Verify(pk, msg, σ)

1. Expand h to $(h_0, \ldots, h_{t-1})$, $0 \le h_i < s$.
2. For all $i = 0, \ldots, t - 1$:
   i. Set $\hat{\mathbf{G}}_i = \mathrm{SF}(\pi_{\mu_i, \nu_i}(\mathbf{G}_{h_i}))$.
3. Compute
   $h' = \mathsf{hash}(\hat{\mathbf{G}}_0, \ldots, \hat{\mathbf{G}}_{t-1}, \mathsf{msg})$.
4. Accept if $h' = h$ or reject otherwise.

Fig. 3. The MEDS Protocol

the overall communication cost scales down proportionally to the value of w. In terms of security, this optimization only entails a small modification in the statement of the Forking Lemma, and it is enough to choose parameters such that $\log_2 \binom{t}{w} \ge \lambda$. Note that this optimization can easily be combined with the previous one, by mandating hash digests in $\mathbb{Z}_{s,w}^t$ and choosing parameters such that $\log_2 \left(\binom{t}{w}(s-1)^w\right) \ge \lambda$. In practice, this can be achieved with a hash function hash : $\{0,1\}^* \to \{0,1\}^\lambda$, by expanding the output to a t-tuple $(h_0, \ldots, h_{t-1})$, $0 \le h_i < s$ of weight w.

Seed Tree. Finally, the signature size can be optimized again using a *seed tree*. This primitive allows to generate the many seeds used throughout the protocol in a recursive way, starting from a master seed mseed and building a binary tree, via repeated PRNG applications, having t seeds as leaves. When the required $t - w$ values need to be retrieved, it is then enough to reveal the appropriate sequence of nodes. This reduces the space required for the seeds from $\lambda(t-w)$ to $\lambda N_{\mathrm{seeds}}$, where N_{seeds} can be upper bounded by $2^{\lceil \log_2(w) \rceil} + w(\lceil \log_2(t) \rceil - \lceil \log_2(w) \rceil - 1)$, as shown in [29]. We refer the reader to Section 2.7 of [12] for more details. As suggested in [12], we are including a 256-bit salt to ward off multi-target collision attacks and the leaf address as identifier for domain separation in the inputs of the seed-tree hash functions.

To give a complete picture, we present the MEDS protocol in Fig. 3, in its final form, including all applicable variants. The various parameters control different optimization: for instance s refers to the number of public keys used, whereas w refers to the fixed weight of the challenge hash string. Parameter choices will be thoroughly discussed in Sect. 7.1.

Public Key and Signature Size. With these various optimizations, we obtain the following public key and signature size for MEDS:

- MEDS public key size: $\lambda + (s-1)((k-2)(mn-k)+n)\lceil \log_2(q)\rceil$
- MEDS signature size:

$$\underbrace{\lambda}_{h} + \underbrace{w(m^2 + n^2)\lceil \log_2(q)\rceil}_{\{\mu_i,\nu_i\}_{h_i=1}} + \underbrace{\lambda N_{\text{seeds}}}_{\{\mu_i,\nu_i\}_{h_i=0}} + \underbrace{2\lambda}_{salt}$$

6 Concrete Security Analysis

In this section, we will mostly use the Big O notation $\mathcal{O}$ to express the complexity of algorithms. Where we are not interested in the polynomial factor we will use $\mathcal{O}^*$. We note that despite the notation, the estimates are quite tight and provide a good basis for choosing parameters.

Recall that the goal of an adversary against MCE is to recover the matrices $\mathbf{A}$ and $\mathbf{B}$, given a description of the matrix codes $\mathcal{C}$ and $\mathcal{D}$. The most naïve attack would be to try every $\mathbf{A} \in \mathrm{GL}_m(q)$ and $\mathbf{B} \in \mathrm{GL}_n(q)$ until we find the correct isometry, amounting to a complexity of $\mathcal{O}(q^{n^2+m^2})$.

The naïve attack can be improved by noting that once one of the matrices $\mathbf{A}$ or $\mathbf{B}$ is known, the resulting problem becomes easy [22]. Hence, we only need to brute-force one of $\mathbf{A}$ or $\mathbf{B}$, so the complexity becomes $\mathcal{O}^*(q^{\min\{m^2,n^2\}})$.

In the rest of the section, we will see that there exist several non-trivial attacks that perform much better than this upper bound.

6.1 Birthday-Based Graph-Theoretical Algorithms for Solving MCE

Recent works [22,45] investigate the hardness of MCE by connecting it to other equivalence problems, namely, the Code Equivalence problem in the Hamming metric [22] and the Quadratic Maps Linear Equivalence problem (QMLE) [45]. The latter provides complexity analysis by viewing MCE as an instance of QMLE. We recap their results here. For better understanding, we include the definition of the related QMLE problem.

Problem 4. QMLE$(k, N, \mathcal{F}, \mathcal{P})$:
Given: Two k-tuples of multivariate polynomials of degree 2

$$\mathcal{F} = (f_1, f_2, \ldots, f_k), \ \mathcal{P} = (p_1, p_2, \ldots, p_k) \in \mathbb{F}_q[x_1, \ldots, x_N]^k.$$

Goal: Find – if any – matrices $\mathbf{S} \in \mathrm{GL}_N(q), \mathbf{T} \in \mathrm{GL}_k(q)$ such that

$$\mathcal{P}(\mathbf{x}) = (\mathcal{F}(\mathbf{xS}))\mathbf{T}.$$

Algorithm 1 Collision-search algorithm

1: **function** BUILDLIST($\mathcal{F}$, $\mathbb{P}$)	8: **function** COLLISIONFIND($\mathcal{F}$, $\mathcal{P}$)
2: $L \leftarrow \emptyset$	9: $L_1 \leftarrow$ BUILDLIST($\mathcal{F}$, $\mathbb{P}$)
3: **repeat**	10: $L_2 \leftarrow$ BUILDLIST($\mathcal{P}$, $\mathbb{P}$)
4: $\mathbf{x} \xleftarrow{\$} \mathbb{F}_q^{(m+n)}$	11: **for all** $(\mathbf{x}, \mathbf{y}) \in \{L_1 \times L_2\}$ **do**
5: **if** $\mathbb{P}(\mathcal{F}, \mathbf{x})$ **then** $L \leftarrow L \cup \{\mathbf{x}\}$	12: $\phi \leftarrow$ INHQMLE($\mathbf{x}, \mathbf{y}$)
6: **until** $|L| = \ell$	13: **if** $\phi \neq \perp$ **then**
7: **return** L	14: **return** solution ϕ
	15: **return** $\perp$

We denote by hQMLE, inhQMLE and BMLE the related problems when the polynomials are homogeneous of degree 2, inhomogeneous and bilinear, respectively. It was shown in [45] that, under the assumption that the two codes $\mathcal{C}$ and $\mathcal{D}$ have trivial automorphism groups (which is believed to be true with overwhelming probability for big enough parameters), MCE($k, n, m, \mathcal{C}, \mathcal{D}$) is equivalent to hQMLE($k, N, \mathcal{F}, \mathcal{P}$) where $N = m + n$. Concretely, an MCE instance with a solution $(\mathbf{A}, \mathbf{B})$ is transformed into an hQMLE instance with a solution $(\mathbf{S}, \mathbf{T})$ where $\mathbf{S} = \begin{bmatrix} \mathbf{A} & \mathbf{0} \\ \mathbf{0} & \mathbf{B}^\top \end{bmatrix}$ and $\mathbf{T}$ corresponds to a change of basis of $\mathcal{D}$. Therefore it is possible to apply algorithms for solving hQMLE to MCE instances such as the graph-theoretic algorithm of Bouillaguet et al. [17]. The algorithm is basically a collision-search algorithm comprised of two steps, as given in Algorithm 1. In the first step we build two lists L_1 and L_2 of size ℓ of elements in $\mathbb{F}_q^{(m+n)}$ that satisfy a predefined distinguishing property $\mathbb{P}$ related to the given systems of polynomials $\mathcal{F}$ and $\mathcal{P}$ and that is preserved under isometry. In the second step, we try to find a collision between the two lists that will lead us to the solution. For the property $\mathbb{P}$, the authors of [17] propose:

$$\mathbb{P}(\mathcal{F}, \mathbf{x}) = \top \Leftrightarrow Dim(Ker(D_\mathbf{x}(\mathcal{F}))) = \kappa$$

for a suitably chosen κ, where $D_\mathbf{x}(\mathcal{F}) : \mathbf{y} \mapsto \mathcal{F}(\mathbf{x} + \mathbf{y}) - \mathcal{F}(\mathbf{x}) - \mathcal{F}(\mathbf{y})$ is the *differential* of $\mathcal{F}$ at a point $\mathbf{x}$. Clearly, the rank of the differential is preserved under isometry, so this is an appropriate choice of $\mathbb{P}$. Other instantiations are possible as well, as long as they are invariant under isometry, although their success depends on the distribution of elements that satisfy the property for varying κ.

Once a collision $(\mathbf{a}, \mathbf{b})$ is found, it can be used to derive an associated *inhomogeneous* QMLE instance inhQMLE $(k, (m + n), \mathcal{F}', \mathcal{P}')$ as $\mathcal{F}'(\mathbf{x}) = \mathcal{F}(\mathbf{x} + \mathbf{a})$, $\mathcal{P}'(\mathbf{x}) = \mathcal{P}(\mathbf{x} + \mathbf{b})$ on which we call an inhomogeneous solver. Since it can not be directly checked whether a pair is a collision, the solver needs to be called for each pair, similar to the guess and check approach in ISD algorithms [41].

The inhomogeneous instance can be solved much more efficiently than the homogeneous one. Heuristic evidence suggests that solving *random* instances of the inhQMLE problem using an algebraic approach takes $\mathcal{O}((m + n)^9)$ operations [27], however, the derived inhQMLE instances from the collision-search attack are not random enough. These specific instances have a solver with a complexity of $\mathcal{O}(q^\kappa)$ [16]. As κ is typically chosen to be small, this approach is still efficient in practice. Following the analysis from [45], the concrete complexity of the algorithm for $k \leqslant 2(m + n)$ follows a birthday argument and is the maximum of the complexity of the two steps, i.e.:

$$\max(\sqrt{q^{(m+n)}/d} \cdot C_\mathbb{P}, dq^{(m+n)} \cdot C_{i\mathsf{Q}}), \tag{1}$$

with success probability of $\approx 63\%$. Here, $C_\mathbb{P}$ denotes the cost of checking whether an element satisfies the property $\mathbb{P}$, d is the proportion of elements satisfying $\mathbb{P}$ and $C_{i\mathsf{Q}}$ denotes the cost of a single query to inhQMLE. Note that d can be calculated as $d = 1/\mathcal{O}(q^{\kappa^2 + \kappa(k-(m+n))})$ and κ is chosen such that it minimizes Eq. (1). Asymptotically, the complexity is $\mathcal{O}^*(q^{\frac{2}{3}(m+n)})$ by balancing the steps [45]. The memory complexity is simply the size of the lists.

It is pointed out in [45] that when $k \geq 2(m + n)$, we can no longer assume that we have any elements satisfying $\mathbb{P}$, which forces us to consider *all* elements in the collision search giving a complexity of $\mathcal{O}(q^{m+n})$. In that case, we can consider choosing arbitrarily one element $\mathbf{x}$ and checking for a collision with all other elements $\mathbf{y} \in \mathbb{F}_q^{m+n}$. Note that this approach was also proposed in [17], and can be applied to any parameter set, thus giving an upper-bound on the complexity of a classical collision-search algorithm.

For a quantum version of Algorithm 1, both BUILDLIST and COLLISIONFIND can be seen as searches of unstructured databases of a certain size, hence Grover's algorithm applies to both: we can build the list L using only $\sqrt{\ell \cdot d^{-1}}$ searches, and we can find a collision using only $\sqrt{|L_1 \times L_2|}$ queries to the solver. This requires both $\mathbb{P}$ and inhQMLE to be performed in superposition. The balance between both sides remains the same. In total, the complexity of the quantum version becomes $\mathcal{O}^*(q^{\frac{1}{3}(m+n)})$.

Collision-Search Algorithm Using Non-trivial Roots. When viewing an MCE instance as an hQMLE instance, it is possible to use certain bilinear properties to improve Algorithm 1. When $n = m$, such instances have approximately q^{2n-k-1} non-trivial roots, which can be used to improve a subroutine of Algorithm 1, and to make it deterministic instead of probabilistic [45]. In practice, such non-trivial roots exist **i)** almost always when $k < 2n$, **ii)** with probability $1/q$ for $k = 2n$, **iii)** with probability $1/q^{k+1-2n}$ for $k > 2n$. The complexity of this approach is $\mathcal{O}^*(q^n)$, if such non-trivial roots exist. This complexity is proven under the assumption that the complexity of the inhomogenous QMLE solver is no greater than $\mathcal{O}(q^n)$, which holds trivially when $k \geq n$ [45], and heuristically when $k < n$. Finding the non-trivial roots can also be done using a bilinear XL algorithm [40]. We do not consider this approach in our analysis, as it is only interesting for a subset of parameters where the systems are (over)determined, i.e. when k is close to $m + n$.

6.2   Algebraic Attacks

Direct Modelling. Recently, in [45], it was shown that MCE is equivalent to BMLE. One of the natural attack avenues is thus to model the problem as an algebraic system of polynomial equations over a finite field. This approach was taken in [27], where the general Isomorphism of Polynomials (IP) problem was investigated. Here, we focus specifically on BMLE and perform a detailed complexity analysis.

First, fix arbitrary bases $(\mathbf{C}^{(1)}, \ldots, \mathbf{C}^{(k)})$ and $(\mathbf{D}^{(1)}, \ldots, \mathbf{D}^{(k)})$ of the codes $\mathcal{C}$ and $\mathcal{D}$ respectively. In terms of the bases, the MCE problem can be rephrased as finding $\mathbf{A} \in \mathrm{GL}_m(q), \mathbf{B} \in \mathrm{GL}_n(q)$ and $\mathbf{T} = (t_{ij}) \in \mathrm{GL}_k(q)$ such that:

$$\sum_{1 \leqslant s \leqslant k} t_{rs}\mathbf{D}^{(s)} = \mathbf{A}\mathbf{C}^{(r)}\mathbf{B}, \quad \forall r, 1 \leqslant r \leqslant k \tag{2}$$

The system (2) consists of knm equations in the $m^2 + n^2 + k^2$ unknown coefficients of the matrices $\mathbf{A}, \mathbf{B}$ and $\mathbf{T}$. The quadratic terms of the equations are always of the form $\gamma a_{ij}b_{i'j'}$ for some coefficients a_{ij} and $b_{i'j'}$ of $\mathbf{A}$ and $\mathbf{B}$ respectively which means the system (2) is bilinear. Note that the coefficients of $\mathbf{T}$ appear only linearly. As previously, we can guess the m^2 variables from $\mathbf{A}$, which will lead us to a linear system that can be easily solved. However, we can do better by exploiting the structure of the equations.

For ease of readability of the rest of the paragraph denote by $\mathbf{M}_{i\_}$ and $\mathbf{M}_{\_i}$ the i-th row and i-th column of a matrix $\mathbf{M}$. Note that, in (2), for $i \neq j$, the unknown coefficients from two rows $\mathbf{A}_{i\_}$ and $\mathbf{A}_{j\_}$ don't appear in the same equation. Symmetrically, the same holds for $\mathbf{B}_{\_i}$ and $\mathbf{B}_{\_j}$, but we will make use of it for the matrix $\mathbf{A}$. Thus, we can consider only part of the system, and control the number of variables from $\mathbf{A}$. The goal is to reduce the number of variables that we need to guess before obtaining an overdetermined linear system, and we want to do this in an optimal way. Consider the first α rows from $\mathbf{A}$. Extracting the equations that correspond to these rows in (2) leads us to the system:

$$\sum_{1 \leqslant s \leqslant k} t_{rs}\mathbf{D}^{(s)}_{i\_} = \mathbf{A}_{i\_}\mathbf{C}^{(r)}\mathbf{B}, \quad \forall r, i, \ 1 \leqslant r \leqslant k, \ 1 \leqslant i \leqslant \alpha. \tag{3}$$

Guessing the αm coefficients from $\mathbf{A}_{i\_}$ leads to a linear system of αkn equations in $n^2 + k^2$ variables. Choosing $\alpha = \lceil \frac{n^2+k^2}{kn} \rceil$, the complexity of the approach becomes $\mathcal{O}(q^{m\lceil \frac{n^2+k^2}{kn} \rceil}(n^2 + k^2)^3)$. For the usual choice of $m = n = k$, this reduces to at least $\alpha = 2$ and a complexity of $\mathcal{O}(q^{2n}n^6)$.

Note that, one can directly solve the bilinear system (3) using for example XL [20] and the analysis for bilinear systems from [40] (similar results can be obtained from [25]). We have verified, however, that due to the large number of variables compared to the available equations, the complexity greatly surpasses the one of the simple linearization attack presented above.

Improved Modelling. In order to improve upon this baseline algebraic attack, we will model the problem differently and completely avoid the t_{rs} variables. This modelling is in the spirit of the minors modellings of MinRank as in [7, 26].

As previously, let $\mathbf{G}$ and $\mathbf{G}'$ be the $k \times mn$ generator matrices of the equivalent codes $\mathcal{C}$ and $\mathcal{D}$ respectively. Then from Lemma 1, $\tilde{\mathbf{G}} = \mathbf{G}(\mathbf{A}^\top \otimes \mathbf{B})$ is a generator matrix of $\mathcal{D}$ for some invertible matrices $\mathbf{A}$ and $\mathbf{B}$. We will take the coefficients of $\mathbf{A}$ and $\mathbf{B}$ to be our unknowns. A crucial observation for this attack is that each row $\tilde{\mathbf{G}}_{i_-}$ of $\tilde{\mathbf{G}}$ is in the span of the rows of $\mathbf{G}'$, since $\mathbf{G}'$ and $\tilde{\mathbf{G}}$ define the same code. This means that adding $\tilde{\mathbf{G}}_{i_-}$ to $\mathbf{G}'$ does not change the code, i.e.,

$$^{(i)}\mathbf{G}' = \begin{pmatrix} \mathbf{G}' \\ \tilde{\mathbf{G}}_{i_-} \end{pmatrix}$$

is not of full rank. From here, all maximal minors $\left| \left({}^{(i)}\mathbf{G}'_{-j_1}\ {}^{(i)}\mathbf{G}'_{-j_2}\ \ldots^{(i)}\mathbf{G}'_{-j_{k+1}} \right) \right|$ of $^{(i)}\mathbf{G}'$, for every $\{j_1, j_2, \ldots, j_{k+1}\} \subset \{1, 2, \ldots, mn\}$, are zero.

Now, as in a minors modeling of MinRank, we can form equations in the unknown coefficients of $\mathbf{A}$ and $\mathbf{B}$ by equating all maximal minors to zero, which amounts to a total of $\binom{mn}{k+1}$ equations. Since the unknown coefficients of $\mathbf{A}$ and $\mathbf{B}$ appear only in the last row of the minors, and only bilinearly, the whole system is also bilinear. Thus we have reduced the problem to solving the bilinear system

$$\left\{ \left| \left({}^{(i)}\mathbf{G}'_{-j_1}\ {}^{(i)}\mathbf{G}'_{-j_2}\ \ldots^{(i)}\mathbf{G}'_{-j_{k+1}} \right) \right| = 0, \ \begin{array}{l} \text{for all } i \in \{1, 2, \ldots, k\} \text{ and all} \\ \{j_1, j_2, \ldots, j_{k+1}\} \subset \{1, 2, \ldots, mn\} \end{array} \right. \quad (4)$$

in the $m^2 + n^2$ unknown coefficients of $\mathbf{A}$ and $\mathbf{B}$.

At first sight, (4) seems to have more than enough equations to fully linearize the system. However, the majority of these equations are linearly dependent. In fact, there are only $(mn - k)k$ linearly independent equations. To see this, fix some i and consider a minor $\left| \left({}^{(i)}\mathbf{G}'_{-j_1}\ {}^{(i)}\mathbf{G}'_{-j_2}\ \ldots^{(i)}\mathbf{G}'_{-j_{k+1}} \right) \right|$ of $^{(i)}\mathbf{G}'$. Since all rows except the first don't contain any variables, the equation

$$\left| \left({}^{(i)}\mathbf{G}'_{-j_1}\ {}^{(i)}\mathbf{G}'_{-j_2}\ \ldots^{(i)}\mathbf{G}'_{-j_{k+1}} \right) \right| = 0$$

basically defines the linear dependence between the columns $^{(i)}\mathbf{G}'_{-j_1}, \ldots^{(i)}\mathbf{G}'_{-j_{k+1}}$. But the rank of the matrix is k, so all columns can be expressed through some set of k independent columns. Thus, in total, for a fixed i we have $mn - k$ independent equations and in total $(mn - k)k$ equations for all i.

Alternatively, we can obtain the same amount of equations from $\tilde{\mathbf{G}}$ and the generator matrix $\mathbf{G}'^\perp$ of the dual code of $\mathcal{D}$. Since $\tilde{\mathbf{G}}$ should also be a generator matrix of $\mathcal{D}$, we construct the system:

$$\mathbf{G}'^\perp \cdot \tilde{\mathbf{G}}^\top = \mathbf{0},$$

which is again a system of $(mn - k)k$ bilinear equations in $n^2 + m^2$ variables.

The complexity of solving the obtained system using either of the modellings strongly depends on the dimension of the code – it is the smallest for $k = mn/2$, and grows as k reduces (dually, as k grows towards mn). In Sect. 7 we give the concrete complexity estimate for solving the system for the chosen parameters using bilinear XL and the analysis from [40].

The attack does not seem to benefit a lot from being run on a quantum computer. Since the costly part comes from solving a huge linear system for which there are no useful quantum algorithms available, the only way is to 'Groverize' an enumeration part of the algorithm. One could enumerate over one set of the variables, either of $\mathbf{A}$ or $\mathbf{B}$, typically the smaller one, and solve a biliner system of less variables. Grover's algorithm could then speed up quadratically this enumeration. However, since in the classical case the best approach is to not use enumeration, this approach only makes sense for quite small values of the field size i.e. only when $q < 4$. In this parameter regime, however, combinatorial attacks perform significantly better, so this approach becomes irrelevant.

6.3   Leon-Like Algorithm Adapted to the Rank Metric

Leon [34] proposed an algorithm against the code equivalence problem in the Hamming metric that relies on the basic property that isometries preserve the weight of the codewords and that the weight distribution of two equivalent codes is the same. Thus, finding the set of codewords of smallest weight in both codes reveals enough information to find a permutation that maps one set to the other, which with high probability is the unknown isometry between the codes. This algorithm is quite unbalanced and heavy on the 'codewords finding' side, since it requires finding all codewords of minimal weight. Beullens [10] proposed to relax the procedure and instead perform a collision based algorithm, much in the spirit of Algorithm 1: Build two lists of elements of the codes of particular weight (the distinguishing property from [10] actually also includes the multiset of entries of a codeword) and find a collision between them. As in Leon's algorithm and Algorithm 1, the 'collision finding' part employs an efficient subroutine for reconstructing the isometry.

The approach from the Hamming metric can be translated to matrix codes and can be used to solve MCE, but some adjustments are necessary. First of all note that finding codewords of a given rank r is equivalent to an instance of MinRank [19,26] for k matrices of size $m \times n$ over $\mathbb{F}_q$. Depending on the parameters, we have noticed that the Kipnis-Shamir modelling [32] and Bardet's modelling [7] perform the best, so we use both in our complexity estimates.

For the collision part, notice that given two codewords $\mathbf{C}_1$ from $\mathcal{C}$ and $\mathbf{D}_1$ from $\mathcal{D}$, it is not possible to determine the isometry $(\mathbf{A}, \mathbf{B})$, as there are many isometries possible between single codewords. Thus, there is no efficient way of checking that these codewords collide nor finding the correct isometry. On the other hand, a pair of codewords is typically enough. For the pairs $(\mathbf{C}_1, \mathbf{C}_2)$ and $(\mathbf{D}_1, \mathbf{D}_2)$ we can form the system of $2mn$ linear equations

$$\begin{cases} \mathbf{A}^{-1}\mathbf{D}_1 = \mathbf{C}_1\mathbf{B} \\ \mathbf{A}^{-1}\mathbf{D}_2 = \mathbf{C}_2\mathbf{B} \end{cases} \tag{5}$$

in the $m^2 + n^2$ unknown coefficients of $\mathbf{A}$ and $\mathbf{B}$. When $m = n$, which is a typical choice, the system is expected to be overdetermined, and thus solved in $\mathcal{O}(n^6)$. In practice, and since $\mathbf{C}_1$, $\mathbf{C}_2$, $\mathbf{D}_1$ and $\mathbf{D}_2$ are low-rank codewords, there are fewer than $2n^2$ linearly independent equations, so instead of a unique solution, we can obtain a basis of the solution space. However, the dimension of the solution space is small enough so that coupling this technique with one of the algebraic modelings in Sect. 6.2 results in a system that can be solved through direct linearization. It is then easy to check whether the obtained isometry maps $\mathcal{C}$ to $\mathcal{D}$. We will thus assume, as a lower bound, that we find collisions between pairs of codewords.

Now, let $C(r)$ denote the number of codewords of rank r in a k-dimensional $m \times n$ matrix code. Then, using a birthday argument, two lists of size $\sqrt{2C(r)}$ of rank r codewords of $\mathcal{C}$ and $\mathcal{D}$ are enough to find two collisions. To detect the two collisions, we need to generate and solve systems as in Eq. (5) for all possible pairs of elements from the respective lists, so $\left(\sqrt{\frac{2C(r)}{2}}\right)^2$ systems in total. Since $C(r) \approx q^{r(n+m-r)-nm+k}$, the total complexity amounts to

$$\mathcal{O}(q^{2(r(n+m-r)-nm+k)}(m^2 + n^2)^\omega).$$

Note that a deterministic variant of this approach has the same asymptotic complexity. Choosing two rank r codewords of $\mathcal{C}$ and checking them for a 2-collision against all pairs of rank r codewords of $\mathcal{D}$ requires solving $\binom{C(r)}{2}$ systems.

Finally, we choose r so that both parts – the MinRank and the collision part are as close to a balance as possible. Section 7 discuses further the complexity of this approach for the chosen parameters of our scheme.

When considering the quantum version of the algorithm, we apply the same reasoning as in the case of the collision based Algorithm 1, and obtain quadratic speedup in the collision part. Because hybridization is also possible for the Min-Rank part, it can also benefit from using Grover, especially for larger fields.

7 Implementation and Evaluation

In this section we give an assessment of the performance of MEDS. We provide concrete parameter choices for MEDS and a first preliminary evaluation of its performance based on a C reference implementation as well as a comparison to related signature schemes. The source code of our implementation is available at https://github.com/MEDSpqc/meds.

For our reference implementation, we simply implemented all finite field arithmetic in $\mathbb{F}_q$ using integer arithmetic modulo q, where q is a prime. We implemented all matrix multiplication, generating random invertible matrices, and computing the systematic form of a matrix in constant time such that their runtime does not depend on secret input.

We are using two different approaches for generating an invertible matrix M: We either generate a random matrix and check if it is invertible by explicitly computing its inverse or we construct an invertible matrix following the approach

Table 1. Cost of the investigated attacks in log scale, and 'SIG' for 'signature size in bytes. Preferred choice in bold.

$\lceil \log_2 q \rceil$	$n = k$	Birthday	Algebraic	Leon	SIG
9	16	235.29	181.55	131.20	13 296
9	17	249.04	194.55	149.65	16 237
10	15	244.62	174.75	130.50	12 428
11	14	250.79	160.24	131.21	12 519
12	14	272.40	160.24	141.17	13 548
13	**13**	**274.10**	**146.76**	**130.41**	**11 586**
14	13	294.10	146.76	134.41	13 632
20	12	383.75	138.46	135.40	16 320

of [47] based on the approach by [43] by generating a random lower-left triangular matrix $\mathbf{L}$ with the diagonal all 1 and an upper-right triangular matrix $\mathbf{U}$ with the diagonal all $\neq 0$ and computing $\mathbf{M}$ as $\mathbf{M} = \mathbf{LU}$ directly. This, however, covers only a subset of $((q-1)/q)^n$ matrices of all invertibe matrices in $\mathbb{F}_q^{n \times n}$. We are using the first approach for key generation, since here we need not only invertible matrices but also their inverses anyways, and the second approach for signing where the inverses of invertible matrices are not explicitly required.

7.1 Parameter Choice and Evaluation

A summary of the cost of the three different attacks described in Sect. 6 is given in Table 1. First, we decide to set $n = k$, as this seems to be the Goldilocks zone for our scheme. For k larger, the algebraic attack becomes significantly better, and the same is true for Leon's attack when k is smaller. Then, for finite fields of different sizes, we find the smallest value of n that achieves the required security level of 128 bits. We see that Leon's algorithm performs the best in most cases, although the algebraic approach is almost as good. Finally, to determine the optimal value for q, we choose the optimization parameters $(s, t, \text{and } w)$ such that the sizes of the public key and the signature are comparable, and we report the signature size in the last column of Table 1. We conclude that the sweet spot for 128-bit security is given for the 13-bit prime $q = 8191$ and $n = k = 13$.

Remark 3. Given these parameters, we heuristically assume that the automorphism group of the codes is trivial with overwhelming probability. It is computationally infeasible to compute the automorphism group of codes of this size; however, data on smaller-sized codes shows that the probability of a random code having a trivial automorphism group grows rapidly as q, n, and m increase.

In this setting, we can vary s, t, and w for different trade-offs of public key and signature sizes as well as performance. We also checked the impact of q if we aim for small public keys or small signatures (instead if balancing these two as in Table 1). In such cases, both 11-bit and 13-bit primes for q seem to perform similarly well. Hence, we stick to the 13-bit prime $q = 8191$ in our discussion.

Table 2. Parameters for MEDS, for $\lambda = 128$ bits of classical security. 'ST' for seed tree. 'PK' for 'public key size' and 'SIG' for 'signature size in bytes, 'FS' for 'Fiat-Shamir' probability logarithmic to base 2.

Parameter Set	q	n	m	k	s	t	w	ST	PK	SIG	FS
MEDS-2826-st	8191	13	13	13	2	256	30	✓	2826	18020	−129.739
MEDS-8445-st-f	8191	13	13	13	4	160	23	✓	8445	13946	−128.009
MEDS-8445-st	8191	13	13	13	4	464	17	✓	8445	10726	−128.764
MEDS-8445-st-s	8191	13	13	13	4	1760	13	✓	8445	8702	−128.162
MEDS-11255-st	8191	13	13	13	5	224	19	✓	11255	11618	−128.451
MEDS-11255	8191	13	13	13	5	224	19	−	11255	13778	−128.451
MEDS-42161-st	8191	13	13	13	16	128	16	✓	42161	9616	−128.849
MEDS-356839-st	8191	13	13	13	128	80	12	✓	356839	7288	−129.64
MEDS-716471-st	8191	13	13	13	256	64	11	✓	716471	6530	−127.374

Table 3. Performance of MEDS in time (ms) and mega cycles (mcyc.) at 1900 MHz on an AMD Ryzen 7 PRO 5850U CPU following the SUPERCOP setup (https://bench. cr.yp.to/supercop.html) computed as median of 16 randomly seeded runs each.

Parameter Set	Key Generation		Signing		Verification	
	(ms)	(mcyc.)	(ms)	(mcyc.)	(ms)	(mcyc.)
MEDS-2826-st	71.128110	135.143409	102.787710	195.296649	98.00434	186.208246
MEDS-8445-st-f	211.447740	401.750706	63.206200	120.09178	60.13987	114.265753
MEDS-8445-st	211.354280	401.573132	185.680270	352.792513	178.42456	339.006664
MEDS-8445-st-s	211.766000	402.3554	697.002740	1324.305206	673.18607	1279.053533
MEDS-11255-st	258.177820	490.537858	88.123950	167.435505	84.46502	160.483538
MEDS-11255	258.988880	492.078872	88.191290	167.563451	84.50302	160.555738
MEDS-42161-st	969.972890	1842.948491	50.544150	96.033885	48.4196	91.99724
MEDS-356839-st	8200.832680	15581.582092	31.630390	60.097741	32.37874	61.519606
MEDS-716471-st	18003.067490	34205.828231	25.568960	48.581024	28.93696	54.980224

Table 2 provides an overview of 128-bit security parameters for MEDS, highlighting different performance and key/signature size trade-offs. The best attack for all parameter set based on $q = 8191$, $n = 13$, and $k = 13$ is the Leon-like attack as shown in Table 1 with an expected cost of slightly over 2^{130} operations. The best quantum attack is obtained by Groverizing Leon's algorithm and has a cost of around 2^{88} operations. We select s, t, and w such that the probability of an attack on the Fiat-Shamir construction is around 2^{-128}. To improve the efficiency of vectorized implementations using SIMD instructions in the future, we select t as multiple of 16. In general, we are using all optimizations discussed in Sect. 5. However, we provide one parameter set without using the seed tree (without '-st' in the name of the parameter set).

Table 3 shows the resulting performance of these parameter sets from our constant-time C reference implementation on an AMD Ryzen 7 PRO 5850U CPU. The C reference implementation follows the implementation discussion

Table 4. Performance comparison to other relevant schemes (mcyc. rounded to three significant figures). Data marked with '(scop)' is from the SUPERCOP website. For SPHINCS+ we list results for the 'simple' variant.

Scheme	pk size (byte)	sig size (byte)	key gen (mcyc.)	sign (mcyc.)	verify (mcyc.)
ed25519 (scop)	32	64	0.048442	0.051300	0.182148
[35] dilithium2 (scop)	1312	2420	0.151339	0.363393	0.162999
[42] falcon512dyn (scop)	897	666	19.520464	0.880309	0.085587
[31] sphincsf128shake256 (scop)	32	16976	6.856442	220.279833	9.905358
[31] sphincss128shake256 (scop)	32	8080	217.958286	3502.227717	4.036804
[11] UOV ov-Ip	278432	128	2.903434	0.105324	0.090336
[8] LESS-I	8748	12728	—	—	—
[6] Wavelet	3236327	930	7403.069461	1644.281062	1.087538
[2] SDitH Var3f	144	12115	—	4.03000	3.0380
[2] SDitH Var3sss	144	5689	—	994.0460	969.2770
MEDS-8445-st-f	8445	13914	401.75	120.09	114.27
MEDS-11255-st	11255	11586	490.54	168.44	160.48
MEDS-42161-st	42161	9584	1842.95	96.03	92.00
MEDS-716471-st	716471	6498	34205.83	48.583	54.98

above but does not apply any further algorithmic or platform-specific optimizations. We expect that optimized and vectorized implementations can significantly increase the performance.

The parameter set MEDS-2826-st with $s = 2$ provides the smallest public key with about 2.8 kB and a signature of about 18 kB. MEDS-8445-st increases the public key size with $s = 4$ to slightly over 8 kB while reducing the signature size to about 10.5 kB. MEDS-8445-st-f is a 'fast' variant of this parameter set with a smaller $t = 160$ but a larger $w = 23$, resulting in a larger signature size of about 14 kB. MEDS-8445-st-s is 'small' and goes the opposite direction, providing a smaller signature size of about 8.5 kB due to a smaller $w = 13$ at a larger computational cost due to $t = 1760$. These three sibling parameter sets illustrate the impact of t and w on performance and signature size.

MEDS-11255-st provides balanced public key and signature sizes, with both around 11 kB, and a small sum of signature and public key size at moderate computational cost for signing and verification due to $t = 224$. Removing the seed tree optimization comes with an increase in signature size of about 2 kB, which illustrates the impact of the seed tree.

Finally, sets MEDS-42161-st, MEDS-356839-st, and MEDS-716471-st push the public key size to an extreme at the expense of key generation time in the pursue of reducing signature size and computational cost for signing and verification. However, we expect that at least the key generation time can significantly be improved by optimizing the computation of solving the medium-size sparse linear system used for partially seeding the public key.

7.2 Comparison to Related Signature Schemes

Table 4 shows a comparison of public key and signature sizes as well as computational performance of our new MEDS scheme with some established schemes and related recent proposals. While the comparison of public key and signature sizes is accurate, the comparison of the performance needs to be taken with a large grain of salt: While we provide numbers in the same performance metric (mega cycles – mcyc.), a direct comparison is still quite hard since not all schemes have received the same degree of optimization and since not all performance data has been obtained on the same CPU architecture.

The performance data from the 'classical' scheme ed25519 as well as from the NIST PQC schemes CRYSTALS-Dilithium [35], Falcon [42], and SPHNICS+ [31] has been obtained from the SUPERCOP website[4]. We selected the performance data from the AMD64 Zen CPU, which is an AMD Ryzen 7 1700 from 2017, i.e., the same microarchitecture (but a different CPU) as we used for our measurements of MEDS. We are reporting median cycles directly from the website.

For UOV [11], LESS [8] and Wavelet [6] we list the performance data as reported in the respective papers unless such data was unavailable. In the case of SDitH [2], only reports of performance data in milliseconds on a 3.1 GHz Intel Core i9-9990K are available. We computed the corresponding number of cycles from this to enable a rough comparison to the other schemes, but note that this data is therefore not entirely accurate.

Table 4 shows that, although code-based schemes do not compete well with pre-quantum or lattice-based PQC schemes, MEDS fills a gap that was not previously available for multivariate or code-based schemes, with a relatively small combined size of public key and signature. Furthermore, its versatility in parameter selection allows for great flexibility for specific applications. In terms of performance, the current implementation of MEDS is still unoptimized. We expect speed-ups of at least one order of magnitude from SIMD parallelization on AVX256 and AVX512 CPUs, since both the data-independent loop of the Fiat-Shamir construction and the matrix arithmetic lend themselves to efficient parallelization. Providing optimized implementations of MEDS for modern SIMD architectures as well as embedded systems is an open task for future work.

References

1. Aguilar Melchor, C., et al.: HQC. NIST PQC Submission (2020)
2. Aguilar-Melchor, C., Gama, N., Howe, J., Hülsing, A., Joseph, D., Yue, D.: The return of the SDitH. Cryptology ePrint Archive, Paper 2022/1645 (2022, to appear at Eurocrypt 2023)
3. Alamati, N., De Feo, L., Montgomery, H., Patranabis, S.: Cryptographic group actions and applications. In: Moriai, S., Wang, H. (eds.) ASIACRYPT 2020. LNCS, vol. 12492, pp. 411–439. Springer, Cham (2020). https://doi.org/10.1007/978-3-030-64834-3_14

---

[4] https://bench.cr.yp.to/results-sign.html – amd64; Zen (800f11); 2017 AMD Ryzen 7 1700; 8 × 3000 MHz; rumba7, supercop-20220506.

4. Albrecht, M.R., et al.: Classic McEliece. NIST PQC Submission (2020)
5. Aragon, N., et al.: BIKE. NIST PQC Submission (2020)
6. Banegas, G., Debris-Alazard, T., Nedeljković, M., Smith, B.: Wavelet: code-based postquantum signatures with fast verification on microcontrollers. Cryptology ePrint Archive, Paper 2021/1432 (2021)
7. Bardet, M., et al.: Improvements of algebraic attacks for solving the rank decoding and MinRank problems. In: Moriai, S., Wang, H. (eds.) ASIACRYPT 2020. LNCS, vol. 12491, pp. 507–536. Springer, Cham (2020). https://doi.org/10.1007/978-3-030-64837-4_17
8. Barenghi, A., Biasse, J.-F., Persichetti, E., Santini, P.: LESS-FM: fine-tuning signatures from the code equivalence problem. In: Cheon, J.H., Tillich, J.-P. (eds.) PQCrypto 2021 2021. LNCS, vol. 12841, pp. 23–43. Springer, Cham (2021). https://doi.org/10.1007/978-3-030-81293-5_2
9. Barenghi, A., Biasse, J.-F., Ngo, T., Persichetti, E., Santini, P.: Advanced signature functionalities from the code equivalence problem. Int. J. Comput. Math. Comput. Syst. Theory **7**(2), 112–128 (2022)
10. Beullens, W.: Not enough LESS: an improved algorithm for solving code equivalence problems over $\mathbb{F}_q$. In: Dunkelman, O., Jacobson, Jr., M.J., O'Flynn, C. (eds.) SAC 2020. LNCS, vol. 12804, pp. 387–403. Springer, Cham (2021). https://doi.org/10.1007/978-3-030-81652-0_15
11. Beullens, W., et al.: Oil and vinegar: modern parameters and implementations. Cryptology ePrint Archive, Paper 2023/059 (2023)
12. Beullens, W., Katsumata, S., Pintore, F.: Calamari and Falafl: logarithmic (linkable) ring signatures from isogenies and lattices. In: Moriai, S., Wang, H. (eds.) ASIACRYPT 2020. LNCS, vol. 12492, pp. 464–492. Springer, Cham (2020). https://doi.org/10.1007/978-3-030-64834-3_16
13. Beullens, W., Kleinjung, T., Vercauteren, F.: CSI-FiSh: efficient isogeny based signatures through class group computations. In: Galbraith, S.D., Moriai, S. (eds.) ASIACRYPT 2019. LNCS, vol. 11921, pp. 227–247. Springer, Cham (2019). https://doi.org/10.1007/978-3-030-34578-5_9
14. Biasse, J.-F., Micheli, G., Persichetti, E., Santini, P.: LESS is more: code-based signatures without syndromes. In: Nitaj, A., Youssef, A. (eds.) AFRICACRYPT 2020. LNCS, vol. 12174, pp. 45–65. Springer, Cham (2020). https://doi.org/10.1007/978-3-030-51938-4_3
15. Bonnetain, X., Schrottenloher, A.: Quantum security analysis of CSIDH. In: Canteaut, A., Ishai, Y. (eds.) EUROCRYPT 2020. LNCS, vol. 12106, pp. 493–522. Springer, Cham (2020). https://doi.org/10.1007/978-3-030-45724-2_17
16. Bouillaguet, C.: Algorithms for some hard problems and cryptographic attacks against specific cryptographic primitives. Ph.D. thesis, Université Paris Diderot (2011)
17. Bouillaguet, C., Fouque, P.-A., Véber, A.: Graph-theoretic algorithms for the "isomorphism of polynomials" problem. In: Johansson, T., Nguyen, P.Q. (eds.) EUROCRYPT 2013. LNCS, vol. 7881, pp. 211–227. Springer, Heidelberg (2013). https://doi.org/10.1007/978-3-642-38348-9_13
18. Castryck, W., Lange, T., Martindale, C., Panny, L., Renes, J.: CSIDH: an efficient post-quantum commutative group action. In: Peyrin, T., Galbraith, S. (eds.) ASIACRYPT 2018. LNCS, vol. 11274, pp. 395–427. Springer, Cham (2018). https://doi.org/10.1007/978-3-030-03332-3_15
19. Courtois, N.T.: Efficient zero-knowledge authentication based on a linear algebra problem MinRank. In: Boyd, C. (ed.) ASIACRYPT 2001. LNCS, vol. 2248, pp. 402–421. Springer, Heidelberg (2001). https://doi.org/10.1007/3-540-45682-1_24

20. Courtois, N., Klimov, A., Patarin, J., Shamir, A.: Efficient algorithms for solving overdefined systems of multivariate polynomial equations. In: Preneel, B. (ed.) EUROCRYPT 2000. LNCS, vol. 1807, pp. 392–407. Springer, Heidelberg (2000). https://doi.org/10.1007/3-540-45539-6_27
21. Couveignes, J.-M.: Hard homogeneous spaces. Cryptology ePrint Archive, Paper 2006/291 (2006)
22. Couvreur, A., Debris-Alazard, T., Gaborit, P.: On the hardness of code equivalence problems in rank metric. CoRR, abs/2011.04611 (2020)
23. De Feo, L., Galbraith, S.D.: SeaSign: compact isogeny signatures from class group actions. In: Ishai, Y., Rijmen, V. (eds.) EUROCRYPT 2019. LNCS, vol. 11478, pp. 759–789. Springer, Cham (2019). https://doi.org/10.1007/978-3-030-17659-4_26
24. Ding, J., et al.: Rainbow. Technical report, National Institute of Standards and Technology (2020)
25. Faugère, J.-C., Din, M.S.E., Spaenlehauer, P.-J.: Gröbner bases of bihomogeneous ideals generated by polynomials of bidegree (1, 1): algorithms and complexity. J. Symb. Comput. **46**(4), 406–437 (2011)
26. Faugère, J.-C., Levy-dit-Vehel, F., Perret, L.: Cryptanalysis of MinRank. In: Wagner, D. (ed.) CRYPTO 2008. LNCS, vol. 5157, pp. 280–296. Springer, Heidelberg (2008). https://doi.org/10.1007/978-3-540-85174-5_16
27. Faugère, J.-C., Perret, L.: Polynomial equivalence problems: algorithmic and theoretical aspects. In: Vaudenay, S. (ed.) EUROCRYPT 2006. LNCS, vol. 4004, pp. 30–47. Springer, Heidelberg (2006). https://doi.org/10.1007/11761679_3
28. Fiat, A., Shamir, A.: How to prove yourself: practical solutions to identification and signature problems. In: Odlyzko, A.M. (ed.) CRYPTO 1986. LNCS, vol. 263, pp. 186–194. Springer, Heidelberg (1987). https://doi.org/10.1007/3-540-47721-7_12
29. Gueron, S., Persichetti, E., Santini, P.: Designing a practical code-based signature scheme from zero-knowledge proofs with trusted setup. Cryptography **6**(1), 5 (2022)
30. Haviv, I., Regev, O.: On the lattice isomorphism problem. In: Chekuri, C. (ed.) SODA 2014, pp. 391–404. ACM SIAM (2014)
31. Hulsing, A., et al.: SPHINCS+. NIST PQC Submission (2020)
32. Kipnis, A., Shamir, A.: Cryptanalysis of the HFE public key cryptosystem by relinearization. In: Wiener, M. (ed.) CRYPTO 1999. LNCS, vol. 1666, pp. 19–30. Springer, Heidelberg (1999). https://doi.org/10.1007/3-540-48405-1_2
33. Kuperberg, G.: Another subexponential-time quantum algorithm for the dihedral hidden subgroup problem. In: Severini, S., Brandão, F.G.S.L. (eds.) TQC 2013. LIPIcs, vol. 22, pp. 20–34. Schloss Dagstuhl (2013)
34. Leon, J.S.: Computing automorphism groups of error-correcting codes. IEEE Trans. Inf. Theory **28**(3), 496–510 (1982)
35. Lyubashevsky, V., et al.: CRYSTALS. NIST PQC Submission (2020)
36. McEliece, R.J.: A public-key cryptosystem based on algebraic coding theory. DSN PR 42-44, California Institute of Technology (1978)
37. Nguyen, P., Wolf, C.: International workshop on post-quantum cryptography (2006)
38. NIST. Post-Quantum Cryptography Standardization (2017). https://csrc.nist.gov/Projects/Post-Quantum-Cryptography
39. Patarin, J.: Hidden fields equations (HFE) and isomorphisms of polynomials (IP): two new families of asymmetric algorithms. In: Maurer, U. (ed.) EUROCRYPT 1996. LNCS, vol. 1070, pp. 33–48. Springer, Heidelberg (1996). https://doi.org/10.1007/3-540-68339-9_4

40. Perlner, R., Smith-Tone, D.: Rainbow band separation is better than we thought. Cryptology ePrint Archive, Paper 2020/702 (2020)
41. Prange, E.: The use of information sets in decoding cyclic codes. IRE Trans. Inf. Theory **8**(5), 5–9 (1962)
42. Prest, T., et al.: FALCON. NIST PQC Submission (2020)
43. Randall, D.: Efficient Generation of Random Nonsingular Matrices. Technical Report UCB/CSD-91-658, EECS Department, UC Berkeley (1991)
44. Regev, O.: On lattices, learning with errors, random linear codes, and cryptography. In: Gabow, H.N., Fagin, R. (eds.) Theory of Computing, pp. 84–93. ACM (2005)
45. Reijnders, K., Samardjiska, S., Trimoska, M.: Hardness estimates of the code equivalence problem in the rank metric. Cryptology ePrint Archive, Paper 2022/276 (2022)
46. Rostovtsev, A., Stolbunov, A.: Public-key cryptosystem based on isogenies. Cryptology ePrint Archive, Paper 2006/145 (2006)
47. Tang, G., Duong, D.H., Joux, A., Plantard, T., Qiao, Y., Susilo, W.: Practical post-quantum signature schemes from isomorphism problems of trilinear forms. In: Dunkelman, O., Dziembowski, S. (eds.) EUROCRYPT 2022. LNCS, vol. 13277, pp. 582–612. Springer, Cham (2022). https://doi.org/10.1007/978-3-031-07082-2_21

Efficient Computation
of $(3^n, 3^n)$-Isogenies

Thomas Decru[1] and Sabrina Kunzweiler[2]([envelope])

[1] imec-COSIC, KU Leuven, Leuven, Belgium
`thomas.decru@kuleuven.be`
[2] Univ. Bordeaux, CNRS, Bordeaux INP, Inria, Bordeaux, France
`sabrina.kunzweiler@math.u-bordeaux.fr`

Abstract. The parametrization of $(3,3)$-isogenies by Bruin, Flynn and Testa requires over 37.500 multiplications if one wants to evaluate a single isogeny in a point. We simplify their formulae and reduce the amount of required multiplications by 94%. Further we deduce explicit formulae for evaluating $(3,3)$-splitting and gluing maps in the framework of the parametrization by Bröker, Howe, Lauter and Stevenhagen. We provide implementations to compute $(3^n, 3^n)$-isogenies between principally polarized abelian surfaces with a focus on cryptographic application. Our implementation can retrieve Alice's secret isogeny in 11 s for the SIKEp751 parameters, which were aimed at NIST level 5 security.

1 Introduction

Elliptic curves have a rich history of being used for cryptographic purposes. Their higher-dimensional variants have also been studied in the context of the discrete logarithm problem, but were deemed not practical or safe enough to be used (see for example [16,27]). With the advent of quantum computers in mind, a lot of this research has shifted towards using isogenies between elliptic curves.

In 2009, Charles, Goren and Lauter (CGL) used isogenies between supersingular elliptic curves over $\mathbb{F}_{p^2}$ to construct a hash function based on their expander graph properties [10]. In 2018, Takashima generalized this construction to supersingular Jacobians of hyperelliptic curves of genus two [28], but this hash function was quickly found to allow many collisions by Flynn and Ti [14]. These collisions were fixed by Castryck, Decru and Smith, and they also argued for the correct generalization to superspecial abelian varieties [8].

In 2011, Jao and De Feo constructed a Diffie–Hellman style key exchange, called Supersingular Isogeny Diffe–Hellman (SIDH), based on the isogeny graph underlying the CGL hash function [17]. The protocol can also be generalized to allow a key exchange when using abelian surfaces instead of elliptic curves, as shown by Flynn and Ti [14]. This higher-dimensional variant was further improved in a follow-up work by Kunzweiler, Ti and Weitkämper [20].

The SIDH protocol was used as the basis for the Supersingular Isogeny Key Encapsulation (SIKE) which was submitted to NIST as a candidate for their

© The Author(s), under exclusive license to Springer Nature Switzerland AG 2023
N. El Mrabet et al. (Eds.): AFRICACRYPT 2023, LNCS 14064, pp. 53–78, 2023.
https://doi.org/10.1007/978-3-031-37679-5_3

post-quantum standardization process. Early July 2022, NIST announced SIKE to be one of only four candidates to advance to round 4 of the post-quantum standardization process for public key exchanges [23]. That same month however, Castryck and Decru published a devastating attack on SIKE, retrieving Bob's private key in minutes to hours depending on the security level [7]. Their attack relied on embedding elliptic curves into abelian surfaces, and used Kani's reducibility criterion [18] as part of their decisional oracle. The attack got improved by a quick series of follow-up works using a direct computational approach [22,24], and finally Robert managed to prove that even if the endomorphism ring of the starting curve in SIDH is unknown, there is always a polynomial-time attack by using abelian eightfolds [25].

Despite these generalizations and the increasing interest in higher-dimensional cryptographic applications, most of the aforementioned implementations restrict themselves to isogenies of very low prime degree. The genus-2 version of the CGL hash function in [8] used $(2,2)$-isogenies only, since they are by far easiest to compute. Kunzweiler improved further on these $(2,2)$-isogeny formulae in [19], and Castryck and Decru provided a $(3,3)$-version based on their multiradical isogeny setting [6]. The (now also broken) genus-2 variant of SIDH in [14] used $(2,2)$- and $(3,3)$-isogenies to obtain a five-minute key exchange on the basic security level. The implementation of the attacks on SIKE in [7] and [22] only target Bob's private key, since this requires only using $(2,2)$-isogenies. In [26], Santos, Costello and Frengley do manage to use up to $(11,11)$-isogenies, but only as a decisional tool to detect (N,N)-split Jacobians.

The reason for these restrictions is that computing isogenies between abelian surfaces is typically a lot harder than isogenies between elliptic curves. The general (ℓ,ℓ)-isogeny formulae by Cosset and Robert [12] have polynomial time complexity $\mathcal{O}(\ell^2)$ or $\mathcal{O}(\ell^4)$, depending on $\ell \bmod 4$, but arithmetic has to be performed in the field extension where the theta coordinates are defined, which can turn expensive quickly for cryptographic purposes. The only other known general parametrization are the $(3,3)$-isogeny formulae by Bruin, Flynn and Testa (BFT) [4], which were used as a basis for both the multiradical $(3,3)$-hash function and the genus-2 variant of SIDH. The parametrization is complete, but the formulae require over 37.500 multiplications if one wants to also evaluate points and not just compute the codomain curve.

Our Contribution. We optimize the BFT-formulae from [4] and reduce the amount of required multiplications by 94%. We also develop concrete and efficient gluing and splitting formulae for $(3,3)$-isogenies, which allow us to evaluate them on points. All of these operations are furthermore done over the ground field. Our implementations and formulae are with cryptographic applications in mind and may not work for some small field characteristics. Additionally, certain exceptional cases occur with probability $\mathcal{O}(p^{-1})$ or less, in which case we do not implement them in generic applications to reduce the overhead. Exceptions to this which are useful for cryptographic purposes - such as the gluing and splitting - are of course exempt from this exclusion. We provide a $(3,3)$-variant of the CGL hash function similar to the one from [6], and implement an attack targeting Alice's secret isogeny in the SIKE protocol. The latter can be done in 11 s for the SIKEp751 parameters, aimed at NIST level 5 security, down from the 1 h computation for Bob's secret isogeny in [24].

Outline. We will provide necessary mathematical preliminaries in Sect. 2. In Sect. 3, we will recap the BFT parametrization and discuss our improvements to it. In Sect. 4 we will discuss isogenies between abelian surfaces of which at least one of the domain or codomain is a product of elliptic curves, followed by the necessary coordinate transformations between these parametrizations in Sect. 5. Our version of the $(3,3)$-hash function and attack on Alice's private key in the SIKE protocol will be discussed in Sect. 6, respectively 7. Finally, we will provide an overview of the auxiliary Magma [2] and SageMath [30] code in Sect. 8, which can be found at https://github.com/KULeuven-COSIC/3_3_isogenies.

2 Preliminaries

Below are some notes on the definitions that we will need later. In general, we assume to work over a field k with nonnegative characteristic $p > 5$, though some of the results generalize beyond this restriction.

2.1 Genus-2 Curves and Their Jacobians

Let $\mathcal{C}$ be an algebraic curve of genus 2. Any such curve is hyperelliptic and admits an affine equation of the form $\mathcal{C} : y^2 = f(x)$, where $f \in k[x]$ is a square-free polynomial of degree 5 or 6. If f is a degree-5 polynomial, then the corresponding genus-2 curve has precisely one point at infinity which we denote by ∞. On the other hand, if the degree of f is 6, then there are two points at infinity and we denote them by ∞_+ and ∞_-. Note that ∞_+ and ∞_- get swapped by the hyperelliptic involution $\tau : \mathcal{C} \to \mathcal{C}, (x, y) \mapsto (x, -y)$, whereas in the degree-5 case, ∞ is a fixed point. In general, points fixed by the involution are referred to as the *Weierstrass points* of $\mathcal{C}$.

While the points on a genus-2 curve do *not* form a group, we will work with Jacobians of such curves. The Jacobian $\mathrm{Jac}(\mathcal{C})$ of a genus-2 curve $\mathcal{C}$ is an abelian surface, i.e. an abelian variety of dimension 2. Moreover it comes equipped with a principal polarization, i.e. an isomorphism to its dual and is therefore considered a *principally polarized abelian surface (p.p.a.s.)*. In general, p.p.a.s. come in two flavours. They are either irreducible and hence the Jacobian of a genus-2 curve, or they are reducible in which case they are the product of two elliptic curves.

To work with elements of the Jacobian $\mathrm{Jac}(\mathcal{C})$, one usually exploits its link to the Picard group of $\mathcal{C}$. Recall that for any field extension k'/k, the group of k'-rational points $\mathrm{Jac}(\mathcal{C})(k')$ is isomorphic to the Picard group $Pic^0_{\mathcal{C}}(k')$. This allows us to represent elements of $\mathrm{Jac}(\mathcal{C})$ as equivalence classes of degree-0 divisors on

$\mathcal{C}$. Moreover, any element $[D] \in \text{Jac}(\mathcal{C})$ has a unique representative of the form $[P_1 + P_2 - D_\infty]$, where

$$D_\infty = \begin{cases} 2 \cdot \infty & \text{if } \deg(f) = 5, \\ \infty_+ + \infty_- & \text{if } \deg(f) = 6, \end{cases}$$

and $P_1 + P_2$ is an effective divisor with affine part in general position, i.e. $P_1 \neq \tau(P_2)$, see [15, Proposition 1]. This facilitates a compact representation in terms of Mumford coordinates. For simplicity, assume that $P_1 = (x_1, y_1)$ and $P_2 = (x_2, y_2)$ are both affine, then the Mumford presentation of $[D]$ is defined as the pair of polynomials $[a, b] \in k[x]^2$ with $a = (x - x_1)(x - x_2)$ and $y = b(x)$ is the line connecting P_1 and P_2. For the general definition, we refer to [11].

2.2   Torsion Subgroups and Isogenies of p.p.a.s.

For an integer $N \in \mathbb{N}$, the N-torsion subgroup of a p.p.a.s. is defined as $\mathcal{A}[N] = \{P \in \mathcal{A} \mid N \cdot P = 0\}$. If N is not divisible by p, then this is a free $\mathbb{Z}/N\mathbb{Z}$-module of rank 4. To describe subgroups defining isogenies between p.p.a.s., it is necessary to take into account the *Weil pairing* which is an alternating, bilinear pairing $e_N : \mathcal{A}[N] \times \mathcal{A}[N] \to \mu_N$, where μ_N denotes the group of N-th roots of unity. A subgroup $G \subset \mathcal{A}[N]$ is called *maximal N-isotropic* if the following two properties are satisfied.

1. The Weil pairing restricts trivially onto G (isotropy).
2. There is no proper subgroup $H \subset \mathcal{A}[N]$ properly containing G (maximality).

Let $G \subset \mathcal{A}[N]$ be a maximal N-isotropic subgroup, then up to isomorphism there exists a unique p.p.a.s. $\mathcal{A}'$ together with an isogeny $\Phi : \mathcal{A} \to \mathcal{A}'$ with kernel $\ker(\Phi) = G$. In our paper, we always consider kernel groups of rank 2, i.e. $G \cong \mathbb{Z}/N\mathbb{Z} \times \mathbb{Z}/N\mathbb{Z}$. In this case, we simply refer to the kernel as an (N, N)-*subgroup* and call the corresponding isogeny an (N, N)-*isogeny*. Indeed, we will only be interested in the case where $N = 3$ or more generally $N = 3^n$.

Since there are two types of p.p.a.s., Jacobians of genus-2 curves and products of elliptic curves, there exist four different types of isogenies of p.p.a.s depending on the nature of the domain and codomain. We distinguish the following cases.

- Generic case: $\Phi : \text{Jac}(\mathcal{C}) \to \text{Jac}(\mathcal{C}')$.
- Splitting case: $\Phi : \text{Jac}(\mathcal{C}) \to E_1' \times E_2'$.
- Gluing case: $\Phi : E_1 \times E_2 \to \text{Jac}(\mathcal{C}')$.
- Product case: $\Phi : E_1 \times E_2 \to E_1' \times E_2'$.

In higher-dimensional isogeny-based cryptography, one almost always works with superspecial abelian varieties, see for example [8]. Given that the superspecial products of elliptic curves only constitute a proportion of $\mathcal{O}(p^{-1})$ of all superspecial p.p.a.s., the generic case occurs most often in cryptographic contexts.

2.3   The Quartic Model of the Kummer Surface

Instead of working with the Jacobian of a genus-2 curve, it is sometimes favourable to work with the associated Kummer surface obtained by taking the quotient by the action of $[-1]$ on $\mathrm{Jac}(\mathcal{C})$. While this results in losing the full picture of the group, it has the geometric advantage that the Kummer surface can be compactly defined as a variety in $\mathbb{P}^3$. In general, the Kummer surface can be seen as the natural analogue to x-only arithmetic often used in elliptic curve cryptography. We now provide some more details on the definition.

Let $\mathcal{C} : y^2 = F(x)$ with $F = \sum_{i=0}^{6} f_i x^i$ be a curve of genus 2 and let $\mathrm{Jac}(\mathcal{C})$ be its Jacobian. Consider the map $\xi : \mathrm{Jac}(\mathcal{C}) \to \mathbb{P}^3$, generically defined as

$$[(x_1, y_1) + (x_2, y_2) - D_\infty] \mapsto (\xi_0 : \xi_1 : \xi_2 : \xi_3),$$

where

$$\xi_0 = 1, \quad \xi_1 = x_1 + x_2, \quad \xi_2 = x_1 x_2, \quad \xi_3 = \frac{\varphi(\xi_0, \xi_1, \xi_2) - 2 y_1 y_2}{\xi_1^2 - 4\xi_0 \xi_2}$$

and

$$\varphi = 2 f_0 \xi_0^3 + f_1 \xi_0^2 \xi_1 + 2 f_2 \xi_0^2 \xi_2 + f_3 \xi_0 \xi_1 \xi_2 + 2 f_4 \xi_0 \xi_2^2 + f_5 \xi_1 \xi_2^2 + 2 f_6 \xi_2^3.$$

The image of the map ξ in $\mathbb{P}^3$ is a quartic surface defined by the equation

$$K(\xi_0, \xi_1, \xi_2, \xi_3) = (\xi_1^2 - 4\xi_0 \xi_2)\xi_3^2 + \varphi(\xi_0, \xi_1, \xi_2)\xi_3 + \eta(\xi_0, \xi_1, \xi_2) = 0,$$

where $\eta \in k[\xi_0, \xi_1, \xi_2]$ is a homogeneous degree-4 polynomial. The image of ξ is called the *Kummer surface* of $\mathcal{C}$ and we denote it as $\mathcal{K}(\mathcal{C})$. While we omit the formulae for η here, we remark that its coefficients lie in $\mathbb{Z}[f_0, \ldots, f_6]$. For an explicit description of η and more details on the definition of the Kummer surface, we refer to [5, Chapter 3].

Remnants of the Group Structure. Applying the map $\xi : \mathrm{Jac}(\mathcal{C}) \to \mathcal{K}(\mathcal{C})$, the group structure gets lost, in particular the Kummer surface is *not* an abelian variety. For instance, consider two elements $T, T' \in \mathrm{Jac}(\mathcal{C})$. Given only $\xi(T)$ and $\xi(T')$, it is not possible to determine $\xi(T + T')$. However, there are some remnants of the group structure of the Jacobian. In particular, multiplication by an integer $n \in \mathbb{Z}$ remains meaningful on the Kummer surface. That is, given $\xi(T)$ for some element $T \in \mathrm{Jac}(\mathcal{C})$, one can compute $n \cdot \xi(T) := \xi(nT)$ (see [5, Chapter 3.6]). Furthermore, one can use differential additions to compute images of points on the Kummer surface that lift to a specific element of the Jacobian. Since our applications do not require this, we shall not elaborate.

Isogenies. An isogeny $\Phi : \mathrm{Jac}(\mathcal{C}) \to \mathrm{Jac}(\mathcal{C}')$ descends to a rational map $\Phi_\mathcal{K} : \mathcal{K}(\mathcal{C}) \to \mathcal{K}(\mathcal{C}')$ which makes the following square commute.

$$
\begin{array}{ccc}
\mathrm{Jac}(\mathcal{C}) & \xrightarrow{\;\Phi\;} & \mathrm{Jac}(\mathcal{C}') \\
\downarrow{\scriptstyle \xi} & & \downarrow{\scriptstyle \xi'} \\
\mathcal{K}(\mathcal{C}) & \dashrightarrow{\;\Phi_\mathcal{K}\;} & \mathcal{K}(\mathcal{C}').
\end{array}
$$

Being a map of Kummer surfaces, $\Phi_\mathcal{K}$ is strictly speaking not an isogeny. However, we slightly abuse notation and refer to $\Phi_\mathcal{K}$ as the isogeny on the level of Kummer surfaces.

3   (3,3)-Isogenies Between Jacobians

In the first part of this section, we summarize the parametrization of genus-2 curves whose Jacobians have a $(3,3)$-torsion subgroup with rational generators, as well as the corresponding isogeny formulae by Bruin, Flynn and Testa from [4]. In the second part, we explain optimizations for the evaluation of these formulae.

3.1   BFT Approach

Consider a genus-2 curve $\mathcal{C}$ and a maximal isotropic group $G = \langle T, T' \rangle \subset \mathrm{Jac}(\mathcal{C})[3](k)$. In [4], the authors show that if the data $(\mathcal{C}, G)$ is sufficiently general, then there exist $r, s, t \in k$ such that $\mathcal{C}$ is isomorphic to the curve

$$\mathcal{C}_{r,s,t} : y^2 = G_{r,s,t}(x)^2 + \lambda H_{r,s,t}(x)^3 = G'_{r,s,t}(x)^2 + \lambda' H'_{r,s,t}(x)^3,$$

where

$$H_{r,s,t}(x) = x^2 + rx + t, \qquad \lambda = 4s,$$
$$G_{r,s,t}(x) = (s - st - 1)x^3 + 3s(r - t)x^2 + 3sr(r - t)x - st^2 + sr^3 + t,$$
$$H'_{r,s,t}(x) = x^2 + x + r, \qquad \lambda' = 4st,$$
$$G'_{r,s,t}(x) = (s - st + 1)x^3 + 3s(r - t)x^2 + 3sr(r - t)x - st^2 + sr^3 - t.$$

The 3-torsion elements T and T' are given by $[H_{r,s,t}(x), G_{r,s,t}(x)]$ respectively $[H'_{r,s,t}(x), G'_{r,s,t}(x)]$.[1] For an explicit description of the full torsion subgroup $\langle T, T' \rangle$, see [4, Theorem 6].

Remark 1. The generality stems from the fact that both T and T' require non-degenerate support. However, due to [4, Lemma 3], it is always possible to choose two generators of $\langle T, T' \rangle$ that satisfy this. The chance of two random generators having degenerate support is $\mathcal{O}(p^{-1})$, so we will not elaborate on those cases.

Remark 2. When considering the isomorphism $(x, y) \mapsto (x, y + G_{r,s,t}(x))$, the parametrization gets a cleaner form which is similar to the well-known parametrization of $X_1(3)$ in the elliptic-curve case. Indeed, the curve is then given by

$$\mathcal{C} : y^2 + G_{r,s,t}(x)y = sH_{r,s,t}(x)^3.$$

The $(3,3)$-subgroup is then generated by $[H_{r,s,t}(x), 0]$ and $[H'_{r,s,t}(x), x^3 - t]$.

---

[1] Remark the slight abuse of notation: the polynomials $G_{r,s,t}(x)$ and $G'_{r,s,t}(x)$ are cubic and hence this is not a Mumford representation. However, they reduce to the correct linear expression modulo $H_{r,s,t}(x)$, respectively $H'_{r,s,t}(x)$.

We consider the $(3,3)$-isogeny $\Phi : \mathrm{Jac}(\mathcal{C}_{r,s,t}) \to \mathrm{Jac}(\mathcal{C}_{r,s,t})/\langle T, T' \rangle$, where we assume $\mathrm{Jac}(\mathcal{C}_{r,s,t})/\langle T, T' \rangle = \mathrm{Jac}(\widetilde{\mathcal{C}})$ is again the Jacobian of a genus-2 curve. Along with the formulae for the codomain curve, the authors of [4] also provide explicit formulae for the induced map $\Phi_{\mathcal{K}} : \mathcal{K}(\mathcal{C}_{r,s,t}) \to \mathcal{K}(\widetilde{\mathcal{C}})$ on the corresponding Kummer surface.[2] Naturally, the map on the Kummer surfaces is of degree three. More precisely, it is of the form

$$\Phi_{\mathcal{K}} : \mathcal{K}(\mathcal{C}_{r,s,t}) \to \mathcal{K}(\widetilde{\mathcal{C}})$$
$$(\xi_0 : \xi_1 : \xi_2 : \xi_3) \mapsto (\widetilde{\xi_0} : \widetilde{\xi_1} : \widetilde{\xi_2} : \widetilde{\xi_3}),$$

with

$$\widetilde{\xi_0} = \sum_{0 \leq i \leq j \leq k \leq 3} a_{i,j,k} \xi_i \xi_j \xi_k, \qquad \widetilde{\xi_1} = \sum_{0 \leq i \leq j \leq k \leq 3} b_{i,j,k} \xi_i \xi_j \xi_k,$$
$$\widetilde{\xi_2} = \sum_{0 \leq i \leq j \leq k \leq 3} c_{i,j,k} \xi_i \xi_j \xi_k, \qquad \widetilde{\xi_3} = \sum_{0 \leq i \leq j \leq k \leq 3} d_{i,j,k} \xi_i \xi_j \xi_k. \tag{1}$$

Note that there are exactly 20 monomials of degree 3 in four variables. There exist expressions $a_{0,0,0}, \ldots, d_{3,3,3} \in \mathbb{Z}[r, s, t]$ for the 80 coefficients. Unfortunately, these expressions are not very compact and their evaluation requires over 37.500 multiplications using a multivariate Horner scheme.

3.2 Improvements

To reduce the number of multiplications in the evaluation of the $(3,3)$-isogeny, we find more compact representations for the coefficients $a_{i,j,k}, b_{i,j,k}, c_{i,j,k}, d_{i,j,k}$ introduced in Eq. 1.

Relations Among the Coefficients. As a first step, we observe that there exist various relations among the $a_{i,j,k}, b_{i,j,k}, c_{i,j,k}, d_{i,j,k}$ from above and the coefficients of the curve equations from $\mathcal{C}_{r,s,t}$ and $\widetilde{\mathcal{C}}$. To make this more explicit, denote $\mathcal{C}_{r,s,t} : y^2 = \sum f_i x^i$ and $\widetilde{\mathcal{C}} : y^2 = \sum g_i x^i$ keeping in mind that we know explicit descriptions of the coefficients from Sect. 3.1. The coefficients of the Kummer surface equations $K_{r,s,t}$ of $\mathcal{K}(\mathcal{C}_{r,s,t})$ can be expressed in terms of $f_0, \ldots, f_6$, and in the same way the coefficients of the equation $\widetilde{K}$ of $K(\widetilde{\mathcal{C}})$ can be expressed in terms of $g_0, \ldots, g_6$. In the following, we interpret the polynomial $\widetilde{K} \in k[\widetilde{\xi_0}, \widetilde{\xi_1}, \widetilde{\xi_2}, \widetilde{\xi_3}]$ as a polynomial in $k[\xi_0, \xi_1, \xi_2, \xi_3]$ via the identities for $\widetilde{\xi_i}$ from Eq. 1. In that setting, $\widetilde{K}$ is a degree-12 polynomial. Further note that $\widetilde{K}$ vanishes at all points $(\xi_0 : \xi_1 : \xi_2 : \xi_3)$ of $\mathcal{K}(\mathcal{C}_{r,s,t})$, hence $\widetilde{K}$ is divisible by $K_{r,s,t}$ and we can write

$$\widetilde{K} = Q_{\mathrm{aux}} \cdot K_{r,s,t} \in k[\xi_0, \xi_1, \xi_2, \xi_3] \tag{2}$$

for a degree-8 polynomial Q_{aux} in $k[\xi_0, \xi_1, \xi_2, \xi_3]$.

While there exist known expressions for $a_{i,j,k}, b_{i,j,k}, c_{i,j,k}, d_{i,j,k}$ we treat them as variables. The only exceptions are $a_{i,3,3}, b_{i,3,3}, c_{i,3,3}, d_{i,3,3}$ with $i \in \{0, 1, 2, 3\}$,

---

[2] They can be found online at http://www.cecm.sfu.ca/~nbruin/c3xc3/.

for which we insert the already known (and compact) expressions. In fact, these are either 0 or Δ, where the latter is a factor of the discriminant of $\tilde{C}$. By comparing coefficients of the identity in Eq. 2, we obtain in total 447 relations among the $a_{i,j,k}, b_{i,j,k}, c_{i,j,k}, d_{i,j,k}$ and the f_i, g_i. Note that these relations also include the 165 coefficients $q_{i_1,\ldots,i_8}$ of the degree-8 polynomial Q_{aux}. However, it is easy to eliminate these unknowns from the system which reduces the number of relations by 165 and leaves us with 282 relations purely between $a_{i,j,k}, b_{i,j,k}, c_{i,j,k}, d_{i,j,k}$ and f_i, g_i. If $K_{r,s,t}$ and $\tilde{K}$ were general degree-4 equations, (almost) all the obtained relations would be quartic in $a_{i,j,k}, b_{i,j,k}, c_{i,j,k}, d_{i,j,k}$. However, given the special form of the Kummer surface equations, we obtain several quadratic and even linear relations. For instance, one immediately obtains

$$a_{2,2,3} = 4(f_6\Delta - g_6).$$

This requires a total of one full and one small-scalar multiplication, compared to 96 multiplications to compute the same coefficient in the original formulae by means of a Horner scheme.

Expressing All Coefficients from These Relations. Despite the relations between the coefficients only being quartic, we still have a system of 282 equations in 80 unknowns. A direct Gröbner basis computation is hence completely out of reach. After clearing the easiest (linear) relations, it becomes evident that one can not simply backsubstitute to obtain easy expressions for all $a_{i,j,k}, b_{i,j,k}, c_{i,j,k}, d_{i,j,k}$, since more of these always show up when trying to introduce new relations for a partial Gröbner basis computation. Nonetheless, looking at the lowest degrees in which the coefficients occur, we can distinguish four sets as follows:

$$\begin{aligned}
S_1 &= \{a_{i,3,3}, b_{i,3,3}, c_{i,3,3} \mid 0 \leq i \leq 3\}, \\
S_2 &= \{a_{i,j,3}, b_{i,j,3}, c_{i,j,3}, d_{i,3,3} \mid 0 \leq i, j \leq 2\}, \\
S_3 &= \{a_{i,j,k}, b_{i,j,k}, c_{i,j,k}, d_{i,j,3} \mid 0 \leq i, j, k \leq 2\}, \\
S_4 &= \{d_{i,j,k} \mid 0 \leq i, j, k \leq 2\}.
\end{aligned}$$

The coefficients in S_1 are easiest to express since they are all either zero or (a small power of) Δ. All coefficients in S_2 satisfy at least one linear relation only involving terms in $S_2 \cup \mathfrak{G}_2$, where $\mathfrak{G}_2 = \{f_i\Delta \mid 0 \leq i \leq 6\} \cup \{g_i \mid 0 \leq i \leq 6\}$. As evident by the example of $a_{2,2,3}$ above, some of these can be expressed directly in terms of $\mathfrak{G}_2$. There are however fewer such linear relations than variables, hence we can not expect this to always be the case. Nonetheless, it seems like $\mathfrak{G}_2$ is a good candidate set to express the elements of S_2 in the following sense.

Let $S_2' \subset S_2$ be the subset of coefficients for which we have already found an (easy) expression. Fix an (arbitrary) ordering for all monomials $r^i s^j t^k$ occurring in $S_2' \cup \mathfrak{G}_2$. Define the matrix A as the one where each row represents an element from $S_2' \cup \mathfrak{G}_2$, and where the column entries correspond to the coefficient at the (fixed ordering) monomial $r^i s^j t^k$ (including a lot of zeros for missing terms).

Choose an element $s \in \mathcal{S}_2$ which is not in $\mathcal{S}_2'$, and express it as a column vector $\vec{s}$ based on that same monomial ordering. Finding an expression for s in terms of $\mathcal{S}_2' \cup \mathfrak{G}_2$ now boils down to finding a solution for the linear system

$$A\vec{x} = \vec{s}.$$

For all but three of the elements of $\mathcal{S}_2$, we could find such solutions $\vec{x}$.[3] However, we are not looking for just *any* solution $\vec{x}$, we are looking for one such that it results in an easy to evaluate expression for the respective s. To find the actual fastest evaluation of s, we would need to know the concrete performance of our hard- and software related to finite field arithmetic. To avoid this being too platform-dependent, we content ourselves by trying to find the $\vec{x}$ such that $||\vec{x}||_0$ is smallest; i.e. we are looking for the sparsest solution $\vec{x}$ out of all options.

If an extremely sparse solution exists (such as in the case of $a_{2,3,3}$), an algebra software package such as Magma may return it directly when asked to solve the system $A\vec{x} = \vec{s}$. Unfortunately, this stops being the case rather quickly. Denoting $\mathcal{L}$ as the lattice of the kernel of A, we can also compute the closest vectors $\vec{v}_i$ to $\mathcal{L}$ for one already-found $\vec{x}$. The difference between $\vec{x}$ and these close vectors yield solutions to the linear system of equations with minimized L_2-norm. Even though a minimal $||\vec{x} - \vec{v}_i||_2$ will not result in a minimal $||\vec{x} - \vec{v}_i||_0$, generically we can still expect the latter to be small as well. Assuming we can enumerate enough close vectors $\vec{v}_i$, we can simply compute all $||\vec{x} - \vec{v}_i||_0$ and choose the one which results in the sparsest solution. Even though this strategy provided some solid results, it - again unfortunately - stops being convenient rather quickly since the close vectors with regard to the L_2-norm stopped yielding sparse solutions. Furthermore, for $\mathcal{S}_3$ and $\mathcal{S}_4$ up ahead, this approach resulted in too large dimensions for $\mathcal{L}$ so we had to resort to other methods.

We are trying to find solutions to $A\vec{x} = \vec{s}$ under the condition that $||\vec{x}||_0$ is minimal. This setting can be translated to the following system of conditions:

$$A\vec{x} = \vec{s}, \qquad y_i \in \{0, 1\},$$
$$\sum_i y_i \le m, \qquad |x_i| \le My_i,$$

where $\vec{y}$ is a vector of boolean predicates with coefficients y_i, the integer m is an upper bound for the amount of nonzero entries in $\vec{x}$, and M is an upper bound for the coefficients in $\vec{x}$. This is a problem that can be solved using Mixed Integer Linear Programming and is used often in machine learning. This problem is NP-hard, but for smallish m, M, and somewhat restricted dimensions of A, this can be solved in reasonable time using Python's built-in function `scipy.optimize.milp`.

Using these methods, we managed to find sparse solutions $\vec{x}$ for all $s \in \mathcal{S}_2$. For $\mathcal{S}_3$ we remark that they stem from quadratic and cubic equations which

---

[3] These three missing expressions seem independent on the order in which we add elements to $\mathcal{S}_2'$. They are still relatively compactly representable however.

always involve a factor Δ, hence we must consider $\Delta S_3 = \{\Delta s \mid s \in S_3\}$ instead. The other terms in the obtained relations are in

$$\mathfrak{G}_3 = S_2^2 \cup \{f_i \Delta s \mid 0 \leq i \leq 6, s \in S_2\} \cup \{g_i s \mid 0 \leq i \leq 6, s \in S_2\},$$

where $S_2^2 = \{s_i s_j \mid s_i, s_j \in S_2\}$. For S_4 the trend continues in a similar fashion, and the other terms in the relation come from

$$\mathfrak{G}_4 = S_2^3 \cup \Delta S_3 \cup \{f_i \Delta s \mid 0 \leq i \leq 6, s \in S_2^2\} \cup \{g_i s \mid 0 \leq i \leq 6, s \in S_2^2\},$$

where $S_2^3 = \{s_i s_j s_k \mid s_i, s_j, s_k \in S_2\}$.

Final Results. Using the methods outlined above, we managed to find expressions for all $a_{i,j,k}, b_{i,j,k}, c_{i,j,k}, d_{i,j,k}$. Replacing a squaring and cubing with one respectively two multiplications, evaluating all of these coefficients now takes 2.234 multiplications, which is a 94% reduction compared to the formulae from [4]. These coefficients can be recycled for each point on the Kummer surface, such that pushing multiple points through at once comes with little overhead compared to pushing through just one point. We emphasize that the obtained expressions do not work for certain small field characteristics, but this imposes no restrictions for cryptographic applications.

4   Non-generic $(3, 3)$-Isogeny Formulae

In this section we will describe formulae for $(3,3)$-isogenies where the domain or the codomain are products of elliptic curves. For the splitting and the gluing case our formulae are based on the parametrization by Bröker, Howe, Lauter and Stevenhagen [3].

4.1 $(3, 3)$-Isogenies Between Elliptic Products

Let $\Phi : E_1 \times E_2 \to E_1' \times E_2'$ be a $(3,3)$-isogeny such that $\ker \Phi$ is diagonal; i.e. it is of the form $\langle (P_1, \infty_{E_2}), (\infty_{E_1}, P_2) \rangle$. Then Φ decomposes as a direct product $\phi_1 \times \phi_2$, where $\phi_i : E_i \to E_i'$ are 3-isogenies for $i \in \{1, 2\}$. Formulae for Φ can hence be obtained from elliptic curves with rational 3-torsion.

Proposition 1. *Let Φ be a $(3,3)$-isogeny between products of elliptic curves, with diagonal kernel which is generated by rational points. Then up to isomorphism, this isogeny is given by*

$$\Phi : E_1 \times E_2 \to E_1' \times E_2'$$
$$(P_1, P_2) \mapsto (\phi_1(P_1), \phi_2(P_2)),$$

where for $i \in \{1, 2\}$ we have

$$E_i : y^2 + a_i xy + b_i y = x^3$$
$$E_i' : y^2 + a_i xy + b_i y = x^3 - 5a_i b_i x - a_i^3 b_i - 7b_i^2$$

and

$$\phi_i(x, y) = \left(\frac{x^3 + a_i b_i x + b_i^2}{x^2}, \frac{x^3 y - a_i^2 b_i x^2 - a_i b_i xy - 2a_i b_i^2 x - 2b_i^2 y - b_i^3}{x^3} \right).$$

Proof. The parametrization of 3-isogenies between elliptic curves is well-known, see for example [9, Section 4]. The evaluation on points is a straightforward computation by using $(0,0)$ as kernel generator in Vélu-style formulae. □

If the kernel of Φ is nondiagonal, then E_1 and E_2 are necessarily connected by a 2-isogeny, which follows from Kani's reducibility criterion [18]. Its parametrization is independent of the rationality of the 3-torsion.

Proposition 2. *Let Φ be a $(3,3)$-isogeny between products of elliptic curves, with nondiagonal kernel. Then this isogeny is an endomorphism given by*

$$\Phi : E_1 \times E_2 \to E_1 \times E_2$$
$$(P_1, P_2) \mapsto (P_1 + \hat{\phi}(P_2), P_2 - \phi(P_1)),$$

where $\phi : E_1 \to E_2$ is a 2-isogeny such that $\ker \Phi = \{(P, \phi(P)) \mid P \in E_1[3]\}$. Up to isomorphism[4], ϕ is given by

$$\phi : E_1 \to E_2$$
$$(x, y) \mapsto \left(\frac{x^2 + b}{x}, y \cdot \frac{x^2 - b}{x^2} \right),$$
$$\hat{\phi} : E_2 \to E_1$$
$$(x, y) \mapsto \left(\frac{x^2 - 4b}{4(x + a)}, y \cdot \frac{x^2 + 2ax + 4b}{8(x + a)^2} \right),$$

where

$$E_1 : y^2 = x^3 + ax^2 + bx, \qquad E_2 : y^2 = x^3 + ax^2 - 4bx - 4ab.$$

Proof. Due to [18, Theorem 2.6], it must hold that E_1 and E_2 are connected by means of a 2-isogeny. Consider the following commutative diagram as in [22, Theorem 1], where ϕ and ϕ' are 2-isogenies:

$$\begin{array}{ccc} E_1 & \xrightarrow{\phi} & E_2 \\ \downarrow{\gamma} & & \downarrow{\gamma'} \\ E_1' & \xrightarrow{\phi'} & E_2' \end{array}$$

Then

$$\Phi : E_1' \times E_2 \to E_1 \times E_2'$$
$$(P_1, P_2) \mapsto (\hat{\gamma}(P_1) + \hat{\phi}(P_2), \gamma'(P_2) - \phi'(P_1))$$

---

[4] If the relevant 2-torsion is not rational, this isomorphism may be defined over a (small) field extension, regardless of the rationality of the 3-torsion.

is a $(\deg\gamma + \deg\phi, \deg\gamma + \deg\phi)$-isogeny which preserves product polarizations. The degree of γ and γ' is then necessarily one if we want to construct a $(3,3)$-isogeny, such that up to isomorphism we can choose $E_i = E_i'$ for $i \in \{1,2\}$, as well as $\phi = \phi'$. The isogeny Φ can then be evaluated as $\Phi(P_1, P_2) = (P_1 + \hat{\phi}(P_2), P_2 - \phi(P_1))$. The parametrization of the 2-isogeny ϕ is such that $\ker\phi = \langle(0,0)\rangle$. $\square$

Remark 3. For a fixed $\mathbb{F}_{p^2}$, there are $\mathcal{O}(p)$ supersingular elliptic curves and all have exactly three outgoing 2-isogenies, yet there are $\mathcal{O}(p^3)$ superspecial p.p.a.s. The ratio of products of 2-isogenous supersingular elliptic curves to superspecial p.p.a.s. is hence $\mathcal{O}(p^{-2})$. Therefore, it is to be expected that in cryptographic applications, isogenies as in Proposition 2 will never be used, unless the protocol is constructed in a particular way to encounter this type.

4.2 Splitting

Here, we consider $(3,3)$-isogenies where the domain is the Jacobian of a genus-2 curve and the codomain is a product of elliptic curves. Such an isogeny is called a $(3,3)$-splitting and it arises from degree-3 covers $\psi_1 : \mathcal{C} \to E_1$ and $\psi_2 : \mathcal{C} \to E_2$. More precisely, it is the product of the push forwards of these maps, i.e. $\Phi = \psi_{1,*} \times \psi_{2,*}$ To make these more explicit, assume that the maps ψ_1 and ψ_2 are compatible with the hyperelliptic involution $\iota : \mathcal{C} \to \mathcal{C}$, i.e. we have $\psi_i(\iota(P)) = -\psi_i(P)$ for all $P \in \mathcal{C}(K)$. In that case, the isogeny is given by

$$
\begin{aligned}
\Phi : \mathrm{Jac}(\mathcal{C}) &\to E_1 \times E_2 \\
[P + Q - D_\infty] &\mapsto (\psi_1(P) + \psi_1(Q), \ \psi_2(P) + \psi_2(Q)).
\end{aligned}
\tag{3}
$$

There exists a complete parametrization for this case and an explicit description of the maps ψ_1 and ψ_2 by Bröker, Howe, Lauter and Stevenhagen [3].

Proposition 3 (Proposition A.2 in [3]). *Let* $a, b, c, d, t \in k$ *satisfy*

$$12ac + 16bd = 1, \quad \Delta_1 = a^3 + b^2 \neq 0, \quad \Delta_2 = c^3 + d^2 \neq 0, \quad t \neq 0.$$

Define polynomials $F_{a,b,c,d,t}, f_1, f_2$ *by*

$$
\begin{aligned}
F_{a,b,c,d,t} &= (x^3 + 3ax + 2b)(2dx^3 + 3cx^2 + 1), \\
f_1 &= x^3 + 12(2a^2d - bc)x^2 + 12(16ad^2 + 3c^2)\Delta_1 x + 512\Delta_1^2 d^3, \\
f_2 &= x^3 + 12(2bc^2 - ad)x^2 + 12(16b^2c + 3a^2)\Delta_2 x + 512\Delta_2^2 b^3,
\end{aligned}
$$

and consider the curves $C_{a,b,c,d,t} : ty^2 = f(x)$ *and* $E_{a,b,c,d,t,i} : ty^2 = f_i(x)$ *for* $i \in \{1,2\}$. *Then there are degree-3 morphisms given by*

$$
\begin{aligned}
\psi_{a,b,c,d,t,i} : \mathcal{C}_{a,b,c,d,t} &\to E_{a,b,c,d,t,i} \\
(x,y) &\mapsto (r_i(x), s_i(x) \cdot y)
\end{aligned}
$$

with

$$r_1(x) = 12\Delta_1 \frac{-dx + e}{x^3 + 3ax + 2b}, \qquad s_1 = \Delta_1 \frac{16dx^3 - 12cx^2 - 1}{(x^3 + 3ax + 2b)^2},$$

$$r_2(x) = 12\Delta_2 \frac{x^2(ax - 2b)}{2dx^3 + 3cx^2 + 1}, \qquad s_2 = \Delta_2 \frac{x^3 + 12ax - 16b}{(2dx^3 + 3cx^2 + 1)^2}.$$

On the other hand, if C is a genus-2 curve whose Jacobian is $(3, 3)$-isogenous to a product of elliptic curves $E_1 \times E_2$, then there exists a quintuple (a, b, c, d, t) as above and isomorphisms $C \to C_{a,b,c,d,t}$ and $E_i \to E_{a,b,c,d,t,i}$ for $i \in \{1, 2\}$.

From now on, we assume that we are in the setting of the above proposition. The determination of the necessary coordinate transformation from C to a curve $C_{a,b,c,d,t}$ will be explained in Sect. 5.2. Using the explicit description of the maps $\psi_{a,b,c,d,t,1}, \psi_{a,b,c,d,t,2}$ one can derive a formula for the map $\Phi : \mathrm{Jac}(C_{a,b,c,d,t}) \to E_{a,b,c,d,t,1} \times E_{a,b,c,d,t,2}$ using the description in Eq. 3. That said, here we focus on the induced map on the level of Kummer varieties.

Proposition 4. *Let $C_{a,b,c,d,t}$ and $E_{a,b,c,d,t,i}$ for $i \in \{1, 2\}$ be as in Proposition 3. Define*

$$\Phi_{\mathcal{K}} : \mathcal{K}(C_{a,b,c,d,t}) \to \mathbb{P}^1 \times \mathbb{P}^1$$

as the induced $(3, 3)$-isogeny on the level of Kummer surfaces. Then the kernel of $\Phi_{\mathcal{K}}$ is given by the subvariety of $\mathcal{K}(C)$ defined by

$$\left\{ \begin{array}{l} 0 = \xi_0^2 + 4c(\xi_1^2 - \xi_0\xi_2) - 8d\xi_1\xi_2 \\ 0 = \xi_2^2 + 4a(\xi_1^2 - \xi_0\xi_2) - 8b\xi_0\xi_1 \end{array} \right\}$$

Moreover, there exist polynomials $g_{x,1}, g_{z,1}, g_{x,2}, g_{z,2} \in \mathbb{Z}[\xi_0, \xi_1, \xi_2, \xi_3]$ such that

$$\Phi_{\mathcal{K}} : (\xi_0 : \xi_1 : \xi_2 : \xi_3) \mapsto ((g_{x,1}, g_{z,1}), (g_{x,2}, g_{z,2})).$$

The explicit formulae for the map are provided in the auxiliary material, see Sect. 8.

Proof. The derivation of the explicit formulae for $\Phi_{\mathcal{K}}$ can be done using a computer algebra package. Here, we sketch the main steps.

Let $\xi = (\xi_0 : \xi_1 : \xi_2 : \xi_3) \in \mathcal{K}(C)$. We write $[P + Q - D_\infty] \in \mathrm{Jac}(C)$ with $P = (x_1, y_1)$ and $Q = (x_2, y_2)$ for a point lying above ξ. To find explicit formulae, we will be working in the ring $\mathbb{Z}[\xi_0, \xi_1, \xi_2, \xi_3, x_1, y_1, x_2, y_2]$, but at least at the final step, the variables x_1, y_1, x_2, y_2 need to be eliminated. While we cannot deduce the explicit coordinates of P and Q from ξ alone, we can use the following identities for this elimination.

$$\begin{aligned} x_1 + x_2 &= \xi_1/\xi_0, \\ x_1 x_2 &= \xi_2/\xi_0, \\ 2y_1 y_2 &= \left(\phi(\xi_0, \xi_1, \xi_2) - \xi_3(\xi_1^2 - 4\xi_0\xi_2) \right)/\xi_0^3. \end{aligned} \tag{4}$$

Denote $\psi_i = \psi_{a,b,c,d,t,i}$ for $i \in \{1,2\}$. The isogeny Φ is equal to the product $\psi_{1,*} \times \psi_{2,*}$, cf. Equation 3. Using the explicit description of $\psi_i : \mathcal{C}_{a,b,c,d,t} \to E_{a,b,c,d,t,i}$ from Proposition 3, we symbolically compute $P_i = \psi_i(P)$ and $Q_i = \psi_i(Q)$ on E_i for $i \in \{1,2\}$. Applying the standard formulae for elliptic curve addition, we then compute $R_i = P_i + Q_i$ for $i \in \{1,2\}$. By construction, the obtained expressions for the coordinates of R_i are invariant under swapping P and Q, hence symmetric in x_1, x_2 and in y_1, y_2. Using the Kummer surface coordinates from Eq. 4, it is therefore possible to completely eliminate x_1 and x_2 from the coordinates. The elimination of y_1 and y_2 is more subtle. While we can express $y_1 y_2$ in Kummer surface coordinates, this is not possible for the symmetric expression $y_1 + y_2$. However, it is still possible to eliminate the variables y_1 and y_2 from the formula for the x-coordinate of R_i, but this is not the case for its y-coordinate.[5]

As a result, we obtain quartic polynomials $g_{x,1}, g_{z,1}, g_{x,2}, g_{z,2} \in \mathbb{Z}[\xi_0, \xi_1, \xi_2, \xi_3]$ defining the map $\Phi_{\mathcal{K}} \to \mathbb{P}^1 \times \mathbb{P}^1$. The polynomials

$$g_{z,1} = \left(\xi_0^2 + 4c(\xi_1^2 - \xi_0\xi_2) - 8d\xi_1\xi_2\right)^2, \qquad g_{z,2} = \left(\xi_2^2 + 4a(\xi_1^2 - \xi_0\xi_2) - 8b\xi_0\xi_1\right)^2$$

define the kernel of the isogeny. Explicit descriptions for $g_{x,1}, g_{x,2}$ and a formal verification can be found in the auxiliary material, see Sect. 8.   □

4.3   Gluing

Let us now consider the case where the domain of the $(3,3)$-isogeny is a product of elliptic curves and its codomain the Jacobian of a genus-2 curve. Such an isogeny is called a $(3,3)$-*gluing*, and it is the dual of the $(3,3)$-split isogeny described above. Similar as in that case, a $(3,3)$-gluing Φ arises from degree-3 covers $\psi_1 : \mathcal{C} \to E_1$ and $\psi_2 : \mathcal{C} \to E_2$. And in this case it is the product of the pull-backs, i.e. $\Phi = \psi_1^* \times \psi_2^* : E_1 \times E_2 \to \mathrm{Jac}(\mathcal{C})$. To derive explicit formulae for this isogeny, we again use the parametrization from [3], cf. Proposition 3.

Proposition 5. *Let $\mathcal{C}_{a,b,c,d,t}$ and $E_{a,b,c,d,t,i}$ for $i \in \{1,2\}$ be as in Proposition 3. Denote*

$$\Phi : E_{a,b,c,d,t,1} \times E_{a,b,c,d,t,2} \to Jac(\mathcal{C}_{a,b,c,d,t})$$

the $(3,3)$-isogeny induced by the maps $\psi_{a,b,c,d,t,1}$ and $\psi_{a,b,c,d,t,2}$. Writing

$$\alpha_1 = x_1 + 8a^2d - 6bc, \qquad \beta_1 = ax_1 + 8d\Delta_1, \qquad \gamma_1 = 48c\Delta_1 - 8bx_1,$$
$$\alpha_2 = x_2 + 8bc^2 - 6ad, \qquad \beta_2 = cx_2 + 8b\Delta_2, \qquad \gamma_2 = 48a\Delta_2 - 8dx_2,$$

we have

$$\psi_{a,b,c,d,t,i}^* : E_{a,b,c,d,t,i} \to Jac(\mathcal{C}_{a,b,c,d,t})$$
$$(x_i, y_i) \mapsto [x^2 + \lambda_{i,1}x + \lambda_{i,0}, -4y_i(\mu_{i,1}x + \mu_{i,0})]$$

---

[5] The element $y_1 + y_2$ can of course be represented in terms of the Mumford coordinates of $[P + Q - D_\infty]$ allowing to deduce a formula for the y-coordinates in that setting as well.

with

$$\lambda_{1,1} = \frac{-4\beta_1}{4\alpha_1^2 + a}, \qquad \lambda_{1,0} = \frac{\gamma_1}{4\alpha_1^2 + a}, \qquad \lambda_{2,1} = \frac{-4\beta_2}{\gamma_2}, \qquad \lambda_{2,0} = \frac{4\alpha_2^2 + c}{\gamma_2}$$

and

$$\mu_{1,1} = \frac{4\alpha_1^3 + 3a\alpha_1 + b}{(4\alpha_1^2 + a)^2}, \qquad \mu_{1,0} = \frac{4\beta_1^2 - \Delta_1}{a(4\alpha_1^2 + a)^2}$$

$$\mu_{2,1} = \frac{-4\Delta_2}{\gamma_2^2}, \qquad \mu_{2,0} = \frac{16\Delta_2(2bc + 3a(x_2 + \alpha_2)) - 8dx_2^2}{\gamma_2^2}.$$

Proof. Denote $\psi_i = \psi_{a,b,c,d,t,i} : \mathcal{C}_{a,b,c,d,t} \to E_{a,b,c,d,t,i}$. Counted with multiplicities, each point $P_i = (x_i, y_i) \in E_{a,b,c,d,t,i}$ has precisely 3 preimages in $\mathcal{C}_{a,b,c,d,t}$. From the explicit description of the maps ψ_i, one can directly read off the preimages of the neutral element on the two elliptic curves. Naturally, these consist of two disjoint sets of the Weierstrass point of the hyperelliptic curve. More precisely,

$$\psi_i^{-1}(\infty) = \{(\alpha, 0) \in \mathcal{C}_{a,b,c,d,t}(\bar{k}) \mid F_i(\alpha) = 0\},$$

where $F_1 = x^3 + 3ax + 2b$ and $F_2 = 2dx^3 + 3cx^2 + 1$ are the two factors of the defining polynomial of $\mathcal{C}_{a,b,c,d,t}$. This means that under the pull-back $\psi_i^* : E_{a,b,c,d,t,i} \to \mathrm{Jac}(\mathcal{C}_{a,b,c,d,t})$, the element $[P_i - \infty]$ gets mapped to

$$\left[\sum_{P' \in \psi_i^{-1}(P_i)} P' - \sum_{F_i(\alpha)=0} (\alpha, 0) \right] = \left[\sum_{P' \in \psi_i^{-1}(P_i)} P' + \sum_{F_i(\alpha)=0} (\alpha, 0) - 3 \cdot D_\infty \right].$$

Our strategy to find explicit formulae of this map is very similar to that in the proof of Proposition 4. That is, we first express the preimage of a general point $P_i = (x_i, y_i) \in E_i$ symbolically. This requires working in the ring $R = \mathbb{Q}[x_i, y_i, u_1, u_2, u_3, v_1, v_2, v_3]$, where (u_j, v_j) represent the coordinates of the points $\{P_j'\}$ in the preimage of P_i. In the final formula, the variables u_j, v_j need to be eliminated. To this end, one uses the explicit description of the maps ψ_i (Proposition 3), more precisely we use the identities

$$r_i(u_j) = x_i \quad \text{and} \quad s_i(u_j)v_j = y_i \tag{5}$$

for all $j \in \{1, 2, 3\}$. In particular, u_1, u_2, u_3 are the roots of a cubic polynomial in $\mathbb{Q}[x_i] \subset R$, hence their elementary symmetric polynomials are in $\mathbb{Q}[x_i]$. The next step is to find the unreduced Mumford coordinates of the divisor

$$D_P = \sum_{P' \in \psi_i^{-1}(P)} P' + \sum_{F_i(\alpha)=0} (\alpha, 0) - 3 \cdot D_\infty.$$

These consist of a pair of polynomials $[A, B]$, where $A \in R[x]$ is a degree-6 polynomial with roots the x-coordinates of the affine points in the support of D_P and $B \in R[x]$ interpolates the points in the support of D_P. For A, one immediately finds an expression with coefficients in $\mathbb{Q}[x_i] \subset R$. It is the product of F_1 and the cubic polynomial with roots u_1, u_2, u_3. The computation of B requires more work. In our approach, we used the standard Newton interpolation method to represent the polynomial in $R[x]$, after which we used the above relations obtained from Eq. 5 to eliminate the variables u_j, v_j.

It remains to compute the reduced Mumford coordinates for $[D_P]$. This can be done in two reduction steps following Cantor's algorithm. The resulting Mumford coordinates are $[x^2 + \lambda_{i,1} x + \lambda_{i,0}, -4y_i(\mu_{i,1} x + \mu_{i,0})]$ as in the statement of the proposition. A formal verification of the correctness of the formulae is provided in the auxiliary material, see Sect. 8.   □

5   Coordinate Transformations

In the two previous sections, we discussed explicit formulae for all 4 types of $(3,3)$-isogenies. In order to apply these formulae to compute a specific $(3,3)$-isogeny, it is necessary to compute a coordinate transformation to a given parametrization. Here, we first discuss coordinate transformations in general and provide explicit formulae for the induced transformation on the Kummer surface. In the second part, we explain the determination of a suitable transformation, given as input a description of the $(3,3)$-kernel.

5.1   Explicit Formulae for Transformations

To fix some notation, we first recall a standard result about the coordinate transformations for hyperelliptic curves, see for example [21, Corollary 7.4.33].

Proposition 6. *Let* $\mathcal{C} : y^2 = f(x), \mathcal{C}' : y'^2 = g(x')$ *be two curves of genus 2 defined over* k. *Then* $\mathcal{C}$ *and* $\mathcal{C}'$ *are* k-*isomorphic iff there exist* $\begin{pmatrix} \alpha & \beta \\ \gamma & \delta \end{pmatrix} \in GL_2(k)$ *and* $\epsilon \in k^\times$ *such that*

$$x' = \frac{\alpha x + \beta}{\gamma x + \delta}, \quad y' = \frac{\epsilon y}{(\gamma x + \delta)^3}.$$

The above proposition describes the effect of coordinate transformations on the points of a hyperelliptic curve $\mathcal{C}$. One can also consider the induced maps on the Mumford coefficients of elements in the Jacobian $\mathrm{Jac}(\mathcal{C})$ or on the Kummer surface $\mathcal{K}(\mathcal{C})$. In our application, the latter type of transformation will be important. The derivation of the induced maps on the Kummer surface can be done by simple algebra. Since we could not find any explicit formulae in the literature, we provide the resulting formulae here.

Proposition 7. *Let* $\mathcal{C} : y^2 = F(x), \mathcal{C}' : y'^2 = G(x')$ *be two* k-*isomorphic genus-2 curves. Assume that the coordinate transformation between the curves is defined* by $\begin{pmatrix} \alpha & \beta \\ \gamma & \delta \end{pmatrix} \in GL_2(k)$ and $\epsilon \in k^\times$ as described in Proposition 6 and set $\vartheta = \alpha\delta + \beta\gamma$, $\varrho = \alpha\beta\gamma\delta$. Then

$$\xi'_0 = \delta^2 \xi_0 + \gamma\delta\xi_1 + \gamma^2\xi_2,$$
$$\xi'_1 = 2\beta\delta\xi_0 + \vartheta\xi_1 + 2\alpha\gamma\xi_2,$$
$$\xi'_2 = \beta^2\xi_0 + \alpha\beta\xi_1 + \alpha^2\xi_2,$$
$$\xi'_3 = \left(\lambda_0\xi_0 + \lambda_1\xi_1 + \lambda_2\xi_2 + (\alpha\delta - \beta\gamma)^4\xi_3\right)/\epsilon^2,$$

with

$$\lambda_0 = -2\alpha^2\gamma^2(3\vartheta^2 - 8\varrho)f_0 + 2\alpha\gamma\vartheta(\vartheta^2 - 2\varrho)f_1 - 4\varrho(\vartheta^2 - 2\varrho)f_2$$
$$+ \beta\delta\vartheta^3 f_3 - 2\beta^2\delta^2\vartheta^2 f_4 + 4\beta^3\delta^3\vartheta f_5 - 8\beta^4\delta^4 f_6,$$
$$\lambda_1 = -4\alpha^3\gamma^3\vartheta f_0 + \alpha^2\gamma^2(\vartheta^2 + 4\varrho)f_1 - 4\alpha\gamma\varrho\vartheta f_2 + \varrho(\vartheta^2 + 4\varrho)f_3$$
$$- 4\beta\delta\varrho\vartheta f_4 + \beta^2\delta^2(\vartheta^2 + 4\varrho)f_5 - 4\beta^3\delta^3\vartheta f_6,$$
$$\lambda_2 = -8\alpha^4\gamma^4 f_0 + 4\alpha^3\gamma^3\vartheta f_1 - 2\alpha^2\gamma^2\vartheta^2 f_2 + \alpha\gamma\vartheta^3 f_3 - 4\varrho(\vartheta^2 - 2\varrho)f_4$$
$$+ 2\beta\delta\vartheta(\vartheta^2 - 2\varrho)f_5 - 2\beta^2\delta^2(3\vartheta^2 - 8\varrho)f_6,$$

defines the corresponding coordinate transformations between the Kummer surfaces $\mathcal{K}(\mathcal{C})$ and $\mathcal{K}(\mathcal{C}')$.

Proof. This can be verified by a direct computation.   □

5.2 Finding the Correct Transformation

Given two generators T_1, T_2 of a $(3,3)$-subgroup of a p.p.a.s., we explain how to compute the coordinate transformation that allows us to apply one of the isogeny formulae from Sect. 3 and Subsect. 4.2. While the exact procedure depends on the type of $(3,3)$-isogeny, we use a Gröbner basis approach as the underlying method in all cases.

Generic Case (Sect. 3). We first consider the generic case, that is we are given two kernel generators $T_1, T_2 \in \mathrm{Jac}(\mathcal{C})$ which define a $(3,3)$-isogeny to the Jacobian of another genus-2 curve. The goal is to find parameters $(\alpha, \beta, \gamma, \delta, \epsilon)$ defining a coordinate transformation as in Proposition 6 and parameters (r, s, t) such that the image curve is in the form of $\mathcal{C}_{r,s,t}$ and the images of the kernel generators are given by T and T' as described in Subsect. 3.1. An efficient method for this has already been developed in the context of a $(3,3)$-based hash function in [6]. We use their implementation for our algorithms as well.

Product Case (Subsect. 4.1). Transformations between products of elliptic curves are products of isomorphisms between elliptic curves. These are well-known and of the form $(x, y) \mapsto (u'^2 x + r', u'^3 y + s'u'^2 x + t')$ for elliptic curves in Weierstraß form, where u' is necessarily a unit (see for example [11, Subsection 4.4.2]).

Splitting Case (Subsect. 4.2). Now assume we are given two kernel generators $T_1, T_2 \in \mathrm{Jac}(\mathcal{C})$ that define a $(3,3)$-isogeny to a product of elliptic curves. In this case, we need to find parameters $(\alpha, \beta, \gamma, \delta, \epsilon)$ defining the transformation together with parameters (a, b, c, d, t) such that the image of the curve $\mathcal{C} : y^2 = f(x)$ under the transformation is equal to $\mathcal{C}_{a,b,c,d,t} : ty^2 = F_{a,b,c,d,t}(x)$ as in Proposition 3. Note that such a transformation only exists if $\mathrm{Jac}(\mathcal{C})$ is indeed $(3,3)$-isogenous to a product of elliptic curves. In this case the splitting is unique with overwhelming probability. One method to (probabilistically) find the correct parameters is to symbolically equate the coefficients of

$$ty^2 = F_{a,b,c,d,t}(x) \quad \text{and} \quad y'^2 = f(x')$$

with

$$x' = \frac{\alpha x + \beta}{\gamma x + \delta}, \quad y' = \frac{\epsilon y}{(\gamma x + \delta)^3}.$$

Together with the conditions on the parameters

$$12ac + 16bd = 1, \quad \Delta_1 = a^3 + b^2 \neq 0, \quad \Delta_2 = c^3 + d^2 \neq 0, \quad t \neq 0,$$

this yields a system of equations in $k[a, b, c, d, t, \alpha, \beta, \gamma, \delta, \epsilon]$ which can be solved by a Gröbner basis computation. As mentioned before, the defined splitting is unique, however there will be in general multiple solutions to the system stemming from an equivalence relation on the set of parameters $\{a, b, c, d, t\}$, as well as on the parameters defining the transformation.

In practice, the Gröbner basis computation can be sped up by providing additional information on the parameters. Here, such information is available by means of the kernel generators T_1, T_2. While we are not aware of explicit formulae for the kernel generators defining the $(3,3)$-isogeny from Proposition 3, we did derive relations for the Kummer coordinates of the kernel generators for exactly the isogeny from Proposition 4. Hence, we add the conditions

$$0 = \left(\xi_0'^2 + 4c(\xi_1'^2 - \xi_0'\xi_2') - 8d\xi_1'\xi_2' \right)^2,$$
$$0 = \left(\xi_2'^2 + 4a(\xi_1'^2 - \xi_0'\xi_2') - 8b\xi_0'\xi_1' \right)^2$$

with $(\xi_0', \xi_1', \xi_2', \xi_3')$ the image of $(\xi_0, \xi_1, \xi_2, \xi_3) \in \{T_1, T_2\}$ computed as in Proposition 7. This not only speeds up the Gröbner basis computation to solve the system by several orders of magnitude, but it also guarantees that we use the correct kernel in the (unlikely) case that there exist two $(3,3)$-splittings.

Gluing Case (Subsect. 4.3). Despite being the dual of the splitting case, finding the coordinate transformation for the gluing is more intricate. Let $E_1 \times E_2$ be a product of elliptic curves. Over the algebraic closure $\bar{k}$, there exist 24 different ways to glue elliptic curves along their 3-torsion.[6] For instance, [3, Algorithm 5.4] explains how to compute all $(3,3)$-isogenous Jacobians of genus-2 curves for a given product of elliptic curves. Here, we are only interested in one specific isogeny defined by a specific $(3,3)$-subgroup $\langle T_1, T_2 \rangle \subset E_1 \times E_2$.

If the elliptic curves are given in general Weierstrass form $y^2 + a_1 xy + a_3 y = x^3 + a_2 x^2 + a_4 x + a_6$, then we first apply the transformation $y' = (y + a_1 x +$

---

[6] In light of Proposition 2, there may be slightly fewer if E_1 and E_2 are 2-isogenous.

$a_3)/2$ to obtain an equation of the form $y'^2 = f(x)$. Now it suffices to consider coordinate transformations of the form $x = \alpha x + \beta$, $y' = \epsilon y$ preserving this form. In that setting, our goal is to find a pair of transformations $(\alpha_i, \beta_i, \epsilon_i)$ for E_i with $i \in \{1, 2\}$ and parameters (a, b, c, d, t) such that after applying the transformations, the elliptic curves are as in Proposition 3. Moreover, we require that (the transformations of) T_1, T_2 are in the kernel of the resulting $(3, 3)$-isogeny.

The first conditions can be imposed by a standard coefficient comparison similar to the splitting case. For the second condition, we use our explicit description of the gluing map from Proposition 5 which yields four additional conditions per kernel generator. More precisely, we require that

$$\psi^*_{a,b,c,d,t,1}(T_i') = -\psi^*_{a,b,c,d,t,2}(T_i') \quad \text{for } i \in \{1, 2\}$$

which provides one condition per Mumford coordinate. The resulting system has a unique solution up to the equivalence relations described in the previous part, and it can be solved efficiently by a Gröbner basis computation.

6   A $(3, 3)$-Variant of the CGL Hash Function

In this section, we will discuss an implementation of a $(3, 3)$-variant of the CGL hash function similar to the one from [6].

6.1   Starting p.p.a.s

In the elliptic-curve case, knowledge of the starting curve's endomorphism ring reveals cycles in the isogeny graph, which can be used to create collisions in the corresponding hash function (see for example [13]). Even though this has not been written down explicitly yet, there is no reason to assume that the same does not hold in higher dimensions. Ideally, our starting p.p.a.s. would thus be sampled randomly from the set of superspecial p.p.a.s. such that its endomorphism ring is unknown. Unfortunately, there is no known way to do this without revealing an isogeny path to a superspecial p.p.a.s. of which the endomorphism ring is known. This connecting isogeny can then be used to reveal the endomorphism ring of the resulting superspecial p.p.a.s. as well. In fact, hashing into the set of supersingular elliptic curves is still an open problem in cryptography.[7]

In our setting, the field characteristic will always be of the form $p = f \cdot 3^n - 1$ for some (necessarily even) cofactor f. This results in the Jacobians of the well-known genus-2 curve $\mathcal{C} : y^2 = x^6 - 1$ to be superspecial, and it is isomorphic to the curve $\mathcal{C}' : y^2 = (x^2 - 1)(x^2 - 2x)(x - 1/2)$ used in [8]. Since we can not randomly sample a superspecial p.p.a.s., we may as well start from $\mathrm{Jac}(\mathcal{C})$. Unfortunately this is a Jacobian which has degenerate 3-torsion elements in the sense of Remark 1. Indeed, one can readily verify that the divisor $D = (0, \sqrt{-1}) - \infty$ is an

---

[7] At least in a trustless set-up; for a trusted set-up variant, see [1].

element in $\mathrm{Jac}(\mathcal{C})[3]$. Given how this would immediately put us in a setting where we would have to deal with overhead occurring with probability $\mathcal{O}(p^{-1})$, we thus choose a different starting p.p.a.s. by taking a random walk in the superspecial $(3,3)$-isogeny graph starting from $\mathrm{Jac}(\mathcal{C})$. The resulting superspecial p.p.a.s. are hardcoded in the accompanying code, one for each level of security. The code also provides a symplectic basis of $\mathrm{Jac}(\mathcal{C})[3^n]$ for each security level such that $(3^n, 3^n)$-groups can be sampled uniformly at random using the methods from [20, Section 2.3].

6.2   Optimal Strategies for $(3^n, 3^n)$-Isogeny Computations

Given a maximal isotropic group $\langle T, T' \rangle \subset \mathrm{Jac}(\mathcal{C})[3^n]$, the following are two possible ways of computing the isogeny with kernel $\langle T, T' \rangle$ as chain of n $(3,3)$-isogenies.

– One can compute $(3^{n-1}T, 3^{n-1}T')$, quotient out the $(3,3)$-subgroup generated by these two elements, and compute the images of T, T' under this initial isogeny Φ_1. In the next step, we can repeat this process, but then with $(3^{n-2}\Phi_1(T), 3^{n-2}\Phi_1(T'))$ and pushing through $(\Phi_1(T), \Phi_1(T'))$. Iteratively repeating this will compute the entire $(3^n, 3^n)$-isogeny.
– One can compute the set of pairs $\{(3^iT, 3^iT') : 0 \le i < n\}$ inductively on the starting Jacobian by iterated multiplication by 3. Starting from the pair $(3^{n-1}T, 3^{n-1}T')$ one can then quotient out the $(3,3)$-subgroup generated by this pair, and push all other pairs of divisors through this initial isogeny Φ_1. This results in immediate access to the pair $(3^{n-2}\Phi_1(T), 3^{n-2}\Phi_1(T'))$ on the codomain Jacobian and we can continue inductively.

The above methods are extreme in the sense that the former computes a maximal amount of multiplications by 3, whereas the latter computes a maximal amount of images under each isogeny. In [17, Section 4], they discuss this in-depth in terms of optimal strategies, where trade-offs can be made to obtain a method in-between the extreme versions described here. They describe optimal strategies in terms of elemental $\mathbb{F}_{p^2}$-operations, which is possible since 2- and 3-isogenies between elliptic curves require a limited amount of such operations and are hence almost surely optimized already.

Unfortunately, this is not the case when working with elements of Jacobians. A first subtlety is that Magma has optimized internal arithmetic for computing a scalar multiple kT for $T \in \mathrm{Jac}(\mathcal{C})$. This internal structure outperforms reimplementing the arithmetic ourselves, which makes it impossible to express things in elemental $\mathbb{F}_{p^2}$-operations. Furthermore, the implemented scalar multiplication on Jacobians is noticeably faster if we compute the scalar $k = 3^{n-i}$ first, compared to repeatedly multiplying T by 3.

Another subtlety is that we push points through on the Kummer surface, and not on the Jacobian. This means that after the first step we do not have access to $(\Phi_1(T), \Phi_1(T'))$ but to their images on the associated Kummer surface. This is not a problem since we are only interested in quotienting out the subgroup generated by these elements, and one can perform scalar multiplications on the Kummer surface as well. The scalar multiplication formulae on our model of the Kummer surface are a lot more involved compared to their Jacobian counterparts however. In practice, one notices that it is often more efficient to lift points on the Kummer surface to an arbitrary preimage on the Jacobian, perform the scalar multiplication there, and then project back to the Kummer surface.

Due to these limitations, it is impossible to reuse the mathematical optimal strategies obtained in [17, Section 4]. Instead, we heuristically try out their well-formed balanced strategies for various pairs of weights. In any case, this leads to an approach that only requires $\mathcal{O}(n \log n)$ computations compared to the $\mathcal{O}(n^2)$ computations in the extreme methods outlined at the start of this subsection. In practice, putting the weights equal seemed to perform extremely well for all fields of cryptographic characteristic. The equal-weight strategy boils down to pushing $(3^{\lfloor n/2 \rfloor} T, 3^{\lfloor n/2 \rfloor} T')$ through the initial isogeny Φ_1, then $(3^{\lfloor 3n/4 \rfloor - 1} \Phi_1(T), 3^{\lfloor 3n/4 \rfloor - 1} \Phi_1(T'))$ through the second isogeny Φ_2, and so on. This resulted in a speed-up of a factor at least two compared to naively using either of the extreme methods.

6.3 Implementation

We ran our $(3, 3)$-variant of the CGL hash function on an Intel Xeon Gold 6248R CPU at 3.00GHz in Magma V2.27-7. For a fair comparison to the $(3, 3)$-variant of [6], we reran their code using this same set-up. The results can be found below.

	$p \approx 2^{86}$	$p \approx 2^{128}$	$p \approx 2^{171}$	$p \approx 2^{256}$
bits of classical security	128	192	256	384
bits of quantum security	86	128	170	256
time per bit processed [6] (reran)	3.23 ms	3.30 ms	3.56 ms	4.09 ms
time per bit processed (this work)	6.81 ms	7.47 ms	7.53 ms	7.96 ms

Even though these results seem dissatisfying, they are not completely unexpected. The difference in approach is that the $(3, 3)$-variant of [6] does not require pushing points through the isogeny, nor does it require computing scalar multiplications on the Jacobians (or lifts from the Kummer to the Jacobian). Our version on the other hand has the benefit of not having to compute three cubic roots at each step in the isogeny chain. Over a field $\mathbb{F}_{p^2}$ with $p = f \cdot 3^n - 1$, the computation of a cubic root requires $O(n)$ multiplications. In contrast to that, our algorithm requires $O(\log(n))$ multiplications at each step. Note that we cannot provide a precise count of operations due to the small Gröbner basis computation involved at each step. This implies that our algorithm scales better with increasing bitsize. From a certain point onwards, it should outperform the one from [6], though only at very high security levels.

We stress that our implementation does not lend itself to an actual practical hash function. Recall that we work over a field with $p = f \cdot 3^n - 1$. With a given symplectic 3^n-torsion basis of the starting Jacobian, we can thus hash $\lfloor \log_2 3^{3n} \rfloor$ bits before having "depleted" the available 3^n-torsion. If we want to hash inputs that are longer, we then have to resample a new symplectic basis, which is a nontrivial operation compared to the hash function itself. The main goal of this implementation is to show how fast we can manoeuvre in the $(3,3)$-isogeny graph with a *given* $(3^n, 3^n)$-subgroup, *whilst* also being able to push points through the isogeny chain. Both of these requirements are needed in certain other applications, such as attacking Alice's private key in SIKE, which is the topic of the next section.

7   Recovering Alice's Private Key in SIKE

In essence, we follow the attack strategy described in [22]. The main difference is that we target the recovery of Alice's secret key. Let $p = 2^a 3^b - 1$ be a SIKE prime and define

$$E_0/\mathbb{F}_{p^2} : y^2 = x^3 + 6x^2 + x$$

to be the starting curve, as is the case in all SIKE instantiations, including fixed bases for its 2^a- and 3^b-torsion; i.e. $E_0[2^a] = \langle P_A, Q_A \rangle$ and $E_0[3^b] = \langle P_B, Q_B \rangle$. Define the curve $E_0'/\mathbb{F}_{p^2} : y^2 = x^3 + x$ with its well-known endomorphism $\iota : E_0' \to E_0'$, $(x, y) \mapsto (-x, iy)$ and define $\rho : E_0 \to E_0'$ as the 2-isogeny connecting these curves.

Let k_A be the private key of Alice, which is used to construct the isogeny $\phi_A : E_0 \to E_A = E_0/\langle P_A + k_A Q_A \rangle$. In the SIDH protocol, Alice then sends the information $(E_A, \phi_A(P_B), \phi_A(Q_B))$ to Bob. To retrieve her private key, we consider the following commutative diagram:

$$
\begin{array}{ccc}
E_0 & \xrightarrow{\phi_A} & E_A \\
\downarrow{\gamma} & & \downarrow{\gamma'} \\
E_0 & \xrightarrow{\phi_A'} & X
\end{array}
$$

with the endomorphism

$$\gamma : E_0 \to E_0$$
$$P \mapsto [u]P + \hat{\rho} \circ \rho \circ [v]P$$

for certain integers u and v. It follows that the endomorphism γ is of degree $c = u^2 + 4v^2$. By [22, Theorem 1], the isogeny

$$\Phi : E_0 \times E_A \to E_0 \times X$$

$$(P, Q) \mapsto (\hat{\gamma}(P) + \hat{\phi}_A(Q), \gamma'(Q) - \phi_A'(P))$$

is a $(2^a + c, 2^a + c)$-isogeny preserving product polarizations. Furthermore, $\ker \Phi = \{([2^a]P, -\phi_A \circ \hat{\gamma}(P) \mid P \in E_0[2^a + c]\}$. We can compute Alice's private key k_A

from the kernel of ϕ_A, which in turn can be computed from $\hat{\phi}_a$. This dual isogeny can be retrieved, since

$$\hat{\phi}_A = E_A \rightarrow E_0 \times E_A \xrightarrow{\Phi} E_0 \times X \rightarrow E_0,$$

where the first map is inclusion and the last map is projection. To efficiently evaluate the $(2^a + c, 2^a + c)$-isogeny Φ using $(3,3)$-isogeny formulae, ideally we have that $c = 3^b - 2^a$. However, we run into two issues:

– the integer $3^b - 2^a$ may be negative;
– if $3^b - 2^a$ has a prime factor ℓ with odd multiplicity such that $\ell \equiv 3 \bmod 4$ then there are no u, v to compute γ.

For all the SIKE parameters, at least one of these is true. To combat this, we can instead look for integers $c' = 3^{b'} - d'2^{a'}$, where

1. if $b' > b$ then we need to guess $b' - b$ additional steps after the $(3^b, 3^b)$-isogeny;
2. if $b' < b$ then we only need to compute a $(3^{b-b'}, 3^{b-b'})$-isogeny;
3. if $a' > a$ then we need to extend Alice's isogeny with a $2^{a'-a}$-isogeny;[8]
4. if $a' < a$ then we need to guess the first $2^{a-a'}$-isogeny component of ϕ_A;
5. d' gives us leeway to extend ϕ_A with an isogeny of degree d'.

Options 2, 3 and 5 seem most interesting because they involve no guessing, but they all come with the side effect that c' is less likely to be positive. Remark that d' needs to be coprime with 3. If we allow d' to be even, then we can always choose $a' \leq a$. Choosing $d' > 1$ will likely result in computing an isogeny with nonrational kernel generator, unless it factors as $2m^2$, in which case one can compute a rational 2-isogeny followed by $[m]$. We suggest the following choices, where we allow d' to be even and thus always have $a' \leq a$.

	b	a	b'	a'	d'
SIKEp434	137	216	138	215	1
SIKEp503	159	250	160	250	4
SIKEp610	192	305	192	301	1
			194	303	1
SIKEp751	239	372	238	372	10

For SIKEp434 this means we need to guess the first step of Alice's chain of 2-isogenies, and then after computing a $(3^{137}, 3^{137})$-isogeny determine the (almost always unique) $(3,3)$-splitting. For SIKEp503 we need to also guess the final $(3,3)$-splitting, but can just extend ϕ_A with $[2]$ instead of having to guess. The options for SIKEp610 are a trade-off: either guess the first 2^4-isogeny component

---

[8] Remark that we may extend by a 2^ε-isogeny which is a part of $\hat{\phi}_A$ for some $\epsilon \leq a' - a$. We would then need to guess the final 2^ε-isogeny of ϕ_A but this is easy for small ε.

of ϕ_A, or only guess the 2^2-isogeny component but then also guess which $(3^2, 3^2)$-isogeny splits after computing a $(3^{192}, 3^{192})$-isogeny.

For the SIKEp751 parameters we can use an endomorphism of degree $3^{238} - 10 \cdot 2^{372}$, which was factored using the number sieve from [29]. This factorisation allows us to avoid any need for guessing, and only requires us to extend Alice's secret isogeny by an (arbitrary) isogeny of degree ten. The 2-torsion is of course rational, and the twist contains rational 5-torsion, which allows for a swift auxiliary 10-isogeny using x-only arithmetic over $\mathbb{F}_{p^2}$. Using the techniques discussed earlier, we manage to retrieve Alice's secret isogeny ϕ_A in 11 s. To the best of our knowledge, the fastest recovery of Bob's secret isogeny is 1 h for this security level [24]. Our computation consists of three nontrivial parts and is pretty consistent with regard to timing: 0.5 s for the Gröbner basis computation to glue the elliptic curves together, 10 s to compute the $(3^{236}, 3^{236})$-isogeny between Jacobians, and 0.5 s for the Gröbner basis computation for the final $(3, 3)$-splitting. All timings are based on using an Intel Xeon Gold 6248R CPU at 3.00 GHz in Magma V2.27-7.

8 Auxiliary Code

The auxiliary material contains the following code and can be found online at https://github.com/KULeuven-COSIC/3_3_isogenies

- `33_hash_BFT.m` contains an implementation of the CGL hash function described in Sect. 6.
- `BFT_verification.m` contains the symbolic formulae verification of the results from Subsect. 3.2.
- `symplectic_basis.m` contains a generating function for symplectic bases, which was used to hardcode the starting torsion of `33hashBFT.m`.
- `SIKEp751_attack.m` includes the attack on Alice's secret isogeny as described in Sect. 7.
- `uv_list.m` contains factorizations relevant to the SIKE attack parameters from Sect. 7.
- `verification_split.sage` contains a script to verify the splitting formulae from Subsect. 4.2.
- `verification_glue.sage` contains a script to verify the gluing formulae from Subsect. 4.3.

Acknowledgements. This work is a result of a workshop during Leuven Isogeny Days 2022, supported by the European Research Council (ERC) under the European Union's Horizon 2020 research and innovation programme (grant agreement ISOCRYPT - No. 101020788). This work was supported in part by CyberSecurity Research Flanders with reference number VR20192203, the DFG under Germany's Excellence Strategy - EXC 2092 CASA - 390781972 and the Agence Nationale de la Recherche under the grant ANR CIAO (ANR-19-CE48-0008). We thank Anna Somoza and Eda Kırımlı for helpful discussions.

References

1. Basso, A., et al.: Supersingular curves you can trust. In: Hazay, C., Stam, M. (eds.) EUROCRYPT 2023. LNCS, vol. 14005, pp. 405–437. Springer, Cham (2023). https://doi.org/10.1007/978-3-031-30617-4_14
2. Bosma, W., Cannon, J., Playoust, C.: The Magma algebra system. I. The user language. J. Symbolic Comput. **24**(3–4), 235–265 (1997). https://doi.org/10.1006/jsco.1996.0125
3. Bröker, R., Howe, E.W., Lauter, K.E., Stevenhagen, P.: Genus-2 curves and Jacobians with a given number of points. LMS J. Comput. Math. **18**(1), 170–197 (2015). https://doi.org/10.1112/S1461157014000461
4. Bruin, N., Flynn, E.V., Testa, D.: Descent via (3, 3)-isogeny on Jacobians of genus 2 curves. Acta Arithmetica **165**(3), 201–223 (2014). http://eudml.org/doc/279018
5. Cassels, J.W.S., Flynn, E.V.: Prolegomena to a middlebrow arithmetic of curves of genus 2, vol. 230. Cambridge University Press (1996). https://doi.org/10.1017/CBO9780511526084
6. Castryck, W., Decru, T.: Multiradical isogenies. In: 18th International Conference Arithmetic, Geometry, Cryptography, and Coding Theory, Contemporary Mathematics, vol. 779, pp. 57–89. American Mathematical Society (2022). https://doi.org/10.1090/conm/779
7. Castryck, W., Decru, T.: An efficient key recovery attack on SIDH. In: Hazay, C., Stam, M. (eds.) EUROCRYPT 2023. LNCS, vol. 14008, pp. 423–447. Springer, Cham (2023). https://doi.org/10.1007/978-3-031-30589-4_15
8. Castryck, W., Decru, T., Smith, B.: Hash functions from superspecial genus-2 curves using Richelot isogenies. J. Math. Cryptol. **14**(1), 268–292 (2020). https://doi.org/10.1515/jmc-2019-0021
9. Castryck, W., Decru, T., Vercauteren, F.: Radical isogenies. In: Moriai, S., Wang, H. (eds.) ASIACRYPT 2020. LNCS, vol. 12492, pp. 493–519. Springer, Cham (2020). https://doi.org/10.1007/978-3-030-64834-3_17
10. Charles, D.X., Lauter, K.E., Goren, E.Z.: Cryptographic hash functions from expander graphs. J. Cryptol. **22**(1), 93–113 (2007). https://doi.org/10.1007/s00145-007-9002-x
11. Cohen, H., et al.: Handbook of Elliptic and Hyperelliptic Curve Cryptography. CRC Press (2005). https://doi.org/10.1201/9781420034981
12. Cosset, R., Robert, D.: Computing (ℓ, ℓ)-isogenies in polynomial time on Jacobians of genus 2 curves. Math. Comput. **84**(294), 1953–1975 (2015). http://www.jstor.org/stable/24489183
13. Eisenträger, K., Hallgren, S., Lauter, K., Morrison, T., Petit, C.: Supersingular isogeny graphs and endomorphism rings: reductions and solutions. In: Nielsen, J.B., Rijmen, V. (eds.) EUROCRYPT 2018. LNCS, vol. 10822, pp. 329–368. Springer, Cham (2018). https://doi.org/10.1007/978-3-319-78372-7_11
14. Flynn, E.V., Ti, Y.B.: Genus two isogeny cryptography. In: Ding, J., Steinwandt, R. (eds.) PQCrypto 2019. LNCS, vol. 11505, pp. 286–306. Springer, Cham (2019). https://doi.org/10.1007/978-3-030-25510-7_16
15. Galbraith, S.D., Harrison, M., Mireles Morales, D.J.: Efficient hyperelliptic arithmetic using balanced representation for divisors. In: van der Poorten, A.J., Stein, A. (eds.) ANTS 2008. LNCS, vol. 5011, pp. 342–356. Springer, Heidelberg (2008). https://doi.org/10.1007/978-3-540-79456-1_23
16. Gaudry, P.: An algorithm for solving the discrete log problem on hyperelliptic curves. In: Preneel, B. (ed.) EUROCRYPT 2000. LNCS, vol. 1807, pp. 19–34. Springer, Heidelberg (2000). https://doi.org/10.1007/3-540-45539-6_2

17. Jao, D., De Feo, L.: Towards quantum-resistant cryptosystems from supersingular elliptic curve isogenies. In: Yang, B.-Y. (ed.) PQCrypto 2011. LNCS, vol. 7071, pp. 19–34. Springer, Heidelberg (2011). https://doi.org/10.1007/978-3-642-25405-5_2

18. Kani, E.: The number of curves of genus two with elliptic differentials. Journal für die reine und angewandte Mathematik **1997**(485), 93–122 (1997). https://doi.org/10.1515/crll.1997.485.93

19. Kunzweiler, S.: Efficient computation of $(2^n, 2^n)$-isogenies. Cryptology ePrint Archive, Paper 2022/990 (2022). https://eprint.iacr.org/2022/990

20. Kunzweiler, S., Ti, Y.B., Weitkämper, C.: Secret keys in genus-2 SIDH. In: AlTawy, R., Hülsing, A. (eds.) SAC 2021. LNCS, vol. 13203, pp. 483–507. Springer, Cham (2022). https://doi.org/10.1007/978-3-030-99277-4_23

21. Liu, Q.: Algebraic Geometry and Arithmetic Curves, vol. 6. Oxford University Press, Oxford (2002)

22. Maino, L., Martindale, C., Panny, L., Pope, G., Wesolowski, B.: A direct key recovery attack on SIDH. In: Hazay, C., Stam, M. (eds.) EUROCRYPT 2023. LNCS, vol. 14008, pp. 448–471. Springer, Cham (2023). https://doi.org/10.1007/978-3-031-30589-4_16

23. National Institute of Standards and Technology (NIST): Post-quantum cryptography standardization process. https://csrc.nist.gov/projects/post-quantum-cryptography

24. Oudompheng, R., Pope, G.: A note on reimplementing the Castryck-Decru attack and lessons learned for SageMath. Cryptology ePrint Archive, Paper 2022/1283 (2022). https://eprint.iacr.org/2022/1283

25. Robert, D.: Breaking SIDH in polynomial time. In: Hazay, C., Stam, M. (eds.) EUROCRYPT 2023. Lecture Notes in Computer Science, vol. 14008, pp. 472–503. Springer, Cham (2023). https://doi.org/10.1007/978-3-031-30589-4_17

26. Santos, M.C.R., Costello, C., Frengley, S.: An algorithm for efficient detection of (N, N)-splittings and its application to the isogeny problem in dimension 2. Cryptology ePrint Archive, Paper 2022/1736 (2022). https://eprint.iacr.org/2022/1736

27. Smith, B.: Isogenies and the discrete logarithm problem in Jacobians of genus 3 hyperelliptic curves. In: Smart, N. (ed.) EUROCRYPT 2008. LNCS, vol. 4965, pp. 163–180. Springer, Heidelberg (2008). https://doi.org/10.1007/978-3-540-78967-3_10

28. Takashima, K.: Efficient algorithms for isogeny sequences and their cryptographic applications. In: Takagi, T., Wakayama, M., Tanaka, K., Kunihiro, N., Kimoto, K., Duong, D.H. (eds.) Mathematical Modelling for Next-Generation Cryptography. MI, vol. 29, pp. 97–114. Springer, Singapore (2018). https://doi.org/10.1007/978-981-10-5065-7_6

29. The CADO-NFS Development Team: CADO-NFS, an implementation of the number field sieve algorithm (2017). http://cado-nfs.inria.fr/, release 2.3.0

30. The Sage Developers: SageMath, the Sage Mathematics Software System (Version 9.0) (2023). https://www.sagemath.org

On the Post-quantum Security of Classical Authenticated Encryption Schemes

Nathalie Lang$^{(\boxtimes)}$ and Stefan Lucks

Bauhaus-Universität Weimar, Weimar, Germany
{nathalie.lang,stefan.lucks}@uni-weimar.de

Abstract. We study the post-quantum security of authenticated encryption (AE) schemes, designed with classical security in mind. Under superposition attacks, many CBC-MAC variants have been broken, and AE modes employing those variants, such as EAX and GCM, thus fail at authenticity. As we show, the same modes are IND-qCPA insecure, i.e., they fail to provide privacy under superposition attacks. However, a constrained version of GCM is IND-qCPA secure, and a nonce-based variant of the CBC-MAC is secure under superposition queries. Further, the combination of classical authenticity and classical chosen-plaintext privacy thwarts attacks with superposition chosen-ciphertext and classical chosen-plaintext queries – a security notion that we refer to as IND-qdCCA. And nonce-based key derivation allows generically turning an IND-qdCCA secure scheme into an IND-qCCA secure scheme.

Keywords: authenticated encryption · post-quantum security

1 Introduction

The advent of quantum computers can be a game-changer for cryptography. This is well-known for current public-key cryptosystems [Sho94], thus the ongoing process to find consensus for new public-key cryptosystems [CJL+16]. The impact of quantum computers on symmetric cryptography is less understood. There are two common attack models for adversaries with a quantum computer: Q1 attacks allow only classical communication between the adversary and the victim (or the "challenger" in attack definitions). In Q2 attacks, the adversary can send queries in superposition to the challenger. Accordingly, the challenger's answers can also be in superposition. By a "common wisdom", symmetric cryptosystems can be made quantum-secure "by doubling the key size". This fails in the Q2 setting, where many symmetric cryptosystems have been broken (e.g., [KLLN16, BLNS21]). Even for the Q1 setting, this "common wisdom" has been disproven: Certain Q1 attacks degrade $2.5k$-bit classical security down to k-bit Q1 security [BSS22, US22].

We focus on the Q2 model. To motivate the practical relevance of the Q2 model, we give an example: Consider sensitive classical data (e.g. medical records), stored in an authenticated and encrypted database. The analysis soft-ware connects to a security module, which decrypts selected database entries, returning insensitive data (e.g., by anonymizing the records and aggregating data). The module can be a subroutine running on the same computer as the analysis software, though with different privileges. If this computer is a quantum computer, queries can be in superposition. The module could force queries to be classical, e.g., by performing measurements, but this would put the reason of using a quantum computer for data analysis into question. In our example, the analysis software only asks for the decryption of chosen ciphertexts, but never for the encryption of any plaintexts. This inspires a constrained variant of Q2 attacks: Q2d ("Q2 decrypt") attacks can make chosen-ciphertext queries in superposition, while chosen-plaintext queries are always classical. Note that Q2 security trivially implies Q2d security, Q2d security trivially implies Q1 security, and, for chosen-plaintext attacks, Q2d and Q1 are equivalent.

Focus of this Paper. We focus on the Q2 and Q2d security of authenticated encryption (AE), motivated by the following question: *"When exposed to super-position queries, which state-of-the-art AE systems maintain a meaningful level of security?"* A "none" answer to this question would imply a difficult transition from legacy to post-quantum cryptosystems, once superposition queries become an issue. Beyond superposition attacks on MACs, which imply some AE sys-tems failing to provide authenticity [KLLN16], this question has, to the best of our knowledge, only been addressed for the OCB mode [MMPR22], and for a sponge-based AE scheme [JS22]. We will consider other modes, but also describe generic conditions for security under superposition attacks.

Related Work. Certain properties, like the no-cloning theorem, require the reconsideration and revision of classical security notions to the quantum sce-nario [AGM18b, AGM18a]. Many well-established classical message authentica-tion codes have been found insecure in the Q2 model: Quantum period finding breaks many message authentication codes (MACs), including common variants of CBC-MAC [KLLN16]. (Though, there are also the positive results for HMAC and NMAC [SY17, HI21].) Quantum linearization pushes quantum period find-ing further, for more attacks [BLNS21]. Authenticated encryption (AE) combines privacy with authenticity, and the above attacks also apply to the authentica-tion aspect of AE modes. [ATTU16] did study the privacy of unauthenticated encryption in the Q2 setting, for chosen-plaintext attacks: Some modes (e.g., counter) are secure in the Q2 sense, even when the underlying block cipher is only Q1 secure. Other modes (e.g., CBC encryption) are secure in the Q2 sense when instantiated with a Q2-secure block cipher. The same paper also describes a wicked block cipher, which we will refer to as $\tilde{E}$, which is a 1PRP but not a qPRP. When instantiated with $\tilde{E}$, CBC encryption is insecure in the Q2 model.

In the current paper, we consider the matching IND-qCPA and IND-qCCA notions from [BZ13b] to model the *privacy aspect* of AE modes. These models assume so-called classical "challenge queries" (two chosen messages, the chal-lenger will encrypt one of them), while "learning queries" (one message which the challenger will encrypt or, in the case of IND-qCCA also decrypt) can be in superposition. [CETU20] proposes stronger security notions for quantum chosen-plaintext security, which also allow to eliminate the distinction between challenge and learning queries. But [CETU20] only deals with chosen-plaintext security, while we will consider both chosen-plaintext and chosen-ciphertext attacks.

We model the *authenticity aspect* of AE modes by the "Plus One" (PO) notion [BZ13a]. We refer to PO security in a Q2 setting as qPO, and to PO security in a Q1 setting as 1PO. The stronger "Blind Unforgeability" (BU) notion [AMRS20] seems to be less natural. Though, we can informally argue that the nonce-prefix MAC, which we analyze in Sect. 5.1, is BU secure since it behaves like a qPRF, which suffices for BU security. An alternative to "classical modes", i.e., to modes proposed for classical security, could be new "quantum" modes, such as QCB, a mode for tweakable block ciphers, which has been proven IND-qCPA and qPO secure [BBC+21]. Most of our security proofs are straightforward reductions. We do not require Zhandry's random oracle recording technique [Zha19]. For some proofs, we we build on the O2H lemma [Unr15, AHU19].

Outline and Contribution

Sections 2 **and** 3 give preliminaries and sum up known ideas and results.

Section 4 studies the privacy in the IND-qCPA sense, of certain AE modes, which are already known to be qPO insecure [KLLN16, BLNS21]:

(A) The generic SIV mode, GCM mode, and EAX mode are IND-qCPA insecure.
(B) A restricted variant of GCM, which, for a block size of n, only allows nonces of size $n - 32$ bit, is IND-qCPA secure.[1]

In Sect. 5 we identify two techniques, which have been employed for classical security, but which happen to also defend against superposition attacks:

(C) The *nonce-prefix variant of the CBC-MAC* shares the security properties of CBC encryption described by [ATTU16]: When instantiated with a Q2-secure block cipher, the nonce-prefix MAC is qPO secure, but, when instantiated with the wicked block cipher $\tilde{E}$ from [ATTU16], the MAC is insecure.
(D) *Nonce-based re-keying* defends against superposition chosen-plaintext queries: It turns an IND-1CPA secure AE system into an IND-qCPA secure one.

Section 6 considers generic AE schemes:

(E) If an authenticated encryption scheme is both IND-1CPA secure and 1PO secure, then it is also IND-qdCCA secure.

---

[1] This seems to be good news for many practical instantiations of GCM, which often employ $n = 128$ and 96-bit nonces. But the attack from [KLLN16] still applies, i.e., even that variant is qPO insecure.

(F) *Nonce-based re-keying* turns an IND-qdCCA and 1PO secure AE system into an IND-qCCA secure one

In Sect. 7 we conclude.

Note that by combining results (E) and (F) we can construct IND-qCCA secure AE from an AE scheme, which is only Q1 secure.

2 Definitions

2.1 Notation

We refer to security against classical adversaries by the prefix "c", to security against Q1 adversaries by "1", to security against Q2 adversaries by the "q", and to security against Q2d adversaries ("Q2 decrypt") by "qd". E.g., we write "IND-qCPA" for Q2 security in a chosen-plaintext setting, "IND-qdCCA" for Q2d security in a chosen-ciphertext setting, "1PO" for authenticity against Q1 adversaries, and "cPRP" for a classically secure PRP. If "P" is a primitive, C[P] denotes the instantiation of a generic construction "C" by P. If S is a set of primitives, Cr[S] denotes all instantiations C[P] for all P $\in S$. We write $s||t$ for the concatenation of bit-strings $s, t \in \{0, 1\}^*$.

Much of our methodological approach is based on reductions. Typically, we assume the existence of a Q2-adversary A_2 against some scheme, and we describe a Q1 adversary A_1 against another scheme, or in a different attack setting. A_1 performs some simple operations to transform superposition queries from A_2 into the classical queries A_1 can make, and to transform the classical responses A_1 receives from its challenger into superposition responses for A_2, and to compute its own final output from A_2's final output. I.e., A_1 is about as efficient as A_2 (though $\text{Adv}(A_1)$ and $\text{Adv}(A_2)$ may be significantly different). We thus propose the following notation:

Definition 1 ($A_1 \hookleftarrow_{\text{wrap}} A_2$). *Consider two adversaries A_1 and A_2. A_2 makes q_2 queries $Q_1^2, \ldots, Q_{q_2}^2$ of total length $\sigma_2 = \sum_{1 \leq i \leq q_2} |Q_i^2|$ and forwards them to A_1 who makes q_1 queries $Q_1^1, \ldots, Q_{q_1}^1$ of total length $\sigma_1 = \sum_{1 \leq i \leq q_1} |Q_i^1|$. We write $T(A_x)$ for the running time of A_x. Then A_2 is a wrapper for A_1, written as $A_1 \hookleftarrow_{wrap} A_2$, if $(\sigma_1 \in O(\sigma_2)$ and $T(A_2) \in T(A_1) + O(\sigma_2))$.*

2.2 Symmetric Schemes

Definition 2 (Encryption). *Let $\mathcal{K}$ be a finite set of secret keys. An encryption scheme $(\mathcal{E}, \mathcal{D})$ is a pair of two efficient algorithms $\mathcal{E}$ and $\mathcal{D}$, in combination with a soundness property. The encryption algorithm $\mathcal{E}$ takes a key $K \in \mathcal{K}$, a nonce N, a header H, and a message $M \neq \perp$ and generates a ciphertext $C = \mathcal{E}_K(N, H, M)$. The decryption algorithm $\mathcal{D}$ takes a key $K \in \mathcal{K}$, a nonce N, a header H, and a ciphertext C and generates a message $M = \mathcal{D}_K(N, H, C)$. The soundness property*

$$\mathcal{D}_K(N, H, \mathcal{E}_K(N, H, M)) = M$$

holds for all $K \in \mathcal{K}$, all nonces N, all headers H and all messages M. Encryption schemes are either unauthenticated, i.e., for all $K \in \mathcal{K}$, all nonces N, all headers H, and ciphertext C, $M = D_K(N, H, C)$ is a valid message, or authenticated, i.e., some triples (N, H, C) are invalid and cannot be decrypted. Then, we write $\perp = \mathcal{D}_K(N, H, C)$, understanding $\perp$ as an error message.

Remark: All authenticated encryption schemes we consider in the current paper have a constant-size expansion, i.e., there exists a constant τ such that $|C| = |M| + \tau$ for all K, N, H, and M and $C = E_K(N, H, M)$.

Definition 3 (Message authentication codes (MACs)). *Let $\mathcal{K}$ be a finite set of secret keys. A MAC $\mathcal{M}$ is a deterministic function, which can be implemented by an efficient algorithm. If $\mathcal{M}$ is nonce-based, it takes a key $K \in \mathcal{K}$, a nonce N, and a message M and computes an authentication tag $T = \mathcal{M}_K(N, M)$. If $\mathcal{M}$ is deterministic, it takes a key $K \in \mathcal{K}$ and a message M and computes an authentication tag $T = \mathcal{M}'_K(M)$.*

Now we formalize the notion of privacy under chosen-plaintext attacks:

Definition 4 (The generic IND-CPA and IND-CCA games). *Let $(\mathcal{E}, \mathcal{D})$ denote a nonce-based encryption scheme with keyspace $\mathcal{K}_\mathcal{E}$ and $\mathcal{A}$ an adversary, making q queries.[2]*
The Generic IND-CCA game consists of the following three steps:

Initialize: *The challenger randomly chooses $K \xleftarrow{\$} \mathcal{K}_\mathcal{E}$ and $b \xleftarrow{\$} \{0, 1\}$.*
  It maintains a set B of "blocked triples", which is initially empty: $B = \{\}$.
Query Phase: *For $i \in \{1, \ldots, q\}$, $\mathcal{A}$ makes either of the following queries:*
  Forward Learning query: *$\mathcal{A}$ chooses a nonce/header/message triple (N_i, H_i, M_i) and receives $C_i = \mathcal{E}_K(N_i, H_i, M_i)$.*
    The challenger sets $B = B \cup \{(N_i, H_i, M_i)\}$.
  Backward Learning query: *$\mathcal{A}$ chooses a nonce/header/ciphertext triple (N_i, H_i, C_i).*
    If $(N_i, H_i, C_i) \in B$, the challenger sends $\perp$ to $\mathcal{A}$.
    Else, the challenger sends $\mathcal{D}_K(N_i, H_i, C_i)$ to $\mathcal{A}$.
  Challenge query: *$\mathcal{A}$ chooses a nonce N_i, two headers $H_{i,0}$ and $H_{i,1}$ and two messages $M_{i,0}$ and $M_{i,1}$, receives ciphertext $C_i = \mathcal{E}_K(N_i, H_{i,b}, M_{i,b})$.*
    The challenger sets $B = B \cup \{(N_i, H_{i,0}, M_{i,0}), (N_i, H_{i,1}, M_{i,1})\}$.
Finalize: *$\mathcal{A}$ outputs a classical bit $b' \in \{0, 1\}$. The event $\mathrm{win}(\mathcal{A})$ occurs if $b' = b$.*
  *The **advantage** of $\mathcal{A}$ is*

$$Adv(\mathcal{A}) = |\Pr[b' = 1 | b = 1] - \Pr[b' = 1 | b = 0]| \tag{1}$$

The Generic IND-CPA game consists of the same steps, except that $\mathcal{A}$ cannot make any backward learning queries.

---

[2] $\mathcal{A}$ is constrained to choose unique nonces for forward learning and challenge queries. This will be formalized in Definition 8 below.

In the next step, we formalize the notion of authenticity:

Definition 5 (The generic PO game). *Let* $(\mathcal{E}, \mathcal{D})$ *denote an encryption scheme (authenticated or not) with key space* $\mathcal{K}_{\mathcal{E}}$. *In this game, the adversary* $\mathcal{A}$ *can make* q *learning queries and no challenge queries.*

Initialize: *The challenger randomly chooses* $K \xleftarrow{\$} \mathcal{K}_{\mathcal{E}}$.
Query Phase: *For* $i \in \{1, \ldots, q\}$, $\mathcal{A}$ *chooses a nonce/header/message triple* (N_i, H_i, M_i) *as a learning query and receives* $C_i = \mathcal{E}_K(N_i, H_i, M_i)$.
Finalize: $\mathcal{A}$ *outputs* $q + 1$ *distinct classical triples* (N_i', H_i', C_i') $(1 \le i \le q + 1)$ *of nonce* N_i', *header* H_i' *and ciphertext* C_i'. $\mathcal{A}$ *wins if all triples are valid, i.e., if*

$$\forall i \in \{1, \ldots, q + 1\} : \quad \mathcal{D}_K(N_i', H_i', C_i') \ne \perp.$$

$\mathcal{A}$'s **advantage** *is* $Adv(\mathcal{A}) = Pr[\mathcal{A} \text{ wins}]$.

The generic PO game extends naturally to an adversary $\mathcal{A}'$ *attacking a deterministic MAC and to an adversary* $\mathcal{A}''$ *attacking a nonce-based MAC. In the query phase,* $\mathcal{A}'$ *chooses a message* M_i *and receives the authentication tag* $T_i = MAC_K(M_i)$. *Next,* $\mathcal{A}''$ *chooses a pair* (N_i, M_i) *of nonce and message and receives* $T_i = MAC_K(N_i, M_i)$. *Upon finalization,* $\mathcal{A}'$ *outputs* $q + 1$ *pairs* (T_j', M_j') *and wins if all pairs are valid.* $\mathcal{A}''$ *outputs* $q + 1$ *triples* (T_j', N_j', M_j') *and wins if all triples are valid.*

Finally, we consider the primitives our modes are built from.

Definition 6 (Generic PRPs/PRFs).
If $\$: \{0,1\}^n \to \{0,1\}^n$ *is a permutation over* n *bit (or* $\$: \{0,1\}^n \to \{0,1\}^m$ *an* n-*bit to* m-*bit function), chosen uniformly at random, and* $P : \{0,1\}^n \to \{0,1\}^n$ *is another permutation (or* $F : \{0,1\}^n \to \{0,1\}^m$ *another function), chosen according to some probability distribution, we define the PRP advantage (PRF-advantage) of* A *by*

$$Adv^{PRP}(A, (P, \$)) = \left| \Pr[A^P = 1] - \Pr[A^\$ = 1] \right|$$

(or $Adv^{PRF}(A(F, \$)) = \left| \Pr[A^F = 1] - \Pr[A^\$ = 1] \right|$*).*

Note that the definition of the PRP advantage allows A to choose x and query for $P(x)$ or $\$(x)$, respectively, but we do not allow A to query for the inverse permutations of P and $\$$. I.e., we do not consider "strong PRPs".

2.3   Quantum Attacks and Types of Adversaries

We assume the reader to be familiar with classical and quantum computers, and their distinction.

Definition 7 (Types of queries). *Let* f *be a function, available by an oracle. In the case of a* classical query, *an adversary chooses* x *and receives* $f(x)$ *as the answer. In the case of a* superposition query, *the adversary chooses* $|x\rangle |y\rangle$ *and receives* $|x\rangle |y \oplus f(x)\rangle$ *as the answer.*

Definition 8 (Types of adversaries). *A* classical adversary *is running a classical computer and its queries are classical.*
A Q1 adversary *is running a quantum computer but only makes classical queries.*
A Q2 adversary *is running a quantum computer and can make superposition learning queries. More precisely, for a forward learning query (N_i, H_i, M_i), the header H_i and the message M_i can be in superposition, and the nonce N_i is classical.[3] For a backward learning query, (N_i, H_i, C_i), the header H_i, the ciphertext C_i and also the nonce N_i can be in superposition.*
Challenge queries are completely classical.
A Q2d adversary *is a Q2 adversary, restricted to classical forward learning queries; only its backward learning queries can be in superposition.[4]*
All adversaries use unique nonces for their challenge and forward learning queries. That is, if for $i \neq j$ neither the i-th nor the j-th query are backward learning queries, and the nonces for either query are N_i and N_j, then $N_i \neq N_j$.[5]

2.4   A Wicked PRP

[ATTU16] proposes a family of permutations over $\{0,1\}^n$, which they prove to be a secure 1PRP, but which they show to be vulnerable under superposition attacks, i.e., it fails to be a secure qPRP. In the current paper, we will refer to this as the "wicked PRP $\tilde{E}$":

Definition 9 (Wicked PRP $\tilde{E}$). $\tilde{E} : \{0,1\}^n \times \{0,1\}^n \to \{0,1\}^n$ *is a family of permutations $\tilde{E}_k(\cdot)$ over $\{0,1\}^n$. There exist efficiently computable functions $f' : \{0,1\}^n \to \{0,1\}^n, f'' : \{0,1\}^n \to \{0,1\}^n, E' : \{0,1\}^n \times \{0,1\}^n \to \{0,1\}^{n-1}$, and $E'' : \{0,1\}^n \times \{0,1\}^n \to \{0,1\}$, such that for every key k, $\tilde{E}_k(x)$ can be written as*

$$\tilde{E}_k(x) = E'_{f'(k)}(x) || E''_{f''(k)}(x).$$

Furthermore, for all x and k, E' satisfies

$$E'_{f'(k)}(x) = E'_{f'(k)}(x \oplus k).$$

See [ATTU16] for a concrete construction of the wicked PRP, based on an $n - 1$-bit PRP and some random oracles. [ATTU16] prove $\tilde{E}$ to be a secure 1PRP. Even though $\tilde{E}$ is a 1PRP, is not a qPRP: The adversary can use Simon's algorithm to find k, and then it is trivial to distinguish $\tilde{E}_k$ from random. Thus, $\tilde{E}$ can be seen as a 1PRP, i.e., secure against Q1-adversaries, but with a built-in backdoor for Q2-adversaries.

---

[3] Prohibiting superposition nonces is the established approach in the related work since the nonce, even though we *model* it as chosen by the adversary, is a counter, a timestamp, or a random value generated by the sender's communication machinery.

[4] Similarly, a Q2e ("Q2 encrypt") adversary can make superposition forward learning queries, but only classical backward learning queries. Though, we do not need Q2e adversaries in our context.

[5] $N_i \neq N_j$ is well-defined, even in the Q2 model with forward learning queries in superposition, since the nonces N_i and N_j are always classical.

3   Known Ideas and Results

We summarize some known ideas and results, which we draw on in subsequent sections: Firstly, we recall Simon's algorithm. Secondly, we consider the security of the Counter- and the CBC-Mode under superposition chosen-plaintext queries [ATTU16]. Thirdly, we consider quantum period finding attacks [KLLN16], using chosen-message queries in superposition to break numerous message authentication codes, such as most variants of the CBC-MAC and MACs based on polynomial hashing. Fourth, we recall quantum linearization attacks [BLNS21], an extension of quantum period finding to break (among other things) beyond-birthday message authentication codes.

3.1   Simon's Problem, -subprogram, and -algorithm

Given oracle access to a function $f : \{0,1\}^m \to \{0,1\}^n$ with $f(x) = f(y) \Leftrightarrow x \oplus y \in \{0,s\}$ for a hidden nonzero "period" $s \in \{0,1\}^m$. Simon's algorithm [Sim97] allows to generically recover s in polynomial time. A classical generic algorithm would require time $\Omega(2^{m/2})$. Here, "generic" means without exploiting any specific property of f, except for the existence of the hidden period s.

The algorithm can be described as running Simon's subprogram $O(m)$ times, and then solving a system of linear equations. Simon's subprogram performs the following steps:

1. Initialize a $2n$-qubit register to a superposition of 2^n values: $2^{-n/2} \sum_x |x\rangle |0\rangle$. (One can do so by initializing the first n qubits to $|0\rangle$ and applying the Hadamard transform to get $2^{-n/2} \sum_x |x\rangle = H^{\oplus n} |0\rangle$.)
2. Call the f-oracle for $2^{-n/2} \sum_x |x\rangle |f(x)\rangle$.
3. Measure the second register. Let v be the result of the measurement. The state in the $2n$-qubit register collapses to a superposition of only two values: $2^{-1/3}(|y\rangle + |y \oplus s\rangle) |v\rangle$.
4. Apply the Hadamard-transform to the first n qubits: $H^{\oplus n}(2^{-1}(|y\rangle + |y+s\rangle) |y\rangle$.
5. Measure the first n qubits. This yields a random z with $z \cdot s = 0$. Return z.

Each evaluation of Simon's subprogram implies one superposition query (cf. step 2). Simon's algorithm runs Simon's subprogram until m linearly independent equations $z_i \cdot s = 0$ have been collected. In the algorithm's final step, one computes s by solving this system. Note that with overwhelming probability, it suffices to call Simon's subprogram $O(m)$ times. Below, we will write $T(\text{Simon}(m))$ for the run time required to recover an m-bit secret this way.

[KLLN16] made two observations, which are helpful for the application of Simon's algorithm for cryptanalytic purposes:

1. Assume many independent functions f_1, f_2, all with the same period s (i.e., $f_i(x) = f_i(y) \Leftrightarrow x \oplus y \in \{0,s\}$). Even if each oracle call provides access to another function f_i, one can apply Simon's algorithm to recover s.

2. One can even apply Simon's algorithm with a relaxed version of Simon's problem. Assume a period s, such that $f(x) = f(y) \Leftarrow x \oplus y \in \{0, s\}$ but allow for certain cases of $f(x) = f(y)$ even if $x \oplus y \notin \{0, s\}$. As long as $\max_{t \in \{0,1\}^m / \{0,s\}} \Pr_x[f(x) = f(x \oplus t)]$ is negligible, Simon's algorithm will provide the period s in $O(m)$ queries with overwhelming probability. E.g., this is the case if, apart from the constraining $f(x) = f(x \oplus s)$, f is chosen randomly.

3.2 Counter- and CBC-Mode Under Superposition Queries [ATTU16]

Definition 10 (Stream cipher). *Assume a pseudorandom function F_K, such that for every input N, $F_K(N) \in \{0,1\}^*$ is an infinite random string of bits. We write $F_K^m(N) \in \{0,1\}^m$ for the first m bits of $F_K(N)$. An F-based stream cipher takes nonces N_i, a messages M_i and computes ciphertext C_i of length $|C_i| = |M_i|$ as $C_i = F_K^{|M_i|}(N_i) \oplus M_i$.*

Theorem 1 (Similar to Lemma 5 of [ATTU16]). *Assume a PRF-based stream cipher and a Q2-adversary A_2 against the stream cipher. Then a Q1-adversary A_1 and a Q2-adversary A_2 against the same stream cipher exists with $A_1 \leftarrow_{wrap} A_2$ and $Adv(A_1) = Adv(A_2)$.*

The proof for Theorem 1 is essentially the same as the proof given in [ATTU16]. But since [ATTU16] only claim polynomial-time equivalence of A_1 and A_2 and assume a random nonce, we provide the proof in the full paper [LL23].

Definition 11 (Counter mode and CBC). *Assume an n-bit block cipher E and a key K. Given a nonce $N < 2^n$, the counter mode key stream is an infinite string $Cnt_K(N) = E_K(N)\|E_K(N+1)\|E_K(N+2)\|\ldots$, where the addition $N+i$ is modulo 2^n. Counter mode encryption is the stream cipher based on Cnt_K. Given an m-block message $M = (M_1, \ldots M_m) \in (\{0,1\}^n)^m$, CBC encryption consists of two steps: first randomly choose $C_0 \in \{0,1\}^n$, then compute $C_i = E_K(M_i \oplus C_{i-1})$. The ciphertext from CBC encryption is the $(m+1)$-block string $(C_0, C_1, \ldots, C_m)$.*
Counter[E] and CBC[E] are the instantiations of the Counter- and the CBC-mode by E.

Definition 12. *Two nonce-message pairs (N, M) and (N', M') with nonempty messages M and M' are counter-overlapping, if $((N \leq N')$ and $(N' - N < |M|/n))$ or $((N \geq N')$ and $(N - N' < |M'|/n))$. Else, they are counter-overlap free.*

According to Theorem 1, *superposition queries fail to provide any benefit at all over classical queries* – for the counter mode:

Theorem 2 (Similar to Theorem 3 of [ATTU16]). *If A_2 is a Q2-adversary on the counter mode, a Q1-adversary $A_1 \leftarrow_{wrap} A_2$ on the counter mode exists with $Adv(A_1) = Adv(A_2)$.*

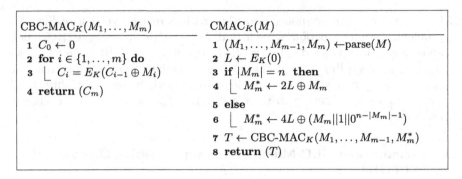

Fig. 1. Pseudocode of CBC-MAC (CBC-MAC by itself is classically insecure when applied to messages where one message is allowed to be a prefix of a longer message. On the other hand, CMAC has been proven secure, assuming the block cipher E to be secure (i.e., a good PRF).) and CMAC (For CMAC, $2L$ and $4L$ are defined as products over $GF(2^n)$, and the "parse" operation splits any nonempty M into n-bit blocks M_1, ..., M_{m-1} and one block M_m with $|M_m| \in \{1, \ldots, n\}$. If M is the empty string, then $\text{parse}(M) = M_1$ with M_1 being an empty block: $|M_1| = 0$.). Both algorithms receive a key K and a message $(M_1, \ldots, M_m)$. For CBC-MAC it holds that $\forall i: M_i \in \{0,1\}^n$.

CBC Encryption. For the CBC-mode, *the adversary can benefit greatly from superposition queries*, except when the underlying block cipher is secure against such queries:

Theorem 3 ([ATTU16]). *CBC[$\tilde{E}$] is IND-1PRP secure. CBC[$\tilde{E}$] is IND-qCPA insecure. CBC[qPRP] is IND-qCPA secure.*

Recall that we write $\tilde{E}$ for the wicked PRP from Definition 9.

3.3   Quantum Period Finding Attacks [KLLN16]

Quantum period finding [KLLN16] applies Simon's algorithm to create forgeries for a variety of message authentication codes (MACs). This also breaks the authenticity of AE schemes employing these MACs. We will outline the attacks on the CMAC and GMAC, due to their relevance for the rest of this paper.

The CBC-MAC and its Variants. Given the learning queries as the interface, the core idea is to define a function f maintaining Simon's promise, such that finding the period s is useful for the adversary. Kaplan et al. [KLLN16] used these to attack the two-key variant of CBC-MAC, but, as they pointed out, the attack applies to many other CBC-MAC variants. Here, we consider the attack on the one-key variant, also dubbed CMAC.

Attacking CMAC [KLLN16]. CMAC is a variant of CBC-MAC see Fig. 1. For the attack we assume a string constant $\sigma \in (\{0,1\}^n)^*$, two constants $\beta_0 \neq \beta_1$ in

$\text{EAX}_K(N, H, M)$	
1 $N' \leftarrow \text{CMAC}_K(\langle 0 \rangle \parallel N)$	4 $C' \leftarrow \text{CMAC}_K(\langle 2 \rangle \parallel C)$
2 $H' \leftarrow \text{CMAC}_K(\langle 1 \rangle \parallel H)$	5 $T \leftarrow N' \oplus H' \oplus C'$
3 $C \leftarrow \text{Ctr}_K(N', M)$	6 **return** (T,C)

Fig. 2. The EAX mode. It takes a key K, nonce N, header H, and message M as input. By $\langle i \rangle \in \{0,1\}^n$, we denote an initial block encoding the number $i \in \{0,1,2\}$.

$\{0,1\}^n$, and the function $f : \{0,1\} \times \{0,1\}^n \to \{0,1\}^n$ by

$$f(b,x) = \text{CMAC}_K(\sigma \parallel \beta_b \parallel x) = E_K(x \oplus 2L \oplus E_K(\overbrace{\beta_b \oplus \text{CBC-MAC}_K(\sigma)}^{\alpha_b})).$$

The secret period s is $s = (1 \parallel E_K(\alpha_0) \oplus E_K(\alpha_1))$, since

$$f(0,x) = f(1,y) \Leftrightarrow x \oplus y = E_K(\alpha_0) \oplus E_K(\alpha_1).$$

Assume finding s did require $q' \in \Omega(n)$ learning queries. The adversary now makes $q' + 1$ queries for $T_i = \text{CMAC}_K(\sigma \parallel \beta_0 \parallel X_i)$, with distinct X_i. Thanks to the secret period $s = 1 \parallel (E_K(\alpha_0) \oplus E_K(\alpha_1))$ we know $T_i = \text{CMAC}_K(\sigma \parallel \beta_1 \parallel X_i)$. In total, we made $q = 2q' + 1$ learning queries and got $q + 1 = 2q' + 2$ pairs (M_i, T_i), thus winning the qPO game.

Attacking EAX. Consider the EAX mode for authenticated encryption, as depicted in Fig. 2. Note that EAX makes three calls to the CMAC. If the message is empty, EAX is essentially a nonce-dependent MAC for the header, and the CMAC attack applies to EAX just as well. Thus, EAX is not qPO secure.

Attacking GMAC/GCM [KLLN16] GCM and its related algorithms are presented in Fig. 3. Unlike EAX, GCM does not employ any variant of CBC-MAC, but rather employs a polynomial hash. When calling GCM with an empty message ϵ, GCM is de facto used as a nonce-based MAC for the header. We will refer to this as $\text{GMAC}_K(N, X) = \text{GCM}_K(N, X, M)$. As it turns out, GMAC, and, by implication, GCM, are not qPO secure. Furthermore, the attack is essentially the same as for CMAC: define $\sigma \in /\{0,1\}^n)^*$, $\beta_0 \neq \beta_1$ in $\{0,1\}^n$ and the $f : \{0,1\} \times \{0,1\}^n \to \{0,1\}^n$ by

$$f_N(b,x) = \text{CMAC}_K(N, \sigma \parallel \beta_b \parallel x). \tag{2}$$

The secret period $s \in \{0,1\}^{n+1}$ is

$$s = 1 \parallel (L\beta_0 \oplus L\beta_1) = 1 \parallel (L(\beta_0 \oplus \beta_1)). \tag{3}$$

Since s does not depend on the nonce N, one can apply Simon's algorithm exactly as in the case of CMAC: "As for the CBC-MAC, repeating these two steps leads to an existential forgery attack" [KLLN16].

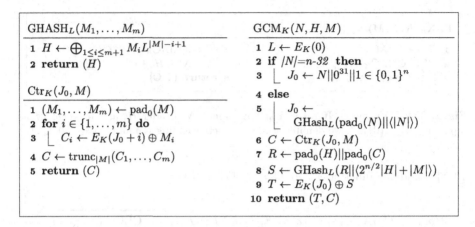

Fig. 3. GHash under key L (L^i denotes exponentiation in $\mathrm{GF}(2^n)$ and $M_i L^i$ is a product in $\mathrm{GF}(2^n)$.) of a message $(M_1, \ldots, M_m)$ of n-bit blocks, Ctr-mode to encrypt a message M with a start counter $J_0 \in \{0, 1\}^n$ and GCM encryption of a message M (The length of messages is restricted to less than 2^{32} blocks.), depending on a key K, nonce N, and a header H. For $S \in \{0, 1\}^*$, the operation $\mathrm{pad}_0(S)$ denotes appending the minimum number of 0-bits, such that the length of the result is a multiple of the block size n. We will refer to $E_K(N), E_K(N + 1), \ldots$ as the *key stream*.

3.4   Quantum Linearization for Beyond-Birthday MACs [BLNS21]

We continue by giving examples for quantum linearization attacks. A deeper understanding of such attacks is not necessary for the reader. However, for further reading we refer to [BLNS21]. Typical Variants of CBC-MAC (e.g. CMAC), and typical MACs based on polynomial hashing (e.g. GMAC), only provide classical security up to the birthday bound of $2^{n/2}$, where n is the block size. Coincidently, many beyond-birthday MACs (against classical adversaries) seem to be save from a straightforward application of period finding. [BLNS21] extended period finding to linearization. At the cost of increasing the size of each query from $\Theta(1)$ blocks to $\Theta(n)$ blocks, quantum linearization allows breaking several beyond-birthday MACs (and also many other schemes).

Attacking the GCM-SIV2 and the GCM-SIV2-MAC. SIV is a mode of operation to perform "deterministic authenticated encryption", i.e., authenticated encryption with minimal damage when nonces are reused [RS06]. Generic SIV is depicted in Fig. 4. Many instantiations of generic SIV have been proposed by different authors. GCM-SIV2 is a beyond-birthday-secure instantiation, combining a beyond-birthday secure MAC with a beyond-birthday secure variant of the counter mode [IM16]. The MAC, which we refer to as GCM-SIV2-MAC, takes two n-bit keys L_1, L_2, four block cipher keys K_1', K_2', K_3', and K_4', a nonce N, a header $H = (H_1, \ldots, H_j)$, and a message $M(M_1, \ldots, M_m)$ and computes a $2n$-bit authentication tag

$$(T_1, T_2) = \mathrm{GCM\text{-}SIV2\text{-}MAC}_{L_1, L_2, K_1', K_2', K_3', K_4'}(N, H, M).$$

GenericSIV$_{K,L}(N, H, M)$
1 $V \leftarrow \text{MAC}_L(I(N, H, M))$ **2** $C \leftarrow \text{Enc}_K(V, M)$,   **3 return** (V, C)

Fig. 4. Pseudocode of the generic SIV encryption, combining a MAC and a nonce-based encryption operation Enc, using two independent keys K and L. $I(N, H, M)$ is an input encoding of a nonce N, header H, and message M, which satisfies $I(N, H, M) \neq I(N', H', M')$ if $(N, H, M) \neq (N', H', M')$. Given (V, C), authenticated SIV decryption first computes $M = \text{Enc}_K^{-1}(V, C)$, and then $V' = \text{MAC}_L(I(N, H, M))$. If $V = V'$, authenticated SIV decryption returns M, else it rejects (V, C).

After parsing the joint input H and M as a sequence $(X_1, \ldots, X_{a+m+1})$ of $a + m + 1$ n-bit blocks, with the last block $(\langle|H|\rangle||\langle|M|\rangle)$ holding encodings of the lengths of H and M, GCM-SIV2-MAC computes intermediate values

$$V_1 = N \oplus \bigoplus_{1 \leq i \leq a+m+1} L_1^i X_i \quad \text{and} \quad V_2 = N \oplus \bigoplus_{1 \leq i \leq a+m+1} L_2^i X_i$$

and then returns

$$T_1 = E_{K_1'}(V_1) \oplus E_{K_3'}(V_2) \quad \text{and} \quad T_2 = E_{K_2'}(V_1) \oplus E_{K_4'}(V_2)$$

Plain quantum period finding fails for the GCM-SIV2-MAC, but quantum linearization succeeds [BLNS21]. To attack the MAC, one generates pairs $(N, H, M) \neq (N, H', M')$ with the same authentication tag

$$T = \text{GCM-SIV2-MAC}_K(N, H, M) = \text{GCM-SIV2-MAC}_K(N, H', M').$$

This not only allows to break the qPO security of the MAC but also of GCM-SIV2 itself: For any such pair, ask for $(C, T) = \text{GCM-SIV2}_K(N, H, M)$. Then decrypting (N, C', H', T) with $C' = C \oplus M \oplus M'$ will return M'.

4   Privacy Under Q2 Attacks (or Lack Theorof)

As we argued in Sect. 3, AE modes, such as EAX, GCM, and GCM-SIV2, directly inherit qPO insecurity from the MAC schemes they are based on. Thus authenticity is lost – but could any of these AE modes still preserve privacy, at least in the IND-qCPA sense?

4.1   GCM-SIV2

Recall the generic SIV mode from Fig. 4. It uses the result of the MAC operation as the nonce for the encryption operation Enc. Thus, when instantiated with any of the MACs studied in Sect. 3, the adversary can force a nonce-reuse for Enc. One such instantiation is GCM-SIV2, which furthermore instantiates Enc by the counter mode. Using the counter mode with the same nonce is insecure. Thus, GCM-SIV2 is IND-qCPA insecure.

4.2 GCM

For GCM, it is easy to recover the internal secret $L = E_K(0)$ from Eq. 3, since β_0, β_1, and i are known to the adversary, and the computations are in GF(2^n)). *But can we exploit knowing L for a qCPA attack?* The answer depends on the nonce length. Observe that GCM treats nonces N of size $|N| = n - 32$ differently from different-sized nonces, cf. lines 2–5 in GCM (Fig. 3). The case $\text{GCM}_{|N|=n-32}$ will be considered below. But, *GCM without restrictions on the nonce-space is not IND-qCPA secure – not even if the block cipher is a qPRP.* If $|N| \neq n - 32$, the initial counter J_0 is derived by calling GHash: $J_0 = \text{GHash}_L(\text{pad}_0(N)||\langle|N|\rangle)$. Knowing L allows us to create overlapping counters efficiently. We present two approaches.

Our first approach employs two nonces N and N', with $|N'| = n - 32 \neq |N|$. We do not need unplausibly long nonces; as a reasonable choice, we set $|N| = n$. Fix N' and $J_0 = N'||0^{31}||1$. Now the adversary just has to compute N with

$$\text{GHash}_L(N||\langle n\rangle) = L^2 N \oplus L\langle n\rangle = J_0,$$

i.e., compute $N = (J_0 \oplus L\langle n\rangle) * L^{-2}$ in GF(2^n). A nonce-respecting adversary uses either N or N' in a learning query, and the other one in the challenge query. Both nonces generate the same J_0 and thus the same key stream.

Our second approach even works for nonces $N \neq N'$ of equal size $|N| = |N'| = n$. We choose N and N' such that $J_0' = J_0 + 1$. This creates a counter overlap. Namely, we fix N', compute J_0' and then solve the equation below for N:

$$\underbrace{L^2 N \oplus L\langle n\rangle}_{J_0} = \underbrace{(L^2 N' \oplus L\langle n\rangle)}_{J_0'} - 1.$$

Due to $J_0' = J_0 + 1$, the keystreams overlap, except for the first output block from the J_0 key stream.

$\text{GCM}_{|N|=n-32}$, *a Restricted Variant of GCM.* If we restrict all nonces N to $|N| = n-32$, the initial counter is set to $J_0 = N||0^{31}||1$, without invoking GHash. As with all variants of GCM, $\text{GCM}_{|N|=n-32}$ fails at authenticity, i.e., is qPO insecure. But the restriction $|N| = n - 32$ preserves privacy: Due to the message length restriction, all nonce-respecting queries are overlap-free. According to Theorem 1, $\text{GCM}_{|N|=n-32}$ is IND-qCPA secure if the block cipher is a 1PRP, even when the adversary knows L.

4.3 EAX

Reconsider CMAC. We aim to recover the key-dependent secret $L = E_K(0)$. Recall lines 3–6 of Algorithm 2. Consider an arbitrary n_1-bit string X and set $X_1 = X||1 \in n\{0,1\}^n$. If $M_m = X$, then $M_m^* = X_1 \oplus 4L$. If $M_m = X_1$, then $M_m^* = X_1 \oplus 2L$. For the attack, we thus assume learning queries with a superposition of two identical messages, except for M_m being either X or X_1.[6] We continue with the attack to recover $6L$ (and by implication: L). Note that this attack is specific to CMAC, and would not apply to most other CBC-MAC variants:

1. Guess $\beta = \mathrm{LSB}(6L)$.
2. Define the function $f_\beta : \{0,1\} \times \{0,1\}^{n-1} \to \{0,1\}^n$ by

$$f_\beta(b,x) = \begin{cases} \mathrm{CMAC}_K(x) & \text{if } b=0 \\ \mathrm{CMAC}_K(x||\beta) & \text{else} \end{cases}.$$

3. Note that if $\beta = \mathrm{LSB}(6L)$, then f is periodic: $f_\beta(0||x) = f_\beta(1||x \oplus \mathrm{MSB}_{n-1}(6L))$.
   Apply Simon's algorithm to recover the period $s = \mathrm{MSB}_{n-1}(6L)$.
4. If Simon's algorithm fails, replace β by $1 - \beta$ and go to step 2.
   Else return $6L = (s||\beta)$

For MAC forgeries, there seems to be no benefit over the attack from Sect. 3.3. But knowing L allows us to mount the following simple IND-qCPA attack:

1. Choose an n-bit nonce $N_0 = L \oplus 2L$, a $2n$-bit nonce $N_1 = (L||N_0)$, a header H and two messages $M_0 \neq M_1$ with $|M_0| = |M_1|$.
2. Make $\begin{cases} \text{a learning query for } (T_1, C_1) = \mathrm{EAX}_K(N_0, H, M_0), \text{ and} \\ \text{a challenge query for } (T_2, C_2) = \mathrm{EAX}_K(N_1, H, M_b) \text{ for unknown } b. \end{cases}$
3. If $C_1 = C_2$ then return 0; else return 1.

As it turns out, this attack succeeds with advantage 1. Namely, we generate the same keystream in either query and thus, if $b = 0$ then $C_1 = C_2$. Also, if $b = 1$ then $C_1 = C_2 \oplus M_1 \oplus M_2 \neq C_1$. To verify this claim, observe

$$\mathrm{CMAC}_K(\langle 0 \rangle || N_0) = \mathrm{CMAC}_K(\langle 0 \rangle || (L \oplus 2L))$$
$$= E_K(E_K(0) \oplus L \oplus 2L \oplus 2L) \qquad = E_K(0) = L$$

and

$$\mathrm{CMAC}_K(\langle 0 \rangle || L || N_0) = \mathrm{CMAC}_K(\langle 0 \rangle || L || (L \oplus 2L))$$
$$= E_K(E_K(E_K(0) \oplus L) \oplus L \oplus 2L \oplus 2L)$$
$$= E_K(E_K(0) \oplus L \oplus 2L \oplus 2L) \qquad = E_K(0) = L.$$

Note that this attack does not work for nonces of equal sizes.

5   Accidential Protection from Q2 Attacks

All AE modes we studied in the context of the current research have been designed and proposed with classical security in the mind. Thus, one must not blame the modes' authors for insecurities under quantum attacks. But we found some design aspects in some of the modes we studied, which happen to protect against Q2 attacks.

---

[6] The design of a quantum interface for the superposition of messages of different lengths may not be obvious. For concreteness, assume a maximum message length μ, and a message of length $m = |M| \leq \mu$ is encoded as a $(\mu + \log_2(\mu))$-qubit string $|M\rangle |0^{\mu-m}\rangle |m\rangle$ of message, padding and message length.

NP-MAC$_K(M)$

---

1 choose nonce $N \in \{0,1\}^n$ at random   3 **return** (T)
2 $T \leftarrow$ CBC-MAC$_K(N, |M|, \text{pad}_0(M))$

Fig. 5. The NP-MAC with a full-block nonce $N \in \{0,1\}^n$; for simplicity, we assume the encoding of the message length $|M| < 2^n$ to be a full-block value $|M| \in \{0,1\}^n$. We write NP-MAC[E] for the instantiation of NP-MAC with a block cipher E.

5.1   The Nonce-Prefix MAC from the CCM Mode

CCM [WHF03] is an early AE mode. Though criticized for a variety of practical undesirabilities [RW03], CCM did inspire the evolution of improved AE modes ("improved" from a classical point of view), such as EAX. We focus on CCM-MAC, which applies CBC-MAC to $(N, |M|, M)$, where N is the nonce, $|M|$ is the message length, and M is the message itself. The original CCM-MAC did allow to squeeze the nonce N of length $|N| \ll n$ and the encoding of $|M|$ into the first input block for the CBC-MAC, while we propose NP-MAC, where the nonce $N \in \{0,1\}^n$ fits exactly into the first block, see Fig. 5. We tried to find possible attacks on NP-MAC by using quantum period finding and quantum linearization. Not only did we not find any feasible attacks, but instead we could even prove that those two techniques would not work in attacking NP-MAC. As we will show below, it is secure when instantiated with a qPRP and used with random nonces, but insecure when instantiated with the wicked 1PRP $\tilde{E}$ (cf. Definition 9), just like CBC encryption.

Theorem 4. *For NP-MAC[$\tilde{E}$] a Q2-Adversary A exists, which recovers the secret key. The accumulated length of all queries from A is $O(n^2)$, and $T(A) \in O(T(Simon(n)))$.*

Proof. Assume a single-block-message $M = \sum_{x \in \{0,1\}^n} |x\rangle$ as the superposition $M = M_1 = \sum_{x \in \{0,1\}^n} |x\rangle$. Note that $|M| = n$ and $\text{pad}_0(M) = M$. Every learning query will be of the form (N_i, M) with a unique nonce N_i and M in superposition[7]. The challenger responds $T = $ CBC-MAC$_K(N_i, |M|, M)$, also in superposition. The first two blocks N_i and $|M|$ are classical values. Thus, $\gamma = $ CBC-MAC$_k(N_i, |M|)$ is a classical constant. The final block is $M = \sum_{x \in \{0,1\}^n} |x\rangle$. Thus, the authentication tag is

$$T = \sum_{x \in \{0,1\}^n} |x\rangle\, |f_{k,N_i}(M)\rangle = \sum_{x \in \{0,1\}^n} |x\rangle\, |\tilde{E}_k(x \oplus \overbrace{\text{CBC-MAC}_k(N_i, |M|)}^{\gamma})\rangle \quad (4)$$

$$= \sum_{x \in \{0,1\}^n} |x\rangle\, |\tilde{E}_k(x)\rangle. \quad (5)$$

---

[7] We would like to point out that there is no need for N_i to be in superposition since the attack already works for classical nonces.

Recall the definition of $\tilde{E}_k$ in Definition 9: The first $n - 1$ bits of $\tilde{E}$ form a subfunction $E'_{f(k)}$, with period k, i.e., $E'_{f(k)}(x) = E'_{f(k)}(y)$ if and only if $x = y$ or $x = y \oplus k$. Thus, the first $n - 1$ bits of f_{k,N_i} also form a function with the same period. This allows a Q2 adversary to recover the secret key k by running Simon's algorithm. The adversary makes $O(n)$ queries, each of length n, so the total query length is $O(n^2)$.[8]

Corollary 1. *NP-MAC[$\tilde{E}$] is qPO insecure.*

Theorem 5. *Let E be a qPRF. For every adversary A_2, distinguishing NP-MAC[E] from random, an adversary $A_1 \leftarrow_{wrap} A_2$ exists, which distinguishes CBC[E_K] from random with $Adv(A_1) = Adv(A_2)$.*

Proof. Let N_i be the random nonce for i-th chosen message $|M_i\rangle$ of length m_i[9] from A_2. For each such $|M_i\rangle$, A_1 creates its own chosen message $M'_i = (0^n \,||\, m_i \,||\, |M_i\rangle)$ and requests the CBC encryption of M'_i from the challenger, using the nonce N_i. A_1 ignores the answer to its query, except for the final block, C_{i,m_i}, which it returns to A_2. Observe $C_{i,m_i} = \text{CBC-MAC}_K(N_i, |M_i\rangle)$. Thus, A_2 receives exactly the answer it expects. $A_1 \leftarrow_{wrap} A_2$, since A_1 extends each query from A_2 by prepending just two blocks, and otherwise, A_1 performs no additional work beyond invoking A_2 and the challenger. Similarly, A_1 succeeds if and only if A_2 succeeds, hence $Adv(A_1) = Adv(A_2)$.

Corollary 2. *NP-MAC[qPRP] is qPO secure, and a quantum-secure MAC.*

We do not claim NP-MAC[qPRP] to *be* a qPRF. NP-MAC is not even a function, as its output depends on the random nonce N chosen in the first step as presented in Fig. 5. But once N has been set, NP-MAC is a function, and if N is chosen at random, the output is indistinguishable from random. In that sense, NP-MAC[qPRP] can be regarded as a "weak qPRF". Here, the next input block, after the nonce, does not actually need to be an encoding of the message length $|M|$. For qPO security, we just need classical security (and, of course, the random nonce as the first block). For the classical security of NP-MAC, any prefix-free encoding of M suffices [Jon02], and $|M| \,||\, M$ is such an encoding.

5.2 Key Derivation, as in AES-GCM-SIV

AES-GCM-SIV is another instantiation of the generic SIV principle (cf. Figure 4). It follows the approach of nonce-based key derivation, see Fig. 6. The goal is to improve the concrete security of GCM-SIV against classical attacks, while maintaining much of the original performance of GCM-SIV. (This is in contrast to GCM-SIV2, which improves the security of GCM-SIV at the performance costs of running GCM-SIV twice.)

---

[8] Here, the query length is counted in bits.

[9] The chosen messages $|M_i\rangle$ can be in superposition, but all messages $|M_i\rangle$ in superposition are of the same length m_i.

KD-Enc$_K(N, H, M)$	KD-Dec$_K(N, H, T, C)$
1 $K_N \leftarrow \mathrm{KD}_K(N)$	**1** $K_N \leftarrow \mathrm{KD}_K(N)$
2 $(T, C) \leftarrow \mathrm{AEnc}_{K_N}(N, H, M)$	**2** $M \leftarrow \mathrm{AEnc}_{K_N}(N, H, T, C)$
3 **return** (T, C)	**3** **return** (M)

Fig. 6. Nonce-based key derivation scheme KD-Enc taking as input a nonce N, header H, and message M. It is based on an authenticated encryption scheme AEnc and a random function KD to derive the temporary key K_N from N and K. We write KD-Enc$[F^{KD}, E^{AE}]$ for the instantiation of the KD-Enc scheme with a key derivation scheme F^{KD} and an authenticated encryption scheme E^{AE}.

Chosen-plaintext queries in the IND-qCPA attack games must use different classical nonces. Nonce-based key derivation thus forces a fresh temporary key for every chosen-plaintext query. This has two implications. The first implication is that we get Q2 security w.r.t. chosen-plaintext attacks, from Q1 security:

Theorem 6. *Let E be a block cipher and assume a Q2-adversary A_2 attacking the IND-qCPA security of KD-Enc$[E, AEnc]$. Then a Q1-adversary A_{1PRF} attacking the 1PRF security of KD and a Q1-adversary $A_{IND\text{-}1CPA}$ attacking the IND-1CPA security of AEnc exist, such that*

$$A_{1PRF} \leftarrow_{wrap} A_2, \text{ and } A_{IND\text{-}1CPA} \leftarrow_{wrap} A_2, \text{ and}$$
$$Adv(A_2) \leq 2Adv(A_{1PRF}) + Adv(A_{IND\text{-}1CPA}).$$

Proof. Let A_2 be given. Define games G_{A_2,A_2}, $G_{KD,KD}$, $G_{\$,KD}$, and $G_{\$,A_2}$. Game G_{A_2,A_2} is plainly running A_2: $Adv(A_2) = |\Pr[A_2 = 1|b = 1] - \Pr[A_2 = 1|b = 0]|$. The other games are defined in Fig. 7. From an adversarial point of view, the games G_{A_2,A_2} and $G_{KD,KD}$ are identical, just that G_{A_2,A_2} employs the challenger's secret key while $G_{KD,KD}$ uses its on key K', thus

$$|\Pr[\mathrm{Exp}(G_{A_2,A_2}, 0) = 1] - \Pr[\mathrm{Exp}(G_{KD,KD}, 0) = 1]| \qquad (6)$$
$$= |\Pr[\mathrm{Exp}(G_{A_2,A_2}, 1) = 1] - \Pr[\mathrm{Exp}(G_{KD,KD}, 1) = 1]| = 0.$$

Similarly to the argument for Eq. 6, the games $G_{\$,KD}$ and $G_{\$,A_2}$ are identical, and thus:

$$|\Pr[\mathrm{Exp}(G_{\$,KD}, 0) = 1] - \Pr[\mathrm{Exp}(G_{\$,A_2}, 0) = 1]|$$
$$= |\Pr[\mathrm{Exp}(G_{\$,KD}, 1) = 1] - \Pr[\mathrm{Exp}(G_{\$,A_2}, 1) = 1]| = 0.$$

Next, we define the adversaries A_{1PRF} and $\mathcal{A}_{IND\text{-}1CPA}$

– A_{1PRF} randomly chooses $b \in \{0,1\}$ and runs either $\mathrm{Exp}(G_{KD,KD}, b)$ or $\mathrm{Exp}(G_{\$,KD}, b)$. The advantage of A_{1PRF} satisfies

$$2 \cdot Adv(A_{1PRF}) \leq |\Pr[\mathrm{Exp}(G_{\$,KD}, 0) = 1] - \Pr[\mathrm{Exp}(G_{KD,KD}, 0) = 1]|$$
$$+ |\Pr[\mathrm{Exp}(G_{\$,KD}, 1) = 1] - \Pr[\mathrm{Exp}(G_{KD,KD}, 1) = 1]|.$$

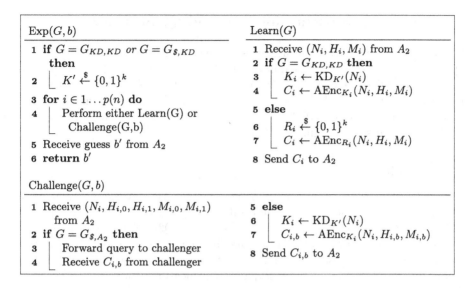

Fig. 7. Experiment run by the adversary. G can be $G_{KD,KD}$, $G_{\$,KD}$, or $G_{\$,A_2}$. Note that here we do not consider $G = G_{A_2,A_2}$.

- $\mathcal{A}_{\text{IND-1CPA}}$ runs $\text{Exp}(G_{\$,A_2}, b)$ for a b chosen by the challenger and unknown to $\mathcal{A}_{\text{IND-1CPA}}$. The resulting advantage is

$$\text{Adv}(\mathcal{A}_{\text{IND-1CPA}}) = \left| \Pr[\text{Exp}(G_{\$,A_2}, 0) = 1] - \Pr[\text{Exp}(G_{\$,A_2}, 1) = 1] \right|.$$

Only learning queries can be in superposition, and all of the games $G_{KD,KD}$, $G_{\$,KD}$ and $G_{\$,A_2}$ compute their response to learning queries on their own, without invoking an oracle. Thus, both $\mathcal{A}_{\text{1PRF}}$ and $\mathcal{A}_{\text{IND-1CPA}}$ are Q1 adversaries. Also, all of these games are wrappers around A_2, thus $\mathcal{A}_{\text{1PRF}} \leftarrow_{\text{wrap}} A_2$, and $\mathcal{A}_{\text{IND-1CPA}} \leftarrow_{\text{wrap}} A_2$. Finally, for the claimed bound on the advantage of A:

$$
\begin{aligned}
\text{Adv}(A_2) = {} & \left| \Pr[\text{Exp}(G_{A_2,A_2}, 0) = 1] - \Pr[\text{Exp}(G_{A_2,A_2}, 1) = 1] \right| \\
\leq {} & \left| \Pr[\text{Exp}(G_{A_2,A_2}, 0) = 1] - \Pr[\text{Exp}(G_{KD,KD}, 0) = 1] \right| \\
& + \left| \Pr[\text{Exp}(G_{KD,KD}, 0) = 1] - \Pr[\text{Exp}(G_{\$,KD}, 0) = 1] \right| \\
& + \left| \Pr[\text{Exp}(G_{\$,KD}, 0) = 1] - \Pr[\text{Exp}(G_{\$,A_2}, 0) = 1] \right| \\
& + \left| \Pr[\text{Exp}(G_{\$,A_2}, 0) = 1] - \Pr[\text{Exp}(G_{\$,A_2}, 1) = 1] \right| \quad (7)\\
& + \left| \Pr[\text{Exp}(G_{\$,A_2}, 1) = 1] - \Pr[\text{Exp}(G_{\$,KD}, 1) = 1] \right| \\
& + \left| \Pr[\text{Exp}(G_{\$,KD}, 1) = 1] - \Pr[\text{Exp}(G_{KD,KD}, 1) = 1] \right| \\
& + \left| \Pr[\text{Exp}(G_{KD,KD}, 1) = 1] - \Pr[\text{Exp}(G_{A_2,A_2}, 1) = 1] \right| \\
\leq {} & 4 \cdot 0 + 2 \cdot \text{Adv}(\mathcal{A}_{\text{1PRF}}) + \text{Adv}(\mathcal{A}_{\text{IND-1CPA}})
\end{aligned}
$$

Corollary 3. *If AEnc is IND-1CPA secure, KD-Enc[1PRP, AEnc] is IND-qCPA secure.*

6   Generic Approaches for Q2d and Q2 Security

We describe how to turn Q1-secure AE schemes into Q2d-secure and even proper Q2-secure AE schemes. The definition of the IND-qdCCA security stems from the generic IND-CCA game (cf. Definition 4) and that of a Q2d adversary (cf. Definition 8). Below, Subsect. 6.1 provides an intuitive and informal overview over core ideas. Subsections 6.2 to 6.4 are more formal and technical. Subsection 6.5 briefly discusses the tightness of the concrete results.

6.1   Intuition

Consider a Q1-secure AE scheme AEnc. Assume that AEnc provides both chosen-plaintext privacy (1CPA) and authenticity (1PO) when all queries are classical. We claim that in such case, AEnc is also Q2d-secure. For instance, it provides privacy even when decryption queries are in superposition. To prove this claim, assume an adversary making decryption queries (N_i, H_i, C_i) in superposition. Imagine to measure one such query. The measurement result (N_i', H_i', C_i') can be old (i.e., C_i' stems from a matching encryption query (N_i', H_i', M_i') for some M_i') or invalid (decryption returns $\perp$). If there is a non-negligible probability for (N_i, H_i, C_i) in superposition to be found neither old nor invalid after a potential measurement, then we refer to (N_i, H_i, C_i) as *pivotal*. Based on this notion, we distinguish two cases: *(1) The adversary makes no pivotal decryption queries.* Then, the ability to choose decryption queries in superposition, or to choose decryption queries at all, does not provide any significant advantage over making only classical encryption queries. A successful attack in this scenario would thus violate 1CPA security. *(2) The adversary makes at least one pivotal decryption query.* By guessing the index of a pivotal query and actually measuring it, one can generate a forgery. A successful attack in this scenario would thus violate 1PO security. The proof of Theorem 7 centers around this idea.

We also claim that key derivation with a 1PRF secure key derivation function can turn a Q2d chosen-ciphertext secure and 1PO secure scheme AEnc into a fully Q2 chosen-ciphertext secure scheme. Thus, if AEnc is secure against adversaries making decryption queries in superposition, then the derived scheme is also secure against adversaries making all queries in superposition. This is the intuition for Theorem 8. For the proof, recall the proof of Theorem 6: The main key is only used to generate nonce-dependent derived keys, and each chosen plaintext is encrypted under another derived key. In this case, it turns out that the benefit from choosing plaintexts in superposition is negligible.

By combining both results, one can create a proper Q2-secure AE scheme (encryption and decryption queries in superposition) from a (seemingly much weaker) Q1-secure AE scheme and a 1PRF.

6.2   The O2H ("One-Way to Hiding") Lemma

To analyze the approach to gather Q2d and Q2 security from Q1 security, we first explain the semi-classical one-way to hiding (O2H) lemma from [AHU19], an improved version of the classical O2H lemma from [Unr15]. At its core are so-called punctured oracles. Consider a subset S from the set of inputs to the oracle H. $H\backslash S$ (H punctured by S) takes a value x as input and computes whether $x \in S$ or not. The event "Find" denotes the case this measurement returns that $x \in S$ is true. When Find does not occur, the outcome of $A^{H/S}$ is independent of $H(x)$ for $x \in S$.

Lemma 1 (Semi-Classical O2H [AHU19]). *Let $S \subset X$ be random. Let $G, H : X \to Y$ be random functions satisfying $\forall x \notin S$. $G(x) = H(x)$. Let z be a random bitstring. $(S, G, H, z$ may have arbitrary joint distribution.) Let A be an oracle algorithm of query depth d (not necessary unitary). Let*

$$P_{left} := \Pr[b = 1 : b \leftarrow A^H(z)], \quad P_{right} := \Pr[b = 1 : b \leftarrow A^G(z)]$$

$$P_{find} := \Pr[Find : A^{G\backslash S}(z)] = \Pr[Find : A^{H\backslash S}(z)]$$

Then

$$|P_{left} - P_{right}| \leq 2\sqrt{(d+1) \cdot P_{find}}, \tag{8}$$

$$|\sqrt{P_{left}} - \sqrt{P_{right}}| \leq 2\sqrt{(d+1) \cdot P_{find}}. \tag{9}$$

This lemma needs to be contextualized. Firstly, the notion "depth d" considers an adversary to perform multiple queries in parallel. In our context, it suffices to point out that $d \leq q$ holds for every q-query adversary.

Secondly, Relationship 8 results in better bounds for our purpose. We deal with Relationship 9 in the full paper [LL23]. Thus, Relationship 8 can be rewritten as

$$P_{\text{left}} \leq 2\sqrt{(d+1) \cdot P_{\text{find}}} + P_{\text{right}}. \tag{10}$$

Thirdly, in the context of that paper, $\Pr[b = 1 : b \leftarrow A^H(z)]$ in the notation of [AHU19] is the same as $\text{win}(A) = \Pr[b = b']$ in our notation, where b' is the output from A and b the challenger's internal choice (cf. Definition 4 and Eq. 1). As we define the advantage of an adversary by $\text{Adv}(A) = |\Pr[b' = 1|b = 1] - \Pr[b' = 1|b = 0]|$, we have

$$\text{win}(A) = (\text{Adv}(A) + 1)/2.$$

6.3 From Q1 Security to Q2d Security

Theorem 7. *Let $AEnc$ be an AE scheme producing an n-bit output and assume a Q2d-adversary A_{qdCCA} attacking the IND-qdCCA security of $AEnc$. Then a Q1-adversary A_{1PO} attacking the 1PO security and a Q1-adversary A_{1CPA} attacking the IND-1CPA security of $AEnc$ exists, such that*

$$A_{1PO} \leftarrow_{wrap} A_{qdCCA} \quad and \quad A_{1CPA} \leftarrow_{wrap} A_{qdCCA} \quad and$$

$$Adv(A_{qdCCA}) \leq 4\sqrt{(q+1)}\sqrt{Adv(A_{1PO})} + Adv(A_{1CPA}).$$

Proof. Consider an IND-qdCCA adversary $\mathcal{A}$, and define the H oracle: H is identical to the Q2d challenger, responding to all queries from $\mathcal{A}$, including backward learning queries in superposition. I.e., A_{qdCCA}, when connected to its challenger, can be written as $\mathcal{A}^H$.

Define S as the set of those backward learning queries, which return a valid message: $S = (N_i, H_i, C_i) : \text{ADec}_K(N_i, H_i, C_i) \neq \perp$. Recall that the set B of "blocked" triples from Definition 4 includes the triples (N_i, H_i, C_i) known from forward learning queries, and, any backward query trying to decrypt a "blocked" triple returns $\perp$. Thus, whenever the event Find occurs, there is a new triple (N_i, H_i, C_i), which has not been known from any other queries. This allows an adversary to win the PO game by measuring $(N_i, H_i, C_i) \notin B$ but $(N_i, H_i, C_i) \in S$. A PO forgery consists of the new triple (N_i, H_i, C_i) and all the known triples. This defines $A_{1\text{PO}}$. Obviously, $A_{1\text{PO}} \hookleftarrow_{\text{wrap}} A_{\text{qdCCA}}$ and $\text{Adv}(A_{1\text{PO}}) = P_{\text{Find}}$.

Let G be an oracle, which relays challenge and forward learning queries to a Q1 challenger, and which responds to all backward learning queries by returning $\perp$. Clearly, $H \backslash S$ and $G \backslash S$ behave identically. We write $A_{1\text{CPA}}$ as $\mathcal{A}^G$. Obviously $A_{1\text{CPA}} \hookleftarrow_{\text{wrap}} A_{\text{qdCCA}}$.

We still have to prove the bound

$$\text{Adv}(A_{\text{qdCCA}}) \leq 2\sqrt{(q+1)}\sqrt{\text{Adv}(A_{1\text{PO}})} + \text{Adv}(A_{1\text{CPA}}).$$

If $\text{Adv}(A_{1\text{CPA}}) \geq \text{Adv}(A_{\text{qdCCA}})$, this is trivial. For the rest of this proof, we assume $\text{Adv}(A_{1\text{CPA}}) < \text{Adv}(A_{\text{qdCCA}})$. In our context, $P_{\text{left}} = \text{win}(A_{\text{qdCCA}})$, $P_{\text{right}} = \text{win}(A_{1\text{CPA}})$, and $P_{\text{find}} = A_{1\text{PO}}$.

Eq. 8 (or rather, the derived Eq. 10) implies

$$\text{win}(A_{\text{qdCCA}}) \leq 2\sqrt{(q+1)}\sqrt{\text{Adv}(A_{1\text{PO}})} + \text{win}(A_{1\text{CPA}}).$$

We apply $\text{win}(A) = (\text{Adv}(A) + 1)/2$ and simplify the expression to

$$\text{Adv}(A_{\text{qdCCA}}) \leq 4\sqrt{(q+1)}\sqrt{\text{Adv}(A_{1\text{PO}})} + \text{Adv}(A_{1\text{CPA}}).$$

Corollary 4. *If AEnc is both IND-1CPA secure and 1PO secure, then AEnc is also IND-qdCCA secure.*

6.4   Transitioning Q2d Security into Q2 Security

Theorem 8. *Let E be a block cipher and assume a q-query Q2-adversary A_2 attacking the IND-qCCA security of KD-Enc[E, AEnc]. Then a Q1-adversary A_{1PRF} attacking the 1PRF security of KD, a Q2d-adversary $A_{Ind\text{-}qdCCA}$ attacking the IND-qdCCA security of AEnc and a Q1-adversary A_{1PO} exists, attacking the 1PO security of AEnc, such that*

$$A_{1PRF} \hookleftarrow_{wrap} A_2, \text{ and } A_{IND\text{-}qdCCA} \hookleftarrow_{wrap} A_2, \text{ and } A_{1PO} \hookleftarrow_{wrap} A_2, \text{ and}$$

$$Adv(A_2) \leq 2\sqrt{(q+1) \cdot (2 \cdot Adv(A_{1PRF}) + Adv(A_{qdCCA}) + 4 \cdot Adv(A_{1PO}))}.$$

Proof (Sketch). The proof resembles the proof of Theorem 6. The core idea – beyond ideas already used to prove Theorem 6 – is to define a "cheating" game where the response to chosen-ciphertext queries (even in superposition) is just $\perp$. We use the semi-classical O2H lemma ([AHU19]; Lemma 1 in the current paper) to argue that any advantage in distinguishing a "cheating" game from one with proper decryptions can be exploited to find a classical chosen-ciphertext query (N, H, C) which decrypts to a message $M \neq \perp$. As all the chosen-plaintext queries are classical, the pair $(M, (N, H, C))$ implies a forgery in the PO sense.

Corollary 5. *If AEnc is IND-qdCCA and 1PO secure, then KD-Enc[1PRP, AEnc] is IND-qCCA secure.*

6.5 On the Tightness of the Reductions

As abstract results, Theorems 7 and 8 and Corollaries 4 and 5 are *very encouraging:* Classical security concerning quantum adversaries (i.e. 1PO and IND-1CPA security) suffices to achieve security even when chosen-ciphertext queries can be in superposition (i.e., IND-qdCCA security).

But, while the other reductions in the current paper are tight, the connection between the required 1PO and IND-1CPA security level and the IND-q(d)CCA security level granted by Theorems 7 and 8 is not. We provide a numerical example for IND-qdCCA (Theorem 7). Consider an AE scheme with a key size of 256 bit, and adversaries restricted to iterate Grover's algorithm about 2^{80} times. The probability to recover the secret key would thus be about $2^{2*80-256} = 2^{-96}$. Assume that the best 1PO or IND-1CPA attack is equivalent to key recovery, i.e., $\text{Adv}(A_{1PO}) = \text{Adv}(A_{1CPA}) = 2^{-96}$. Under these assumptions, and for $q < 2^{20}$, the bound from Theorem 7 is

$$\text{Adv}(A_{\text{qdCCA}}) \leq 4 \cdot \sqrt{(q+1)}\sqrt{\text{Adv}(A_{1PO})} + \text{Adv}(A_{1CPA})$$
$$\leq 4 \cdot 2^{10}2^{-48} + 2^{-96} \qquad\qquad \approx 2^{-36}.$$

If we increase the limit on the number of queries to, say, $q < 2^{50}$, the same calculation gives the bound $\text{Adv}(A_{\text{qdCCA}}) \leq 4 \cdot 2^{25}2^{-48} + 2^{-96} \approx 2^{-21}$. This should still be fine for most practical purposes. Nevertheless, given the ultra-strong bounds of 2^{-96} each for the 1PO and the IND-1CPA advantage, the bounds on $\text{Adv}(A_{\text{qdCCA}})$ may be surprising.

7 Final Remarks

Recall our motivating question: *"When exposed to superposition queries, which state-of-the-art AE systems maintain a meaningful level of security?"* The first answers are negative: EAX, GCM, and variants of SIV do not only fail at authenticity (as known before), but they also fail at privacy under chosen-plaintext queries. We conclude that all of those modes fail to provide any meaningful level of security under superposition queries. Other answers are positive:

A restricted variant of GCM avoids the vulnerability to superposition chosen-plaintext attacks. The nonce-prefix MAC is secure under superposition attacks, and can thus be used as a building block for superposition-resistant AE systems. Theorem 7 provides a path from chosen-plaintext privacy and authenticity in the Q1 model (IND-1CPA and 1PO security) to chosen-ciphertext security in the Q2d model (IND-qdCCA). If we also consider Theorem 8 (i.e., if we apply nonce-based key-derivation), the path leads to chosen-ciphertext privacy in the unrestricted Q2 model (IND-qCCA). To some degree, Theorems 7 and 8 resemble results from [BN00], which provide a generic path from classical chosen-plaintext privacy and classical authenticity to classical chosen-ciphertext privacy.

Based on our findings, new questions arise: (1) By definition, the nonce-prefix MAC requires random nonces. *Could a variant of the nonce-prefix MAC, with nonces chosen by a nonce-respecting adversary, also be qPO secure?* (2) The concrete bounds for IND-q(d)CCA security from Theorems 7 and 8 are a bit unsatisfactory. *Is there a matching attack? Or can one improve the concrete bounds?* An answer to either question might require different methods than ours, or, perhaps, a stronger variant of the O2H Lemma.

References

[AGM18a] Alagic, G., Gagliardoni, T., Majenz, C.: Can you sign a quantum state? CoRR, abs/1811.11858 (2018)

[AGM18b] Alagic, G., Gagliardoni, T., Majenz, C.: Unforgeable quantum encryption. In: Nielsen, J.B., Rijmen, V. (eds.) EUROCRYPT 2018. LNCS, vol. 10822, pp. 489–519. Springer, Cham (2018). https://doi.org/10.1007/978-3-319-78372-7_16

[AHU19] Ambainis, A., Hamburg, M., Unruh, D.: Quantum security proofs using semi-classical oracles. In: Boldyreva, A., Micciancio, D. (eds.) CRYPTO 2019. LNCS, vol. 11693, pp. 269–295. Springer, Cham (2019). https://doi.org/10.1007/978-3-030-26951-7_10

[AMRS20] Alagic, G., Majenz, C., Russell, A., Song, F.: Quantum-access-secure message authentication via blind-unforgeability. In: Canteaut, A., Ishai, Y. (eds.) EUROCRYPT 2020. LNCS, vol. 12107, pp. 788–817. Springer, Cham (2020). https://doi.org/10.1007/978-3-030-45727-3_27

[ATTU16] Anand, M.V., Targhi, E.E., Tabia, G.N., Unruh, D.: Post-quantum security of the CBC, CFB, OFB, CTR, and XTS modes of operation. In: Takagi, T. (ed.) PQCrypto 2016. LNCS, vol. 9606, pp. 44–63. Springer, Cham (2016). https://doi.org/10.1007/978-3-319-29360-8_4

[BBC+21] Bhaumik, R., et al.: QCB: efficient quantum-secure authenticated encryption. In: Tibouchi, M., Wang, H. (eds.) ASIACRYPT 2021. LNCS, vol. 13090, pp. 668–698. Springer, Cham (2021). https://doi.org/10.1007/978-3-030-92062-3_23

[BLNS21] Bonnetain, X., Leurent, G., Naya-Plasencia, M., Schrottenloher, A.: Quantum linearization attacks. In: Tibouchi, M., Wang, H. (eds.) ASIACRYPT 2021. LNCS, vol. 13090, pp. 422–452. Springer, Cham (2021). https://doi.org/10.1007/978-3-030-92062-3_15

[BN00] Bellare, M., Namprempre, C.: Authenticated encryption: relations among notions and analysis of the generic composition paradigm. In: Okamoto,

T. (ed.) ASIACRYPT 2000. LNCS, vol. 1976, pp. 531–545. Springer, Heidelberg (2000). https://doi.org/10.1007/3-540-44448-3_41

[BSS22] Bonnetain, X., Schrottenloher, A., Sibleyras, F.: Beyond quadratic speedups in quantum attacks on symmetric schemes. In: Dunkelman, O., Dziembowski, S. (eds.) EUROCRYPT 2022. LNCS, vol. 13277, pp. 315–344. Springer, Cham (2022). https://doi.org/10.1007/978-3-031-07082-2_12

[BZ13a] Boneh, D., Zhandry, M.: Quantum-secure message authentication codes. In: Johansson, T., Nguyen, P.Q. (eds.) EUROCRYPT 2013. LNCS, vol. 7881, pp. 592–608. Springer, Heidelberg (2013). https://doi.org/10.1007/978-3-642-38348-9_35

[BZ13b] Boneh, D., Zhandry, M.: Secure signatures and chosen ciphertext security in a quantum computing world. In: Canetti, R., Garay, J.A. (eds.) CRYPTO 2013. LNCS, vol. 8043, pp. 361–379. Springer, Heidelberg (2013). https://doi.org/10.1007/978-3-642-40084-1_21

[CETU20] Carstens, T.V., Ebrahimi, E., Tabia, G.N., Unruh, D.: On quantum indistinguishability under chosen plaintext attack. IACR Cryptology ePrint Archive, p. 596 (2020)

[CJL+16] Chen, L., et al.: Breaking the quadratic barrier: quantum cryptanalysis of milenage, telecommunications' cryptographic backbone (2016)

[HI21] Hosoyamada, A., Iwata, T.: On tight quantum security of HMAC and NMAC in the quantum random oracle model. In: Malkin, T., Peikert, C. (eds.) CRYPTO 2021. LNCS, vol. 12825, pp. 585–615. Springer, Cham (2021). https://doi.org/10.1007/978-3-030-84242-0_21

[IM16] Iwata, T., Minematsu, K.: Stronger security variants of GCM-SIV. IACR Trans. Symmetric Cryptol. **2016**(1), 134–157 (2016)

[Jon02] Jonsson, J.: On the security of CTR + CBC-MAC. In: Nyberg, K., Heys, H. (eds.) SAC 2002. LNCS, vol. 2595, pp. 76–93. Springer, Heidelberg (2003). https://doi.org/10.1007/3-540-36492-7_7

[JS22] Janson, C., Struck, P.: Sponge-based authenticated encryption: Security against quantum attackers. IACR Cryptology ePrint Archive, p. 139 (2022)

[KLLN16] Kaplan, M., Leurent, G., Leverrier, A., Naya-Plasencia, M.: Breaking symmetric cryptosystems using quantum period finding. In: Robshaw, M., Katz, J. (eds.) CRYPTO 2016. LNCS, vol. 9815, pp. 207–237. Springer, Heidelberg (2016). https://doi.org/10.1007/978-3-662-53008-5_8

[LL23] Lang, N., Lucks, S.: On the post-quantum security of classical authenticated encryption schemes. Cryptology ePrint Archive, Paper 2023/218 (2023). https://eprint.iacr.org/2023/218

[MMPR22] Maram, V., Masny, D., Patranabis, S., Raghuraman, S.: On the quantum security of OCB. IACR Cryptology ePrint Archive, p. 699 (2022)

[RS06] Rogaway, P., Shrimpton, T.: A provable-security treatment of the key-wrap problem. In: Vaudenay, S. (ed.) EUROCRYPT 2006. LNCS, vol. 4004, pp. 373–390. Springer, Heidelberg (2006). https://doi.org/10.1007/11761679_23

[RW03] Rogaway, P., Wagner, D.A.: A critique of CCM. IACR Cryptology ePrint Archive, p. 70 (2003)

[Sho94] Shor, P.W.: Algorithms for quantum computation: discrete logarithms and factoring. In: 35th Annual Symposium on Foundations of Computer Science, Santa Fe, New Mexico, USA, 20–22 November 1994, pp. 124–134. IEEE Computer Society (1994)

[Sim97] Simon, D.: On the power of quantum computation. SIAM J. Comput. **26**(5), 1474–1483 (1997)

[SY17] Song, F., Yun, A.: Quantum security of NMAC and related constructions. In: Katz, J., Shacham, H. (eds.) CRYPTO 2017. LNCS, vol. 10402, pp. 283–309. Springer, Cham (2017). https://doi.org/10.1007/978-3-319-63715-0_10

[Unr15] Unruh, D.: Revocable quantum timed-release encryption. J. ACM **62**(6), 49:1–49:76 (2015)

[US22] Ulitzsch, V., Seifert, J.-P.: IARR eprint 2022/733 (2022)

[WHF03] Whiting, D., Housley, R., Ferguson, N.: Counter with CBC-MAC (CCM). RFC 3610, 1–26 (2003)

[Zha19] Zhandry, M.: How to record quantum queries, and applications to quantum indifferentiability. In: Boldyreva, A., Micciancio, D. (eds.) CRYPTO 2019. LNCS, vol. 11693, pp. 239–268. Springer, Cham (2019). https://doi.org/10.1007/978-3-030-26951-7_9

A Side-Channel Attack Against *Classic McEliece* When Loading the Goppa Polynomial

Boly Seck[1,2]($\boxtimes$)(ID), Pierre-Louis Cayrel[2](ID), Vlad-Florin Dragoi[3](ID), Idy Diop[1](ID), Morgan Barbier[4], Jean Belo Klamti[5](ID), Vincent Grosso[2](ID), and Brice Colombier[2](ID)

[1] ESP, Laboratoire d'imagerie médicale et de Bio-informatique, Dakar, Senegal
idy.diop@esp.sn, seck.boly@ugb.edu.sn
[2] Univ Lyon, UJM-Saint-Etienne, CNRS, Laboratoire Hubert Curien UMR 5516, 42023 Saint-Etienne, France
{pierre.louis.cayrel,vincent.grosso,b.colombier}@univ-st-etienne.fr
[3] Faculty of Exact Sciences, Aurel Vlaicu University, Arad, Romania
vlad.dragoi@uav.ro
[4] ENSICAEN, Groupe de recherche en informatique et instrumentation de Caen, CNRS, Boulevard Maréchal Juin 14 000, Caen, France
morgan.barbier@ensicaen.fr
[5] Department of Electrical and Computer Engineering, University of Waterloo, Ontario, Canada
jbklamti@uwaterloo.ca

Abstract. The NIST Post-Quantum Cryptography (PQC) standardization challenge was launched in December 2016 and recently, has released its first results. The whole process has given a considerable dynamic to the research in post-quantum cryptography, in particular to practical aspects, such as the study of the vulnerabilities of post-quantum algorithms to side-channel attacks. In this paper, we present a realistic template attack against the reference implementation of *Classic McEliece* which is a finalist of the 4th round of NIST PQC standardization. This profiled attack allowed us to accurately find the Hamming weight of each coefficient of the Goppa polynomial. With only one decryption, this result enables us first, to find directly the Goppa polynomial in the case of weak keys with the method of Loidreau and Sendrier (P. Loidreau and N. Sendrier, "Weak keys in the McEliece public-key cryptosystem", *IEEE Trans. Inf. Theory*, 2001). Then, in the case of "slightly less weak keys", we also find this polynomial with an exhaustive search with low complexity. Finally, we propose the best complexity reduction for exhaustive Goppa polynomial search on $\mathbb{F}_{2^m}$. We attack the constant-time implementation of *Classic McEliece* proposed by Chen *et al.* This implementation, which follows the NIST specification, is realized on a stm32f4-Discovery microcontroller with a 32-bit ARM Cortex-M4.

Keywords: NIST PQC standardization · Classic McEliece · Side-Channel Attack · Template Attack · Goppa Polynomial

© The Author(s), under exclusive license to Springer Nature Switzerland AG 2023
N. El Mrabet et al. (Eds.): AFRICACRYPT 2023, LNCS 14064, pp. 105–125, 2023.
https://doi.org/10.1007/978-3-031-37679-5_5

1   Introduction

In recent years, research on quantum computers has accelerated considerably [TF19, GI19, Lar+21]. These computers can theoretically solve difficult number theory problems (the integer factorization problem and the discrete logarithm problem) in polynomial time [Fey18, DJ92, Gro96, Sho94]. Thus, if large-scale quantum computers are built, they will be able to break most current asymmetric systems such as RSA, ECDSA and ECDH. This would severely compromise the confidentiality and integrity of all digital communications. As a result, the cryptographic community has turned its attention to credible alternatives for dealing with quantum computing. Thus, in 2016, the National Institute of Standards and Technology (NIST) announced a call for proposals to standardize post-quantum cryptography (PQC) primitives [CML17]. This standardization process consists of several rounds, and only those applicants that best meet NIST's requirements in each round are selected to proceed to the next round.

On the fifth of July, 2022, NIST released the first four winning algorithms (a key establishment algorithm named CRYSTALS-Kyber, and three digital signature algorithms named CRYSTALS-Dilithium, FALCON, and SPHINCS+). The first three of these algorithms are based on structured lattices and the last one, SPHINCS+ is a hash-based signature scheme. These future standards are expected to be used by defaultc for selecting post-quantum algorithms in the majority of security products. Provided that these post-quantum algorithms are also combined with proven classical algorithms through hybrid mechanisms. The main goal of the process started by NIST is to replace three standards that are considered the most vulnerable to quantum attacks, $i.e.$, FIPS 186-4[1] (for digital signatures), NIST SP 800-56A[2], and NIST SP 800-56B[3] (both for keys establishment in public-key cryptography).

Beside the four winners, an extension of the NIST PQC standardization campaign (4th round) is planned for key establishment algorithms: BIKE, HQC, *Classic McEliece* [Cho+20] (all three based on error-correcting codes). *Classic McEliece* was the first selected finalist for code-based cryptography as a Key Encapsulation Mechanism (KEM), while BIKE and HQC were two alternatives.

In addition to defining secure schemes and choosing secure parameters, an important issue, in the standardization process, is the impact of a scheme's implementation on its security. A general requirement on the implementation of a scheme is that the execution time of operations does not vary with the secret information (e.g., the secret key or plaintext). This is called a constant-time implementation. However, there are other side-channel attacks beside timing attacks that can allow an attacker to access secret information. Other side-channels include power consumption and electromagnetic, photonic, and acoustic emissions. For many PQC systems, it is still unclear which side-channel attacks are feasible in practice and how to be protected against them. That

---

[1] https://nvlpubs.nist.gov/nistpubs/FIPS/NIST.FIPS.186-4.PDF.

[2] https://nvlpubs.nist.gov/nistpubs/SpecialPublications/NIST.SP.800-56Ar2.PDF.

[3] https://nvlpubs.nist.gov/nistpubs/SpecialPublications/NIST.SP.800-56Br1.PDF.

is why the side-channel topic has become recurrent in the NIST PQC seminar[4] [Saa22, Rav+22]. In the past, code-based cryptosystems were subject to side-channel attacks even before NIST started the standardisation process [CD10, HMP10, Mol+11, Ava+11, Che+16]. However, the end of the first round of this challenging process defined the beginning of a side-channel race for physical security assesment. Indeed, *Classic McEliece* KEM oriented attacks appeared in a series of articles, where either the security of session key or of the private key was investigated [Lah+20, Cay+21, GJJ22, Col+22a, Sec+22, Gro+23, Col+23]. Here we make another step in this direction.

Contribution: In this work, we focus on the constant-time implementation of *Classic McEliece* which is one of the finalists of the NIST PQC extended campaign. This is a KEM, which is conservatively built from a Public Key Encryption (PKE) designed for One-way under Chosen-Plaintext Attack (OW-CPA) security, namely Niederreiter's dual version of McEliece's PKE using Goppa binary codes, as described in Sect. 2.2. First, we perform a template attack during decryption in *Classic McEliece* to find the Hamming weights of the Goppa polynomial coefficients. Since the Goppa polynomial is loaded from memory during this step, we were able to track the execution step of the algorithm and measure the corresponding power consumption. With this information at hand, we have built a profile for each possible weight and deployed, using a single trace, our attack. At the end of this step, each weight was detected with an almost perfect accuracy. Finally, we have used this information to find the Goppa polynomial. In the case of weak keys with binary coefficients, the polynomial was retrieved directly from the Hamming weight. In the case of "slightly less weak keys", we show that in polynomial time one can compute the Goppa polynomial. Moreover, we have significantly improved the complexity of the best attack to find the Goppa polynomial on $\mathbb{F}_{2^m}$ from 2^{1615} to 2^{1174} for $m = 13$, $n = 8192$ and $t = 128$. Finally, we show that our attack is realistic compared to other side-channel attacks on *Classic McEliece*.

Organization: The paper is organized as follows: Sect. 2 provides some background information on code-based cryptography and briefly describes *Classic McEliece* scheme. Section 3 presents a detailed description of our template attack on the constant-time implementation of *Classic McEliece* on ARM Cortex-M4 [CC21] to recover the Hamming weights of the Goppa polynomial coefficients. In Sect. 4, we use this result to find the Goppa polynomial directly in the case of weak keys and reduce the complexity of the exhaustive search for the Goppa polynomial on $\mathbb{F}_{2^m}$. Section 5 compares our attack with a recent side-channel attack of Guo *et al.* [GJJ22] on *Classic McEliece* and finally, we conclude this paper in Sect. 6.

---

[4] https://csrc.nist.gov/Projects/post-quantum-cryptography/workshops-and-timeline/pqc-seminars.

2   Theoretical Background

2.1   Preliminaries

Let us first recall basic definitions and notations used in coding theory. A linear code $\mathcal{C}$ over $\mathbb{F}_q$ is a vector subspace of $\mathbb{F}_q^n$ of dimension k and the elements of $\mathcal{C}$ are called codewords. A generator matrix of $\mathcal{C}$ is a matrix $\boldsymbol{G} \in \mathbb{F}_q^{k \times n}$ such that its lines form a basis of the vector space $\mathcal{C}$ such that $\mathcal{C} = \{\boldsymbol{x}\boldsymbol{G} | \boldsymbol{x} \in \mathbb{F}_q^k\}$. A parity-Check matrix is a matrix $\boldsymbol{H} \in \mathbb{F}_q^{(n-k) \times n}$ such that $\mathcal{C} = \{\boldsymbol{y} \in \mathbb{F}_q^n | \boldsymbol{H}\boldsymbol{y}^T = 0\}$.

To perform error detection and correction, a code $\mathcal{C}$ uses a norm, the most common one being the Hamming weight $wt(\boldsymbol{y}) = \#\{i, \boldsymbol{y}_i \neq 0\}$. Any linear code possesses a minimum distance, i.e.,

$$d(\mathcal{C}) = \min\{wt(\boldsymbol{c}) \mid \boldsymbol{c} \in \mathcal{C}, \boldsymbol{c} \neq 0\}. \tag{1}$$

The majority of structured codes with Hamming distance d can correct any error $\boldsymbol{e}$ of Hamming weight $wt(\boldsymbol{e}) \leq \lfloor (d-1)/2 \rfloor$. This quantity, which we will refer to as t in the following, refers to the correction capacity of $\mathcal{C}$.

Several families of codes were proposed in the literature as possible solutions in a cryptographic context such as the McEliece cryptosystem [Sid94, Nie86, SK14, Mis+13]. However, many of these were completely broken [CB14, Cou+14, Bar+16, OK15]. The original proposal by McEliece that uses binary Goppa codes remains unbroken. Thus, we will remind here some properties of Goppa codes used in *Classic McEliece*.

Goppa Codes

Definition 1 (Goppa code). *Let* $g(x) = g_t x^t + \cdots + g_2 x^2 + g_1 x + g_0 \in \mathbb{F}_{q^m}[x]$, *and let* $L = \{\alpha_1, \alpha_2, ..., \alpha_n\} \subseteq \mathbb{F}_{q^m}$ *such that,* $g(\alpha_i) \neq 0$, *for all* $\alpha_i \in L$. *Then the code defined by*

$$\mathcal{C} = \left\{(\boldsymbol{c}_1, \boldsymbol{c}_2, \ldots, \boldsymbol{c}_n) \in \mathbb{F}_q^n : \sum_{i=1}^{n} \frac{c_i}{x - \alpha_i} \equiv 0 \mod g(x)\right\} \tag{2}$$

is called Goppa code with parameters L *and* $g(x)$, *denoted by* $\Gamma(L, g)$.

For each i, $\gcd(x - \alpha_i, g(x)) = 1$ since $g(\alpha_i) \neq 0$, the value of $(x - \alpha_i)^{-1}$ is computed into $\frac{\mathbb{F}_{q^m}[x]}{\langle g(x) \rangle}$.

Theorem 1 [MS77]. *The multiplicative of* $(x - \alpha_i)$ *inverse exists in the quotient ring* $\frac{\mathbb{F}_{q^m}[x]}{\langle g(x) \rangle}$; *the value of* $(x - \alpha_i)^{-1}$ *in* $\frac{\mathbb{F}_{q^m}[x]}{\langle g(x) \rangle}$ *is* $\left(\frac{g(\alpha_i) - g(x)}{x - \alpha_i}\right) g(\alpha_i)^{-1}$. *A vector* $\boldsymbol{c} \in \Gamma(L, g)$ *if and only if* $\sum_i c_i \left(\frac{g(\alpha_i) - g(x)}{x - \alpha_i}\right) g(\alpha_i)^{-1} \equiv 0 \mod g(x)$.

Using this result, we can derive the following important corollary:

Corollary 1 [MS77]. *For a Goppa code $\Gamma(L, g)$, the parity check matrix over $\mathbb{F}_{q^m}$ is*

$$
H = \begin{bmatrix}
g(\alpha_1)^{-1} & g(\alpha_2)^{-1} & \cdots & g(\alpha_n)^{-1} \\
\alpha_1 g(\alpha_1)^{-1} & \alpha_2 g(\alpha_2)^{-1} & \cdots & \alpha_n g(\alpha_n)^{-1} \\
\vdots & \vdots & \vdots & \vdots \\
\alpha_1^{t-1} g(\alpha_1)^{-1} & \alpha_2^{t-1} g(\alpha_2)^{-1} & \cdots & \alpha_n^{t-1} g(\alpha_n)^{-1}
\end{bmatrix}_{t \times n}.
\tag{3}
$$

If we consider the elements of $\mathbb{F}_{q^m}$ as vectors of length m over $\mathbb{F}_q$ by vector space isomorphism, we have a parity check matrix H for $\Gamma(L, g)$ over $\mathbb{F}_q$ to be a $mt \times n$ matrix, with at least t linearly independent columns over $\mathbb{F}_q$. Therefore, the Hamming distance of the Goppa code, $d(\Gamma(L, g)) \geq t + 1$. Since at most mt rows are linearly independent, $\text{Rank}(H) \leq mt$ therefore, the dimension of the Goppa code is $k \geq n - mt$.

Definition 2 (Primitive polynomial). *An irreducible polynomial $p(z)$ of degree m over $\mathbb{F}_q$ is called a primitive polynomial if its roots form primitive elements of $\mathbb{F}_{q^m}$.*

Remark 1. The number of irreducible polynomials of degree t with coefficients in $\mathbb{F}_{q^m}$ is approximately $\frac{q^{mt}}{t}$.

2.2 Code-Base Cryptography

We briefly present the McEliece cryptosystem [McE78] and its variant, Niederreiter [Nie86], and the KEM *Classic McEliece* whose implementation on ARM Cortex-M4 is the target of our attack.

McEliece Cryptosystem. The McEliece cryptosystem was introduced by Robert J. McEliece in 1978. The basic idea of this cryptosystem is to use binary Goppa code ($q = 2$) with an efficient decoding algorithm that can correct up to t errors. The public key is a matrix $G = SG'P$ where G' is a generator matrix of the Goppa code, S (resp. P) is a random $k \times k$ non-singular (resp. $n \times n$ permutation) matrix. The code length n, the code dimension k, and the Hamming weight of the error $wt(e) = t$ are public parameters, but the Goppa code $\Gamma(L, g)$, matrices S and P are secrets. The encryption works by computing a code word for the plaintext x using the generator matrix G and by adding an error e. The ciphertext $\tilde{c}$ is therefore computed as $\tilde{c} = xG \oplus e$. The receiver corrects the error by applying the decoding algorithm with G' and recovers x. The security of the system is based on the hardness of decoding a general linear code, a problem known to be $\mathcal{NP}$−complete [BMVT78].

Niederreiter Cryptosystem. This cryptosystem is a dual version of the McEliece cryptosystem. It was published by Harald Niederreiter in 1986. The main difference between the McEliece and the Niederreiter scheme is that the public key in Niederreiter's scheme is a parity check matrix instead of a generator matrix. In the Niederreiter scheme, the ciphertext is a syndrome $\tilde{c} = \boldsymbol{H}\boldsymbol{e}^T$ where the error vector $\boldsymbol{e}$ is the image of the plaintext $\boldsymbol{x}$ by an encoding function ϕ. Therefore, an efficient syndrome decoding algorithm is used for decryption. In what follows, we will focus on the instantiation of Niederreiter using binary Goppa codes as in *Classic McEliece* [Cho+20] (see also [BCS13] and [Cho17] for more details).

Classic McEliece. *Classic McEliece* is a code-based a KEM introduced by Bernstein *et al.* [Ber+17]. It is composed of three algorithms (key generation, encapsulation and decapsulation) described below.

Key Generation. The key pair generation in *Classic McEliece* is described as follows:

1. Construct a parity check matrix $\boldsymbol{H}'$ for a Goppa code $\Gamma(L, g)$;
2. Transform $\boldsymbol{H}'$ into a $mt \times n$ binary matrix $\boldsymbol{H}$ by replacing each $\mathbb{F}_{2^m}$-entry by a m-bit column;
3. Compute the systematic form $[\boldsymbol{I}_{mt}|\boldsymbol{T}]$ of $\boldsymbol{H}$ and return $\{g(x), \alpha_1, \alpha_2, \ldots, \alpha_n\}$ as the secret key and $\boldsymbol{T}$ as the public key.

Encapsulation. The session key K and its encapsulation are generated as follows:

1. Generate a random $\boldsymbol{e} \in \mathbb{F}_2^n$ with $wt(\boldsymbol{e}) = t$;
2. Compute the matrix $\boldsymbol{H} = [\boldsymbol{I}_{mt}|\boldsymbol{T}]$ by appending $\boldsymbol{T}$ to the identity matrix $\boldsymbol{I}_{mt}$ and then a vector $\tilde{c}_0 = \boldsymbol{H}\boldsymbol{e}^T$;
3. Compute $\tilde{c}_1 = \text{H}(2|\boldsymbol{e})$ and generate ciphertext $\tilde{c} = (\tilde{c}_0|\tilde{c}_1)$, H represents the hash function SHAKE256;
4. Compute a 256-bit session key $K = \text{H}(1|\boldsymbol{e}|\tilde{c})$.

Decapsulation. Recovering the session key K' from a ciphertext $\tilde{c}$ can be done as follows:

1. Split $\tilde{c}$ as $(\tilde{c}_0|\tilde{c}_1)$, with $\tilde{c}_0 \in \mathbb{F}_2^{mt}$ and $\tilde{c}_1 \in \mathbb{F}_2^{256}$;
2. Use the underlying decoding algorithm for Niederreiter scheme to recover $\boldsymbol{e}$ such that $wt(\boldsymbol{e}) = t$ and $\tilde{c}_0 = \boldsymbol{H}\boldsymbol{e}^T$;
3. Compute $\tilde{c}_1' = \text{H}(2|\boldsymbol{e})$, and checks if $\tilde{c}_1' = \tilde{c}_1$;
4. Compute the session key $K' = \text{H}(1|\boldsymbol{e}|\tilde{c})$.

If there is no failure at any stage during the decapsulation process and $\tilde{c}_1' = \tilde{c}_1$, then surely the session key K' will be identical to K. In this scenario, the same session key is established. Table 1 shows the parameters of *Classic McEliece* proposed in [Cho+20].

The main component of decapsulation in *Classic McEliece* is inspired by Chou *et al.* [Cho17]. This paper presents a fast constant-time implementation of the "McBits" proposed by Bernstein *et al.* [BCS13]. They use the FFT (Fast Fourier Transform) algorithms for root finding and syndrome computation, the Beneš network algorithm for secret permutation, and bitslicing for low-level operations.

Table 1. Parameter sets: sizes of public keys, secret keys and ciphertexts in bytes

Variant of KEM	m	n	t	Sec. level	Public key	Secret key	Ciphertext
mceliece348864	12	3488	64	1	261120	6492	128
mceliece460896	13	4608	96	3	524160	13608	188
mceliece6688128	13	6688	128	5	1044992	13932	240
mceliece6960119	13	6960	119	5	1047319	13948	226
mceliece8192128	13	8192	128	5	1357824	14120	240

3 Template Attack on *Classic McEliece*

Side-channel attacks are powerful tools for accessing secret information (passwords, secret keys, etc.) and pose a threat to cryptographic algorithm implementations. One of the most powerful techniques for evaluating side-channel information, template attack, was presented by Chari, Rao, and Rohatgi in [CRR02]. The general idea of template attacks is to rely on a multivariate model of side-channel traces to break secure implementations. In this section, we will first give a theoretical overview of template attacks, then we will show the information leakage related to the loading function of the coefficients of the Goppa polynomial during the decryption step of *Classic McEliece* and finally, we will present our template attack principle and results.

3.1 Template Attacks

Multivariate-Gaussian Model. We consider the case where the electronic noise at each point of a power trace follows a normal distribution. This power consumption model does not take into account the correlation between neighboring points. To take into account this correlation between points, it is necessary to model a power trace t_r as a *multivariate normal distribution*. The multivariate normal distribution is a generalization of the normal distribution to higher dimensions. It can be described by a covariance matrix C and a mean vector μ. The Probability Density Function (PDF) of the multivariate normal distribution is given below.

$$PDF(t_r; (\mu, C)) = \frac{1}{\sqrt{(2\pi)^\ell \times \det(C)}} \exp\left(-\frac{1}{2}(t_r - \mu)^T C^{-1}(t_r - \mu)\right) \quad (4)$$

where ℓ is the number of samples in the power trace t_r.

The covariance matrix C essentially characterizes the fluctuations in the power traces such as electronic noise. However, the multivariate normal distribution can also be used to characterize other components of power consumption. One of the problems with using the multivariate normal distribution is the cost of computing the covariance matrix C which grows quadratically with ℓ. Therefore, in practice, only small parts of the power traces are characterized.

General Description. Template attacks exploit that the power consumption also depends on the data that is being processed. In contrast to other types of power analysis attacks like Simple Power Analysis (SPA) [KJJ99] or Differential Power Analysis (DPA) [KJJ99]), template attacks consist of two phases. A *building phase*, in which the characterization of power consumption takes place, and a *matching phase*, in which the characterization is used to determine the secret information.

In template attack, the power traces can be characterized by a multivariate normal distribution, which is fully defined by a mean vector μ and covariance matrix C. This couple (μ, C) is called a *template*. We can characterize the attacked device to determine the templates of some instruction sequences. In the *building phase*, we use another device of the same type as the one being attacked that we can fully control. On this device, we execute these instruction sequences with different data d_i and key k_j to record the resulting power consumption. Then, we aggregate the traces that correspond to a pair of (d_i, k_j), and estimate μ and C. Thus, we obtain a template h for every pair (d_i, k_j).

$$h_{d_i, k_j} = (\mu, C)_{d_i, k_j}.$$

As mentioned above the size of the covariance matrix grows quadratically with the number of points in the trace. The inverse of C, which is needed to compute the PDF, can be numerically problematic for large ℓ as shown by the authors in [EPW10]. We need to find a strategy to determine the points that contain the most information about the characterized instruction. This is called Points of Interest (POI) and we denote the number of POI by N_{POI}. There are several methods to find the POIs, such as the Sum of Differences [RO04] that we will use in this paper, the Sum Of Squared Differences (SOSD) [GLRP06], the Signal to Noise Ratio (SNR) [MOP08], the Principal Component Analysis (PCA) [Arc+06] etc.

Next, we use the characterization and a power trace of the attacked device to determine the key. In this *matching phase*, we evaluate the probability density function of the multivariate normal distribution with (μ, C_{d_i, k_j}) and the power trace of the attacked device. In other words, given a power trace t_r of the attacked device, and a template h_{d_i, k_j}, we compute the PDF:

$$PDF(t_r; (\mu, C_{d_i, k_j})) = \frac{1}{\sqrt{(2\pi)^{N_{POI}} \times \det(C)}} \exp\left(-\frac{1}{2}(t_r - \mu)^T C^{-1}(t_r - \mu)\right).$$

(5)

We do this for every template. As a result, we get the PDFs

$$PDF(t_r; (\mu, C)_{d_1, k_1}), \ldots, PDF(t_r; (\mu, C)_{d_D, k_K}).$$

The probabilities measure how well the templates match a given trace t_r and the highest value indicates the correct template. Since each template is associated with a key, we get an indication of the correct key. If all keys are equiprobable, the decision rule that minimizes the probability of a wrong decision is to decide for h_{d_i, k_j} if

$$PDF(t_r; h_{d_i, k_j}) > PDF(t_r; h_{d_i, k_v}) \forall v \neq j.$$

This is the Maximum Likelihood (ML) decision rule.

Templates with Power Models. In addition to building templates for data and key pairs, there are other strategies. For example, if a device leaks the Hamming weight of the data, then moving the value 1 will result in the same power consumption as moving the value 2. Therefore, the template associated with value 1 will correspond to a trace in which value 1 is moved as well as the template associated with value 2. Thus, it is possible to build templates for values with different Hamming weights. Suppose we want to build templates for the output of a single-byte instruction sequence. We can simply build templates from 0 to 8 per byte. This is the approach we will take to build our templates for a decryption sequence in *Classic McEliece* implementation.

3.2   Measurement Setup and Leakage Analysis

For our experiments, we used *Classic McEliece* variant mceliece8192128 ($m = 13, n = 8192, t = 128$) where the coefficients of the Goppa polynomial are represented on m bits. But for the purpose of the implementation in [CC21], each coefficient will be represented on 2 bytes instead of 1 byte and 5 bits. We attack a software implementation of the decapsulation algorithm (loading function of the coefficients of the Goppa polynomial, irr_load_32x) running on an STM32F415RGT6 microcontroller [CC21]. The microcontroller features a 32-bit ARM Cortex-M4 core with 1 MB Flash memory and 192 kB SRAM.

The traces are acquired using the ChipWhisperer-Pro (CW1200) [OC14] which is an open-source embedded security analysis platform for recording and analyzing power consumption. All traces are acquired at a sample rate 105×10^6 samples per second (105 MS/s). Data acquisition is controlled by scripts running on PC. The ChipWhisperer measures power consumption during loading of the coefficients of the Goppa polynomial $g(x)$ of degree t. Once the acquisition is finished, the PC stores the measured trace on the hard disk. The measurement process is repeated depending on the desired number of traces. In traces, we can distinguish four patterns Fig. 1. These patterns are caused by the bitsliced representation used in the loading function irr_load_32x. Bitslicing is a simulation of hardware implementations in software. It is an implementation trick to speed up software implementations. It was introduced by Biham [Bih97] in 1997 for DES. The basic idea of bitslicing is to represent n-bit data as a bit in n distinct registers. On 32-bit registers, there are 31 unused bits in each register, which can be filled in the same fashion by taking 31 other independent n-bit data and putting each of their n bits in one of the registers. Bitwise operators on 32-bit (e.g. AND, OR, XOR) then act as 32 parallel operators. The bitslicing in this loading function irr_load_32x consists of transposing 32 16-bit coefficients into 16 different 32-bit registers for each round of the main loop. This loading function (Fig. 2) consists of the main loop to load the 128 coefficients in steps of 32 (hence the four patterns in Fig. 1) nested in two consecutive loops. These two loops each load 16 16-bit coefficients. Then, each of these 16 coefficients is transposed into 16 different 32-bit registers. Finally, a kind of assembly operation of

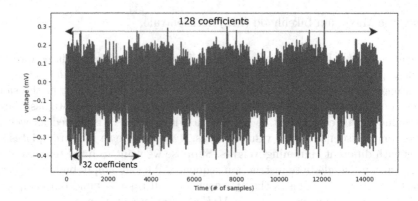

Fig. 1. Power consumption of the loading function of the Goppa polynomial.

these two groups is performed to have the 32 16-bit coefficients in 16 different 32-bit registers. The Fig. 3 shows the power consumption of this implementation strategy.

```
 1  static inline void irr_load_32x(uint32_t out[][GFBITS], const
 2  unsigned char * in, int len )
 3  {
 4    int i, j;
 5    uint32_t mat[16];
 6    uint16_t *mat16 = (uint16_t*)&mat[0];
 7    for(i=0;i<len;i+=32) {
 8        for(j=0;j<16;j++) mat16[j] = load_gf(in + (i+j)*2);
 9        for(j=0;j<16;j++) mat16[16+j] = load_gf(in + (i+j+16)*2);
10        transpose_16x16( mat16 , mat16 );
11        transpose_16x16( (mat16+16), (mat16+16) );
12        bs16_to_bs32( out[i>>5] , mat16 , mat16+16 , GFBITS );
13    }
14  }
```

Fig. 2. Loading function of the coefficients of the Goppa polynomial $g(x)$ in [CC21]

We will now perform a power consumption analysis on the loading function irr_load_32x. The hypothesis is that small variations in power level may be observed in a trace based on the output of this function.

We analyze how the power consumption of the load function depends on the least significant bit (LSB) of 16-bit data with its transpose operation. If the LSB output produced by irr_load_32x is 1 then, in theory, the device under test should consume more power in comparison with a 0 value. If the hypothesis holds, we may exploit this fact to deduce the Hamming weights of the coefficients during

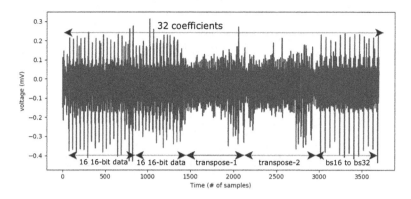

Fig. 3. Zoom on a pattern in power consumption of loading function of the coefficients of $g(x)$.

loading operations. It should be noted that this variation in power consumption is very small. The technique of differential power analysis used to determine the effect of the LSB on power consumption is the Difference Of Means (DOM). We measured the power consumption of the microcontroller when loading 10 000 random coefficients. We obtain 10 000 power traces, then sort them into two subsets (5 000 power traces for LSB = 1 and 5 000 power traces for LSB = 0) and calculate the average of each subset. The DOM between each subset will infer whether the proposed hypothesis is significant. In the case of a significant hypothesis, the DOM between the two subsets will highlight the change in power consumption when LSB of 0 is compared to LSB of 1. The average of each subset is calculated point by point. Thus, the difference of means can then be calculated by simply subtracting the points in the first subset from the points in the second subset. The result of this DOM is shown in Fig. 4.

3.3 Principle and Results

We have two significant peaks easily discernible. These two peaks reveal the moments when the power consumption of the microcontroller depends on the LSB. Thus this loading function `irr_load_32x` leaks information. The transpose function also processes the same data as the loaded data and therefore the bit-sliced representation according to this result also leads to information leakage. We now exploit this property in a power analysis attack to determine the Hamming weights of the Goppa polynomial coefficients $g(x)$. Recall that in *Classic McEliece*, the secret key consists of the Goppa polynomial and the support. Therefore, recovering the secret key corresponds to recovering $g(x)$ and L. It should also be noted that this experiment was done for the other 15 bits of the coefficient and the result is the same.

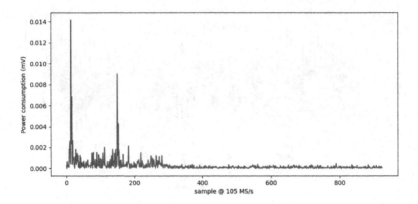

Fig. 4. Difference of means of power traces for LSB = 1 and LSB = 0.

In what follows, we will only use the loading of the first coefficient of $g(x)$ without the transposition for the template attack. In this section, we present the template attack on loading the first 16-bit coefficient of $g(x)$. We describe how to generate the templates from the random coefficient traces. Our template will attempt to recognize the Hamming weight of each coefficient at the output of the loading function `irr_load_32x`. The goal of our attack is to find the Hamming weights of all 128 coefficients of $g(x)$. This information will significantly reduce the complexity of the exhaustive search for the Goppa polynomial on $\mathbb{F}_{2^m}$. For our experiment, we used the same device for *building* and *matching phases*.

As we said at the end of Sect. 3.1, we will build templates in Hamming weights. Since each coefficient of $g(x)$ is represented on 16 bits in [CC21], we will build 17 templates for each coefficient. A key point with template attacks is that they require a large amount of data to make good templates. We recall that each output of this load function is unique, so there is only one output with a Hamming weight of 0 and one with a weight of 16. This means that using random inputs, there is only a $1/(256)^2$ probability of having a trace with a Hamming weight of 0 or 16.

In our experiment, we have efficiently used 350 000 traces which allowed us to have a good distribution to build our templates. We then examine a trace and decide what its Hamming weight is. To set up the templates, we need to sort our template traces into 17 groups. The first group will consist of all traces that have a Hamming weight of 0. The next group has a Hamming weight of 1, etc., and the last group has a Hamming weight of 16. After sorting the traces by their Hamming weights, we look for the "average trace" for each weight. We create an array that contains 17 of these averages. We can always plot these averages to make sure that the average traces are correct. We will now use these average traces to find the POIs using the Sum of Differences method in Fig. 5. This method shows where these average traces have a lot of variances and the POIs are the highest peaks. In our case, we have one POI (sample 13). In the case where we had more peaks in the Sum of Differences, we cannot simply

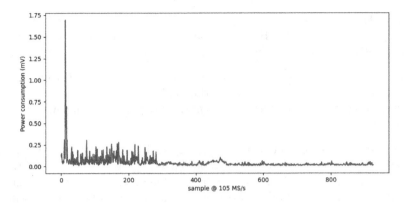

Fig. 5. Sum of Differences for 350 000 traces.

sort an array and choose the highest points. We have to make sure that the points are separated by some space. We can now construct our multivariate normal distribution for each Hamming weight. We need to write the $1 \times N_{POI}$ mean vector μ and the $N_{POI} \times N_{POI}$ covariance matrix C at this POI for each Hamming weight. In our case $N_{POI} = 1$, the mean is a scalar and the covariance matrix is reduced to the variance.

Our templates are ready, so we can use them to perform the *matching phase* now. For a decryption, using a random ciphertext, we recorded 17 power traces on the attacked device during the loading of the first coefficient of $g(x)$. These 17 power traces correspond to the loading of the coefficients with Hamming weights set from 0 to 16. We load our 17 template traces for each coefficient with a fixed Hamming weight and apply the *PDF* for each target trace to check which template fits best. We were able to find the Hamming weight of the first coefficient of the Goppa polynomial on the device attacked during decryption with a success rate of 99.86% after 1000 simulations. This *matching phase* with one target trace takes about 4 s on an 8-core processor running at 3.6 GHz. Thus we manage with our templates to find the Hamming weight of the first coefficient of $g(x)$ when it is loaded from memory. To find the Hamming weights of the remaining $t - 1$ coefficients, it is necessary to construct $t - 1$ groups of $m+1$ templates in Hamming weights. We proceed in the same way as for the first coefficient, except that the position of the POI(s) will change because it depends on the position of the coefficient during loading. The knowledge of the Hamming weights of the coefficients of $g(x)$ allowed us to improve the complexity of the exhaustive search for the Goppa polynomial on $\mathbb{F}_{2^m}$.

4 Complexity of the Goppa Polynomial Search

In this section, we have given the complexity of finding the secret Goppa polynomial in the original McEliece with the knowledge of Hamming weights of its coefficients. Indeed, the key recovery attack against McEliece using irreducible

Goppa code consists of recovering the Goppa polynomial g and the support $L = \{\alpha_1, \alpha_2, ..., \alpha_n\} \in \mathbb{F}_{2^m}^n$. However, the best way to proceed is described as follows [LS01]:

1. *Step 1:* Find an monic irreducible polynomial g of degree t such that the Goppa code $\Gamma(L, g)$ is equivalent to the public code $\mathcal{C}$.
2. *Step 2:* Find the permutation by using the Support Splitting Attack (SSA) algorithm.

The cost of a such enumerative attack is given by $Cost = \lambda n^3 \mathcal{C}_{irr}$ where n is the code length and λ is a small constant depending on the implementation of the attack [LS01]. $\mathcal{C}_{irr}$ is the number of irreducible polynomials over $\mathbb{F}_{2^m}$ i.e. the cardinal of search space. In the case of an extended code of Goppa, the value of $\mathcal{C}_{irr}$ is given by [LS01]

$$\mathcal{C}_{irr} \approx \frac{2^{m(t-3)}}{mt}. \tag{6}$$

With the knowledge of Hamming weights δ_j of the Goppa polynomial coefficients g_j, and by assuming that irreducible monic polynomials over $\mathbb{F}_{2^m}$ have a uniform distribution, the cardinal of the search space is given by

$$\#\text{Search Space} = \frac{\prod\limits_{j=0}^{t-1} \binom{m}{\delta_j}}{t}. \tag{7}$$

In fact, to the best of our knowledge, there is no specific algorithm to construct an irreducible polynomial by knowing the Hamming weights of its coefficients. Therefore finding such polynomials corresponds in practice to search in the set of all monic polynomials with corresponding coefficients Hamming weights set. Note that, in the case that the Goppa polynomial is an irreducible binary polynomial that corresponds to a weak key in [LS01], with the knowledge of the Hamming weight of coefficients, the cardinal of the search space is equal to 1. Indeed, all coefficients with non-zero Hamming weight have their value equal to 1 thus, we can directly reconstruct the Goppa polynomial without searching (Table 2). While it was shown in [LS01] that the computation time to find this irreducible binary polynomial for an instance where $m = 10$, $n = 1024$, and $t = 50$ with their implementation should be 500 years. We can also imagine a scenario in which the user generates non-binary polynomials with fixed weights for all coefficients (to speed up the generation of the public key).

This technique only speeds up the generation of the public key offline but not the decryption process. We call this second case "slightly less weak keys". In the Table 2, we show the expression of the size of search space for two particular cases of "slightly less weak keys". It is sufficient to perform an exhaustive low-complexity search to recover the Goppa polynomial. Thus with the information on the Hamming weights of the coefficients of the Goppa polynomial, we have increased the set of weak keys proposed in [LS01].

For non-binary irreducible polynomials where the extension degree is larger than 8, each finite field element is implemented at least on 2 bytes. Thus, for

Table 2. Size of the search space in the case of Weak keys

key level	#Search Space
Weak keys in [LS01]	$\frac{2^{m(t-3)}}{mt}$
Weak keys with knowledge of coefficients Hamming weight	1
Slightly less weak keys with coefficients Hamming weight equal to 1	$\frac{\binom{m}{1}^t}{t}$
Slightly less weak keys with coefficients Hamming weight equal to 2	$\frac{\binom{m}{2}^t}{t}$

suitable values $0 \leq i_j \leq \delta_j$, one can look for polynomials whose coefficients have Hamming weight i_j on the first byte and $\delta_j - i_j$ on the remaining $m - 8$ bits. With this technique, the cardinality of the search space (7) becomes

$$\#\text{Search Space} = \frac{\prod_{j=0}^{t-1} \binom{8}{i_j}\binom{m-8}{\delta_j - i_j}}{t} \leq \frac{\binom{8}{4}^t \left(\lfloor \frac{m-8}{2} \rfloor\right)^t}{t}. \tag{8}$$

When extended code is implemented in the attack, this number should be divided by $2^m(2^m - 1)m$. Indeed there are $2^m(2^m - 1)m$ polynomial g' such that the extended codes of the Goppa codes $\Gamma(L, g')$ are equivalent to that of $\Gamma(L, g)$. Therefore, we can upper bound the number $\tilde{C}_{irr}$ of irreducible polynomials with the knowledge of the Hamming weights of the polynomial coefficients by

$$\tilde{C}_{irr} \leq \frac{\binom{8}{4}^t \left(\lfloor \frac{m-8}{2} \rfloor\right)^t}{2^m(2^m - 1)mt}. \tag{9}$$

With our template attack on the implementation of *Classic McEliece*, we significantly reduced the cost of the exhaustive search of the Goppa polynomial in $\mathbb{F}_{2^m}$. As shown in Table 3, the knowledge of the Hamming weights of the Goppa polynomial coefficients allowed us for example to divide the size of the search space by 2^{441} for the variant of *Classic McEliece* with $m = 13$, $n = 8192$ and $t = 128$ from 2^{1615} to 2^{1174}. To date, we propose here the best complexity reduction for an exhaustive Goppa polynomial search.

5   Comparison with Other Key Recovery Attacks

We recall that the decryption in *Classic McEliece* is equivalent to the syndrome decoding of Goppa binary codes, including the steps of computing the syndrome polynomial and the error locator polynomial and that of its evaluation at points in $\mathbb{F}_{2^m}$. This polynomial evaluation over $\mathbb{F}_{2^m}$ is realized thanks to the implementation of the additive FFT after having calculated the error locator polynomial with the Berlekamp-Massey (BM) algorithm. Recently, Guo *et al.* [GJJ22] proposed a key-recovery side-channel attack on reference implementations (on FPGA and ARM Cortex-M4) [CC21, WSN18] of *Classic McEliece*. They design an attack algorithm in which they submit special ciphertexts to the decryption

Table 3. Complexity to find Goppa polynomial with the knowledge of the Hamming weights of its coefficients from template attack against parameters of *Classic McEliece* [Cho+20]

m	t	n	$\log_2(\mathcal{C}_{irr})$	$\log_2(\tilde{\mathcal{C}}_{irr})$				$\log_2(\mathcal{C}_{irr}/\tilde{\mathcal{C}}_{irr})$
				$\delta_j = 1$	$\delta_j = 2$	$\delta_j = 3$	$\delta_j = m/2$	
12	64	3488	725	158	274	338	534	191
13	96	4608	1199	251	425	521	871	328
13	128	6688	1615	347	578	706	1174	441
13	119	6960	1498	320	535	654	1089	409
13	128	8192	1615	347	578	706	1174	441

oracle that correspond to single error cases in the plaintexts. They exploited a leak in the additive FFT with a fixed input error before using a machine learning-based classification algorithm to determine the error locator polynomial. They choose a plaintext or error e of Hamming weight equal to 1 before encrypting it. Then, the profiled attack allows them to find the secret polynomial of the error locator among the 2^m possibilities and thus obtain an element of the support L. Finally, they designed new algorithms to recover the Goppa irreducible polynomial and then the full secret key.

Table 4. Profiled side-channel attacks on *Classic McEliece*

Attack	Hamming weight	Target
Guo *et al.* [GJJ22]	1	The FFT additive and BM algorithm
Our attack	no constraints	Loading function of Goppa polynomial coefficients

Countermeasures for the GJJ Attack. The main drawback of the key-recovery side-channel attack on *Classic McEliece* by Guo *et al.* [GJJ22] is the constraint on the Hamming weight of the plaintexts. This attack requires decrypting ciphertexts with Hamming weights of 1 to recover the secret in *Classic McEliece*. However, one can easily notice that with the systematic form of $\boldsymbol{H}$, we can detect the problem of bad ciphertexts with Hamming weights less than or equal to t. This is not the only step where this attack could be compromised. Recall that the error locator polynomial is obtained with the Berlekamp-Massey algorithm. At this point, the error locator polynomial, via its degree, directly reflects any intentional error or misformated chipertext. Indeed, when this polynomial is of degree lower than t the decryption must stop and thus one can avoid the GJJ attack. All of these point out towards the fact that the GJJ attack to find the secret key in *Classic McEliece* is not realistic.

Positive Points in Our Attack. Our template attack to find the Hamming weights of the Goppa polynomial coefficients on *Classic McEliece* is realistic compared to the key-recovery side-channel attack of Guo *et al.* for the variant mceliece8192128 as shown in the Table 4. First, we have no constraints on the Hamming weight of the ciphertext and use fewer traces to recover the Hamming weight of Goppa polynomial coefficients. Secondly, we just follow the steps of the decryption execution in the implementation of *Classic McEliece* and we measure the trace of power consumption corresponding to the loading of the coefficients of the Goppa polynomial. Finally, our method has the particularity to be extended on other steps of decryption in *Classic McEliece* or other cryptosystems. Indeed, the loading of a vector of evaluation points is also performed just before the additive FFT for the evaluation of the error locator polynomial. If the setup is such that our attack can be reproduced we could gain the same information (Hamming weight) about the evaluation points. Also, notice that any decoding algorithm for binary Goppa codes has to use this/similar function for loading the Goppa polynomial and the points of evaluation. This information on the Hamming weights of the evaluation points, combined with our current results on the coefficients of the Goppa polynomial, will greatly improve our knowledge of the secret in *Classic McEliece*. We can also use this information on the evaluation points to apply the decoding method with a hint from [KM22] to directly recover the Goppa polynomial.

Common Countermeasure Fail Against Our Attack. We recall that our attack on the loading function of the Goppa polynomial coefficients is performed on the optimized reference implementation of *Classic McEliece* on ARM-Cortex M4 [CC21]. This reference implementation represents the side-channel attack target of several recent papers [Cay+21, Col+22b, GJJ22]. Shuffling is nowadays one of the most common and effective countermeasure techniques against most side-channel attacks [CMJ22]. However, in our attack, shuffling does not work because loading the coefficients in a random order will not affect their Hamming weights. In general, we have shown in this work that this loading function is not appropriate for secret variables in *Classic McEliece*. Moreover, our proposal is a first step towards much more powerful and potentially generic possible attacks. Indeed, the loading of a list of secret coefficients is performed at several places in the decryption of a code-based cryptographic scheme, and if we can isolate the exact moment when such functions are loaded then we could imagine applying our attack.

6   Conclusion

In this paper, we have presented a side-channel attack against the reference implementation of *Classic McEliece* on ARM Cortex-M4. The side channel here corresponds to loading the coefficients of the Goppa polynomial from memory during decryption. The *phase of matching* of our profiled attack is very fast (about 4 s) and allows us to find the Hamming weights of the coefficients of the

Goppa polynomial that is an important part of the secret key of *Classic McEliece*. First, this result allowed us to directly find the Goppa polynomial in the case of weak keys with the method of Loidreau and Sendrier. In the case of "slightly less weak keys", we manage to find this polynomial with a low-complexity exhaustive search. Thus, we increase the set of weak keys compared to the method of Loiderau and Sendrier. Then, this information about the Hamming weights of the coefficients also allowed us to give the best complexity reduction for Goppa polynomial search on $\mathbb{F}_{2^m}$. Finally, we have shown that our attack is realistic (we only need a decryption of a random ciphertext) compared to other side-channel attacks on *Classic McEliece*. We also hope to apply it during in-memory loading of evaluation points to improve recent side-channel attack results on post-quantum cryptosystem implementations.

Acknowledgments. The author Jean Belo Klamti was supported by a grant of the Ripple Impact Fund/Silicon Valley Community Foundation (Grant 2018-188473).

References

[Arc+06] Archambeau, C., Peeters, E., Standaert, F.-X., Quisquater, J.-J.: Template attacks in principal subspaces. In: Goubin, L., Matsui, M. (eds.) CHES 2006. LNCS, vol. 4249, pp. 1–14. Springer, Heidelberg (2006). https://doi.org/10.1007/11894063_1

[Ava+11] Avanzi, R., Hoerder, S., Page, D., Tunstall, M.: Side-channel attacks on the McEliece and Niederreiter public-key cryptosystems. J. Cryptograh. Eng. **1**(4), 271–281 (2011)

[Bar+16] Bardet, M., Chaulet, J., Dragoi, V., Otmani, A., Tillich, J.-P.: Cryptanalysis of the McEliece public key cryptosystem based on polar codes. In: Takagi, T. (ed.) PQCrypto 2016. LNCS, vol. 9606, pp. 118–143. Springer, Cham (2016). https://doi.org/10.1007/978-3-319-29360-8_9

[BCS13] Bernstein, D.J., Chou, T., Schwabe, P.: McBits: fast constant-time code-based cryptography. In: Bertoni, G., Coron, J.-S. (eds.) CHES 2013. LNCS, vol. 8086, pp. 250–272. Springer, Heidelberg (2013). https://doi.org/10.1007/978-3-642-40349-1_15

[Ber+17] Bernstein, D.J., et al.: Classic McEliece: conservative code-based cryptography. In: NIST submissions (2017)

[Bih97] Biham, E.: A fast new DES implementation in software. In: Biham, E. (ed.) FSE 1997. LNCS, vol. 1267, pp. 260–272. Springer, Heidelberg (1997). https://doi.org/10.1007/BFb0052352

[BMVT78] Berlekamp, E., McEliece, R., Van Tilborg, H.: On the inherent intractability of certain coding problems (corresp.). IEEE Trans. Inf. Theory **24**(3), 384–386 (1978)

[Cay+21] Cayrel, P.-L., Colombier, B., Drăgoi, V.-F., Menu, A., Bossuet, L.: Message-recovery laser fault injection attack on the *Classic McEliece* cryptosystem. In: Canteaut, A., Standaert, F.-X. (eds.) EUROCRYPT 2021. LNCS, vol. 12697, pp. 438–467. Springer, Cham (2021). https://doi.org/10.1007/978-3-030-77886-6_15

[CB14] Chizhov, I.V., Borodin, M.A.: Effective attack on the McEliece cryptosystem based on Reed-Muller codes. Discrete Appl. Math. **24**(5), 273–280 (2014)

[CC21]   Chen, M.-S., Chou, T.: Classic McEliece on the ARM cortex-M4. IACR Trans. Crypt. Hardware Embed. Syst., 125–148 (2021)

[CD10]   Cayrel, P.-L., Dusart, P.: McEliece/Niederreiter PKC: sensitivity to fault injection. In: International Conference on Future Information Technology, Busan, South Korea (2010)

[Che+16] Chen, C., Eisenbarth, T., von Maurich, I., Steinwandt, R.: Horizontal and vertical side channel analysis of a McEliece cryptosystem. IEEE Trans. Inf. Forensics Secur. **11**(6), 1093–1105 (2016)

[Cho17]   Chou, T.: McBits revisited. In: Fischer, W., Homma, N. (eds.) CHES 2017. LNCS, vol. 10529, pp. 213–231. Springer, Cham (2017). https://doi.org/10.1007/978-3-319-66787-4_11

[Cho+20] Chou, T., et al.: Classic McEliece: conservative code-based cryptography 10 October 2020 (2020)

[CMJ22]   Chen, Z., Ma, Y., Jing, J.: Low-cost shuffling countermeasures against side-channel attacks for NTT-based post-quantum cryptography. IEEE Trans. Comput.-Aided Design Integr. Circ. Syst. **42**(1), 322–326 (2022)

[CML17]   Chen, L., Moody, D., Liu, Y.: NIST post-quantum cryptography standardization (2017)

[Col+22a] Colombier, B., Dragoi, V.-F., Cayrel, P.-L., Grosso, V.: Physical security of code-based cryptosystems based on the syndrome decoding problem. In: Cryptarchi Workshop, Porquerolles, France (2022)

[Col+22b] Colombier, B., Drăgoi, V.-F., Cayrel, P.-L., Grosso, V.: Profiled side-channel attack on cryptosystems based on the binary syndrome decoding problem. IEEE Trans. Inf. Forensics Secur. (2022)

[Col+23] Colombier, B., Grosso, V., Cayrel, P.-L., Drăgoi, V.-F.: Horizontal correlation attack on classic McEliece. Cryptology ePrint Archive, Paper 2023/546 (2023)

[Cou+14] Couvreur, A., Gaborit, P., Gauthier-Umaña, V., Otmani, A., Tillich, J.-P.: Distinguisher-based attacks on public-key cryptosystems using Reed-Solomon codes. Designs Codes Cryptogr. **73**(2), 641–666 (2014)

[CRR02]   Chari, S., Rao, J.R., Rohatgi, P.: Template attacks. In: Kaliski, B.S., Koç, K., Paar, C. (eds.) CHES 2002. LNCS, vol. 2523, pp. 13–28. Springer, Heidelberg (2003). https://doi.org/10.1007/3-540-36400-5_3

[DJ92]   Deutsch, D., Jozsa, R.: Rapid solution of problems by quantum computation. Proc. R. Soc. London Ser. A: Math. Phys. Sci. **439**(1907), 553–558 (1992)

[EPW10]   Eisenbarth, T., Paar, C., Weghenkel, B.: Building a side channel based disassembler. In: Gavrilova, M.L., Tan, C.J.K., Moreno, E.D. (eds.) Transactions on Computational Science X. LNCS, vol. 6340, pp. 78–99. Springer, Heidelberg (2010). https://doi.org/10.1007/978-3-642-17499-5_4

[Fey18]   Feynman, R.P.: Simulating physics with computers. In: Feynman and Computation, pp. 133–153. CRC Press (2018)

[GI19]   Gyongyosi, L., Imre, S.: A survey on quantum computing technology. Comput. Sci. Rev. **31**, 51–71 (2019)

[GJJ22]   Guo, Q., Johansson, A., Johansson, T.: A key-recovery side-channel attack on classic McEliece implementations. IACR Trans. Cryptogr. Hardw. Embed. Syst. 800–827 (2022)

[GLRP06] Gierlichs, B., Lemke-Rust, K., Paar, C.: Templates vs. stochastic methods. In: Goubin, L., Matsui, M. (eds.) CHES 2006. LNCS, vol. 4249, pp. 15–29. Springer, Heidelberg (2006). https://doi.org/10.1007/11894063_2

[Gro+23] Grosso, V., Cayrel, P., Colombier, B., Dragoi, V.: Punctured syndrome decoding problem - efficient side-channel attacks against classic McEliece. In: Kavun, E.B., Pehl, M. (eds.) COSADE 2023. LNCS, vol. 13979, pp. 170–192. Springer, Cham (2023). https://doi.org/10.1007/978-3-031-29497-6_9

[Gro96] Grover, L.K.: A fast quantum mechanical algorithm for database search. In: Proceedings of the Twenty-Eighth Annual ACM Symposium on Theory of Computing, pp. 212–219 (1996)

[HMP10] Heyse, S., Moradi, A., Paar, C.: Practical power analysis attacks on software implementations of McEliece. In: Sendrier, N. (ed.) PQCrypto 2010. LNCS, vol. 6061, pp. 108–125. Springer, Heidelberg (2010). https://doi.org/10.1007/978-3-642-12929-2_9

[KJJ99] Kocher, P., Jaffe, J., Jun, B.: Differential power analysis. In: Wiener, M. (ed.) CRYPTO 1999. LNCS, vol. 1666, pp. 388–397. Springer, Heidelberg (1999). https://doi.org/10.1007/3-540-48405-1_25

[KM22] Kirshanova, E., May, A.: Decoding McEliece with a hint - secret Goppa key parts reveal everything. In: Galdi, C., Jarecki, S. (eds.) SCN 2022. LNCS, vol. 13409, pp. 3–20. Springer International Publishing, Cham (2022). https://doi.org/10.1007/978-3-031-14791-3_1

[Lah+20] Lahr, N., Niederhagen, R., Petri, R., Samardjiska, S.: Side channel information set decoding using iterative chunking. In: Moriai, S., Wang, H. (eds.) ASIACRYPT 2020. LNCS, vol. 12491, pp. 881–910. Springer, Cham (2020). https://doi.org/10.1007/978-3-030-64837-4_29

[Lar+21] Larsen, M.V., Guo, X., Breum, C.R., Neergaard-Nielsen, J.S., Andersen, U.L.: Deterministic multi-mode gates on a scalable photonic quantum computing platform. Nat. Phys. 17(9), 1018–1023 (2021)

[LS01] Loidreau, P., Sendrier, N.: Weak keys in the McEliece publickey cryptosystem. IEEE Trans. Inf. Theory 47(3), 1207–1211 (2001)

[McE78] McEliece, R.J.: A public-key cryptosystem based on algebraic. Coding Thv 4244, 114–116 (1978)

[Mis+13] Misoczki, R., Tillich, J.-P., Sendrier, N., Barreto, P.S.L.M.: MDPC-McEliece: new McEliece variants from Moderate Density Parity-Check codes. In: Proceedings of the IEEE International Symposium Information Theory - ISIT, pp. 2069–2073 (2013)

[Mol+11] Molter, H.G., Stöttinger, M., Shoufan, A., Strenzke, F.: A simple power analysis attack on a McEliece cryptoprocessor. J. Cryptogr. Eng. 1(1), 29–36 (2011)

[MOP08] Mangard, S., Oswald, E., Popp, T.: Power Analysis Attacks: Revealing the Secrets of Smart Cards, vol. 31. Springer, Cham (2008). https://doi.org/10.1007/978-0-387-38162-6

[MS77] MacWilliams, F.J., Sloane, N.J.A.: The theory of error correcting codes, vol. 16. Elsevier, Amsterdam (1977)

[Nie86] Niederreiter, H.: Knapsack-type cryptosystems and algebraic coding theory. Prob. Contr. Inform. Theory 15(2), 157–166 (1986)

[OC14] O'Flynn, C., Chen, Z.D.: ChipWhisperer: an open-source platform for hardware embedded security research. In: Prouff, E. (ed.) COSADE 2014. LNCS, vol. 8622, pp. 243–260. Springer, Cham (2014). https://doi.org/10.1007/978-3-319-10175-0_17

[OK15] Otmani, A., Kalachi, H.T.: Square code attack on a modified Sidelnikov cryptosystem. In: El Hajji, S., Nitaj, A., Carlet, C., Souidi, E.M. (eds.)

C2SI 2015. LNCS, vol. 9084, pp. 173–183. Springer, Cham (2015). https://doi.org/10.1007/978-3-319-18681-8_14

[Rav+22] Ravi, P., Chattopadhyay, A., D'Anvers, J.P., Baksi, A.: Side-channel and Fault-injection attacks over lattice-based postquantum schemes (Kyber, Dilithium): survey and new results. Cryptology ePrint Archive, Paper 2022/737. 2022

[RO04] Rechberger, C., Oswald, E.: Practical template attacks. In: Lim, C.H., Yung, M. (eds.) WISA 2004. LNCS, vol. 3325, pp. 440–456. Springer, Heidelberg (2005). https://doi.org/10.1007/978-3-540-31815-6_35

[Saa22] Saarinen, M.-J.O.: WiP: applicability of ISO standard side-channel leakage tests to NIST post-quantum cryptography. In: 2022 IEEE International Symposium on Hardware Oriented Security and Trust (HOST), pp. 69–72 (2022)

[Sec+22] Seck, B., et al.: Key-recovery by side-channel information on the matrix-vector product in code-based cryptosystems. In: International Conference on Information Security and Cryptology, Seoul, South Korea (2022)

[Sho94] Shor, P.W.: Algorithms for quantum computation: discrete logarithms and factoring. In: Proceedings 35th Annual Symposium on Foundations of Computer Science, pp. 124–134. IEEE (1994)

[Sid94] Sidelnikov, V.M.: A public-key cryptosytem based on Reed-Muller codes. Discrete Appl. Math. **4**(3), 191–207 (1994)

[SK14] Shrestha, S.R., Kim, Y.-S.: New McEliece cryptosystem based on polar codes as a candidate for post-quantum cryptography. In: 2014 14th International Symposium on Communications and Information Technologies (ISCIT), pp. 368–372. IEEE (2014)

[TF19] Takeda, S., Furusawa, A.: Toward large-scale fault-tolerant universal photonic quantum computing. APL Photon. **4**(6), 060902 (2019)

[WSN18] Wang, W., Szefer, J., Niederhagen, R.: FPGA-based Niederreiter cryptosystem using binary Goppa codes. In: Lange, T., Steinwandt, R. (eds.) PQCrypto 2018. LNCS, vol. 10786, pp. 77–98. Springer, Cham (2018). https://doi.org/10.1007/978-3-319-79063-3_4

Symmetric Cryptography

Universal Hashing Based on Field Multiplication and (Near-)MDS Matrices

Koustabh Ghosh[(✉)] [iD], Jonathan Fuchs[iD], Parisa Amiri Eliasi[iD], and Joan Daemen[iD]

Digital Security Group, Radboud University, Nijmegen, The Netherlands
{koustabh.ghosh,jonathan.fuchs,parisa.amirieliasi,joan.daemen}@ru.nl

Abstract. In this paper we propose a new construction for building universal hash functions, a specific instance called *multi-265*, and provide proofs for their universality. Our construction follows the key-then-hash parallel paradigm. In a first step it adds a variable length input message to a secret key and splits the result in blocks. Then it applies a fixed-length public function to each block and adds their results to form the output. The innovation presented in this work lies in the public function: we introduce the *multiply-transform-multiply*-construction that makes use of field multiplication and linear transformations. We prove upper bounds for the universality of key-then-hash parallel hash functions making use of a public function with our construction provided the linear transformation are maximum-distance-separable (MDS). We additionally propose a concrete instantiation of our construction multi-265, where the underlying public function uses a near-MDS linear transformation and prove it to be 2^{-154}-universal. We also make the reference code for multi-265 available.

Keywords: Primitive · Keyed hashing · Parallel · Forgery · Multi-265

1 Introduction

Message authentication code (MAC) functions strive to provide protection against forgery where forgery is defined according to the following scenario. An adversary gains access to a generation oracle and a verification oracle, where the generation oracle returns a tag given an input of a message (and nonce) and the verification oracle for a given tag, message (and nonce) returns whether the tag is valid or not. Forgery consists of a successfull verification query where the message (and nonce) was not used in any generation query.

There are two mainstream approaches to build MAC functions: the nonce based Wegman-Carter-Shoup (WCS) construction [18, 20] or hash-then-encrypt construction [11]. In both approaches MAC functions consist of two phases: a compression phase that converts a variable-length input into a fixed-size state under a secret key and a scrambling phase that takes this state and turns it into an output by the use of a pseudorandom function (PRF) or permutation (PRP).

© The Author(s), under exclusive license to Springer Nature Switzerland AG 2023
N. El Mrabet et al. (Eds.): AFRICACRYPT 2023, LNCS 14064, pp. 129–150, 2023.
https://doi.org/10.1007/978-3-031-37679-5_6

In this paper we consider only the compression phase and will refer to it as a *keyed hash function.*

The security of the compression phase of a hash-then-encrypt MAC function $F_\mathbf{K}$ depends on the success probability, taken over the key space of an optimal attacker, to generate collisions at the output of F_K: Finding $\mathbf{M}$ and $\mathbf{M}^*$ such $F_K(\mathbf{M}) = F_K(\mathbf{M}^*)$. The ε-universality [19] of $F_\mathbf{K}$ upper bounds the probability of obtaining such a collision. This can further be generalised to ε-Δuniversality [19], which is an upper bound for the success probability, taken over the key space of an optimal attacker, to find a particular output difference at the output of $F_\mathbf{K}$: Finding $\mathbf{M}$ and $\mathbf{M}^*$ such $F_K(\mathbf{M}) - F_K(\mathbf{M}^*) = \Delta$. The latter is relevant for the security of WC(S) MAC functions.

In the literature we see three main categories of keyed hash function constructions. The first category builds them as modes of strong cryptographic primitive, like constructions based on cryptographic hash functions such as HMAC [2] and NMAC [2], or block ciphers such as CBC-MAC [3], CMAC [6] and PMAC [7]. The second category builds more efficient functions by applying simple algebraic constructions using multiplication and addition in a finite field such as GHASH [16] and Poly1305 [4]. The third category does the same but in a different way: by using public permutations with a relatively small number of rounds.

In keyed hash functions of this third category, a message of variable length is parsed into blocks of a fixed size and added block-by-block to a long key. The latter is typically generated from a short key by means of a stream cipher or a key-schedule like computation. The resulting string can be processed in essentially two ways: parallel or serial. The parallel construction applies the public permutation to the blocks in parallel and adds the corresponding results to form the output. We see this construction in the compression phases of Kravatte [5] and Xoofff [8]. The serial construction applies the permutation serially to each block with the permutation result of the previous block added to it, much like CBC-MAC. This construction is an idealized version of the compression phase of Pelican-MAC [9], in the sense that in Pelican-MAC there is no key added to the message prior to compression, but rather it starts from a secret IV.

Fuchs et al. investigated the security of both constructions in [11]. They show that the universality of the parallel construction is at least as good as that of the serial construction, and can be much better. Moreover, both constructions have the same workload per block but the serial construction cannot be parallelized and therefore the parallel construction is superior.

In this paper we study a variant of the permutation-based parallel keyed hashing: instead of a public permutation we make use of a public function that is not invertible.

1.1 Our Contribution

In this paper we first generalize the results of [11] to the parallelization of a public function. The main innovation in this work lies in the public function: we introduce the *multiply-transform-multiply*-construction that makes use of field multiplication and linear transformations. We prove upper bounds for the universality of key-then-hash parallel hash functions making use of a public function with our construction provided the linear transformations are maximum-distance-separable (MDS) [10]. We prove that they are $2/p^n$-Δuniversal with the multiplication taking place in the field with p elements, where p is a prime, provided that the linear transformations employed are $n \times n$ MDS matrices.

In secure multi-party computation (MPC), fully homomorphic encryption (FHE), zero-knowledge (ZK) schemes, data is typically encoded in large prime fields. In various application, part of such a function or circuit call on symmetric cryptographic primitives such as a PRF, a symmetric encryption scheme, or a collision resistant keyed hash function. In such applications, the main bottleneck comes from the number of field applications in the underlying primitive [1,12]. The computational cost of our construction per input word, where word is an element of the chosen prime field, is only one field multiplication and a small number of field additions depending on the chosen linear transformation. Therefore, our construction, with a very low multiplicative cost, is especially suitable for use as a collision-resistant keyed hash function in such applications.

Furthermore this low multiplicative cost is also beneficial when masking is applied as protection against differential power analysis (DPA) [15]. In masking, each variable x is encoded in a number of shares $x_0, x_1, \ldots, x_{d-1}$, such that $x = x_0 + x_1 + \ldots + x_{d-1}$, where any subset of $d-1$ shares have a random distribution with the addition taking place in the underlying field. The linear parts of the algorithm, such as the MDS matrix and the key additions, can be performed on the shares separately. There are two main approaches for computing multiplications: the Ishai-Sahai-Wagner (ISW) approach [14] and threshold implementations [17]. In both techniques, the total computational cost increases quadratically with the number of shares d and linearly with the number of multiplications. Furthermore, ISW requires randomness, which also increases quadratically with the number of shares and linearly with the number of multiplications.

The additive cost of our construction can be further optimized by using specific types of near-MDS matrices, instead of MDS matrices. To that end we additionally propose a concrete instantiation of our construction called *multi-265*. Its public function makes use of the prime field with p elements, where $p = 2^{26} - 5$ and a 6×6 lightweight circulant near-MDS matrix with branch number 6. We prove it gives rise to a keyed hash function that is 2^{-154}-Δuniversal. Despite the fact that its matrix is not MDS, it is still $2/p^6$-Δuniversal.

1.2   Outline of the Paper

This paper is organised as follows. In Sect. 2, we remind the readers of key-then-hash functions and their universalities [11]. In Sect. 3, we generalize the parallel construction of a public permutation [11] to a public function. In Sect. 4, we introduce the notations that will be used throughout this paper. In Sect. 5 we describe the propagation properties of field multiplication. In Sect. 6 we look at a simple construction for the public function that we call the duplicated field multiplication. In Sect. 7 we introduce the multiply-transform-multiply and prove bounds on its universality if the underlying linear transformation is MDS. In Sect. 8 we introduce our proposed keyed hash function multi-265, study its security and report on the implementation aspects.

2   Preliminaries

Security analysis in this work builds upon the results of [11] and to that end we adopt a terminology similar to that paper. We denote a public function as $f: G \rightarrow G'$ where G and G' are abelian groups $\langle G, + \rangle$ and $\langle G', + \rangle$.

The elements of G are called *blocks*. The set containing ℓ-block string is denoted as G^{ℓ}, i.e., $G^{\ell} = \{(x_0, x_1, \ldots, x_{\ell-1}) \mid x_i \in G \text{ for each } i = 0, 1, \ldots, \ell-1\}$. The set of strings of length 1 upto κ is denoted as $BS(G, \kappa) = \cup_{\ell=1}^{\kappa} G^{\ell}$. We denote strings in bold uppercase letters, like $\mathbf{M}$, its blocks by M_i, where indexing starts from 0 and the length of that string by $|\mathbf{M}|$.

Let $X \in G$ be a discrete random variable that has a value that depends on the key K. We denote the probability that a variable X has value x by $\Pr(X = x)$. In words, $\Pr(X = x)$ is the fraction of the keyspace for which variable X has value x. We call two variables independent if $\Pr(X = x, X' = x') = \Pr(X = x)\Pr(X' = x')$ for all $x, x' \in G$.

The probability mass function (PMF) of a variable X, denoted as g_X, is the array of values $\Pr(X = x)$ over all values x. We have $g_X(x) = \Pr(X = x)$. Clearly, $\forall x : 0 \leq g_X(x) \leq 1$ and $\sum_x g_X(x) = 1$. As such, a PMF can be seen as a mapping $g: G \rightarrow [0, 1]$.

For two independent random variables X and Y, let $Z = X + Y$. The PMF g_Z is given by the convolution of two PMFs g_X, g_Y and is denoted as $g_X * g_Y$.

$$g_Z = g_X * g_Y \iff \forall z : g_Z(z) = \sum_x g_X(x) g_Y(x - z),$$

with $-$ is determined by the group operation of G and the summation done over $\mathbb{R}$. We further let g_X^{*n} with $n \in \mathbb{N}$ denote the convolution of g_X n-times.

2.1 ε and ε-Δuniversality

Let $F_{\mathbf{K}}$ denote a keyed hash function where the key $\mathbf{K}$ is sampled uniformly at random from the key space. The security of a keyed hash function is measured by the probability of generating a collision at the output of $F_{\mathbf{K}}$: distinct $\mathbf{M}, \mathbf{M}^*$ such that $F_{\mathbf{K}}(\mathbf{M}) = F_{\mathbf{K}}(\mathbf{M}^*)$. This probability is upper-bounded by the so called ε-universality. We further look at an even stronger notion of universality: ε-Δuniversality, which gives an upper-bound on the probability taken over all keys of two distinct inputs strings exhibiting a specific output difference.

Definition 1 (ε-universality[19]). == *A keyed hash function* F *is said to be* ε-universal *if for any distinct strings* $\mathbf{M}, \mathbf{M}^*$

$$\Pr[F_{\mathbf{K}}(\mathbf{M}) = F_{\mathbf{K}}(\mathbf{M}^*)] \leq \varepsilon.$$

Definition 2 (ε-Δuniversality[19]). *A keyed hash function* F *is said to be* ε-Δ*universal if for any distinct strings* $\mathbf{M}, \mathbf{M}^*$ *and for all* $\Delta \in G$

$$\Pr[F_{\mathbf{K}}(\mathbf{M}) - F_{\mathbf{K}}(\mathbf{M}^*) = \Delta] \leq \varepsilon.$$

2.2 Key-then-Hash Functions

We study keyed hash functions that take as input elements of $BS(G, \kappa)$ and return an element of G'. The keys are elements of G^κ. When processing an input, the key is first added to the input and then an unkeyed function is applied to the result. This is a special case of keyed hash functions and such functions are called key-then-hash functions. A key-then-hash function is defined as: $F \colon BS(G, \kappa) \to G'$ with $F_{\mathbf{K}}(\mathbf{M}) := F(\mathbf{K} + \mathbf{M})$. The addition of two strings $\mathbf{M} = (M_0, M_1, \ldots, M_{|\mathbf{M}|-1})$ and $\mathbf{M}^* = (M_0^*, M_1^*, \ldots, M_{|\mathbf{M}^*|-1}^*)$ with $|\mathbf{M}| \leq |\mathbf{M}^*|$ is defined as $\mathbf{M}' := \mathbf{M} + \mathbf{M}^* = (M_0 + M_0^*, M_1 + M_1^*, \ldots, M_{|\mathbf{M}|-1} + M_{|\mathbf{M}|-1}^*)$ with $|\mathbf{M}'| = |\mathbf{M}|$. In Sect. 3 we demonstrate how to build such functions using a public function as the underlying primitive.

3 Parallel Universal Hashing

We first note that ε-universality of a key-then-hash function is upper bounded by the ε-Δuniversality of that function. To that end we now see how a public function can be parallelized to form a key-then-hash function and further prove upper bound on the ε-Δuniversality of such construction.

The analysis of a parallel universal hash construction using public permutations has been presented by Fuchs et al. in [11]. Using a similar approach, we generalize their results to a parallel universal hash construction built on a public function as its underlying primitive.

3.1 Construction

We adapt the parallelization of a public permutation to public functions in Algorithm 1 and depict it in Fig. 1. The construction takes as parameters a public function $f \colon G \to G'$ and a maximum string length κ. The inputs to the construction are a key $\mathbf{K} \in G^\kappa$ and a string $\mathbf{M} \in BS(G, \kappa)$. The construction returns a digest $h \in G'$.

Given any public function f, its parallelization is the key-then-hash function denoted as Parallel [f]. Since these are the key-then-hash functions we study, for the rest of the paper F and Parallel [f] will be used interchangeably to denote parallelized public functions. The key space of Parallel [f] is G^κ and as such we assume the existence of long keys with independent key blocks.

Algorithm 1: The parallelization Parallel[f]
___
Parameters: A public function f: G → G′ and a maximum string length κ
Inputs   : A key **K** ∈ G^κ and a message **M** ∈ BS(G, κ)
Output   : A digest h ∈ G′

x ← **M** + **K**
h ← 0
for i ← 0 **to** |**M**| − 1 **do**
  | h ← h + f(x_i)
end
return h
___

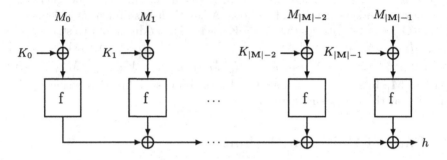

Fig. 1. The parallelization Parallel[f] adapted from [11].

3.2 Propagation Probabilities of Fixed-Length Functions

Before we can investigate the universality of Parallel[f], we first look at the differential properties of the underlying fixed length function f.

Classically, a differential defined over the fixed input-length public function f: G → G′ is the tuple (A, Δ), where $A \in G/\{0\}$ is called the input difference and $\Delta \in G′$ is called the output difference. We now remind the reader of differential probability of a differential over fixed-length public functions.

Definition 3 (Differential probability). *Let* f: G → G′ *be a public function. The differential probability of a differential* (A, Δ) *of* f, *denoted as* $\mathsf{DP}_f(A, \Delta)$, *is:*

$$\mathsf{DP}_f(A, \Delta) = \frac{\#\{X \in G \mid f(X + A) - f(X) = \Delta\}}{\#G}.$$

We say that input difference A propagates to output difference Δ *with probability* $\mathsf{DP}_f(A, \Delta)$.

The universality of a parallelized public permutation depends on the uniformity of the public permutation by Lemma 3 [11]. Unlike a public permutation, the relative frequency of outputs of a non-bijective public function f is not constant. Thus in order to generalize the universality of parallelized public permutation to public function, we introduce the definition of *image probability* of f.

Definition 4 (Image probability). *Let* $f: G \to G'$ *be a public function. The image probability of an output* $Z \in G'$ *of* f*, denoted as* $\mathsf{IP}_f(Z)$*, is the number of inputs that* f *maps to* Z *divided by the total number of possible inputs, namely,*

$$\mathsf{IP}_f(Z) = \frac{\#\{X \in G \mid f(X) = Z\}}{\#G}.$$

To obtain the ε-Δuniversality of $F = \text{Parallel}[f]$, we need to obtain an upper bound of the maximum possible value of DP_f and IP_f over all differentials and outputs of the underlying fixed length public function f respectively. As such we denote them as:

$$\text{MDP}_f = \max_{(A,\Delta)} \mathsf{DP}_f(A, \Delta) \quad \text{and} \quad \text{MIP}_f = \max_{Z} \mathsf{IP}_f(Z).$$

Furthermore we denote by DP_A and IP the probability mass functions $\mathsf{DP}_f(A, Z)$ with $A \in G$ fixed and $\mathsf{IP}_f(Z)$ respectively.

3.3   Differentials over Parallel[f] and Their Differential Probability

The inputs to $F = \text{Parallel}[f]$ are of variable lengths and as such the classical definition of differentials no longer work since two distinct strings may now differ in both value and length. With this distinction in mind, a difference between two strings is defined in [11] that is relevant to our approach.

Definition 5 (Difference between two strings [11]). *The difference between two strings* $\mathbf{M}$*,* $\mathbf{M}^*$ *with* $|\mathbf{M}| \le |\mathbf{M}^*|$ *is defined as the pair* $(\mathbf{A}, \lambda) \in G^{|\mathbf{M}|} \times \mathbb{Z}_{\ge 0}$*, where* $\mathbf{A} = \mathbf{M} - \mathbf{M}^* = (M_0 - M_0^*, M_1 - M_1^*, \dots, M_{|\mathbf{M}|-1} - M_{|\mathbf{M}|-1}^*)$ *and* $\lambda = |\mathbf{M}^*| - |\mathbf{M}|$.

Now, given two strings $\mathbf{M}$ and $\mathbf{M}^*$, the probability that the strings result in an output difference Δ through F is determined by the difference between the strings.

Proposition 1 (Proposition 1 [11]). *Given two strings* $\mathbf{M}, \mathbf{M}^*$ *with* $|\mathbf{M}| \le |\mathbf{M}^*|$*, the probability that the strings result in an output difference* Δ *through* $F_{\mathbf{K}}$ *is given by:*

$$\Pr[F_{\mathbf{K}}(\mathbf{M}) - F_{\mathbf{K}}(\mathbf{M}^*) = \Delta] = \frac{\#\{\mathbf{K} \in G^{\kappa} \mid F(\mathbf{A} + \mathbf{K}) - F(0^{|\mathbf{A}|+\lambda} + \mathbf{K}) = \Delta\}}{\#G^{\kappa}},$$

where $(\mathbf{A}, \lambda)$ *is the difference between the strings* $\mathbf{M}$ *and* $\mathbf{M}^*$.

This naturally leads to the following definitions of generalised differentials and their DP.

Definition 6 (Generalized differentials and their DP [11]). *Given an input difference* $(\mathbf{A}, \lambda)$ *and output difference* Δ*, the differential probability of the differential* $(\mathbf{A}, \lambda, \Delta)$ *over* F*, denoted as* $\mathsf{DP}_F(\mathbf{A}, \lambda, \Delta)$ *is given by*

$$\mathsf{DP}_F(\mathbf{A}, \lambda, \Delta) = \frac{\#\{\mathbf{K} \in G^{\kappa} \mid F(\mathbf{A} + \mathbf{K}) - F(0^{|\mathbf{A}|+\lambda} + \mathbf{K}) = \Delta\}}{\#G^{\kappa}}.$$

Lemma 1 (DP of differentials over Parallel [f]). *The differential probability of a differential* $(\mathbf{A}, \lambda, \Delta)$ *over Parallel* [f] *is given by*

$$\mathsf{DP}_F(\mathbf{A}, \lambda, \Delta) = \mathsf{DP}_{A_0} * \mathsf{DP}_{A_1} * \ldots * \mathsf{DP}_{A_{|\mathbf{A}|-1}} * \mathsf{IP}^{*\lambda}(\Delta).$$

Proof. Since the keys that are added to each of the blocks are mutually independent, the difference in the outputs of the first $|\mathbf{A}|$ blocks can be seen as the outcomes of independent stochastic variables whose distributions are given by the PMFs DP_{A_i} respectively, while the outputs of the last λ blocks can be seen as the outcomes of independent stochastic variables whose distribution is given by the PMF IP. Naturally the PMF of the input difference (A, λ) to F denoted as $\mathsf{DP}_F(A, \lambda)$ is given by

$$\mathsf{DP}_F(A, \lambda) = \mathsf{DP}_{A_0} * \mathsf{DP}_{A_1} * \ldots * \mathsf{DP}_{A_{|\mathbf{A}|-1}} * \mathsf{IP}^{*\lambda}.$$

□

Theorem 1 (ε-Δuniversality of Parallel [f]). *The parallelization of a public function* f, *Parallel* [f], *is* $\max \{\mathsf{MDP}_f, \mathsf{MIP}_f\}$-$\Delta$*universal.*

Proof. We first note that if for independent random variables g_X, g_Y and g_Z, $g_Z = g_X * g_Y$, then it follows directly from the definition of g_Z, that

$$\max_z g_Z(z) \leq \max \left(\max_x g_X(x), \max_y g_Y(y) \right).$$

By applying this relation to Lemma 1, we can upper bound DP_F as

$$\max_{\mathbf{A}, \lambda, \Delta} \mathsf{DP}_F(\mathbf{A}, \lambda, \Delta) \leq \max \left\{ \max_{A, \Delta \in G} \mathsf{DP}_f(A, \Delta), \max_{Z \in G'} \mathsf{IP}_f(Z) \right\}$$
$$= \max \{\mathsf{MDP}_f, \mathsf{MIP}_f\}.$$

□

The tightness of the ε-Δuniversality bound in Theorem 1 depends solely on the tightness of the bounds for MDP_f and MIP_f of the underlying public function f since for single block inputs, Parallel [f] = f. Furthermore the bound obtained for the ε-Δuniversality in Theorem 1 is consistent with the results obtained by Fuchs et al. for the ε-Δuniversality of a parallelized public permutation in Theorem 2 [11]. Indeed when f is a public permutation, the PMF IP for f is simply the uniform distribution and as such, the ε-Δuniversality of a parallelized public permutation is determined solely by its MDP_f.

4   Notations

$\mathbb{F}_p$ denotes the prime field with p elements and $\mathbb{F}_p^{2n}$ denotes the cartesian product of $\mathbb{F}_p$ $2n$-times. For the public functions proposed in this paper, $G = \mathbb{F}_p^{2n}$ and $G' = \mathbb{F}_p^{2n}$ for some prime p and integer $n \geq 1$. As such the input and the output to our public function are both $2n$-tuples, where all elements of the tuple are elements from the finite field $\mathbb{F}_p$ and the block string space is $\mathrm{BS}(\mathbb{F}_p^{2n}, \kappa)$.

We represent $X \in G = \mathbb{F}_p^{2n}$ as $X = (x_0, x_1, \ldots, x_{n-1}, y_0, y_1, \ldots, y_{n-1})^\mathsf{T}$. For simplicity, we slightly abuse the notations to denote $X = (\mathbf{x}, \mathbf{y})$, where $\mathbf{x} = (x_0, x_1, \ldots, x_{n-1})^\mathsf{T} \in \mathbb{F}_p^n$ and $\mathbf{y} = (y_0, y_1, \ldots, y_{n-1})^\mathsf{T} \in \mathbb{F}_p^n$. Similarly input differences and key blocks are denoted as $A = (\mathbf{a}, \mathbf{b})$ and $K = (\mathbf{h}, \mathbf{k})$ respectively. An output $Z \in G' = \mathbb{F}_p^{2n}$ is denoted as $Z = (z_0, z_1, \ldots, z_{2n-1})^\mathsf{T}$ and similarly output difference Δ is given by $\Delta = (\delta_0, \delta_1, \ldots, \delta_{2n-1})$.

The number of non-zero components in a vector $\mathbf{x} \in \mathbb{F}_p^n$ is the hamming weight of $\mathbf{x}$ that is denoted as $\mathrm{w}(\mathbf{x})$ and we denote $(0, 0, \ldots, 0)^\mathsf{T} \in \mathbb{F}_p^n$ as 0^n. Since multiplication in $\mathbb{F}_p$ is an integral part of our public function, we first look at its differential properties.

5   Differential Properties of Field Multiplication

We first consider as public function $\mathrm{f} \colon \mathbb{F}_p \times \mathbb{F}_p \to \mathbb{F}_p$ to denote the multiplication in $\mathbb{F}_p$. We remind the reader of the differential properties of field multiplication.

Lemma 2. *When* f *is the field multiplication, the image probabilities of its outputs are given by*

$$\mathrm{IP}_\mathrm{f}(Z) = \begin{cases} \frac{2p-1}{p^2}, & \text{when } Z = 0 \\ \frac{p-1}{p^2}, & \text{otherwise.} \end{cases}$$

Proof. For $Z = 0$, $f(x, y) = xy = 0$ implies $x = 0$ or $y = 0$. So $\mathrm{IP}_\mathrm{f}(0) = \frac{2p-1}{p^2}$. For $Z = z \neq 0$, $xy = z$ implies $x = z/y$ with $y \neq 0$ and thus $\mathrm{IP}_\mathrm{f}(Z) = \frac{p-1}{p^2}$.   □

So, for field multiplication we have $\mathrm{MIP}_\mathrm{f} = \frac{2p-1}{p^2}$ and is achieved only for $Z = 0$.

Lemma 3. *When* f *is the field multiplication,* $\mathrm{DP}_\mathrm{f}(A, \Delta) = \frac{1}{p}$ *for any* $A \in \mathbb{F}_p^2$ *and any* $\Delta \in \mathbb{F}_p$.

Proof. An input difference $A = (a, b)$ propagates to the output difference $\Delta = \delta$ under a key $K = (h, k)$ for f if:

$$(a + h)(b + k) - hk = \delta \quad \Longrightarrow \quad bh + ak + ab = \delta. \tag{1}$$

(1) describes a line in $\mathbb{F}_p \times \mathbb{F}_p$ with p points and thus $\mathrm{DP}(A, \Delta) = 1/p$.   □

So, when f is the field multiplication, $\mathrm{MDP}_\mathrm{f} = 1/p$ and $\mathrm{MIP}_\mathrm{f} = (2p - 1)/p^2$. Thus by Theorem 1, we see that Parallel $[\mathrm{f}]$ is ε-Δuniversal, where $\varepsilon = \frac{2p-1}{p^2}$.

6   Duplicated Multiplication as Public Function

In our quest to build a public function based on field multiplication, we now look at a slightly more complicated public function, that we call *duplicated field multiplication*. It is defined as follows:

$$f\colon \mathbb{F}_p^2 \to \mathbb{F}_p^2 : f(x, y) = (xy, (x + u)(y + v)). \tag{2}$$

for some constants $u, v \in \mathbb{F}_p \backslash \{0\}$. Here instead of computing only one multiplication, we compute two multiplications in parallel, where the input of the second multiplication is offset by (u, v).

Lemma 4. *When* f *is the duplicated multiplication,* $\max_{Z \in \mathbb{F}_p^2} \mathsf{IP}_f(Z) = \frac{2}{p^2}$

Proof. Let $Z = 0^2 = (0, 0)$. $f(x, y) = (0, 0)$ implies $(xy, (x + u)(y + v)) = (0, 0)$. Thus

$$xy = 0 \quad \text{and} \quad (x + u)(y + v) = 0.$$

This holds only for $(0, -v)$ and $(-u, 0)$. Thus, in this case the $\mathsf{IP}_f(0^2) = \frac{2}{p^2}$. When $Z = (z_0, z_1) \neq (0, 0)$, $f(x, y) = Z$ implies $xy = z_0$ and $(x + u)(y + v) = z_1$. Now since $u \neq 0$,

$$(x + u)(y + v) = z_1 \implies y = u^{-1}(z_1 - z_0 - vx - uv).$$

Substituting the value of y in $xy = z_0$, we obtain a quadratic equation in y. This has at most 2 solutions. So for $Z \neq (0, 0)$, $\mathsf{IP}_f(Z) \leq \frac{2}{p^2}$.   □

So, for the duplicated field multiplication, $\mathsf{MIP}_f = \frac{2}{p^2}$, which is indeed achieved for $Z = 0^2$.

Lemma 5. *When* f *is the duplicated multiplication,* $\mathsf{DP}_f(A, \Delta)$ *is given by:*

$$\mathsf{DP}_f(A, \Delta) = \begin{cases} \frac{1}{p}, & \text{when } va + ub = \delta_2 - \delta_1 \\ 0, & \text{otherwise.} \end{cases}$$

Proof. An input difference $A = (a, b)$ propagates to an output difference $\Delta = (\delta_1, \delta_2)$ under a key $K = (h, k)$ if

$$(a + h)(b + k) - hk = \delta_1,$$
$$(a + h + u)(b + k + v) - (h + u)(k + v) = \delta_2.$$

This simplifies to

$$bh + ak + ab = \delta_1 \quad \text{and} \quad va + ub = \delta_2 - \delta_1. \tag{3}$$

Thus $\mathsf{DP}_f(A, \Delta) > 0$ iff $va + ub = \delta_2 - \delta_1$ and in that case we must have $bh + ak + ab = \delta_1$, which again describes a line in $\mathbb{F}_p \times \mathbb{F}_p$, i.e., $\mathsf{DP}_f(A, Z) = 1/p$.   □

So $\mathsf{MDP}_f = \frac{1}{p} > \mathsf{MIP}_f = \frac{2}{p^2}$. Thus we conclude by Theorem 1 that parallelized duplicated multiplication is $1/p$-Δuniversal.

7   The Multiply-Transform-Multiply Construction

We now define a construction for building a public function from finite field multiplication and two linear transformations, that we call the *multiply-transform-multiply* (MTM) construction. We show that instances of this construction with maximum-distance-separable (MDS) linear transformations provide very good uniformity in the parallelization. As such we briefly remind the reader of the branch number of a matrix [10] and the definition of MDS matrices in terms of their branch numbers.

Definition 7 (Branch number). *Given a $n \times n$ matrix N defined over a field $\mathbb{F}_p$, its branch number is defined as* $\min\limits_{\mathbf{x} \in \mathbb{F}_p^n / \{0^n\}} (\mathrm{w}(\mathbf{x}) + \mathrm{w}(N \cdot \mathbf{x}))$.

We have a trivial upper-bound for the branch number of a matrix given by: branch number of $N \leq n + 1$.

Definition 8 (MDS matrix). *An $n \times n$ matrix N defined over a over a field $\mathbb{F}_p$ is said to be MDS if N has branch number $n + 1$.*

Before looking at the multiply-transform-multiply construction, we define the coordinate-wise product of vectors that will help us to explain the construction.

Definition 9 (Coordinate-wise product). *Given $\mathbf{x} = (x_0, x_1, \ldots, x_{n-1})^\mathsf{T}$ and $\mathbf{y} = (y_0, y_1, \ldots, y_{n-1})^\mathsf{T}$, their coordinate wise product denoted as $\mathbf{x} \odot \mathbf{y}$ is given by*

$$\mathbf{x} \odot \mathbf{y} = (x_0 y_0, x_1 y_1, \ldots, x_{n-1} y_{n-1})^\mathsf{T}.$$

Definition 10 (MTM(n, p)). *For a positive integer $n > 1$ and prime p such that $\log_2 p \geq n$, MTM(n, p) denotes a family of functions where any function $\mathrm{f}[\alpha, \beta] \in \mathrm{MTM}(n, p)$ is given by:*

$$\mathrm{f}[\alpha, \beta] \colon \mathbb{F}_p^{2n} \mapsto \mathbb{F}_p^{2n} \colon \mathrm{f}[\alpha, \beta](X) = \mathrm{f}[\alpha, \beta](\mathbf{x}, \mathbf{y}) = (\mathbf{x} \odot \mathbf{y}, N_\alpha \cdot \mathbf{x} \odot N_\beta \cdot \mathbf{y}),$$

where N_α, N_β are any $n \times n$ matrices.

To simplify notations, we will denote $N_\alpha \cdot \mathbf{x} = \mathbf{p}$ and $N_\beta \cdot \mathbf{y} = \mathbf{q}$, which means $\mathrm{f}[\alpha, \beta](\mathbf{x}, \mathbf{y}) = (\mathbf{x} \odot \mathbf{y}, \mathbf{p} \odot \mathbf{q})$. The matrices N_α and N_β are denoted as $N_\alpha = \begin{bmatrix} \alpha_{i,j} \end{bmatrix}$ and $N_\beta = \begin{bmatrix} \beta_{i,j} \end{bmatrix}$ with $0 \leq i, j \leq n - 1$.

We now provide an intuitive design rationale for our construction. Our goal is to build a key-then-hash function that is close to $1/p^n$-Δuniversal, i.e., by Theorem 1 we must have $\mathrm{MDP}_{\mathrm{f}[\alpha, \beta]} \leq \frac{1}{p^n}$ and $\mathrm{MIP}_{\mathrm{f}[\alpha, \beta]} \leq \frac{1}{p^n}$. $\mathrm{f}[\alpha, \beta]$ computes a total of $2n$ multiplications and this requires that for any input difference A to $\mathrm{f}[\alpha, \beta]$, that difference propagates to maximal number of multiplications in $\mathrm{f}[\alpha, \beta]$.

Definition 11 (Active multiplication). *A multiplication in* $f[\alpha, \beta]$ *is said to be active corresponding to an input difference if that multiplication has a non-zero input difference in at least one of its multiplicands as a result of propagation of that difference inside* $f[\alpha, \beta]$.

The minimum number of active multiplications over all possible input differences is determined by the minimum of the branch numbers of N_α and N_β. To that end, we show that when N_α and N_β are both MDS, Parallel $[f[\alpha, \beta]]$ is $2/p^n$-Δuniversal.

$\varepsilon = 2/p^n$ instead of $1/p^n$ is due to the fact that $\mathrm{MIP}_{f[\alpha,\beta]} = 2/p^n$ by Corollary 1. As we saw in Sect. 6, the maximum value of $\mathrm{IP}_{f[\alpha,\beta]}$ can indeed be reduced if the entries to some of the multiplications were offset by a non-zero quantity, or in other words, if we used affine maps instead of the linear maps N_α and N_β. However such an offset will not have any bearing on the DP of the differentials and thus by using offsets ε is only improved by a factor of 2. So the gain by having an offset is insignificant and thus we decided that none of the multiplications in $\mathrm{MTM}(n, p)$ family of functions will have any offsets.

For the remainder of this section, we assume $f[\alpha, \beta] \in \mathrm{MTM}(n, p)$ is chosen such that the underlying matrices N_α and N_β are both MDS.

7.1   Maximum Image Probability of $f[\alpha, \beta]$

In this section we obtain the value of $\mathrm{MIP}_{f[\alpha,\beta]}$ and show that the value is obtained when output $Z = 0^{2n}$.

Lemma 6. *Let* $f[\alpha, \beta] \in \mathrm{MTM}(n, p)$ *be chosen such that both* N_α *and* N_β *are MDS. Then,* $\mathrm{IP}_{f[\alpha,\beta]}(0^{2n}) = \frac{2p^n-1}{p^{2n}}$.

Proof. We prove that $f[\alpha, \beta](\mathbf{x}, \mathbf{y}) = 0^{2n}$ if and only if $\mathbf{x} = 0^n$ or $\mathbf{y} = 0^n$.

If $\mathbf{x} = 0^n$, then we must have $\mathbf{p} = 0^n$ and if $\mathbf{y} = 0^n$, we must have $\mathbf{q} = 0^n$ since the matrices N_α and N_β, being MDS, are invertible. Thus if $\mathbf{x} = 0^n$ or $\mathbf{y} = 0^n$, then $\mathbf{x} \odot \mathbf{y} = 0^n$ and $\mathbf{p} \odot \mathbf{q} = 0^n$, i.e., $f[\alpha, \beta](\mathbf{x}, \mathbf{y}) = 0^{2n}$.

We now show that if both $\mathbf{x} \neq 0^n$, $\mathbf{y} \neq 0^n$, then $f[\alpha, \beta](\mathbf{x}, \mathbf{y}) \neq 0^{2n}$. Indeed,

$$f[\alpha, \beta](\mathbf{x}, \mathbf{y}) = (\mathbf{x} \odot \mathbf{y}, \mathbf{p} \odot \mathbf{q}) = 0^{2n} \implies \mathbf{x} \odot \mathbf{y} = 0^n \text{ and } \mathbf{p} \odot \mathbf{q} = 0^n.$$

Let $w(\mathbf{x}) = w$ for some some $w \in \{1, \ldots, n\}$. We will argue only on the basis of $w(\mathbf{x})$ and thus we assume without loss of generality that $x_0, x_1, \ldots, x_{w-1} \neq 0$ and $x_w = x_{w+1} = \ldots = x_{n-1} = 0$. Thus for $\mathbf{x} \odot \mathbf{y} = 0^n$, we must have $y_0 = y_1 = \ldots = y_{w-1} = 0$, which means $w(\mathbf{y}) \leq n - w$. Now N_α and N_β are both $n \times n$ MDS matrix. Thus we have

$$w(\mathbf{x}) + w(\mathbf{p}) \geq n + 1 \implies w(\mathbf{p}) \geq n - w + 1, \qquad (4.1)$$

$$w(\mathbf{y}) + w(\mathbf{q}) \geq n + 1 \text{ and } w(\mathbf{y}) \leq n - w \implies w(\mathbf{q}) \geq w + 1. \qquad (4.2)$$

But, (4.1) together with $\mathbf{p} \odot \mathbf{q} = 0^n$ implies that $w(\mathbf{q}) \leq w - 1$, a contradiction with (4.2). Thus $f[\alpha, \beta](\mathbf{x}, \mathbf{y}) = 0^{2n}$ iff either $\mathbf{x} = 0^n$ or $\mathbf{y} = 0^n$. Hence, $\mathrm{IP}_{f[\alpha,\beta]}(0^{2n}) = \frac{p^n + p^n - 1}{p^{2n}} = \frac{2p^n - 1}{p^{2n}}$. $\square$

Lemma 7. *Let* $f[\alpha, \beta] \in \text{MTM}(n, p)$ *be chosen such that both* N_α *and* N_β *are MDS. Then, for any* $Z \neq 0^{2n}$, $\text{IP}_{f[\alpha,\beta]}(Z) \leq \frac{2(2p-1)^{n-1}+p-3}{p^{2n}}$.

Proof. Since $Z \neq 0^{2n}$, $z_i \neq 0$ for some $i \in \{0, \ldots, 2n-1\}$. First let $z_i \neq 0$ for some $i \in \{0, \ldots n-1\}$. Without loss of generality we assume $z_0 \neq 0$. This implies $y_0 = z_0/x_0$. The $(n-1)$ equations $x_i y_i = z_i$ for $i = 1, \ldots, (n-1)$ can have at most $(2p-1)^{n-1}$ solutions. Let one such solution be

$$x_i = \lambda_i, \quad y_i = \mu_i \text{ for } i = 1, \ldots (n-1). \tag{5}$$

Now, we see that all the variables x_i, y_i for $i \in \{1, 2, \ldots, n-1\}$ have been evaluated and the only unknowns are x_0 and y_0. We now find out the number of possible values of x_0 and y_0 corresponding to each solution in (5).

Substituting the values of x_i, y_i for $i \in \{1, \ldots, n-1\}$ from (5) and $y_0 = z_0/x_0$ in $p_i q_i = z_{n+i}$ for $i \in \{0, 1, \ldots, n-2\}$, we have a system of $n-1$ equations, where the i-th equation is given by:

$$(\alpha_{i,0} x_0 + \alpha_{i,1} \lambda_1 + \ldots + \alpha_{i,n-1} \lambda_{n-1})(\beta_{i,0} \frac{z_0}{x_0} + \beta_{i,1} \mu_1 + \ldots + \beta_{i,n-1} \mu_{n-1}) = z_{n+i}. \tag{6}$$

Now, for $i \in \{0, 1, \ldots, n-2\}$ let us denote by $\alpha_i = \alpha_{i,1} \lambda_1 + \ldots + \alpha_{i,n-1} \lambda_{n-1}$ and $\beta_i = \beta_{i,1} \mu_1 + \ldots + \beta_{i,n-1} \mu_{n-1}$. Then the set of $(n-1)$ linear equations in (6) converts to:

$$(\alpha_{i,0} x_0 + \alpha_i)(\beta_{i,0} \frac{z_0}{x_0} + \beta_i) = z_{n+i} \text{ for } i \in \{0, 1, \ldots, n-2\}. \tag{7}$$

Now, whenever one of $\alpha_i \neq 0$ or $\beta_i \neq 0$, $(\alpha_{i,0} x_0 + \alpha_i)(\beta_{i,0} \frac{z_0}{x_0} + \beta_i) = z_{n+i}$ describes a quadratic equation. But whenever both $\alpha_i = 0$ and $\beta_i = 0$, this becomes independent of x_0. This leads to the following two possibilities:

1. $\alpha_i = \beta_i = 0 \ \forall \ i \in \{0, \ldots n-2\}$.
2. $\exists 0 \leq i \leq n-2$ such that $\alpha_i \neq 0$ or $\beta_i \neq 0$.

We first look at the case $\alpha_i = \beta_i = 0$ for each $i \in \{0, \ldots n-2\}$. Let $\lambda = (\lambda_1, \lambda_2, \ldots, \lambda_{n-1})^\mathsf{T} \in \mathbb{F}_p^{n-1}$, $\mu = (\mu_1, \mu_2, \ldots \mu_{n-1})^\mathsf{T} \in \mathbb{F}_p^{n-1}$. Furthermore let N_α' and N_β' denote the $(n-1) \times (n-1)$ submatrices of N_α and N_β respectively, where N_α' and N_β' are obtained by removing the 0-th column and $(n-1)$-th row from N_α and N_β respectively. So, $N_\alpha' = \begin{bmatrix} \alpha_{i,j} \end{bmatrix}$ and $N_\beta' = \begin{bmatrix} \beta_{i,j} \end{bmatrix}$ with $0 \leq i \leq n-2$, $1 \leq j \leq n-1$. Now the set of $(n-1)$ linear equations $\alpha_i = \beta_i = 0$ for $i \in \{0, \ldots n-2\}$ can be written as:

$$N_\alpha' \cdot \lambda = 0^n \text{ and } N_\beta' \cdot \mu = 0^n. \tag{8}$$

N_α' and N_β' are submatrices of the MDS matrices N_α and N_β. Thus from (8), N_α' and N_β' both must be invertible. Thus $\lambda = \mu = 0^n$. In this case (7) converts to $\alpha_{i,0} \beta_{i,0} z_0 = z_{n+i}$ for $i \in \{0, \ldots, n-2\}$, i.e., the equations are independent of x_0. Thus, the number of solutions, if it exists, is bounded by the number of solutions to $x_0 y_0 = z_0$, i.e., $p - 1$. In other words when each of $x_i = y_i = 0$ for $i \in \{1, \ldots, n-1\}$, there can be at most $(p-1)$ values of the pair (x_0, y_0)

When there exists $0 \le i \le n-2$ such that $\alpha_i \ne 0$ or $\beta_i \ne 0$, for that value of i, (9) is a quadratic equation.

$$(\alpha_{i,0} x_0 + \alpha_i)(\beta_{i,0} \frac{z_0}{x_0} + \beta_i) = z_{n+i}. \tag{9}$$

Thus (9) has at most 2 solutions and this holds true for each solution from (5) except when each $x_i = y_i = 0$ for $i \in \{1, \ldots, n-1\}$.

Now, each $x_i = y_i = 0$ for $i \in \{1, \ldots, n-1\}$ implies that $z_i = 0$ for each $i \in \{1, \ldots, n-1\}$. Thus we can conclude that for a $Z \ne 0^{2n}$,

$$\mathrm{IP}_{f[\alpha,\beta]}(Z) \le \begin{cases} \frac{2(2p-1)^{n-1} + p - 3}{p^{2n}} & , \text{ if } z_i \ne 0 \text{ for exactly one } i \in \{0, \ldots, n-1\} \\ \frac{2(2p-1)^{n-1}}{p^{2n}} & , \text{ if } z_i \ne 0 \text{ for more than one } i \in \{0, \ldots, n-1\}. \end{cases}$$

Now let $z_i \ne 0$ for some $i \in \{n, \ldots, 2n-1\}$. Since inverse of an MDS matrix is necessarily MDS and invertible, we can apply the same arguments as when $z_i \ne 0$ for some $i \in \{0, \ldots, n-1\}$ to obtain a solution in p_i, q_i and the number of such solutions is again at most $\frac{2(2p-1)^{n-1} + p - 3}{p^{2n}}$. Since N_α^{-1} and N_β^{-1} are both invertible, each solution in p_i, q_i corresponds to a unique solution in x_i, y_i and hence for such a Z as well $\mathrm{IP}_{f[\alpha,\beta]}(Z) \le \frac{2(2p-1)^{n-1} + p - 3}{p^{2n}}$. $\square$

Corollary 1. *For any* $f[\alpha, \beta] \in \mathrm{MTM}(n, p)$, *where* N_α *and* N_β *are both MDS,* $\mathrm{MIP}_{f[\alpha,\beta]} = \frac{2p^n - 1}{p^{2n}} \le \frac{2}{p^n}$

Proof. By Lemmas 6 and 7, we see that $\mathrm{IP}_{f[\alpha,\beta]}(0^{2n}) = \frac{2p^n - 1}{p^{2n}}$ and for any $Z \ne 0^{2n}$, $\mathrm{IP}_{f[\alpha,\beta]}(Z) \le \frac{2(2p-1)^{n-1} + p - 3}{p^{2n}}$. Now, since p is chosen such that $\log_2 p > n$, we have

$$2p^n - 2(2p-1)^{n-1} > 2p^{n-1}(p - 2^{n-1}) > 2^n p^{n-1} > p - 2.$$

So, $2p^n - 1 > 2(2p-1)^{n-1} + p - 3$ and thus $\mathrm{MIP}_{f[\alpha,\beta]} = \frac{2p^n - 1}{p^{2n}} \le \frac{2}{p^n}$. $\square$

7.2   Maximum Differential Probability of $f[\alpha, \beta]$

Before looking into the differential probability of $f[\alpha, \beta]$, we introduce some new notation. For an input difference $A = (\mathbf{a}, \mathbf{b})$, we denote $N_\alpha \cdot \mathbf{a} = \mathbf{c} = (c_0, c_1, \ldots, c_{n-1})$ and $N_\beta \cdot \mathbf{b} = \mathbf{d} = (d_0, d_1, \ldots, d_{n-1})$ respectively. Due to N_α, N_β being MDS, for any choice of $\mathbf{a}$ and $\mathbf{b}$, we must have $\mathrm{w}(\mathbf{a}) + \mathrm{w}(\mathbf{c}) \ge (n+1)$ and $\mathrm{w}(\mathbf{b}) + \mathrm{w}(\mathbf{d}) \ge (n+1)$. For any vector $\mathbf{x} \in \mathbb{F}_p^n$, $D_\mathbf{x}$ denotes the $n \times n$ diagonal matrix with i-th diagonal entry being x_i.

Lemma 8. *An input difference* $A = (\mathbf{a}, \mathbf{b})$ *propagates to the output difference* $\Delta = (\delta_0, \delta_1, \ldots, \delta_{2n-1})^\mathsf{T}$ *under* $f[\alpha, \beta]$ *for a key* $K = (\mathbf{h}, \mathbf{k})$ *if*

$$N_A \cdot K + O_A = \Delta. \tag{10}$$

Here N_A *and* O_A *are given by:*

$$N_A = \begin{bmatrix} D_{\mathbf{b}} & D_{\mathbf{a}} \\ N_\alpha \cdot D_{\mathbf{d}} & N_\beta \cdot D_{\mathbf{c}} \end{bmatrix},$$

$$O_A = \begin{bmatrix} a_0 b_0 & \dots & a_{n-1}b_{n-1} & c_0 d_0 & \dots & c_{n-1}d_{n-1} \end{bmatrix}^\mathsf{T}.$$

Proof. An input difference $A = (\mathbf{a}, \mathbf{b})$ propagates to an output difference $\Delta = (\delta_0, \delta_1, \dots, \delta_{2n-1})^\mathsf{T}$ under a key $K = (\mathbf{h}, \mathbf{k})$ if

$$f[\alpha, \beta](\mathbf{h} + \mathbf{a}, \mathbf{k} + \mathbf{b}) - f[\alpha, \beta](\mathbf{h}, \mathbf{k}) = \Delta.$$

From the definition of $f[\alpha, \beta]$ we have,

$$((\mathbf{h} + \mathbf{a}) \odot (\mathbf{k} + \mathbf{b}), N_\alpha \cdot (\mathbf{h} + \mathbf{a}) \odot N_\beta \cdot (\mathbf{k} + \mathbf{b})) - (\mathbf{h} \odot \mathbf{k}, N_\alpha \cdot \mathbf{h} \odot N_\beta \cdot \mathbf{k}) = \Delta.$$

This leads to two sets of n equations, where for $i \in \{0, \dots, n-1\}$ the i-th such equations are given by:

$$(h_i + a_i) \cdot (k_i + b_i) - h_i \cdot k_i = \delta_i,$$

$$\left(\sum_{j=0}^{n-1} \alpha_{i,j}(h_j + a_j)\right) \cdot \left(\sum_{j=0}^{n-1} \beta_{i,j}(k_j + b_j)\right) - \left(\sum_{j=0}^{n-1} \alpha_{i,j} h_j\right) \cdot \left(\sum_{j=0}^{n-1} \beta_{i,j} k_j\right) = \delta_{n+i}.$$

For each $0 \le i \le n - 1$, these sets of equations respectively simplify to:

$$b_i h_i + a_i k_i + a_i b_i = \delta_i,$$

$$d_i \sum_{j=0}^{n-1} \alpha_{i,j} h_i + c_i \sum_{j=0}^{n-1} \beta_{i,j} k_j + c_i d_i = \delta_{n+i}.$$

Thus, we now have a set of $2n$ linear equations in $2n$ variables h_i, k_i. Writing this set of equations in terms of matrices, we arrive at our desired lemma. □

We call the matrix N_A the *difference matrix* corresponding to the input difference A. Given any A we denote by $\mathcal{C}_A$ the column space generated by N_A.

Corollary 2. *Given a differential* (A, Δ) *to* $f[\alpha, \beta]$, $\mathsf{DP}_{f[\alpha,\beta]}(A, \Delta)$ *is given by:*

$$\mathsf{DP}_{f[\alpha,\beta]}(A, \Delta) = \begin{cases} 0, & when\ (\Delta - O_A) \notin \mathcal{C}_A \\ \frac{1}{p^r}, & otherwise. \end{cases}$$

Here r *denotes the rank of* N_A.

Proof. When $(\Delta - O_A) \notin \mathcal{C}_A$, (10) is inconsistent and thus $\mathsf{DP}_{f[\alpha,\beta]}(A, \Delta) = 0$. Otherwise (10) has p^{2n-r} solutions and hence $\mathsf{DP}_{f[\alpha,\beta]}(A, \Delta) = \frac{p^{2n-r}}{p^{2n}} = \frac{1}{p^r}$. □

Lemma 9. *Given any input difference A to $f[\alpha, \beta]$ where the underlying matrices are MDS, the rank of N_A is at least n.*

Proof. Since $A \neq 0^{2n}$, at least one of $\mathbf{a}$ and $\mathbf{b}$ must be non-zero. Let us assume without loss of generality that $\mathbf{b} \neq 0$. For $i \in \{0, 1, \ldots, n-1\}$, let C_i denote the i-th column of N_A, i.e.,

$$C_i = \begin{bmatrix} 0 \ldots b_i \ldots 0 \; \alpha_{0,i}d_0 \ldots \alpha_{i,i}d_i \ldots \alpha_{n-1,i}d_{n-1} \end{bmatrix}^{\mathsf{T}}.$$

We show that $\{C_0, C_1, \ldots, C_{n-1}\}$ is a set of n linearly independent column vectors and thus $\text{rank}(N_A) \geq n$. So, we show that for scalars $\lambda_0, \lambda_1, \ldots, \lambda_{n-1} \in \mathbb{F}_p$

$$\lambda_0 C_0 + \lambda_1 C_1 + \ldots + \lambda_{n-1} C_{n-1} = 0^n \quad \Longrightarrow \quad \lambda_0 = \lambda_1 = \ldots = \lambda_{n-1} = 0.$$

Now, $\sum_{i=0}^{n-1} \lambda_i C_i = 0^n$ simplifies to:

$$\begin{bmatrix} \lambda_0 b_0 \\ \lambda_1 b_1 \\ \vdots \\ \lambda_{n-1} b_{n-1} \\ (\lambda_0 \alpha_{0,0} + \lambda_1 \alpha_{0,1} + \ldots \lambda_{n-1} \alpha_{0,n-1})d_0 \\ (\lambda_0 \alpha_{1,0} + \lambda_1 \alpha_{1,1} + \ldots \lambda_{n-1} \alpha_{1,n-1})d_1 \\ \vdots \\ (\lambda_0 \alpha_{n-1,0} + \lambda_1 \alpha_{n-1,1} + \ldots \lambda_{n-1} \alpha_{n-1,n-1})d_{n-1} \end{bmatrix} = \begin{bmatrix} 0 \\ 0 \\ \vdots \\ 0 \\ 0 \\ 0 \\ \vdots \\ 0 \end{bmatrix}. \tag{11}$$

Let $w(\mathbf{b}) = w$ for some $w \in \{1, \ldots, n\}$. Without loss of generality we assume that $b_0, b_1, \ldots, b_{w-1} \neq 0$. Then clearly from (11) we see that $\lambda_0 = \lambda_1 = \ldots = \lambda_{w-1} = 0$. Thus (11) now reduces to the following set of n linear equations in $n - w$ variables $\lambda_w, \lambda_{w+1}, \ldots, \lambda_{n-1}$.

$$\begin{bmatrix} (\lambda_w \alpha_{0,w} + \lambda_{w+1} \alpha_{0,w+1} + \ldots \lambda_{n-1} \alpha_{0,n-1})d_0 \\ (\lambda_w \alpha_{1,w} + \lambda_{w+1} \alpha_{1,w+1} + \ldots \lambda_{n-1} \alpha_{1,n-1})d_1 \\ \vdots \\ (\lambda_w \alpha_{n-1,w} + \lambda_{w+1} \alpha_{n-1,w+1} + \ldots \lambda_{n-1} \alpha_{n-1,n-1})d_{n-1} \end{bmatrix} = \begin{bmatrix} 0 \\ 0 \\ \vdots \\ 0 \end{bmatrix}. \tag{12}$$

Since, $w(\mathbf{b}) = w$ and $w(\mathbf{b}) + w(\mathbf{d}) \geq n + 1$, at least $n - w + 1$ components of $\mathbf{d}$ must be non-zero. Again for simplicity we assume $d_0, d_1, \ldots, d_{n-w} \neq 0$. But this would imply

$$\begin{bmatrix} \alpha_{0,w} & \alpha_{0,w+1} & \cdots & \alpha_{0,n-1} \\ \vdots & \vdots & \ddots & \vdots \\ \alpha_{n-w,w} & \alpha_{n-w,w+1} & \cdots & \alpha_{n-w,n-1} \end{bmatrix} \cdot \begin{bmatrix} \lambda_w \\ \vdots \\ \lambda_{n-1} \end{bmatrix} = \begin{bmatrix} 0 \\ \vdots \\ 0 \end{bmatrix}. \tag{13}$$

But, the $(n-w+1) \times (n-w)$ matrix in the left hand side of (13) is a submatrix of N_α and thus has full rank, i.e., rank of this matrix is $n-w$. Thus this system of equations has a unique solution given by: $\lambda_w = \ldots = \lambda_{n-1} = 0$.

Thus, we have shown that $\{C_0, \ldots, C_{n-1}\}$ is a set of n linearly independent column vectors. Hence rank(N_A)$\geq n$. $\qquad\square$

Corollary 3. *For any* $f[\alpha, \beta]$ *where the underlying matrices are MDS,* $\mathrm{MDP}_{f[\alpha,\beta]} = \frac{1}{p^n}$.

Proof. It follows from Corollary 2 that for any differential (A, Δ) to $f[\alpha, \beta]$, $\mathrm{DP}_{f[\alpha,\beta]}(A, \Delta) \leq \frac{1}{p^r}$ where rank(N_A) = r. By Lemma 9 it follows that $r \geq n$ and consequently $\mathrm{DP}_{f[\alpha,\beta]}(A, \Delta) \leq \frac{1}{p^n}$.

This bound is also attained for a well chosen differential. Indeed it can be seen that if A is chosen such that $\mathbf{a} = 0^n$, then rank(N_A) = n. In this case if Δ is chosen such that $(\Delta - O_A) \in \mathcal{C}_A$ (in particular one can choose $\Delta = 0^{2n}$), then $\mathrm{DP}_{f[\alpha,\beta]}(A, \Delta) = \frac{1}{p^n}$. $\qquad\square$

7.3 ε-Δuniversality of Parallel $[f[\alpha, \beta]]$

Theorem 2. *Let* $f[\alpha, \beta] \in \mathrm{MTM}(n,p)$ *be such that its underlying matrices are MDS. Then Parallel*$[f[\alpha, \beta]]$ *is* $\frac{2}{p^n}$-Δ*universal.*

Proof. From Corollaries 1 and 3 it follows that for such a $f[\alpha, \beta]$, $\mathrm{MIP}_{f[\alpha,\beta]} \leq \frac{2}{p^n}$ and $\mathrm{MDP}_{f[\alpha,\beta]} \leq \frac{1}{p^n}$. Thus it follows from Theorem 1 that Parallel $[f[\alpha, \beta]]$ is $\frac{2}{p^n}$-Δuniversal. $\qquad\square$

Thus, whenever N_α and N_β are MDS, Parallel $[f[\alpha, \beta]]$ is $\frac{2}{p^n}$-Δuniversal. However while the matrices being MDS is sufficient to obtain this universality, it is not strictly necessary. It is possible to choose a member of $\mathrm{MTM}(n,p)$, whose parallelization is $\frac{2}{p^n}$-Δuniversal, but the underlying matrices N_α and N_β are not MDS. However this requires more detailed security analysis. We look at such a public function in the next section.

8   Multi-265

We now introduce the key-then-hash function multi-265 . This is the parallelization of a public function that we denote as f-265 belonging to $\mathrm{MTM}(6, 2^{26} - 5)$, i.e., multi-265 $=$ Parallel $[$f-265$]$. The specifications of f-265 is as follows.

Definition 12. *The public function of multi-265 denoted as f-265 is defined as:*

$$f\text{-}265 \colon \mathbb{F}_p^{12} \mapsto \mathbb{F}_p^{12} \colon f\text{-}265(X) = f\text{-}265(\mathbf{x}, \mathbf{y}) = (\mathbf{x} \odot \mathbf{y}, N \cdot \mathbf{x} \odot N \cdot \mathbf{y}),$$

where N is the 6×6 circulant matrix whose first row is given by $\begin{pmatrix} 1 & 1 & 3 & 1 & 3 & 0 \end{pmatrix}$.

We will now motivate the design choices we made. We want to use fast 32-bit integer multiplication instructions and apply lazy modular reductions. Therefore we take a prime significantly smaller than 2^{32}. Still, we want this modular reduction to be efficient and for that purpose we take the prime of our field to be a pseudo-mersenne prime [13], i.e., of the form $2^l - \lambda$, for a small λ and we chose for $p = 2^{26} - 5$. Now, for the dimension n, we wanted $\varepsilon = 2/p^n$ to be smaller than 2^{-128}, i.e., $n \geq 5$ for our chosen prime p. Thus a 5×5 MDS matrix would guarantee $\varepsilon = 2p^{-5} \approx 2^{-129}$. However, these dimensions are not well suited in the SIMD architecture and therefore we chose for 6×6 matrices. Now, a 6×6 MDS matrix is quite expensive and thus we instead looked for a 6×6 matrix with branch number 6. Any 6×6 matrix with branch number 6 however does not assure us of $\varepsilon = 2p^{-6}$. Thus another added restriction, as we will soon see, is that matrices should have branch number at least 7 when restricted to inputs with weight at least 3.

So, we finally chose N to be a circulant matrix and chose both the matrices in f-265 to be the same to simplify our security analysis. We limited the entries in N to the set $\{-1, 0, 1, 2, 3\}$ so matrix multiplication can be efficiently implemented with only addition and subtraction. We found N by exhaustive search over all candidates checking the branch number is 6 and then selecting the ones that have branch number 7 when restricted to inputs with weight 3 or more. We did this by finding all full rank matrices having at most one entry 0 such that all 3×3, 4×4 and 5×5 submatrices have full rank. Sage code to find all matrices that satisfy these requirements can be found at https://github.com/KoustabhGhosh/Multi-265.

In this section, we use similar notations as in Sect. 7. So we have $N \cdot x = p$, $N \cdot y = q$ and for an input difference $A = (a, b)$, $N \cdot a = c$ and $N \cdot b = d$.

8.1   Maximum Image Probability of f-265

In this section we show that similar to f$[\alpha, \beta]$, MIP$_{\text{f-265}} \leq \frac{2}{p^6}$ and is obtained for the output 0^{12}.

Lemma 10. *For the public function* f-265, $\text{IP}_{f\text{-}265}(0^{12}) = \frac{2p^6 - 1}{p^{12}}$.

Proof. We show that f-265$(x, y) = 0^{12}$ if and only if $x = 0^6$ or $y = 0^6$. Clearly if $x = 0^6$ or $y = 0^6$, f-265$(X) = 0^{12}$

We now show that when both $x \neq 0^6$ and $y \neq 0^6$, f-265$(x, y) \neq 0^{12}$. Let $w(x) = w$ for some some $w \in \{1, \ldots, 6\}$.

When $w \geq 3$, since N has branch number 7 for all inputs with weight at least 3, we have

$$w(x) + w(p) \geq 7 \qquad \Longrightarrow \qquad w(p) \geq 7 - w. \tag{14}$$

From (14), $x \odot y = 0^6$ and $p \odot q = 0^6$ we see that

$$w(y) \leq 6 - w, \tag{15.1}$$

$$w(q) \leq 6 - (7 - w) = w - 1. \tag{15.2}$$

But, (15.1) together with the fact that N has branch number 6 implies that $w(\mathbf{q}) \geq 6 - (6 - w) = w$, a contradiction with (15.2).

When $w < 3$, we have

$$w(\mathbf{x}) + w(\mathbf{p}) \geq 6 \quad \Longrightarrow \quad w(\mathbf{p}) \geq 6 - w.$$

From $\mathbf{p} \odot \mathbf{q} = 0^6$ it follows that

$$w(\mathbf{q}) \leq 6 - (6 - w) = w.$$

But, $w(\mathbf{q}) \leq w < 3$ implies that $w(\mathbf{y})$ must also be greater than 3 due to N having branch number 6. But since $w(\mathbf{y}) > 3$, we must have

$$w(\mathbf{y}) + w(\mathbf{q}) \geq 7 \quad \Longrightarrow \quad w(\mathbf{y}) \geq 7 - w. \tag{16}$$

From $\mathbf{x} \odot \mathbf{y} = 0^6$ we have $w(\mathbf{y}) \leq 6 - w$, a contradiction with (16).

Thus $f\text{-}265(X) = 0^{12}$ iff either $\mathbf{x} = 0^6$ or $\mathbf{y} = 0^6$. □

Lemma 11. *Let $Z \neq 0^{12}$. Then for the public function $f\text{-}265$, $\mathsf{IP}_{f\text{-}265}(Z) \leq \frac{2(2p-1)^5 + p - 3}{p^{12}}$.*

Proof. When $Z \neq 0^{12}$, $\mathsf{IP}_{f\text{-}265}(Z) \leq \frac{2(2p-1)^5 + p - 3}{p^{12}}$ follows directly from Lemma 7. The only property of $n \times n$ MDS matrices that we used in proof to Lemma 11 was that the MDS matrix itself and all its $(n-1) \times (n-1)$ are invertible. N follows these properties since N itself and all its 5×5 submatrices are invertible. □

Corollary 4. *For the public function $f\text{-}265$, $\mathrm{MIP}_{f\text{-}265} = \frac{2p^6 - 1}{p^{12}} \leq \frac{2}{p^6}$.*

Proof. The proof follows directly from Lemmas 10 and 11. □

8.2   Maximum Differential Probability of f-265

By applying Lemma 8, we see that an input difference $A = (\mathbf{a}, \mathbf{b})$ propagates to the output difference $\Delta = (\delta_0, \delta_1, \ldots, \delta_{11})$ under f-265 for a key $K = (\mathbf{h}, \mathbf{k})$ if $N_A \cdot K + O_A = \Delta$. For f-265, N_A is given by

$$N_A = \begin{bmatrix}
b_0 & 0 & 0 & 0 & 0 & 0 & a_0 & 0 & 0 & 0 & 0 & 0 \\
0 & b_1 & 0 & 0 & 0 & 0 & 0 & a_1 & 0 & 0 & 0 & 0 \\
0 & 0 & b_2 & 0 & 0 & 0 & 0 & 0 & a_2 & 0 & 0 & 0 \\
0 & 0 & 0 & b_3 & 0 & 0 & 0 & 0 & 0 & a_3 & 0 & 0 \\
0 & 0 & 0 & 0 & b_4 & 0 & 0 & 0 & 0 & 0 & a_4 & 0 \\
0 & 0 & 0 & 0 & 0 & b_5 & 0 & 0 & 0 & 0 & 0 & a_5 \\
d_0 & d_0 & 3d_0 & d_0 & 3d_0 & 0 & c_0 & c_0 & 3c_0 & c_0 & 3c_0 & 0 \\
0 & d_1 & d_1 & 3d_1 & d_1 & 3d_1 & 0 & c_1 & c_1 & 3c_1 & c_1 & 3c_1 \\
3d_2 & 0 & d_2 & d_2 & 3d_2 & d_2 & 3c_2 & 0 & c_2 & c_2 & 3c_2 & c_2 \\
d_3 & 3d_3 & 0 & d_3 & d_3 & 3d_3 & c_3 & 3c_3 & 0 & c_3 & c_3 & 3c_3 \\
3d_4 & d_4 & 3d_4 & 0 & d_4 & d_4 & 3c_4 & c_4 & 3c_4 & 0 & c_4 & c_4 \\
d_5 & 3d_5 & d_5 & 3d_5 & 0 & d_5 & c_5 & 3c_5 & c_5 & 3c_5 & 0 & c_5
\end{bmatrix}.$$

We know by Corollary 2 that for a differential (A, Δ), its DP is upper bounded by $1/p^r$, where r is the rank of N_A. Before we can obtain a lower bound for N_A, we first look at an important property of N.

Lemma 12. *For $r \in \{1, 2, 3, 4, 5\}$, all the $(r+1) \times r$ submatrices of N have rank r.*

Proof. For $r = 1$, all 2×1 submatrices of N has rank 1 since $\begin{bmatrix} 0 & 0 \end{bmatrix}^{\mathsf{T}}$ is not a submatrix of N. For $r = 2$, all 3×2 submatrices must have rank 2 since otherwise there must exist a 3×3 submatrix with rank 2, a contradiction. For $r \geq 3$, the proof is trivial since all $r \times r$ submatrices of N have rank r for $r \geq 3$.   □

Lemma 13. *Given any input difference A, rank $(N_A) \geq 6$.*

Proof. Since $A = (\mathbf{a}, \mathbf{b}) \neq 0^{12}$, we assume without loss of generality that $\mathbf{b} \neq 0^6$.

Let $w(\mathbf{b}) = w$. In the proof to Lemma 9 we used the following facts about the underlying $n \times n$ MDS matrix N_α of $f[\alpha, \beta]$:

1. For any $\mathbf{b}$ with $w(\mathbf{b}) = w$, we must have $w(\mathbf{d}) \geq n - w + 1$.
2. Every $(n - w + 1) \times (n - w)$ submatrix of N_α has rank $(n - w)$.

In this case, N however is not MDS and has branch number 6. But, we can use the fact that for $w \geq 3$, its branch number is 7.

Indeed when $w < 3$, we must have $w(\mathbf{d}) \geq 6 - w > 3$. Consequently arguing similarly to the proof of Lemma 9, we see that instead of requiring that every $(7 - w) \times (6 - w)$ submatrix of N have rank $(6 - w)$, we instead require that each $(6 - w) \times (6 - w)$ submatrix of N must have rank $6 - w$. This is true since for $w < 3$, all $(6 - w) \times (6 - w)$ submatrices of N have full rank by design.

For $w \geq 3$, since N has branch number 7, we only require that each $(7 - w) \times (6 - w)$ have rank $6 - w$, which is indeed true by Lemma 12.   □

8.3 ε-Δuniversality of Multi-265

Theorem 3. *multi-265 is 2^{-154}-Δuniversal.*

Proof. From Lemmas 10 and 13, it follows that $\mathrm{MIP}_{\text{f-265}} \leq \frac{2}{p^6}$ and $\mathrm{MDP}_{\text{f-265}} \leq \frac{1}{p^6}$. Now, since $\frac{2}{p^6} = \frac{2}{(2^{26}-5)^6} \leq 2^{-154}$, it follows from Theorem 1 that multi-265 is 2^{-154}-Δuniversal.   □

8.4   Implementation Aspects

Multi-265 can be implemented on any platform with SIMD architecture. These instructions process vectors of the same type elements that are packed together in parallel. As a result, operations like addition, multiplication etc. can be performed on multiple entries at the same time and this increases the performance of the implementation. Newer SIMD architecture has 128-bit vector registers that can be seen as 16, 8, 4, or 2 elements with size 8, 16, 32, and 64 bits respectively by defining the arrangement-specifier accordingly. This specifier determines the packing unit of data.

A message block being an element of $\mathbb{F}_p^{12}$ can be treated as 288-bits since $p = 2^{26} - 5$. Now, each message block can be stored in 3 128-bit vector registers. Thus, a rearranging procedure is done after loading each block of message from memory. The first byte of each 32-bit word in the Neon vectors is set to zero and the remaining 3-bytes are filled with the corresponding 3-bytes of the message block.

Each 32-bit word contains 24-bits of data initially. So we can defer modular reductions for all the linear operations to the output of each call to f-265 and we are only required to do 12 modular reductions at the end of each round. Moreover our choice of prime $p = 2^{26} - 5$, being a pseudo mersenne prime, means that the reduction can be done very efficiently [13].

The reference code for multi-265 in a keyless setting is available at https://github.com/KoustabhGhosh/Multi-265.

Acknowledgements. Koustabh Ghosh is supported by the Netherlands Organisation for Scientific Research (NWO) under TOP grant TOP1.18.002 SCALAR, Joan Daemen and Jonathan Fuchs are supported by the European Research Council under the ERC advanced grant agreement under grant ERC-2017-ADG Nr. 788980 ESCADA and Parisa Amiri Eliasi is supported by the Cryptography Research Center of the Technology Innovation Institute (TII), Abu Dhabi (UAE), under the TII-Radboud project with title Evaluation and Implementation of Lightweight Cryptographic Primitives and Protocols.

References

1. Albrecht, M., Grassi, L., Rechberger, C., Roy, A., Tiessen, T.: MiMC: efficient encryption and cryptographic hashing with minimal multiplicative complexity. In: Cheon, J.H., Takagi, T. (eds.) ASIACRYPT 2016, Part I. LNCS, vol. 10031, pp. 191–219. Springer, Heidelberg (2016). https://doi.org/10.1007/978-3-662-53887-6_7

2. Bellare, M., Canetti, R., Krawczyk, H.: Keying hash functions for message authentication. In: Koblitz, N. (ed.) CRYPTO 1996. LNCS, vol. 1109, pp. 1–15. Springer, Heidelberg (1996). https://doi.org/10.1007/3-540-68697-5_1

3. Bellare, M., Kilian, J., Rogaway, P.: The security of cipher block chaining. In: Desmedt, Y.G. (ed.) CRYPTO 1994. LNCS, vol. 839, pp. 341–358. Springer, Heidelberg (1994). https://doi.org/10.1007/3-540-48658-5_32

4. Bernstein, D.J.: The Poly1305-AES message-authentication code. In: Gilbert, H., Handschuh, H. (eds.) FSE 2005. LNCS, vol. 3557, pp. 32–49. Springer, Heidelberg (2005). https://doi.org/10.1007/11502760_3

5. Bertoni, G., Daemen, J., Hoffert, S., Peeters, M., Assche, G.V., Keer, R.V.: The authenticated encryption schemes Kravatte-SANE and Kravatte-SANSE. IACR Cryptol. ePrint Arch., p. 1012 (2018)

6. Black, J., Rogaway, P.: CBC MACs for arbitrary-length messages: the three-key constructions. In: Bellare, M. (ed.) CRYPTO 2000. LNCS, vol. 1880, pp. 197–215. Springer, Heidelberg (2000). https://doi.org/10.1007/3-540-44598-6_12

7. Black, J., Rogaway, P.: A block-cipher mode of operation for parallelizable message authentication. In: Knudsen, L.R. (ed.) EUROCRYPT 2002. LNCS, vol. 2332, pp. 384–397. Springer, Heidelberg (2002). https://doi.org/10.1007/3-540-46035-7_25

8. Daemen, J., Hoffert, S., Assche, G.V., Keer, R.V.: The design of Xoodoo and Xoofff. IACR Trans. Symmetric Cryptol. **2018**(4), 1–38 (2018)

9. Daemen, J., Rijmen, V.: The Pelican MAC Function. IACR Cryptol. ePrint Arch., p. 88 (2005)

10. Daemen, J., Rijmen, V.: The Design of Rijndael - The Advanced Encryption Standard (AES). Information Security and Cryptography, 2nd edn. Springer, Cham (2020)

11. Fuchs, J., Rotella, Y., Daemen, J.: On the security of keyed hashing based on an unkeyed block function. IACR Cryptol. ePrint Arch., p. 1172 (2022)

12. Grassi, L., Rechberger, C., Rotaru, D., Scholl, P., Smart, N.P.: MPC-friendly symmetric key primitives. In: Proceedings of the 2016 ACM SIGSAC Conference on Computer and Communications Security, Vienna, Austria, 24–28 October 2016, pp. 430–443. ACM (2016)

13. Greuet, A., Montoya, S., Vermeersch, C.: Quotient approximation modular reduction. Cryptology ePrint Archive, Paper 2022/411 (2022)

14. Ishai, Y., Sahai, A., Wagner, D.: Private circuits: securing hardware against probing attacks. In: Boneh, D. (ed.) CRYPTO 2003. LNCS, vol. 2729, pp. 463–481. Springer, Heidelberg (2003). https://doi.org/10.1007/978-3-540-45146-4_27

15. Kocher, P., Jaffe, J., Jun, B.: Differential power analysis. In: Wiener, M. (ed.) CRYPTO 1999. LNCS, vol. 1666, pp. 388–397. Springer, Heidelberg (1999). https://doi.org/10.1007/3-540-48405-1_25

16. McGrew, D.A., Viega, J.: The security and performance of the galois/counter mode (GCM) of operation. In: Canteaut, A., Viswanathan, K. (eds.) INDOCRYPT 2004. LNCS, vol. 3348, pp. 343–355. Springer, Heidelberg (2004). https://doi.org/10.1007/978-3-540-30556-9_27

17. Nikova, S., Rijmen, V., Schläffer, M.: Secure hardware implementation of nonlinear functions in the presence of glitches. J. Cryptol. **24**(2), 292–321 (2011)

18. Shoup, V.: On fast and provably secure message authentication based on universal hashing. In: Koblitz, N. (ed.) CRYPTO 1996. LNCS, vol. 1109, pp. 313–328. Springer, Heidelberg (1996). https://doi.org/10.1007/3-540-68697-5_24

19. Stinson, D.R.: On the connections between universal hashing, combinatorial designs and error-correcting codes. Electron. Colloquium Comput. Complex. **TR95-052** (1995)

20. Wegman, M.N., Carter, J.: New hash functions and their use in authentication and set equality. J. Comput. Syst. Sci. **22**(3), 265–279 (1981)

Invertible Quadratic Non-linear Functions over $\mathbb{F}_p^n$ via Multiple Local Maps

Ginevra Giordani[1] , Lorenzo Grassi[2,3] , Silvia Onofri[4(✉)] ,
and Marco Pedicini[5]

[1] Università degli Studi dell'Aquila, L'Aquila, Italy
`ginevra.giordani@graduate.univaq.it`
[2] Ruhr University Bochum, Bochum, Germany
`Lorenzo.Grassi@ruhr-uni-bochum.de`
[3] Ponos Technology, Zug, Switzerland
[4] Scuola Normale Superiore, Pisa, Italy
`silvia.onofri@sns.it`
[5] Università degli Studi Roma Tre, Rome, Italy
`marco.pedicini@uniroma3.it`

Abstract. The construction of invertible non-linear layers over $\mathbb{F}_p^n$ that minimize the multiplicative cost is crucial for the design of symmetric primitives targeting Multi Party Computation (MPC), Zero-Knowledge proofs (ZK), and Fully Homomorphic Encryption (FHE). At the current state of the art, only few non-linear functions are known to be invertible over $\mathbb{F}_p$, as the power maps $x \mapsto x^d$ for $\gcd(d, p-1) = 1$. When working over $\mathbb{F}_p^n$ for $n \geq 2$, a possible way to construct invertible non-linear layers $\mathcal{S}$ over $\mathbb{F}_p^n$ is by making use of a local map $F : \mathbb{F}_p^m \to \mathbb{F}_p$ for $m \leq n$, that is, $\mathcal{S}_F(x_0, x_1, \ldots, x_{n-1}) = y_0 \| y_1 \| \ldots \| y_{n-1}$ where $y_i = F(x_i, x_{i+1}, \ldots, x_{i+m-1})$. This possibility has been recently studied by Grassi, Onofri, Pedicini and Sozzi at FSE/ToSC 2022. Given a quadratic local map $F : \mathbb{F}_p^m \to \mathbb{F}_p$ for $m \in \{1, 2, 3\}$, they proved that the shift-invariant non-linear function $\mathcal{S}_F$ over $\mathbb{F}_p^n$ defined as before is never invertible for any $n \geq 2 \cdot m - 1$.

In this paper, we face the problem by generalizing such construction. Instead of a single local map, we admit multiple local maps, and we study the creation of nonlinear layers that can be efficiently verified and implemented by a similar shift-invariant lifting. After formally defining the construction, we focus our analysis on the case $\mathcal{S}_{F_0,F_1}(x_0, x_1, \ldots, x_{n-1}) = y_0 \| y_1 \| \ldots \| y_{n-1}$ for $F_0, F_1 : \mathbb{F}_p^2 \to \mathbb{F}_p$ of degree at most 2. This is a generalization of the previous construction using two alternating functions F_0, F_1 instead of a single F. As main result, we prove that (i) if $n \geq 3$, then $\mathcal{S}_{F_0,F_1}$ is never invertible if both F_0 and F_1 are quadratic, and that (ii) if $n \geq 4$, then $\mathcal{S}_{F_0,F_1}$ is invertible if and only if it is a Type-II Feistel scheme.

Keywords: Invertible Quadratic Functions · Local Maps · Type-II Feistel

N. El Mrabet et al. (Eds.): AFRICACRYPT 2023, LNCS 14064, pp. 151–176, 2023.
https://doi.org/10.1007/978-3-031-37679-5_7

1 Introduction

The study of substitutive transformations in the Boolean case (the S-Boxes), $\mathcal{S}: \mathbb{F}_2^n \to \mathbb{F}_2^n$ has led to the discovery of many families of functions with properties crucial to cryptography, including non-linearity [28], algebraic immunity [27], and arithmetic complexity. These properties play a significant role in cryptography, as they can be used to design cryptographic functions with desirable security properties. From the cryptographic point of view, important classes of non-linear functions include the (almost) perfect non-linear ((A)PN) ones [28,29]. Given a function $\mathcal{F}$ over $\mathbb{F}_2^n$, let

$$\Delta_{\mathcal{F}} := \max_{a \neq 0, b \in \mathbb{F}_2^n} |\{x \in \mathbb{F}_2^n \mid \mathcal{F}(x+a) + \mathcal{F}(x) = b\}|.$$

$\mathcal{F}$ is said to be $\Delta_{\mathcal{F}}$-differentially uniform. In particular, $\mathcal{F}$ is perfect non-linear if $\Delta_{\mathcal{F}} = 1$, and almost perfect non-linear if $\Delta_{\mathcal{F}} = 2$.

Finding APN functions for n odd is easy. For example, APN functions include the Gold map [17] $x \mapsto x^{2^l+1}$ for $\gcd(l,n) = 1$, the inverse map [5] $x \mapsto x^{-1} \equiv x^{2l}$ for $n = 2l+1$, and many others. However, finding APN permutations for n even is less trivial. In fact, when $n \geq 8$ is even, this task is an open problem which has been nicknamed the *Big APN Problem*. Several works have been carried on in order to solve it, including [4,8–12] among many others.

The research of APN functions is justified by the fact that, if used as S-Boxes, APN functions provide optimal resilience against differential attacks [6]. Given pairs of inputs with some fixed input differences, differential cryptanalysis considers the probability distribution of the corresponding output differences produced by the cryptographic primitive. Hence, it is natural to consider functions with low differential probability for preventing it. At the same time, it is well known that the security against differential (and more generally, statistical) attacks is achieved by a combination of the linear and the non-linear layers. As a concrete example, consider the case of the wide-trail design strategy [14], proposed by Daemen and Rijmen for designing the round transformation of key-alternating block ciphers that combines efficiency and resistance against linear and differential cryptanalysis. Instead of spending most of its resources for looking for large S-Boxes with "good" statistical properties, the wide-trail strategy aims at designing the round transformation(s) in order to maximize the minimum number of active S-Boxes over multiple rounds. Thus, in symmetric primitives designed by the wide trail strategy, the idea is to look for linear layers that guarantee a large number of active S-Boxes over several rounds. This fact together with the existence of 4-differentially uniform invertible functions for every $n \geq 3$ may imply that the big APN problem previously recalled could be considered a more theoretical rather than a practical open problem in symmetric cryptography.

At the opposite, the research of low-multiplicative[1] non-linear functions over prime fields $\mathbb{F}_p$ for $p \geq 3$ prime is currently very relevant for symmetric encryp-

---

[1] In this paper, we use the term "$\mathbb{F}_p$-multiplication" – or simply, "multiplication" – to refer to a non-linear operation over $\mathbb{F}_p$.

tion schemes designed for applications like Multi Party Computation (MPC), Zero-Knowledge proofs (ZK), and Fully Homomorphic Encryption (FHE). MPC allows different users that do not necessarily trust each other to evaluate a function on a shared secret without revealing it. FHE allows a user to operate on encrypted data without decrypting them. Finally, ZK is a technique that allows to authenticate a secret information without disclosing it. The number of possible applications of these techniques is countless, including e.g. crypto-currency as probably the most well known one. In the recent years, several symmetric primitives over prime fields have been proposed for these applications, including MiMC [2], GMiMC [1], *Rescue* [3], HADESMiMC/POSEIDON [22], Ciminion [15], PASTA [16], REINFORCED CONCRETE [21], NEPTUNE [24], GRIFFIN [20], Anemoi [7], HYDRA [25], among others.

These MPC-/FHE-/ZK-friendly symmetric primitives are characterized by the following:

- they are usually defined over prime fields $\mathbb{F}_p^t$ for a huge prime $p \approx 2^{128}$ (or even bigger), whereas classical schemes are defined over binary fields $\mathbb{F}_2^n$;
- they can be described via a simple algebraic expression over their natural field, whereas classical schemes usually admit a very complex algebraic structure.

In order to be efficient in MPC, FHE, and ZK protocols/applications, the number of multiplications or/and the multiplication depth necessary to evaluate/verify the considered symmetric primitive should be minimum. Moreover, besides that, unlike the case of traditional primitives, the size of the field over which the scheme is defined does not impact the cost of the performed operations. Apart from that, due to the large size of the field p, any sub-component (as the non-linear S-Boxes) that defines the symmetric primitive must be computed on the fly, that is, it cannot be pre-computed and stored as a look-up table. In both cases, a simple algebraic structure is in general the most convenient choice for achieving the best possible performances.

At the current state of the art, only few invertible non-linear functions over prime fields are known, recalled in the following section. In this paper, we analyze the possibility to set up invertible quadratic functions over $\mathbb{F}_p^n$ for MPC-/FHE-/ZK-friendly symmetric schemes via cyclic shift-invariant functions induced by multiple local maps.

1.1 Related Works: Shift-Invariant Lifting Functions Induced by a Local Map

Well known examples of invertible non-linear functions over $\mathbb{F}_p$ for a prime integer $p \geq 3$ include (i) the power maps $x \mapsto x^d$, which are invertible if and only if $\gcd(d, p - 1) = 1$, and (ii) the Dickson polynomials

$$x \mapsto \mathcal{D}_\alpha(x) := \sum_{i=0}^{\lfloor \frac{d}{2} \rfloor} \frac{d}{d - i} \binom{d - i}{i} (-\alpha)^i x^{d-2i},$$

which are invertible for $\gcd(d, p^2 - 1) = 1$. Other classes of invertible non-linear functions constructed via the Legendre symbol and/or the $x \mapsto (-1)^x$ function have been recently proposed in [23,31], but it is currently not clear if they can be efficiently used for MPC, FHE, and ZK protocols/applications.

When working over $\mathbb{F}_p^n$ for $n \geq 2$, a possible way to set up non-linear invertible functions is by exploiting the Feistel and/or the Lai-Massey [19,26,32] approach. Another approach has been recently considered by Grassi et al. [24] at FSE/ToSC 2022, and it is inspired by the chi-function, which was introduced in the setting of cellular automata cryptography in [33] and studied by Joan Daemen in his PhD thesis "Cipher and Hash Function Design Strategies based on linear and differential cryptanalysis" [13]. The chi-function over $\mathbb{F}_2^n$ is a nonlinear shift-invariant transformation (i.e., a transformation which does not change its output when the input is shifted) that can be defined in terms of the local map $\chi(x_0, x_1, x_2) = x_0 \oplus (x_1 \oplus 1) \cdot x_2$. The *shift-invariant* chi-transformation is then applied to a binary sequence by taking triplets of the input sequence, with bits from the beginning of the sequence being used when the end of the input sequence is reached.

The general scheme with a single local map $F : \mathbb{F}_p^m \rightarrow \mathbb{F}_p$ is specified as the substitutive transformation over $\mathbb{F}_p^n$ such that for each $(x_0, x_1, \ldots, x_{n-1}) \in \mathbb{F}_p^n$, we have

$$\mathcal{S}_F(x_0, x_1, \ldots, x_{n-1}) := y_0 \| y_1 \| \ldots \| y_{n-1} \quad \text{where} \quad y_i = F(x_0, x_1, \ldots, x_{m-1}).$$

In [24], authors proved that, given any quadratic function $F : \mathbb{F}_p^2 \rightarrow \mathbb{F}_p$, the corresponding function $\mathcal{S}_F$ over $\mathbb{F}_p^n$ for $n \geq 3$ as defined in Definition 3 is never invertible. An equivalent similar result holds when considering quadratic functions $F : \mathbb{F}_p^3 \rightarrow \mathbb{F}_p$ and the corresponding function $\mathcal{S}_F$ over $\mathbb{F}_p^n$ for $n \geq 5$.

Later on, Grassi considered the possibility to exploit non-invertible non-linear functions as building blocks for MPC-/FHE-/ZK-friendly schemes *in which the internal state is obfuscated by a secret (e.g., a secret key)*. In [18], he proved that the function $\mathcal{S}_F$ induced by $F : \mathbb{F}_p^2 \rightarrow \mathbb{F}_p$ defined as $F(x_0, x_1) = x_0^2 + x_1$ (or equivalent) minimizes the probability that a collision occurs among all $\mathcal{S}_F$ over $\mathbb{F}_p^n$ induced by any quadratic function $F : \mathbb{F}_p^m \rightarrow \mathbb{F}_p$ for $m \in \{1, 2\}$. Such probability is upper bounded by p^{-n}.

1.2   Our Contribution

The just mentioned recent results by Grassi concerning non-invertible non-linear functions cannot be used for setting up symmetric primitives in which the internal state is *not* obfuscated by a secret, as the case of a sponge hash function. Indeed, the absence of a secret key could potentially allow the attacker to control the inputs in order to ensure that they trigger a collision. Hence, the problem of constructing invertible non-linear functions with minimal multiplicative complexity remains crucial.

In this paper we adopt the same design to extend the construction: *instead of a single local map, we admit multiple local maps, and we study the creation of nonlinear layers that can be efficiently verified and implemented by a similar shift-invariant lifting.* The general scheme with multiple local maps is specified as

$$\mathcal{S}_{F_0,F_1,\ldots,F_{n-1}}(x_0,x_1,\ldots,x_{n-1}) := y_0\|y_1\|\cdots\|y_{n-1}$$

where

$$y_i = F_i(x_0,x_1,\ldots,x_{m-1}) \qquad \text{for each } i \in \{0,\ldots,n-1\}$$

and $F_i : \mathbb{F}_p^m \to \mathbb{F}_p$ are possibly distinct functions. Instead of working with a generic function $\mathcal{S}$, in this paper we limit ourselves to consider the case in which each value y_i is specified by cyclically using h fixed local maps $F_0,F_1,\ldots,F_h :$ $\mathbb{F}_p^m \to \mathbb{F}_p$ which depend on m components of the domain vector $x_0,x_1,\ldots,x_{n-1}$ for $m \leq n$, also these variables are taken by shifting the components, namely:

$$y_i = F_{i \bmod h}(x_i,x_{i+1},\ldots x_{i+m-1}),$$

where indices of variables x_i are taken modulo n. We distinguish the case $h = 2$ that we call the *alternating shift-invariant lifting* (ASI-liftings), from the case $h > 2$ that we call *cyclic shift-invariant lifting* (CSI-liftings), see Definition 3 in Sect. 2. In there, we give a notion of similarity between families of local maps for which invertibility holds for the entire equivalent class, which allows us to simplify the proof of invertibility of ASI-liftings to a representative function of the equivalence class.

In this paper, we limit ourselvses to consider the case $h = 2$ with $F_0,F_1 :$ $\mathbb{F}_p^2 \to \mathbb{F}_p$ both quadratic, or one linear and one quadratic. In such a case, we prove that the Feistel Type-II functions [30,34] are the *only* ones in which the scheme we called alternating shift-invariant lifting functions is invertible over $\mathbb{F}_p^n$. More formally, our main result can be summarized as following:

Theorem 1. *Let $p \geq 3$ be a prime integer, and let $n \geq 3$. Let $F_0,F_1 : \mathbb{F}_p^2 \to \mathbb{F}_p$ be two functions. Let $\mathcal{S}_{F_0,F_1} : \mathbb{F}_p^n \to \mathbb{F}_p$ be defined as $\mathcal{S}_{F_0,F_1}(x_0,x_1,\ldots,x_{n-1}) :=$ $y_0\|y_1\|\cdots\|y_{n-1}$ where*

$$y_i = F_{i \bmod 2}(x_i,x_{i+1},\ldots,x_{i+m-1}) \qquad \text{for each } i \in \{0,1,\ldots,n-1\}.$$

Then:

- *if F_0 and F_1 are both of degree 2, then $\mathcal{S}_{F_0,F_1}$ is never invertible;*
- *if F_0 is linear and F_1 is quadratic, then $\mathcal{S}_{F_0,F_1}$ is invertible for $n \geq 4$ if and only if it is a Feistel Type-II function, e.g.,*

$$y_i = \begin{cases} x_{i-1} & \text{if } i \text{ odd} \\ x_{i-1} + x_{i-2}^2 & \text{otherwise (if } i \text{ even)} \end{cases}.$$

If $n = 3$, $\mathcal{S}_{F_0,F_1}$ is invertible also in the case in which F_0 is a linear function of the form $F_0(x_0,x_1) = \alpha_{1,0;0} \cdot x_0 + \alpha_{0,1;0} \cdot x_1$ with $\alpha_{1,0;0},\alpha_{0,1;0} \neq 0$, and F_1 is a quadratic function of the form $F_1(x_0,x_1) = \gamma \cdot \left(\frac{\alpha_{0,1;0}}{\alpha_{1,0;0}} \cdot x_0 - \frac{\alpha_{1,0;0}}{\alpha_{0,1;0}} \cdot x_1 \right)^2 + \alpha_{1,0;1} \cdot x_0 + \alpha_{0,1;1} \cdot x_1$, where $\gamma \in \mathbb{F}_p$ and $\alpha_{1,0;1} \cdot \alpha_{1,0;0}^2 \neq -\alpha_{0,1;1} \cdot \alpha_{0,1;0}^2$.

Note that we focus on the case $n \geq 3$, since there exist *invertible* SI-lifting functions $\mathcal{S}_F(x_0, x_1)$ over $\mathbb{F}_p^2$ induced by quadratic local maps $F : \mathbb{F}_p^2 \to \mathbb{F}_p$, as $F(x_0, x_1) = \gamma_2 \cdot (x_0 - x_1)^2 + \gamma_1 \cdot x_1 + \gamma_0 \cdot x_0$, with $\gamma_0 \neq \pm\gamma_1$ and $\gamma_2 \neq 0$ – see [24] for details.

The proof of the previous Theorem is divided in two parts:

– in Sect. 4, we study the case where both F_0, F_1 are quadratic;
– in Sect. 5, we study the mixed case, where one function is linear and the other one is quadratic.

The problem of setting up a substitutive transformation quadratic and invertible over $\mathbb{F}_p^n$ for generic prime $p \geq 3$ and n remains open. Potential ideas for solving this problem are discussed in Sect. 6.

2   Preliminary: Notation and Related Works

2.1   Notation

From now on, let $p \geq 3$ be a prime number. Let $\mathbb{F}_p$ denote the field of integer numbers modulo p. We use small letters to denote either parameters/indexes or variables and greek letters to denote fixed elements in $\mathbb{F}_p$. Given $x \in \mathbb{F}_p^n$, we denote by x_i its i-th component for each $i \in \{0, 1, \ldots, n-1\}$, that is, $x = (x_0, x_1, \ldots, x_{n-1})$. We use capital letters to denote functions from $\mathbb{F}_p^m$ to $\mathbb{F}_p$ for $m \geq 1$, e.g., $F : \mathbb{F}_p^m \to \mathbb{F}_p$ and the calligraphic font to denote functions over $\mathbb{F}_p^n$ for $n \geq 1$, e.g., $\mathcal{S} : \mathbb{F}_p^n \to \mathbb{F}_p^n$. Given a matrix $M^T \in \mathbb{F}_p^{c \times r}$, we denote by $M^T \in^{c \times r}$ its transpose. We formally define the term "collision" as:

Definition 1 (Collision). *Let $\mathbb{F}$ be a generic field, and let $\mathcal{F}$ be a function defined over $\mathbb{F}^n$ for $n \geq 1$. A pair $x, y \in \mathbb{F}^n$ is a collision for $\mathcal{F}$ if and only if $\mathcal{F}(x) = \mathcal{F}(y)$ and $x \neq y$.*

2.2   Related Works: Invertibility of $\mathcal{S}_F$ over $\mathbb{F}_p^n$ via a Quadratic Local Map $F : \mathbb{F}_p^m \to \mathbb{F}_p$

As already mentioned in the introduction, Grassi et al. [24] studied the invertibility of *shift-invariant lifting functions*:

Definition 2 (Shift-Invariant lifting). *Let $p \geq 3$ be a prime integer, and let $1 \leq m \leq n$. Let $F : \mathbb{F}_p^m \to \mathbb{F}_p$ be a local map. The shift-invariant lifting (SI–lifting) function $\mathcal{S}_F$ over $\mathbb{F}_p^n$ induced by the local map F is defined as*

$$\mathcal{S}_F(x_0, \ldots, x_{n-1}) = y_0\|y_1\|\ldots\|y_{n-1} \quad \text{such that} \quad y_i = F(x_i, \ldots, x_{i+m-1})$$

where indexes i of x_i are taken modulo n.

In particular, they considered shift-invariant lifting functions $\mathcal{S}_F$ induced over $\mathbb{F}_p^n$ by a *quadratic* local map $F : \mathbb{F}_p^m \to \mathbb{F}_p$ for $m \in \{2, 3\}$. As a main result, they proved the following theorem regarding the impossibility to set up permutations for (i) $m = 2$ and $n \geq 3$ and (ii) $m = 3$ and $n \geq 5$. More formally,

Theorem 2 ([24, **Theorems 2 & 3**]). *Let $p \geq 3$ be a prime integer, and let $1 \leq m \leq n$. Given $F : \mathbb{F}_p^m \to \mathbb{F}_p$ a quadratic local map, then the SI–lifting function $\mathcal{S}_F$ induced by F over $\mathbb{F}_p^n$ is not invertible neither if $m = 2$ and $n \geq 3$ nor if $m = 3$ and $n \geq 5$.*

For the cases $(m,n) \in \{(2,2),(3,3),(3,4)\}$ they presented some local quadratic maps F for which $\mathcal{S}_F$ over $\mathbb{F}_p^n$ is invertible. In particular, in the case $(m,n) = (2,2)$, invertibility can be achieved *only* with the shift-invariant lifting induced by a local map having the Lai–Massey structure:

Lemma 1 ([24, **Proposition 8**]). *Let $G : \mathbb{F}_p^2 \to \mathbb{F}_p$ a quadratic local map. Let $\gamma_0, \gamma_1 \in \mathbb{F}_p$ be such that $\gamma_0 \neq \pm\gamma_1$. The shift-invariant lifting function $\mathcal{S}_G$ induced by G over $\mathbb{F}_p^n$ is invertible if and only if*

$$G(x_0, x_1) = \gamma_0 \cdot x_0 + \gamma_1 \cdot x_1 + \gamma_2 \cdot (x_0 - x_1)^2.$$

3 Alternating/Cyclic Shift-Invariant Lifting Functions via Multiple Local Maps

In this section, we introduce the concept of shift-invariant functions induced by *multiple* local maps, which generalizes the shift-invariant lifting functions recalled before.

Definition 3 (Cyclic Shift-Invariant Lifting). *Let $p \geq 3$ be a prime integer and let $1 \leq m, h \leq n$. For each $i \in \{0, 1, \ldots, h - 1\}$, let $F_i : \mathbb{F}_p^m \to \mathbb{F}_p$ be a local map. The cyclic shift-invariant lifting (CSI-lifting) function $\mathcal{S}_{F_0, F_1, \ldots, F_{h-1}}$ induced by the family of local maps $(F_0, \ldots, F_{h-1})$ over $\mathbb{F}_p^n$ is defined as*

$$\mathcal{S}(x_0, x_1, \ldots, x_{n-1}) = y_0 \| y_1 \| \ldots \| y_{n-1} \qquad where$$
$$y_i := F_{i \bmod h}(x_i, x_{i+1}, \ldots, x_{i+m-1})$$

for each $i \in \{0, 1, \ldots, n - 1\}$, where the sub-indexes are taken modulo n.

For the follow-up, we use a notation similar to the one introduced in [24], that is, we denote the d-degree local map F_j as

$$F_j(x_0, x_1, \ldots, x_{m-1}) := \sum_{\substack{0 \leq i_0, \ldots, i_{m-1} \leq d \text{ s.t.} \\ i_0 + \ldots + i_{m-1} \leq d}} \alpha_{i_0, \ldots, i_{m-1}; j} \cdot x_0^{i_0} \cdot \ldots \cdot x_{m-1}^{i_{m-1}} \qquad (1)$$

for each $j \in \{0, 1, \ldots, h - 1\}$.

The previous definition corresponds to the one proposed in [24] for the case $h = 1$. In there, it was pointed out that the function $\mathcal{S}_F$ is shift-invariant in the sense that $\mathcal{S}_F \circ \Pi = \Pi \circ \mathcal{S}_F$ for each *translation permutation* Π over $\mathbb{F}_p^n$, that is, a map Π over $\mathbb{F}_p^n$ defined as

$$\Pi(x_0, x_1, \ldots, x_{n-1}) := x_{\pi(0)} \| x_{\pi(1)} \| \ldots \| x_{\pi(n-1)} \qquad where$$
$$\forall j \in \{0, 1, \ldots, n - 1\} : \qquad \pi(j) := j + i \mod n$$

for a certain $i \in \{0, 1, \ldots, n-1\}$. Here, a similar property holds. The function $\mathcal{S}_{F_0,F_1,\ldots F_{h-1}}$ is "cyclic shift-invariant" in the sense that

$$\Pi \circ \mathcal{S}_{F_0,F_1,\ldots,F_{h-1}}(x) = \mathcal{S}_{F_{\pi(0)},F_{\pi(1)},\ldots,F_{\pi(h-1)}} \circ \Pi(x)$$

where the sub-indexes of F are computed modulo h. Hence, note that the π in the sub-index of F is useless if i is a multiple of h (as for the case $h = 1$).

In the rest of the paper, we mainly focus on the case $h = 2$, i.e., functions $\mathcal{S}_{F_0,F_1}(x_0, x_1, \ldots, x_{n-1}) = y_0 \| y_1 \| \ldots \| y_{n-1}$ where

$$y_i = \begin{cases} F_0(x_i, x_{i+1}, \ldots, x_{i+m-1}) & \text{if } i \text{ is even} \\ F_1(x_i, x_{i+1}, \ldots, x_{i+m-1}) & \text{otherwise (if } i \text{ is odd)} \end{cases} \tag{2}$$

for each $i \in \{0, 1, \ldots, n-1\}$, where the sub-indexes of x_i are taken modulo n. We refer to the alternating shift-invariant function $\mathcal{S}_{F_0,F_1}$ over $\mathbb{F}_p^n$ defined via the local maps $F_0 : \mathbb{F}_p^m \to \mathbb{F}_p$ and $F_1 : \mathbb{F}_p^m \to \mathbb{F}_p$ as the "alternating shift-invariant (m,n)-lifting $\mathcal{S}_{F_0,F_1}$ induced by the pair (F_0, F_1)" (for simplicity, we usually make use of the abbreviation "ASI-lifting function $\mathcal{S}_{F_0,F_1}$").

3.1 Balanced Functions and Class of Equivalence

First, we recall the definition of balanced functions in order to prove a necessary condition for $\mathcal{S}_{F_0,F_1,\ldots,F_{h-1}}$ to be invertible. As first thing, we recall a necessary condition that the functions $F_0, F_1, \ldots, F_{h-1}$ must satisfy for $\mathcal{S}_{F_0,F_1,\ldots,F_{h-1}}$ being invertible.

Definition 4 (Balanced Function). *Let $p \geq 3$ be a prime integer and let $F : \mathbb{F}_p^m \to \mathbb{F}_p$. We say that F is **balanced** if and only if*

$$\forall y \in \mathbb{F}_p : \qquad |\{x \in \mathbb{F}_p^m \mid F(x) = y\}| = p^{m-1}.$$

Proposition 1. *Let $p \geq 3$ be a prime integer, and let $1 \leq m, h \leq n$. Let $\mathcal{S}_{F_0,F_1,\ldots,F_{h-1}} : \mathbb{F}_p^n \to \mathbb{F}_p^n$ be the cyclic shift-invariant lifting function induced by $F_0, F_1, \ldots, F_{h-1} : \mathbb{F}_p^m \to \mathbb{F}_p$ over $\mathbb{F}_p^n$. If at least one function among $F_0, \ldots, F_{h-1}$ is not balanced, then $\mathcal{S}_{F_0,F_1,\ldots,F_{h-1}}$ is not invertible.*

This is a well known result, and its proof is a simple generalization of the one provided in [24, Proposition 3].

Next, we introduce an equivalence relation for classifying families of local maps with similar properties that generalizes the one given in [24].

Definition 5 (Class of Equivalence). *Let $p \geq 3$ be a prime integer, and let $1 \leq m, h \leq n$. Let $\{F_i : \mathbb{F}_p^m \to \mathbb{F}_p\}_{1 \leq i < h}$ and $\{F_i' : \mathbb{F}_p^m \to \mathbb{F}_p\}_{1 \leq i < h}$ two indexed sets of functions. We say that the two indexed sets of functions are **similar** – denoted as $(F_0, F_1, \ldots, F_{h-1}) \sim (F_0', F_1', \ldots, F_{h-1}')$ – if and only if there exist*

- *a factor $\mu \in \mathbb{F}_p \setminus \{0\}$;*
- *a vector $\bar{\nu} = \nu \| \nu \| \ldots \| \nu \in \mathbb{F}_p^m$;*

– h values $\omega_i \in \mathbb{F}_p \setminus \{0\}$ and h values $\psi_i \in \mathbb{F}_p$ for $i \in \{0, 1, \ldots, h-1\}$;

such that we have

$$F_i'(x) = \omega_i \cdot F_i(\mu \cdot x + \bar{\nu}) + \psi_i \qquad \text{for all } x \in \mathbb{F}_p^m \text{ and for any integer } 0 \le i < h.$$

The following holds:

Lemma 2. *The relation $\sim$ introduced in Definition 5 is an equivalence relation, i.e., it satisfies the following properties: reflexivity, symmetry, and transitivity.*

The proof of this Lemma is equivalent to the one given in [24], where similarity relation is shown to be an equivalence relation.

We show that in the case of cyclic shift-invariant lifting functions, invertibility is an invariant by similarity of the two families of functions which induce the lifting:

Proposition 2. *Let $p \ge 3$ be a prime integer, and let $1 \le m, h \le n$. Let $F_0, F_1, \ldots, F_{h-1} : \mathbb{F}_p^m \to \mathbb{F}_p$ and $F_0', F_1', \ldots, F_{h-1}' : \mathbb{F}_p^m \to \mathbb{F}_p$ be two similar families of functions. Let*

$$\mathcal{S}_{F_0, F_1, \ldots, F_{h-1}} : \mathbb{F}_p^n \to \mathbb{F}_p^n, \qquad (\text{resp.,} \ \mathcal{S}_{F_0', F_1', \ldots, F_{h-1}'} : \mathbb{F}_p^n \to \mathbb{F}_p^n)$$

be the cyclic SI-lifting function induced by $(F_0, \ldots, F_{h-1})$ (resp., $(F_0', \ldots, F_{h-1}')$). Then, $\mathcal{S}_{F_0, F_1, \ldots, F_{h-1}}$ is invertible if and only if $\mathcal{S}_{F_0', F_1', \ldots, F_{h-1}'}$ is invertible.

Proof. By definition of F_i' and $\mathcal{S}_{F_i'}$, we have that

$$[\mathcal{S}_{F_i'}(x_0, \ldots, x_{n-1})]_i = F_i'(x_i, \ldots, x_{i+m-1}),$$

where the sub-indexes are taken modulo n. Since $F_i'(x) = \omega_i \cdot F_i(\mu \cdot x + \bar{\nu}) + \psi_i$ for each $x \in \mathbb{F}_p^m$, it follows that

$$\mathcal{S}_{F_i'}(x) = \omega_{i \bmod h} \cdot \mathcal{S}_{F_i}(\mu \cdot x + \bar{\nu}) + \bar{\psi}$$

where $\bar{\psi} \in \mathbb{F}_q^n$ such that $\bar{\psi}_i = \psi_{i \bmod h}$. That is, $\mathcal{S}_{F_i'}$ is equal to $\mathcal{S}_{F_i}$ pre-composed and post-composed with two invertible affine functions. This implies that $\mathcal{S}_{F_i'}$ is invertible if and only if $\mathcal{S}_{F_i}$ is invertible.   □

3.2 Necessary Conditions for Quadratic Functions $F_0, F_1, \ldots, F_{h-1} : \mathbb{F}_p^2 \to \mathbb{F}_p$

As next step, we introduce some necessary conditions that the quadratic functions $F_0, F_1, \ldots, F_{h-1} : \mathbb{F}_p^2 \to \mathbb{F}_p$ should satisfy in order to build an invertible alternating or cyclic shift-invariant lifting $\mathcal{S}_{F_0, F_1, \ldots, F_{h-1}}$.

Lemma 3. *Let $p \geq 3$ be a prime integer, and let $n \geq 2$ be an integer. Let $F_0, F_1, \ldots, F_{h-1} : \mathbb{F}_p^2 \to \mathbb{F}_p$ be $1 \leq h \leq n$ be quadratic functions. For each $j \in \{0, 1, \ldots, h-1\}$ and for each $i \in \{0, 1, 2\}$, let*

$$\alpha_j^{(i)} := \sum_{\substack{0 \leq i_0, i_1, \ldots, i_{h-1} \leq i \ s.t. \\ i_0 + i_1 + \ldots + i_{h-1} = i}} \alpha_{i_0, i_1, \ldots, i_{h-1}; j} \tag{3}$$

be the sum of the coefficients of the monomials of degree i of the function F_j.

Let $\mathfrak{I} \subseteq \{0, 1, \ldots, h-1\}$ be the set of indices such that, for each $i \in \mathfrak{I}$, $\alpha_i^{(1)} = \alpha_i^{(2)} = 0$. If

$$\forall i, j \in \{0, 1, \ldots, h-1\} \setminus \mathfrak{I} : \qquad \alpha_j^{(1)} \cdot \alpha_i^{(2)} = \alpha_j^{(2)} \cdot \alpha_i^{(1)},$$

*then the cyclic SI-lifting $\mathcal{S}_{F_0, F_1, \ldots, F_{h-1}}$ over $\mathbb{F}_p^n$ for $n \geq 3$ is **not** invertible.*

Proof. We prove such result by proposing collisions via inputs of the form $(x, x, \ldots, x)$ and $(y, y, \ldots, y)$ for $x \neq y$. A collision occurs if $F_j(x, x) = F_j(y, y)$ for each $j \in \{0, 1, \ldots, h-1\}$. By denoting $d = x - y \neq 0$ and $s = x + y$, these conditions hold if

$$\forall j \in \{0, 1, \ldots, h-1\} : \qquad s \cdot \alpha_j^{(2)} + \alpha_j^{(1)} = 0.$$

It follows that

- if $\alpha_i^{(1)} = \alpha_i^{(2)} = 0$ for a certain $i \in \{0, 1, \ldots, h-1\}$, then such condition is always satisfied independently of s;
- otherwise, if for each $i, j \in \{0, 1, \ldots, h-1\} \setminus \{\mathfrak{I}\}$, there exists $\gamma_{i,j} \in \mathbb{F}_p \setminus \{0\}$ such that (i) $\alpha_j^{(1)} = \gamma_{i,j} \cdot \alpha_i^{(1)}$ and simultaneously (ii) $\alpha_i^{(2)} = \gamma_{i,j} \cdot \alpha_j^{(2)} \neq 0$, then the system reduces to a single equation, and a collision can be found.

Note that the existence of $\gamma_{i,j}$ is equivalent to the condition $\alpha_j^{(1)} \cdot \alpha_i^{(2)} = \alpha_j^{(2)} \cdot \alpha_i^{(1)}$ to hold. $\qquad \square$

Another important requirement is that the quadratic functions $F_0, \ldots, F_{h-1}$ should not depend on a single variable, otherwise the alternating or cyclic shift-invariant lifting $\mathcal{S}_{F_0, \ldots, F_{h-1}}$ is not invertible.

Lemma 4. *Let $p \geq 3$ be a prime integer, and let $n \geq 2$ be an integer. Let $F_0, F_1, \ldots, F_{h-1} : \mathbb{F}_p^2 \to \mathbb{F}_p$ be $1 \leq h \leq n$ quadratic functions. If there exists $l \leq h$ such that the quadratic function F_l depends on a single variable, i.e.,*

$$F_l(x_0, x_1) = \alpha_{2 \cdot (1-i), 2i; l} \cdot x_i^2 + \alpha_{1-i, i; l} \cdot x_i + \alpha_{0, 0; l},$$

*for $i \in \{0, 1\}$ and where $\alpha_{2 \cdot (1-i), i; l} \neq 0$, then the cyclic SI-lifting $\mathcal{S}_{F_0, F_1, \ldots, F_{h-1}}$ defined over $\mathbb{F}_p^n$ for $n \geq 3$ is **not** invertible.*

Proof. As it is well known, a function of the form $x \mapsto \gamma_2 \cdot x^2 + \gamma_1 \cdot x + \gamma_0$ for $\gamma_2 \neq 0$ is not invertible and not balanced (indeed, there are $(p-1)/2$ $\mathbb{F}_p$ elements with two pre-images, $(p-1)/2$ $\mathbb{F}_p$ elements with zero pre-image, and 1 $\mathbb{F}_p$ element with one pre-image). Since this implies that $F_l(x_0, x_1)$ is not balanced as well, we can immediately conclude that $\mathcal{S}_{F_0, F_1, \ldots, F_{h-1}}$ is not invertible due to Proposition 1. $\qquad \square$

4   Invertible Functions $\mathcal{S}_{F_0,F_1}$ over $\mathbb{F}_p^n$ via Quadratic $F_0, F_1 : \mathbb{F}_p^2 \to \mathbb{F}_p$

In this section, we show an impossibility result: given two quadratic local maps $F_0, F_1 : \mathbb{F}_p^2 \to \mathbb{F}_p$, we prove that it is not possible to build an invertible ASI-lifting $\mathcal{S}_{F_0,F_1} : \mathbb{F}_p^n \to \mathbb{F}_p^n$ for $n \geq 3$. We recall that for $n = 2$ there exist quadratic functions for which $\mathcal{S}$ is invertible, e.g., $F_0(x_0, x_1) = F_1(x_0, x_1) = x_0 + (x_0 - x_1)^2$.

The following proposition represents the main result of this section.

Proposition 3. *Let $p \geq 3$ be a prime integer. Let $F_0, F_1 : \mathbb{F}_p^2 \to \mathbb{F}_p$ be two quadratic functions. Then the ASI-lifting $\mathcal{S}_{F_0,F_1}$ over $\mathbb{F}_p^n$ for $n \geq 3$ is **not** invertible.*

We divide the proof of the proposition in two parts:

– the case $n \geq 4$ even in Sect. 4.1;
– the case $n \geq 3$ odd in Sect. 4.2.

We study the case $n \geq 4$ even and the case $n \geq 3$ odd separately since the numbers of repetitions of F_0 and F_1 in $\mathcal{S}_{F_0,F_1}$ is different if n is odd. Then, collisions we find in order to prove the non-invertibility of $\mathcal{S}_{F_0,F_1}$ are slightly different.

4.1   Proof of Proposition 3 for the Case n Even

We separate the proof for the case n even in three lemmas:

– Lemma 5: $\alpha_{1,1;0} \neq 0, \alpha_{1,1;1} \neq 0$;
– Lemma 6: $\alpha_{1,1;0} = 0, \alpha_{1,1;1} \neq 0$ (or $\alpha_{1,1;0} \neq 0, \alpha_{1,1;1} = 0$);
– Lemma 7: $\alpha_{1,1;0} = \alpha_{1,1;1} = 0$.

Together, these lemmas show collisions for each possible ASI-lifting $\mathcal{S}_{F_0,F_1}$ where $F_0, F_1 : \mathbb{F}_p^2 \to \mathbb{F}_p$ are quadratic and $n \geq 4$ is even, proving Proposition 3.

Lemma 5. *Let $p \geq 3$ be a prime integer, and let $n \geq 4$ be an even number. Let F_0, F_1 be two quadratic functions such that $\alpha_{1,1;0} \neq 0, \alpha_{1,1;1} \neq 0$. Then, the corresponding ASI-lifting $\mathcal{S}_{F_0,F_1}$ over $\mathbb{F}_p^n$ is not invertible.*

Proof. Consider inputs $(x_0, x_1, x_2, x_3, \ldots, x_{n-1})$ and $(y_0, y_1, y_2, y_3, \ldots, y_{n-1}) = (x_0, x_1, y_2, x_3, \ldots, x_{n-1})$, i.e., *two inputs that differ only for the values of x_2, y_2, while the others are equal*. Then, the system $\mathcal{S}_{F_0,F_1}(x_0, x_1, x_2, x_3, \ldots, x_{n-1}) = \mathcal{S}_{F_0,F_1}(x_0, x_1, y_2, x_3, \ldots, x_{n-1})$ reduces to the two equations

$$F_1(x_1, x_2) = F_1(x_1, y_2) \quad \text{and} \quad F_0(x_2, x_3) = F_0(y_2, x_3),$$

while the other equations are obviously satisfied (since the inputs are equal). Such two equations are equal to

$$\alpha_{0,2;1} \cdot d_2 \cdot s_2 + \frac{\alpha_{1,1;1}}{2} \cdot d_2 \cdot s_1 + \alpha_{0,1;1} \cdot d_2 = 0,$$

$$\alpha_{2,0;0} \cdot d_2 \cdot s_2 + \frac{\alpha_{1,1;0}}{2} \cdot d_2 \cdot s_3 + \alpha_{1,0;0} \cdot d_2 = 0,$$

via the change of variables

$$d_i = x_i - y_i \qquad \text{and} \qquad s_i = x_i + y_i. \tag{4}$$

Since $d_2 \neq 0$, the system can be written in matrix form as

$$\begin{bmatrix} \frac{\alpha_{1,1;1}}{2} & 0 \\ 0 & \frac{\alpha_{1,1;0}}{2} \end{bmatrix} \times \begin{bmatrix} s_1 \\ s_3 \end{bmatrix} = - \begin{bmatrix} \alpha_{0,2;1} \cdot s_2 + \alpha_{0,1;1} \\ \alpha_{2,0;0} \cdot s_2 + \alpha_{1,0;0} \end{bmatrix}.$$

The determinant of the left hand side (l.h.s., for short) matrix $\frac{\alpha_{1,1;1} \cdot \alpha_{1,1;0}}{4}$ is always different from zero, given that $\alpha_{1,1;0} \neq 0, \alpha_{1,1;1} \neq 0$. Then, the system is compatible and the solution provides a collision for $\mathcal{S}_{F_0,F_1}$. $\square$

Lemma 6. *Let $p \geq 3$ be a prime integer, and let $n \geq 4$ be an even number. Let F_0, F_1 be two quadratic functions such that $\alpha_{1,1;0} = 0, \alpha_{1,1;1} \neq 0$ (or viceversa). Then, the corresponding ASI-lifting $\mathcal{S}_{F_0,F_1}$ over $\mathbb{F}_p^n$ is not invertible.*

Proof. First, note that, since $\alpha_{1,1;0} = 0$, at least one between $\alpha_{2,0;0}, \alpha_{0,2;0}$ is non-zero, otherwise F_0 would be linear. Let's first consider the case where $\alpha_{2,0;0} \neq 0$, and let's consider again inputs of the form $(x_0, x_1, x_2, x_3, \ldots, x_{n-1})$ and $(y_0, y_1, y_2, y_3, \ldots, y_{n-1}) = (x_0, x_1, y_2, x_3, \ldots, x_{n-1})$, with $x_2 \neq y_2$. Using the change of variables (4) and considering that $d_2 \neq 0$, the system can be written as

$$\begin{bmatrix} \frac{\alpha_{1,1;1}}{2} & \alpha_{0,2;1} \\ 0 & \alpha_{2,0;0} \end{bmatrix} \times \begin{bmatrix} s_1 \\ s_2 \end{bmatrix} = \begin{bmatrix} -\alpha_{0,1;1} \\ -\alpha_{1,0;0} \end{bmatrix},$$

The determinant of the l.h.s. matrix is $\frac{\alpha_{1,1;1}}{2} \cdot \alpha_{2,0;0} \neq 0$, then the system is compatible, i.e., it has a solution that is a collision for $\mathcal{S}_{F_0,F_1}$.

On the other side, if $\alpha_{0,2;0} \neq 0$, we set up a collision by considering the inputs $(x_0, x_1, x_2, \ldots, x_{n-1})$ and $(y_0, y_1, y_2, \ldots, y_{n-1}) = (x_0, y_1, x_2, \ldots, x_{n-1})$, where $x_1 \neq y_1$ and $d_i = 0$ for all $i \neq 1$. The system $\mathcal{S}_{F_0,F_1}(x_0, x_1, x_2, \ldots, x_{n-1}) = \mathcal{S}_{F_0,F_1}(x_0, y_1, x_2, \ldots, x_{n-1})$ reduces to the equations $F_0(x_0, x_1) = F_0(x_0, y_1)$ and $F_1(x_1, x_2) = F_0(y_1, x_2)$, while the other equations are obviously satisfied. Using that $d_1 \neq 0$, it corresponds to

$$\begin{bmatrix} \alpha_{0,2;0} & 0 \\ \alpha_{2,0;1} & \frac{\alpha_{1,1;1}}{2} \end{bmatrix} \times \begin{bmatrix} s_1 \\ s_2 \end{bmatrix} = \begin{bmatrix} -\alpha_{0,1;0} \\ -\alpha_{1,0;1} \end{bmatrix}.$$

Since the determinant of the l.h.s. matrix is $\alpha_{0,2;0} \cdot \frac{\alpha_{1,1;1}}{2} \neq 0$, then the system has a solution, i.e., the ASI-lifting has a collision.

The case where $\alpha_{1,1;0} \neq 0, \alpha_{1,1;1} = 0$ is equivalent: we can find the collisions for $\mathcal{S}_{F_0,F_1}$ starting from inputs $(x_0, x_1, x_2, \ldots, x_{n-1}), (y_0, y_1, y_2, y_3, \ldots, y_{n-1}) = (x_0, y_1, x_2, \ldots, x_{n-1})$ if $\alpha_{2,0;1} \neq 0$, while if $\alpha_{0,2;1} \neq 0$ we work with inputs $(x_0, x_1, x_2, x_3, \ldots, x_{n-1}), (y_0, y_1, y_2, y_3, \ldots, y_{n-1}) = (x_0, x_1, y_2, x_3, \ldots, x_{n-1})$. $\square$

Lemma 7. *Let $p \geq 3$ be a prime integer, and let $n \geq 4$ be an even number. Let F_0, F_1 be two quadratic functions such that $\alpha_{1,1;0} = \alpha_{1,1;1} = 0$. Then, the corresponding ASI-lifting $\mathcal{S}_{F_0,F_1}$ over $\mathbb{F}_p^n$ is not invertible.*

Proof. In order to prove the lemma, we set up a collision by working with the system $\mathcal{S}_{F_0,F_1}(x_0,\ldots,x_{n-1}) = \mathcal{S}_{F_0,F_1}(y_0,\ldots,y_{n-1})$, that is,

$$
\begin{bmatrix}
\alpha_{2,0;0}\cdot d_0 & \alpha_{0,2;0}\cdot d_1 & 0 & 0 & \cdots & 0 & 0 \\
0 & \alpha_{2,0;1}\cdot d_1 & \alpha_{0,2;1}\cdot d_2 & 0 & \cdots & 0 & 0 \\
0 & 0 & \alpha_{2,0;0}\cdot d_2 & \alpha_{0,2;0}\cdot d_3 & \cdots & 0 & 0 \\
\vdots & & & & \ddots & \ddots & \vdots \\
0 & 0 & 0 & 0 & \cdots & \alpha_{2,0;1}\cdot d_{n-2} & \alpha_{0,2;1}\cdot d_{n-1} \\
\alpha_{0,2;1}\cdot d_0 & 0 & 0 & 0 & \cdots & 0 & \alpha_{2,0;1}\cdot d_{n-1}
\end{bmatrix}
\times
\begin{bmatrix}
s_0 \\ s_1 \\ s_2 \\ \vdots \\ s_{n-2} \\ s_{n-1}
\end{bmatrix}
$$

$$
= -
\begin{bmatrix}
\alpha_{1,0;0}\cdot d_0 + \alpha_{0,1;0}\cdot d_1 \\
\alpha_{1,0;1}\cdot d_1 + \alpha_{0,1;1}\cdot d_2 \\
\alpha_{1,0;0}\cdot d_2 + \alpha_{0,1;0}\cdot d_3 \\
\vdots \\
\alpha_{1,0;0}\cdot d_{n-2} + \alpha_{0,1;0}\cdot d_{n-1} \\
\alpha_{1,0;1}\cdot d_{n-1} + \alpha_{0,1;1}\cdot d_0
\end{bmatrix}
\tag{5}
$$

where d_i and s_i are defined as in Eq. (4). The determinant of the l.h.s. matrix is $\left(\alpha_{2,0;0}^{\frac{n}{2}}\cdot\alpha_{2,0;1}^{\frac{n}{2}} - \alpha_{0,2;0}^{\frac{n}{2}}\cdot\alpha_{0,2;1}^{\frac{n}{2}}\right)\cdot\prod_{i=0}^{n-1} d_i$. Then, by taking $d_i \neq 0$ for all i, the determinant is different from zero if $\alpha_{2,0;0}^{\frac{n}{2}}\cdot\alpha_{2,0;1}^{\frac{n}{2}} - \alpha_{0,2;0}^{\frac{n}{2}}\cdot\alpha_{0,2;1}^{\frac{n}{2}} \neq 0$. Otherwise, if $\alpha_{2,0;0}^{\frac{n}{2}}\cdot\alpha_{2,0;1}^{\frac{n}{2}} = \alpha_{0,2;0}^{\frac{n}{2}}\cdot\alpha_{0,2;1}^{\frac{n}{2}}$, the rows of the matrix are linearly dependent, i.e., there exists a linear combination among the rows that is equal to zero. This means that the same linear combination holds for the rows of the right hand side (r.h.s., for short) vector, i.e., there exist $\{\lambda_i\}_{i\in\{0,\ldots,n-1\}} \in \mathbb{F}_p\backslash\{0\}$ such that

$$
\sum_{i=0}^{n-1} \lambda_i \cdot \left(\alpha_{1,0;\,i\bmod 2}\cdot d_i + \alpha_{0,1;\,i\bmod 2}\cdot d_{i+1}\right) = 0.
$$

Let d_0 be the variable that satisfies such combination. Then, we can rewrite the system as

$$
\begin{bmatrix}
\alpha_{2,0;1}\cdot d_1 & \alpha_{0,2;1}\cdot d_2 & 0 & \cdots & 0 & 0 \\
0 & \alpha_{2,0;0}\cdot d_2 & \alpha_{0,2;0}\cdot d_3 & \cdots & 0 & 0 \\
\vdots & & & \ddots & \ddots & \vdots \\
0 & 0 & 0 & \cdots & \alpha_{2,0;0}\cdot d_{n-2} & \alpha_{0,2;0}\cdot d_{n-1} \\
0 & 0 & 0 & \cdots & 0 & \alpha_{2,0;1}\cdot d_{n-1}
\end{bmatrix}
\times
\begin{bmatrix}
s_1 \\ s_2 \\ \vdots \\ s_{n-2} \\ s_{n-1}
\end{bmatrix}
$$

$$
= -
\begin{bmatrix}
\alpha_{1,0;1}\cdot d_1 + \alpha_{0,1;1}\cdot d_2 \\
\alpha_{1,0;0}\cdot d_2 + \alpha_{0,1;0}\cdot d_3 \\
\vdots \\
\alpha_{1,0;0}\cdot d_{n-2} + \alpha_{0,1;0}\cdot d_{n-1} \\
\alpha_{1,0;1}\cdot d_{n-1} + d_0\cdot(\alpha_{0,1;1} + \alpha_{0,2;1}\cdot s_0)
\end{bmatrix},
$$

where s_0 is a free variable. The determinant of the l.h.s. matrix is $\left(\alpha_{2,0;1}^{\frac{n}{2}}\cdot\alpha_{2,0;0}^{\frac{n}{2}-1}\right)\cdot \prod_{i=1}^{n-1} d_i$, which is non-null if and only if $\alpha_{2,0;0} \neq 0$ and $\alpha_{2,0;1} \neq 0$. In such a case, a collision exists.

SubCase: $\alpha_{2,0;1} = 0$ *and* $\alpha_{2,0;0} \neq 0$. In such a case, the linear system (5) is equal
to

$$
\begin{bmatrix}
\alpha_{2,0;0} \cdot d_0 \, \alpha_{0,2;0} \cdot d_1 & 0 & 0 & \cdots & 0 & 0 \\
0 & 0 & \alpha_{0,2;1} \cdot d_2 & 0 & \cdots & 0 & 0 \\
0 & 0 & \alpha_{2,0;0} \cdot d_2 \, \alpha_{0,2;0} \cdot d_3 & \cdots & 0 & 0 \\
\vdots & & & \ddots & \ddots & \vdots & \vdots \\
0 & 0 & 0 & 0 & \cdots & \alpha_{2,0;0} \cdot d_{n-2} \, \alpha_{0,2;0} \cdot d_{n-1} \\
\alpha_{0,2;1} \cdot d_0 & 0 & 0 & 0 & \cdots & 0 & 0
\end{bmatrix}
\times
\begin{bmatrix}
s_0 \\ s_1 \\ s_2 \\ \vdots \\ s_{n-2} \\ s_{n-1}
\end{bmatrix}
$$

$$
= -
\begin{bmatrix}
\alpha_{1,0;0} \cdot d_0 + \alpha_{0,1;0} \cdot d_1 \\
\alpha_{1,0;1} \cdot d_1 + \alpha_{0,1;1} \cdot d_2 \\
\alpha_{1,0;0} \cdot d_2 + \alpha_{0,1;0} \cdot d_3 \\
\vdots \\
\alpha_{1,0;0} \cdot d_{n-2} + \alpha_{0,1;0} \cdot d_{n-1} \\
\alpha_{1,0;1} \cdot d_{n-1} + \alpha_{0,1;1} \cdot d_0
\end{bmatrix}.
$$

The determinant of the l.h.s. matrix is $- \left(\alpha_{0,2;0}^{\frac{n}{2}} \cdot \alpha_{0,2;1}^{\frac{n}{2}} \right) \cdot \prod_{i=0}^{n-1} d_i$. Since $\alpha_{0,2;1} \neq$
0, otherwise F_1 would be linear, the determinant is not null unless $\alpha_{0,2;0} = 0$. In
such a case, consider $\mathcal{S}_{F_0,F_1}(x_0, x_1, \ldots, x_{n-1}) = \mathcal{S}_{F_0,F_1}(y_0, y_1, \ldots, y_{n-1})$, that is

$$
\begin{bmatrix}
\alpha_{2,0;0} \cdot d_0 \, \alpha_{0,1;0} & 0 & \cdots & 0 & 0 \\
0 & \alpha_{1,0;1} \, \alpha_{0,2;1} \cdot d_2 & \cdots & 0 & 0 \\
\vdots & & \ddots & \ddots & \vdots & \vdots \\
0 & 0 & 0 & \cdots & \alpha_{2,0;0} \cdot d_{n-2} \, \alpha_{0,1;0} \\
\alpha_{0,2;1} \cdot d_0 & 0 & 0 & \cdots & 0 & \alpha_{1,0;1}
\end{bmatrix}
\times
\begin{bmatrix}
s_0 \\ d_1 \\ \vdots \\ s_{n-2} \\ d_{n-1}
\end{bmatrix}
= -
\begin{bmatrix}
\alpha_{1,0;0} \cdot d_0 \\
\alpha_{0,1;1} \cdot d_2 \\
\vdots \\
\alpha_{1,0;0} \cdot d_{n-2} \\
\alpha_{0,1;1} \cdot d_0
\end{bmatrix}.
$$

We solve this system of n equations with respect to the variables s_i for even
i and d_i for odd i, that gives the set of variables $\{s_0, d_1, s_2, d_3 \ldots, s_{n-2}, d_{n-1}\}$.
We leave the other d_i's as free variables.

The determinant of the l.h.s. matrix is

$$
\prod_{i \text{ even}} d_i \cdot \left(\alpha_{2,0;0}^{\frac{n}{2}} \cdot \alpha_{1,0;1}^{\frac{n}{2}} + \alpha_{0,2;1}^{\frac{n}{2}} \cdot \alpha_{0,1;0}^{\frac{n}{2}} \right).
$$

If $\left(\alpha_{2,0;0}^{\frac{n}{2}} \cdot \alpha_{1,0;1}^{\frac{n}{2}} + \alpha_{0,2;1}^{\frac{n}{2}} \cdot \alpha_{0,1;0}^{\frac{n}{2}} \right) \neq 0$ and if we choose $d_i \neq 0$ for all i, the system
is compatible and there is a collision for the ASI-lifting. Otherwise, there is a
linear combination among the rows of the matrix that is equal to zero, i.e., there
exist $\{\lambda_i\}_{i \in \{0,\ldots,n-1\}} \in \mathbb{F}_p \setminus \{0\}$ such that

$$
\sum_{i \text{ even}} \left(\lambda_i \cdot \alpha_{1,0;0} \cdot d_i + \lambda_{i+1} \cdot \alpha_{0,1;1} \cdot d_{i+2} \right) = 0.
$$

Then, suppose that d_1 satisfies this combination. We can rewrite the system as

$$
\begin{bmatrix}
\alpha_{2,0;0} \cdot d_0 & 0 & 0 & 0 & \cdots & 0 & 0 \\
0 & \alpha_{2,0;0} \cdot d_2 & \alpha_{0,1;0} & 0 & \cdots & 0 & 0 \\
0 & 0 & \alpha_{1,0;1} & \alpha_{0,2;1} \cdot d_4 & \cdots & 0 & 0 \\
\vdots & & & & \ddots & \ddots & \vdots \\
0 & 0 & 0 & 0 & \cdots & \alpha_{2,0;0} \cdot d_{n-2} & \alpha_{0,1;0} \\
\alpha_{0,2;1} \cdot d_0 & 0 & 0 & 0 & \cdots & 0 & \alpha_{1,0;1}
\end{bmatrix}
\times
\begin{bmatrix}
s_0 \\
s_2 \\
d_3 \\
\vdots \\
s_{n-2} \\
d_{n-1}
\end{bmatrix}
$$

$$
= -[\alpha_{1,0;0} \cdot d_0 ; \alpha_{0,1;1} \cdot d_2 + \alpha_{1,0;1} \cdot d_1 ; \alpha_{1,0;0} \cdot d_2 ; \ldots ; \alpha_{1,0;0} \cdot d_{n-2} ; \alpha_{0,1;1} \cdot d_0]^T.
$$

The determinant of the l.h.s. matrix is $\prod_{i \text{ even}} d_i \cdot \left(\alpha_{2,0;0}^{\frac{n}{2}} \cdot \alpha_{1,0;1}^{\frac{n}{2}-1} \right)$. Since $\alpha_{2,0;0} \neq 0$ (otherwise F_0 would be linear), this determinant is non-zero if $\alpha_{1,0;1} \neq 0$. If $\alpha_{1,0;1} = 0$, F_1 is non-balanced due to Lemma 4, then $\mathcal{S}_{F_0,F_1}$ is always non-invertible. The case where $\alpha_{2,0;1} \neq 0$ and $\alpha_{2,0;0} = 0$ is analogous.

SubCase: $\alpha_{2,0;1} = \alpha_{2,0;0} = 0$. In such a case, the linear system (5) reduces to

$$
\forall i \in \{1, 3, \ldots, n-1\} : \qquad \alpha_{0,2;0} \cdot d_i \cdot s_i = -\alpha_{1,0;0} \cdot d_{i-1} - \alpha_{0,1;0} \cdot d_i
$$
$$
\forall i \in \{0, 2, \ldots, n-2\} : \qquad \alpha_{0,2;1} \cdot d_i \cdot s_i = -\alpha_{1,0;1} \cdot d_{i-1} - \alpha_{0,1;1} \cdot d_i.
$$

Note that $\alpha_{0,2;1} \neq 0$ and $\alpha_{0,2;0} \neq 0$, otherwise F_0, F_1 would be linear. By taking $d_i \neq 0$ for all i, a solution of such system of equations is given by

$$
\forall i \in \{1, 3, \ldots, n-1\} : \qquad s_i = -\frac{\alpha_{1,0;0} \cdot d_{i-1} + \alpha_{0,1;0} \cdot d_i}{\alpha_{0,2;0} \cdot d_i}
$$
$$
\forall i \in \{0, 2, \ldots, n-2\} : \qquad s_i = \frac{\alpha_{1,0;1} \cdot d_{i-1} + \alpha_{0,1;1} \cdot d_i}{\alpha_{0,2;1} \cdot d_i},
$$

which corresponds to a collision for the analyzed ASI-lifting function. □

4.2 Proof of Proposition 3 for the Case n Odd

In order to prove Proposition 3 in the case n odd, we separate the proof again in three lemmas:

- Lemma 8: $\alpha_{1,1;0} \neq 0$;
- Lemma 9: $\alpha_{1,1;0} = 0, \alpha_{1,1;1} \neq 0$;
- Lemma 10: $\alpha_{1,1;0} = \alpha_{1,1;1} = 0$.

As before, these lemmas analyze each possible $\mathcal{S}_{F_0,F_1}$ for $F_0, F_1 : \mathbb{F}_p^2 \to \mathbb{F}_p$ are quadratic functions and n is odd, showing the non-invertibility of the ASI-lifting.

Lemma 8. *Let $p \geq 3$ be a prime integer, and let $n \geq 3$ be an odd number. Let F_0, F_1 be two quadratic functions such that $\alpha_{1,1;0} \neq 0$. Then, the corresponding ASI-lifting $\mathcal{S}_{F_0,F_1}$ over $\mathbb{F}_p^n$ is not invertible.*

Proof. Consider inputs of the form $(x_0, x_1, \ldots, x_{n-1})$ and $(y_0, y_1, \ldots, y_{n-1}) = (y_0, x_1, \ldots, x_{n-1})$, i.e., inputs that differ just in the first element. Referring to the change of variables in Eq. (4), we suppose $d_0 \neq 0$, while $d_i = 0$ for all $i \in \{1, 2, \ldots, n-1\}$. Then, the system $\mathcal{S}_{F_0, F_1}(x_0, x_1, \ldots, x_{n-1}) = \mathcal{S}_{F_0, F_1}(y_0, x_1, \ldots, x_{n-1})$ can be represented as

$$\begin{bmatrix} \frac{\alpha_{1,1;0}}{2} & 0 \\ 0 & \frac{\alpha_{1,1;0}}{2} \end{bmatrix} \times \begin{bmatrix} s_1 \\ s_{n-1} \end{bmatrix} = -\begin{bmatrix} \alpha_{2,0;0} \cdot s_0 + \alpha_{1,0;0} \\ \alpha_{0,2;0} \cdot s_0 + \alpha_{0,1;0} \end{bmatrix}.$$

Since the determinant of the l.h.s. matrix is $\left(\frac{\alpha_{1,1;0}}{2}\right)^2 \neq 0$, the system is compatible, i.e., it is always possible to find a collision for the ASI-lifting. $\square$

Lemma 9. *Let $p \geq 3$ be a prime integer, and let $n \geq 3$ be an odd number. Let F_0, F_1 be two quadratic functions such that $\alpha_{1,1;0} = 0, \alpha_{1,1;1} \neq 0$. Then, the corresponding ASI-lifting $\mathcal{S}_{F_0, F_1}$ over $\mathbb{F}_p^n$ is not invertible.*

Proof. Let start from inputs $(x_0, x_1, x_2, \ldots, x_{n-1})$ and $(y_0, y_1, y_2, \ldots, y_{n-1}) = (x_0, y_1, x_2, \ldots, x_{n-1})$, where only $x_1 \neq y_1$, while the others are equal. In such a case, by using the change of variables defined in Eq. (4) and the fact that $d_1 \neq 0$, the system $\mathcal{S}_{F_0, F_1}(x_0, x_1, x_2, \ldots, x_{n-1}) = \mathcal{S}_{F_0, F_1}(x_0, y_1, x_2, \ldots, x_{n-1})$ can be written as

$$\begin{bmatrix} \alpha_{0,2;0} & 0 \\ \alpha_{2,0;1} & \frac{\alpha_{1,1;1}}{2} \end{bmatrix} \times \begin{bmatrix} s_1 \\ s_2 \end{bmatrix} = -\begin{bmatrix} \alpha_{0,1;0} \\ \alpha_{1,0;1} \end{bmatrix}.$$

Since the determinant of the l.h.s. matrix is $\alpha_{0,2;0} \cdot \frac{\alpha_{1,1;1}}{2}$ and $\alpha_{1,1;1} \neq 0$, the system is compatible if and only if $\alpha_{0,2;0} \neq 0$. Otherwise, we can find a collision for $\mathcal{S}_{F_0, F_1}$ using inputs $(x_0, x_1, x_2, x_3, \ldots, x_{n-1})$ and $(y_0, y_1, y_2, y_3, \ldots, y_{n-1}) = (x_0, x_1, y_2, x_3, \ldots, x_{n-1})$, i.e., with $d_2 \neq 0$ and $d_i = 0$ for $i \neq 2$. Then, the system is

$$\begin{bmatrix} \frac{\alpha_{1,1;1}}{2} & \alpha_{0,2;1} \\ 0 & \alpha_{2,0;0} \end{bmatrix} \times \begin{bmatrix} s_1 \\ s_2 \end{bmatrix} = -\begin{bmatrix} \alpha_{0,1;1} \\ \alpha_{1,0;0} \end{bmatrix}.$$

The determinant of the l.h.s. matrix is $\alpha_{2,0;0} \cdot \frac{\alpha_{1,1;1}}{2} \neq 0$, since $\alpha_{2,0;0} \neq 0$, otherwise F_0 would be a linear function. $\square$

Lemma 10. *Let $p \geq 3$ be a prime integer, and let $n \geq 3$ be an odd number. Let F_0, F_1 be two quadratic functions such that $\alpha_{1,1;0} = \alpha_{1,1;1} = 0$. Then, the corresponding ASI-lifting $\mathcal{S}_{F_0, F_1}$ over $\mathbb{F}_p^n$ is not invertible.*

Proof. The proof is analogous to the one provided to prove Lemma 7. $\square$

5   Invertible Functions $\mathcal{S}_{F_0, F_1}$ over $\mathbb{F}_p^n$ via Linear F_0 and Quadratic F_1 (or Vice-Versa)

In this section, we analyse the ASI-lifting functions $\mathcal{S}_{F_0, F_1}$ over $\mathbb{F}_p^n$ induced by a linear local map $F_0 : \mathbb{F}_p^2 \to \mathbb{F}_p$ and a quadratic one $F_1 : \mathbb{F}_p^2 \to \mathbb{F}_p$, or vice-versa. The main result is given in the following proposition.

Proposition 4. *Let $p \geq 3$ be a prime integer, and let $n \geq 3$. Let $F_0 : \mathbb{F}_p^2 \to \mathbb{F}_p$ be a linear function and $F_1 : \mathbb{F}_p^2 \to \mathbb{F}_p$ a quadratic function, or vice-versa. If $n > 3$, then $\mathcal{S}_{F_0,F_1}$ is invertible if and only if it is a Type-II Feistel scheme, that is,*

- *F_0 (resp., F_1) depends on one variable only, and*
- *$F_1(x_0, x_1) = \alpha_{1-i,i;1} \cdot x_i + H(x_{1-i})$ for $i \in \{0, 1\}$, where $H : \mathbb{F}_p \to \mathbb{F}_p$ is a quadratic function (resp., $F_0(x_0, x_1) = \alpha_{1-i,i;0} \cdot x_i + H(x_{1-i})$).*

If $n = 3$, then $\mathcal{S}_{F_0,F_1}$ is invertible if and only if

- *it is a Type-II Feistel scheme (as before), or*
- *$F_0(x_0, x_1) = \alpha_{1,0;0} \cdot x_0 + \alpha_{0,1;0} \cdot x_1$, $\alpha_{1,0;0}, \alpha_{0,1;0} \neq 0$, and $F_1(x_0, x_1) = \gamma \cdot \left(\frac{\alpha_{0,1;0}}{\alpha_{1,0;0}} \cdot x_0 - \frac{\alpha_{1,0;0}}{\alpha_{0,1;0}} \cdot x_1 \right)^2 + \alpha_{1,0;1} \cdot x_0 + \alpha_{0,1;1} \cdot x_1$, with $\gamma \in \mathbb{F}_p$ and $\alpha_{1,0;1} \cdot \alpha_{1,0;0}^2 \neq -\alpha_{0,1;1} \cdot \alpha_{0,1;0}^2$.*

The proof is organized as follows:

- first, for $n \geq 4$, we show that if one of the two functions is linear and depends on a single variable only, then the only invertible ASI-liftings are the Type-II Feistel schemes;
- in Sect. 5.1, we study the case $n \geq 4$ even, showing that no ASI-lifting $\mathcal{S}_{F_0,F_1}$ is invertible besides the Type-II Feistel one;
- in Sect. 5.2, we study the case $n \geq 3$ odd. We divide the proof in two subcases: Lemma 13 deals with the case where F_0 is quadratic and F_1 linear, while Lemma 14 proves the proposition for F_0 linear and F_1 quadratic, including the special result for the case $n = 3$.

As we did in the previous section, we study the cases n even and n odd separately, since the numbers of repetitions of F_0 and F_1 in $\mathcal{S}_{F_0,F_1}$ is different if n is odd. Moreover, due to Definition 5, we assume $\alpha_{0,0;0} = \alpha_{0,0;1} = 0$, and we usually work with a linear function of the form $F_l(x_0, x_1) = x_0 + \alpha \cdot x_1$ or $F_l(x_0, x_1) = x_1 + \alpha \cdot x_0$ for $\alpha \in \mathbb{F}_p$ and $l \in \{0, 1\}$.

Type-II Feistel Schemes for $n \geq 4$. First of all, we consider the case in which one function is linear and depends on a single variable only. In the next lemma, we prove that the only functions $\mathcal{S}_F$ of this form that are invertible are the Type-II Feistel schemes [30,34].

Lemma 11. *Let $p \geq 3$ be a prime integer, and let $n \geq 4$. Let $F_j(x_0, x_1) = x_i$ for $i, j \in \{0, 1\}$ be a linear function over $\mathbb{F}_p$ that depends on one variable only. The corresponding ASI-lifting function $\mathcal{S}_{F_0,F_1}$ over $\mathbb{F}_p^n$ for $n \geq 4$ is invertible if and only if F_{1-j} is linear in one of the two variables, that is, $F_{1-j}(x_0, x_1) = x_l + H(x_{1-l})$ for $l \in \{0, 1\}$.*

We point out that the previous scheme corresponds to a Type-II Feistel scheme. We emphasize that for $n = 3$ there exist ASI-lifting functions $\mathcal{S}_{F_0,F_1}$ that are invertible even if (i) F_0 (resp., F_1) is linear and does not depend on a single variable and (ii) $\mathcal{S}_{F_0,F_1}$ is not a Type-II Feistel scheme – see Lemma 14.

Proof. We limit ourselves to propose the proof for the case $n \geq 4$ even only. The proof for the case $n \geq 5$ odd is analogous, independently of the fact that F_0 or F_1 is linear.

W.l.o.g., let $F_0(x_0, x_1) = x_0$ (i.e., $\alpha_{0,1;0} = 0$) – the other cases are analogous since n is even. Then, given a generic quadratic function F_1, we have that $y = S_{F_0,F_1}(x)$ corresponds to

$$y_i = \alpha_{2,0;1} \cdot x_i^2 + \alpha_{1,1;1} \cdot x_i \cdot x_{i+1} + \alpha_{0,2;1} \cdot x_{i+1}^2 + \alpha_{1,0;1} \cdot x_i + \alpha_{0,1;1} \cdot x_{i+1},$$

$$y_{i+1} = x_{i+1},$$

for each $i \in \{1, 3, \ldots, n-1\}$. By replacing the second equation in the first one, we get

$$\alpha_{2,0;1} \cdot x_i^2 + (\alpha_{1,1;1} \cdot y_{i+1} + \alpha_{1,0;1}) \cdot x_i + (\alpha_{0,2;1} \cdot y_{i+1}^2 + \alpha_{0,1;1} \cdot y_{i+1} - y_i) = 0$$

for each $i \in \{1, 3, \ldots, n-1\}$. Note that each equation depends on a different variable x_i. By working independently on each one of such equations, it follows that the ASI-lifting function S_{F_0,F_1} is always invertible if and only if

- the coefficient of the monomial x_i^2 is zero, that is, $\alpha_{2,0;1} = 0$;
- the coefficient of the monomial x_i is non-null, that is, $\alpha_{1,1;1} \cdot y_{i+1} + \alpha_{1,0;1} \neq 0$.

Since y_{i+1} can take any possible value, then the second condition is satisfied only by $\alpha_{1,1;1} = 0$ and $\alpha_{1,0;1} \neq 0$. This concludes the proof.

□

5.1   Proof of Proposition 4 for the Case n Even

In this subsection, we only consider the case F_0 linear and F_1 quadratic. We emphasize that the case F_0 quadratic and F_1 linear is equivalent, since n is even.

Lemma 12. *Let $p \geq 3$ be a prime integer, and let $n \geq 4$ be an even number. Let $F_0(x_0, x_1) = \alpha_{1,0;0} \cdot x_0 + \alpha_{0,1;0} \cdot x_1$ be a linear function over $\mathbb{F}_p$, while let $F_1(x_0, x_1)$ be a quadratic function over $\mathbb{F}_p$. Then, the corresponding ASI-lifting S_{F_0,F_1} over $\mathbb{F}_p^n$ is invertible if and only if*

1. *$\alpha_{1,0;0} = 0$ or $\alpha_{0,1;0} = 0$;*
2. *$F_1(x_0, x_1) = \alpha_{1-i,i;1} \cdot x_i + H(x_{1-i})$ for $i \in \{0, 1\}$, where $H : \mathbb{F}_p \to \mathbb{F}_p$ is a quadratic function.*

Proof. We already proved in Lemma 11 that, if $\alpha_{1,0;0} = 0$ or $\alpha_{0,1;0} = 0$, Type-II Feistel are the only invertible ASI-liftings. For this reason, we consider the case $F_0(x_0, x_1) = x_0 + \alpha_{0,1;0} \cdot x_1$ with $\alpha_{0,1;0} \neq 0$. Here, we prove that the corresponding S_{F_0,F_1} is never invertible by constructing a collision. Let $y = S_{F_0,F_1}(x)$, then

$$y_i = \alpha_{2,0;1} \cdot x_i^2 + \alpha_{1,1;1} \cdot x_i \cdot x_{i+1} + \alpha_{0,2;1} \cdot x_{i+1}^2 + \alpha_{1,0;1} \cdot x_i + \alpha_{0,1;1} \cdot x_{i+1},$$

$$y_{i+1} = x_{i+1} + \alpha_{0,1;0} \cdot x_{i+2}$$

for each $i \in \{1, 3, 5, \ldots, n-1\}$. By replacing $x_{i+1} = y_{i+1} - \alpha_{0,1;0} \cdot x_{i+2}$, we get equations of the form

$$\alpha_{2,0;1} \cdot x_i^2 - \alpha_{1,1;1} \cdot \alpha_{0,1;0} \cdot x_i \cdot x_{i+2} + \alpha_{0,2;1} \cdot \alpha_{0,1;0}^2 \cdot x_{i+2}^2$$
$$+ x_i \cdot (\alpha_{1,1;1} \cdot y_{i+1} + \alpha_{1,0;1}) + x_{i+2} \cdot (-2 \cdot \alpha_{0,2;1} \cdot \alpha_{0,1;0} \cdot y_{i+1} - \alpha_{0,1;1} \cdot \alpha_{0,1;0})$$
$$+ \alpha_{0,2;1} \cdot y_{i+1}^2 + \alpha_{0,1;1} \cdot y_{i+1} - y_i = 0.$$

Note that each equation can be interpreted as a local map on the variables x_i, x_{i+2}. Hence, let's fix the values of $y_0, y_2, \ldots, y_{2j}, \ldots, y_{n-2} \in \mathbb{F}_p$ such that

$$y' = y_0 = y_2 = \ldots = y_{2j} = \ldots = y_{n-2}$$

for a certain $y' \in \mathbb{F}_p$, and let's introduce the function $G_{y'} : \mathbb{F}_p^2 \to \mathbb{F}_p$ defined as

$$G_{y'}(x_0, x_1) = \beta_{2,0} \cdot x_0^2 + \beta_{1,1} \cdot x_0 \cdot x_1 + \beta_{0,2} \cdot x_1^2 + \beta_{1,0} \cdot x_0 + \beta_{0,1} \cdot x_1,$$

where

$$\beta_{2,0} = \alpha_{2,0;1}, \qquad \beta_{1,1} = -\alpha_{1,1;1} \cdot \alpha_{0,1;0}, \qquad \beta_{0,2} = \alpha_{0,2;1} \cdot \alpha_{0,1;0}^2,$$
$$\beta_{1,0} = \alpha_{1,1;1} \cdot y' + \alpha_{1,0;1}, \qquad \beta_{0,1} = -2 \cdot \alpha_{0,2;1} \cdot \alpha_{0,1;0} \cdot y' - \alpha_{0,1;1} \cdot \alpha_{0,1;0}.$$

Let's now consider the SI-lifting $\mathcal{S}_{G_{y'}}$ over $\mathbb{F}_p^{n/2}$ defined via the local map $G_{y'}$. Note that a collision for $\mathcal{S}_{G_{y'}}$ implies a collision on $\mathcal{S}_{F_0, F_1}$ over $\mathbb{F}_p^n$ as well, i.e., $\mathcal{S}_{G_{y'}}(x_0, x_1, \ldots, x_{n/2-1}) = \mathcal{S}_{G_{y'}}(x_0', x_1', \ldots, x_{n/2-1}')$ implies

$$\mathcal{S}_{F_0, F_1}(y' - \alpha_{0,1;0} \cdot x_0, x_0, y' - \alpha_{0,1;0} \cdot x_1, x_1, \ldots, y' - \alpha_{0,1;0} \cdot x_{n/2-1}, x_{n/2-1})$$
$$= \mathcal{S}_{F_0, F_1}(y' - \alpha_{0,1;0} \cdot x_0', x_0', y' - \alpha_{0,1;0} \cdot x_1', x_1', \ldots, y' - \alpha_{0,1;0} \cdot x_{n/2-1}', x_{n/2-1}').$$

Hence, in order to prove our result, it is sufficient to show that $\mathcal{S}_{G_{y'}}$ is *not* invertible over $\mathbb{F}_p^{n/2}$: this immediately implies that $\mathcal{S}_{F_0, F_1}$ cannot be invertible.

Due to Theorem 2, such S-Box $\mathcal{S}_{G_{y'}}$ is not invertible for $\frac{n}{2} \geq 3$, i.e., $n \geq 6$. In the case $n/2 = 2$, the S-Box $\mathcal{S}_{G_{y'}}$ is invertible if

$$G_{y'}(x_0, x_1) = \gamma_0 \cdot x_0 + \gamma_1 \cdot x_1 + \gamma_2 \cdot (x_0 - x_1)^2$$

with $\gamma_0 \neq \pm\gamma_1$, as proved in Lemma 1.

Then, by the definition of our local map, the SI-lifting is invertible if

1. $\beta_{2,0} = \beta_{0,2}$, that is, $\alpha_{2,0;1} = \alpha_{0,2;1} \cdot \alpha_{0,1;0}^2$;
2. $\beta_{1,1} = -2 \cdot \beta_{2,0}$, that is, $\alpha_{1,1;1} = \frac{2 \cdot \alpha_{2,0;1}}{\alpha_{0,1;0}} = 2 \cdot \alpha_{0,2;1} \cdot \alpha_{0,1;0}$;
3. $\beta_{1,0} \neq \pm\beta_{0,1}$, that is, $y' \cdot (\alpha_{1,1;1} \pm 2 \cdot \alpha_{0,2;1} \cdot \alpha_{0,1;0}) \neq -\alpha_{1,0;1} \mp \alpha_{0,1;1} \cdot \alpha_{0,1;0}$,

where the third condition is satisfied if

3.a $\pm 2 \cdot \alpha_{0,2;1} \cdot \alpha_{0,1;0} = -\alpha_{1,1;1}$ (note that y' can take any possible value);
3.b $\pm\alpha_{0,1;1} \cdot \alpha_{0,1;0} \neq -\alpha_{1,0;1}$.

By replacing the second condition in (3.a) and since $\alpha_{0,1;0} \neq 0$, we get the condition $\pm 2 \cdot \alpha_{0,2;1} = -2 \cdot \alpha_{0,2;1}$, which is satisfied if and only if $\alpha_{0,2;1} = 0$. By the first condition, we also have $\alpha_{2,0;1} = 0$. By the second condition, it follows that $\alpha_{1,1;1} = 0$. Since $\alpha_{2,0;1} = \alpha_{1,1;1} = \alpha_{0,2;1} = 0$, we have that F_1 must be linear in order to get invertibility for n even. Hence, the ASI-lifting $\mathcal{S}_{F_0, F_1}$ is never invertible for $n \geq 4$ if F_1 is quadratic and if $\alpha_{1,0;0}, \alpha_{0,1;0} \neq 0$. $\qquad \square$

5.2   Proof of Proposition 4 for the Case $n \geq 3$ Odd

We are going to consider separately the following two cases: Lemma 13 covers the case where F_0 is a quadratic function and F_1 is linear, while Lemma 14 deals with F_0 linear and F_1 quadratic. In the case $n \geq 5$, the only invertible non-linear functions $\mathcal{S}_{F_0,F_1}$ are the ones with a Feistel structure. Note that in the case $n = 3$ there is an extra case in which the function $\mathcal{S}_{F_0,F_1}$ is invertible without being a Type-II Feistel scheme – see Lemma 14.

Lemma 13. *Let $p \geq 3$ be a prime integer, and let $n \geq 3$ be an odd number. Let F_0 be a quadratic function over $\mathbb{F}_p$, while let $F_1(x_0, x_1) = \alpha_{1,0;1} \cdot x_0 + \alpha_{0,1;1} \cdot x_1$ be a linear function over $\mathbb{F}_p$. Then, the corresponding ASI-lifting $\mathcal{S}_{F_0,F_1}$ over $\mathbb{F}_p^n$ is invertible if and only if it is a Type-II Feistel Scheme, that is,*

- $\alpha_{1,0;1} = 0$ or $\alpha_{0,1;1} = 0$;
- $F_0(x_0, x_1) = \alpha_{i,1-i;0} \cdot x_i + H(x_i)$ for $i \in \{0,1\}$, where $H : \mathbb{F}_p \to \mathbb{F}_p$ is a quadratic function.

Proof. Since the invertibility of Type-II Feistel schemes in the case $F_1(x_0, x_1) = x_0$ or $F_1(x_0, x_1) = x_1$ is treated in Lemma 11, we focus on $F_1(x_0, x_1) = \alpha_{1,0;1} \cdot x_0 + \alpha_{0,1;1} \cdot x_1$, with $\alpha_{1,0;1}, \alpha_{0,1;1} \neq 0$. We show that, in such a case, a collision always occurs for $\mathcal{S}_{F_0,F_1}$.

In order to find the collision, let consider the inputs $(x_0, x_1, \ldots, x_{n-1})$ and $(y_0, y_1, \ldots, y_{n-1}) = (y_0, x_1, \ldots, x_{n-1})$, where $y_0 \neq x_0$. Then, the system representing $\mathcal{S}_{F_0,F_1}(x_0, x_1, \ldots, x_{n-1}) = \mathcal{S}_{F_0,F_1}(y_0, x_1, \ldots, x_{n-1})$ reduces to

$$\alpha_{2,0;0} \cdot d_0 \cdot s_0 + \frac{\alpha_{1,1;0}}{2} \cdot d_0 \cdot s_1 + \alpha_{1,0;0} \cdot d_0 = 0,$$

$$\alpha_{0,2;0} \cdot d_0 \cdot s_0 + \frac{\alpha_{1,1;0}}{2} \cdot d_0 \cdot s_{n-1} + \alpha_{0,1;0} \cdot d_0 = 0,$$

via the variables d_i, s_i introduced in (4). If $\alpha_{1,1;0} \neq 0$, the system admits the solution

$$s_1 = -2\frac{\alpha_{1,0;0} + \alpha_{2,0;0} \cdot s_0}{\alpha_{1,1;0}} \quad \text{and} \quad s_{n-1} = -2\frac{\alpha_{0,1;0} + \alpha_{0,2;0} \cdot s_0}{\alpha_{1,1;0}}$$

which corresponds to a collision for the analysed ASI-lifting function. If otherwise $\alpha_{1,1;0} = 0$, then one between $\alpha_{2,0;0}$ and $\alpha_{0,2;0}$ should be non-zero, otherwise F_0 would be linear. We study separately these two subcases.

SubCase: $\alpha_{1,1;0} = 0$, $\alpha_{2,0;0} \neq 0$. In such a case, using the change of variables introduced in (4), the collision $\mathcal{S}_{F_0,F_1}(x_0, x_1, \ldots, x_{n-1}) = \mathcal{S}_{F_0,F_1}(y_0, y_1, \ldots, y_{n-1})$ corresponds to the linear system

$$
\begin{bmatrix}
\alpha_{2,0;0} \cdot d_0 & \alpha_{0,2;0} \cdot s_1 + \alpha_{0,1;0} & 0 & 0 & \cdots & 0 & 0 \\
0 & \alpha_{1,0;1} & 0 & 0 & \cdots & 0 & 0 \\
0 & 0 & \alpha_{2,0;0} \cdot d_2 & \alpha_{0,1;0} & \cdots & 0 & 0 \\
\vdots & & & & \ddots & \ddots & \vdots \\
0 & 0 & 0 & 0 & \cdots & \alpha_{1,0;1} & 0 \\
\alpha_{0,2;0} \cdot d_0 & 0 & 0 & 0 & \cdots & 0 & \alpha_{2,0;0} \cdot d_{n-1}
\end{bmatrix}
\times
\begin{bmatrix}
s_0 \\ d_1 \\ s_2 \\ d_3 \\ \vdots \\ d_{n-2} \\ s_{n-1}
\end{bmatrix}
$$

$$
= -
\begin{bmatrix}
\alpha_{1,0;0} \cdot d_0 \\
\alpha_{0,1;1} \cdot d_2 \\
\alpha_{1,0;0} \cdot d_2 \\
\alpha_{0,1;1} \cdot d_3 \\
\vdots \\
\alpha_{0,1;1} \cdot d_{n-1} \\
\alpha_{1,0;0} \cdot d_{n-1} + \alpha_{0,1;0} \cdot d_0
\end{bmatrix}.
$$

We solve this system of n equations with respect to the variables s_i for even i and d_i for odd i, that gives the set of variables $\{s_0, d_1, s_2, d_3 \ldots, s_{n-1}\}$. We leave the others as free variables.

The determinant of the l.h.s. matrix is $\alpha_{2,0;0}^{\frac{n+1}{2}} \cdot \alpha_{1,0;1}^{\frac{n-1}{2}} \cdot \prod_{i \text{ even}} d_i$. Then, if we take $d_i \neq 0$ for all even i, the system is compatible and the ASI-lifting has a collision if $\alpha_{2,0;0} \neq 0$ (since $\alpha_{1,0;1} \neq 0$). The last case to analyse is when $\alpha_{2,0;0} = \alpha_{1,1;0} = 0$ (and so $\alpha_{0,2;0} \neq 0$).

SubCase: $\alpha_{1,1;0} = \alpha_{2,0;0} = 0$, $\alpha_{0,2;0} \neq 0$. Working as before, the system of equations corresponding to the collision is given by

$$
\begin{bmatrix}
\alpha_{0,2;0} \cdot d_1 & 0 & 0 & \cdots & 0 & 0 \\
0 & \alpha_{0,1;1} & 0 & \cdots & 0 & 0 \\
0 & \alpha_{1,0;0} & \alpha_{2,0;0} \cdot d_3 & \cdots & 0 & 0 \\
\vdots & & \ddots & \ddots & & \vdots \\
0 & 0 & 0 & \cdots & \alpha_{0,1;1} & 0 \\
0 & 0 & 0 & \cdots & \alpha_{1,0;0} & \alpha_{0,2;0} \cdot d_0
\end{bmatrix}
\times
\begin{bmatrix}
s_1 \\ d_2 \\ s_3 \\ \vdots \\ d_{n-1} \\ s_0
\end{bmatrix}
= -
\begin{bmatrix}
\alpha_{1,0;0} \cdot d_0 + \alpha_{0,1;0} \cdot d_1 \\
\alpha_{1,0;1} \cdot d_1 \\
\alpha_{0,1;0} \cdot d_3 \\
\vdots \\
\alpha_{1,0;1} \cdot d_{n-2} \\
\alpha_{0,1;0} \cdot d_0
\end{bmatrix}.
$$

This time, we solve this system of n equations with respect to the variables $\{s_1, d_2, s_3 \ldots, d_{n-1}, s_0\}$. We leave the others as free variables. In such a case, the determinant of the l.h.s. matrix is $\alpha_{0,2;0}^{\frac{n+1}{2}} \cdot \alpha_{0,1;1}^{\frac{n-1}{2}} \cdot d_0 \cdot \prod_{i \text{ odd}} d_i$. Then, by taking $d_i \neq 0$ for $i = 0$ and for each i odd, the determinant is always non-zero. As a result, the system is compatible and we can find a collision for the ASI-lifting. $\square$

Lemma 14. *Let $p \geq 3$ be a prime integer, and let $n \geq 3$ be an odd number. Let $F_0(x_0, x_1) = \alpha_{1,0;0} \cdot x_0 + \alpha_{0,1;0} \cdot x_1$ be a linear function over $\mathbb{F}_p$, while let F_1 be a quadratic function over $\mathbb{F}_p$.*

If $n \geq 5$, then the corresponding ASI-lifting S_{F_0, F_1} defined over $\mathbb{F}_p^n$ is invertible if and only if it is a Type-II Feistel Scheme, that is,

- *$\alpha_{1,0;0} = 0$ or $\alpha_{0,1;0} = 0$;*
- *$F_1(x_0, x_1) = \alpha_{i,1-i;0} \cdot x_i + H(x_i)$ for $i \in \{0, 1\}$, where $H : \mathbb{F}_p \to \mathbb{F}_p$ is a quadratic function.*

If $n = 3$, then $\mathcal{S}_{F_0,F_1}$ is invertible if and only if either (i) the condition just given holds, or (ii) $F_0(x_0, x_1) = \alpha_{1,0;0} \cdot x_0 + \alpha_{0,1;0} \cdot x_1$ for $\alpha_{1,0;0}, \alpha_{0,1;0} \neq 0$ and

$$F_1(x_0, x_1) = \gamma \cdot \left(\frac{\alpha_{0,1;0}}{\alpha_{1,0;0}} \cdot x_0 - \frac{\alpha_{1,0;0}}{\alpha_{0,1;0}} \cdot x_1 \right)^2 + \alpha_{1,0;1} \cdot x_0 + \alpha_{0,1;1} \cdot x_1$$

where $\gamma \in \mathbb{F}_p$ and $\alpha_{1,0;1} \cdot \alpha_{1,0;0}^2 \neq -\alpha_{0,1;1} \cdot \alpha_{0,1;0}^2$.

Proof. Again, the case $F_0(x_0, x_1) = x_0$ or $F_0(x_0, x_1) = x_1$ follows from Lemma 11, so we limit ourselves to consider the case $F_0(x_0, x_1) = \alpha_{1,0;0} \cdot x_0 + \alpha_{0,1;0} \cdot x_1$ with $\alpha_{1,0;0}, \alpha_{0,1;0} \neq 0$. We start by showing that for $n \geq 5$ the ASI-lifting is never invertible, i.e., we can always find a collision.

In order to prove it, let's start by considering $(x_0, x_1, x_2, x_3, x_4, \ldots, x_{n-1})$ and $(y_0, y_1, y_2, y_3, y_4, \ldots, y_{n-1}) = (x_0, x_1, y_2, y_3, x_4, \ldots, x_{n-1})$, i.e., two inputs that differ just in $y_2 \neq x_2$ and $y_3 \neq x_3$. Using the change of variables of Eq. (4), the system reduces to

$$d_2 \cdot \left(\alpha_{0,2;1} \cdot s_2 + \frac{\alpha_{1,1;1}}{2} \cdot s_1 + \alpha_{0,1;1} \right) = 0,$$

$$\alpha_{1,0;0} \cdot d_2 + \alpha_{0,1;0} \cdot d_3 = 0,$$

$$d_3 \cdot \left(\alpha_{2,0;1} \cdot s_3 + \frac{\alpha_{1,1;1}}{2} \cdot s_4 + \alpha_{1,0;1} \right) = 0.$$

Since $\alpha_{1,0;0}, \alpha_{0,1;0} \neq 0$, the second equation is satisfied by $d_2 = -\frac{\alpha_{0,1;0}}{\alpha_{1,0;0}} \cdot d_3$. By taking $d_2, d_3 \neq 0$, the other equations reduce to

$$\alpha_{0,2;1} \cdot s_2 + \frac{\alpha_{1,1;1}}{2} \cdot s_1 = -\alpha_{0,1;1},$$

$$\alpha_{2,0;1} \cdot s_3 + \frac{\alpha_{1,1;1}}{2} \cdot s_4 = -\alpha_{1,0;1}.$$

If $\alpha_{1,1;1} \neq 0$, then the system admits a solution, which corresponds to a collision. Similar result holds for $\alpha_{1,1;1} = 0$ and $\alpha_{0,2;1}, \alpha_{2,0;1} \neq 0$. Hence, the only remaining cases to analyse are (i) $\alpha_{1,1;1} = \alpha_{0,2;1} = 0$ and $\alpha_{2,0;1} \neq 0$, or (ii) $\alpha_{1,1;1} = \alpha_{2,0;1} = 0$ and $\alpha_{0,2;1} \neq 0$. We limit ourselves to analyse the first case, since the other one is analogous.

SubCase: $\alpha_{1,1;1} = \alpha_{2,0;1} = 0$, $\alpha_{0,2;1} \neq 0$. By using the change of variables of Eq. (4), the system $\mathcal{S}_{F_0,F_1}(x_0, \ldots, x_{n-1}) = \mathcal{S}_{F_0,F_1}(y_0, \ldots, y_{n-1})$ is equal to

$$\begin{bmatrix} \alpha_{1,0;0} & \alpha_{0,1;0} & 0 & 0 & \cdots & 0 & 0 \\ 0 & \alpha_{1,0;1} & \alpha_{0,2;1} \cdot d_2 & 0 & \cdots & 0 & 0 \\ 0 & 0 & 0 & \alpha_{0,1;0} & \cdots & 0 & 0 \\ \vdots & & & & \ddots & \ddots & \vdots \\ 0 & 0 & 0 & 0 & \cdots & \alpha_{1,0;1} & \alpha_{0,2;1} \cdot d_{n-1} \\ \alpha_{0,1;0} & 0 & 0 & 0 & \cdots & 0 & 0 \end{bmatrix} \times \begin{bmatrix} d_0 \\ d_1 \\ s_2 \\ d_3 \\ \vdots \\ d_{n-2} \\ s_{n-1} \end{bmatrix} = - \begin{bmatrix} 0 \\ \alpha_{0,1;1} \cdot d_2 \\ \alpha_{0,1;0} \cdot d_3 \\ \alpha_{1,0;0} \cdot d_2 \\ \vdots \\ \alpha_{0,1;1} \cdot d_{n-1} \\ \alpha_{1,0;0} \cdot d_{n-1} \end{bmatrix}.$$

We solve this system with respect to the variables $\{d_0, d_1, s_2, d_3, \ldots, d_{n-2}, s_{n-1}\}$, i.e., variables d_i for odd i and for d_0 and variables s_i for even $i \geq 2$. We leave the others as free variables.

Since the determinant of the l.h.s. matrix is $-\alpha_{0,1;0}^{\frac{n+1}{2}} \cdot \alpha_{0,2;1}^{\frac{n-1}{2}} \cdot \prod_{i \geq 2 \text{ even}} d_i$, if we choose each $d_i \neq 0$ for $i \geq 2$ even, then the system is compatible and the ASI-lifting is not invertible.

SubCase: $n = 3$. Finally, we prove the result for $n = 3$. Given $F_0(x_0, x_1) = \alpha_{1,0;0} \cdot x_0 + \alpha_{0,1;0} \cdot x_1$ for $\alpha_{0,1;0}, \alpha_{1,0;0} \neq 0$, the system $y = \mathcal{S}_{F_0,F_1}(x)$ is

$$\alpha_{1,0;0} \cdot x_0 + \alpha_{0,1;0} \cdot x_1 = y_0,$$
$$\alpha_{2,0;1} \cdot x_1^2 + \alpha_{0,2;1} \cdot x_2^2 + \alpha_{1,1;1} \cdot x_1 \cdot x_2 + \alpha_{1,0;1} \cdot x_1 + \alpha_{0,1;1} \cdot x_2 = y_1,$$
$$\alpha_{1,0;0} \cdot x_2 + \alpha_{0,1;0} \cdot x_0 = y_2.$$

By replacing $x_1 = \frac{y_0 - \alpha_{1,0;0} \cdot x_0}{\alpha_{0,1;0}}, x_2 = \frac{y_2 - \alpha_{0,1;0} \cdot x_0}{\alpha_{1,0;0}}$ in the second equation, we get

$$x_0^2 \cdot \left(\frac{\alpha_{2,0;1} \cdot \alpha_{1,0;0}^2}{\alpha_{0,1;0}^2} + \frac{\alpha_{0,2;1} \cdot \alpha_{0,1;0}^2}{\alpha_{1,0;0}^2} + \alpha_{1,1;1} \right) + x_0 \cdot \left(y_0 \cdot \left(-2 \cdot \frac{\alpha_{2,0;1} \cdot \alpha_{1,0;0}}{\alpha_{0,1;0}^2} - \frac{\alpha_{1,1;1}}{\alpha_{1,0;0}} \right) \right.$$
$$+ y_2 \cdot \left(-2 \cdot \frac{\alpha_{0,2;1} \cdot \alpha_{0,1;0}}{\alpha_{1,0;0}^2} - \frac{\alpha_{1,1;1}}{\alpha_{0,1;0}} \right) - \frac{\alpha_{1,0;1} \cdot \alpha_{1,0;0}}{\alpha_{0,1;0}} - \frac{\alpha_{0,1;1} \cdot \alpha_{0,1;0}}{\alpha_{1,0;0}} \right)$$
$$+ \frac{\alpha_{2,0;1}}{\alpha_{0,1;0}^2} \cdot y_0^2 + \frac{\alpha_{0,2;1}}{\alpha_{1,0;0}^2} \cdot y_2^2 + \frac{\alpha_{1,1;1}}{\alpha_{0,1;0} \cdot \alpha_{1,0;0}} \cdot y_0 \cdot y_2 + \frac{\alpha_{1,0;1}}{\alpha_{0,1;0}} \cdot y_0 + \frac{\alpha_{0,1;1}}{\alpha_{1,0;0}} \cdot y_2 - y_1 = 0.$$

Working as in the proof of Lemma 11, the ASI-lifting is always invertible if and only if

- the coefficient of the monomial x_0^2 is zero, that is, $\alpha_{2,0;1} \cdot \alpha_{1,0;0}^4 + \alpha_{0,2;1} \cdot \alpha_{0,1;0}^4 + \alpha_{1,1;1} \cdot \alpha_{1,0;0}^2 \cdot \alpha_{0,1;0}^2 = 0$;
- the coefficient of the monomial x_0 is non-null, that is,
  1. $-2 \cdot \alpha_{1,0;0}^2 \cdot \alpha_{2,0;1} - \alpha_{1,1;1} \cdot \alpha_{0,1;0}^2 = 0$,
  2. $-2 \cdot \alpha_{0,2;1} \cdot \alpha_{0,1;0}^2 - \alpha_{1,1;1} \cdot \alpha_{1,0;0}^2 = 0$,
  3. $\alpha_{1,0;1} \cdot \alpha_{1,0;0}^2 \neq -\alpha_{0,1;1} \cdot \alpha_{0,1;0}^2$.

By combining these conditions, we get that the ASI-lifting is invertible if

$$F_1(x_0, x_1) = \gamma \cdot \left(\frac{\alpha_{0,1;0}}{\alpha_{1,0;0}} \cdot x_0 - \frac{\alpha_{1,0;0}}{\alpha_{0,1;0}} \cdot x_1 \right)^2 + \alpha_{1,0;1} \cdot x_0 + \alpha_{0,1;1} \cdot x_1$$

where $\gamma \in \mathbb{F}_p$ and $\alpha_{1,0;1} \cdot \alpha_{1,0;0}^2 \neq -\alpha_{0,1;1} \cdot \alpha_{0,1;0}^2$.   □

6   Summary and Open Problems for Future Work

In this paper, we show that it is impossible to have invertibility of alternating shift-invariant lifting functions $\mathcal{S}_{F_0,F_1}$ over $\mathbb{F}_p^n$ induced by two local quadratic maps $F_0, F_1 : \mathbb{F}_p^2 \to \mathbb{F}_p$. When we relax conditions and we take one of the two local maps to be linear, we find some invertible functions. Unfortunately, for each $n \geq 4$, we get only the already known Type-II Feistel schemes.

Our findings provide some insights, though it leaves open for future research the problem of setting up invertible quadratic non-linear functions over $\mathbb{F}_p^n$

induced by local maps. An obvious possible way to solve it is to consider local maps $F_0, F_1, \ldots, F_{h-1} : \mathbb{F}_p^m \to \mathbb{F}_p$ defined over a larger input domain by taking $m \geq 3$. Another strategy may consist of generalizing the current construction. E.g., let's focus on the case of the SI-lifting function $\mathcal{S}_F$ over $\mathbb{F}_p^n$ for $F : \mathbb{F}_p^m \to \mathbb{F}_p$. In the current definition, the function F takes in input consecutive elements $x_i, x_{i+1}, \ldots, x_{i+m-1}$. A possible way to generalize such definition consists of allowing for non-consecutive inputs, as formally given in the following definition.

Definition 6. *Let $p \geq 3$ be a prime integer, and let $1 \leq m \leq n$ be two positive integers. Let $F : \mathbb{F}_p^m \to \mathbb{F}_p$, and let $j_1, j_2, \ldots, j_{m-1} \in \{1, 2, \ldots, n-1\}$ be $m-1$ **distinct** integers. We define $\mathcal{S}_{F,[j_1,j_2,\ldots,j_{m-1}]}$ over $\mathbb{F}_p^n$ as*

$$\mathcal{S}_{F,[j_1,j_2,\ldots,j_{m-1}]}(x_0, x_1, \ldots, x_{n-1}) = y_0 \| y_1 \| \ldots \| y_{n-1}$$

where

$$y_i = F(x_i, x_{i+j_1}, x_{i+j_2}, \ldots, x_{i+j_{m-1}}) \qquad \text{for each } i \in \{0, 1, \ldots, n-1\}.$$

A similar construction can be proposed for cycling and alternating shift-invariant functions as well. We leave the problem to study their invertibility as future work.

Acknowledgement. Lorenzo Grassi was supported by the German Research Foundation (DFG) within the framework of the Excellence Strategy of the Federal Government and the States – EXC 2092 CaSa – 39078197.

References

1. Albrecht, M.R., et al.: Feistel structures for MPC, and more. In: Sako, K., Schneider, S., Ryan, P.Y.A. (eds.) ESORICS 2019. LNCS, vol. 11736, pp. 151–171. Springer, Cham (2019). https://doi.org/10.1007/978-3-030-29962-0_8
2. Albrecht, M., Grassi, L., Rechberger, C., Roy, A., Tiessen, T.: MiMC: efficient encryption and cryptographic hashing with minimal multiplicative complexity. In: Cheon, J.H., Takagi, T. (eds.) ASIACRYPT 2016. LNCS, vol. 10031, pp. 191–219. Springer, Heidelberg (2016). https://doi.org/10.1007/978-3-662-53887-6_7
3. Aly, A., Ashur, T., Ben-Sasson, E., Dhooghe, S., Szepieniec, A.: Design of symmetric-key primitives for advanced cryptographic protocols. IACR Trans. Symmetric Cryptol. **2020**(3), 1–45 (2020)
4. Beierle, C., Carlet, C., Leander, G., Perrin, L.: A further study of quadratic APN permutations in dimension nine. Finite Fields Their Appl. **81**, 102049 (2022)
5. Beth, T., Ding, C.: On almost perfect nonlinear permutations. In: Helleseth, T. (ed.) EUROCRYPT 1993. LNCS, vol. 765, pp. 65–76. Springer, Heidelberg (1994). https://doi.org/10.1007/3-540-48285-7_7
6. Biham, E., Shamir, A.: Differential cryptanalysis of DES-like cryptosystems. In: Menezes, A.J., Vanstone, S.A. (eds.) CRYPTO 1990. LNCS, vol. 537, pp. 2–21. Springer, Heidelberg (1991). https://doi.org/10.1007/3-540-38424-3_1
7. Bouvier, C., et al.: New design techniques for efficient arithmetization-oriented hash functions: anemoi permutations and jive compression mode. Cryptology ePrint Archive, Paper 2022/840 (2022). https://eprint.iacr.org/2022/840

8. Budaghyan, L., Calderini, M., Carlet, C., Davidova, D., Kaleyski, N.S.: On two fundamental problems on APN power functions. IEEE Trans. Inf. Theory **68**(5), 3389–3403 (2022)
9. Budaghyan, L., Carlet, C., Leander, G.: Constructing new APN functions from known ones. Finite Fields Their Appl. **15**(2), 150–159 (2009)
10. Carlet, C.: Relating three nonlinearity parameters of vectorial functions and building APN functions from bent functions. Des. Codes Cryptogr. **59**(1–3), 89–109 (2011)
11. Carlet, C.: Boolean functions. In: Handbook of Finite Fields. Discrete Mathematics and Its Applications, pp. 241–252. CRC Press (2013)
12. Carlet, C.: On APN exponents, characterizations of differentially uniform functions by the Walsh transform, and related cyclic-difference-set-like structures. Des. Codes Cryptogr. **87**(2–3), 203–224 (2019)
13. Daemen, J.: Cipher and hash function design, strategies based on linear and differential cryptanalysis, Ph.D. thesis. K.U. Leuven (1995). http://jda.noekeon.org/
14. Daemen, J., Rijmen, V.: The wide trail design strategy. In: Honary, B. (ed.) Cryptography and Coding 2001. LNCS, vol. 2260, pp. 222–238. Springer, Heidelberg (2001). https://doi.org/10.1007/3-540-45325-3_20
15. Dobraunig, C., Grassi, L., Guinet, A., Kuijsters, D.: CIMINION: symmetric encryption based on Toffoli-gates over large finite fields. In: Canteaut, A., Standaert, F.-X. (eds.) EUROCRYPT 2021. LNCS, vol. 12697, pp. 3–34. Springer, Cham (2021). https://doi.org/10.1007/978-3-030-77886-6_1
16. Dobraunig, C., Grassi, L., Helminger, L., Rechberger, C., Schofnegger, M., Walch, R.: Pasta: a case for hybrid homomorphic encryption. Cryptology ePrint Archive, Report 2021/731 (2021), https://ia.cr/2021/731. Accepted at TCHES 2023
17. Gold, R.: Maximal recursive sequences with 3-valued recursive crosscorrelation functions. IEEE Trans. Inform. Theory **14**, 154–156 (1968)
18. Grassi, L.: Bounded surjective quadratic functions over $\mathbb{F}_p{}^n$ for MPC-/ZK-/HE-friendly symmetric primitives. Cryptology ePrint Archive, Paper 2022/1313 (2022). https://eprint.iacr.org/2022/1313
19. Grassi, L.: On generalizations of the lai-massey scheme: the blooming of amaryllises. Cryptology ePrint Archive, Paper 2022/1245 (2022). https://eprint.iacr.org/2022/1245
20. Grassi, L., Hao, Y., Rechberger, C., Schofnegger, M., Walch, R., Wang, Q.: Horst meets fluid-SPN: griffin for zero-knowledge applications. Cryptology ePrint Archive, Report 2022/403 (2022). https://ia.cr/2022/403
21. Grassi, L., Khovratovich, D., Lüftenegger, R., Rechberger, C., Schofnegger, M., Walch, R.: Reinforced concrete: a fast hash function for verifiable computation. In: Proceedings of the 2022 ACM SIGSAC Conference on Computer and Communications Security, CCS 2022, pp. 1323–1335. ACM (2022)
22. Grassi, L., Khovratovich, D., Rechberger, C., Roy, A., Schofnegger, M.: POSEIDON: a new hash function for zero-knowledge proof systems. In: USENIX Security 2021. USENIX Association (2021)
23. Grassi, L., Khovratovich, D., Rønjom, S., Schofnegger, M.: The legendre symbol and the modulo-2 operator in symmetric schemes over $(\mathbb{F}_p)^n$. IACR Trans. Symmetric Cryptol. **2022**(1), 5–37 (2022)
24. Grassi, L., Onofri, S., Pedicini, M., Sozzi, L.: Invertible quadratic non-linear layers for MPC-/FHE-/ZK-friendly schemes over $\mathbb{F}_p{}^n$ - application to POSEIDON. IACR Trans. Symmetric Cryptol. **2022**(3), 20–72 (2022)

25. Grassi, L., Øygarden, M., Schofnegger, M., Walch, R.: From farfalle to Mega-fono via Ciminion: the PRF hydra for MPC applications. In: Hazay, C., Stam, M. (eds.) EUROCRYPT 2023. LNCS, vol. 14007, pp. 255–286. Springer, Cham (2023). https://doi.org/10.1007/978-3-031-30634-1_9
26. Lai, X., Massey, J.L.: A proposal for a new block encryption standard. In: Damgård, I.B. (ed.) EUROCRYPT 1990. LNCS, vol. 473, pp. 389–404. Springer, Heidelberg (1991). https://doi.org/10.1007/3-540-46877-3_35
27. Meier, W., Pasalic, E., Carlet, C.: Algebraic attacks and decomposition of boolean functions. In: Cachin, C., Camenisch, J.L. (eds.) EUROCRYPT 2004. LNCS, vol. 3027, pp. 474–491. Springer, Heidelberg (2004). https://doi.org/10.1007/978-3-540-24676-3_28
28. Meier, W., Staffelbach, O.: Nonlinearity criteria for cryptographic functions. In: Quisquater, J.-J., Vandewalle, J. (eds.) EUROCRYPT 1989. LNCS, vol. 434, pp. 549–562. Springer, Heidelberg (1990). https://doi.org/10.1007/3-540-46885-4_53
29. Nyberg, K.: S-boxes and round functions with controllable linearity and differential uniformity. In: Preneel, B. (ed.) FSE 1994. LNCS, vol. 1008, pp. 111–130. Springer, Heidelberg (1995). https://doi.org/10.1007/3-540-60590-8_9
30. Nyberg, K.: Generalized feistel networks. In: Kim, K., Matsumoto, T. (eds.) ASIACRYPT 1996. LNCS, vol. 1163, pp. 91–104. Springer, Heidelberg (1996). https://doi.org/10.1007/BFb0034838
31. Szepieniec, A.: On the use of the legendre symbol in symmetric cipher design. Cryptology ePrint Archive, Report 2021/984 (2021). https://ia.cr/2021/984
32. Vaudenay, S.: On the Lai-Massey scheme. In: Lam, K.-Y., Okamoto, E., Xing, C. (eds.) ASIACRYPT 1999. LNCS, vol. 1716, pp. 8–19. Springer, Heidelberg (1999). https://doi.org/10.1007/978-3-540-48000-6_2
33. Wolfram, S.: Cryptography with cellular automata. In: Williams, H.C. (ed.) CRYPTO 1985. LNCS, vol. 218, pp. 429–432. Springer, Heidelberg (1986). https://doi.org/10.1007/3-540-39799-X_32
34. Zheng, Y., Matsumoto, T., Imai, H.: On the construction of block ciphers provably secure and not relying on any unproved hypotheses. In: Brassard, G. (ed.) CRYPTO 1989. LNCS, vol. 435, pp. 461–480. Springer, New York (1990). https://doi.org/10.1007/0-387-34805-0_42

POSEIDON2: A Faster Version of the POSEIDON Hash Function

Lorenzo Grassi[1,2], Dmitry Khovratovich[3], and Markus Schofnegger[4(✉)]

[1] Ponos Technology, Zug, Switzerland
`lorenzo@ponos.technology`
[2] Ruhr University Bochum, Bochum, Germany
[3] Ethereum Foundation, Esch-sur-Alzette, Luxembourg
[4] Horizen Labs, Austin, USA
`mschofnegger@horizenlabs.io`

Abstract. Zero-knowledge proof systems for computational integrity have seen a rise in popularity in the last couple of years. One of the results of this development is the ongoing effort in designing so-called *arithmetization-friendly* hash functions in order to make these proofs more efficient. One of these new hash functions, POSEIDON, is extensively used in this context, also thanks to being one of the first constructions tailored towards this use case. Many of the design principles of POSEIDON have proven to be efficient and were later used in other primitives, yet parts of the construction have shown to be expensive in real-word scenarios.

In this paper, we propose an optimized version of POSEIDON, called POSEIDON2. The two versions differ in two crucial points. First, POSEIDON is a sponge hash function, while POSEIDON2 can be either a sponge or a compression function depending on the use case. Secondly, POSEIDON2 is instantiated by new and more efficient linear layers with respect to POSEIDON. These changes allow to decrease the number of multiplications in the linear layer by up to 90% and the number of constraints in Plonk circuits by up to 70%. This makes POSEIDON2 the currently fastest arithmetization-oriented hash function without lookups.

Besides that, we address a recently proposed algebraic attack and propose a simple modification that makes both POSEIDON and POSEIDON2 secure against this approach.

Keywords: POSEIDON · POSEIDON2 · ZK Application · Sponge/Compression Mode

1 Introduction

The area of zero-knowledge proof systems has seen a rise in popularity during the last couple of years. Arithmetization techniques such as R1CS used in Groth16 [31], AIR used for FRI-based commitments [9,10], and Plonk [22] and Plonk-style arithmetizations (e.g., [21] used in halo2 [47]) make it possible to efficiently verify the correctness of a computation.

© The Author(s), under exclusive license to Springer Nature Switzerland AG 2023
N. El Mrabet et al. (Eds.): AFRICACRYPT 2023, LNCS 14064, pp. 177–203, 2023.
https://doi.org/10.1007/978-3-031-37679-5_8

Most of these proof systems internally use hash functions for the purpose of polynomial (Merkle tree) commitments. These hash functions are rather different compared to more traditional primitives. Indeed, while the latter are often optimized for plain performance in software or hardware implementations, constructions for proof systems mostly focus on minimizing the number of *constraints* (similar to gates) when writing them down in a specific circuit language. This fact has led to new symmetric designs, exhibiting sometimes unusual symmetric building blocks (e.g., sacrificing plain performance in order to obtain a simpler description in a certain proof system).

In the literature, hash functions fulfilling these properties are often described as being *arithmetization-oriented*, which refers to their focus towards use cases of computational integrity. Besides POSEIDON [24], examples of such constructions include MiMC/GMiMC [2,3], *Rescue* [4], NEPTUNE [28], Anemoi [16], and GRIFFIN [23]. In the last years, the knowledge of designing arithmetization-oriented hash functions has evolved, and more specific design goals are known today. For example, while minimizing the number of nonlinear operations was deemed the main target several years ago, many more performance metrics are taken into account now. Some of these metrics are the plain performance and the circuit complexity, which can play a significant role in the final proof composition.

The Origin of Poseidon. In this paper, we mostly focus on the POSEIDON hash function. First described in 2019 [26], it is heavily based on the HADESMiMC family of block ciphers [27]. The key property of HADESMiMC is that it uses two different round functions, one containing a full nonlinear layer with S-boxes applied to the entire state, and one containing a partial nonlinear layer with the S-boxes only affecting part of the state. This approach was chosen in order to provide convincing security arguments against statistical attacks using the full rounds while at the same time increasing the degree efficiently (i.e., by using a smaller number of S-boxes) using the partial rounds. However, HADESMiMC was designed with MPC use cases in mind, which has very different properties and optimization goals compared to modern proof systems. Most importantly, all linear operations can be computed locally by every party in an MPC protocol. Since the final efficiency of such a protocol depends on the number of communication rounds and no communication is needed for linear operations, the main optimization goal of HADESMiMC was to minimize the number of nonlinear operations. As a result, the final number of linear operations turned out to be comparatively high, mainly due to many multiplications with matrices of large sizes. In particular, each round of HADESMiMC contains a multiplication of a t-element state with a dense and unstructured $t \times t$ matrix over $\mathbb{F}_p$, where p is a comparatively large prime. Hence, this operation results in a number of multiplications in $\mathcal{O}(t^2)$ over $\mathbb{F}_p$.

Similar to MPC use cases, in some arithmetization techniques (e.g., R1CS used in Groth16 [31]), the number of nonlinear operations is also the main bottleneck. Hence, building a hash function based on the HADESMiMC permutation seemed like an efficient approach. This idea led to the specification of POSEIDON, which is essentially a sponge hash function using an internal permutation similar to the one used in HADESMiMC (with minor differences such as the omission of a key addition). POSEIDON has since been implemented and used in many different proving frameworks, including e.g. Ginger-lib [32] and Plonky2 [41].

Plain Performance and the Plonk Arithmetization. Since the design of POSEIDON, various new optimization goals emerged. For example, it became clear that plain performance must not be neglected, since among other things it plays a crucial role when building the commitments outside of the respective circuits. Recent hash function designs in this area acknowledge this fact and try to also optimize for plain performance.

Moreover, the variety of different arithmetization techniques has increased in the last couple of years. While R1CS was the main target for the original POSEIDON, nowadays also the so-called algebraic intermediate representation (AIR) [11] for FRI-based proof systems [9] or Plonk [22] and "Plonkish" representations are popular approaches. Particularly, in Plonk linear operations also contribute to the final cost. Note that this is a clear distinction between Plonk and R1CS.

The POSEIDON hash function, while widely used and arguably efficient in some use cases, exhibits a large number of linear operations. This makes it expensive in terms of plain performance and when considering a Plonk-style arithmetization.

1.1   Our Goals

Our first goal for POSEIDON2$^\pi$ is to achieve a simpler and more efficient version of POSEIDON$^\pi$. At the same time, we want to stay close to the original description, which allows us to benefit from years of third-party cryptanalysis applied to POSEIDON$^\pi$. In particular, our modifications allow us to achieve significant performance improvements while keeping the same round numbers, i.e., the same number of nonlinear operations. This is beneficial in concrete use cases in computational integrity. Indeed, the number of constraints does not increase when choosing POSEIDON2$^\pi$ instead of POSEIDON$^\pi$, while at the same time the plain performance is better. For example, Merkle trees, a prominent building block in many proof systems, can be computed significantly faster.

The updated POSEIDON2$^\pi$ will show similarities to other primitives, for example NEPTUNE. Still, the algorithmic description is much closer to POSEIDON$^\pi$. We chose this approach since POSEIDON$^\pi$ is widely used in practice, and reusing components from the original design reduces implementation efforts.

Remark 1. We emphasize that we do not propose changes to the original permutation, and we do not propose a new security analysis for it either. Instead, our modification POSEIDON2$^\pi$ can be thought of as a new and optimized version of POSEIDON$^\pi$.

1.2 Our Contributions and Results

Security Issue for Poseidon $^\pi$. We address a security problem with the original POSEIDON$^\pi$ permutation. Indeed, as has been observed in [8], the first two nonlinear layers can be skipped when mounting an algebraic attack on POSEIDON$^\pi$. This results in equation systems of lower degrees and a more efficient attack. This approach can be mitigated by adding an additional linear layer to the beginning of the permutation. We discuss this issue in Sect. 7.3.

Poseidon2$^\pi$. As the main contribution, we consider various optimizations in order to make POSEIDON faster and more efficient in recent proof systems. In particular, compared to the original POSEIDON$^\pi$ permutation, our modification called POSEIDON2$^\pi$ has

(1) an additional linear layer at the beginning of the permutation,
(2) different linear layer matrices,
(3) round constants only applied to the first word in the internal rounds, and
(4) the same number of rounds for many instantiations used in practice.

Regarding the last point, we compare the statistical and the algebraic security of POSEIDON2$^\pi$ with that of POSEIDON$^\pi$. We also emphasize that our new modified permutation is very similar in nature to the original one, and thus inherits the trust gained from the third-party cryptanalysis of POSEIDON. A full specification of the new linear layers and of POSEIDON2$^\pi$ is given in Sect. 5 and Sect. 6.

Modes of Operation. In many computational integrity proof systems, the construction of Merkle trees is a crucial part. For example, it is used to compute commitments to polynomials or to prove membership. When building a Merkle tree, the next hash is computed using a fixed number of previous (hash) outputs. For this purpose, the sponge function has often been used in the past, albeit with only one permutation call. In this paper, depending on the use case, we suggest to use either the classical sponge hash function or a generic compression function which computes a single new output using an arbitrary number of inputs and only one permutation call. We discuss both modes of operation specified for POSEIDON2$^\pi$ in Sect. 3.1.

Performance Comparison. Following the description of our new permutation POSEIDON2$^\pi$, we discuss its performance characteristics in Sect. 8. We focus on the plain performance and on the number of Plonk constraints, and provide benchmarks from a Rust implementation for various state sizes. We also compare POSEIDON2$^\pi$ to the original version and to other similar primitives, and we provide a new Plonkish arithmetization technique which is compatible with both POSEIDON2$^\pi$ and POSEIDON$^\pi$.

2 Preliminaries: Modern Arithmetization Techniques

Our focus in this paper is on use cases in the area of computational integrity proof systems. In such a scenario, a prover wants to convince a verifier to have correctly run an arbitrary computation, without making the verifier recompute the result. Many such proof systems exist in practice [11,22,31], and they also allow for zero-knowledge versions where the verifier does not learn any private details of the provided proof.

In general, a proof can be split into two steps. First, the computation has to be represented as a number of polynomials, which is usually called *arithmetization*. Then, a polynomial commitment scheme is used in order to finalize the proof. In this paper, we focus on the arithmetization step, and for this purpose we briefly describe popular techniques. The aim when applying these is to keep the number of constraints as low as possible.

R1CS. A rank-1 constraint satisfaction system (R1CS) consists of n equations in the variables $v_0, v_1, \ldots, v_m$ defined by $\left(\sum_{i=0}^{m} a_i^{(n)} v_i \right) \cdot \left(\sum_{i=0}^{m} b_i^{(n)} v_i \right) = \left(\sum_{i=0}^{m} c_i^{(n)} v_i \right)$, where v_i are elements from a finite field $\mathbb{F}$, $v_0 \in 0, 1$, and $a_i^{(n)}, b_i^{(n)}, c_i^{(n)}$ are field elements describing the n-th constraint.

Note that these equations are of degree 2 in $\{v_i\}_{i=0}^{m}$. They are derived from the statement to prove, which in many cases is a hash function evaluation. Then, minimizing the number of constraints generally leads to more efficient proofs. As an example, using high-degree functions in the hash specification results in a larger number of constraints, which is why many recent arithmetization-oriented designs rely on low-degree components.

Plonk and Variants. The Plonk [22] arithmetization results in a table-like representation for the execution trace. However, the constraints are not restricted to describe entire state transitions, and in general more freedom is offered to the designer. In particular, every constraint is of the form

$$q_{L_i} \cdot a_{L_i} + q_{R_i} \cdot a_{R_i} + q_{O_i} \cdot a_{O_i} + q_{M_i} \cdot (a_{L_i} a_{R_i}) + q_{C_i} = 0,$$

where $a_{L_i}, a_{R_i}, a_{O_i}$ are witness variables describing two inputs and an output of a gate, and $q_{L_i}, q_{R_i}, q_{O_i}, q_{M_i}, q_{C_i}$ are set such that a specific gate constraint (e.g., an addition or a multiplication) is enforced. Note that this is only a basic description of Plonk, and subsequent variants such as [21] make it possible to increase the "width" of the gate (e.g., the number of inputs).

A notable difference in Plonk when compared to R1CS is that linear gates (e.g., additions) also require constraints of their own. Hence, linear operations are not "for free" anymore. This can make expensive linear operations, such as matrix multiplications, not only inefficient in a plain evaluation, but also with regards to the arithmetization.

Plonkish and AIR. Both Plonkish [47] and AIR [11] are more powerful representations compared to R1CS and regular Plonk. Like Plonk, both Plonkish and AIR describe a computation trace as a matrix, but allow high-degree polynomial relations to represent the state transformation.

The set of states is a $T \times w$ matrix, where T is the number of states and w is the width (or the number of registers). Focusing on a hash function evaluation, for example w is set to the state size of the hash primitive and each new state describes the values obtained after applying a round function to the previous state. In contrast to R1CS, the constraint polynomials are not required to be of degree 2, but the efficiency of the arithmetization still depends on the maximum degree d in the constraint polynomials. The prover time is proportional to $T \cdot w \cdot d$, whereas the proof size is an affine function of the maximal number of variables q in the constraints. Hence, more efficient Plonkish/AIR proofs are delivered by smaller degrees and/or fewer variables in the constraints.

3   Preliminaries: ZK-Friendly Symmetric Primitives

3.1   Modes of Operation

Hash functions are crucial in the context of zero-knowledge protocols, e.g., to build Merkle trees for a polynomial commitment. Given a hash function $\mathcal{H} : \mathbb{F}_p^\star \to \mathbb{F}_p^\infty$ for a prime $p \geq 2$, it must be computationally hard to find

(collision resistance) x, x' such that $\mathcal{H}(x) = \mathcal{H}(x')$,
(preimage resistance) x given y such that $\mathcal{H}(x) = y$,
(second-preimage resistance) x' given $x \neq x'$ such that $\mathcal{H}(x') = \mathcal{H}(x)$.

In this paper, we mainly focus on the sponge mode, which has also been used in many of the recent arithmetization-oriented designs.

While hash functions are perfectly usable and allow to make strong security arguments, they are often more generic. For many classical applications (e.g., ordinary hashing of arbitrary-length inputs) this is not a major issue. However, when building a Merkle tree with small fixed-size input lengths, we often only need a single permutation call to process the entire input and compute the desired output. In this case, the construction is not used as a hash function in a traditional sense, but rather as a compression function.

The concept of compression functions is well-known in cryptography, and they can also be used to build general-purpose hash functions [18,40]. For our use case, however, we focus on single calls to compression functions, precisely matching our need for building a Merkle tree and supporting so-called t-to-n compressions, i.e., compressing a vector of size t into one of size n. As for the case of hash functions, a compression function $C : \mathbb{F}_p^t \to \mathbb{F}_p^n$ must guarantee resistance against collision and (second-)preimage attacks.

Sponge Hash Functions. A sponge hash function [12] is built using an internal cryptographic permutation or function. It accommodates for both arbitrarily sized inputs and arbitrarily sized outputs. Let $\mathcal{P}$ be a permutation over $\mathbb{F}_p^t$, and let $t = r + c$, where c denotes the capacity and r the rate. A sponge function then works as follows.

1. The input message $m \in \mathbb{F}_p^*$ is padded with $10*$ such that its size is a multiple of r, that is, $m = m_0 \parallel m_1 \parallel \cdots \parallel m_{\mu-1} \in (\mathbb{F}_p^r)^\mu$.
2. The capacity is initialized with $IV \in \mathbb{F}_p^c$.
3. The message blocks are compressed one-by-one into a $\mathbb{F}_p^t$ state such that

$$\forall i \in \{0, 1, \ldots, \mu - 1\}: \quad h_i = h_{i-1} + P(m_i \parallel 0^c),$$

where $0^c := 0 \parallel \cdots \parallel 0 \in \mathbb{F}_p^c$ and $h_{-1} := 0^r \parallel IV \in \mathbb{F}_p^t$.
4. After processing the last message block, the output is of the form $\mathrm{Tr}_r(h_\mu) \parallel \mathrm{Tr}_r(h_{\mu+1}) \parallel \cdots$, where the truncation function Tr_r yields the first r elements of the input.

In this paper, we adapt the SAFE padding rule proposed in [7], consisting of adding the smallest number $< r$ of zeroes such that the size of $m \parallel 0^*$ is a multiple of r, where $IV = H(IO, D)$ with H being a 128-bit hash function, IO being the pattern of absorbing to and squeezing elements to the sponge (for plain ℓ-input hashing one sets $IO = 2^{63} + \ell 2^{32} + 1$), and D being a domain separator.

Security. As proven in [12], if the inner permutation resembles a random one, the sponge construction is indifferentiable from a random oracle up to around $p^{c/2}$ queries. Equivalently, in order to provide κ bits of security, $p^{c/2} \geq 2^\kappa$.[1]

Cryptographic Compression Functions. Let $\mathcal{P}$ be a permutation over $\mathbb{F}_p^t$. Several strategies can be used to construct a compression function. Here we focus on compression functions defined by combining the truncation function with the feed-forward operation, i.e.,

$$x \in \mathbb{F}_p^t \mapsto \mathcal{C}(x) := \mathrm{Tr}_n(\mathcal{P}(x) + x) \in \mathbb{F}_p^n,$$

where Tr_n yields the first n elements of the inputs. Several schemes proposed in the literature reduce to this model, including Haraka [37] and the Jive mode of operation proposed in [16].

Security of $\mathcal{C}$. As discussed e.g. in [23], this approach can be seen as a permutation-based variant of the Davies-Meyer mode [15,42] which, like the latter, crucially relies on a feed-forward operation for one-wayness. For a security level of κ bits and assuming $\mathcal{P}$ behaves like a pseudo-random (known) permutation, $\mathcal{C}$ is a secure compression function with respect to collisions and (second-)preimages if

(1) $p^n \geq 2^{2\kappa}$ due to the birthday bound attack whose cost is in $\mathcal{O}(2^{-n/2} = 2^{-\kappa})$,
(2) $p^{t-n} \geq 2^\kappa$ in order to avoid a guessing attack on the truncated part.

---

[1] We assume that the output consists of at least $2\kappa/\log_2(p)$ elements in order to prevent birthday bound attacks.

3.2 The Poseidon$^\pi$ Permutation

Since our optimization is strongly based on the POSEIDON$^\pi$ permutation, we recall its definition here. We refer to the original paper [24,26] for more details.

Remark 2. We emphasize that the round numbers given in the following are based on the updated security analysis proposed in [26], where the designers make corrections to the original bounds. This also includes the recent results from [6]. However, to the best of our knowledge, such results should not impact the round number of any instance of POSEIDON$^\pi$ (due to the restriction on the value of p, t and κ). For this reason, we do not consider it in this work.

Let $p > 2^{30}$ be a prime number and let $t \geq 2$ (in the following, let $n \approx \log_2(p)$). The POSEIDON$^\pi$ permutation $\mathcal{P}$ over $\mathbb{F}_p^t$ is defined by

$$\mathcal{P}(x) = \mathcal{E}_{R_F-1} \circ \cdots \circ \mathcal{E}_{R_F/2} \circ \mathcal{I}_{R_P-1} \circ \cdots \circ \mathcal{I}_0 \circ \mathcal{E}_{R_F/2-1} \circ \cdots \circ \mathcal{E}_0(x),$$

where $\mathcal{E}$ is an external (full) round, $\mathcal{I}$ is an internal (partial) round, R_F is the number of external rounds, and R_P is the number of internal rounds. For a security level of κ bits with $2^{80} \leq 2^\kappa \leq \min\{2^{256}, p^{t/3}\}$ (due to the security of the sponge hash function and compression function given before),

$$R_F = 2 \cdot R_f = 8,$$

$$R_P \geq \left\lceil 1.125 \cdot \left\lceil \max\left\{ \frac{\min\{\kappa, \log_2(p)\}}{\log_2(d)} + \log_d(t) - 5, R_{\mathrm{GB}} \right\} \right\rceil \right\rceil, \tag{1}$$

where R_{GB} is related to the Gröbner basis attack and given by[2]

$$R_{\mathrm{GB}} \geq \max\Bigg\{ \log_d(2) \cdot \min\{\kappa, \log_2(p)\} - 6,$$

$$t - 7 + \log_d(2) \cdot \min\left\{ \frac{\kappa}{t+1}, \frac{\log_2(p)}{2} \right\}, \frac{M}{\log_2(3)} - t - 1 \Bigg\}.$$

The security level consists of 2 external/full rounds and 12.5% more internal/partial rounds. The external round $\mathcal{E}$ is defined by

$$\mathcal{E}_i(x) = M \cdot \left((x_0 + c_0^{(i)})^d, (x_1 + c_1^{(i)})^d, \ldots, (x_{t-1} + c_{t-1}^{(i)})^d \right)$$

for $i \in \{0, 1, \ldots, R_F - 1\}$, where $d \geq 3$ is the smallest positive integer that satisfies $\gcd(d, p - 1) = 1$ and where $c_j^{(i)}$ is the j-th round constant in the i-th external round. The internal round is defined by

$$\mathcal{I}_i(x) = M \cdot \left((x_0 + c_0^{(i)})^d, x_1 + c_1^{(i)}, \ldots, x_{t-1} + c_{t-1}^{(i)} \right)$$

---

[2] The attack presented in [6] is prevented if $\binom{\mathcal{V}+D_{\mathrm{reg}}}{D_{\mathrm{reg}}}^2 \geq 2^M$, where $\mathcal{V} = (R_F - 2) \cdot t + R_P + 2r$ and $D_{\mathrm{reg}} \approx r \cdot \frac{R_F}{2} + R_P + \alpha$. We remark that – to the best of our knowledge – this attack does not affect the instances considered in this paper.

for $i \in \{0, 1, \dots, R_P - 1\}$, where d is defined as before and where $c_j^{(i)}$ is the j-th round constant in the i-th internal round.

In both cases, M is a $t \times t$ MDS matrix fulfilling particular properties in order to prevent arbitrarily long subspace trails. We refer to [30] and to Sect. 5.3 for more details regarding the condition for preventing arbitrarily long subspace trails. Here we limit ourselves to recall that such a condition is satisfied if the minimal polynomials of $M, M^2, \dots, M^\ell$ are irreducible and of maximum degree. One way to set up an MDS matrix is by using a Cauchy matrix, whose element in the j-th column of the i-th row is defined by $M_{i,j} = 1/(x_i + y_j)$ for pairwise distinct $\{x_i\}_{i=1}^t$ and $\{y_i\}_{i=1}^t$, where $x_i + y_j \neq 0$.

Efficient Implementation. The POSEIDON$^\pi$ permutation allows for an optimized implementation, where the round constant additions and the matrix multiplications in the partial rounds can be replaced by more efficient equivalent operations. The approach is described in detail in [26, Appendix B]. We use this method in our benchmarks for POSEIDON$^\pi$.

Security Argument. The security argument of POSEIDON$^\pi$ is based on the HADES design strategy [27]. In particular, the external rounds together with the wide trail strategy are used to obtain simple and convincing arguments against statistical attacks. On the other hand, the internal rounds are mainly responsible for the security against algebraic attacks. The motivation is that the degree grows equally in the external and the internal round, but internal rounds are more efficient in the target use cases.

4   Security: Initial and Final Matrix Multiplications

In the case of a block cipher, it is well known that the initial and the final affine layer do not (usually) affect the security. Indeed, it is sufficient to swap the initial/final affine layer with the initial/final key addition. Having done that, one can simply consider an equivalent version of the cipher without the initial/final affine layer, which is applied directly to the plaintext/ciphertext.

The situation is different for the case of a sponge function. In the following, we discuss the impact of the initial and final linear layers in the case of a permutation that instantiates a sponge hash function and/or a compression one.

Remark 3. The following considerations only hold for SPN schemes. They do not hold in general for schemes in which a nonlinear diffusion takes place.

Case: Sponge Hash Function. In the case of a sponge hash function, the inner part is initialized with an initial value IV. Since the S-boxes of the nonlinear layer work independently from each other over $\mathbb{F}_p$, it is sufficient to replace IV with the corresponding value IV' computed via the nonlinear layer in order to remove the first nonlinear layer. In this case, the collision/preimage found for the sponge hash function instantiated with the modified permutation without the initial nonlinear layer can be easily extended to a collision/preimage for the sponge hash function instantiated with the original permutation. This attack has been discussed in [8] for the case of POSEIDON$^\pi$ and *Rescue*. Interestingly, the recent sponge hash function Tip5 [46] exhibits a similar problem, since its internal SPN permutation starts with a nonlinear layer instead of a linear one.

A similar conclusion holds for the final linear layer as well. We recall that in the sponge hash function, a truncation takes place in the final step. The final linear layer guarantees that the truncated part depends on all the outputs of the final nonlinear layer. If the linear layer is omitted, then no diffusion takes place. Working in the same way just described for the initial layer, it is simple to observe that the final nonlinear layer does not have any impact on the security, and it can simply be removed.

Case: Compression Function. The situation for the compression function is slightly different. As discussed in [23], given invertible linear layers $M', M'', \hat{M}$, the security of the two constructions

$$x \mapsto M' \times \mathcal{P}(M'' \times x) + \hat{M} \times x \qquad \text{and} \qquad x' \mapsto \mathcal{P}'(x') + x'$$

is identical for $\mathcal{P}'(\cdot) := M' \times \mathcal{P}(M'' \times \hat{M}^{-1} \times \cdot)$ and $x' := \hat{M} \times x$. For this reason, we are not aware of any concrete impact of the initial and/or final linear layer on the security of the compression function $x \mapsto \mathrm{Tr}_n(\mathcal{P}(x) + x)$.

Conclusion. When designing an SPN permutation for a sponge hash function, it is paramount that it starts and finishes with a linear layer that provides diffusion. Since these linear layers do not decrease the security when used with a compression function, we suggest to do the same in this case.

5   More Efficient Linear Layers

Using the wide trail strategy and matrices with large branch numbers allows the designer to use convincing arguments regarding the statistical security of a permutation. However, POSEIDON$^\pi$ is mostly used together with large prime numbers, which in combination with low-degree nonlinear functions provide strong statistical properties. Therefore, large branch numbers are not strictly needed in order to achieve the advertised level of security, and we can instead focus on more efficient matrices.

In this section, we propose several new linear layers to be used together with the POSEIDON$^\pi$ permutation. All of these are built in order to provide the same security level as the original specification. However, we take into account the plain performance and the number of constraints in a Plonkish arithmetization (for the latter, recall that linear constraints are not free and are indeed part of the final cost). In particular,

(1) for the plain performance, we want to minimize the number of constant multiplications, and

(2) we aim for small matrix entries, such that multiplications can be replaced by addition chains in many cases.

Both of these optimizations also result in fewer reductions being necessary, further speeding up the computation. To summarize, our main goals are to provide the same security level of POSEIDON$^\pi$, while at the same time having linear layers which require significantly fewer operations to compute.

In the following, we show how to use non-MDS matrices for the external and internal rounds, denoted respectively by $M_\mathcal{E}$ and $M_\mathcal{I}$. Since POSEIDON$^\pi$ is defined to use MDS matrices and hence this goes against the original specification of POSEIDON, we will later show that this modification has no impact regarding the final security. We also give the efficiency in terms of Plonk constraints, noting that even more efficient representations can be derived when supporting extended versions of Plonk (e.g., Plonkish).

5.1 Matrix for the External Round

Let us focus on the case $t = 4 \cdot t'$ for $t' \in \mathbb{N}$ (the cases $t \in \{2, 3\}$ are discussed separately later). For the external rounds, we propose to instantiate $M_\mathcal{E}$ via the efficient matrices proposed for GRIFFIN-π in [23] as

$$M_\mathcal{E} = \mathrm{circ}(2 \cdot M_4, M_4, \ldots, M_4) \in \mathbb{F}_p^{t \times t},$$

where M_4 is a 4×4 MDS matrix. We define M_4 to be

$$M_4 = \begin{pmatrix} 5 & 7 & 1 & 3 \\ 4 & 6 & 1 & 1 \\ 1 & 3 & 5 & 7 \\ 1 & 1 & 4 & 6 \end{pmatrix},$$

which corresponds to the matrix $M_{4,4}^{8,4}$ from [19], setting $\alpha = 2$. This matrix is MDS for all primes we consider (that is, $p > 2^{31}$).

As shown in [19], we can compute the multiplication of 4 input elements with M_4 by using only 8 additions and 4 constant multiplications.

Plonk Arithmetization. We assume the use of 2-fan-in gates. The arithmetization in Plonk is then similar to the plain computation, with various small differences. First, only 8 constraints are needed for each M_4 computation. Secondly, only t constraints are needed for the finalization of $M_\mathcal{E}$. In total, we need $8 \cdot (t/4) + t = 3t$ constraints.

5.2 Matrix for the Internal Round

In the original POSEIDON$^\pi$ specification, the security argument against statistical attacks purely takes into account the external rounds and the number of active

S-boxes in these rounds. The main reason for this is that the wide trail design strategy [17] is only applicable if the number of S-boxes in each round is at least $\lceil t/2 \rceil$ for a state size t. This is not the case for the partial rounds of POSEIDON$^\pi$, where only a single S-box is used.

Hence, for the partial rounds, the MDS property is not required anymore, and we can set up the matrix $M_\mathcal{I}$ focusing only on providing full diffusion, breaking arbitrarily long subspace trails, and ensuring that the polynomial representation of the scheme is dense. This is exactly the approach introduced in the NEPTUNE scheme [28]. For this reason, we suggest to instantiate $M_\mathcal{I}$ with the matrix proposed for NEPTUNE, that is,

$$
M_\mathcal{I} = \begin{pmatrix} \mu_0 & 1 & \cdots & 1 \\ 1 & \mu_1 & \cdots & 1 \\ \vdots & \vdots & \ddots & \vdots \\ 1 & 1 & \cdots & \mu_{t-1} \end{pmatrix},
$$

where $\mu_0, \mu_1, \ldots, \mu_{t-1}$ are random elements from $\mathbb{F}_p \setminus \{0, 1\}$ such that the matrix is invertible and no arbitrarily long subspace trails exist (see Sect. 5.3). We suggest to choose these elements in order to make the multiplications efficient (e.g., small values or powers of 2, which make multiplications fast).

Plain Efficiency. Note that we can store the sum of the input vector in a single variable, which needs $t-1$ additions. Then, storing $\mu_i - 1$ for $i \in \{1, 2, \ldots, t-1\}$, we can compute each vector element with one multiplication and one addition. In total, we need $t - 1 + t = 2t - 1$ additions and t multiplications. The performance benefit is significant especially for larger t, which is a popular choice in STARK-based proof systems (e.g., Plonky2 [41]).

Plonk Arithmetization. Again, we assume the use of 2-fan-in gates. The matrix multiplication with a vector $(x_0, x_1, \ldots, x_{t-1})$ can be written down as

$$
s = x_0 + x_1 + \cdots + x_{t-1},
$$
$$
y_i = (\mu_i - 1)x_i + s \quad \text{for} \quad i \in \{0, 1, \ldots, t-1\},
$$

where s represents the precomputed sum and $(y_0, y_1, \ldots, y_{t-1})$ is the output vector. This method needs $t - 1 + t = 2t - 1$ constraints. Note that instead of storing $\mu_0, \mu_1, \ldots, \mu_{t-1}$, it is better to directly store $\mu_0 - 1, \mu_1 - 1, \ldots, \mu_{t-1} - 1$ as public constants.

5.3   Preventing Arbitrarily Long Subspace Trails

Before going on, we discuss which conditions the matrix $M_\mathcal{I}$ must satisfy to prevent arbitrarily long subspace trails.

Definition 1 ([29]). *Let $t \geq 2$ be an integer and let $p \geq 2$ be a prime integer. Let $\mathfrak{U}_0, \ldots, \mathfrak{U}_r \subseteq \mathbb{F}_p^t$ be $r + 1$ subspaces such that $\dim(\mathfrak{U}_i) \leq \dim(\mathfrak{U}_{i+1}) < t$ for each $i \in \{0, 1, \ldots, r-1\}$. $(\mathfrak{U}_0, \ldots, \mathfrak{U}_r)$ is a subspace trail of length $r \geq 1$ for a function $\mathcal{F}$ over $\mathbb{F}_p^t$ if for each $i \in \{0, \ldots, r-1\}$ and for each $\varphi_i \in \mathbb{F}_p^t$ there exists $\varphi_{i+1} \in \mathbb{F}_p^t$ such that $F(\mathfrak{U}_i + \varphi_i) := \{\mathcal{F}(x) \mid \forall x \in \mathfrak{U}_i + \varphi_i\} \subseteq \mathfrak{U}_i + \varphi_{i+1}$. We say that it is an invariant subspace trail if $\mathfrak{U}_i = \mathfrak{U}_j$ for each $i, j \in \{0, 1, \ldots, r\}$.*

Since the nonlinear layer in a partial round of POSEIDON$^\pi$ contains only a single nonlinear S-box, there exists a subspace that is invariant through it. More generally, independent of the details of the linear layer $M_\mathcal{I}$, there exists a subspace that is invariant for up to $t - 1$ rounds. Depending on the details of the linear layer $M_\mathcal{I}$, such a subspace can be used as a starting point for a subspace trail over an arbitrary number of rounds. In this case, an attack can be set up, as concretely shown by Beyne et al. [13] at Crypto 2020, and by Keller et al. [35] at Eurocrypt 2021.

Hence, it is crucial to choose the linear layer correctly. For a complete analysis regarding this problem we refer to [30]. In there, the authors show that if the minimal polynomials of the matrices $M_\mathcal{I}, M_\mathcal{I}^2, M_\mathcal{I}^3, \ldots$ are irreducible and of maximum degree, no arbitrarily long subspace trail exists.

We emphasize that this is a sufficient condition, but not a necessary one. In the following, we always assume that $M_\mathcal{I}$ satisfies the given condition. In particular, we suggest to use the tools provided in [30] for a given $M_\mathcal{I}$.

6   POSEIDON$^\pi$ Specification

POSEIDON2$^\pi$ is a permutation over $\mathbb{F}_p^t$, where p as in POSEIDON$^\pi$ (that is, $p > 2^{30}$) and $t \in \{2, 3, 4, \ldots, 4 \cdot t', \ldots, 24\}$ for $t' \in \mathbb{N}$. These values are sufficient for our use case. The POSEIDON2$^\pi$ permutation $\mathcal{P}_2$ over $\mathbb{F}_p^t$ is defined as

$$\mathcal{P}_2(x) = \mathcal{E}_{R_F-1} \circ \cdots \circ \mathcal{E}_{R_F/2} \circ \mathcal{I}_{R_P-1} \circ \cdots \circ \mathcal{I}_0 \circ \mathcal{E}_{R_F/2-1} \circ \cdots \circ \mathcal{E}_0(M_\mathcal{E} \cdot x),$$

where the number of rounds is the same as in POSEIDON$^\pi$ (see Eq. (1)). Similar to POSEIDON$^\pi$, the external round is defined by

$$\mathcal{E}_i(x) = M_\mathcal{E} \cdot \left((x_0 + c_0^{(i)})^d, (x_1 + c_1^{(i)})^d, \ldots, (x_{t-1} + c_{t-1}^{(i)})^d \right),$$

where $d \geq 3$ is the smallest positive integer that satisfies $\gcd(d, p-1) = 1$ and $c_j^{(i)}$ is the j-th round constant in the i-th external round. The internal round is defined by

$$\mathcal{I}_i(x) = M_\mathcal{I} \cdot \left((x_0 + \hat{c}_0^{(i)})^d, x_1, \ldots, x_{t-1} \right),$$

where $d \geq 3$ as before and $\hat{c}_0^{(i)}$ is the round constant in the i-th internal round. All round constants are generated as in POSEIDON$^\pi$.

Remark 4. In contrast to POSEIDON$^\pi$, we are only applying a single round constant in the internal rounds. The motivation for this change comes from the fact that an optimized (equivalent) implementation of POSEIDON$^\pi$ also uses only one round constant during the internal rounds, and hence the security is not affected.

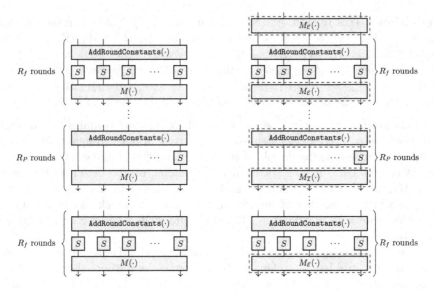

Fig. 1. POSEIDON$^\pi$ (left) and POSEIDON2$^\pi$ (right) with changes in red. (Color figure online)

Linear Layers. The linear layers of POSEIDON2$^\pi$ are defined as follows.

Case: $t = 4 \cdot t' \geq 4$. For $t = 4k$, the matrices $M_{\mathcal{E}}$ and $M_{\mathcal{I}}$ are set up using the approach described in Sect. 5. We emphasize that $M_{\mathcal{I}}$ must be chosen in order to prevent arbitrarily long subspace trails, as described before.

Case: $t \in \{2,3\}$. For $t \in \{2,3\}$ we first compute $M_{\mathcal{I}}$ as before. By imposing the additional condition that $M_{\mathcal{I}}$ is MDS, we can simply set $M_{\mathcal{E}} = M_{\mathcal{I}}$, which reduces code complexity. For $M_{\mathcal{I}}$ to be MDS, we require all of its submatrices to be invertible. For $t = 2$ this is achieved if $\mu_0\mu_1 - 1 \neq 0$ and $\mu_0, \mu_1 \neq 0$. For $t = 3$, this is achieved if $\mu_0\mu_1\mu_2 - \mu_0 - \mu_1 - \mu_2 + 2 \neq 0$ and

$$\mu_0, \mu_1, \mu_2 \neq 0, \quad \mu_0\mu_1 - 1 \neq 0, \quad \mu_0\mu_2 - 1 \neq 0, \quad \mu_1\mu_2 - 1 \neq 0.$$

By choosing $\mu_i \in \{2, 3, \ldots, p/4\}$, the MDS condition is always fulfilled (indeed, $xy \neq 1$ for $x, y \in \{2, 3, \ldots, p/4\}$).

Poseidon$^\pi$ versus Poseidon2$^\pi$. Compared to the original POSEIDON$^\pi$ specification recalled in Sect. 3.2, three differences arise.

1. A linear layer $M_{\mathcal{E}}$ is applied at the input of POSEIDON2$^\pi$ (see Sect. 4).
2. Two different linear layers are used in POSEIDON2$^\pi$ for $t \geq 4$.
3. Only one round constant is applied in each internal round.

A graphical overview of the differences between POSEIDON$^\pi$ and POSEIDON2$^\pi$ is given in Fig. 1.

From an implementation point of view, we emphasize that the optimized representation of the internal rounds, as used in POSEIDON$^\pi$, is not needed for POSEIDON2$^\pi$. Indeed, it would make the computation slightly more expensive. This makes POSEIDON2$^\pi$ simpler and more memory-efficient than POSEIDON$^\pi$.

7 Security Analysis

Changing the matrix, and especially removing the MDS requirement, may have an impact on the final security of the permutation. In this section, we assess the security level of the newly obtained POSEIDON2$^\pi$ permutation.

Remark 5. Due to the similarities between POSEIDON$^\pi$ and POSEIDON2$^\pi$, we emphasize that (almost) all the attacks work in the same way for the two schemes. This means that we are going to adapt the security analysis of POSEIDON$^\pi$ and POSEIDON2$^\pi$, focusing only on the possible differences that can arise between the two cases.

Remark 6. For the cases $t \in \{2, 3\}$, POSEIDON2$^\pi$ is just a special case of POSEIDON$^\pi$ in which the MDS matrix has been fixed for achieving optimal performances. For this reason, we only focus on the case $t \geq 4$ in the following.

7.1 Statistical Attacks

Differential Attacks. Given pairs of inputs with some fixed input differences, differential cryptanalysis [14] considers the probability distribution of the corresponding output differences produced by the cryptographic primitive. Let $\Delta_I, \Delta_O \in \mathbb{F}_p^t$ be respectively the input and the output differences through a permutation $\mathcal{P}$ over $\mathbb{F}_p^t$. The differential probability (DP) of having a certain output difference Δ_O given a particular input difference Δ_I is equal to

$$\mathrm{Prob}(\Delta_I \to \Delta_O) = \max_{\Delta_I, \Delta_O \neq 0} \frac{|\{x \in \mathbb{F}_p^t \mid \mathcal{P}(x + \Delta_I) - \mathcal{P}(x) = \Delta_O\}|}{p^t}.$$

In the case of iterated schemes, a cryptanalyst searches for ordered sequences of differences over any number of rounds that are called differential characteristics/trails. Assuming the independence of the rounds, the DP of a differential trail is the product of the DPs of its one-round differences.

As in POSEIDON$^\pi$, we make used of the wide trail design strategy on the external rounds of POSEIDON2$^\pi$ for ensuring security against this attack. As it is well known, $\mathrm{DP}_{\max}(x \mapsto x^d) = (d-1)/p$. Based on the result proposed in [23, Prop. 1], the branch number of $M_{\mathcal{E}}$ assuming an MDS matrix for M_4 is $b = t/4 + 4 \equiv t' + 4 \geq 5$. Hence, following the wide trail strategy at least b S-boxes are active in 2 consecutive external (full) rounds of the permutation. When considering two consecutive rounds three times,

$$\left(\frac{d-1}{p}\right)^{3(t'+4)} \leq \frac{(d-1)^{3(t'+4)}}{p^{12}} \cdot 2^{-9/4\kappa} \ll 2^{-2\kappa},$$

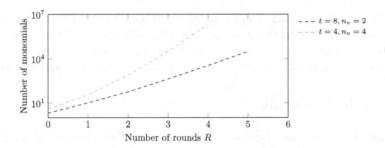

Fig. 2. The number of monomials reached in POSEIDON2$^\pi$ after R rounds, where $d = 3$. We observed no significant difference between $\mathcal{E}$ and $\mathcal{I}$. Moreover, the numbers reached match the maximum theoretical number of monomials.

where $p^{-t/3} = p^{-4t'/3} \leq 2^{-\kappa}$ and where $d \ll p$ (usually, $\log_2(d) \leq 4$ compared to $\log_2(p) > 30$). The factor 2 is crucial for avoiding clustering effects.

As a result, 6 external rounds of POSEIDON2$^\pi$ are sufficient for guaranteeing security against differential attacks, exactly as in POSEIDON$^\pi$, where 2 external rounds are used as a security margin. Note that this is a pessimistic estimate. Indeed, as has been shown in previous works (e.g., [35]), the internal rounds can also be taken into account, which is ignored in this discussion.

Other Statistical Attacks. Due to the facts that no entry of $M_\mathcal{E}$ is equal to zero and $M_\mathcal{E}$ provides full diffusion after one round, a similar conclusion holds for other statistical attacks, such as linear attacks [38], truncated differential attacks [36], rebound attacks [39], among others.

7.2   Algebraic Attacks

Changing the matrices in the linear layers may have an impact on the density of the resulting polynomials. This may weaken the resistance against certain attacks like interpolation attacks and Gröbner basis attacks, which also depend on the number of monomials found in the final representations. For this purpose, we first investigate the density and the degrees of the equations generated. Then, we focus on the security with respect to Gröbner basis attacks.

Interpolation Attack: Degrees and Density. The interpolation attack [34] aims to construct an interpolation polynomial that describes the function. Such polynomial can be used in order to set up a distinguisher and/or an attack on the symmetric scheme. The attack does not work if the number of unknown monomials is sufficiently large (e.g., larger than the data available for the attack). In the MitM scenario, the attacker constructs two polynomials, one that involves the input(s) and one that involve the output(s), that must match in the middle.

The maximum possible degrees are reached for both POSEIDON$^\pi$ and POSEIDON2$^\pi$. It remains to determine the density. For this purpose, we implemented both permutations (including the four different round functions) in Sage and tested the density after increasing numbers of rounds. The results of this experiment for POSEIDON2$^\pi$ are given in Fig. 2. We note that the reached number of monomials corresponds to the maximum number of possible monomials $\#_{n_v,d}$ for n_v variables of total degree d, which is given by

$$\#_{n_v,d} = \sum_{i=1}^{d} \binom{n_v + i - 1}{i}.$$

As a result, the security of POSEIDON$^\pi$ and POSEIDON2$^\pi$ with respect to the interpolation attack is comparable.

Gröbner Basis Attacks. In a Gröbner basis attack, the adversary first writes down the function in consideration as an equation system and tries to solve this system for the unknowns. Like in the original POSEIDON paper, here we focus on the CICO problem, and quickly recall it here.

Definition 2. *A permutation $\mathcal{P}$ is (λ, x_2, y_1)-secure with respect to the CICO problem if there is no algorithm with expected complexity less than lambda that for given x_2, y_1 finds x_1, y_2 such that $\mathcal{P}(x_1 \parallel x_2) = y_1 \parallel y_2$.*

Usually, we set the number of elements in the x_1 part to be the same as the number of elements in the y_1 part. In other words, we leave a certain size of the input variable and require the same size in the output to fulfill some property. Then, the expected complexity for a random permutation is proportional to the size of x_1. For the sponge mode using only a single permutation call, solving the CICO problem directly translates to a preimage attack on the sponge, and conversely a preimage attack on the sponge mode is a solution to the CICO problem. Solving CICO is also sufficient to break the compression mode, but an attack on the compression mode does not necessarily result in a solution to the CICO problem. Still, the CICO problem gives a good estimate of the strength of a cryptographic permutation, and of how much it deviates from a strong one.

The equations for the CICO problem can be written down in a straightforward way. First, we fix part of the input and use unknowns for the remainder. Then, we apply the permutation to this input state, using an algebraic description of our choice. At the end, we enforce part of the output to fulfill a certain property, for example to be equal to a known value. Then the attacker has to follow three steps, which as a first step include computing the Gröbner basis (we refer to [1,44] for a more detailed description of these steps). As is customary in the literature [4,16] and has also been done in POSEIDON, here we focus on this first step. For this purpose, we compare the degrees reached during Gröbner basis computations between POSEIDON$^\pi$ and POSEIDON2$^\pi$. Similar degrees imply a similar cost of the attacks for POSEIDON$^\pi$ and POSEIDON2$^\pi$.

In our experiments, we set $p \approx 2^{16}$, $t = 12$, and we use two input variables. We then apply two strategies. In the first one we represent the permutation with full-round equations, hence reaching a maximum equation degree of $d^{R_F+R_P}$. In the second one, we introduce intermediate variables for each S-box, hence reaching a maximum equation degree of only d. Further, we tested the external (full) and internal (partial) rounds separately, in order to get a better understanding of the impact of our new linear layers.

In none of the tested cases we could observe a significant difference between POSEIDON$^\pi$ and POSEIDON2$^\pi$. In particular, the maximum degrees reached during the Gröbner basis computation were the same, the degrees of the final univariate polynomials (after conversion) were the same, and the FGLM [20] time differences were negligible. We also tried solving the system in Sage, and again the solving time differences we observed were negligible. This is particularly true when testing only the internal (partial) rounds and introducing intermediate variables in each step.

Following our experimental results from both the density and Gröbner basis tests, we conclude that POSEIDON2$^\pi$ is no less secure against algebraic attacks than POSEIDON$^\pi$. This means that the strongest attack vector remains the interpolation one, and that security against this one implies security against Gröbner basis attacks also in the case of POSEIDON2$^\pi$.

7.3   Attack from Bariant et al. [8]

Finally, we point out a recent attack proposed by Bariant et al. [8] at ToSC 2022. In there, the authors propose a strategy for skipping the first round of POSEIDON$^\pi$ when attempting to solve the CICO problem. The idea is the following. Given a permutation $\mathcal{P}$, we split it into two parts s.t. $\mathcal{P}(\cdot) = \mathcal{P}_2 \circ \mathcal{P}_1(\cdot)$. The idea is to find an affine subspace $\mathcal{3} \subseteq \mathbb{F}_p^t$ s.t. for each entry $z \in \mathcal{3}$, $\mathcal{P}_1^{-1}(z)$ satisfies the input condition of the CICO problem with probability 1. Given such a subspace $\mathcal{3}$, it is possible to reduce the CICO problem from $\mathcal{P}$ to $\mathcal{P}_2$. In an analogous way, this approach can be exploited to reduce the interpolation attack from $\mathcal{P}$ to $\mathcal{P}_2$.

In the case of POSEIDON$^\pi$, the authors present an attack if $\mathcal{P}_1$ is equal to the first two rounds without the final linear operation (equivalently, the first full round plus the next nonlinear layer). To be precise, the first nonlinear layer is skipped by using the strategy recalled in Sect. 4. Hence, the attack reduces to the case of one round defined as one linear layer followed by one nonlinear layer. One crucial condition for the attack to work is that the S-box S over $\mathbb{F}_p$ satisfies

$$\forall x, y \in \mathbb{F}_p : \quad S(x \cdot y) = S(x) \cdot S(y).$$

This is always the case if S is a power map, as for POSEIDON and *Rescue* (but not e.g. for NEPTUNE, whose S-box is constructed via the Lai–Massey scheme).

In order to prevent the attack, one possibility is to consider an S-box that is not a monomial. This includes S-boxes based on the Legendre functions and/or the powers $(-1)^x$ described in [25], or a Dickson polynomial defined as

$$x \mapsto D_d(x, \alpha) = \sum_{i=0}^{\lfloor \frac{d}{2} \rfloor} \frac{d}{d-i} \binom{d-i}{i} (-\alpha)^i x^{d-2i},$$

where $\alpha \in \mathbb{F}_p$. Both options are not suitable for our goals. First of all, the S-boxes based on the Legendre functions and/or the powers $(-1)^x$ are more expensive than simple power maps in ZK applications/protocols (see [45] for details). Moreover, a Dickson polynomial is invertible if $\gcd(p^2 - 1, d) = 1$. Then, if $\gcd(d, p - 1) = \gcd(d, p + 1) = 1$, the power map can be replaced by a Dickson polynomial of the same degree. However, its computation requires several additions which impact the cost in Plonk applications. If $\gcd(d, p-1) = 1$ and $\gcd(d, p + 1) \neq 1$, the degree of the Dickson polynomial is higher than the corresponding degree of the power map, and then more constraints are needed.

The attack from [8] affects the security of both POSEIDON$^\pi$ and POSEIDON2$^\pi$. However, since we apply an initial linear layer in POSEIDON2$^\pi$, its advantage decreases to only 1 round. Moreover, the security margin of POSEIDON2$^\pi$ consists of two external rounds and 12.5% more internal rounds. Hence, even without increasing the number of rounds of POSEIDON$^\pi$ or changing the nonlinear layer, the scheme remains secure. Therefore, we decided that modifications of the nonlinear layer are not needed in our case.

8   Performance Evaluation

Here we first give a theoretical comparison with the original POSEIDON$^\pi$ permutation in terms of the number of additions, multiplications, and Plonk constraints. Since we only change the linear layers, we focus only on the linear layers, i.e., we ignore the impact of the nonlinear layer. Then, we present an implementation of both the original POSEIDON$^\pi$ and our new POSEIDON2$^\pi$, and we assess the impact of our optimizations. In all our comparisons we use the efficient representation of POSEIDON$^\pi$ described in detail in [26, Appendix B].

We note that our main goal was to increase the performance in a plain implementation and with classical Plonk constraints. Indeed, POSEIDON2$^\pi$ is similar to POSEIDON$^\pi$ when considering the cost in R1CS or AIR. We therefore omit these metrics and instead refer to recent comparisons given e.g. in [23].

8.1   Theoretical Comparison

We first focus on the number of arithmetic operations and on the number of Plonk constraints needed to evaluate all linear layers of POSEIDON2$^\pi$ and its predecessor POSEIDON2$^\pi$. The results are shown in Fig. 3. Taking these numbers, and considering for example an instance where $\log_2(p) \approx 64$, we observe that the number of operations in the linear layers can be reduced significantly. This is especially due to the larger number of operations needed for the external linear layers in the original POSEIDON$^\pi$.

8.2   Implementation and Benchmarks

We implemented the new POSEIDON2$^\pi$ in Rust and compared it with other similar permutations using efficient implementations from [33]. The code and an

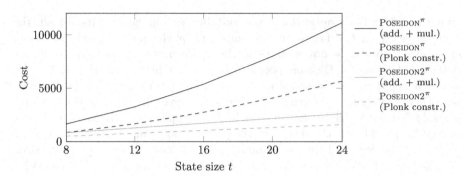

Fig. 3. Number of operations and Plonk constraints needed for the linear layers of POSEIDON$^\pi$ and POSEIDON2$^\pi$, where $p \approx 2^{64}$.

instance generation script are available online.[3] All benchmarks were run on an Intel i7-6700K CPU. Moreover, we focus only on primitives without any high-degree components. For example, *Rescue* needs the computation of $x \mapsto x^{1/d}$ in its nonlinear layer, which is of high degree in large fields if d is small. Hence, these computations become the bottleneck in the plain performance, which makes *Rescue* significantly slower than POSEIDON$^\pi$ or POSEIDON2$^\pi$. The same is also true for Anemoi and GRIFFIN-π.

In our benchmarks we focus on three different primes, namely the 255-bit BLS12 one p_{BLS12}, the 64-bit Goldilocks one $p_{\text{Goldilocks}}$ (used in e.g. Plonky2 [41]), and the 31-bit Babybear one p_{Babybear} used in Risc0 [43].[4] The results for some instances are shown in Table 1, where we emphasize that we use the optimized representation of POSEIDON$^\pi$ described in detail in [26, Appendix B]. We chose often used compression ratios such as 2-to-1, 4-to1, and 8-to-1 for the various field sizes. From this comparison, we can see that we can improve the performance of the original version by a factor of up to 4 for the 24-word instance. We emphasize that the advantage increases for larger state sizes, which is mainly due to the expensive matrix multiplication in the external rounds of POSEIDON$^\pi$. However, even in the 3-word case we can observe an improvement by a factor of more than 2.

8.3   Efficient Plonkish Version

There are many possible Plonk arithmetizations and many tradeoffs a circuit builder can choose, especially when extending the classical Plonk framework with custom gates. One such approach [5] has recently been applied to POSEIDON$^\pi$, and potentially it can also be used for POSEIDON2$^\pi$.

In this section, however, we revisit the Plonkish representation of POSEIDON$^\pi$ in [26, Appendix E]. We demonstrate a more optimal version which requires

---

[3] https://github.com/HorizenLabs/poseidon2.

[4] $p_{\text{BLS12}} = \text{0x73eda753299d7d483339d80809a1d80553bda402fffe5bfefffffffff00000001}$,
$p_{\text{Goldilocks}} = \text{0xffffffff00000001}$, $p_{\text{Babybear}} = \text{0x78000001}$.

Table 1. Plain performance of various permutations in μs using `Rust`, where $n = \lceil \log_2(p) \rceil$.

Permutation	$t = 2$	$t = 3$	$t = 4$	$t = 8$	$t = 12$	$t = 16$	$t = 20$	$t = 24$
p_{BLS12}, $\lceil \log_2(p) \rceil = 255$								
POSEIDON$^\pi$	11.78	16.99	22.26	53.46	–	–	–	–
NEPTUNE	–	–	17.45	30.05	–	–	–	–
GMiMC	20.63	21.86	22.96	26.97	–	–	–	–
POSEIDON2$^\pi$	**6.49**	**7.30**	**13.30**	**22.12**	–	–	–	–
$p_{\text{Goldilocks}}$, $\lceil \log_2(p) \rceil = 64$								
POSEIDON$^\pi$	–	–	–	4.25	7.00	12.03	15.33	–
NEPTUNE	–	–	–	3.65	6.22	9.94	12.31	–
GMiMC	–	–	–	3.26	7.01	13.57	26.72	–
POSEIDON2$^\pi$	–	–	–	**2.06**	**2.81**	**3.57**	**4.42**	–
p_{Babybear}, $\lceil \log_2(p) \rceil = 31$								
POSEIDON$^\pi$	–	–	–	–	–	7.06	–	15.01
NEPTUNE	–	–	–	–	–	5.62	–	10.17
GMiMC	–	–	–	–	–	10.33	–	23.59
POSEIDON2$^\pi$	–	–	–	–	–	**2.09**	–	**3.53**

$(t - 1)$ polynomial equations to express the state variables that do not undergo S-boxes, in contrast to t equations in [26, Appendix E]. The resulting representation is suitable for both POSEIDON$^\pi$ and POSEIDON2$^\pi$ and makes the prover's work more efficient due to fewer polynomials being used.

Let us introduce auxiliary notation. For round r we denote

(1) the input to `AddRoundConstants` by $A_1^r, A_2^r, \ldots, A_t^r$,
(2) the output of `AddRoundConstants` by $B_1^r, B_2^r, \ldots, B_t^r$, and
(3) the input to M by $C_1^r, C_2^r, \ldots, C_t^r$.

Therefore we have that in full rounds $C_i^r = S(B_i^r)$ and in partial rounds

$$C_i^r = \begin{cases} B_i^r & i < t, \\ S(B_i^r) & i = t. \end{cases}$$

Now we proceed as follows.

1. Note that C_i^{r-1} are linear functions of $\{A_i^r\}$.
2. Going through the constant layer we obtain that C_i^{r-1} are *affine* functions of $\{B_i^r\}$.
3. Using the fact that $B_i^r = C_i^r$ for $i < t$ we get that

$$\{C_i^{r-1}\}_{1 \leq i \leq t} \text{ are affine functions of } \{C_i^r\}_{1 \leq i \leq t-1} \text{ and } B_t^r. \tag{2}$$

4. Repeatedly apply the same statement to $\{C_i^{r-1}\}_{1 \leq i \leq t}$ and further up for $k = 1, 2, \ldots, t-1$:

$$\{C_i^{r-k}\}_{1 \leq i \leq t} \text{ are affine functions of } \{C_i^r\}_{1 \leq i \leq t-1} \text{ and } \{B_t^j\}_{r-k < j \leq r}. \quad (3)$$

5. Restrict Eq. (3) to S-box outputs:

$$\{C_t^{r-k}\}_{1 \leq k \leq t-1} \text{ are affine functions of } \{C_i^r\}_{1 \leq i \leq t-1} \text{ and } \{B_t^{r-k}\}_{0 \leq k < t-1}. \quad (4)$$

6. Now rearrange $(t-1)$ equations Eq. (4) so that $\{C_i^r\}_{1 \leq i \leq t-1}$ are now expressed through the others:

$$\{C_i^r\}_{1 \leq i \leq t-1} \text{ are affine functions of } \{C_t^{r-k}\}_{1 \leq k \leq t-1} \text{ and } \{B_t^{r-k}\}_{0 \leq k < t-1}. \quad (5)$$

7. Now go further from round r. Similarly to Eq. (2), derive:

$$\{B_i^{r+1}\}_{1 \leq i \leq t} \text{ are affine functions of } \{B_i^r\}_{1 \leq i \leq t-1} \text{ and } \{C_t^r\}. \quad (6)$$

8. Recursively applying Eq. (6), we get that for any $r' > r$

$$\{B_i^{r'}\}_{1 \leq i \leq t} \text{ are affine functions of } \{B_i^r\}_{1 \leq i \leq t-1} \text{ and } \{C_t^j\}_{r \leq j < r'}. \quad (7)$$

9. Restraining Eq. (7) to $i = t$ we get

$$\{B_t^{r+k}\}_{1 \leq k \leq t-1} \text{ are affine functions of } \{B_i^r\}_{1 \leq i \leq t-1} \text{ and } \{C_t^{r+k}\}_{0 \leq k < t-1}. \quad (8)$$

10. Now rearrange $(t-1)$ equations Eq. (8) so that $\{B_i^r\}_{1 \leq i \leq t-1}$ are now expressed through the others:

$$\{B_i^r\}_{1 \leq i \leq t-1} \text{ are affine functions of } \{B_t^{r+k}\}_{1 \leq k \leq t-1} \text{ and } \{C_t^{r+k}\}_{0 \leq k < t-1}. \quad (9)$$

11. As $\{B_i^r\}_{1 \leq i \leq t-1}$ and $\{C_i^r\}_{1 \leq i \leq t-1}$ are identical, we get

$$\{C_i^r\}_{1 \leq i \leq t-1} \text{ are affine functions of } \{B_t^{r+k}\}_{1 \leq k \leq t-1} \text{ and } \{C_t^{r+k}\}_{0 \leq k < t-1}. \quad (10)$$

12. Combining Eq. (5) and Eq. (10) we get that

$$t-1 \text{ affine equations of } \{B_t^{r-k}, C_t^{r-k-1}, B_t^{r+k+1}, C_t^{r+k}\}_{0 \leq k \leq t-2}. \quad (11)$$

13. Replacing C_t^i variables with degree-d power functions of B_t^i we get $(t-1)$ equations of degree d over $2t-1$ variables $B_t^{r-t+1}, B_t^{r-t+2}, \ldots, B_t^{r+t-1}$.

So we get a group of $(t-1)$ constraints that link inputs and outputs of S-boxes over $(2t-1)$ rounds. The process is illustrated in Fig. 4.

A reader should ask immediately whether we have derived Eq. (5) correctly, as it could have happened that the system does not have rank $t-1$ w.r.t. C_i^r.

Proposition 1. *If the matrix $\mathcal{M}$ of* POSEIDON2$^\pi$ *does not have an invariant subspace trail, then the state $\{C_i^r\}_{1 \leq i \leq t}$ is uniquely determined by S-box inputs in t preceding rounds $\{B_t^{r-k}\}_{0 \leq k < t}$.*

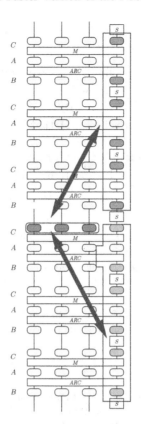

Fig. 4. Expressing the round state (pink) via S-box inputs and outputs as per Eq. (5) (orange) and Eq. (10) (green). (Color figure online)

Proof. Obviously B_t^r bijectively maps to C_t^r as it is the S-box mapping. Now consider the rest of the state. Imagine the mapping is not bijective, then there exist two executions of POSEIDON2$^\pi$ with different substates $\{C_i^r\}_{1 \le i \le t-1}$ and $\{C_i^{r\prime}\}_{1 \le i \le t-1}$ but identical $\{B_t^{r-k}\}_{0 \le k < t}$. Then the difference $\delta \ne \mathbf{0}$ between the two states is contained in the elements $1, 2, \ldots, t-1$. Moreover, as there is no difference in $\{B_t^{r-k}\}_{0 \le k < t}$, we get that all $t-1$ vectors

$$\mathcal{M}^{-1} \cdot \delta, \mathcal{M}^{-2} \cdot \delta, \ldots, \mathcal{M}^{-t+1} \cdot \delta$$

are 0 in the t-th component. This only happens if δ belongs to some invariant subspace, which is forbidden, so we get a contradiction. This concludes the proof.   □

The natural question is how the constraint groups should overlap in order to uniquely determine the state in POSEIDON2$^\pi$ and POSEIDON$^\pi$. For this we recall that by Eq. (10) any t consecutive S-box inputs and outputs determine all C variables in the round. Therefore, it is sufficient that constraint groups overlap by t variables B_t^i.

Putting everything together, in order to cover R_F full and R_P partial rounds we need (all constraints of degree d):

- $tR_F/2$ constraints that link inputs and outputs of a single full round for the first group of full rounds. In the last round we replace $C_j^{R_F/2}$ with degree-d functions of $B_t^{R_F/2+1}, B_t^{R_F/2+2}, \ldots, B_t^{R_F/2+t-1}$ as per Eq. (10).
- $(t-1)\lceil \frac{R_P}{t-1} - 1 \rceil$ constraints Eq. (11) that link $B_t^r, B_t^{r+1}, \ldots, B_t^{r+2t-1}$ for $r = R_F/2, R_F/2 + 2t - 1, R_F/2 + 4t - 2, \ldots$.
- $tR_F/2$ constraints that link inputs and outputs of a single full round for the last group of full rounds. In the first round of those we replace $A_j^{R_F/2+R_P+1}$ with degree-d functions of $B_t^{R_F/2+R_P}, B_t^{R_F/2+R_P-1}, \ldots, B_t^{R_F/2+R_P-t+1}$ as per Eq. (5).

In total we need about $t \cdot R_F + R_P - t + 1$ constraints of degree d. Note that even though it is one constraint more than in [26, Appendix E], the constraints for the partial rounds depend on fewer variables and are thus cheaper to build overall.

Acknowledgements. We thank Nicholas Mainardi for making improvements to the original code. We also thank the anonymous reviewers for their helpful suggestions.

References

1. Albrecht, M.R., et al.: Algebraic cryptanalysis of STARK-friendly designs: application to MARVELLOUS and MiMC. In: Galbraith, S.D., Moriai, S. (eds.) ASIACRYPT 2019. LNCS, vol. 11923, pp. 371–397. Springer, Cham (2019). https://doi.org/10.1007/978-3-030-34618-8_13
2. Albrecht, M.R., Grassi, L., Perrin, L., Ramacher, S., Rechberger, C., Rotaru, D., Roy, A., Schofnegger, M.: Feistel structures for MPC, and more. In: Sako, K., Schneider, S., Ryan, P.Y.A. (eds.) ESORICS 2019. LNCS, vol. 11736, pp. 151–171. Springer, Cham (2019). https://doi.org/10.1007/978-3-030-29962-0_8
3. Albrecht, M., Grassi, L., Rechberger, C., Roy, A., Tiessen, T.: MiMC: efficient encryption and cryptographic hashing with minimal multiplicative complexity. In: Cheon, J.H., Takagi, T. (eds.) ASIACRYPT 2016. LNCS, vol. 10031, pp. 191–219. Springer, Heidelberg (2016). https://doi.org/10.1007/978-3-662-53887-6_7
4. Aly, A., Ashur, T., Eli Ben-Sasson, Dhooghe, S., Szepieniec, A.: Design of symmetric-key primitives for advanced cryptographic protocols. IACR Trans. Symmetric Cryptol. **2020**(3), 1–45 (2020)
5. Ambrona, M., Schmitt, A., Toledo, R.R., Willems, D.: New optimization techniques for PlonK's arithmetization. IACR Cryptol. ePrint Arch., p. 462 (2022)
6. Ashur, T., Buschman, T., Mahzoun, M.: Algebraic cryptanalysis of POSEIDON. IACR Cryptol. ePrint Arch., p. 537 (2023)
7. Aumasson, J.P., Khovratovich, D., Mennink, B., Quine, P.: SAFE (sponge API for field elements) - a toolbox for ZK hash applications (2022). https://hackmd.io/bHgsH6mMStCVibM_wYvb2w
8. Bariant, A., Bouvier, C., Leurent, G., Perrin, L.: Algebraic attacks against some arithmetization-oriented primitives. IACR Trans. Symmetric Cryptol. **2022**(3), 73–101 (2022)

9. Ben-Sasson, E., Bentov, I., Horesh, Y., Riabzev, M.: Fast reed-solomon interactive oracle proofs of proximity. In: 45th International Colloquium on Automata, Languages, and Programming (ICALP 2018). Leibniz International Proceedings in Informatics (LIPIcs), vol. 107, pp. 14:1–14:17. Schloss Dagstuhl-Leibniz-Zentrum fuer Informatik (2018)

10. Ben-Sasson, E., Bentov, I., Horesh, Y., Riabzev, M.: Scalable, transparent, and post-quantum secure computational integrity. Cryptology ePrint Archive, Report 2018/46 (2018)

11. Ben-Sasson, E., Bentov, I., Horesh, Y., Riabzev, M.: Scalable zero knowledge with no trusted setup. In: Boldyreva, A., Micciancio, D. (eds.) CRYPTO 2019. LNCS, vol. 11694, pp. 701–732. Springer, Cham (2019). https://doi.org/10.1007/978-3-030-26954-8_23

12. Bertoni, G., Daemen, J., Peeters, M., Van Assche, G.: On the indifferentiability of the sponge construction. In: Smart, N. (ed.) EUROCRYPT 2008. LNCS, vol. 4965, pp. 181–197. Springer, Heidelberg (2008). https://doi.org/10.1007/978-3-540-78967-3_11

13. Beyne, T., et al.: Out of oddity – new cryptanalytic techniques against symmetric primitives optimized for integrity proof systems. In: Micciancio, D., Ristenpart, T. (eds.) CRYPTO 2020. LNCS, vol. 12172, pp. 299–328. Springer, Cham (2020). https://doi.org/10.1007/978-3-030-56877-1_11

14. Biham, E., Shamir, A.: Differential cryptanalysis of DES-like cryptosystems. In: Menezes, A.J., Vanstone, S.A. (eds.) CRYPTO 1990. LNCS, vol. 537, pp. 2–21. Springer, Heidelberg (1991). https://doi.org/10.1007/3-540-38424-3_1

15. Black, J., Rogaway, P., Shrimpton, T.: Black-box analysis of the block-cipher-based hash-function constructions from PGV. In: Yung, M. (ed.) CRYPTO 2002. LNCS, vol. 2442, pp. 320–335. Springer, Heidelberg (2002). https://doi.org/10.1007/3-540-45708-9_21

16. Bouvier, C., et al.: New design techniques for efficient arithmetization-oriented hash functions: anemoi permutations and jive compression mode. IACR Cryptol. ePrint Arch., p. 840 (2022)

17. Daemen, J., Rijmen, V.: The wide trail design strategy. In: Honary, B. (ed.) Cryptography and Coding 2001. LNCS, vol. 2260, pp. 222–238. Springer, Heidelberg (2001). https://doi.org/10.1007/3-540-45325-3_20

18. Damgård, I.B.: A design principle for hash functions. In: Brassard, G. (ed.) CRYPTO 1989. LNCS, vol. 435, pp. 416–427. Springer, New York (1990). https://doi.org/10.1007/0-387-34805-0_39

19. Duval, S., Leurent, G.: MDS matrices with lightweight circuits. IACR Trans. Symmetric Cryptol. 2018(2), 48–78 (2018)

20. Faugère, J., Gianni, P.M., Lazard, D., Mora, T.: Efficient computation of zero-dimensional Gröbner bases by change of ordering. J. Symb. Comput. 16(4), 329–344 (1993)

21. Gabizon, A., Williamson, Z.J.: Turbo-PLONK (2022). https://docs.zkproof.org/pages/standards/accepted-workshop3/proposal-turbo_plonk.pdf

22. Gabizon, A., Williamson, Z.J., Ciobotaru, O.: PLONK: permutations over lagrange-bases for oecumenical noninteractive arguments of knowledge. Cryptology ePrint Archive, Report 2019/953 (2019)

23. Grassi, L., Hao, Y., Rechberger, C., Schofnegger, M., Walch, R., Wang, Q.: A new feistel approach meets fluid-SPN: griffin for zero-knowledge applications. IACR Cryptol. ePrint Arch., p. 403 (2022)

24. Grassi, L., Khovratovich, D., Rechberger, C., Roy, A., Schofnegger, M.: POSEI-DON: a new hash function for zero-knowledge proof systems. In: USENIX Security Symposium, pp. 519–535. USENIX Association (2021)
25. Grassi, L., Khovratovich, D., Rønjom, S., Schofnegger, M.: The legendre symbol and the modulo-2 operator in symmetric schemes over $\mathbb{F}_p{}^n$ preimage attack on full grendel. IACR Trans. Symmetric Cryptol. **2022**(1), 5–37 (2022)
26. Grassi, L., Khovratovich, D., Roy, A., Rechberger, C., Schofnegger, M.: POSEI-DON: a new hash function for zero-knowledge proof systems. IACR Cryptol. ePrint Arch., p. 458 (2019)
27. Grassi, L., Lüftenegger, R., Rechberger, C., Rotaru, D., Schofnegger, M.: On a generalization of substitution-permutation networks: the HADES design strategy. In: Canteaut, A., Ishai, Y. (eds.) EUROCRYPT 2020. LNCS, vol. 12106, pp. 674–704. Springer, Cham (2020). https://doi.org/10.1007/978-3-030-45724-2_23
28. Grassi, L., Onofri, S., Pedicini, M., Sozzi, L.: Invertible quadratic non-linear layers for MPC-/FHE-/ZK-friendly schemes over $\mathbb{F}_p{}^n$ application to POSEIDON. IACR Trans. Symmetric Cryptol. **2022**(3), 20–72 (2022)
29. Grassi, L., Rechberger, C., Rønjom, S.: Subspace trail cryptanalysis and its applications to AES. IACR Trans. Symmetric Cryptol. **2016**(2), 192–225 (2016)
30. Grassi, L., Rechberger, C., Schofnegger, M.: Proving resistance against infinitely long subspace trails: how to choose the linear layer. IACR Trans. Symmetric Cryptol. **2021**(2), 314–352 (2021)
31. Grassi, L., Lüftenegger, R., Rechberger, C., Rotaru, D., Schofnegger, M.: On a generalization of substitution-permutation networks: the HADES design strategy. In: Canteaut, A., Ishai, Y. (eds.) EUROCRYPT 2020. LNCS, vol. 12106, pp. 674–704. Springer, Cham (2020). https://doi.org/10.1007/978-3-030-45724-2_23
32. Horizen Labs: ginger-lib: a RUST library for recursive SNARKs using Darlin (2022). https://github.com/HorizenOfficial/ginger-lib
33. IAIK: Hash functions for Zero-Knowledge applications Zoo (2021). https://extgit.iaik.tugraz.at/krypto/zkfriendlyhashzoo. IAIK, Graz University of Technology
34. Jakobsen, T., Knudsen, L.R.: The interpolation attack on block ciphers. In: Biham, E. (ed.) FSE 1997. LNCS, vol. 1267, pp. 28–40. Springer, Heidelberg (1997). https://doi.org/10.1007/BFb0052332
35. Keller, N., Rosemarin, A.: Mind the middle layer: the HADES design strategy revisited. In: Canteaut, A., Standaert, F.-X. (eds.) EUROCRYPT 2021. LNCS, vol. 12697, pp. 35–63. Springer, Cham (2021). https://doi.org/10.1007/978-3-030-77886-6_2
36. Knudsen, L.R.: Truncated and higher order differentials. In: Preneel, B. (ed.) FSE 1994. LNCS, vol. 1008, pp. 196–211. Springer, Heidelberg (1995). https://doi.org/10.1007/3-540-60590-8_16
37. Kölbl, S., Lauridsen, M.M., Mendel, F., Rechberger, C.: Haraka v2 - efficient short-input hashing for post-quantum applications. IACR Trans. Symmetric Cryptol. **2016**(2), 1–29 (2016)
38. Matsui, M.: Linear cryptanalysis method for DES cipher. In: Helleseth, T. (ed.) EUROCRYPT 1993. LNCS, vol. 765, pp. 386–397. Springer, Heidelberg (1994). https://doi.org/10.1007/3-540-48285-7_33
39. Mendel, F., Rechberger, C., Schläffer, M., Thomsen, S.S.: The rebound attack: cryptanalysis of reduced whirlpool and Grøstl. In: Dunkelman, O. (ed.) FSE 2009. LNCS, vol. 5665, pp. 260–276. Springer, Heidelberg (2009). https://doi.org/10.1007/978-3-642-03317-9_16

40. Merkle, R.C.: A certified digital signature. In: Brassard, G. (ed.) CRYPTO 1989. LNCS, vol. 435, pp. 218–238. Springer, New York (1990). https://doi.org/10.1007/0-387-34805-0_21
41. Polygon: Introducing Plonky2 (2022). https://blog.polygon.technology/introducing-plonky2/
42. Preneel, B., Govaerts, R., Vandewalle, J.: Hash functions based on block ciphers: a synthetic approach. In: Stinson, D.R. (ed.) CRYPTO 1993. LNCS, vol. 773, pp. 368–378. Springer, Heidelberg (1994). https://doi.org/10.1007/3-540-48329-2_31
43. RISC Zero: RISC Zero: General-Purpose Verifiable Computing (2023). https://www.risczero.com/
44. Sauer, J.F., Szepieniec, A.: SoK: Gröbner basis algorithms for arithmetization oriented ciphers. IACR Cryptol. ePrint Arch., p. 870 (2021)
45. Szepieniec, A.: On the use of the legendre symbol in symmetric cipher design. IACR Cryptol. ePrint Arch., p. 984 (2021)
46. Szepieniec, A., Lemmens, A., Sauer, J.F., Threadbare, B.: The Tip5 hash function for recursive STARKs. Cryptology ePrint Archive, Paper 2023/107 (2023). https://eprint.iacr.org/2023/107
47. Zcash: halo2 (2022). https://zcash.github.io/halo2/index.html

From Unbalanced to Perfect: Implementation of Low Energy Stream Ciphers

Jikang Lin[1,2], Jiahui He[1,2], Yanhong Fan[1,2,3(✉)], and Meiqin Wang[1,2,3]

[1] Key Laboratory of Cryptologic Technology and Information Security,
Ministry of Education, Shandong University, Jinan, China
{linjikang,hejiahui2020}@mail.sdu.edu.cn, {yanhongfan,mqwang}@sdu.edu.cn
[2] School of Cyber Science and Technology, Shandong University, Qingdao, China
[3] Quan Cheng Shandong Laboratory, Jinan, China

Abstract. Low energy is an important aspect of hardware implementation. For energy-limited battery-powered devices, low energy stream ciphers can play an important role. In `IACR ToSC 2021`, Caforio et al. proposed the Perfect Tree energy model for stream cipher that links the structure of combinational logic circuits with state update functions to energy consumption. In addition, a metric given by the model shows a negative correlation with energy consumption, i.e., the higher the balance of the perfect tree, the lower the energy consumption. However, Caforio et al. didn't give a method that eliminate imbalances of the unrolled strand tree for the existing stream ciphers.

In this paper, based on the Perfect Tree energy model, we propose a new redundant design model that improve the balances of the unrolled strand tree for the purpose of reducing energy consumption. In order to obtain the redundant design, we propose a search algorithm for returning the corresponding implementation scheme. For the existing stream ciphers, the proposed model and search method can be used to provide a low-power redundancy design scheme. To verify the effectiveness, we apply our redundant model and search method in the stream ciphers (e.g., `Trivium` and `Kreyvium`) and conducted a synthetic test. The results of the energy measurement demonstrate that the proposed model and search method can obtain lower energy consumption.

Keywords: Low Energy · Stream Cipher · Hardware Implementation · `Trivium`

1 Introduction

Hardware implementations of symmetric ciphers focus on several hardware performance index such as low latency, low area, low power and low energy consumption. For battery-powered devices, such as portable devices, medical implant devices or RFID tags, the implementation of low energy consumption plays an important role.

© The Author(s), under exclusive license to Springer Nature Switzerland AG 2023
N. El Mrabet et al. (Eds.): AFRICACRYPT 2023, LNCS 14064, pp. 204–226, 2023.
https://doi.org/10.1007/978-3-031-37679-5_9

Power and energy are correlated physical variables, energy is essentially the integral of power over time, and power is the amount of energy consumed per unit of time, i.e.,

$$E = \int P dt.$$

The energy consumption of semiconductor circuits reflects the total work done by the voltage source during the execution of any operation. The low energy consumption design reduces battery consumption, which is important in battery-driven devices with limited energy supply. In the last few years, there have been a series of works [2–4,7–9,12,14,20–22] on the energy consumption of symmetric ciphers.

For block ciphers, the authors in [2] investigated the architectural design of each component (S-box, MixColumn), the clock frequency and the impact of serialization or unrolling design strategy on energy consumption. To explain the relation between the degree of unrolling and energy efficiency, the authors gave a model that illustrated the energy consumption in each clock cycle as a quadratic function of the degree of unrolling r, with the following expression

$$E(r) = \left(Ar^2 + Br + C\right) \cdot \left(1 + \left\lceil \frac{R}{r} \right\rceil\right),$$

where $\left(Ar^2 + Br + C\right)$ denotes the energy consumed per cycle and $\left(1 + \left\lceil \frac{R}{r} \right\rceil\right)$ is the total clock cycles required for encryption[1]. Based on this model, the degree of unrolling of the energy-efficient optimal block ciphers implementation can be predicted. They concluded that the degree of unrolling $r = 2$ was the optimal configuration for lightweight block ciphers (e.g., Present [6], TWINE [24] and Simon [5]), while for other block ciphers (e.g., AES [12], Noekeon [11] and Piccolo [23]), the degree of unrolling $r = 1$ was optimal. Based on the above model of energy consumption in any r-round unrolled block cipher architecture, the authors developed energy-efficient linear and non-linear layers, and proposed a block cipher for low energy called Midori in [1].

For encrypting significantly large data, the stream cipher is a better scheme than the block cipher. In [3], the authors showed that an unrolled stream cipher circuit was more energy-efficient when the encryption of multiple data blocks was considered instead of a single block. The authors found that a Trivium [13] implementation at degree of unrolling $r = 160$ was about 9 times more energy efficient than any block cipher-based large data encryption scheme, implying that unrolled stream ciphers generally outperformed block ciphers.

For optimizing the energy consumption of stream ciphers, the literature [9] proposed an energy model (i.e., Perfect Tree model) that links the underlying algebraic structure of the state update function to the energy consumptive characteristic. The authors divided the whole circuit into smaller circuit strands, which mainly comprise of the logic functions related to one register update.

---

[1] Where A, B, C are constants, R is the number of iterations of the round function specified in the design of the cipher, and r is the degree of unrolling of the cipher.

Since these strands are interconnected, they seem like a tree. By observing the variation of the power consumption of the circuit strands in the above tree, the authors found that power consumption was related to the balance degree of the tree, i.e., if the balance degree of the tree is higher, the corresponding energy consumption of the tree circuit is lower.

However, the implementation in [9] did not take into account the elimination of imbalances in the unrolled strand tree for the exiting stream ciphers, the imbalances can lead to more glitches. In this paper, we propose a redundant design model for reducing these glitches, and give a method to search the redundant design scheme.

Our Contributions. In this paper, based on a new redundant design model, we propose a search algorithm for implementation scheme of the stream cipher, and reimplement r-round unrolled stream cipher circuits under the redundant scheme. Moreover, we conduct a synthetic test to obtain the results of the energy measurements. We now list our contributions as follows.

1. **A redundant design model for reducing glitches:** We discuss the factors influencing energy consumption in semiconductor circuits, of which toggle rate is the one focused on in this paper, and illustrate the relation between glitches and toggle rate. These discussions demonstrate that we can improve energy efficiency by reducing glitches. The glitches in the circuit are produced by inconsistent input delays of the combinational logic circuit modules, so we can reduce the glitches by balancing the delays of all the inputs of the modules.

   According to the definition of Perfect Tree energy model in [9], each circuit strand (combinational logic module) corresponds to an unrolled strand tree, and the balance of this tree corresponds to the input delay balance of the strand. If we want to convert an unbalanced tree into a balanced one, a natural idea is to add child nodes to the unbalanced tree. Corresponding to the circuit, this means adding additional combinational logic modules to the circuit, which we call redundant modules.

2. **A search algorithm for implementation schemes:** The essence of our redundant design is to optimize the input ports with lower delay, i.e., to connect these input ports to the redundant modules. The optimization method of the ports depend on the parameters of the update function of the ciphers. We build a set of mappings of the circuit strand to their input ports as a way to present the entire scheme of implementation. We present our generic search algorithm, which takes the tap locations of the register as input and the implementation scheme of the circuit strand as output.

3. **Apply our model and search method in the stream ciphers:** To verify the efficiency of our model and algorithm, we apply them to Trivium [13] and Kreyvium [10]. We obtain the implementation scheme with redundant design using the search algorithm, and describe the circuit in VHDL. Then we use Synopsys Design Compiler and Synopsys VCS to complete the synthesis, post-synthesis simulation and energy analysis. As shown in

Table 1, the results of the energy measurements demonstrate our redundant design model and search method can obtain lower energy consumption. VHDL codes for describing redundant design schemes are available at https://github.com/JKLinsdu/RedundantDesign.

Table 1. Part of power/energy measurements in this paper. w/: With redundant design, w/o: Without redundant design (corresponding to the implementation in [9]), Lib.1: TSMC 90 nm, Lib.2: UMC 55 nm

Lib	Cipher	Design	Total Power (uW)	Energy (nJ/Mbit)
Lib.1	Trivium	w/o	2552.9	93.0
	(r = 288)	w/	2394.7	87.2
	Kreyvium	w/o	2848.4	116.7
	(r = 256)	w/	2723.5	111.6
Lib.2	Trivium	w/o	2758.1	100.4
	(r = 288)	w/	2577.9	93.9
	Kreyvium	w/o	2637.0	108.1
	(r = 256)	w/	2454.5	100.6

Outline of the Paper. The rest of the paper is organized as follows. Section 2 gives the specification of Perfect Tree energy model including the definition of circuit strand, unrolled strand tree and perfect m-ary tree, in addition, the energy consumption in semiconductor circuits is also discussed. In Sect. 3, we discuss the glitches in semiconductor circuits and gives a redundant design model that reduces glitches. Section 4 gives an algorithm for searching for ports to which the outputs of redundant modules should be connected. In Sect. 5, We apply the redundant design to stream ciphers and give some test result to illustrate the effectiveness of the proposed model and search method. Finally, we conclude the paper in Sect. 6.

2 Preliminaries

In this section, we first review the definition of circuit strand and illustrate the role of the Restricted directive for circuits, using Trivium as an example. We then further review the relation between the circuit strand and tree to introduce the concepts of Perfect m-ary Tree in Perfect Tree energy model. Finally, we describe the energy consumption in semiconductor circuits, and point out the direction for further optimization.

2.1 Circuit Strand

Definition 1 (Circuit Strand [9]). *Update functions of a stream cipher correspond to different combinational logic circuit modules. the combinational logic circuit module can be denoted as circuit strand.*

In the case of `Trivium`, it consists of the following three update functions

$$t_1 \leftarrow s_{65} + (s_{90} \cdot s_{91}) + s_{92} + s_{170}$$
$$t_2 \leftarrow s_{161} + (s_{174} \cdot s_{175}) + s_{176} + s_{263}$$
$$t_3 \leftarrow s_{242} + (s_{285} \cdot s_{286}) + s_{287} + s_{68},$$

where s_i $(1 \le i \le 288)$ are the bits in the state register.

Thus, the update functions of `Trivium` correspond to three independent circuit strands (combinational logic circuit modules). These circuit strands can be represented as

$$x_1 + x_2 + (x_3 \cdot x_4) + x_5.$$

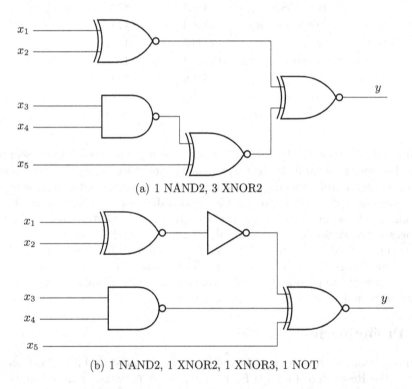

(a) 1 NAND2, 3 XNOR2

(b) 1 NAND2, 1 XNOR2, 1 XNOR3, 1 NOT

Fig. 1. The combinational logic circuit module that corresponds to the circuit strand.

For the circuit strand above, there are many circuit implementation schemes. Figure 1 gives two schemes with four gates (i.e., Fig. 1a and Fig. 1b). Take a `Trivium` implementation at degree of unrolling $r = 288$ as an example, when using the Restricted directive of Synopsys Design Compiler, there will be $288 \times 3 = 864$ of such modules at the gate-level netlist. And these modules are connected to each other, but without breaking individual boundaries.

The Synopsys Design Compiler has a variety of compilation directives, which choose different mappings and optimization for the circuit. The experiments in [9] show that for the circuits compiled under the Restricted directive, the power consumption was much lower than for circuits compiled under the Regular or Ultra directives. When using the Restricted directive, the state update circuit for $r = 1$ is simply replicated for higher degrees of unrolling, i.e., each circuit strand has the same gates and structure, and the output of each strand may be the input of other modules and the input of each strand may be the output of other modules.

2.2   Unrolled Strand Tree and Perfect m-ary Tree

In [9], an energy model applied to stream ciphers is proposed which uses a tree structure to portray energy efficiency, i.e., a good shaped tree corresponds to high energy efficiency, while a bad shaped tree corresponds to low energy efficiency. According to Definition 1, the update function of Trivium consists of three strands

$$t_1 = s_{66} + s_{93} + (s_{91} \cdot s_{92}) + s_{171}$$
$$t_2 = s_{162} + s_{177} + (s_{175} \cdot s_{176}) + s_{264}$$
$$t_3 = s_{243} + s_{288} + (s_{286} \cdot s_{287}) + s_{69}.$$

Definition 2 (Strand in the r-th Unrolled Round [9]). $t_i(r)$ *denotes the strand for equation t_i in the r-th unrolled round, where $i \in \{1, 2, 3\}$, and when $r \in \{1, \ldots, 288\}$, $t_i(r)$ can be written in recursive form for* Trivium *as*

$$t_1(r) = t_3(r - 66) + t_3(r - 93) + [t_3(r - 91) \cdot t_3(r - 92)] + t_1(r - 78)$$
$$t_2(r) = t_1(r - 69) + t_1(r - 84) + [t_1(r - 82) \cdot t_1(r - 83)] + t_2(r - 87)$$
$$t_3(r) = t_2(r - 66) + t_2(r - 111) + [t_2(r - 109) \cdot t_2(r - 110)] + t_3(r - 69),$$

where $t_1(r) = s_{94-r}{}^2$, $t_2(r) = s_{178-r}$ and $t_3(r) = s_{1-r}$ when $r \leq 0$.

Definition 3 (Unrolled Strand Tree [9]). *A strand $t_i(r)$ can be written in a recursive form, i.e., a strand $t_i(r)$ can be represented as a unrolled strand tree $T_i(r)$ with the root node as the output bit whose subtrees are other unrolled strand trees or leaf nodes.*

In general, the leaf nodes of the unrolled strand tree represent the states in the register, and the non-leaf nodes represent the outputs of strands. As shown in Fig. 2, we take the example of $t_1(66)$ and $t_1(67)$, whose corresponding unrolled strand trees are $T_1(66)$ and $T_1(67)$.

Definition 4 (Perfect m-ary Tree [9]). *A perfect m-ary tree is a tree in which all non-leaf nodes have m children and all leaf nodes are at the same depth.*

---

[2] We denote the state bits in the register by s_i $(1 \leq i \leq 288)$.

It is noted that not all unrolled strand trees are perfect m-ary trees. The model in [9] determines whether the circuit strand corresponding to the unrolled strand tree is highly energy efficient precisely by distinguishing whether the unrolled strand tree is a perfect m-ary tree, in other words, the perfect m-ary tree is the tree of good shape in the model.

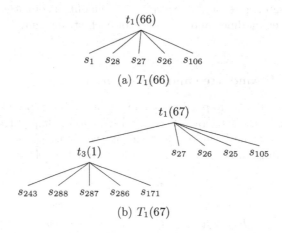

(a) $T_1(66)$

(b) $T_1(67)$

Fig. 2. The unrolled strand tree that corresponds to the circuit strand. $T_1(66)$ is perfect tree, but $T_1(67)$ is not. This means that $t_1(66)$ is energy-efficient and $t_1(67)$ is inefficient.

Since a strand corresponds to an unrolled strand tree, we can estimate the total number of perfect trees in any r-round unrolled implementation of `Trivium`. The total number of perfect trees is a metric given by [9], and this metric shows a negative correlation with energy consumption. Therefore, we can improve energy efficiency by increasing this metric, and more specifically, we can convert an unbalanced unrolled strand tree into a perfect tree.

2.3   Energy Consumption in Semiconductor Circuits

In semiconductor circuits, there are two mainly reasons for producing energy consumption:

(a) *Dynamic dissipation.* Dynamic dissipation is due to the charging and discharging of load capacitances and the short-circuit current in semiconductor circuits. on the frequency of the clock driving the circuit.
(b) *Static dissipation.* Static dissipation is due to leakage current and other current drawn continuously from the power supply.

In detail, the total energy dissipation for a CMOS gate can be written as

$$E = E_{switching} + E_{internal} + E_{leakage},$$

where $E_{internal}$ is internal energy, $E_{switching}$ is switching energy and $E_{leakage}$ is leakage energy. And dynamic dissipation consists of $E_{internal}$ and $E_{switching}$, and static dissipation mainly contains $E_{leakage}$.

Each $0 \rightarrow 1/1 \rightarrow 0$ transition contributes to $E_{switching}$, it is the energy dissipated for charging and discharging the capacitive load of a CMOS gate when output transitions occur. For the capacitive load C_L, the switching power is given as

$$P_{switching} = \frac{1}{2} C_L V_{DD}^2 T_r,$$

where V_{DD} is the internal operating voltage of the device and T_r is the toggle rate (The amount of $0 \rightarrow 1/1 \rightarrow 0$ transitions per unit time). $E_{internal}$ is due to the short-circuit current in a CMOS gate, i.e., the pn Junction loses its unidirectional conductivity and becomes a non-resistive circuit during a $0 \rightarrow 1/1 \rightarrow 0$ transition, and the internal power is given as

$$P_{internal} = \frac{1}{2}(P_{rise} + P_{fall}) T_r,$$

where P_{rise} and P_{fall} depend on the input transition time and the total output net capacitance load.

$E_{leakage}$ is due to leakage current, and it increases with any increase in the physical time required to complete an operation, this means that if we decrease the frequency, $E_{leakage}$ will increase (the frequency is inversely proportional to the clock cycle). When the frequency is high, the value of $E_{leakage}$ is very small and negligible compared with the values of $E_{switching}$ and $E_{internal}$. Thus, our energy optimization is mainly centered on dynamic dissipation.

According to the expressions $E_{switching}$ and $E_{internal}$, both of these physical variables are related to the toggle rate. Therefore, we can optimize the energy by reducing the toggle rate.

3   Redundant Design for Reducing Glitches

The Perfect Tree energy model in [9] used the total number of perfect trees as a metric, which is negatively correlated with energy consumption, and proposed low energy variants of the stream ciphers based on this metric by changing the tap locations. In this section, an alternative idea for reducing energy consumption based on this metric is presented, we analyze the relation between the glitches and the unbalanced unrolled strand tree, and propose a redundant design to reduce glitches.

3.1   Glitches and Unbalanced Unrolled Strand Tree

According to Definition 3, a circuit strand $t_i(r)$ corresponds to an unrolled strand tree $T_i(r)$, the vertex of an unrolled strand tree $T_i(r)$ is the output value of $t_i(r)$, and the child nodes of $t_i(r)$ correspond to the inputs to $t_i(r)$. And $t_i(r)$ has five different inputs from the register storing the state values s_i or other strands.

We classify the type of input according to the distance to the register (i.e., the height of the subtree corresponding to $t_i(r)$), and different types of input have different delays. When the types of the inputs to $t_i(r)$ are different, this can make the delay unbalanced, which is the reason why glitches are produced.

According to Definition 1, each circuit strand corresponds to a combinational logic circuit module, and for `Trivium`, the expressions of all the corresponding strands are exactly the same, which means that these strands have the same gates and structure and, more importantly, the same delay. When using the Synopsys Design Compiler's Restricted directive to prevent the optimization between strands, the boundary of each strand is respected and the internal structure is maintained. Thus, we can convert the problem related to the delay about the entire combinatorial logic circuit consisting of these strands into the problem of computing the height and depth of an unrolled strand tree. For example, there are two typical computational problems related to the delay.

(a) *Estimating the delay of the circuit strand.* First, we compute the delay of a single combinational logic circuit module. Then, the height of the unrolled strand tree corresponding to the circuit strand is observed. According to the product of the above delay and height, we obtain the overall delay of the circuit strand. When two different circuit strands correspond to unrolled strand trees of the same height, it means that the two circuit strands have the same delay.

(b) *Judging whether the input delay of the circuit strand is balanced.* We observe whether all the nodes of the unrolled strand tree corresponding to the circuit strand meet the definition of the perfect m-ary tree (Definition 4). If an unrolled strand tree satisfies the definition of the perfect m-ary tree, it means that all the input delays of its corresponding circuit strand are balanced.

For combinational logic circuits, at any given moment, the output state is determined only by the combination of all the input states at the same moment, independent of the previous state of the circuit, and independent of the state at any other time. This means that for a combinational logic circuit module, if one of the inputs arrives faster or slower than the others, it may temporarily change the output of it, which is not the output after the circuit is stabilized, we claim that glitches are produced in the circuit at this time. The glitches reflect the increase in toggle rate, which leads to an increase in internal energy consumption and switching energy consumption.

In a word, the unbalanced unrolled strand tree, the glitches, and the power consumption are the same phenomenon from different perspectives. As shown in Fig. 2, $T_1(66)$ is a perfect tree, while $T_1(67)$ is not. This means that the input delay of $t_1(67)$ is unbalanced and the input $t_3(1)$ arrives slower than the other inputs, which will cause the output of a to be in an unstable state. Therefore $t_1(67)$ has more glitches, resulting in greater power consumption for $t_1(67)$ than $t_1(66)$, which is shown in Fig. 5.

3.2   Redundant Modules with the Same Delay

According to the analysis results in Sect. 3.1, glitches are the cause of the increased power consumption. Therefore, we can try to reduce glitches. From the viewpoint of Perfect Tree energy model, not all unrolled strand trees satisfy the definition of perfect tree. The reason for the imbalance of the unrolled strand tree is that its leaf nodes are not at the same depth, which means that the input delays of the corresponding circuit strand are inconsistent. Therefore, the problem of reducing glitches is equivalent to the problem of how to convert an unbalanced unrolled strand tree $T_i(r)$ into a perfect tree. A natural idea is to add child nodes for the leaf nodes with smaller depths until all the leaf nodes are at the same depth.

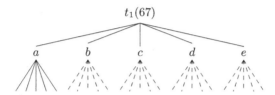

Fig. 3. The adjusted $T_1(67)$. The dashed lines connect the newly added child nodes, corresponding to the five inputs of the redundant module.

According to Definition 3, the leaf nodes of $T_i(r)$ represent the state values in the register, and the non-leaf nodes represent the output values of strands. As shown in Fig. 3, taking the circuit strand $t_1(67)$ as an example, we can adjust the unbalanced unrolled strand tree $T_1(67)$ into a perfect tree by adding child nodes, where a, b, c, d and e denote the five child nodes of $t_1(67)$. This means that the input ports corresponding to b, c, d and e change from direct connections to the states of the register into connections to the outputs of other strands (combinational logic circuit modules). For reducing glitches and improving energy efficiency, the following requirements for redundant module design are required.

(a) The value of the signal arriving at the input port of $t_i(r)$ cannot be changed, only the arrival time is changed, i.e., the outputs of the redundant modules have to be the same as the state values in the register.
(b) The delays of the redundant modules have to be consistent with the delays of the other circuit strands, which ensures that the input delays of the circuit strands are consistent.
(c) The addition of redundant modules will bring additional leakage of power consumption, and it is important to make this part of the power consumption as small as possible.

An intuitive scheme for the above requirements is to use the structure in Fig. 1 and set its input values to ensure that its output value is the same as the state value in the register. If we set $x_1 = s_i$, $x_2 = 0$, $x_3 = 0$, $x_4 = 0$ and $x_5 = 0$, where s_i denotes the state in the register, the output value will be $y = s_i$. We apply this redundant module to $t_1(67)$, this redundant module design scheme uses the same gates and structure as the other circuit strands, ensuring that the signal of a, b, c, d and e arrive at the input port at the same time. In addition, this scheme makes sure that the values b, c, d and e of the signal arriving at the input port is not changed. These redundant modules added between the input ports with low delays and the register states avoid the delay imbalance caused by the direct connection of the two, thus achieving the goal of reducing glitches.

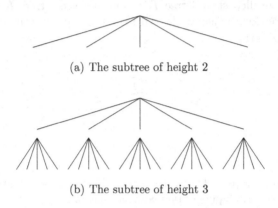

(a) The subtree of height 2

(b) The subtree of height 3

Fig. 4. Optimizing an input port with lower delay corresponding to a tree of height 4 is equivalent to converting a subtree of height 2 to a subtree of height 3. This adjustment requires an additional 25 child (leaf) nodes and generates an additional 5 non-leaf nodes, implying the requirement of five redundant modules.

For other unbalanced unrolled strand trees, we can also optimize input ports with lower delay of circuit strands using redundant modules. For the input ports that need to be optimized, we propose a search algorithm in Sect. 4 to obtain these ports with lower delay. In general, we only adjust unbalanced unrolled strand trees of height 3. After adjusting the tree of height 3, for a tree $T_i(r)$ of height 4, the subtrees of strand $t_i(r)$ are trees of height 2 or 3 and meet the definition of the perfect tree. As shown in Fig. 4, a subtree corresponds to an input port of $t_i(r)$, so in order to adjust an input port with lower delay for a circuit strand corresponding to a tree of height 4, we need to add five additional redundant modules, while for a tree of height 3 only one redundant module is needed. And so on, adjusting the tree for heights greater than 4 requires more redundant modules. The addition of redundant modules is not cost-free, but brings an increase in area and leakage power consumption. The essence of our redundant design is to trade an increase in area for a decrease in total power consumption, and we need to make trade-offs for each hardware metric.

In addition, the corresponding input ports to be optimized are different for different circuit strands, i.e., all input ports have to be selected between the state in the register and the output of the redundant module. When considering the hardware implementation, the layout of the circuit needs to be chosen in a targeted way. VHDL's `if-generate` statement allows us to conditionally include blocks of code in the design, we can use this statement to make a selection on the input port.

4 Search Algorithm

In this section, we propose a generic search algorithm, which is used to search the input ports of the circuit strands that need to be connected to the outputs of the redundant modules. According to Definition 3, the vertex of an unrolled strand tree $T_i(r)$ is the corresponding circuit strand $t_i(r)$'s output value, and the child nodes of $t_i(r)$ correspond to the inputs to $t_i(r)$, which possibly have different delays. By filtering the ports of these circuit strands, we can determine the corresponding implementation rules and the input types of circuit strands in different classes which can ensure that the optimized unrolled strand tree will be balanced, i.e., the optimized unrolled strand tree will meet the definition of the perfect tree. In other words, the implementation rules for $t_i(r)$ indicate the type of all the input ports. Based on the type of input ports, we can determine where to add the redundant modules to reach the goal of balancing delays and reducing glitches.

Our search algorithm takes the tap locations involved in the recursive expressions (in Definition 2) of circuit strand as inputs, and outputs the implementation rule of the circuit strand. For different strands, the corresponding search algorithm can also be derived by changing the tap locations parameters.

Before introducing the search method, we give the notations used in this section as follows.

- r: The degree of unrolling.
- X_i: The tap locations involved in the recursive expressions of circuit strand.
- x_i: The input ports for circuit strand.
- $\mathcal{T}$: The set of register's tap locations.
- $\mathcal{M}$: The mapping set of register's tap locations to input ports for corresponding circuit strand.
- $\mathcal{E}$: The mapping set of circuit strands to their input ports.

Our search method is applicable to stream ciphers. In stream ciphers, their update functions can be described using a series of tap location parameters. Definition 2 gives the recursive form of the circuit strand, from the correspondence between the expression for $t_i(r)$ and the unrolled strand tree, we can observe that the shape of the tree depends on the numerical comparisons of the degree of unrolling and the tap locations involved in the recursive expressions. And according to Sect. 3.2, we only need to adjust the unrolled strand trees with height 3 for the trade-off of each hardware metric. The essence of the implementation scheme of the redundant design is to optimize the input ports with lower delays, therefore, we propose Algorithm 1 to search for these input ports.

Algorithm 1: $\mathcal{E} = \texttt{SearchPorts}(\mathcal{T}, \mathcal{M})$

Input: The sets $\mathcal{T}$ and $\mathcal{M}$
Output: The set $\mathcal{E}$ of ports with redundant modules as inputs with the
         tap locations in $\mathcal{M}$

1 $\mathcal{E} \leftarrow \phi$
2 **for** i *in range(1,r)* **do**
3 $\quad$ $w \leftarrow 0$
4 $\quad$ **foreach** *element X in $\mathcal{T}$* **do**
5 $\quad\quad$ **if** $i > X$ **then**
6 $\quad\quad\quad$ $w \leftarrow w + 1$
7 $\quad\quad$ **end**
8 $\quad$ **end**
9 $\quad$ $v \leftarrow \texttt{sizeof}(\mathcal{T})$
10 $\quad$ **if** $w \neq 0$ **and** $w \neq v$ **then**
11 $\quad\quad$ **foreach** *element X in $\mathcal{T}$* **do**
12 $\quad\quad\quad$ **if** $i \leq X$ **then**
13 $\quad\quad\quad\quad$ $x \leftarrow \texttt{mapping}(X, \mathcal{M})$
14 $\quad\quad\quad\quad$ $\mathcal{E} \leftarrow \mathcal{E} \cup \{(i, x)\}$
15 $\quad\quad\quad$ **end**
16 $\quad\quad$ **end**
17 $\quad$ **end**
18 **end**
19 **return** $\mathcal{E}$

Algorithm 1 consists of two steps: (a) Step 1. Determine whether the delays of the inputs of $t_i(r)$ are balanced. This determination can be done by the above numerical comparison used to observe the shape of the tree, and this step corresponds to **Line 2–8** in Algorithm 1. (b) Step 2. Filter the input ports with lower delays corresponding to $t_i(r)$ with delay imbalance in Step 1, this step also uses numerical comparisons and corresponds to **Line 10–17** in Algorithm 1. Next, we explain Algorithm 1 line by line:

Line 1 Initialize the set $\mathcal{E}$ as an empty set.
Line 2 For the circuit at degree of unrolling r, there are r strands for equation t_i being iterated.
Line 3 Initialize the counter w as 0. We denote the result of a numerical comparison by 0 and 1, and accumulate the results. The total result after accumulation is related to the balance of the unrolled strand tree, i.e., the tree

is balanced when the counter has a value of 0 or the number of elements in the set $\mathcal{T}$. In a word, this counter reflects the balance of the unrolled strand tree corresponding to the circuit strand.

Line 4–8 Iterate through the five taps to get the result of the comparison with the numerical value of i, and accumulate the results.

Line 9 The `sizeof()` is used to return the number of elements in the set.

Line 10 Filter unbalanced unrolled strand trees.

Line 11–16 The input ports are classified in more detail, and the ports that need to be optimized are added to the set $\mathcal{E}$. Where `mapping()` is used to return the mapping value of an element X in the set $\mathcal{M}$.

Line 19 Return the set $\mathcal{E}$ of mappings of circuit strands to their inputs.

Taking `Trivium` as an example, as shown in Fig. 1, a circuit strand corresponds to five input ports, so we can create a mapping from the circuit strand to the input ports that need to be optimized to present a specific implementation scheme. When considering an implementation of the cipher, we connect the input ports of the mappings in the set to redundant modules.

Example: Implementation rule for $t_1(67)$. As shown in Fig. 2, $T_1(67)$ is an unbalanced tree, thus there are a portion of input ports with lower delays, and we use Algorithm 1 to filter them. It is noted that the tap locations involved in the recursive expressions of the circuit strand $t_1(67)$ are $X_1 = 66$, $X_2 = 93$, $X_3 = 91$, $X_4 = 92$ and $X_5 = 78$, where the value of X_1 is less than 67, so $w = 1$. Because $w \neq 0$ and $w \neq 5$, we further filter the input port for $t_1(67)$. Since the values of X_2, X_3, X_4 and X_5 are greater than 67, and $(X_1, x_1) \in \mathcal{M}$, $(X_2, x_2) \in \mathcal{M}$, $(X_3, x_3) \in \mathcal{M}$, $(X_4, x_4) \in \mathcal{M}$, $(X_5, x_5) \in \mathcal{M}$, so $(67, x_2) \in \mathcal{E}$, $(67, x_3) \in \mathcal{E}$, $(67, x_4) \in \mathcal{E}$ and $(67, x_5) \in \mathcal{E}$. Thus, the input ports x_2, x_3, x_4 and x_5 of $t_1(67)$ is to be connected to the redundant module.

5   Applications to Stream Ciphers

In this section, we apply the proposed model and search method in two `Trivium`-like stream ciphers: `Trivium` [13] and `Kreyvium` [10]. The most significant characteristic of `Trivium`-like ciphers is that the strands corresponding to the update functions are approximately the same. For `Trivium`-like ciphers, our redundant design model can play a positive role in energy optimization. In order to verify the effectiveness of our model and algorithm, we conduct synthetic tests and give the experimental results.

We take the tap location parameters of the stream cipher as the input of the search algorithm and get the mappings of circuit strands to its ports as the implementation scheme. Based on these mappings, we describe the layout of the circuit in VHDL, i.e., the input ports of each circuit strand should be connected to which part of the entire circuit. Then, we use Synopsys Design Compiler to convert the circuit described by VHDL into a gate-level netlist based on the standard cell library, and the two standard cell libraries we used in our experiments are TSMC 90 nm and UMC 55 nm. We then use Synopsys VCS to run post-synthesis simulation of gate-level netlist, with the aim of collecting the switching activity of each gate of the circuit and generating SAIF files containing the information about the toggle counts. In the last step, the SAIF files are sent back to the synthesis tool together with the gate-level netlist from the initial synthesis to run power analysis.

5.1   Application to Trivium

Trivium [13] is a hardware-oriented synchronous stream cipher, which still has a large margin of security [17–19,25], its update functions and their corresponding circuit strands are given in Sect. 2.1, and these circuit strands are exactly the same.

We use the Synopsys design compiler's restriction directive to compile the circuit to ensure that the boundaries of the circuit strands are not broken, so we can conduct a separate energy analysis for each circuit strand. Power measurements for all circuit strands $t_i(r)$ without redundant design of the two standard cell libraries (TSMC 90 nm and UMC 55 nm) are shown in Fig. 5. And we can observe that the power consumption of the circuit strands corresponding to the perfect trees are relatively low, and the power consumption of the circuit strands corresponding to the unbalanced unrolled strand trees are relatively high, where data points with colors close to blue correspond to circuit strand with low energy consumption, while data points with colors close to red are circuit strand with high energy consumption. Take the circuit strands $t_1(r)$ ($1 \leq r \leq 93$) as examples, where the unrolled strand trees corresponding to circuit strands $t_1(r)$ for $1 \leq r \leq 66$ are perfect trees, while the unrolled strand trees corresponding to circuit strands $t_1(r)$ for $67 \leq r \leq 93$ are imbalanced trees. We can observe a sudden rise between the data points corresponding to the two parts of the circuit strands mentioned above in Fig. 5a, more specifically, there is a significant discontinuity between $t_1(66)$ and $t_1(67)$. Another phenomenon of interest is that the data points corresponding to the circuit strands do not rise monotonically as r rises, but there are sudden drops, and the data points that drop suddenly correspond to the circuit strands corresponding to the perfect trees as well, which reminds us that converting an unbalanced tree into a perfect one is an idea for optimizing power consumption, specifically, this can be achieved by introducing redundant design to the circuit.

For redundant design, we also synthesize the circuit using Synopsys Design Compile's Restriction directive. From the gate-level netlist, the circuit with redundant design has some more combinational logic circuit modules (redundant modules) than the circuit without redundant design. Thanks to Restriction directive, the boundary of each circuit strand is not broken, so we can also use the power analysis tool to measure the power consumption of each circuit strand of the circuit with redundant design. Based on the power measurement figures of the circuit with and without redundant design, we can observe the role of the redundant modules by comparing the two. Note that according to the analysis in Sect. 3, we only optimize for unbalanced unrolled strand trees of height 3.

As shown in Fig. 5 and Fig. 6, the values of the data points corresponding to all circuit strands are reduced to different degrees, where the decrease in the values of the data point corresponding to circuit strands $t_1(r)$ for $67 \leq r \leq 93$ is particularly significant. The main reason for this significant decrease is that the power consumption of the circuit strands corresponding to the unbalanced unrolled strand trees of height 3 is reduced due to the fact that we have adjusted these trees to satisfy the definition of the perfect tree. Taking $t_1(66)$ and $t_1(67)$ as examples, in Fig. 5, there is a obvious discontinuity between the two, while in Fig. 6, there is a continuity between the two, which implies that the redundant modules play the role in reducing glitches. And compared with Fig. 5, the sudden rise that exists between circuit strands $t_1(r)$ for $1 \leq r \leq 66$ and circuit strands $t_1(r)$ for $67 \leq r \leq 93$ is eliminated.

Then, we conducted energy measurements on Trivium's circuit with and without redundant design, and compared the results in these two cases. In Fig. 7, we render the energy measurement of the process of encrypting 1 Mbit data results by using two standard cell libraries (TSMC 90 nm and UMC 55 nm) over 100 Mhz, and the energy consumption is computed as the product of the average power and the total time required for the encryption process. Our energy measurement figure shows the energy consumed to encrypt 1 Mbit of data at different degree of unrolling. It is noted that for lower degree of unrolling, since the number of glitches is small and the effect of redundant design is not obvious, the two lines in the figure overlap. As shown in Fig. 7, the energy measurement figure first drops sharply and then tends to be stable. Considering throughput and the impact of the degree of unrolling r on energy consumption, we take $r = 288$ as the optimal parameter. Take the circuit based on TSMC 90 nm as an example, at degree of unrolling $r = 288$, the energy consumption of the implementations with and without redundant design are 87.2 nJ/Mbit (Corresponding dynamic power consumption is 2335.5 uW and leakage power consumption is 59.2 uW) and 93.0 nJ/Mbit (Corresponding dynamic power consumption is 2497.7 uW and leakage power consumption is 55.2 uW) as shown in Fig. 7 and Table 2, respectively, which indicates a reduction in energy consumption of about 6.2%. Another example is based on UMC 55 nm, at degree of unrolling $r = 288$, the energy consumption of the implementations with and without redundant design are 93.9 nJ/Mbit (Corresponding dynamic power consumption is 2569.1 uW and leakage power consumption is 8.8 uW) and 100.4 nJ/Mbit (Corresponding dynamic power consumption is 2749.9 uW and leakage power consumption is 8.2 uW), respectively, which indicates a reduction in energy consumption of about 6.5%. According to the comparison results of dynamic and leakage power consumption in Table 2, we can find that the redundant design increases leakage power consumption, but reduces dynamic power consumption. The reason for this is that our redundant scheme reduces glitch by adding redundant circuits to balance the dynamic and leakage power consumption, so as to reduce the power consumption of the whole scheme.

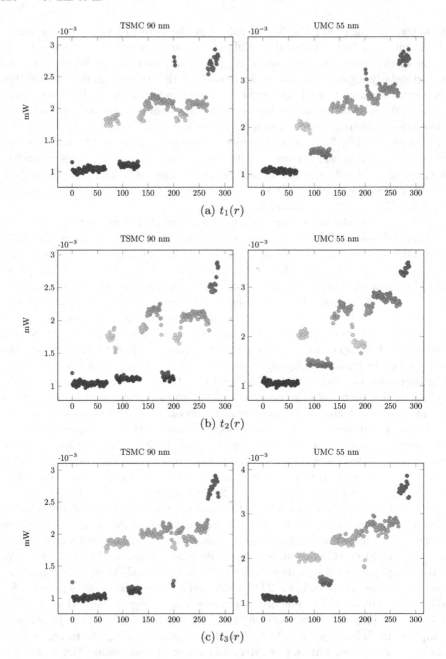

Fig. 5. Trivium power measurements for all the circuit strands for the TSMC 90 nm and UMC 55 nm cell libraries without redundant design.

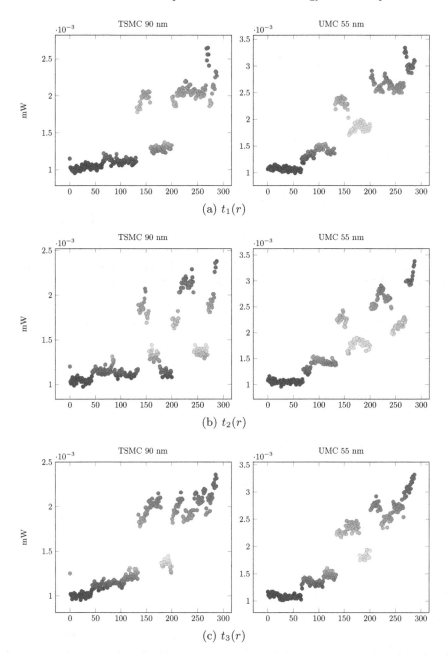

Fig. 6. Trivium power measurements for all the circuit strands for the TSMC 90 nm and UMC 55 nm cell libraries with redundant design.

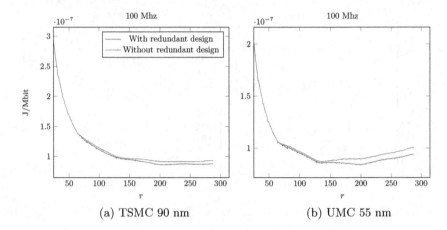

Fig. 7. Trivium energy measurements for the TSMC 90 nm and UMC 55 nm cell libraries. For 100 Mhz, the implementation with redundant design is more advantageous than the implementation without redundant design.

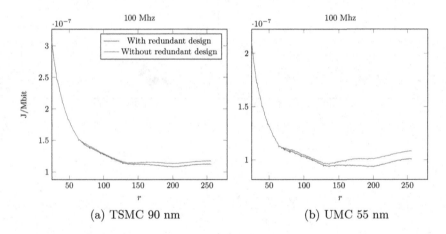

Fig. 8. Kreyvium energy measurements for the TSMC 90 nm cell libraries.

5.2 Application to Kreyvium

Kreyvium [10] is a stream cipher designed to be applied to fully homomorphic encryption schemes. Compared with Trivium, Kreyvium's security [15–17] is improved from 80-bit to 128-bit. Although Kreyvium and Trivium have the same structure and taps, the three circuit strands corresponding to Kreyvium's update functions are not exactly the same. According to Definition 1 and the description of Kreyvium, the update functions of Kreyvium consists of three strands

$$t_1 = s_{66} + s_{93} + (s_{91} \cdot s_{92}) + s_{171} + IV_0^*$$
$$t_2 = s_{162} + s_{177} + (s_{175} \cdot s_{176}) + s_{264}$$
$$t_3 = s_{243} + s_{288} + (s_{286} \cdot s_{287}) + s_{69} + K_0^*,$$

where IV_0^* and K_0^* denote the bits from IV and key.

Table 2. Part of power/energy measurements at 100 Mhz. w/: With redundant design, w/o: Without redundant design (corresponding to the implementation in [9]), Lib.1: TSMC 90 nm, Lib.2: UMC 55 nm

Lib	Cipher	Design	Total Power (uW)	Dynamic Power (uW)	Leakage Power (uW)	Energy (nJ/Mbit)
Lib.1	Trivium	w/o	2552.9	2497.7	55.2	93.0
	(r = 288)	w/	2394.7	2335.5	59.2	87.2
	Kreyvium	w/o	2848.4	2791.7	56.7	116.7
	(r = 256)	w/	2723.5	2662.8	60.7	111.6
Lib.2	Trivium	w/o	2758.1	2749.9	8.2	100.4
	(r = 288)	w/	2577.9	2569.1	8.8	93.9
	Kreyvium	w/o	2637.0	2628.7	8.3	108.1
	(r = 256)	w/	2454.5	2445.6	8.9	100.6

We apply the proposed model and search method to the Kreyvium to give a redundant design scheme and describe it using VHDL. Based on the Synopsys Design Compiler and two cell libraries (i.e., TSMC 90 nm and UMC 55 nm), we synthesise the hardware implementation scheme, and the results of our energy analysis based on encrypted 1 Mbit data are shown in Fig. 8 and Table 2. We can also observe that as the degree of unrolling r increases, the energy line first has a significant drop, and then fluctuates in a small range in Fig. 8. And as the degree of unrolling r increases, the advantages of our redundant design become more and more apparent. Considering the throughput and the impact of degree of unrolling on energy (when greater than a certain value, the impact of degree of unrolling on energy consumption is small), we take $r = 256$ as the optimal. At degree of unrolling $r = 256$, for TSMC 90 nm, the energy consumption of the implementations with and without redundant design are 111.6 nJ/Mbit (Corresponding dynamic power consumption is 2662.8 uW and leakage power consumption is 60.7 uW) and 116.7 nJ/Mbit (Corresponding dynamic power consumption is 2791.7 uW and leakage power consumption is 56.7 uW), respectively, which indicates a reduction in energy consumption of about 4.4%; for UMC 55nm, the energy consumption of the implementations with and without redundant design are 100.6 nJ/Mbit (Corresponding dynamic power consumption is 2445.6 uW and leakage power consumption is 8.9 uW) and 108.1 nJ/Mbit (Corresponding dynamic power consumption is 2628.7 uW and leakage power consumption is 8.3

uW), respectively, which indicates a reduction in energy consumption of about 6.9%. These results indicate that our redundant design trades a portion of the increase in leakage power consumption for a reduction in dynamic power consumption, and that our design shows an advantage when the latter reduction is greater than the former increase.

6   Conclusion

In this paper, we investigated the hardware implementation of low energy stream ciphers. Based on Perfect Tree energy model, we propose a redundant design model for reducing glitches. In fact, the intuitive scheme in this paper is not the only scheme for redundant module, as long as the combined logic circuit modules that meet requirements of delay balance can be used as redundant modules. We have not yet found a better design scheme for redundant modules, so there remains an open problem of finding a better delay balancing scheme. In addition, we present a search algorithm used to return the implementation scheme. And we reimplemented the different stream ciphers using the redundant design, the experimental results show that the energy consumption of the circuit with redundant design was reduced.

From the experimental results, we can find that applying the redundant design to Trivium-like ciphers worked well because the strands of the Trivium-like cipher are approximately the same, which means that the redundant module is easier to construct. Therefore, from the perspective of energy optimization, we suggest that cipher designers consider setting the circuit strands corresponding to the update functions of the stream ciphers to be approximately the same.

Acknowledgement. This work was partially supported by the National Natural Science Foundation of China (Grant No. 62272273, Grant No. 62002201, Grant No. 62032014), the National Key Research and Development Program of China (Grant No. 2018YFA0704702), and the Major Basic Research Project of Natural Science Foundation of Shandong Province, China (Grant No. ZR202010220025).

References

1. Banik, S., et al.: Midori: a block cipher for low energy. In: Iwata, T., Cheon, J.H. (eds.) ASIACRYPT 2015. LNCS, vol. 9453, pp. 411–436. Springer, Heidelberg (2015). https://doi.org/10.1007/978-3-662-48800-3_17
2. Banik, S., Bogdanov, A., Regazzoni, F.: Exploring energy efficiency of lightweight block ciphers. In: Dunkelman, O., Keliher, L. (eds.) SAC 2015. LNCS, vol. 9566, pp. 178–194. Springer, Cham (2016). https://doi.org/10.1007/978-3-319-31301-6_10
3. Banik, S., et al.: Towards low energy stream ciphers. IACR Trans. Symmetric Cryptology **2018**(2), 1–19 (2018). https://doi.org/10.13154/tosc.v2018.i2.1-19
4. Batina, L., et al.: Dietary recommendations for lightweight block ciphers: power, energy and area analysis of recently developed architectures. In: Hutter, M., Schmidt, J.-M. (eds.) RFIDSec 2013. LNCS, vol. 8262, pp. 103–112. Springer, Heidelberg (2013). https://doi.org/10.1007/978-3-642-41332-2_7

5. Beaulieu, R., Shors, D., Smith, J., Treatman-Clark, S., Weeks, B., Wingers, L.: The Simon and speck families of lightweight block ciphers. Cryptology ePrint Archive, Paper 2013/404 (2013). https://eprint.iacr.org/2013/404

6. Bogdanov, A., et al.: PRESENT: an ultra-lightweight block cipher. In: Paillier, P., Verbauwhede, I. (eds.) CHES 2007. LNCS, vol. 4727, pp. 450–466. Springer, Heidelberg (2007). https://doi.org/10.1007/978-3-540-74735-2_31

7. Caforio, A., Balli, F., Banik, S.: Energy analysis of lightweight AEAD circuits. In: Krenn, S., Shulman, H., Vaudenay, S. (eds.) CANS 2020. LNCS, vol. 12579, pp. 23–42. Springer, Cham (2020). https://doi.org/10.1007/978-3-030-65411-5_2

8. Caforio, A., Balli, F., Banik, S., Regazzoni, F.: A deeper look at the energy consumption of lightweight block ciphers. In: 2021 Design, Automation & Test in Europe Conference & Exhibition (DATE), pp. 170–175. IEEE (2021). https://doi.org/10.23919/DATE51398.2021.9474018

9. Caforio, A., et al.: Perfect trees: designing energy-optimal symmetric encryption primitives. IACR Trans.. Symmetric Cryptology **2021**(4), 36–73 (2021). https://doi.org/10.46586/tosc.v2021.i4.36-73

10. Canteaut, A., et al.: Stream ciphers: a practical solution for efficient homomorphic-ciphertext compression. In: Peyrin, T. (ed.) FSE 2016. LNCS, vol. 9783, pp. 313–333. Springer, Heidelberg (2016). https://doi.org/10.1007/978-3-662-52993-5_16

11. Daemen, J., Peeters, M., Van Assche, G., Rijmen, V.: Nessie proposal: NOEKEON. In: First Open NESSIE Workshop, pp. 213–230 (2000). http://gro.noekeon.org/Noekeon-spec.pdf

12. Daemen, J., Rijmen, V.: The Design of Rijndael, vol. 2. Springer, Cham (2002). https://doi.org/10.1007/978-3-662-60769-5

13. De Cannière, C., Preneel, B.: Trivium. In: Robshaw, M., Billet, O. (eds.) New Stream Cipher Designs. LNCS, vol. 4986, pp. 244–266. Springer, Heidelberg (2008). https://doi.org/10.1007/978-3-540-68351-3_18

14. Feldhofer, M., Wolkerstorfer, J., Rijmen, V.: AES implementation on a grain of sand. IEE Proc.-Inf. Secur. **152**(1), 13–20 (2005). https://doi.org/10.1049/ip-ifs:20055006

15. Hao, Y., Jiao, L., Li, C., Meier, W., Todo, Y., Wang, Q.: Links between division property and other cube attack variants. IACR Trans. Symmetric Cryptology **2020**(1), 363–395 (2020). https://doi.org/10.13154/tosc.v2020.i1.363-395

16. Hao, Y., Leander, G., Meier, W., Todo, Y., Wang, Q.: Modeling for three-subset division property without unknown subset. In: Canteaut, A., Ishai, Y. (eds.) EUROCRYPT 2020. LNCS, vol. 12105, pp. 466–495. Springer, Cham (2020). https://doi.org/10.1007/978-3-030-45721-1_17

17. He, J., Hu, K., Preneel, B., Wang, M.: Stretching cube attacks: improved methods to recover massive superpolies. In: Agrawal, S., Lin, D. (eds.) Advances in Cryptology - ASIACRYPT 2022, pp. 537–566. Springer, Cham (2022). https://doi.org/10.1007/978-3-031-22972-5_19

18. Hu, K., Sun, S., Todo, Y., Wang, M., Wang, Q.: Massive superpoly recovery with nested monomial predictions. In: Tibouchi, M., Wang, H. (eds.) ASIACRYPT 2021. LNCS, vol. 13090, pp. 392–421. Springer, Cham (2021). https://doi.org/10.1007/978-3-030-92062-3_14

19. Hu, K., Sun, S., Wang, M., Wang, Q.: An algebraic formulation of the division property: revisiting degree evaluations, cube attacks, and key-independent sums. In: Moriai, S., Wang, H. (eds.) ASIACRYPT 2020. LNCS, vol. 12491, pp. 446–476. Springer, Cham (2020). https://doi.org/10.1007/978-3-030-64837-4_15

20. Kerckhof, S., Durvaux, F., Hocquet, C., Bol, D., Standaert, F.-X.: Towards green cryptography: a comparison of lightweight ciphers from the energy viewpoint. In: Prouff, E., Schaumont, P. (eds.) CHES 2012. LNCS, vol. 7428, pp. 390–407. Springer, Heidelberg (2012). https://doi.org/10.1007/978-3-642-33027-8_23

21. Moradi, A., Poschmann, A., Ling, S., Paar, C., Wang, H.: Pushing the limits: a very compact and a threshold implementation of AES. In: Paterson, K.G. (ed.) EUROCRYPT 2011. LNCS, vol. 6632, pp. 69–88. Springer, Heidelberg (2011). https://doi.org/10.1007/978-3-642-20465-4_6

22. Satoh, A., Morioka, S., Takano, K., Munetoh, S.: A compact Rijndael hardware architecture with S-box optimization. In: Boyd, C. (ed.) Advances in Cryptology – ASIACRYPT 2001, ASIACRYPT 2001, vol. 2248, pp. 239–254. Springer, Berlin (2001). https://doi.org/10.1007/3-540-45682-1_15

23. Shibutani, K., Isobe, T., Hiwatari, H., Mitsuda, A., Akishita, T., Shirai, T.: *Piccolo*: an ultra-lightweight blockcipher. In: Preneel, B., Takagi, T. (eds.) CHES 2011. LNCS, vol. 6917, pp. 342–357. Springer, Heidelberg (2011). https://doi.org/10.1007/978-3-642-23951-9_23

24. Suzaki, T., Minematsu, K., Morioka, S., Kobayashi, E.: *TWINE*: a lightweight block cipher for multiple platforms. In: Knudsen, L.R., Wu, H. (eds.) SAC 2012. LNCS, vol. 7707, pp. 339–354. Springer, Heidelberg (2013). https://doi.org/10.1007/978-3-642-35999-6_22

25. Ye, C.D., Tian, T.: Algebraic method to recover superpolies in cube attacks. IET Inf. Secur. **14**(4), 430–441 (2020). https://doi.org/10.1049/iet-ifs.2019.0323

Cryptanalysis

The Special Case of Cyclotomic Fields in Quantum Algorithms for Unit Groups

Razvan Barbulescu[1]([⊠]) and Adrien Poulalion[2]

[1] Univ. Bordeaux, CNRS, Bordeaux INP, IMB, UMR 5251,
33400 Talence, France
razvan.barbulescu@u-bordeaux.fr
[2] Alice & Bob, Corps des Mines, France
adrien.poulalion@mines.org

Abstract. Unit group computations are a cryptographic primitive for which one has a fast quantum algorithm, but the required number of qubits is $\tilde{O}(m^5)$. In this work we propose a modification of the algorithm for which the number of qubits is $\tilde{O}(m^2)$ in the case of cyclotomic fields. Moreover, under a recent conjecture on the size of the class group of $\mathbb{Q}(\zeta_m + \zeta_m^{-1})$, the quantum algorithm is much simpler because it is a hidden subgroup problem (HSP) algorithm rather than its error estimation counterpart: continuous hidden subgroup problem (CHSP). We also discuss the (minor) speed-up obtained when exploiting Galois automorphisms thanks to the Buchmann-Pohst algorithm over $\mathcal{O}_K$-lattices.

1 Introduction

The difficulty to compute the class group and its cardinality, the class number, plays an important role in cryptography. Notably, they are at the foundation of a time commitments protocol [49], a scheme of homomorphic encryption [15] and a verifiable delay function [50]. Note that the particular cases play an important role as the former two examples use quadratic fields and for the latter the cyclotomic case can be the fastest.

From a perspective of theoretical computer science, these schemes are broken because there exists a quantum algorithm of polynomial time complexity [10]. However, from a cryptographic point of view it is required to obtain a more precise estimation of the number of qubits and quantum gates, as it was done for the other primitives of public key cryptography [4,6,7,29,40,44,45,51].

Let us recall the chronology of the works addressing this question. Note that, both in the classical and quantum algorithms, the class-and-unit group computations are very similar and are sometimes done simultaneously in order to have a halting condition, as in the classical algorithm of Buchmann and McCurley. In 1994, Shor designed a quantum algorithm to factor integers and, respectively, solve the discrete log problem in cyclic groups [48]. Kitaev [33] reformulated the

R. Barbulescu—The first author has been funded by the Hybrid quantum initiative (HQI) of the France 2030 program.

algorithms by reducing both problems to finding the set of periods of functions defined over $\mathbb{Z}^r$ with fixed r and taking values in a finite set; this is the hidden subgroup problem (HSP). Note that the parameter r affects the time and space complexity only in a polynomial manner.

In 2002, Hallgren [28][1] reduced the computation of a fundamental unit of a real quadratic field to finding the set of periods of a function defined over $\mathbb{R}$. More generally, if a function defined over $\mathbb{R}^m$ has a lattice (discrete subgroup) of periods, then finding the set of periods is the continuous hidden subgroup problem (CHSP). As for factoring and discrete log, the unit group is sub-exponential on a classical computer and polynomial on a quantum one.

When $m = 1$, the main difference between HSP and CHSP is the problem of finding $\alpha \in \mathbb{R}$ when given approximations of $k\alpha$ and $\ell\alpha$ for two integers k and ℓ ; this is solved using continued fractions. To compute fundamental units for a family of number fields of constant degree, one has to solve CHSP for $m \geq 1$ bounded by a constant. In contemporary works, Hallgren [27] and Schmidt [46] replaced the continued fractions by an LLL-based algorithm of Buchmann and Pohst [13].

To this point, CHSP and HSP have an identical quantum part and differ in the classical post-treatment. When the degree of the number fields is free to be unbounded in a family of discriminants going to infinity, one has to solve CHSP for unbounded parameters m, possibly as large as the logarithm of the discriminants. In this case, the previous algorithms [27,46] require an exponential time in m, the degree of the number fields, as it was shown by Biasse and Song in [11, Prop. B.2][2].

In 2014, Eisenträger et al. [21][3] achieved to make this algorithm polynomial-time for arbitrary degree number fields. For this the periodic function is multiplied by a Gaussian. Before the full version [22] of this work was made public, a second team, de Boer et al. [19], worked on a more thorough analysis of the algorithm and established in 2019 the precise complexities (space and time) for the CHSP.

Our Contribution and Cryptographic Recommendations. The goal of this article is to make possible a precise resource comparison between computing unit and class groups on one side and breaking symmetric cryptosystems like AES on the other side, as requested by the NIST specifications [43]. Indeed, experts in the technology of quantum computers study the NISQ scenario in which error-corrected quantum computers with 100-to-1000 qubits become available whereas a quantum computer with 10^{20} qubits remains unfeasible or too expensive to be considered. In this context, the estimation of the number of qubits as "polynomial" in [22] is not enough. We instantiate the case of unit and class group in the general frame of CHSP [19] and obtain that the number of qubits is $\tilde{O}(m^5)$, e.g. when $m = 10000$ a quantum attack requires 10^{20} error-corrected qubits.

---

[1] The version of 2002 had 6 pages whereas the version published in 2007 has 19 pages.

[2] The proposition has number 2 in the version of 2015.

[3] The 10-page-long original version of 2014 doesn't contain the proofs, which were made public only in the 47-page-long version of 2019.

We continue by investigating possible weak number fields K: is it a security problem if K has automorphisms? Is it a weakness if K is cyclotomic?

In Sect. 3.3 we explain that automorphisms allow to implement LLL over $\mathcal{O}_K$ and obtain a speed-up which is at most polynomial in the number of automorphisms.

In the case of cyclotomic fields, the speed-up is not automatic: if one runs the general algorithm on these fields, the number of qubits is $O(m^5 \log m)$. However, we make the following observation: **Assume that L is an unknown lattice, $M \subset L$ is known and has a short basis, and one has an algorithm to produce vectors near L^*. Then one can use the short basis of M to bring any vector near L^* to their nearest vector of M^* and they will automatically be in L^* (illustrated in Fig. 1).**

Cryptographic recommendations. A precise estimation of the resources to compute class and unit groups shows that they are more resistant than symmetric cryptosystems if one avoids weak keys. If one wants to use class group based (CGP-based) cryptography then:

- one must avoid fixed degree fields as they use $O(m)$ qubits,
- one must avoid cyclotomic fields as they use $O(m^2 \log m)$ qubits, also a HSP-based algorithm exists,
- one might prefer to use fields with automorphisms to speed-up the computations as they require $\Omega(m^3)$ qubits and the speed-up concerns only the Buchmann-Pohst algorithm and is polynomial in the number of automorphisms.

Roadmap. The article is organized as follows. In Sect. 2 , we explain our improvement as a general problem of lattices, outside the context of unit groups and quantum computing. Then, in Sect. 3 we make a detailed presentation of the quantum algorithms for unit groups and combine results to state the complexity of the algorithms for arbitrary number fields. We exploit the automorphisms in Subsect. 3.3. In Sect. 4 we instantiate the previous complexities in the case of cyclotomic and abelian fields, and compare with our improvement from Sect. 2. Finally, in Sect. 4.2 we make an attempt to reduce the unit-group computations to HSP instead of CHSP, this reduces massively the number of qubits needed, especially for cyclotomic fields of conductor p^k for small primes p.

2   Our Improvement Seen as a Lattice Problem

Let $\langle x, y \rangle$ denote the dot product of two vectors $x, y \in \mathbb{C}^n$. Given a (full rank) lattice $L \subset \mathbb{R}^m$, we call dual of L the lattice

$$L^* = \{y \in \mathbb{R}^m \mid \forall x \in L, \langle x, y \rangle \in \mathbb{Z}^n\}.$$

Let us recall a series of properties of L^* (see [3] for a reference).

Lemma 2.1. *1. If L is generated by the rows of a matrix B then L^* is generated by the rows of $(B^t)^{-1}$; in particular $\det L^* = 1/\det L$;*
2. If M is a sublattice of L then $L^* \subset M^*$ and $[L : M] = [M^* : L^*]$.

2.1 Informal Presentation

The CHSP algorithm to compute unit groups calls L the lattice of units and follows the following strategy:

1. Use a quantum procedure to generate vectors of $\mathbb{C}^n$ in a small ball around each vector of a set of generators of L^*.
2. Apply the Buchmann-Pohst algorithm (which is classical of polynomial time) and the previously found vectors to find a basis of L^*.
3. Invert the matrix of the previously found basis to obtain a basis of L (this is classical of polynomial time).

A characteristic of Buchmann-Pohst's algorithm is that it has a large precision decrease[4], namely one needs a large number of bits of precision on the vectors computed in Step 1 in order to have much fewer bits of precision on the basis of L^*. Given a precision requirement τ, i.e. $\log \tau$ bits of precision, in [19] one computes that the input of Buchmann-Pohst must have precision which depends on the number of generators (and we need a large number of them to be sure we generate the lattice). In this work we reduce the number of qubits required by Step 1.

In the case of cyclotomic fields, one has a basis for the lattice of cyclotomic units $M \subset L$. This allows to compute a basis of M^* which contains the unknown lattice L^*. Our idea is as follows: when given a vector sufficiently close to L^*, solve CVP with respect to M^* and automatically it will be in L^*. In more detail, let $m_1, \ldots, m_n$ be a basis of L. We do Step 1 at low precision and obtain $\tilde{y}$ and then we correct it into y so that $\langle y, m_i \rangle \in \mathbb{Z}^n$ for all $i = 1, 2, \ldots, n$. At this point we have a generating set of L^* at high precision. This avoids any LLL-reduction as one can use the Hermite normal form.

2.2 Precise Statement

Step 1 produces vectors $\tilde{y}$ close to L^* such that $y := \mathrm{CVP}(\tilde{y}, L^*)$ follow a continuous distribution on $\mathbb{R}^m$ which is close to a discrete Gaussian distribution c on L^*. The following definition is a precise description of its output and focuses on the properties of c used in the following sections.

Definition 2.2 (Dual lattice sampler of parameters (η, δ, r)). *Let $1/4 > \eta > 0$, $1/2 > \delta > 0$ and $r > 0$ be three parameters. Let $c : L^* \to \mathbb{C}$ be a map such that $\sum_{\ell^* \in L^*} |c_{\ell^*}|^2 = 1$ satisfying:*

1. **Uniformity property:** *there exists $\epsilon \leq 1/4$ such that, for every strict sublattice $N \subsetneq L^*$:*

$$\sum_{\ell^* \in N} |c_{\ell^*}|^2 < \frac{1}{2} + \epsilon.$$

---

[4] See Th 10 in [19] for a precise estimation.

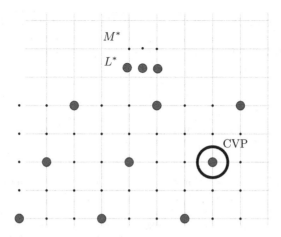

Fig. 1. Illustration of Lemma 2.6. The black lattice of small dots is known and its basis is short so that one can solve CVP for it. One has an oracle producing points $\widetilde{y}$ in the little disk around the bold blue dots. Then, if one brings $\widetilde{y}$ to the small dot y, then y will automatically be in a bold dot. (Color figure online)

2. **Concentration property:** *There exists p such that $0 < p < \frac{1}{2} - \epsilon - \eta$ and*

$$\sum_{|\ell^*| > r} |c_{\ell^*}|^2 < p.$$

An algorithm is a dual lattice sampler of parameters (η, δ, r) if it outputs a vector $x \in \mathbb{R}^m$ such that, for any finite set $S \subset L^*$, one has

$$\mathrm{Prob}\left(y \in \bigcup_{\ell^* \in S} B(\ell^*, \delta\lambda_1^*)\right) \geq \sum_{\ell^* \in S} |c_{\ell^*}|^2 - \eta.$$

We can now define the problem we tackle.

Problem 2.1. Let $M \subset L \subset \mathbb{R}^m$ be two lattices. We are given

- a basis of M;
- an upper bound on $[L : M]$;
- a dual lattice sampler for L of parameters (η, δ, r) of our choice.

Compute a basis $(z_1, \ldots, z_m) \in L$. The basis will be specified by giving the value of $[L : M]$ and the coordinates of the vectors z_i in a basis of $\frac{1}{[L:M]}M$.

Let B_M be the matrix whose rows are the basis $(z_1, \ldots, z_m)$ of M. We propose the following solution to this problem, where we will make precise later the value of δ so that the time complexity is polynomial.

Algorithm 1. Full computation of L using the dual lattice sampler.

Input: – upper bound of $\det L$ of the lattice L and a lower bound on λ_1^*
       – $\eta, \delta, r > 0$ and a dual sampler of L of these parameters;
       – a basis of a sublattice $M \subset L$

Output: a basis of L

1: $k \leftarrow m \log_2 r + \log_2(\det L))$ ▷ Value from [19, Th 3]

2: **for** $i = 1, 2, \ldots, k$ **do**   ▷ Step 1 - Quantum

3:     $\widetilde{y}_i \leftarrow$ output(dual lattice sampler, $\boxed{\delta \lambda_1^*(L) = 1/(2 \|B_M\|)}$)

4:     $\boxed{y_i \leftarrow \text{BDD}(\widetilde{y}_i, M^*, 1/(2 \|B_M\|))}$

5: **end for**

6: ~~Use Buchmann-Pohst algorithm on $(y_1, \ldots, y_t)$.~~ Compute the Hermite normal form to find a basis $(y_1', \ldots, y_m')$ of L^* from $(y_1, \ldots, y_k)$. Here the vectors have exact integer coordinates in a basis of M^*.   ▷ Step 2 - Classical

7: Compute the Smith normal form (SNF) of $(y_1', \ldots, y_m')$ to obtain the exact value of $[L : M]$. Output $(B^{-1})^t \in \frac{1}{[L:M]} \text{Mat}_m(\mathbb{Z})$, where $B \in \text{Mat}_m(\mathbb{Z})$ is the matrix a basis of L^* written in a basis of M^*.   ▷ Step 3 - Classical

---

Notation 2.3. *For any matrix* $B \in \text{GL}_m(\mathbb{C})$ *and any* $\alpha, \beta \in \mathbb{R}_+ \bigcup \{\infty\}$ *the operator norm is*

$$\|B\|_{\alpha, \beta} = \max\{\|Bv\|_\alpha \mid \|v\|_\beta \leq 1\}.$$

When $\alpha = \beta$ *we simply write* $\|B\|_\alpha$. *Then*

$$\|B\|_\infty = \max_j \sum_i |B_{i,j}|,$$

and $\|B\| = \|B\|_\infty$ *when we drop the index.*[5]
     Note also that $\|B\|_{\infty,1} = \max_{i,j} |B_{i,j}| = \|B^t\|_{\infty,1}$ *and finally that,*

$$\forall 1 \leq \alpha, \beta \leq \infty, \quad m \|B\|_{\infty,1} \geq \|B\|_{\alpha,\beta} \geq \|B\|_{\infty,1}.$$

In this article, the complexity of the algorithms depends on $O(\log \|B\|_\infty) = O(\log \|B\|_{\infty,1} + \log m)$. *Since* $\log \|B\| = \Omega(m)$, *this justifies that we don't pay attention to the indices of the operator norm.*

Theorem 2.4. *Algorithm 1 solves Problem 2.1 if* $\delta \lambda_1^*(M) < 1/(2 \|B_M\|_2)$. *The number of qubits is* $O(Qm)$ *with* Q *given in Equation* (1).

We prepare the proof with two lemmas.

Lemma 2.5 (Lemma 5 in [19]). *We note* $k = \alpha(m + m \log_2 r + \log_2(\det L))$, *for an absolute constant* $\alpha > 1$.

---

[5] The norm operator used in the analysis of the Buchmann-Pohst algorithm [19, Appendix B] is $\|\cdot\|_\infty$ and our notations, which are classical, agree with all the cited articles, in particular with [19].

Let $\widetilde{y}_1, \widetilde{y}_2, \ldots, \widetilde{y}_k$ be the first k vectors output by a dual basis sampler. For $i = 1, 2, \ldots, k$ put $y_i = \mathrm{CVP}(\widetilde{y}_i, L)$. Then for any value of the absolute constant $\alpha > 2$ we have

$$\mathrm{Prob}(y_1, \ldots, y_k \text{ generate } L) \geq 1 - \kappa^m,$$

where $\kappa < 1$ is an explicitly computable constant.

From now on, we fix such a k, and we use it in Algorithm 1.

Algorithm 2. Babai's BDD solver.

Input: $\widetilde{y} \in \mathbb{R}^m$ such that $d(\widetilde{y}, M^*) < 1/(2\,\|B_M\|)$
Output: $\mathrm{CVP}(\widetilde{y}, M^*)$, as a vector and as coordinates in a basis of M^*
    compute $\widetilde{z} := B_M^t \widetilde{y}$;
    round $z = (z_1, \ldots, z_n) := (\lfloor \widetilde{z_1} \rceil, \ldots, \lfloor \widetilde{z_n} \rceil)$
    return $y := B_{M^*} z \in M^*$ and $z \in \mathbb{Z}^m$.

The parameter δ of the dual lattice sampler is our choice. We will do so in order to have: $d(\widetilde{y}, L^*) \geq \delta \lambda_1^*(M)$. The following result can be seen as a reformulation of a result of Babai.

Lemma 2.6 ([2] **Eq. (4.3)**). *Algorithm 2 solves* $\mathrm{BDD}(\widetilde{y}, M^*, \delta \lambda_1^*(M))$ *in classical polynomial time when $\delta \lambda_1^*(M) < 1/(2\,\|B_M\|_2)$, where B_M is the matrix of a basis of M.*

Proof. We claim that $\lfloor B_M^t \widetilde{y} \rceil = B_M^t y'$ where $y' = \mathrm{CVP}(\widetilde{y}, M^*)$. Indeed

$$\left\| B_M^t \widetilde{y} - B_M^t y' \right\|_\infty \leq \left\| B_M^t \widetilde{y} - B_M^t y' \right\|_2 \leq \|B_M\|_2 \cdot \left\| \widetilde{y} - y' \right\|_2 = \|B_M\|_2\, \delta \lambda_1^*(M) < 1/2.$$

Since $\lfloor B_M^t \widetilde{y} \rceil = B_M^t y'$, by Lemma 2.1, $y = B_{M^*} z = ((B_M)^t)^{-1}(B_M^t y') = y'$, so the algorithm is correct.

Proof (Proof of Theorem 2.4.a)). We structure the proof in several steps.

step 1. We apply Lemma 2.5 to the lattice L^*. Then, with probability $1 - c^m$, the vectors $y_1, y_2, \ldots, y_k$ generate L^*.

step 2. Let us fix $i \in \{1, 2, \ldots, k\}$. By the definition of the dual sampler, with probability greater than $1 - \eta$, $\mathrm{dist}(\widetilde{y}_i, L^*) < \delta \lambda_1^*(M^*)$. Hence Lemma 2.6 applies and Line 4 is executed in classical polynomial time.

Since $L^* \subset M^*$, $y_i' := \mathrm{CVP}(\widetilde{y}_i, L^*)$ belongs to M^*. Since $d(\widetilde{y}_i, M^*) \leq d(\widetilde{y}_i, L^*) < \lambda_1^*(M)/2$, y_i' is the closest vector of M^* to $\widetilde{y}_i$, or equivalently $y_i' = y_i$. We summarize this by $y_i = \mathrm{CVP}(\widetilde{y}_i, L)$.

step 3. Algorithm 2 can output z in addition to y. This means that the vectors $y_i \in L^*$ are given by their integer coordinates with respect to a basis of M^*.

In Line 6, one computes the HNF [16, Sec 2.4.2] by manipulating integer coefficients only. This is done in classical polynomial time without loss of precision.

step 4. Since $B_M \in \mathrm{Mat}_k(\mathbb{Z})$, $(B_M^{-1}) \in \frac{1}{\det B_M}\mathrm{Mat}_k(\mathbb{Z})$. Finally, B_M and its SNF [16, Sec. 2.4.4] have the same determinant, which equals $[L : M]$. Hence, the last step computes $[L : M]$ in polynomial time.

3 Previous Results on the Quantum Unit-Group Calculation

3.1 A Summary on CHSP

We first define the Continuous Hidden Subgroup Problem to which the problem of computing the unit group can be reduced.

Definition 3.1 (Continuous Hidden Subgroup Problem - CHSP [22]).
*Let $f : \mathbb{R}^m \to \mathcal{S}$, where $\mathcal{S} = \oplus_{i \in \{0,1\}^n} \mathbb{C}|i\rangle$ is the space of states of n qubits. The function f is **an (a, r, ε)-oracle hiding the full-rank lattice** L if and only if it verifies the following conditions:*

1. *L is the period of f, i.e. $\forall x \forall \ell \in L, f(x + \ell) = f(x)$. (periodicity)*
2. *The function f is a-Lipschitz. (Lipschitz condition)*
3. *$\forall x, y \in \mathbb{R}^m$ such that $\operatorname{dist}(x - y, L) \geq r$, we have $|\langle f(x) \mid f(y)\rangle| \leq \varepsilon$. (strong periodicity)*

Given an efficient quantum algorithm to compute f, compute the hidden lattice of periods L.

Let us now recall the algorithm which solves CHSP. We mimic the technique which solve the Hidden Subgroup Problem (HSP). For this latter, let $g : G \to \mathcal{S}$, with G a finite cyclic group. The solution goes as follows:

1. compute the superposition $\sum_{x \in G} |x\rangle$ and then apply g to obtain the superposition of the values of g: $|\psi(g)\rangle = \sum_{x \in G} g(x)|x\rangle$;
2. apply the Quantum Fourier Transform (see [48]) to obtain $\sum_{y \in G} \hat{g}(y)|y\rangle$; this expression is equal to $\sum_{y \in H^\perp} \hat{g}(y)|y\rangle$
3. measure the state to obtain an element $g \in H^\perp$.

A few iterations of the algorithm allow to have a set of generators of $H^\perp$ and hence to compute H.

Coming back to the continuous case, if we were able to implement the Fourier Transform, we would be able to draw random vectors of L^*. If a set of generators is known, then one can extract a basis to completely describe L^*. Then L would be obtained thanks to Lemma 2.1. The obstacle is here that $\mathbb{R}^m$ is infinite and the Fourier Transform (QFT) is now an integral instead of a finite sum so we cannot compute the QFT precisely. As a way around, we do an approximate computation of the QFT by the means of a Riemann sum, which amounts to restrict the domain to a segment and to discretize it. Set $\rho_\sigma(x) = \exp(-\frac{\pi^2 \|x\|^2}{\sigma^2})$.

Lemma 3.2 (Theorem 2 in [19]). *There exists dual lattice sampler quantum algorithm of polynomial time which uses $Qm + n$ qubits, where*

$$Q = O\left(m \log\left(m \log \frac{1}{\eta}\right)\right) + O\left(\log\left(\frac{\operatorname{Lip}(f)}{\eta \delta \lambda_1^*}\right)\right). \tag{1}$$

Algorithm 3. A CHSP solver

Input: A function f which can be computed in polynomial time, as in Definition 3.1 having a hidden period lattice L. We require $\det L$ up to one bit of precision and $\mathrm{Lip}(f)$. A parameter τ of required precision.

Output: $(\tilde{x}_1, \ldots, \tilde{x}_m)$ such that $(x_1, \ldots, x_m)$ is a basis of L for $x_i = \mathrm{CVP}(\tilde{x}_i)$ and $\|x_i - \tilde{x}_i\| \le \tau$

1: $k \mapsto \log_2(\sqrt{m}\, \mathrm{Lip}(f)) + \log_2(\det L)$ $\triangleright$ value from [19, th 3]
2: **for** $i = 1, 2, \ldots, k$ **do** $\triangleright$ Step 1 - Quantum

3:     $\tilde{y}_i \leftarrow$ output(dual lattice sampler: $\boxed{\delta \lambda_1^* = \dfrac{(\lambda_1^*)^3 (\det L)^{-1}}{2^{O(mk)} \|B_{L^*}\|_\infty^m}}$) $\triangleright$ value from [19,
     Appendix B.3 Th 4]
4:     pass $\triangleright$ compare to Algorithm 1
5: **end for**
6: Apply the Buchmann-Pohst algorithm on $(\tilde{y}_1, \ldots, \tilde{y}_k)$ and obtain $(\tilde{y}_1, \ldots, \tilde{y}'_m)$ so that $\mathrm{CVP}(\tilde{y}_i, L^*)_{i=1,m}$ is a basis of L^* $\triangleright$ Step 2 - Classical
7: Output the rows of $(B^{-1})^t$ where B has rows $\tilde{u}'_i$. $\triangleright$ Step 3 - Classical

---

Theorem 3.3 (Space complexity of the CHSP solver, Theorem 1 of [19]). We set[6] $\eta = 1/k^2$. Let N_f be the amount of qubits necessary to encode f. We fix τ the error expected on basis' vectors. Then, Algorithm 3 is correct and requires a number of qubits:

$$N_{qubits} = O(m^3 \cdot \log(m)) + O(m^3 \cdot \log(\mathrm{Lip}(f))) + O(m^2 \cdot \log(\det(L)))$$
$$+ O\left(m \cdot \log \frac{\mathrm{Lip}(f)}{\lambda_1^*}\right) + O\left(m \cdot \log \tau^{-1}\right) + O(mN_f). \tag{2}$$

The complexity of the algorithm depends on λ_1^* which has the advantage that it is an invariant of the lattice. However, λ_1^* is difficult to lower bound and in some applications one has bounds on the coefficients of B_L, the matrix of some basis of L.

Lemma 3.4. $2^{-3m} \|B_L^t\|_\infty \le \frac{1}{\lambda_1^*} \le \|B_L\|_{1,2} \le m \|B_L\|_2$.

Proof. The first inequality is [19, Corollary 6 in Appendix B.1].

The second inequality is direct. Let $v \in L^*$ such that $\|v\|_2 = \lambda_1^*$. By Notation 2.3 we have $\|B_L v\|_1 \le \|B_L\|_{1,2} \|v\|_2$. Since $v \in L^*$, $v \ne 0$, $B_L v \in \mathbb{Z}^n \backslash \{0\}$ and then $\|B_L v\|_1 \ge 1$, so

$$1 \le \|B_L\|_{1,2}\, \lambda_1^*,$$

which proves the second inequality. By the argument of Notation 2.3, $\|B_L\|_{1,2} \le m \|B_L\|_2$.

---

[6] The complexity of the CHSP solver depends on $\log 1/\eta$ and not on η itself. Hence the contribution of η is hidden in the $\tilde{O}$ notation.

3.2   Reduction of the Computation of the Unit Group to CHSP

In this subsection, we present the method of [22] to reduce the computation of the unit group to the CHSP. For completeness, we reproduce the description of [10, Sec 3]. Let $G := \mathbb{R}^{n_1+n_2} \times (\mathbb{Z}/2\mathbb{Z})^{n_1} \times (\mathbb{R}/\mathbb{Z})^{n_2}$, and the mapping $\varphi : G \to \mathbb{R}^{2(n_1+n_2)}$,

$$\varphi(u_1, \ldots, u_{n_1+n_2}, \mu_1, \ldots, \mu_n, \theta_1, \ldots, \theta_{n_2})$$
$$= ((-1)^{\mu_1} e^{u_1}, \ldots, (-1)^{\mu_{n_1}} e^{u_{n_1}}, e^{2i\pi\theta_1} e^{u_{n_1+1}}, \ldots, e^{2i\pi\theta_{n_2}} e^{u_{n_1+n_2}})$$

Let $\sigma_1, \ldots, \sigma_{n_1}$ and respectively $\sigma_{n_1+1}, \ldots, \sigma_{n_1+n_2}$ be the real and the complex embeddings of K. We consider the Cartesian ring

$$E = \sigma_1(\mathcal{O}_K) \times \cdots \times \sigma_{n_1+n_2}(\mathcal{O}_K).$$

An E-ideal is a sub-$\mathbb{Z}$-lattice Λ of E which is such that $\forall x \in E, x\Lambda \subset \Lambda$.
    We define

$$g : G \to \{E\text{-ideals}\}$$
$$x \mapsto \varphi(x)E.$$

Definition 3.5 (Ex. 5.3 of [22]). *Set* $\mathcal{H} = \otimes_{i \in \mathbb{N}} \mathbb{C}|i\rangle$, $\mathcal{H}_Q = \otimes_{i=0}^{Q} \mathbb{C}|i\rangle$ *and* $\pi_Q : \mathcal{H} \to \mathcal{H}_Q$ *the projection on the first* $Q+1$ *qubits. We define the straddle encodings of parameter* $\nu > 0$, $\mathrm{str}_\nu : \mathbb{R} \to \mathcal{H}$, $\mathrm{str}_{m,\nu} : \mathbb{R}^m \to \mathcal{H}^m$ *and* $f : \{lattices\ of\ \mathbb{R}^m\} \to \mathcal{H}^m$ *as follows:*

- $|\mathrm{str}_\nu(x)\rangle = \cos(\frac{\pi}{2}t)|k\rangle + \sin(\frac{\pi}{2}t)|k+1\rangle$, *where* $k = \lfloor x/\nu \rfloor$, $t = x/\nu - k$;
- $|\mathrm{str}_{m,\nu}(x_1, \ldots, x_m)\rangle = \otimes_{i=1}^{m} |\mathrm{str}_\nu(x_i)\rangle$;
- $|f(x)\rangle = |\mathrm{str}_{lattice,m,\nu}(L)\rangle = \gamma^{-1/2} \sum_{x \in L} e^{-\pi\|x\|^2/s} |\mathrm{str}_{m,\nu}(x)\rangle$
  with $\gamma = \sum_{x \in L} e^{-2\pi\|x\|^2/s^2}$.

Note that computing $\mathrm{str}_{lattice,m,\nu}$ *up to an error* τ *requires* $O(m\nu \log \tau)$ *qubits. In Appendix A we propose an alternative function* f *which can be used for totally real* K *and doesn't use the straddle encoding.*

Finally, one defined f as follows:

$$f : G \xrightarrow{g} \{E\text{-ideals}\} \xrightarrow{|\mathrm{str}\rangle} \{\text{quantum states}\} = \mathcal{H}_Q^m. \qquad (3)$$

The following result is the conjunction of several results from [22].

Theorem 3.6 (Theorems 5.5, D.4 and B.3 of [22]). *Let* K *be a number field of degree* n, *discriminant* D, *unit rank* m *and regulator* R. *Let* $L := \mathrm{Log}\,\mathcal{O}_K^*$ *which is the hidden period of the function* f *of Equation (3).*
    Set $s = 3 \cdot 2^{2n} \sqrt{nD}$ *and* $\nu = 1/(4n(s\sqrt{n})^{2n})$. *Then* $f_5 = \otimes^5 f$ *is an* (r, a, ε)-*oracle with* $\varepsilon = 243/1024$, $\mathrm{Lip}(f) = a = \frac{\sqrt{\pi n s}}{4\nu} + 1$ *and* $r = s\sqrt{n}^{n-1} 2\nu\sqrt{m}$, *where* c *is an explicitly computable constant. In particular,* $\varepsilon < 1/4$, $r < \lambda_1(L)/6$ *and*

$$\log_2 \mathrm{Lip}(f) = O\left(m^2 + m \log D\right).$$

Proof. Note first that if $K = \mathbb{Q}$ or is quadratic imaginary then $m = 0$ and there is nothing to be computed. Also note that $n/2 - 1 \leq m \leq n - 1$ so we can interchange $O(m)$ and $O(n)$ in the asymptotic complexity.

By [22, Th 5.5] f is an (r, ∞, ε)-oracle hiding the lattice $L = \log \mathcal{O}_K^*$ with $r = (s\sqrt{n})^{n-1}2\nu\sqrt{n}$ and $\varepsilon' = 3/4$.

By [22, Th D.4] f is a-Lipschitz with $a = \frac{\sqrt{\pi n}s}{4\nu} + 1$.

By [22, Lem E.1] $f_5 := f \otimes f \otimes f \otimes f \otimes f$ is an $(5 \operatorname{Lip}(f), r, (\varepsilon')^5)$-oracle hiding the same lattice.

In particular, $(\varepsilon')^5 = 243/1024 < 1/4$ satisfies the requirements of the CHSP solver (see Definition 2.2).

The condition $r < \lambda_1(L)/6$ is satisfied as $\lambda_1(L) \geq 1/2$ by [22, Lem B.3] and

$$r = O\left(\frac{s\sqrt{n}^{n-1}2}{4n(s\sqrt{n})^{2n}}\right) \leq \frac{1}{2s^{n-1}} \leq \frac{1}{6 \cdot 2^n \sqrt{d}} < \frac{1}{12}.$$

Finally, we have

$$\log_2 \operatorname{Lip}(f) = O(ms) = O(m^2 + m \log D).$$

Corollary 3.7. *Let K be a number field of discriminant D and unit rank m. For any error bound $\tau > 0$. There exists a quantum algorithm of time* $\operatorname{poly}(m, \log D, \log \tau)$ *using a number of qubits*

$$N_{qubits} = O(m^5 + m^4 \log D) + O(m \log \tau^{-1})$$

which, for a set of units $\mu, \varepsilon_1, \ldots, \varepsilon_m$ such that μ is a root of unity and the other have infinite order and

$$\mathcal{O}_K^* \simeq \mu^{\mathbb{Z}/\omega} \times \varepsilon_1^{\mathbb{Z}} \times \cdots \times \varepsilon_m^{\mathbb{Z}},$$

the algorithm outputs $\log(\sigma_j(\varepsilon_i))_{1 \leq i \leq m, 1 \leq j \leq n} + \tau_{i,j}$ with $\tau_{i,j} \in \mathbb{R}$ such that $|\tau_{i,j}| \leq \tau$.

Proof. By Theorem 3.6, there exists a function f which hides $\operatorname{Log} \mathcal{O}_K^*$ and which is an (a, r, ε)-oracle such that $r \leq \lambda_1(L)/6$ and $\varepsilon < 1/4$. By Theorem 3.3 there exists a polynomial-time algorithm which uses a number of qubits as in Equation (2).

In the CHSP solver one stores the values of f on Qm qubits, so the $O(N_f) = O(Qm)$. We are left with estimating Q. For this, the main part is Lemma 2.1:

$$O(\log(1/\lambda_1^*)) = \log_2(\|B_L\|) = O\left(m + \frac{1}{m}\log D\right).$$

We used the fact that L admits an LLL-reduced basis, which is enough to bound $1/\lambda_1^*$, but this cannot be computed because we have no basis of L until the end of the CHSP algorithm. We inject this in Equation (2) and obtain the announced value.

Given $\mathrm{Log}\,\mathcal{O}_K^*$, we are left with computing $\mu, \varepsilon_1, \ldots, \varepsilon_m$. Let ω be the number of roots of unity of K and recall that ω divides D. By multiplying the time by $\log D$, we can enumerate the divisors of D, so we can assume that we know ω.

By Dirichlet's Theorem, an m-tuple such that $\mathrm{Vol}(\mathrm{Log}(\varepsilon_j)) = R$ and a root of unity of order ω, form a basis of the unit group.[7]

Remark 3.8. [8] *The analytic class number formula states that $Rh = \sqrt{D}^{1+o(1)}$. Very little is known on the distribution of h but no conjecture, e.g. the Cohen-Lenstra heuristic, is contradictory with the fact that $h = 1$ and $R = \sqrt{D}^{1+o(1)}$ for a proportion of $1 - o(1)$ of the number fields. Hence, $\max_i(\|\mathrm{log}\,\varepsilon_i\|) \sim R^{1/m}$ and the unit group is fully determined only when $\log \tau = \Omega(\sqrt{D})$. In that case CHSP doesn't compute the full unit group in polynomial-time.*

Note however that in the case of classical algorithms there is no algorithm which computes a partial information on the regulator without fully computing it (see for instance [12]). So the algorithm studied in this article suggests a quantum advantage in the case of unit groups.

Example 3.1. 1. If $K = \mathbb{Q}(\zeta_n)$ with prime n then $m = (n-1)/2$ and $\log_2 D = (m-2)\log_2 m$. If one applies Algorithm 1 without taking notes that it is a very particular case, the algorithm uses $O(m^5 \log m)$ qubits.
2. If K is a Kummer extension, i.e. $K = \mathbb{Q}(\sqrt[n]{D})$ for some integer without powers D, then $O(\log \mathrm{disc}\,K) = O(\log D)$ and the number of qubits is $O(n^5 + n^4 \log D)$. The value of n and D are independent. When n is fixed, i.e; the case of real quadratic fields, the number of qubits is $O(\mathrm{disc}\,K)$. When $n \sim \log D$, the number of qubits is $(\log D)^5/(\log \log D)^4$.

The large number qubits used by the present algorithm is in contrast with Shor's algorithm, which requires $2m + O(1)$ qubits in the case of factorization and discrete logarithms and $7m + O(1)$ in the case of elliptic curve discrete logarithms. The paragraph "Conclusion and Research Directions" at the end of [19, Sec 1] states that, even if the complexity in $\log D$ is ignored and one uses approximation techniques in the quantum Fourier transform, the algorithm requires $\Omega(m^3)$ qubits. We refer to Appendix B for an informal discussion about the security levels one can propose in the case of quantum algorithms.

3.3 Exploiting Automorphisms

In this section we tackle the case of cyclotomic fields without using the cyclotomic units. Instead we use the fact that K has Galois automorphisms.

The main impact of this section is to reduce the practical cost of the Buchmann-Pohst step (which is non-quantum). Indeed, this step consists in applying LLL to a lattice L which has more algebraic structure: it is a $\mathbb{Z}[\zeta_k]$-module for an integer k. From an asymptotic point of view, Fieker and Stehlé [24]

---

[7] We used here a different proof than in [22] where one reduces the case of CHSP defined on arbitrary abelian groups to the case of CHSP over $\mathbb{R}^m$.

[8] We are indebted to Bill Allombert who has made this objection.

proved that, if one is to find a new $\mathbb{Z}[\zeta_k]$-basis of L which is shorter in a sense to be specified later, one has the best asymptotic complexity up to a polynomial factor if one follows the steps:

1. forget the $\mathbb{Z}[\zeta_k]$-module structure;
2. reduce the basis of the underlying $\mathbb{Z}$-lattice;
3. compute again the $\mathbb{Z}[\zeta_k]$-module structure.

From a practical point of view though, we shall explain that it is faster to work directly with the $\mathbb{Z}[\zeta_k]$-module structure.

The structure of $\mathbb{Z}[G]$-lattice. In the following, a lattice which has a structure of R-module for some ring R is called a R-lattice. When $G := \mathrm{Aut}(K/\mathbb{Q})$, the group of Galois automorphisms, is abelian, as it is the case for cyclotomic fields, $\mathcal{O}_K^*/(\mathcal{O}_K^*)_{\mathrm{tors}}$ has a structure of $\mathbb{Z}[G]$-lattice. Indeed, for $\sigma \in G$ and $u \in \mathcal{O}_K^*$ we set $\sigma \cdot u = \sigma(u)$ and for set $\sigma_1, \ldots, \sigma_k \in G$ of ring generators of $\mathbb{Z}[G]$, and any $\lambda = \sum_{e_1, \ldots, e_k} c_{e_1, \ldots, e_k} \sigma_1^{e_1} \cdots \sigma_k^{e_k}$ we set

$$u^\lambda = \prod_{e_1, \ldots, e_k} (\sigma_1^{e_1}(u) \cdots \sigma_k^{e_k}(u))^{c_{e_1, \ldots, e_k}}.$$

Lemma 3.9. *Let $G := \mathrm{Aut}(F/\mathbb{Q})$ and $\sigma \in G$ of order k.*

1. *Then $\mathcal{O}_F^*$ is an $\mathbb{Z}[\zeta_k]$-lattice.*
2. *If k is not of the form*

$$k = 2^\varepsilon \prod p_i^{e_i} \text{ with } \varepsilon \in \{0, 1\} \text{ and } p_i \equiv 1 \pmod 4$$

then $\mathcal{O}_F^*$ is a $\mathcal{O}_{\mathbb{Q}(i\sqrt{d})}$-lattice for some divisor d of k.

Proof. 1. If $\sigma \in G$, every $\mathbb{Z}[G]$-lattice is a $\mathbb{Z}[\sigma]$-lattice. In order to prove that Φ_k is the minimal polynomial of the endomorphism associated to σ, let $u \in \mathcal{O}_F^*$ and set $v = u^{\Phi_k(\sigma)}$. Then $v^{\sigma-1} = u^{\sigma^k-1} = u/u = 1$ and further $\sigma(v) = v$. But $\sigma \in \mathrm{Aut}(F/\mathbb{Q})$, so $v \in \mathcal{O}_F^* \cap \mathbb{Q} = \pm 1 \in (\mathcal{O}_F^*)_{\mathrm{tors}}$. Equivalently, $\Phi_k(\sigma)(u) \in (\mathcal{O}_F^*)_{\mathrm{tors}}$ and Φ_k is an annihilating polynomial of σ. Since it is irreducible, it is the minimal polynomial of σ. But ζ_k has the same minimal polynomial, so $\mathbb{Z}[\sigma] \simeq \mathbb{Z}[\zeta_k]$.
2. It is a classical result that, if one sets $p^* = (-1)^{\frac{p-1}{2}} p$ for a prime p, then

$$\mathbb{Q}(\sqrt{p^*}) \subset \mathbb{Q}(\zeta_p).$$

When $k' \mid k$ one has $\mathbb{Q}(\zeta_{k'}) \subset \mathbb{Q}(\zeta_k)$. Hence if k is divisible by 4 or a prime $p \equiv 3 \pmod 4$, one can take $d = 4$ or $d = p$ in the statement of the lemma.

Norm-Euclidean Rings $\mathcal{O}_k$. Recall that $\mathbb{Z}[i] = \mathbb{Z}[\zeta_4]$ and $\mathcal{O}_{\mathbb{Q}(i\sqrt{3})} = \mathbb{Z}[\zeta_3]$ are norm-Euclidean: let $k = 3$ or 4, in order to divide $a \in \mathbb{Z}[\zeta_k]$ by $b \in \mathbb{Z}[\zeta_k]$ one rounds each coordinate of $a/b \in \mathbb{Q}[\zeta_k]$ and denotes the result by q, and then one sets $r = a - bq$; if $N_{K/\mathbb{Q}}(r) < N_{K/\mathbb{Q}}(b)$ for all a, b we say that $\mathbb{Z}[\zeta_k]$ is norm-Euclidean. Napias [42] showed that the LLL algorithm extends naturally to the norm-Euclidean rings $\mathbb{Z}[i]$ and $\mathbb{Z}[\zeta_3]$.

Definition 3.10 (norm-Euclidean ring, Prop 1.2.5 of [14], Def 2 of [32]).
The Euclidean minimum of a number field K is

$$\mathfrak{M}_K := \max_{x \in K} \min_{y \in \mathcal{O}_K} N_{K/\mathbb{Q}}(x - y).$$

In particular, when K is imaginary quadratic, $\mathfrak{M}_K = \max_{x \in \mathbb{C}} \min_{y \in \mathcal{O}_K} |x - y|^2$.
If $\mathfrak{M}_K < 1$ we say that K is norm-Euclidean.

Example 3.2 (Prop 1.2.4 of [14],Prop 3 of [32]). The following fields are norm-Euclidean:

- $\mathbb{Q}(\zeta_k)$ for $k \in \{1, 3, 4, 5, 7, 8, 9, 11, 12, 15, 16, 20, 24\}$;
- $\mathbb{Q}(i\sqrt{d})$ for $d \in \{1, 2, 3, 7, 11\}$.

Definition 3.11. *($\mathcal{O}_K$-LLL-reduced basis) Let $K = \mathbb{Q}(i\sqrt{d})$ be an imaginary quadratic field. We identify K with its embedding in $\mathbb{C}$ such that $\sqrt{-d}$ is mapped to a complex number of positive imaginary part.*
    We consider the dot product $\langle \cdot, \cdot \rangle$ of $\mathbb{C}^m$ and we set $\|x\| = \sqrt{\langle x, x \rangle}$, which is a norm.
    Let $b_1, b_2, \ldots, b_m$ be independent in $\mathbb{C}^m$. We say that $L := \oplus_{j=1}^m \mathbb{Z}[\zeta_k]b_j$ is a $\mathbb{Z}[\zeta_k]$-lattice and $\{b_j\}$ is a basis. Let $\{b_1^* = b_1, b_2^*, \ldots, b_m^*\}$ be the Gram-Schmidt orthogonalization of $\{b_j\}$ with respect to the dot product. We set $\mu_{i,j} = \langle b_i, b_j^* \rangle / \|b_j^*\|^2$. We say that $\{b_j\}$ is $\mathcal{O}_K$-LLL-reduced with respect to $\mathfrak{M}_K < \delta < 1$ if the following two conditions hold:

1. $\|\mu_{i,j}\| \leq \mathfrak{M}_K$ for $1 \leq j < i \leq m$;   *(size reduced)*
2. $\|b_i^*\|^2 + \|\mu_{i,i-1}\|^2 \|b_{i-1}^*\|^2 \geq \delta \|b_{i-1}^*\|^2$.   *(Lovász condition)*

    In two contemporary works Kim and Lee [32] and Camus [14] extended LLL to all norm-Euclidean rings $\mathbb{Z}[\zeta_k]$ and $\mathcal{O}_{\mathbb{Q}(i\sqrt{D})}$. In particular, when K is a norm-Euclidean quadratic imaginary field, [14, Th. 1.3.8] states that any $\mathcal{O}_K$-reduced basis $b_1, \ldots, b_m$ of L is such that

$$\|b_j\| \leq \left(\frac{1}{\delta - \mathfrak{M}_K} \right)^{j-1} (\det L)^{1/m}.$$

    A direct application of $\mathcal{O}_K$-LLL is the $\mathcal{O}_K$ variant of Buchmann-Pohst algorithm, that we propose in Algorithm 4.

Theorem 3.12 (adaptation to $\mathcal{O}_K$-lattices of Theorem 3.1 in [13]). *Algorithm 4 is correct and terminates in $O\left((k + m)^6(m + \log(D^{1/m}/\mu))\right)$ operations on a classical computer.*

Proof. The proof is a verbatim translation of the correctness proof in the case of $\mathbb{Z}$-lattices. By Eq. 3.3, if $b_1, \ldots, b_m$ is a reduced basis of a lattice such that $\det L \leq D$, then $\max(\|b_1\|, \ldots, \|b_m\|) \leq B$. This is used in the proof of [13, Prop 2.2] to show that the successive minima of the lattice generated by the columns of the matrix in Algorithm 4 are bounded by $\tilde{M}$. We use the upper bound of the

Algorithm 4. Buchmann-Pohst over $\mathcal{O}_K$

Input: a $\mathcal{O}_K$-lattice $L \subset \mathbb{C}^m$ given by approximations $\widetilde{g}_1, \dots, \widetilde{g}_k \in \mathbb{C}^m$ of $g_1, \dots, g_k \in \mathbb{C}^m$ which $\mathcal{O}_K$-span L; a lower bound μ of $\lambda_1(L)$; an upper bound D on $\det L$

Output: approximations of a basis $b_1, \dots, b_m$ over $\mathcal{O}_K$ of L

1: $B \;\leftarrow\; c_K^m D^{1/m}$; $\; C \;\leftarrow\; (B/\mu)^m \gamma_m^{1/2}$; $\; \tilde{M} \;\leftarrow\; (k\sqrt{m}/2 + \sqrt{k})C$; $\; q \;\leftarrow\; \lceil \log_2\left((\sqrt{mk} + 2)\tilde{M}2^{(k-1)/2}/\mu \right)\rceil$

2: the the $\mathcal{O}_K$-LLL-reduction of the following matrix on the left to obtain the matrix on the right

$$\begin{pmatrix} \boxed{\lfloor \widetilde{g}_1 2^q \rfloor} & \cdots & \boxed{\lfloor \widetilde{g}_k 2^q \rfloor} \\ 1 & & \\ & \ddots & \\ & & 1 \end{pmatrix} \rightsquigarrow \begin{pmatrix} \boxed{\widetilde{c}_1} & \cdots & \boxed{\widetilde{c}_k} \\ \boxed{\mathbf{m}_1} & \cdots & \boxed{\mathbf{m}_k} \end{pmatrix}$$

3: **return** $\widetilde{c}_{k-m+2}, \widetilde{c}_2, \dots, \widetilde{c}_k$

norm of an $\mathcal{O}_K$-reduced basis of [14, Prop 1.3.8] instead of [38, (1.12)] to obtain the equivalent of [13, Eq (9)]:

$$\|\widetilde{c}_j\| \leq 2^{(k-1)/2}\tilde{M} \qquad 1 \leq j \leq k - m. \tag{4}$$

For any vector $(\widetilde{c}, \mathbf{m}) \in \oplus_{j=1}^k \mathbb{Z}(\widetilde{c}_j, \mathbf{m}_j)$ such that $\mathbf{m} = (\mathbf{m}^{(1)}, \dots, \mathbf{m}^{(k)})$ is not a relation of $b_1, \dots, b_k$, i.e. $\mathbf{m} \notin L^*$, i.e. $\sum_{j=}^k \mathbf{m}^{(j)}\widetilde{b}_j \neq 0$. Then, the arguments in the proof of [13, Th 3.1] can be copied in a verbatim manner to obtain:

$$\|\widetilde{c}_j\| > 2^{(k-1)/2}\tilde{M} \qquad 1 \leq j \leq k. \tag{5}$$

Since Equations (4) and (5) are contradictory for $1 \leq j \leq k - m$, the only possibility is that $\mathbf{m} \in L^*$. We do the same transformations on the matrix with b_j instead of $\widetilde{b}_j$ and call c_j the vectors which replace $\widetilde{c}_j$ in this case. What we have proved is that $c_1 = c_2 = \cdot = c_{k-m} = 0$.

Since the transformations done in the LLL algorithm on the columns of the matrix are reversible, they preserve the rank of any subset of rows of the matrix. The rank of the first m rows of this matrix is $\dim L = m$. Since $c_1 = c_2 = \cdot = c_{k-m} = 0$, the vectors $c_{k-m+1}, \dots, c_k$ form a basis of L.

LLL over $\mathcal{O}_{\mathbb{Q}(i\sqrt{d})}$ as a Practical Improvement. The constant hidden in the big Oh of implementation is (inverse) proportional to $\log \delta$, which is (inverse) proportional to $\log(\delta - \mathfrak{M}_K)$. Hence the difference is of only a few percentages. The dependence of the time in the rank is quartic, so we replace a number of operations of high-precision real numbers by $2^4 = 16$ times less complex numbers at the same level of precision. Finally, using the Karatsuba trick, a multiplication of complex numbers costs 3 multiplications of real numbers, so the overall gain is a factor $16/3 \approx 5.33$. An implementation [23] of $\mathbb{Z}[i\sqrt{d}]$-LLL shows that the reduction of an $\mathcal{O}_K$-lattice is ≈ 5 times faster when its algebraic structure is used when compared to forgetting it and using only the underlying structure of $\mathbb{Z}$-lattice: they used $\mathcal{O}_K = \mathbb{Z}[i]$, the coordinates of the basis vectors have 512 bits and $\delta = 0.99$ both over $\mathbb{Z}$ and $\mathbb{Z}[i]$.[9]

Consequences in Cryptography. Given our current contribution, the speed-up due to automorphisms is 5.33. It is an open question to extend it to a larger class of $\mathcal{O}_K$-rings (e.g. [37] investigate if LLL can be extended to arbitrary $\mathcal{O}_K$ by solving CVP instances in dimension $[\mathcal{O}_K : \mathbb{Z}]$.). If Buchmann-Pohst can be extended, the best speed-up that one can target is $[\mathcal{O}_K : \mathbb{Z}]^3$. Indeed, the dependence of LLL in the dimension is quartic whereas the cost of the arithmetic over $\mathcal{O}_K$ is quadratic or quasi-linear if fast arithmetic is used

The speed-up due to the automorphisms is polynomial in the number of automorphisms. This is a familiar situation because a similar speed-up happens for automorphisms in the case of classical algorithms for factorization, discrete logarithms in finite fields and discrete logarithms on elliptic curves (see e. g. [30, Sect. 4.3],[5, Sect. 5.3]). For instance, the attacks in [20] against ECDSA using endomorphisms of the curve achieved a polynomial speed-up in an algorithm of exponential complexity. The community reacted by suggesting to use elliptic curves with endomorphisms as their effect was now considered to be benign, e.g. [25]. In a similar manner, if the security of the class group of a given degree and determinant is considered sufficient, we suggest to use fields with automorphisms in order to speed-up the protocol, e.g. it has been done by XTR in cryptosystems based on discrete logarithms in finite fields [39].

4   A New Algorithm Using Cyclotomic Units

When $K = \mathbb{Q}(\zeta_m)$ for an arbitrary integer m we define the group of cyclotomic units to be the subgroup C of K^* generated by -1, ζ_m and $\zeta_m^j - 1$ with $j = 1, 2, \ldots, m-1$, intersected with the group of units $\mathcal{O}_K^*$. We follow the notations of [18, Sec. 3], in particular m and k don't have the same meaning as in the other sections. Factor $m = p_1^{\alpha_1} p_2^{\alpha_2} \cdots p_k^{\alpha_k}$ and, for each index i, put $m_i = m/p_i^{\alpha_i}$.

For $j = 1, \ldots, m-1$ we set

$$v_j = \begin{cases} 1 - \zeta_m^j, & \text{if for all } i \text{ we have } m_i \nmid j, \\ \frac{1 - \zeta_m^j}{1 - \zeta_m^{m_i}}, & \text{otherwise for the unique } i \text{ such that } m_i \mid j. \end{cases}$$

4.1   Unconditional Results

Lemma 4.1 (Theorem 4.2 in [35]). *The lattice $M := \mathrm{Log}\, C$ admits the system of generators $\{b_j = \mathrm{Log}(v_j) \mid j = 1, 2, \ldots, m-1\}$.*

---

[9] A similar speed-up was obtained in the case of $\mathbb{Z}[\zeta_k]$-LLL in [32]: an example took 20 s over $\mathbb{Z}[\zeta_k]$ compared to 75 s over $\mathbb{Z}$.

Lemma 4.2 (Lemma 3.5 in [18]). *For any integer $j \in \{1, 2, \ldots, m-1\}$ we have $\left\| 1 - \zeta_m^j \right\|_2 = O(\sqrt{m})$. Hence $\left\| B_M \right\|_2 = O(\sqrt{m})$.*

Theorem 4.3. *Algorithm 1 computes a basis of the unit group of $\mathbb{Q}(\zeta_m)$ in* $\mathrm{poly}(m)$ *time and uses* $O(m^2 \log m)$ *qubits.*

Proof. The only quantum step of Algorithm 1 is the dual lattice sampler, whose parameters are $\delta = \left\| B_L \right\| / \lambda_1^*(L)$ and $\eta = 1/k^2$ where

$$k = \log_2(\sqrt{m}\, \mathrm{Lip}(f)) + \log_2(\det L))$$

is given in step 1 of the algorithm. In this section m is not necessarily equal to the rank m' of $\mathbb{Z}[\zeta]^*$ but $O(m') = O(m)$ so that we use m and m' interchangeably. By Lemma 3.2, the sampler used $O(Qm)$ qubits with Q as below. We write $a \ll b$ for $a = O(b)$. We use Theorem 3.6: $\log \mathrm{Lip}(f) \ll m^2 + m \log D$ and then $k \ll m^2 + m \log D$. We also use Lemma 4.2: $\log 1/(\delta \lambda_1^*(L)) \ll \log(1/\left\| B_M \right\|) \ll \log m$ and $\log D = (m-2) \log m \ll m \log m$.

$$\begin{aligned} Q &\ll m \log(m \log \tfrac{1}{\eta})) + \log \tfrac{1}{\delta \lambda_1^*(L)} + \log(\mathrm{Lip}(f)) \\ &\ll (m \log m + m \log \log k) + \log m + m^2 + m \log D \\ &\ll m \log m + m \log \log D + \log m + m^2 + m \log D \\ &\ll m^2 + m \log D \\ &\ll m^2 \log m. \end{aligned}$$

This is to be compared to the $O(m^5 + m^4 \log D)$ qubits used by number fields in general (Corollary 3.7) and $O(m^5 \log m)$ used by cyclotomic field if the Algorithm 3 were used without taking profit of the cyclotomic units (Example 3.1).

Remark 4.4. *Our improvement can be used whenever the lattice of units has a sublattice admitting a short basis and this is not limited to the cyclotomic fields and, more generally, abelian fields. For instance, Kihel [31] proposed a family of fields with dihedral Galois group which have a full-rank subgroup of units which are short. Although one expects a speed-up in all these cases, the cyclotomic case is even more special. Indeed, the parameter $\delta \leq \left\| B_M \right\| / \lambda_1^*(L)$ depends in a large extent on the index $[L : M]$. By [36, Ex 8.5] (see also [17, Th 2.8]), in the case of cyclotomic fields of prime conductor, $[L : M] = h^+(m)$. By Conjecture 4.1 this is small, so the impact of the full-rank subgroup is more important in this case.*

4.2   Consequences of a Recent Conjecture for Cyclotomic Fields

One denotes $h(m)$ the class number of $\mathbb{Q}(\zeta_m)$, $h^+(m)$ the class number of its maximal real subfield, i.e. $K := \mathbb{Q}(\zeta_m + \zeta_m^{-1})$, and one sets $h^-(m) = h(m)/h^+(m)$. A folklore conjecture states that $h^-(m)$ is large but easy to compute whereas $h^+(m)$ is small but hard to compute. A recent work compiled existing conjectures and pushed further the numerical computations, so one can give a precise form to the folklore conjecture.

Conjecture 4.1. (Assumption 2 in [18]*).* For all integers m,

$$h^+(m) \leq \text{poly}(m)$$

for a fixed polynomial *poly*.

Consequence of the Conjecture: Class Number in Real Cubic Fields Without Quantum Computers. Marie-Nicole Gras [26] proposed an algorithm to compute class numbers of cyclic cubic fields in polynomial time with respect to a bound on h. If m is the conductor of a cyclic cubic field, then Conjecture 4.1 implies that h is polynomial in m. Note also that Schoof [47] proposed an algorithm for $\mathbb{Q}(\zeta_m)^+$ with prime m which is faster when a small bound on $h^+(m)$ is known.

Reduction of unit group computation to HSP

Theorem 4.5. *Under Conjecture 4.1 the unit group of* $K = \mathbb{Q}(\zeta_m)^+$ *and its class group can be computed by an HSP algorithm in polynomial time and space.*

Proof. Let $N = \text{poly}(m)!$ and note that Conjecture 4.1 implies that $\mathcal{O}_K^* \subset C^{1/N}$. Let $m' = \varphi(m)/2 - 1$ and let $\varepsilon_1, \ldots, \varepsilon_{m'}$ be a basis of $C/\langle \zeta_m, -1 \rangle$. Note that it can be computed using the HNF algorithm from the vectors v_j of Lemma 4.1. Since K is totally real, its only roots of unity are ± 1. For any $c \in C$, we call vectorization of c and denote vect(c) the unique $(m'+1)$-tuple in $(e_0, e_1, \ldots, e_{m'}) \in \mathbb{Z}/2\mathbb{Z} \times (\mathbb{Z}/N\mathbb{Z})^{m'}$ such that $c = (-1)^{e_0} \prod_{j=1}^{m'} \varepsilon_j^{e_j}$.

We set

$$f : \mathbb{Z}/2\mathbb{Z} \times (\mathbb{Z}/N\mathbb{Z})^{m'} \rightarrow \left\{ \begin{array}{c} \text{canonical representations} \\ \text{of Kummer extensions} \end{array} \right\} \tag{6}$$

$$(e_0, e_1, \ldots, e_{m'}) \mapsto K(\zeta_N, \sqrt[N]{(-1)^{e_0} \prod_{j=1}^{m'} \varepsilon_j^{e_j}}))$$

We claim that the period of f is

$$\text{period}(f) = \{\text{vect}(u) \mid u \in (\mathcal{O}_K)^*\}.$$

Indeed, let (e_j) and (z_j) be such that $f(e_0, \ldots, e_{m'}) = f(e_0 + z_0, \ldots, e_m + z_{m'})$ and set $\varepsilon = (-1)^{e_0} \prod_j \varepsilon_j^{e_j}$ and $\zeta = (-1)^{z_0} \prod_j \varepsilon_j^{z_j}$.

We have $K(\zeta_N, \sqrt[N]{\varepsilon}) = K(\zeta_N, \sqrt[N]{\varepsilon\zeta})$. Let $d := [K(\zeta_N, \sqrt[N]{\varepsilon}) : K(\zeta_N)]$. Then the criterion of isomorphism of Kummer extensions [34, page 58] states that $\sqrt[d]{\zeta}$ belongs to $K(\zeta_N)$. But $\sqrt[d]{\zeta} \in \mathbb{R}$ and the maximal real subfield of $K(\zeta_N)$ is K, so $\sqrt[d]{\zeta} \in \mathcal{O}_K^*$. Conversely, if $\sqrt[d]{\zeta} \in \mathcal{O}_K^*$ it is direct that $(z_0, \ldots, z_{m'})$ is a period of f.

Finally, to compute the complexity of the algorithm, we write $a = \mathcal{P}(b)$ for $a = b^{O(1)}$ and $a = \text{polylog}(b)$ for $a = (\log b)^{O(1)}$. By [33], the cost of the HSP is polylog(N). Since, for any n, $n! \leq n^n$, we have

$$\text{time} = \text{polylog}(N) = \mathcal{P}(\text{poly}(m) \log(\text{poly}(m))) = \mathcal{P}(\mathcal{P}(m)) = \mathcal{P}(m).$$

5   Conclusion and Open Questions

1. The unit group algorithms follow a parallel path to those of other problems like the class group e.g Buchmann's algorithm computes the two groups together and the quantum algorithm for class groups [9] is a generalization of the one of Hallgren et al [22]. It is interesting to have a precise estimation of the number of qubits for class groups depending on the bound on the class number, on the computation of discrete logarithms in the class group etc.
2. The idea of a small dual basis can be generalized: a) to all abelian fields; b) to Galois fields with simple group of automorphisms and known units e.g. [31].
3. The possibility of exploiting automorphisms of arbitrary order depends on the possibility of a Buchmann-Pohst algorithm for $\mathcal{O}_K$ -lattices. One might explore such an algorithm which reduces the size of the norms on average but can locally increase them.
4. The quantum algorithms being probabilistic, the output is not certified. Can one do a classical algorithm to prove that a given set of units generate a subgroup which is ℓ-saturated?
5. The technology of quantum computers is very new and it is not known how many physical qubits correspond to a given number of logical ones. Have the gates used by a HSP algorithms less errors and hence require less error-correction? A precise analysis goes beyond the scope of this article.

A   An Alternative Function Hiding the Units

We place ourselves in the case where K is totally real. As before we call n its degree. Let P_K be a polynomial which defines K and let $\alpha_1, \ldots, \alpha_n$ be the n roots of P_K in $\mathbb{R}$. Let

$$w : \{P \in \mathbb{R}[x] \mid \deg P \le n - 1\} \to \mathbb{R}^n$$
$$P \mapsto (P(\alpha_1), \ldots, P(\alpha_n)).$$

Clearly, w is a linear isomorphism.

Assume that $\mathrm{disc}(f)$ is squarefree and then $\mathcal{O}_K = \mathbb{Z}[x]/P_K$. Let $\mathbb{R}_n$ (resp. $\mathbb{Z}_n[x]$) denote the set of elements of $\mathbb{R}[x]$ (resp. $\mathbb{Z}[x]$) of degree at most n. We define

$$f : \mathbb{R}^n \to (\mathbb{R}_n[x] \bmod \mathbb{Z}_n[x]) \times (\mathbb{R}_n[x] \bmod \mathbb{Z}_n[x])$$
$$(x_1, \ldots, x_n) \mapsto (w^{-1}(e^{x_1}, \ldots, e^{x_n}), w^{-1}(e^{-x_1}, \ldots, e^{-x_n})) \bmod \mathbb{Z}_n[x]^2.$$

We claim that the set of periods of f form a lattice Λ such that

$$2 \operatorname{Log} \mathcal{O}_K^* \subset \Lambda \subset \operatorname{Log} \mathcal{O}_K^*.$$

Indeed, let ε be in $\mathcal{O}_K^*$ and set $(x_1, \ldots, x_n) = \operatorname{Log}(\varepsilon^2)$. Then $w^{-1}(e^{x_1}, \ldots, e^{x_n})$ is the representative of ε^2 in the normal basis of K. The coordinates are all integers because ε^2 is in $\mathcal{O}_K = \mathbb{Z}[x]/\langle P_K \rangle$. Similarly, $w^{-1}(e^{-x_1}, \ldots, e^{-x_n})$ is the

Table 1. Classification of cryptographic primitives w.r.t. the resources of quantum attacks: factorization, discrete logarithms, elliptic curve (EC) discrete logarithms, class group of orders of imaginary quadratic fields (IQC), supersingular isogenies, lattices, error correction cryptosystems and class group (CGP) computations.

	polynomial time	subexponential time	exponential time
$O(m)$ qubits	factorization discrete log EC discrete log IQC		lattices error correction codes
$O(m^5 \log m)$ qubits	high degree CGP		
superpolynomial space		isogenies	

representative of ε^{-2} in the normal basis. Its coordinates are integers because $\varepsilon^{-2} \in_O \mathcal{O}_K^*$.

Conversely, let $(x_1, \ldots, x_n)$ be such that $f(x_1, \ldots, x_n) = (0, \ldots, 0)$ and let $\varepsilon = w^{-1}(e^{x_1}, \ldots, e^{x_n})$. Since $f(x_1, \ldots, x_n) = 0$, the coordinates of ε in the normal basis are integers, so $\varepsilon \in \mathcal{O}_K$. Similarly, $\varepsilon^{-1} \in \mathcal{O}_K$, so ε is a unit.

Finally, given Λ, one solves a linear system over $\mathbb{Z}/2\mathbb{Z}$ to find $\mathrm{Log}\,\mathcal{O}_K^*$. Since K is totally real, its roots of unity are ± 1 and $\mathrm{Log}\,\mathcal{O}_K^*$ completely determines $\mathcal{O}_K^*$.

B   A Discussion on Quantum Security Levels

The NIST post-quantum challenge [43] is willingly open on the definition of the computational resources on a quantum computer:

> "Here, computational resources may be measured using a variety of different metrics (e.g., number of classical elementary operations, quantum circuit size, etc.)"

A study conducted by Mosca et al. [41] revealed that part of the experts consider that on the medium term one should not consider attacks which uses billions of qubits but one should protect against attacks which use hundred qubits. A similar situation happens in the case of classical algorithms: in 2015 the recommendations of the standardisation agencies (NIST, ANSSI, etc.) was to use 2048-bit RSA keys. However, in [1] the authors made a precise estimation that RSA 1024 can be broken with their implementation of NFS on a million cores and they made a study that 98% of a sample of million+ servers use RSA 1024. Moreover, more than 30% were supporting RSA 768 which had been broken since 2009.

It is then necessary to be more precise on the quantum resources. We propose a classification on the time complexity and the number of qubits, as in Table 1 (for a review of the quantum attacks on the various public-key primitives see e.g. [8]). In this light, a verifiable delay function [50] based on the class group of a number field of high-degree and non-cyclotomic is more secure than RSA.

References

1. Adrian, D., et al.: Imperfect forward secrecy: how Diffie-Hellman fails in practice. In: Proceedings of the 22nd ACM SIGSAC Conference on Computer and Communications Security (2015)
2. Babai, L.: On Lovász' lattice reduction and the nearest lattice point problem. Combinatorica **6**(1), 1–13 (1986)
3. Banaszczyk, W.: New bounds in some transference theorems in the geometry of numbers. Math. Ann. **296**(1), 625–635 (1993)
4. Banegas, G., Bernstein, D.J., Van Hoof, I., Lange, T.: Concrete quantum cryptanalysis of binary elliptic curves. In: IACR Transactions on Cryptographic Hardware and Embedded Systems, pp. 451–472 (2021)
5. Barbulescu, R., Gaudry, P., Guillevic, A., Morain, F.: Improving NFS for the discrete logarithm problem in non-prime finite fields. In: Oswald, E., Fischlin, M. (eds.) EUROCRYPT 2015. LNCS, vol. 9056, pp. 129–155. Springer, Heidelberg (2015). https://doi.org/10.1007/978-3-662-46800-5_6
6. Beauregard, S.: Circuit for Shor's algorithm using 2n+ 3 qubits. Quantum Inf. Comput. **3**(2), 175–185 (2003)
7. Bernstein, D.J., Lange, T., Martindale, C., Panny, L.: Quantum circuits for the CSIDH: optimizing quantum evaluation of isogenies. In: Ishai, Y., Rijmen, V. (eds.) EUROCRYPT 2019. LNCS, vol. 11477, pp. 409–441. Springer, Cham (2019). https://doi.org/10.1007/978-3-030-17656-3_15
8. Biasse, J.F., Bonnetain, X., Kirshanova, E., Schrottenloher, A., Song, F.: Quantum algorithms for attacking hardness assumptions in classical and post-quantum cryptography. IET Inf. Secur. **17**(2), 171–209 (2023)
9. Biasse, J.F., Song, F.: On the quantum attacks against schemes relying on the hardness of finding a short generator of an ideal in $\mathbb{Q}(\zeta_{p^n})$. Technical report, CACR 2015–12 (2015)
10. Biasse, J.F., Song, F.: Efficient quantum algorithms for computing class groups and solving the principal ideal problem in arbitrary degree number fields. In: Proceedings of the Twenty-seventh Annual ACM-SIAM Symposium on Discrete Algorithms, pp. 893–902. SIAM (2016)
11. Biasse, J.F., Song, F.: On the quantum attacks against schemes relying on the hardness of finding a short generator of an ideal in $\mathbb{Q}(\zeta_{2^k})$. J. Math. Cryptology **13**(3) (2019)
12. Buchmann, J.: A subexponential algorithm for the determination of class groups and regulators of algebraic number fields. Séminaire de théorie des nombres, Paris **1989**(1990), 27–41 (1988)
13. Buchmann, J., Pohst, M.: Computing a lattice basis from a system of generating vectors. In: Davenport, J.H. (ed.) EUROCAL 1987. LNCS, vol. 378, pp. 54–63. Springer, Heidelberg (1989). https://doi.org/10.1007/3-540-51517-8_89
14. Camus, T.: Méthodes algorithmiques pour les réseaux algébriques. PhD thesis, Université Grenoble Alpes (2017)
15. Castagnos, G., Laguillaumie, F.: Linearly homomorphic encryption from DDH. In: Nyberg, K. (ed.) CT-RSA 2015. LNCS, vol. 9048, pp. 487–505. Springer, Cham (2015). https://doi.org/10.1007/978-3-319-16715-2_26

16. Cohen, H.: A Course in Computational Algebraic Number Theory. Graduate Texts in Mathematics (1996)
17. Cramer, R., Ducas, L., Peikert, C., Regev, O.: Recovering short generators of principal ideals in cyclotomic rings. In: Fischlin, M., Coron, J.-S. (eds.) EUROCRYPT 2016. LNCS, vol. 9666, pp. 559–585. Springer, Heidelberg (2016). https://doi.org/10.1007/978-3-662-49896-5_20
18. Cramer, R., Ducas, L., Wesolowski, B.: Mildly short vectors in cyclotomic ideal lattices in quantum polynomial time. J. ACM **68**(2), 1–26 (2021)
19. de Boer, K., Ducas, L., Fehr, S.: On the quantum complexity of the continuous hidden subgroup problem. In: Canteaut, A., Ishai, Y. (eds.) EUROCRYPT 2020. LNCS, vol. 12106, pp. 341–370. Springer, Cham (2020). https://doi.org/10.1007/978-3-030-45724-2_12
20. Duursma, I., Gaudry, P., Morain, F.: Speeding up the discrete log computation on curves with automorphisms. In: Lam, K.-Y., Okamoto, E., Xing, C. (eds.) ASIACRYPT 1999. LNCS, vol. 1716, pp. 103–121. Springer, Heidelberg (1999). https://doi.org/10.1007/978-3-540-48000-6_10
21. Eisenträger, K., Hallgren, S., Kitaev, A., Song, F.: A quantum algorithm for computing the unit group of an arbitrary degree number field. In: Proceedings of the Forty-sixth Annual ACM Symposium on Theory of Computing, pp. 293–302 (2014)
22. Eisenträger, K., Hallgren, S., Kitaev, A., Song, F.: Long version of the submission to STOC 2014 for A quantum algorithm for computing the unit group of an arbitrary degree number field (2019). https://www.cse.psu.edu/~sjh26/units-stoc-submission.pdf
23. Elbaz-Vincent, P., Marcatel, E.: An extension of the fpLLL library to Hermitian lattices. ACM Commun. Comput. Algebra **55**(2), 54–58 (2021)
24. Fieker, C., Stehlé, D.: Short bases of lattices over number fields. In: Hanrot, G., Morain, F., Thomé, E. (eds.) ANTS 2010. LNCS, vol. 6197, pp. 157–173. Springer, Heidelberg (2010). https://doi.org/10.1007/978-3-642-14518-6_15
25. Gallant, R.P., Lambert, R.J., Vanstone, S.A.: Faster point multiplication on elliptic curves with efficient endomorphisms. In: Kilian, J. (ed.) CRYPTO 2001. LNCS, vol. 2139, pp. 190–200. Springer, Heidelberg (2001). https://doi.org/10.1007/3-540-44647-8_11
26. Gras, M.N.: Méthodes et algorithmes pour le calcul numérique du nombre de classes et de unités des extensions cubiques cycliques de Q. J. für die reine und angewandte Mathematik (1975)
27. Hallgren, S.: Fast quantum algorithms for computing the unit group and class group of a number field. In: Proceedings of the Thirty-Seventh Annual ACM Symposium on Theory of Computing (2005)
28. Hallgren, S.: Polynomial-time quantum algorithms for Pell's equation and the principal ideal problem. J. ACM (JACM) **54**(1), 1–19 (2007)
29. Häner, T., MRoetteler, M., Svore, K.M.: Factoring using $2n + 2$ qubits with Toffoli based modular multiplication. Quantum Inf. Comput. **17**(7–8) (2017)
30. Joux, A., Lercier, R., Smart, N., Vercauteren, F.: The number field sieve in the medium prime case. In: Dwork, C. (ed.) CRYPTO 2006. LNCS, vol. 4117, pp. 326–344. Springer, Heidelberg (2006). https://doi.org/10.1007/11818175_19
31. Kihel, O.: Groupe des unités pour des extensions diédrales complexes de degré 10 sur Q. J. théorie des nombres de Bordeaux **13**(2), 469–482 (2001)
32. Kim, T., Lee, C.: Lattice reductions over Euclidean rings with applications to cryptanalysis. In: O'Neill, M. (ed.) IMACC 2017. LNCS, vol. 10655, pp. 371–391. Springer, Cham (2017). https://doi.org/10.1007/978-3-319-71045-7_19

33. Kitaev, A.Y.: Quantum measurements and the abelian stabilizer problem. arXiv preprint quant-ph/9511026 (1995)
34. Koch, H.: Algebraic Number Theory, volume 62 of Encyclopedia of Mathematical Sciences. Springer, Cham (1997). https://doi.org/10.1007/978-3-662-03983-0
35. Kučera, R.: On bases of the Stickelberger ideal and of the group of circular units of a cyclotomic field. J. Number Theory 40(3), 284–316 (1992)
36. Lawrence, C.: Introduction to Cyclotomic Fields, volume 83 of Graduate Texts in Mathematics. Springer, Cham (1997). https://doi.org/10.1007/978-1-4612-1934-7
37. Lee, C., Pellet-Mary, A., Stehlé, D., Wallet, A.: An LLL algorithm for module lattices. In: Galbraith, S.D., Moriai, S. (eds.) ASIACRYPT 2019. LNCS, vol. 11922, pp. 59–90. Springer, Cham (2019). https://doi.org/10.1007/978-3-030-34621-8_3
38. Lenstra, A.K., Lenstra, H.W., Lovász, L.: Factoring polynomials with rational coefficients. Math. Ann. 261, 515–534 (1982)
39. Lenstra, A.K., Verheul, E.R.: The XTR public key system. In: Bellare, M. (ed.) CRYPTO 2000. LNCS, vol. 1880, pp. 1–19. Springer, Heidelberg (2000). https://doi.org/10.1007/3-540-44598-6_1
40. Liu, X., Yang, H., Yang, L.: CNOT-count optimized quantum circuit of the Shor's algorithm. arXiv preprint arXiv:2112.11358 (2021)
41. Mosca, M., Piani, M.: 2021 quantum threat timeline report (2022). https://info.quintessencelabs.com/hubfs/Quantum-Threat-Timeline-Report-2021-full-report-final%20(1).pdf
42. Napias, H.: A generalization of the LLL-algorithm over Euclidean rings or orders. J. théorie des nombres de Bordeaux 8(2), 387–396 (1996)
43. NIST. Submission requirements and evaluation criteria for the post-quantum cryptography standardization process (2016). https://csrc.nist.gov/CSRC/media/Projects/Post-Quantum-Cryptography/documents/call-for-proposals-final-dec-2016.pdf
44. Proos, J.: Shor's discrete logarithm quantum algorithm for elliptic curves. Quantum Inf. Comput. 3(4) (2003)
45. Roetteler, M., Naehrig, M., Svore, K.M., Lauter, K.: Quantum resource estimates for computing elliptic curve discrete logarithms. In: Takagi, T., Peyrin, T. (eds.) ASIACRYPT 2017. LNCS, vol. 10625, pp. 241–270. Springer, Cham (2017). https://doi.org/10.1007/978-3-319-70697-9_9
46. Schmidt, A., Vollmer, U.: Polynomial time quantum algorithm for the computation of the unit group of a number field. In: Proceedings of the Thirty-seventh Annual ACM Symposium on Theory of Computing, pp. 475–480 (2005)
47. Schoof, R.: Class numbers of real cyclotomic fields of prime conductor. Math. Comput. 72(242), 913–937 (2003)
48. Shor, P.W.: Algorithms for quantum computation: discrete logarithms and factoring. In: Proceedings 35th Annual Symposium on Foundations of Computer Science, pp. 124–134. IEEE (1994)
49. Thyagarajan, S.A.K., Castagnos, G., Laguillaumie, F., Malavolta, G.: Efficient CCA timed commitments in class groups. In: Proceedings of the 2021 ACM SIGSAC Conference on Computer and Communications Security (2021)
50. Wesolowski, B.: Efficient verifiable delay functions. In: Ishai, Y., Rijmen, V. (eds.) EUROCRYPT 2019. LNCS, vol. 11478, pp. 379–407. Springer, Cham (2019). https://doi.org/10.1007/978-3-030-17659-4_13
51. Zalka, C.: Shor's algorithm with fewer (pure) qubits. arXiv preprint quant-ph/0601097 (2006)

Improved Cryptanalysis
of the Multi-Power RSA Cryptosystem
Variant

Abderrahmane Nitaj[1]($\boxtimes$) and Maher Boudabra[2]

[1] Normandie Univ, UNICAEN, CNRS, LMNO, 14000 Caen, France
abderrahmane.nitaj@unicaen.fr
[2] Department of Mathematics, King Fahd University of Petroleum and Minerals,
Dhahran, Saudi Arabia
maher.boudabra@kfupm.edu.sa

Abstract. The multi-power RSA cryptosystem is a variant of RSA where the modulus is in the form $N = p^r q^s$ with $\max(r, s) \geq 2$. In the multi-power RSA variant, the decryption phase is much faster than the standard RSA. While RSA has been intensively studied, the security of the multi-power RSA variant needs to be deeply investigated.

In this paper, we consider a multi-power RSA cryptosystem with a modulus $N = p^r q^s$, and propose a method to solve the modular polynomial equations of the form $F(x) \equiv 0 \pmod{W p^u q^v}$ where $F(x)$ is a polynomial with integer coefficients, W is a positive integer, and u, v are integers satisfying $0 \leq u \leq r$, $0 \leq v \leq s$, and $su - rv \neq 0$. Our method is based on Coppersmith's method and lattice reduction techniques.

We show that the new results retrieve or supersede the former results. Moreover, we apply the new method to study various instances of the multi-power RSA cryptosystem, especially when the private exponent is small, when the prime factors have a specific form, and when the least significant or the most significant bits of the private exponent are known.

Keywords: RSA · Factorization · Lattice reduction · Coppersmith's method

1 Introduction

In 1978, Rivest, Shamir and Adleman [21] designed the RSA cryptosystem, one of the most popular asymmetric cryptosystems. Since then, RSA has been intensively studied for vulnerabilities. This includes Diophantine approximation attacks such as the attack of Wiener [24], lattice based attacks such as the attack of Coppersmith [6], and side channel attacks such as the attack of Kocher [10] (see [3,8] for more attacks). The main parameters in RSA are the modulus N, the public exponent e and the private exponent d. The modulus N is the product of two large prime numbers p and q, that is $N = pq$, and the exponents satisfy $ed \equiv 1 \pmod{(p-1)(q-1)}$. During the last decades, various variants of RSA have been proposed. A typical variant of RSA was proposed by Takagi [23] in 1997 where the modulus is in the form $N = p^r q$ with $r \geq 2$. Such

© The Author(s), under exclusive license to Springer Nature Switzerland AG 2023
N. El Mrabet et al. (Eds.): AFRICACRYPT 2023, LNCS 14064, pp. 252–269, 2023.
https://doi.org/10.1007/978-3-031-37679-5_11

kind of moduli have been then applied in various schemes. In 1998, Okamoto and Uchiyama [19] proposed a cryptosystem, formalized in the sequel as EPOC and ESIGN Algorithms in [20], where the modulus is of the form $N = p^2q$. In 2005, the same moduli were used by Schmidt-Samoa [22] to build a trapdoor one-way permutation based on the hardness of factoring integers. In 2000, Lim, Kim, Yie and Lee [13] proposed a variant of RSA with a modulus of the form $N = p^r q^s$ where $r, s \geq 2$. The variants with such moduli are called multi-power variants of RSA.

In the last two decades, the security of the multi-power variants of RSA has been studied only by a few researchers. For an RSA variant with a modulus $N = p^r q$, most of the attacks use one of the key equations $ed \equiv 1 \pmod{(p-1)(q-1)}$ or $ed \equiv 1 \pmod{p^{r-1}(p-1)(q-1)}$, where e is the public exponent, and d is the private exponent. In 1998, Takagi showed that N can be factored if $d < N^{\frac{1}{2(r+1)}}$. In 2004, May [17] improved the bound to $d < N^{\max\left(\frac{r}{(r+1)^2}, \frac{(r-1)^2}{(r+1)^2}\right)}$, and in 2015, Lu et al. [14] improved it to $d < N^{\frac{r(r-1)}{(r+1)^2}}$.

For the multi-power RSA variant with a modulus $N = p^r q^s$ with $r, s \geq 2$, Lu, Peng and Sarkar [15] presented two attacks. The first attack is based on the equation $ed \equiv 1 \pmod{p^{r-1}q^{s-1}(p-1)(q-1)}$, and the bound on d is $d < N^{1-\frac{3r+s}{(r+s)^2}}$. The second attack is based on the equation $ed \equiv 1 \pmod{(p-1)(q-1)}$, and the bound is $d < N^{\frac{7-2\sqrt{7}}{3(r+s)}}$. At Africacrypt 2022, Nitaj, Susilo and Tonien [18] presented an attack when $N = p^r q^s$, and the public exponent satisfies an equation of the form $ex_0 \equiv z_0 \pmod{p^{r-1}q^{s-1}(p-1)(q-1)}$ with $|x_0 z_0| < N^{1+\frac{2(r-s)}{r(r+s)^2}}\sqrt{s(r+s)-\frac{2(2r-s)}{r(r+s)}}$. Recently, in [1], Alquié, Chassé, and Nitaj studied the equation $a_1 x_1 + a_2 x_2 \equiv 0 \pmod{p^u q^v}$ where $0 \leq u < r$, $0 \leq v < s$, p^u and q^v are unknown factors of N, and a_1, a_2 are integers satisfying $\gcd(a_1 a_2, N) = 1$. They showed that the former equation can be efficiently solved and N can be factored if $|x_1 x_2| < N^{\frac{ru+sv+2\min(su,rv)}{(r+s)^2}}$. They adapted their method to the multi-power RSA variant with the equation $ed \equiv 1 \pmod{p^{r-1}q^{s-1}(p-1)(q-1)}$ and retrieved the bounds of [15] and [18].

In this paper, we push further the cryptanalysis of the multi-power RSA variant with a modulus $N = p^r q^s$ where $\max(r, s) \geq 2$. Specifically, we present the following results.

- Let W be an integer with $\gcd(W, N) = 1$. We consider a polynomial $F(x) = b_{d_0} x^{d_0} + b_{d_0-1} x^{d_0-1} + \ldots + b_0 \in \mathbb{Z}[x]$ with $\gcd(b_{d_0}, WN) = 1$, and present a method to find the small solutions of the modular equation $F(x) \equiv 0 \pmod{W p^u q^v}$ where $0 \leq u \leq r$, $0 \leq v \leq s$, and $su - rv \neq 0$. We show that one can solve this equation and factor N whenever

$$|x| < W^{\frac{1}{d_0}} N^{\frac{ru+sv+2rv}{d_0(r+s)^2}}.$$

- We apply our method in the situation $W = 1$, $u = r$, $v = s$, and show that one can solve the equation $F(x) \equiv 0 \pmod{N}$ if $|x| < N^{\frac{1}{d_0}}$. This retrieves a famous result of Coppersmith [6].

- We apply our method with $u = 1$, $v = 0$, and show that the equation $F(x) \equiv 0 \pmod{Wp}$ can be solved if $|x| < W^{\frac{1}{d_0}} N^{\frac{r}{d_0(r+s)^2}}$ which improves a former result of Blömer and May [2].
- We apply our method with $W = 1$, $v = 0$, and show that the equation $F(x) \equiv 0 \pmod{p^u}$ can be solved if $|x| < N^{\frac{ru}{d_0(r+s)^2}}$ which retrieves a former result of Lu et al. [14].
- Let e be a public exponent. Then for all u, v with $0 \le u \le r$, $0 \le v \le s$ and $su - rv \ne 0$, there exists an integer $d_{u,v}$ with $ed_{u,v} \equiv 1 \pmod{p^u q^v}$. We apply our method in this situation and show that one can find $d_{u,v}$ and factor N if

$$d_{u,v} < N^{\frac{ru+sv+2rv}{d_0(r+s)^2}}.$$

This situation is possible even if the private exponent d satisfying $ed \equiv 1 \pmod{(p-1)(q-1)}$ or $ed \equiv 1 \pmod{p^{r-1}q^{s-1}(p-1)(q-1)}$ is of arbitrary size.

- Assume that in the modulus $N = p^r q^s$ the prime factors satisfy $p = 2^{k_1} p_1 + 1$ and $q = 2^{k_2} q_1 + 1$, where k_1 and k_2 are known. We apply our method in this situation and show that the private exponent d satisfying $ed \equiv \pmod{p^{r-1}q^{s-1}(p-1)(q-1)}$ can be found and N can be factored if

$$d < 2^{k_1+k_2} N^{1-\frac{3r+s}{(r+s)^2}}.$$

- We consider the situation where the public e and the private exponent d are such that $ed \equiv 1 \pmod{p^{r-1}q^{s-1}(p-1)(q-1)}$, and an approximation $\tilde{d}$ of d is known. We apply our method and show that if

$$|d - \tilde{d}| < N^{1-\frac{3r+s}{(r+s)^2}},$$

then one can find d and factor N. This situation happens when an amount of the most significant bits of d is known.

- We also consider the situation where an amount of the least significant bits of d is known, that is $d = 2^{k_0} d_1 + \tilde{d}$ with known k_0 and $\tilde{d}$. We apply our method and show that if $d \approx N$, and

$$k_0 \ge \frac{3r+s}{(r+s)^2} \log_2(N),$$

then one can find d and factor N.

- In [4], Boudabra and Nitaj proposed a variant of the multi-power RSA using the arithmetic of elliptic curves. In this scheme, the modulus is $N = p^r q^s$, and the public exponent e and the private exponent d satisfy $ed \equiv 1 \pmod{p^{r-1}q^{s-1}(p+1)(q+1)}$. In [5], the same authors proposed a variant of RSA which is based on Edwards curves with the same key equation. In both cases, we apply our method and show that, if $ed_{u,v} \equiv 1 \pmod{p^u q^u}$ and

$$d_{u,v} < N^{\frac{ru+sv+2rv}{d_0(r+s)^2}},$$

for some positive integer $d_{u,v}$ with $0 \le u \le r$, $0 \le v \le s$, $su - rv \ne 0$, then one can find $d_{u,v}$ and factor N.

The rest of this paper is organized as follows. In Sect. 2, we present the mathematical concepts and tools that are used in the paper. In Sect. 3, we present three useful lemmas that will be used in the method. In Sect. 4, we introduce the main attack. In Sect. 5, we present a detailed comparison between our method and existing methods. In Sect. 6, we present various applications of the new method. We conclude the paper in Sect. 7.

2   Preliminaries

Let $b_1, \cdots, b_\omega \in \mathbb{R}^n$ be ω linearly independent vectors. The lattice $\mathcal{L}$ spanned by $b_1, \cdots, b_\omega$ is the discrete subgroup with the form

$$\mathcal{L} = \left\{ \sum_{i=1}^{\omega} \lambda_i b_i \mid \lambda_i \in \mathbb{Z} \right\}.$$

Sometimes, a matrix B is used to represent $\mathcal{L}$ where each row corresponds to a basis vector $b_1, \cdots, b_\omega$. The integer ω is the rank of $\mathcal{L}$, and n is its dimension. The lattice $\mathcal{L}$ is called full-rank if $\omega = n$. The determinant of $\mathcal{L}$ is defined as $\det(\mathcal{L}) = \sqrt{|\det(BB^t)|}$ where B^t is the transpose of B. If $\mathcal{L}$ is full-rank, then $\det(\mathcal{L}) = |\det(B)|$.

Lattices are used conjointly for the security of some cryptosystems such as LWE and NTRU, and for the cryptanalysis of others such as GGH and RSA. In both cases, short vectors in the lattice are involved. In 1982, Lenstra, Lenstra and Lovász [12] proposed a polynomial time algorithm, known as LLL, to reduce a lattice and find short vectors. The following form is often used for LLL [16].

Theorem 1 (LLL Algorithm).   *Let $\mathcal{L}$ be a lattice of rank ω. The LLL algorithm finds a basis $\{b'_1, \cdots, b'_\omega\}$ satisfying*

$$\|b'_1\| \leq \|b'_2\| \leq \cdots \leq \|b'_i\| \leq 2^{\frac{\omega(\omega-1)}{4(\omega+1-i)}} \det(\mathcal{L})^{\frac{1}{\omega+1-i}},$$

for $1 \leq i \leq \omega$.

In 1996, Coppersmith [6] presented two methods to solve polynomial equations. The first method finds the small solutions of a modular equation of the form $f(x) \equiv 0 \pmod{N}$, and the second one finds the small solutions of an equation of the form $f(x, y) = 0$. In both cases, the coefficients of the polynomials are integers. In 1997, Howgrave-Graham [9] reformulated the method of Coppersmith for the modular equation. The same idea can be used to find the small solutions of a modular equation of the form $f(x_1, \ldots, x_n) \equiv 0 \pmod{N}$.

Theorem 2 (Howgrave-Graham).   *Let M be an integer. Let $f(x_1, \ldots, x_n) = \sum_{i_1 \cdots i_n} a_{i_1 \cdots i_n} x_1^{i_1} \cdots x_n^{i_n} \in \mathbb{Z}[x_1, \ldots, x_n]$ be a polynomial with at most ω monomials. Suppose that $X_1, \cdots, X_n$ are positive numbers, and $y_1, \cdots, y_n$ are integers satisfying*

$$f(y_1, \ldots, y_n) \equiv 0 \pmod{M},$$
$$|y_1| < X_1, \ldots, |y_n| < X_n,$$
$$\|f(x_1 X_1, \ldots, x_n X_n)\| < \frac{M}{\sqrt{\omega}},$$

where $\|f(x_1X_1,\ldots,x_nX_n)\| = \sqrt{\sum_{i_1\cdots i_n} X_i^2 a_{i_1\cdots i_n}^2}$. Then $f(y_1,\ldots,y_n) = 0$ holds over the integers.

If n polynomials satisfy the conditions of Theorem 2 with the same solution $(y_1,\cdots,y_n)$, then using Gröbner basis techniques, or resultant computations, one can extract $(y_1,\cdots,y_n)$. The main condition for using such techniques is based on the assumption that the polynomials satisfying Theorem 2 are algebraically independent. This is widely used for the cryptanalysis of RSA in connection with Coppersmith's method, so we work within the frame of the following assumption.

Assumption 1. *The polynomials produced by the LLL algorithm are algebraically independent.*

3 Useful Lemmas

In this section, we present three lemmas that will be used in our method to solve a modular polynomial equation of the form $F(x) \equiv 0 \pmod{Wp^uq^v}$.

Lemma 1. *Let $N = p^rq^s$ be a multi-power RSA modulus and let u and v be integers with $0 \le u \le r$, $0 \le v \le s$ and $su - rv > 0$. Let t_1 and t_2 be positive integers satisfying $t_1 \le t_2$, and $sut_1 - rvt_2 \ge 0$. Let $k_0 = \frac{sut_1 - rvt_2}{su - rv}$. Then $0 \le k_0 \le t_1$, and*

$$\max\left(0, \left\lceil\frac{u(t_1-k)}{r}\right\rceil, \left\lceil\frac{v(t_2-k)}{s}\right\rceil\right) = \begin{cases} 0 & \text{if } t_2 \le k, \\ \left\lceil\dfrac{v(t_2-k)}{s}\right\rceil & \text{if } k_0 \le k < t_2, \\ \left\lceil\dfrac{u(t_1-k)}{r}\right\rceil & \text{if } k < k_0. \end{cases}$$

Proof. Suppose that $t_2 \ge t_1$, $su - rv > 0$, and $sut_1 - rvt_2 \ge 0$. Define

$$k_0 = \frac{sut_1 - rvt_2}{su - rv}.$$

Then $k_0 \ge 0$, and

$$t_1 - k_0 = \frac{vr(t_2 - t_1)}{su - rv} \ge 0,$$

that is $t_1 \ge k_0$.
Next, we consider the following cases.
Case 1. Suppose that $t_2 \le k$. Then $t_1 - k \le t_2 - k \le 0$ and

$$\max\left(0, \left\lceil\frac{u(t_1-k)}{r}\right\rceil, \left\lceil\frac{v(t_2-k)}{s}\right\rceil\right) = 0.$$

Case 2. Suppose that $t_1 \le k < t_2$. Then $t_1 - k \le 0 < t_2 - k$, and

$$\max\left(0, \left\lceil\frac{u(t_1-k)}{r}\right\rceil, \left\lceil\frac{v(t_2-k)}{s}\right\rceil\right) = \left\lceil\frac{v(t_2-k)}{s}\right\rceil.$$

Case 3. Suppose that $k_0 \leq k < t_1$, then $0 < t_1 - k \leq t_2 - k$, and

$$\frac{v(t_2-k)}{s} - \frac{u(t_1-k)}{r} = \frac{su-rv}{rs}\left(k - \frac{sut_1 - rvt_2}{su-rv}\right) = \frac{su-rv}{rs}(k-k_0) \geq 0.$$

Hence $0 < \frac{u(t_1-k)}{r} \leq \frac{v(t_2-k)}{s}$, and

$$\max\left(0, \left\lceil\frac{u(t_1-k)}{r}\right\rceil, \left\lceil\frac{v(t_2-k)}{s}\right\rceil\right) = \left\lceil\frac{v(t_2-k)}{s}\right\rceil.$$

Case 4. Suppose that $k < k_0$, then $0 < t_1 - k \leq t_2 - k$, and

$$\frac{u(t_1-k)}{r} - \frac{v(t_2-k)}{s} = \frac{su-rv}{rs}\left(\frac{sut_1 - rvt_2}{su-rv} - k\right) = \frac{su-rv}{rs}(k_0-k) > 0.$$

Hence $0 < \frac{v(t_2-k)}{s} < \frac{u(t_1-k)}{r}$, and

$$\max\left(0, \left\lceil\frac{u(t_1-k)}{r}\right\rceil, \left\lceil\frac{v(t_2-k)}{s}\right\rceil\right) = \left\lceil\frac{u(t_1-k)}{r}\right\rceil.$$

This terminates the proof. □

Lemma 2. *Let $N = p^r q^s$ be a multi-power RSA modulus and let u and v be integers with $0 \leq u \leq r$, $0 \leq v \leq s$, and $su - rv > 0$. Let t_1, and t_2 be positive integers with and $t_1 > t_2$. Let $k_0 = \frac{sut_1-rvt_2}{su-rv}$. Then $k_0 > t_1$, and*

$$\max\left(0, \left\lceil\frac{u(t_1-k)}{r}\right\rceil, \left\lceil\frac{v(t_2-k)}{s}\right\rceil\right) = \begin{cases} 0 & \text{if } t_1 \leq k, \\ \left\lceil\frac{u(t_1-k)}{r}\right\rceil & \text{if } k < t_1. \end{cases}$$

Proof. Suppose that $t_1 > t_2$, and $su - rv > 0$. Define

$$k_0 = \frac{sut_1 - rvt_2}{su - rv}.$$

Then

$$k_0 - t_1 = \frac{rv(t_1-t_2)}{su-rv} > 0,$$

from which we deduce $k_0 > t_1$.
Next, consider the following cases.

Case 1. Suppose that $k \geq t_1$. Then $t_2 - k < t_1 - k \leq 0$ and

$$\max\left(0, \left\lceil\frac{u(t_1-k)}{r}\right\rceil, \left\lceil\frac{v(t_2-k)}{s}\right\rceil\right) = 0.$$

Case 2. Suppose that $t_1 > k > t_2$. Then $t_2 - k < 0 < t_1 - k$, and

$$\max\left(0, \left\lceil \frac{u(t_1 - k)}{r} \right\rceil, \left\lceil \frac{v(t_2 - k)}{s} \right\rceil\right) = \left\lceil \frac{u(t_1 - k)}{r} \right\rceil.$$

Case 3. Suppose that $k \leq t_2$. Then $k < k_0$, and

$$\frac{u(t_1 - k)}{r} - \frac{v(t_2 - k)}{s} = \frac{su - rv}{rs}\left(\frac{sut_1 - rvt_2}{su - rv} - k\right) = \frac{su - rv}{rs}(k_0 - k) \geq 0.$$

Hence $0 \leq \frac{v(t_2 - k)}{sr} \leq \frac{u(t_1 - k)}{r}$, and

$$\max\left(0, \left\lceil \frac{u(t_1 - k)}{r} \right\rceil, \left\lceil \frac{v(t_2 - k)}{s} \right\rceil\right) = \left\lceil \frac{u(t_1 - k)}{r} \right\rceil.$$

This terminates the proof. $\qquad\square$

Lemma 3. *Let $N = p^r q^s$ be a multi-power RSA modulus and let u and v be integers with $0 \leq u \leq r$, $0 \leq v \leq s$, and $su - rv > 0$. Let t_1 and t_2 be positive integers with , $t_1 < t_2$, and $sut_1 - rvt_2 > 0$. Let $k_0 = \frac{sut_1 - rvt_2}{su - rv}$. Let $f(x_1, x_2, \ldots, x_n) \in \mathbb{Z}[x_1, x_2, \ldots, x_n]$ be a polynomial and $(y_1, y_2, \ldots, y_n) \in \mathbb{Z}^n$ such that*

$$f(y_1, y_2, \ldots, y_n) \equiv 0 \pmod{p^u q^v}.$$

Then for all integers k, we have

$$f(y_1, y_2, \ldots, y_n)^k N^{\max\left(0, \left\lceil \frac{u(t_1-k)}{r} \right\rceil, \left\lceil \frac{v(t_2-k)}{s} \right\rceil\right)} \equiv 0 \pmod{p^{ut_1} q^{vt_2}}.$$

Proof. Suppose that $t_1 < t_2$, and $f(y_1, y_2, \ldots, y_n) \equiv 0 \pmod{p^u q^v}$. Then, using Lemma 1, we consider the following cases.
Case 1. If $t_2 \leq k$, then

$$f(y_1, y_2, \ldots, y_n)^k N^{\max\left(0, \left\lceil \frac{u(t_1-k)}{r} \right\rceil, \left\lceil \frac{v(t_2-k)}{s} \right\rceil\right)} = f(y_1, y_2, \ldots, y_n)^k$$
$$\equiv 0 \pmod{p^{uk} q^{vk}}$$
$$\equiv 0 \pmod{p^{ut_1} q^{vt_2}}.$$

Case 2. If $k_0 \leq k < t_2$, then $\left\lceil \frac{u(t_1-k)}{r} \right\rceil \leq \left\lceil \frac{v(t_2-k)}{s} \right\rceil$, and

$$f(y_1, y_2, \ldots, y_n)^k N^{\max\left(0, \left\lceil \frac{u(t_1-k)}{r} \right\rceil, \left\lceil \frac{v(t_2-k)}{s} \right\rceil\right)}$$
$$= f(y_1, y_2, \ldots, y_n)^k N^{\left\lceil \frac{v(t_2-k)}{s} \right\rceil}$$
$$\equiv 0 \left(\bmod\ p^{uk} q^{vk} p^{r\left\lceil \frac{v(t_2-k)}{s} \right\rceil} q^{s\left\lceil \frac{v(t_2-k)}{s} \right\rceil}\right)$$
$$\equiv 0 \left(\bmod\ p^{uk} q^{vk} p^{r\left\lceil \frac{u(t_1-k)}{r} \right\rceil} q^{s\left\lceil \frac{v(t_2-k)}{s} \right\rceil}\right)$$
$$\equiv 0 \left(\bmod\ p^{uk+u(t_1-k)} q^{vk+v(t_2-k)}\right)$$
$$\equiv 0 \pmod{p^{ut_1} q^{vt_2}}.$$

Case 3. If $k < k_0$, then $\left\lceil \frac{u(t_1-k)}{r} \right\rceil \geq \left\lceil \frac{v(t_2-k)}{s} \right\rceil$, and

$$f(y_1, y_2, \ldots, y_n)^k N^{\max\left(0, \left\lceil \frac{u(t_1-k)}{r} \right\rceil, \left\lceil \frac{v(t_2-k)}{s} \right\rceil \right)}$$

$$= f(y_1, y_2, \ldots, y_n)^k N^{\left\lceil \frac{u(t_1-k)}{r} \right\rceil}$$

$$\equiv 0 \ \left(\bmod \ p^{uk} q^{vk} p^{r \left\lceil \frac{u(t_1-k)}{r} \right\rceil} q^{s \left\lceil \frac{u(t_1-k)}{r} \right\rceil} \right)$$

$$\equiv 0 \ \left(\bmod \ p^{uk} q^{vk} p^{r \left\lceil \frac{u(t_1-k)}{r} \right\rceil} q^{s \left\lceil \frac{v(t_2-k)}{s} \right\rceil} \right)$$

$$\equiv 0 \ \left(\bmod \ p^{uk+u(t_1-k)} q^{vk+v(t_2-k)} \right)$$

$$\equiv 0 \ \left(\bmod \ p^{ut_1} q^{vt_2} \right).$$

This proves the lemma. $\qquad \qquad \qquad \qquad \qquad \qquad \qquad \qquad \qquad \qquad \Box$

4 Solving the Polynomial Equation

Let $N = p^r q^s$ be a multi-power RSA modulus with $\gcd(r, s) = 1$ and $\max(r, s) \geq 2$. Let W be a positive integer such that $\gcd(W, N) = 1$. Let $F(x) = b_d x^d + b_{d-1} x^{d-1} + \ldots + b_0 \in \mathbb{Z}[x]$ with $\gcd(b_d, WN) = 1$. In this section, we present a method to find the small solutions of the modular equation $F(x) \equiv 0 \pmod{p^u q^v}$ where $0 \leq u \leq r$, $0 \leq v \leq s$, and $su - rv \neq 0$.

Observe that if $su - rv < 0$, then by switching p^r and q^s as well as p^u and q^v, the modulus is $N = q^s p^r$, and the modular equation becomes $F(x) \equiv 0 \pmod{q^v p^u}$ with $rv - su > 0$. As a consequence, we only consider the situation where $N = p^r q^s$, and $F(x) \equiv 0 \pmod{p^u q^v}$ with $0 \leq u \leq r$, $0 \leq v \leq s$, and $su - rv > 0$. The situation $u = r$ and $v = s$ will be derived as a byproduct of the main result.

Theorem 3. *Let $N = p^r q^s$ be a multi-power RSA modulus with unknown factorization. Let u and v be integers such that $0 \leq u \leq r$, $0 \leq v \leq s$, and $su - rv > 0$. Let W be a positive integer with $\gcd(W, N) = 1$. Let $F(x)$ be a polynomial of degree d_0 with integer coefficients whose leading coefficient is coprime to WN. Then one can find the solutions y of the equation $F(x) \equiv 0 \pmod{W p^u q^v}$ with*

$$|y| < W^{\frac{1}{d_0}} N^{\frac{ru+sv+2rv}{d_0(r+s)^2}},$$

and the factorization of N can be found.

Proof. Let $F(x) = b_{d_0} x^{d_0} + b_{d_0-1} x^{d_0-1} + \ldots + b_0$ be a polynomial with integer coefficients and $\gcd(b_{d_0}, WN) = 1$. The equation $F(x) \equiv 0 \pmod{W p^u q^v}$ can be transformed into

$$f(x) = x^{d_0} + a_{d_0-1} x^{d_0-1} + \ldots + a_0 \equiv 0 \pmod{W p^u q^v},$$

where $a_i \equiv b_i b_{d_0}^{-1} \pmod{WN}$.

Let m, t_1, and t_2 be positive integers satisfying $t_1 < t_2$. For $k = 0, \ldots, m$, and $i = 0, \ldots, d_0 - 1$, consider the polynomials

$$G_{k,i}(x) = x^i f(x)^k W^{m-k} N^{\max\left(0, \left\lceil \frac{u(t_1-k)}{r} \right\rceil, \left\lceil \frac{v(t_2-k)}{s} \right\rceil\right)}.$$

Then, by Lemma 3, we have $G_{k,i}(x) \equiv 0 \pmod{W^m p^{ut_1} q^{vt_2}}$ for all k and i.

Let $X = N^\delta$ be an upper bound for x. Consider the lattice $\mathcal{L}$ where a basis is built by using the coefficients of the polynomials $G_{k,i}(xX)$, $k = 0, \ldots, m$, and $i = 0, \ldots, d_0 - 1$. The rows are sorted with the rule that $G_{k,i}(xX) \prec G_{l,j}(xX)$ if $k < l$ or if $k = l$ and $i < j$. Similarly, the columns are sorted with the rule that $x^k \prec x^l$ if $k < l$. Table 1 presents an example of the basis of the lattice with the polynomial $f(x) = x^3 + a_2 x^2 + a_1 x + a_0$ for $m = 3$, $r = 3$, $s = 2$, $t_1 = 3$, $t_2 = 5$, $u = 2$, $v = 1$. The entries marked with a $\star$ are non-zero terms which do not contribute to the determinant of the lattice.

Table 1. The matrix of the lattice with $f(x) = x^3 + a_2 x^2 + a_1 x + a_0$, $m = 3$, $r = 3$, $s = 2$, $t_1 = 3$, $t_2 = 5$, $u = 2$, $v = 1$.

	1	x	x^2	x^3	x^4	x^5	x^6	x^7	x^8	x^9	x^{10}	x^{11}
$G_{0,0}(xX)$	$W^3 N^3$	0	0	0	0	0	0	0	0	0	0	0
$G_{0,1}(xX)$	0	$W^3 N^3 X$	0	0	0	0	0	0	0	0	0	0
$G_{0,2}(xX)$	0	0	$W^3 N^3 X^2$	0	0	0	0	0	0	0	0	0
$G_{1,0}(xX)$	$\star$	$\star$	$\star$	$W^2 N^2 X^3$	0	0	0	0	0	0	0	0
$G_{1,1}(xX)$	0	$\star$	$\star$	$\star$	$W^2 N^2 X^4$	0	0	0	0	0	0	0
$G_{1,2}(xX)$	0	0	$\star$	$\star$	$\star$	$W^2 N^2 X^5$	0	0	0	0	0	0
$G_{2,0}(xX)$	$\star$	$\star$	$\star$	$\star$	$\star$	$\star$	$W N^2 X^6$	0	0	0	0	0
$G_{2,1}(xX)$	0	$\star$	$\star$	$\star$	$\star$	$\star$	$\star$	$W N^2 X^7$	0	0	0	0
$G_{2,2}(xX)$	0	0	$\star$	$\star$	$\star$	$\star$	$\star$	$\star$	$W N^2 X^8$	0	0	0
$G_{3,0}(xX)$	$\star$	$\star$	$\star$	$\star$	$\star$	$\star$	$\star$	$\star$	$\star$	$N X^9$	0	0
$G_{3,1}(xX)$	0	$\star$	$\star$	$\star$	$\star$	$\star$	$\star$	$\star$	$\star$	$\star$	$N X^{10}$	0
$G_{3,2}(xX)$	0	0	$\star$	$\star$	$\star$	$\star$	$\star$	$\star$	$\star$	$\star$	$\star$	$N X^{11}$

The matrix of the lattice is triangular. Hence its determinant is the product of the diagonal terms

$$\det(\mathcal{L}) = X^{e_X} W^{e_W} N^{e_N}, \tag{1}$$

where

$$e_X = \sum_{k=0}^{m} \sum_{i=0}^{d_0-1} (d_0 k + i) = \frac{1}{2}(m+1)(d_0 m + d_0 - 1)d_0,$$

$$e_W = \sum_{k=0}^{m} \sum_{i=0}^{d_0-1} (m - k) = \frac{1}{2} m(m+1)d_0.$$

Let $k_0 = \frac{s u t_1 - r v t_2}{s u - r v}$. By Lemma 1, we have $0 \leq k_0 \leq t_1$. Then

$$e_N = \sum_{k=0}^{\lceil k_0 \rceil - 1} \sum_{i=0}^{d_0-1} \left\lceil \frac{u(t_1 - k)}{r} \right\rceil + \sum_{k=\lceil k_0 \rceil}^{m} \sum_{i=0}^{d_0-1} \left\lceil \frac{v(t_2 - k)}{s} \right\rceil.$$

To ease the estimation of e_N, we set $t_1 = \tau_1 m$ and $t_2 = \tau_2 m$. Then, the dominant parts of e_X, e_W, and e_N are

$$
\begin{aligned}
e_X &= \frac{1}{2}d_0^2 m^2 + o\left(m^2\right), \\
e_W &= \frac{1}{2}d_0 m^2 + o\left(m^2\right), \\
e_N &= \frac{d_0 u\left(su\tau_1^2 - 2rv\tau_1\tau_2 + rv\tau_2^2\right)}{2r(su - rv)} m^2 + o\left(m^2\right).
\end{aligned}
\tag{2}
$$

Finally, the lattice has dimension

$$
\omega = \sum_{k=0}^{m}\sum_{i=0}^{d_0-1} 1 = (m+1)d_0 = md_0 + o(m).
$$

To apply the LLL algorithm and find a link between m, τ_1, and τ_2, we combine Theorem 1 and Theorem 2 with the condition

$$
2^{\frac{\omega(\omega-1)}{4(\omega+1-i)}}\det(\mathcal{L})^{\frac{1}{\omega+1-i}} < \frac{W^m p^{ut_1} q^{vt_2}}{\sqrt{\omega}},
$$

where $i = 1$. This is equivalent to

$$
\det(\mathcal{L}) < \frac{1}{\left(2^{\frac{\omega-1}{4}}\sqrt{\omega}\right)^\omega}\left(W^m p^{ut_1} q^{vt_2}\right)^\omega.
$$

Set $W = N^\mu$ with $\mu \geq 0$. Using (1), $X = N^\delta$, and $p \approx q \approx N^{\frac{1}{r+s}}$, we get

$$
N^{\delta e_X} N^{\mu e_W} N^{e_N} < \frac{1}{\left(2^{\frac{\omega-1}{4}}\sqrt{\omega}\right)^\omega} N^{m\mu\omega} N^{\frac{(ut_1+vt_2)\omega}{r+s}},
$$

which leads to

$$
\delta e_X < -\mu e_W - e_N + m\mu\omega + \frac{(ut_1 + vt_2)\omega}{r+s} - \frac{\omega\ln\left(2^{\frac{\omega-1}{4}}\sqrt{\omega}\right)}{\ln(N)}.
$$

Now, we use the dominant parts as in (2), and let the right term as $-\varepsilon$ for a small $\varepsilon > 0$. Then we get

$$
\frac{1}{2}d_0^2 \delta m^2 < -\frac{1}{2}\mu d_0 m^2 - \frac{d_0 u\left(su\tau_1^2 - 2rv\tau_1\tau_2 + rv\tau_2^2\right)}{2r(su - rv)} m^2 + \mu d_0 m^2 + \frac{u\tau_1 + v\tau_2}{r+s}d_0 m^2 - \varepsilon,
$$

Neglecting ε, we get $\delta < g(\tau_1, \tau_2)$ where

$$
g(\tau_1, \tau_2) = \frac{1}{d_0}\mu - \frac{u\left(su\tau_1^2 - 2rv\tau_1\tau_2 + rv\tau_2^2\right)}{d_0 r(su - rv)} + \frac{2(u\tau_1 + v\tau_2)}{d_0(r+s)}.
$$

To optimize τ_1 and τ_2, we solve the equations $\frac{\partial g}{\partial \tau_1}(\tau_1, \tau_2) = 0$ and $\frac{\partial g}{\partial \tau_2}(\tau_1, \tau_2) = 0$, and get

$$\tau_1 = \frac{r(u+v)}{u(r+s)}, \qquad \tau_2 = 1.$$

Observe that since $rv - su > 0$, the conditions of Lemma 1 are satisfied, namely $t_1 < t_2$, and $sut_1 > rvt_2$. Using the former optimal values, we get

$$\delta < g\left(\frac{r(u+v)}{u(r+s)}, 1\right) = \frac{\mu}{d_0} + \frac{ru + sv + 2rv}{d_0(r+s)^2}.$$

This implies

$$|x| < N^{\frac{\mu}{d_0} + \frac{ru+sv+2rv}{d_0(r+s)^2}} = W^{\frac{1}{d_0}} N^{\frac{ru+sv+2rv}{d_0(r+s)^2}}.$$

Under the former inequality, Theorem 2 ensures that $G_{k,i}(x) = 0$ over the integers for some integers k and i with $0 \leq k \leq m$, $0 \leq i \leq d_0 - 1$. Let y be a solution satisfying $F(y) \equiv 0 \pmod{p^u q^v}$. Then

$$G = \gcd(F(y), N) = p^u q^v,$$

which leads to

$$p = \left(\frac{G^s}{N^v}\right)^{\frac{1}{su-rv}}, \qquad q = \left(\frac{N^u}{G^r}\right)^{\frac{1}{su-rv}}.$$

This terminates the proof. $\qquad\qquad\qquad\qquad\qquad\qquad\qquad\qquad\qquad\square$

As a consequence of Theorem 3, we have the following result which deals with the situation when $u = r$ and $v = s$.

Corollary 1. *Let $N = p^r q^s$ be a multi-power RSA modulus with unknown factorization. Let $F(x)$ be a polynomial with integer coefficients of degree d_0 whose leading coefficient is coprime to N. Then one can find the solutions of the equation $F(x) \equiv 0 \pmod{N}$ with*

$$|x| < N^{\frac{1}{d_0}}.$$

Proof. The proof is similar to that of Theorem 3 with the conditions $W = 1$, $u = r$, $v = s$, and $t_1 \leq t_2$. Moreover, we assume that $m \leq t_2$. Then the exponent e_N becomes

$$e_N = \sum_{k=0}^{m} \sum_{i=0}^{d_0-1} \left\lceil \frac{v(t_2 - k)}{s} \right\rceil = \frac{(m+1)(2t_2 - m)d_0}{2}.$$

Setting $t_1 = \tau_1 m$, and $t_2 = \tau_2 m$ with $\tau_1 \leq \tau_2$, the dominant part of e_N is

$$e_N = \frac{(2\tau_2 - 1)d_0}{2}m^2 + o\left(m^2\right).$$

Pursuing the computation as in the proof of Theorem 3, we get the condition

$$\delta < \frac{2r(\tau_1 - \tau_2) + r + s}{(r+s)d_0},$$

which is optimized with $\tau_1 = \tau_2 = 1$, and leads to $\delta < \frac{1}{d_0}$. $\qquad\qquad\square$

5   Comparison with Former Methods

In this section, we compare the bound in Theorem 3 with three former bounds related to the solutions of the equation $F(x) \equiv 0 \pmod{Wp^u q^v}$.

5.1   Comparison with the Original Method of Coppersmith

In [6], Coppersmith presented a method to find the small solutions of the modular equation $F(x_0) \equiv 0 \pmod{N}$ where $F(x) \in \mathbb{Z}[x]$ is a polynomial of degree d_0, and N is an integer of unknown factorization. The method works when $|x_0| < N^{\frac{1}{d_0}}$.

If we consider the situation of a multi-power RSA modulus $N = p^r q^s$ with unknown factorization, then one can apply our bound in Corollary 1 with $u = r$, $v = s$, and can find all solutions with $|x_0| < N^{\frac{1}{d_0}}$, which retrieves the bound of Coppersmith.

5.2   Comparison with the Method of Blömer and May

In [2] (Theorem 13), Blömer and May presented a method to find the small solutions of the equation $F(x) \equiv 0 \pmod{Wp}$ where $F(x)$ is a polynomial with integer coefficients and degree d_0, $W = N^\mu$ is a known integer, and p is a factor of N with $p \geq N^{\beta_0}$. They showed that one can find the solutions y such that

$$|y| \leq N^{\frac{(\beta_0 + \mu)^2}{(1 + \mu)d_0}}.$$

To compare this bound with the bound in Theorem 3 for the modulus $N = p^r q^s$ with $p \approx q$, we set $\beta_0 = \frac{1}{r+s}$, $u = 1$, and $v = 0$. Then the bound in Theorem 3 becomes

$$|y| < N^{\frac{\mu}{d_0} + \frac{ru + sv + 2rv}{d_0(r+s)^2}} = N^{\frac{\mu + r\beta_0^2}{d_0}}.$$

Comparing the exponents and using $r \geq 1$, we get

$$\frac{\mu + r\beta_0^2}{d_0} - \frac{(\beta_0 + \mu)^2}{(1 + \mu)d_0} \geq \frac{\mu + \beta_0^2}{d_0} - \frac{(\beta_0 + \mu)^2}{(1 + \mu)d_0} = \frac{(1 - \beta_0)^2 \mu}{1 + \mu} > 0.$$

This shows that our bound in Theorem 3 is larger than the bound obtained with the method of Blömer and May.

5.3   Comparison with the Method of Lu et al.

In [14], Lu et al. considered the situation where the modulus N has a divisor p^r where $p > N^{\beta_0}$, and showed that if $F(x)$ is a polynomial with integer coefficients and degree d_0, then one can find the solutions x_0 of the equation $F(x) \equiv 0 \pmod{p^u}$ with $u \geq 1$ under the condition $|x_0| < N^{\frac{ru\beta_0^2}{d_0}}$.

To compare this result with the result of Theorem 3 for the modulus $N = p^r q^s$ with $p \approx q$, we set $\beta_0 = \frac{1}{r+s}$, $v = 0$, and $W = 1$. Then the bound in Theorem 3 becomes

$$|x_0| < W^{\frac{1}{d_0}} N^{\frac{ru+sv+2rv}{d_0(r+s)^2}} = \frac{ru}{d_0(r+s)^2} = \frac{ru\beta_0^2}{d_0}.$$

This shows that the method of Lu et al. [14] is a special case of Theorem 3.

5.4   Comparison with the Method of Lu, Peng, and Sarkar

In [15], Lu, Peng, and Sarkar presented an attack on RSA with a multi-power RSA modulus $N = p^r q^s$ when the public exponent e and the private exponent d satisfy the modular key equation $ed \equiv 1 \pmod{p^{r-1}q^{s-1}(p-1)(q-1)}$. They showed that one can find d if $d < N^{1 - \frac{3r+s}{(r+s)^2}}$.

The modular key equation implies that $ed - 1 \equiv 0 \pmod{p^{r-1}q^{s-1}}$. In Theorem 3, using $W = 1$, $F(x) = ex - 1$, $u = r - 1$, $v = s - 1$, $d_0 = 1$, one can find the private exponent d if

$$|d| < N^{\frac{ru+sv+2rv}{d_0(r+s)^2}} = N^{1 - \frac{3r+s}{(r+s)^2}}.$$

This shows that our method is an extension of the method of Lu, Peng, and Sarkar [15].

6   Applications of the New Method

In this section, we apply the method presented in Theorem 3 to several variants of the RSA cryptosystem.

6.1   Application to the Small RSA Private Exponents

We consider the situation where the public exponent e satisfies $ed_{u,v} \equiv 1 \pmod{p^u q^v}$ for some integers u, v and a small $d_{u,v}$.

Theorem 4. *Let $N = p^r q^s$ be an RSA multi-power modulus. Let u and v be integers with $0 \leq u \leq r$, $0 \leq v \leq s$, and $su - rv > 0$. Let e be a public exponent. If there exists an integer $d_{u,v}$ such that $ed_{u,v} \equiv 1 \pmod{p^u q^v}$ with*

$$d_{u,v} < N^{\frac{ru+sv+2rv}{d_0(r+s)^2}},$$

then one can factor N in polynomial time.

Proof. If $ed_{u,v} \equiv 1 \pmod{p^u q^v}$, then $d_{u,v}$ is a solution of the modular equation $ex - 1 \equiv 0 \pmod{p^u q^v}$. Hence, using Theorem 3 with $W = 1$, one can find the solution $d_{u,v}$ if

$$d_{u,v} < N^{\frac{ru+sv+2rv}{d_0(r+s)^2}}.$$

Using $d_{u,v}$, we can compute

$$G = \gcd(ed_{u,v} - 1, N) = p^u q^v.$$

Then

$$p = \left(\frac{G^s}{N^v}\right)^{\frac{1}{su-rv}}, \quad q = \left(\frac{N^u}{G^r}\right)^{\frac{1}{su-rv}},$$

which gives the factorization of N. □

Observe that Theorem 4 can be applied even when the private exponent d satisfying $ed \equiv 1 \pmod{p^{r-1}q^{s-1}(p-1)(q-1)}$ is larger than the bound $N^{1-\frac{3r+s}{(r+s)^2}}$ presented by Lu, Peng, and Sarkar in [15].

6.2   Application to the Small RSA Private Exponents with Specific Prime Factors

We consider the situation where the prime factors p and q are of a specific shape.

Theorem 5. *Let $N = p^r q^s$ be an RSA multi-power modulus with a public exponent e, and a private exponent d satisfying $ed \equiv 1 \pmod{p^{r-1}q^{s-1}(p-1)(q-1)}$. Suppose that $p = 2^{k_1}p_1 + 1$, and $q = 2^{k_2}q_1 + 1$ where k_1 and k_2 are known integers. If*

$$d < 2^{k_1+k_2}N^{1-\frac{3r+s}{(r+s)^2}}.$$

then one can factor N in polynomial time.

Proof. If $p = 2^{k_1}p_1 + 1$ and $q = 2^{k_2}q_1 + 1$ where k_1 and k_2 are known integers, then the key equation $ed \equiv 1 \pmod{p^{r-1}q^{s-1}(p-1)(q-1)}$ implies that

$$ed - 1 \equiv 0 \pmod{2^{k_1+k_2}p^{r-1}q^{s-1}}.$$

Set $F(x) = ex - 1$. Then d is a solution of the modular equation $F(x) \equiv 0 \pmod{2^{k_1+k_2}p^{r-1}q^{s-1}}$. This situation can be processed by the method of Theorem 3 with $d_0 = 1$, $W = 2^{k_1+k_2}$, $u = r - 1$, and $v = s - 1$. Hence, one can find the solution d if

$$d < W^{\frac{1}{d_0}}N^{\frac{ru+sv+2rv}{d_0(r+s)^2}} = 2^{k_1+k_2}N^{1-\frac{3r+s}{(r+s)^2}}.$$

This terminates the proof. □

Theorem 5 shows the danger of using prime factors of the form $p = 2^{k_1}p_1 + 1$, and $q = 2^{k_2}q_1 + 1$ since the attack can be launched on larger private exponents.

6.3 Application for Known Most Significant Bits of the RSA Private Exponent

We consider an RSA multi-power modulus $N = p^r q^s$ with a private exponent d for which an approximation $\tilde{d}$ is known. This corresponds to the situation where an amount of the most significant bits of d are known.

Theorem 6. *Let $N = p^r q^s$ be an RSA multi-power modulus with a public exponent e, and a private exponent d satisfying $ed \equiv 1 \pmod{p^{r-1}q^{s-1}(p-1)(q-1)}$. Let $\tilde{d}$ be an approximation of d. If*

$$|d - \tilde{d}| < N^{1 - \frac{3r+s}{(r+s)^2}},$$

then one can factor N in polynomial time.

Proof. Let $d = \tilde{d} + x_0$ with known $\tilde{d}$, and unknown d and x_0. Then the equation $ed \equiv 1 \pmod{p^{r-1}q^{s-1}(p-1)(q-1)}$ implies that $ex_0 + e\tilde{d} - 1 \equiv 0 \pmod{p^{r-1}q^{s-1}}$. We can apply Theorem 3 with $F(x) = ex + e\tilde{d} - 1$, $d_0 = 1$, $u = r - 1$, $v = s - 1$, and $W = 1$. Hence, on can find x_0 if

$$|x_0| = |d - \tilde{d}| < N^{\frac{ru+sv+2rv}{d_0(r+s)^2}} = N^{1 - \frac{3r+s}{(r+s)^2}}.$$

Using x_0, we get $d = \tilde{d} + x_0$, and $ed - 1 = kp^{r-1}q^{s-1}(p-1)(q-1)$. Let $g = \gcd(N, ed-1)$. Then $g = p^{r-1}q^{s-1}$, and $pq = \frac{N}{g} = M$. Combining with $N = p^r q^s$, we get

$$p = \left(\frac{N}{M^s}\right)^{\frac{1}{r-s}}, \quad q = \frac{M}{p}.$$

This completes the proof. □

In [14], Lu et al. presented a similar attack when the modulus is $N = p^r q$. They showed that one can find d if $|d - \tilde{d}| < N^{\frac{r(r-1)}{(r+1)^2}}$. This is a special case of Theorem 6 with $s = 1$.

6.4 Application with Known Least Significant Bits of the RSA Private Exponent

Here we consider an RSA multi-power modulus $N = p^r q^s$ with a private exponent d for which two integers k_0 and $\tilde{d}$ are known such that $d = 2^{k_0}d_1 + \tilde{d}$. This corresponds to the situation where an amount of the least significant bits of d are known.

Theorem 7. *Let $N = p^r q^s$ be an RSA multi-power modulus with a public exponent e, and a private exponent d satisfying $ed \equiv 1 \pmod{p^{r-1}q^{s-1}(p-1)(q-1)}$. Let k_0 and $\tilde{d}$ be integers such that $d = 2^{k_0}d_1 + \tilde{d}$. If $d \approx N$, and*

$$k_0 \geq \frac{3r+s}{(r+s)^2} \log_2(N),$$

then one can factor N in polynomial time.

Proof. Let $d = 2^{k_0} d_1 + \tilde{d}$. The equation $ed \equiv 1 \pmod{p^{r-1} q^{s-1}(p-1)(q-1)}$ implies that $2^{k_0} ed_1 + e\tilde{d} - 1 \equiv 0 \pmod{p^{r-1} q^{s-1}}$. Then one can apply Theorem 3 with $F(x) = 2^{k_0} ex + e\tilde{d} - 1$, $u = r - 1$, $v = s - 1$, $W = 1$, and $d_0 = 1$. Hence, one can find d_1 if

$$d_1 < N^{\frac{ru+sv+2rv}{d_0(r+s)^2}} = N^{1 - \frac{3r+s}{(r+s)^2}}.$$

Suppose that $d \approx N$. Then $2^{k_0} d_1 \approx N$, and $2^{k_0} \approx \frac{N}{d_1}$, which is true if

$$k_0 \geq \frac{3r+s}{(r+s)^2} \log_2(N).$$

Using d_1, one can compute $d = 2^{k_0} d_1 + \tilde{d}$, and using d, one can factor N. This completes the proof. □

In [14], Lu et al. presented a similar attack when the modulus is $N = p^r q$. They showed that one can find d if $k_0 \geq \frac{3r+1}{(r+1)^2} \log_2(N)$. As we can see, this is a special case of Theorem 7 with $s = 1$.

6.5 Application to the Small Private Exponent in Two Variants of RSA Based on Elliptic and Edwards Curves

In [4], Boudabra and Nitaj proposed a variant of the multi-power RSA which is based on elliptic curves. The scheme is an extension of the KMOV [11] cryptosystem to the situation where the modulus is of the form $p^r q^s$ for which the public exponent is a positive integer e and the private exponent is a positive integer d with $ed \equiv 1 \pmod{p^{r-1} q^{s-1}(p+1)(q+1)}$. Later on, the same authors [5] proposed a variant of the multi-power RSA cryptosystem based on Edwards curves with the same key equation. For all u and v with $0 \leq u \leq r$, $0 \leq v \leq s$, $su - rv \neq 0$, one can apply Theorem 4 to find all integers $d_{u,v}$ such that $ed_{u,v} \equiv 1 \pmod{p^u q^u}$ whenever

$$d_{u,v} < N^{\frac{ru+sv+2rv}{d_0(r+s)^2}},$$

which leads to the factorization of N.

7 Conclusion

In this paper, we have considered an integer W, a multi-power RSA modulus $N = p^r q^s$, and presented a new method to find the small solutions of a modular equation of the form $F(x) \equiv 0 \pmod{W p^u q^v}$ where $F(x)$ is a polynomial with integer coefficients, $0 \leq u \leq r$, $0 \leq v \leq s$, and $su - rv \neq 0$. The new method enabled us to retrieve several former results related to the security of the multi-power RSA variant. Moreover, we have applied the new method to study the security of several variants of RSA when the modulus is $N = p^r q^s$, especially in the small secret exponent attacks, and in the partial key attacks.

References

1. Alquié, D., Chassé, G., Nitaj, A.: Cryptanalysis of the multi-power RSA cryptosystem variant. In: Beresford, A.R., Patra, A., Bellini, E. (eds.) Cryptology and Network Security. CANS 2022. LNCS, vol. 13641, pp. 245–257. Springer, Cham (2022). https://doi.org/10.1007/978-3-031-20974-1_12
2. Blömer, J., May, A.: A tool kit for finding small roots of bivariate polynomials over the integers. In: Cramer, R. (ed.) EUROCRYPT 2005. LNCS, vol. 3494, pp. 251–267. Springer, Heidelberg (2005). https://doi.org/10.1007/11426639_15
3. Boneh, D.: Twenty years of attacks on the RSA cryptosystem. Not. Amer. Math. Soc. **46**(2), 203–213 (1999)
4. Boudabra, M., Nitaj, A.: A new generalization of the KMOV cryptosystem. J. Appl. Math. Comput. **57**(1-2), 229–245 (2017)
5. Boudabra, M., Nitaj, A.: A new public key cryptosystem based on Edwards curves. J. Appl. Math. Comput. **61**, 431–450 (2019)
6. Coppersmith, D.: Small solutions to polynomial equations, and low exponent RSA vulnerabilities. J. Cryptol. **10**(4), 233–260 (1997)
7. The EPOC and the ESIGN Algorithms. IEEE P1363: Protocols from Other Families of Public-Key Algorithms (1998)
8. Hinek, M.: Cryptanalysis of RSA and Its Variants. Chapman & Hall/CRC, Cryptography and Network Security Series, Boca Raton (2009)
9. Howgrave-Graham, N.: Finding small roots of univariate modular equations revisited. In: Darnell, M. (ed.) Cryptography and Coding 1997. LNCS, vol. 1355, pp. 131–142. Springer, Heidelberg (1997). https://doi.org/10.1007/BFb0024458
10. Kocher, P.C.: Timing attacks on implementations of Diffie-Hellman, RSA, DSS, and other systems. In: Koblitz, N. (ed.) CRYPTO 1996. LNCS, vol. 1109, pp. 104–113. Springer, Heidelberg (1996). https://doi.org/10.1007/3-540-68697-5_9
11. Koyama, K., Maurer, U.M., Okamoto, T., Vanstone, S.A.: New public-key schemes based on elliptic curves over the ring $\mathbb{Z}_n$. In: Feigenbaum, J. (ed.) CRYPTO 1991. LNCS, vol. 576, pp. 252–266. Springer, Heidelberg (1992). https://doi.org/10.1007/3-540-46766-1_20
12. Lenstra, A.K., Lenstra, H.W., Lovász, L.: Factoring polynomials with rational coefficients. Math. Ann. **261**, 513–534 (1982)
13. Lim, S., Kim, S., Yie, I., Lee, H.: A generalized Takagi-cryptosystem with a modulus of the form $p^r q^s$. In: Roy, B., Okamoto, E. (eds.) INDOCRYPT 2000. LNCS, vol. 1977, pp. 283–294. Springer, Heidelberg (2000). https://doi.org/10.1007/3-540-44495-5_25
14. Lu, Y., Zhang, R., Peng, L., Lin, D.: Solving linear equations modulo unknown divisors: revisited. In: Iwata, T., Cheon, J.H. (eds.) ASIACRYPT 2015. LNCS, vol. 9452, pp. 189–213. Springer, Heidelberg (2015). https://doi.org/10.1007/978-3-662-48797-6_9
15. Lu, Y., Peng, L., Sarkar, S.: Cryptanalysis of an RSA variant with moduli $N = p^r q^l$. J. Math. Cryptol. **11**(2), 117–130 (2017)
16. May, A.: New RSA Vulnerabilities Using Lattice Reduction Methods, Ph.D. thesis, University of Paderborn (2003). http://www.cits.rub.de/imperia/md/content/may/paper/bp.ps
17. May, A.: Secret exponent attacks on RSA-type schemes with moduli $N = p^r q$. In: Bao, F., Deng, R., Zhou, J. (eds.) PKC 2004. LNCS, vol. 2947, pp. 218–230. Springer, Heidelberg (2004). https://doi.org/10.1007/978-3-540-24632-9_16

18. Nitaj, A., Susilo, W., Tonien, J.: A generalized attack on the multi-prime power RSA. In: Batina, L., Daemen, J. (eds.) Progress in Cryptology – AFRICACRYPT 2022. AFRICACRYPT 2022. LNCS, vol. 13503, pp. 537–549. Springer, Cham (2022). https://doi.org/10.1007/978-3-031-17433-9_23

19. Okamoto, T., Uchiyama, S.: A new public-key cryptosystem as secure as factoring. In: Nyberg, K. (ed.) EUROCRYPT 1998. LNCS, vol. 1403, pp. 308–318. Springer, Heidelberg (1998). https://doi.org/10.1007/BFb0054135

20. Okamoto, T., Uchiyama, U., Fujisaki, E.: EPOC: efficient probabilistic public-key encryption (1998)

21. Rivest, R., Shamir, A., Adleman, L.: A Method for obtaining digital signatures and public-key cryptosystems. Commun. ACM **21**(2), 120–126 (1978)

22. Schmidt-Samoa, K.: A new Rabin-type trapdoor permutation equivalent to factoring. Electron. Notes Theor. Comput. Sci. **157**(3), 79–94. Elsevier (2006). https://eprint.iacr.org/2005/278.pdf

23. Takagi, T.: Fast RSA-type cryptosystem modulo $p^k q$. In: Krawczyk, H. (eds.) Advances in Cryptology – CRYPTO '98. CRYPTO 1998. LNCS, vol. 1462, pp. 318–326. Springer, Berlin, Heidelberg (1998). https://doi.org/10.1007/BFb0055738

24. Wiener, M.: Cryptanalysis of short RSA secret exponents. IEEE Trans. Inf. Theory **36**, 553–558 (1990)

Blockchain

The Curious Case of the Half-Half Bitcoin ECDSA Nonces

Dylan Rowe[1]([✉]), Joachim Breitner[2][iD], and Nadia Heninger[1][iD]

[1] University of California, San Diego, La Jolla, CA, USA
`drowe@ucsd.edu, nadiah@cs.ucsd.edu`
[2] Freiburg, Germany
`mail@joachim-breitner.de`

Abstract. We report on a new class of ECDSA signature vulnerability observed in the wild on the Bitcoin blockchain that results from a signature nonce generated by concatenating half of the bits of the message hash together with half of the bits of the secret signing key. We give a lattice-based attack for efficiently recovering the secret key from a single signature of this form. We then search the entire Bitcoin blockchain for such signatures, and identify and track the activities of an apparently custom ECDSA/Bitcoin implementation that has been used to empty hundreds of compromised Bitcoin addresses for many years.

1 Introduction

It is well known in the cryptography community that the ECDSA signature scheme is *fragile* against nonce generation vulnerabilities. An attacker can recover a signer's ECDSA private key if they know the nonce used to generate a single signature; if a signer signs two distinct messages with the same nonce; if a signer signs multiple messages with unexpectedly short nonces; if the attacker can learn the most significant bits of many signature nonces, and so on.

In this paper, we report on an apparently new class of vulnerable ECDSA signature nonces that we discovered in the wild on the Bitcoin blockchain: nonces k of the form

$$k = h_{\mathrm{msb}} \,||\, d_{\mathrm{msb}}$$

where h_{msb} are the most significant half (128 bits) of the transaction hash, and d_{msb} are the most significant half (128 bits) of the signer's private key.

We give a lattice-based algorithm to recover the private key from a *single signature* generated with a nonce of this form in around one core-second of computation time, with almost 100% success rate. While our attack is a variant of existing ECDSA key recovery attacks, the particular vulnerability, the problem formulation we give to exploit it, and the fact that it is exploitable with only a single signature appear to be new observations.

We then search the Bitcoin blockchain for signatures of this form and find nearly 90,000 such signatures generated by around 900 addresses. These signatures have been in use from 2015 until now, and have been used to move 222 Bitcoin.

© The Author(s), under exclusive license to Springer Nature Switzerland AG 2023
N. El Mrabet et al. (Eds.): AFRICACRYPT 2023, LNCS 14064, pp. 273–284, 2023.
https://doi.org/10.1007/978-3-031-37679-5_12

Nearly all of the transactions emptied funds from addresses whose private keys had been exposed on the web in some fashion: brainwallets with compromised passwords, pathologically short private keys, addresses given as examples in online documentation, and so on.

We hypothesize that these signatures are an artifact of a custom ECDSA implementation used by a thief to steal these funds. A number of Bitcoin forum postings link addresses receiving these funds to a particular individual who is relatively public about these activities, in addition to other scams.

While significant attention has been paid in the literature to using transaction graph analysis to trace funds and deanonymize users on the Bitcoin network, our work illustrates a case of a novel cryptanalytic attack allowing us to identify a peculiar ECDSA implementation mistake that apparently allows unique identification of a malicious user.

2   Background and Related Work

2.1   Bitcoin

Bitcoin uses the Elliptic Curve Digital Signature Algorithm (ECDSA) to authenticate the sending party of a transaction. These transactions are validated by nodes in the network and published publicly on the Bitcoin blockchain. A Bitcoin address is derived from an ECDSA public key by repeatedly hashing the public key with the SHA-256 and RIPEMD-160 hash functions. Any party who learns the ECDSA private key corresponding to an address can create a transaction moving any funds associated with that address to an account that they control, and authenticate the transaction by creating a valid signature with the private key.

2.2   ECDSA

In the ECDSA signature scheme, public global parameters include an elliptic curve E together with a generator point G that generates a group of order n on E. A signer's private key is an integer d modulo n, and the corresponding public key is the point $Q = dG$. The security of the scheme rests on the presumed difficulty of the elliptic curve discrete log problem (finding d given only G and Q over certain elliptic curves).

To sign a message with hash h, the signer generates an integer nonce k modulo n. The signature is the pair (r, s), where r is the x coordinate of kG and

$$s = k^{-1}(h + dr) \bmod n. \tag{1}$$

To verify the signature, the recipient tests for equality between r and the x coordinate of the point $(hs^{-1})G + (rs^{-1})Q$.

Nonce Generation. While initial descriptions of the ECDSA algorithm specified that the nonce k should be generated at random, there has been a long history of catastrophic vulnerabilities caused by random number generation failures. A single compromised signature nonce k reveals the secret key d by solving Eq. 1 for this value. Repeated (EC)DSA nonces used to sign distinct messages with the same key allow straightforward recovery of the private key by solving the two relations given by Eq. 1 for each signature for the two unknowns d and k. Reused nonces have been observed repeatedly since 2013 on the Bitcoin blockchain in academic works [4–7], and there appear to be systematic thefts from keys compromised in this way[1].

Modern ECDSA implementations (including Bitcoin core, Ethereum, and other cryptocurrencies) generate *deterministic* nonces, for example following RFC 6979 and instantiating HMAC_DRBG with the secret key d and the hash h. Nevertheless, use of such an algorithm is impossible to enforce, and observations from prior work demonstrate that custom implementations still use a variety of methods to generate nonces [5].

Signature Normalization. The signatures (r, s) and $(r, -s)$ are both valid for the same message given the above scheme. To ensure that signatures are unique, Bitcoin and other cryptocurrencies use the convention that only the smaller of the values $-s$ and s is valid. This has the effect of negating the nonce k for some signatures.

2.3   Lattice Problems and Algorithms

A lattice is a discrete additive subgroup of $\mathbb{R}^m$. Explicitly, a lattice $L(B)$ is generated from integer linear combinations of a set of basis vectors $B = \{b_1, \ldots b_m\}$ with $b_i \in \mathbb{R}^m$. The problem of computing the shortest vector (SVP) in a lattice given an arbitrary basis is NP-hard, and hard to approximate for constant factors.

The Lenstra Lenstra Lovász (LLL) lattice reduction algorithm [11] gives an exponential approximation for the shortest vector in polynomial time; the Block Korkine-Zolotarev (BKZ) algorithm [13,14] can be used to solve exact SVP albeit in exponential time; more generally one can interpolate between these extremes to achieve intermediate approximation factors by adjusting the BKZ block size.

2.4   Hidden Number Problem

Boneh and Venkatesan formulated the hidden number problem to study hardcore bits for Diffie-Hellman [3]. In the *hidden number problem*, the goal is to reconstruct a "hidden number" α given only the top bits a_i of samples $t_i \cdot \alpha$ mod p (where t_i is also known). Explicitly, we are searching for α satisfying the equations

$$t_i \cdot \alpha = a_i + b_i \bmod p$$

---

[1] https://bitcointalk.org/index.php?topic=581411.msg9809990#msg9809990 posted December 11, 2014 by Jochen Hoenicke (johoe), retrieved March 2, 2023.

with some fixed bound B on the (unknown) lower bits such that $b_i < B < p$. In Boneh and Venkatesan's work introducing the hidden number problem, they construct a lattice basis using the sample data and solve the CVP (closest vector problem) on that lattice. It is standard in practice to use Kannan's embedding to use an SVP algorithm to solve the problem instead [1,2]. In this formulation the lattice is generated by the rows of

$$
B = \begin{bmatrix}
p & & & & \\
& p & & & \\
& & \ddots & & \\
& & & p & \\
t_1 & t_2 & \dots & t_m & B/p \\
a_1 & a_2 & \dots & a_m & & B
\end{bmatrix}
$$

Most presentations hope that the target vector $v_t = (b_1, b_2, \dots b_m, B\alpha/p, B)$ is short enough to be found by an algorithm like BKZ that solves SVP; this vector can then be used to construct α. We expect this algorithm to succeed when the ℓ_2 norm of v_t is less than the Gaussian Heuristic gh($\cdot$) for $L(B)$, which gives the expected length of the shortest vector of a random lattice. This is approximately $\text{gh}(L(B)) \approx \sqrt{\dim L/(2\pi e)} \det L(B)^{1/\dim L}$ (where $L = L(B)$). It is possible to use sieving and enumeration techniques to increase the probability of success for this approach after applying the optimizations below [1].

2.5   ECDSA as a Hidden Number Problem

Howgrave-Graham and Smart [9] and Nguyen and Shparlinski [12] showed that the above lattice-based algorithm for solving the hidden number problem could be used to recover an (EC)DSA secret key from most significant bits of nonces from many signatures.

In an implementation of ECDSA that leaks the most significant bits of the nonces k_i, we can recover the secret key d as follows. Given signatures (r_i, s_i) and corresponding hashes h_i, each signature satisfies the equation

$$
-s_i h_i + k_i = s_i^{-1} r_i \cdot d \bmod n
$$

This gives an instance of the hidden number problem with $\alpha = d$, $a_i = -s_i h_i$, $t_i = s_i^{-1} r_i$, $b_i = k_i$, and $p = n$. Thus, with enough signatures, we can construct the lattice basis B as above and recover d.

Lattice Attacks on Applications of ECDSA. The above algorithm is commonly used for ECDSA cryptanalysis in the context of side-channel attacks [2,8,10,16]. Breitner and Heninger [5] applied the lattice-based algorithm for the hidden number problem to compute ECDSA private keys in cryptocurrencies from signatures on the blockchain that had been generated with poorly generated nonces. These attacks all required multiple signatures with vulnerable nonces to have been generated from a given key to enable key recovery; in the most common case observed in the wild, it was possible to recover a private signing key from two signatures whose nonces were shorter than 128 bits. Since it is not possible to tell in advance which signatures might be vulnerable, an attacker searching for vulnerable signatures may need to test all pairs of signatures from each key.

No general attack of this form was possible for keys associated with only one signature.

3 Half Nonce Attack

The starting point for our attack is the observation of signatures in the Bitcoin blockchain whose nonces appear to have been generated by concatenating the high bits of h together with the high bits of d. That is, the nonce k satisfies

$$k = 2^\ell h_{\mathrm{msb}} + d_{\mathrm{msb}} \tag{2}$$

where ℓ is the length of d_{msb} (in the context of Bitcoin, $\ell = 128$).

Fifty four of these signature nonces appear in the data of Breitner and Heninger [5], who noted having recovered signature nonces that shared least significant bits of the nonce with d, but apparently did not notice the shared bits with the hash h. Their attack required multiple signatures with nonces of this form to recover the private key, and testing all possible combinations of signatures for keys that had generated large numbers of signatures on the blockchain was prohibitively expensive.

We observe that it is possible to recover the private key from a signature generated with a nonce of this form *from a single signature* using a lattice-based attack.

3.1 Setup and Main Attack

From Eq. 2 defining k and Eq. 1 defining s, we can derive the equation

$$\underbrace{(2^\ell - sr^{-1})}_{A} d_{\mathrm{msb}} + d_{\mathrm{lsb}} + \underbrace{(h - 2^\ell sh_{\mathrm{msb}})r^{-1}}_{b} = 0 \bmod n \tag{3}$$

This is an affine equation in d_{msb} and d_{lsb} over $\mathbb{Z}_n$, where we can expect $d_{\mathrm{msb}}, d_{\mathrm{lsb}}$ to both be smaller than 2^ℓ, and $2\ell \leq \lg n$. The lattice generated by the rows of the basis

$$B = \begin{bmatrix} n & 0 & 0 \\ A & 1 & 0 \\ b & 0 & 2^\ell \end{bmatrix} \tag{4}$$

will contain the target vector $v_t = (d_{\mathrm{lsb}}, d_{\mathrm{msb}}, 2^\ell)$ by construction. We have $\det L(B) = \det B = n2^\ell$, $\dim L = 3$, and $|v_t|_2 \leq \sqrt{3}2^\ell$. The Gaussian Heuristic criteria is very close to but not quite satisfied since we need $\sqrt{3}2^\ell < \sqrt{3/(2\pi e)}2^\ell$. Thus we expect the target vector to be the closest vector in the lattice only a fraction of the time. Empirically, without further optimizations, this lattice construction succeeded with probability 27.1%.

We can increase the success probability by applying the optimizations below, and brute forcing a few bits or using sieving or enumeration with predicate techniques [1] to find the target vector.

3.2 Optimizations

In order to increase our success probability, we apply two optimizations.

Recentering. The recentering optimization observes that the variables d_{msb} and d_{lsb} are always positive, while lattice vectors can take positive or negative values. We define the variables $d'_{\mathrm{msb}} = d_{\mathrm{msb}} - 2^{\ell-1}$ and $d'_{\mathrm{lsb}} = d_{\mathrm{lsb}} - 2^{\ell-1}$ which recenter the values of the unknowns around zero, and then set the bottom right entry of B in Eq. 4 to $2^{\ell-1}$ and redefine A and b in Eq. 3 accordingly. Then, we expect the shortest vector in the lattice to take the form $(d'_{\mathrm{lsb}}, d'_{\mathrm{msb}}, 2^{\ell-1})$ (up to sign). This one-bit change significantly improves the success rate of the algorithm at nearly no cost to running time: with this optimization alone we achieve a success probability of 76.2%.

Brute Forcing. The success rate can also be improved by brute forcing the top few bits of d_{lsb} and d_{msb} to make the unknown values smaller, at a cost of having to run 2^t instances when t bits are brute forced. We ended up brute forcing four bits total, split evenly between d_{msb} and d_{lsb}. This number was chosen as a practical trade-off between running time and success rate.

Since nonces can be negated by the signature normalization process, we also brute force both positive and negative values for the resulting nonces, resulting in $2 \cdot 2^4 = 32$ total lattice reductions for each signature.

Applying both recentering and brute forcing, our algorithm achieved a 99.6% success rate on synthetic data. At this success rate, the algorithm is likely to detect almost all vulnerable signatures when run on the entire Bitcoin blockchain.

Sieving with Predicate. Using the Sieving with Predicate algorithm from [1] with recentering and no brute forcing, we were able to achieve 99.99% success rate on synthetic data, at an even faster average rate of 0.48 s per signature per core on our real data. This also allowed us to recover an additional 440 signatures, including signatures from August 2022 that suggest that the attacker below is still active. However, these extra signatures are not included in the analysis below due to time constraints.

4 Implementation

We implemented the algorithm in Sage [15] using the above optimizations and G6K's implementation of the BKZ algorithm. A single signature takes 0.688 s to test on an Intel Xeon E5-2699A v4 CPU core.

To collect the dataset of 2.14 billion signatures from the Bitcoin blockchain, we instrumented the signature verification code in the official Bitcoin client to

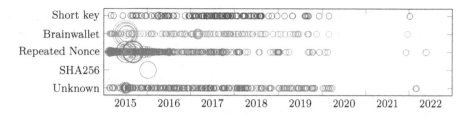

Fig. 1. Compromised signature classification. We plot signatures with compromised nonces over time, grouped by the likely reason the source address is known to be compromised. Larger circles correspond to more transaction inputs on a given date.

write the data from each signature (message hash, signature, public key and transaction id) to a separate file, and re-validated the full Bitcoin blockchain, up to block height 738173 (May 2022).

We then tested each signature using our attack. Since we can verify success using the public key, there are no false positives. Each lattice reduction only requires a single signature, so the attack is perfectly parallellizable; we ran the algorithm on around 1000 physical cores using Slurm [17]. A single core was able to test 120,000 signatures per day. The computation completed in roughly 49 cpu-years, or 18 calendar days.

5   Analysis

We found 88,230 vulnerable signatures from 873 unique secret keys. These were part of 7,242 transactions. Of these, 5,010 had multiple inputs. The transactions transfer funds from 893 unique input addresses[2] to 53 unique output addresses, and 37 addresses occur both as input and as output.

We found a total of 222 Bitcoin that were moved in these transactions. Of these, 55 Bitcoin were moved to an address that is *not* also an input address in these transactions. None of the compromised addresses had any funds as of this writing.

We observe compromised signatures between 2015-02-14 and 2022-05-24. The plot in Fig. 1 shows very high activity in 2015, a break from 2020 to 2021, and a few occurrences again in 2022 before we stopped collecting data.

5.1   Source Address Analysis

Further inspection of the 893 source addresses shows that most of these were known to be compromised prior to our work. We were able to identify the following vulnerable categories:

– **Short keys:** some addresses belong to private keys that are short ($d < 2^{128}$). For example the address 1EHNa6Q4Jz2uvNExL497mE43ikXhwF6kZm corresponds to a private key of $d = 1$.

---

[2] There can be multiple addresses formed from a single private key.

– **Brainwallet:** A brainwallet is a way to generate a private key from a passphrase that one can remember. This makes such Bitcoin addresses susceptible to brute-force attacks, and there exist databases of Bitcoin addresses that arise from weak or compromised brainwallet keyphrases[3].
– **Repeated nonces:** As explained above, re-using a nonce in a signature makes key recovery quite simple. Jochen Hoenicke publishes a list of addresses leaked that way,[4] which we use to identify these addresses.
– **SHA256 inversion hash:** We found one non-ECDSA address, 3GfLKx6ius6MwUetY6gAqeabvoUZJ2qheQ, among the inputs to transactions that contained vulnerable nonces. This address is protected by a simple hash: Its "pkscript" allows anyone who knows the preimage to a certain SHA256 hash to withdraw funds from this address, revealing the preimage in the process.

We were able to attribute most of the source addresses associated with these vulnerable transactions into at least one of these categories of compromised addresses. See Table 1. Many of the remaining unclassified addresses appear on the web, for example as example addresses in Bitcoin-related libraries or tools. It is well known that bots sweep funds from such compromised addresses on the blockchain. Figure 2 shows the flow of Bitcoin through these transactions.

Short key	96
Brainwallet	89
Repeated nonce	512
SHA256	1
Unknown	195
Total	893

Table 1. Source addresses

5.2   Attribution

The unusual prevalence of well-publicized vulnerabilities that can be exploited to reveal the private keys corresponding to the source addresses of these transactions leads us to the hypothesis that these transactions represent an attacker stealing funds from the original owners of these addresses. The quirky signature nonce construction that has revealed the source address private keys to *us* may be an implementation artifact of custom-written attack script that this attacker is using to snatch funds from addresses with compromised private keys, as well as to transfer funds between intermediary addresses.

We have found evidence linking this activity to the person behind the pseudonym "amaclin" on https://bitcointalk.org and https://bitcoin.stackexchange.com.

– Amaclin is said to have "a long history of scamming other users via double-spends and other technical blockchain tricks, and even ground Bitcoin itself

---

[3] We used https://eli5.eu/brainwallet/, which contains 18,982 addresses, but is incomplete.

[4] https://johoe.mooo.com/bitcoin/broken.txt.

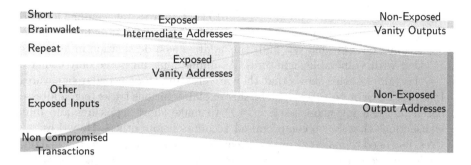

Fig. 2. Flow of Bitcoin through Compromised Transactions. We were able to recover the private keys for every input address in every transaction that contained a vulnerable signature. The vulnerable transactions moved funds from 893 compromised input addresses, through a set of 37 compromised intermediate addresses (most of which were vanity addresses following a recognizable pattern), to 16 output addresses whose keys have not been exposed through vulnerable signatures.

to a near halt with blockchain malleability attacks,"[5] which fits the observations in the previous section. Amaclin was interviewed about the mentioned malleability attack by bitcoinmagazine.com[6] and vice.com[7].

- 32 of the destination addresses of transactions with vulnerable signatures are vanity addresses starting with 1aa or 1xy, and there are indications that these amaclin creates and uses such addresses, and that these addresses are used in draining compromised accounts:

  - For example, transaction 77dd8a24288aa87a7976adeff0579d60ac50b384 b8a28bd589a47459573c9345 from 30 December 2014 (which is not among those with a vulnerable signatures) has among its 17 input addresses 15 such vanity addresses, but also 1ENnzep2ivWYqXjAodTueiZscT6 kunAyYs, which amaclin put on their StackExchange profile page[8].

  - In the aftermath of a reused-nonce incident on blockchain.info[9], Jochen Hoenicke writes[10] that amaclin is among those grabbing funds, and that 1aa and 1xy addresses were used (without explicitly linking these two).

---

[5] https://bitcointalk.org/index.php?topic=5154360.0, posted June 14, 2019 by eddie13, retrieved March 3, 2023.

[6] https://bitcoinmagazine.com/culture/the-who-what-why-and-how-of-the-ongoing-transaction-malleability-attack-1444253640, Oct 7, 2015, retrieved March 2, 2023.

[7] https://www.vice.com/en/article/pga7m9/i-broke-bitcoin, October 7, 2015, retrieved March 2, 2023.

[8] https://bitcoin.stackexchange.com/users/12983/amaclin.

[9] https://web.archive.org/web/20141225032628/http://blog.blockchain.com/2014/12/08/blockchain-info-security-disclosure/, posted December 8, 2014.

[10] https://bitcointalk.org/index.php?topic=581411.msg9888800#msg9888800, posted December 19, 2014, retrieved March 2, 2023.

- Amaclin claims on September 14, 2015 that address 1aa5cmqmvQq8YQT EqcTmW7dfBNuFwgdCD is his[11], used to collect "dust" while a "game" is going on. Our analysis finds this address as a destination in a transaction with vulnerable signatures. Assuming amaclin is the only owner of this address, this shows that they are creating these peculiar signatures.
- In a post on Sept 16, 2015[12], he further explains various tricks (e.g. addresses based on hash inversion, see Sect. 5.1) to make short signatures and build transactions that sweep compromised accounts before others. He writes: "Yes, you need to make the miners prefer my transaction over the original one. To do this, you need to either give more commissions or make the transaction smaller. In short, so that the commission-per-kilobyte would be maximum. This trick allows you to reduce the length of the signature. It cannot always be used for signing because the private key becomes known. But in this case, I don't care that someone recognizes the key. It was already published, so whether it will be known not by a thousand people, but by three thousand - it does not matter. It is important to have time to transfer the loot to your address before others."

The connections between the vulnerable signatures and addresses that can be attributed to amaclin lead us to the hypothesis that code written and used by them is creating the pecular signatures. We reached out to this individual by email in October 2022 and did not receive a response. So far, we have not seen evidence of another source for transactions with vulnerable signatures.

6   Conclusion

This attack has a simple countermeasure: deterministic ECDSA nonce generation as described in, for example, RFC 6979, which is implemented in the core library for Bitcoin, Ethereum, and other cryptocurrencies.

Our much more powerful and exact lattice attack has allowed us to identify 90,000 vulnerable signatures in the Bitcoin blockchain by exploiting this previously unnoticed vulnerable nonce pattern, where the methods of Breitner and Heninger were only able to identify 54 signatures of this form.

Our analysis also illustrates how vulnerabilities in a custom ECDSA implementation can not only reveal private keys, but can also be used to compromise Bitcoin-pseudonymity and addresses to (online) personas.

This is also a nice example of a cryptographic implementation mistake leading to interesting cryptanalysis: our attack easily extends to other nonce constructions from contiguous chunks of d.

Acknowledgements. We are grateful to Jochen Hoenicke for helpful discussions.

---

[11] https://bitcointalk.org/index.php?topic=1179542.msg12417028#msg12417028, retrieved March 3, 2023.

[12] https://bitcointalk.org/index.php?topic=1179542.msg12434341#msg12434341 retrieved March 3, 2023. Translation from Russian using Google Translate.

References

1. Albrecht, M.R., Heninger, N.: On bounded distance decoding with predicate: breaking the lattice barrier for the hidden number problem. In: Canteaut, A., Standaert, F.-X. (eds.) EUROCRYPT 2021. LNCS, vol. 12696, pp. 528–558. Springer, Cham (2021). https://doi.org/10.1007/978-3-030-77870-5_19
2. Benger, N., van de Pol, J., Smart, N.P., Yarom, Y.: Ooh Aah... just a little bit?: a small amount of side channel can go a long way. In: Batina, L., Robshaw, M. (eds.) CHES 2014. LNCS, vol. 8731, pp. 75–92. Springer, Heidelberg (2014). https://doi.org/10.1007/978-3-662-44709-3_5
3. Boneh, D., Venkatesan, R.: Hardness of computing the most significant bits of secret keys in Diffie-Hellman and related schemes. In: Koblitz, N. (ed.) CRYPTO 1996. LNCS, vol. 1109, pp. 129–142. Springer, Heidelberg (1996). https://doi.org/10.1007/3-540-68697-5_11
4. Bos, J.W., Halderman, J.A., Heninger, N., Moore, J., Naehrig, M., Wustrow, E.: Elliptic curve cryptography in practice. In: Christin, N., Safavi-Naini, R. (eds.) FC 2014. LNCS, vol. 8437, pp. 157–175. Springer, Heidelberg (2014). https://doi.org/10.1007/978-3-662-45472-5_11
5. Breitner, J., Heninger, N.: Biased nonce sense: lattice attacks against weak ECDSA signatures in cryptocurrencies. In: Goldberg, I., Moore, T. (eds.) FC 2019. LNCS, vol. 11598, pp. 3–20. Springer, Cham (2019). https://doi.org/10.1007/978-3-030-32101-7_1
6. Brengel, M., Rossow, C.: Identifying key leakage of bitcoin users. In: Bailey, M., Holz, T., Stamatogiannakis, M., Ioannidis, S. (eds.) RAID 2018. LNCS, vol. 11050, pp. 623–643. Springer, Cham (2018). https://doi.org/10.1007/978-3-030-00470-5_29
7. Courtois, N.T., Emirdag, P., Valsorda, F.: Private key recovery combination attacks: on extreme fragility of popular bitcoin key management, wallet and cold storage solutions in presence of poor RNG events. Cryptology ePrint Archive, Report 2014/848 (2014). https://eprint.iacr.org/2014/848
8. Genkin, D., Nissan, N., Schuster, R., Tromer, E.: Lend me your ear: passive remote physical side channels on PCs. In: 31st USENIX Security Symposium (USENIX Security 22). pp. 4437–4454. USENIX Association, Boston, MA, August 2022. https://www.usenix.org/conference/usenixsecurity22/presentation/genkin
9. Howgrave-Graham, N.A., Smart, N.P.: Lattice attacks on digital signature schemes. Des. Codes Cryptogr. **23**(3), 283–290 (2001). https://doi.org/10.1023/A:1011214926272
10. Jancar, J., Sedlacek, V., Svenda, P., Sys, M.: Minerva: the curse of ECDSA nonces. IACR TCHES **2020**(4), 281–308 (2020). https://doi.org/10.13154/tches.v2020.i4.281-308, https://tches.iacr.org/index.php/TCHES/article/view/8684
11. Lenstra, A.K., Lenstra, H.W., Lovasz, L.: Factoring polynomials with rational coefficients. Math. Ann. **261**, 515–534 (1982)
12. Nguyen, P.Q., Shparlinski, I.E.: The insecurity of the elliptic curve digital signature algorithm with partially known nonces. Des. Codes Cryptogr. **30**(2), 201–217 (2003). https://doi.org/10.1023/A:1025436905711
13. Schnorr, C.P.: A hierarchy of polynomial time lattice basis reduction algorithms. Theor. Comput. Sci. **53**(2-3), 201–224 (1987). https://doi.org/10.1016/0304-3975(87)90064-8, http://dx.doi.org/10.1016/0304-3975(87)90064-8
14. Schnorr, C.P., Euchner, M.: Lattice basis reduction: improved practical algorithms and solving subset sum problems. Math. Program. **66**(2), 181–199 (Sep 1994). https://doi.org/10.1007/BF01581144, http://dx.doi.org/10.1007/BF01581144

15. The Sage Developers: SageMath, the Sage Mathematics Software System (Version 8.7) (2022). https://www.sagemath.org
16. Weiser, S., Schrammel, D., Bodner, L., Spreitzer, R.: Big numbers - big troubles: systematically analyzing nonce leakage in (EC)DSA implementations. In: Capkun, S., Roesner, F. (eds.) USENIX Security 2020, pp. 1767–1784. USENIX Association, August 2020
17. Yoo, A.B., Jette, M.A., Grondona, M.: SLURM: simple Linux utility for resource management. In: Feitelson, D., Rudolph, L., Schwiegelshohn, U. (eds.) JSSPP 2003. LNCS, vol. 2862, pp. 44–60. Springer, Heidelberg (2003). https://doi.org/10.1007/10968987_3

Maravedí: A Secure and Practical Protocol to Trade Risk for Instantaneous Finality

Mario Larangeira[1,2]([⊠])[iD] and Maxim Jourenko[1]

[1] Department of Mathematical and Computing Science, School of Computing, Tokyo Institute of Technology,W8-55, 2-12-1 Ookayama, Meguro-ku, Tokyo, Japan
mario@c.titech.ac.jp, jourenko.m.ab@m.titech.ac.jp
[2] Input Output Global, Singapore, Singapore
mario.larangeira@iohk.io
http://iohk.io

Abstract. The efficiency of blockchain systems is often compared to popular credit card networks with respect to the transactions per second rate. This seems to be an unfair comparison since these networks do not complete a transaction from beginning to end. Rather they buy the risk and settle it much later. Typically transactions have only two players, the *payer* and the *payee*, and the settlement of this transaction requires time since it depends on basic properties of the consensus protocol. In practice, the payee, very often, needs to wait for confirmation in order to ship the traded goods. Alternatively, the payee, or merchant, can ship it in faith that the transaction will be confirmed. Our contribution, the Maravedí Protocol, introduces a third player to minimize the risk of the payee to be left without the payment even without the consensus layer confirmation. The main idea is that the third player can work similarly to a *credit card* company. That is, it buys the risk from the merchant, by a small discount, and allows the third player to pay it instantaneously via a payment-channel like protocol. In parallel, the third player receives the regular payment transaction from the payer that can be settled on the chain, thus, after waiting the consensus/blockchain required time. Moreover, the on-chain transaction pays the full amount, allowing the third player to cash in the discount. Hence, on the side of the merchant, our protocol puts forth *instantaneous finality* in a novel way to the best of our knowledge.

1 Introduction

The most widely known application for blockchain based systems is cryptocurrency. One of the main bottlenecks for mass adoption boils down to the number of transactions per second (TPS) rate such systems can process. New transactions are confirmed by the system as new blocks are added to the blockchain,

---

This work was supported by Input Output Global and JST CREST JPMJCR2113, Japan.

and the same chain is agreed among all the honest nodes of the network via a Nakamoto style consensus protocol. The design and security of the consensus protocol plays a major role in the transaction validation process because it dictates the rate of block creation either in Proof of Stake (PoS) or Proof of Work (PoW) systems. Different protocols implement different refresh rates. Therefore, in order to confirm a transaction, *i.e.,* beyond the non-negligible probability of disappearing from the blockchain, it is necessary to wait a few blocks. At the end of this confirmation period, the systems offer *finality, i.e.,* informally, a period of time that a user needs to wait in order to be sure the transaction cannot be reversed. The time requirement for such desirable property varies depending on the system, for example, Bitcoin [20] needs on average every 60 min (or 6 blocks), Ethereum [27] requires 2,5 min (or 10 blocks), Cardano/Ouroboros theoretically requires one time-slot which is 20 s (however for *true immutability of the chain* according to the newest setting can be 36 h) [4,8]. In general, pure blockchain based consensus protocols are slower than BFT systems, *e.g.,* PBFT [3]. Therefore, in order to circumvent this crucial limitation in distributed systems, hybrid protocols, *i.e.,* combination of blockchain and BFT approaches, were suggested, *e.g.,* Algorand [9] and Thunder [21]. However the proposed protocols still require some waiting for the confirmation time in order to achieve finality.

Concretely, the confirmation time for the transferred funds can be particularly risky to settle a transaction. Namely, after the Customer performs a payment, *i.e.,* the payer, how to assure, quickly, to the Merchant, *i.e.,* the payee, that it is safe to deliver the purchased goods. In practice, within a distributed environment with confirmation time, the Merchant can deliver the goods in the optimistic case, *i.e.,* on faith that the transaction will be finalized, after the issue of the payment. Technically, in this scenario, the Merchant is under the risk that the transaction will not be finalized given the waiting time of the consensus protocol. In other words, the Merchant is left without any guarantees of receiving the payment. Researchers and practitioners have allocated effort, which has not yet produced a clear definitive solution to the described limitation. In particular, businesses that rely on cryptocurrency are keen to know whether transactions can be securely confirmed much faster.

An earlier attempt to improve the TPS ratio is based on protocols that do not perform most of its transactions on the chain, *i.e.,* an off-chain protocol. The most widely used is the Lightning Protocol [24] which establishes a channel between two parties and limits the interaction with the blockchain. While the work in [24] does offer a way to issue instantaneous, and verifiable, transactions between the two parties, the initial establishment of the channel requires the interaction with the blockchain, and, therefore, it is necessary to wait for the confirmation time. Thus it is not suitable to the case of several parties, as every new payment should trigger the creation of a new channel.

An Unfair Comparison. It is well known that centralized payment methods like debit cards, Paypal or Payment Hubs [11] are orders of magnitude faster than blockchain based systems, and they do offer instantaneous (with the disclaimer we do not consider card information checking, receipt issuing, etc., which in fact make it not strictly "instantaneous"). However, when discussing the transaction throughput of cryptocurrencies, a very common comparison often appears between the decentralized ledger technology and credit card networks. Whereas the former most known example, *i.e.*, Bitcoin, carries 7 TPS [25], the latter handles tens of thousands per second [25]. This alarming difference can be explained by the centralized nature of the network of the credit card company. Since decentralized ledger technology is mostly *decentralized*, it imposes significant overhead in the processing speed. To the best of our knowledge, another often overlooked difference is that credit card companies do not *only* intermediate the transaction between Customer and Merchant, they, in fact, buy the risk, *i.e.*, the credit risk, from the Merchant by a profit. In the light of this description, this *credit card model* does not seem to have a counterpart in the cryptocurrency realm. More concretely, in the physical world, a Customer would ask for the credit card company, which we denote Risk Buyer, to pay the Merchant, while in a future date the Customer pays the Risk Buyer back.

In this setting, the Merchant is assured, given the prior deal with the Risk Buyer, that it will receive the funds even if the Customer does not fulfill its part of the deal. In the real world, the Risk Buyer would require extra information from the Customer to build confidence and, therefore, *buy the risk*. Concrete examples of extra information are typically background check, spending history, reputation, etc. Moreover Risk Buyer would also require some discount from the Merchant. By paying the Merchant in advance, the Risk Buyer receives a profit in order to engage in the deal in the first place. The crucial term is "in advance". That is, how quick, and guaranteed, this payment should be performed in order to satisfy the *finality* property in the eyes of the Merchant.

Instantaneous Payment Over Blockchain. Not all types of payments require confirmation time in the blockchain realm. In fact, several protocols put forth instantaneous confirmation payments via payment/state channels [6,13], *i.e.*, depend virtually on the network speed, and the already mentioned [24]. Typically, these protocols need an initial phase which indeed requires confirmation time. Subsequent payments, under certain values, are *instantaneous* between payer and payee, albeit they are not reflected in the consensus protocol immediately. The result of these payments are reflected in the underlying ledger when the channel is closed which requires, again, the confirmation time in order to persist the final state of the channel.

Our approach takes this natural property of payment channels, *i.e.*, instantaneous payments, and combines it with blockchain aided transaction, in order to provide instantaneous settlement, *i.e.*, *finality*, to the receiver of the funds, *i.e.*, the Merchant, in an ad-hoc transaction, *i.e.*, without prior interaction to the Costumer. Our approach is in sharp contrast to the existing protocols as we put forth a novel approach: a hybrid design for protocols, and a relaxed notion of finality, *i.e.*, only applies for the Merchant.

Related Work. As already outlined, early attempts to increase the TPS rate of blockchain based systems rely on the establishment of *payment channels*. Such protocols, in general, work by locking funds from two participants, *i.e.*, the capacity of the channel, by standard transactions registered in the ledger, after the confirmation of such a transactions, they interact directly, *i.e.,* without the ledger. Such an approach, effectively allows these participants to carry out numerous direct transactions without time limitations from the consensus protocol. Such transactions are settled instantaneously, although they are not registered in the blockchain/ledger until the channel is closed. It is important to notice that, although the transaction is not present in the ledger, by the time of its settlement, the participants cannot revert it due to mechanisms of the typical payment channel protocol, *e.g.,* [24]. Such a class of protocols, named layer-2 (layer-1 being the consensus layer), has already a large body of work [12].

The protocol in [24] had received a formal treatment by Kiayias *et al.* [16], which also showed evidence that common ledger functionalities (in the UC sense) introduced in the literature do not seem to be realizable (for instantaneous finality) under realistic network assumptions. In particular, they remark that [6,7,17] presents a model that settles every submitted transaction immediately which does not seem to be realistic for existing network models. A significant reminder of the need for protocols that offer quick finality which motivates our novel approach and suggested protocol. A later work by Dinsdale-Young*et al.* [5] tackles the slow consensus drawback by introducing a concrete finality layer. The work relies on the formal properties of blockchain, *i.e.,* common-prefix, chain-growth and chain-quality. Despite its ingenuity, it cannot offer quick finality.

On a similar topic, Miller *et al.* [18] introduced Sprites, a variant of payment-channels, which reduces the worst-case "collateral cost" that each hop in the payment network may incur. In a nutshell, this work leverages on the use of smart contracts, hence their use is restricted to "state channels", to reduce the attack surface and speed up the closing of the channel. More recently, Jourenko *et al.* [14] improved on the technique to close multi-hop payment channels, but without the use of smart-contracts, making it compatible with systems without smart contract capabilities, such as the Bitcoin. In comparison, although our work has three participants, we do not consider a multi-hop payment channel. In fact, our setting is simpler, given that only the Merchant and the Risk Buyer maintain the channel, making it an "almost" regular channel in the sense of [24]. The only difference is the change we introduce to the construction of the channel, which we describe next. This change virtually makes no significant difference in the efficiency of concrete implementation of [24], but allows us to introduce the third player as our model requires.

Our Contribution. This work introduces the study of finality via risk trade. To the best of our knowledge, it is the first time this approach is suggested. We discuss the desiderata for such an approach. Furthermore, we present the Maravedí Protocol which takes this fundamentally different approach to implement *finality*. Namely, it puts forth *instantaneous finality* to the receiver of the funds (which in our jargon is the "Merchant"). Our design sidesteps the drawback of distributed systems, *i.e.,* the confirmation time of the blockchain systems, by allowing a "pre-processing" phase which is mainly the establishment of a pairwise payment channel. The channel bridges the Merchant and the participant who pays in advance, therefore buying the risk, (which in our model is the "Risk Buyer"). Hence the payment to the Merchant is timely performed via the already established payment channel, taking advantage of the existing property of the cited protocol [16,24], *i.e.,* instantaneous payment. Note that the channel creation requires the confirmation time from the ledger. However, made in advance, the required time does not interfere in the instantaneous interaction between the Risk Buyer and the Merchant.

Our design allows any Customer to approach the Merchant in an ad hoc manner, *i.e.,* without any previous interaction, a desirable property. The Customer issues a regular transaction to the Merchant, *i.e.,* "regular" means it requires time to settle in the ledger, however it is assigned to the Risk Buyer. The Merchant forwards the transaction to the Risk Buyer conditioned with a payment under its jointly created payment channel. A technical issue we solve in our construction is conditionally fixing the regular payment and the payment channel transferring of funds, without requiring trust between the two participants, *i.e.,* Risk Buyer and Merchant. We adapted the Hash Time Lock Contract (HTLC) technique used in the Lightning Network [16,24] by allowing the Risk Buyer to keep the value x while delivering $y = H(x)$ to the Merchant (which forwards it to the Costumer), for a hash function H. The transaction issued by the Customer is conditioned to the disclosing of x, which happens when the final payment is done via the payment channel or the ledger.

More concretely, in our construction the HTLC technique is leveraged to provide *atomicity* between the transaction to be published in the ledger and the one performed in the payment-channel. Anytime the Risk Buyer publishes the received blockchain transaction, it also discloses x which allows the Merchant to also cash in the funds in the channel. We remark that the instantaneous finality provided by our protocol relies on the combination of the ledger transaction and the payment-channel transferring of funds. Despite the funds being locked in the channel, the Merchant is assured to receive it given that the "pre-processing" phase within the channel was established. The guarantee provided by the channel construction is more desirable than solely relying on the optimistic heuristic that nodes will reach an eventual consensus in the blockchain based system. Note, for example, that a naive construction would be requiring Risk Buyer to pay the Merchant right away, via the payment channel, and just wait for the transaction (from the Customer) to be confirmed. However, in this case, there is no guarantee that the Merchant would cooperate by, for example, publishing the transaction or sending it to the Risk Buyer. It may be the case, that the Risk Buyer, relying on some reputation registry, may no longer want to do business with the Merchant, however, our construction does not need to rely on such strategy. It enforces payment by design.

In summary our contributions are

- We start by a discussion of the desiderata for risk trade in order to obtain finality for the point of view of the Merchant. A notion we introduce in this work in the best of our knowledge;

- We propose the Maravedí Protocol which concretely illustrates this novel approach to put forth instantaneous finality for the Merchant;
- Finally, we describe the main property of our protocol, namely, the Merchant and the Risk Buyer redeem the respective payment securely.

We remark our protocol is quite practical since we adapted an already existing construction, the Lighting Protocol [16,24]. We also show chase that our approach does not require any sort of collateral, smart-contract capability or checkpoints, e.g., [15]. Furthermore, we believe that the adaptation we propose for the HTLC can be easily implemented taking the original source [24] code as a blueprint for the construction.

Roadmap. One of our main contributions is presented in Sect. 3, *i.e.*, the desiderata of a three-participant trade risk. Section 4 outlines the main phases of our construction, and provides an intuition for the approach, while Sect. 5.2 describes the concrete construction. We provide the security analysis in Sect. 6 along with a discussion with respect to the early introduced desiderata. The last section, *i.e.*, Sect. 7, presents our final comments.

2   Preliminaries

Our protocol relies on the payment-channel protocol for the risk trade for the payment to the Risk Buyer. It is convenient to review the UTXO Model and the Lighting Network design. In addition, for completeness, it is necessary to recall the digital signature primitives used in our construction. However we first start by the primitive which allows us to derive new keys. From now, let λ be the security parameter, while $negl(\lambda)$ is the standard negligible function and $x \xleftarrow{r} \mathcal{X}$ is the sampling algorithm for x from a uniform distribution $\mathcal{X}$.

2.1   Pseudorandom Function

Each payment performed within the channel, a new set of keys are generated from the original set of master keys. From now, we present a formal definition for the Pseudorandom Function (PRF) and its security notion.

Definition 1 (PRF). *Let $\lambda \in \mathbb{N}$, an index, which defines the family, $s \in \{0,1\}^*$, $p : \mathbb{N} \to \mathbb{N}$ and f_s be a family of functions from $\{0,1\}^{p(|s|)}$ to $\{0,1\}^{p(|s|)}$. Furthermore, let Func_λ be the uniform distribution over the set of all $\{0,1\}^\lambda \to \{0,1\}^\lambda$ functions. We say that f_s is a pseudorandom function family if:*

- *$\forall s \in \{0,1\}^*, \forall x \in \{0,1\}^{p(|s|)}, \exists$ PPT algorithm, denoted $\mathrm{PRF}(x,s)$, that computes $f_s(x)$ for the input x*
- *$\forall \lambda \in \mathbb{N}, \forall$ PPT $\mathcal{A}$,*

$$\left| \Pr_{\substack{s \xleftarrow{r} \{0,1\}^\lambda \\ \mathcal{A}' scoins}} [\mathcal{A}^{f_s(\cdot)}(1^\lambda) = 1] - \Pr_{\substack{\mathrm{PRF} \xleftarrow{r} \mathsf{Func}_\lambda \\ \mathcal{A}' scoins}} [\mathcal{A}^{\mathrm{PRF}(\cdot)}(1^\lambda) = 1] \right| = negl(\lambda),$$

where $\mathcal{A}$ is given oracle access to $f_s(\cdot)$ and PRF in each of the probability expressions above respectively.

2.2   Digital Signature Schemes

Typically, the standard digital signature scheme is the main cryptographic primitive for transaction frameworks. Furthermore, payment channel [16,24] relies on two extra signature schemes, namely, Identity Based Signature and Combined Signature. It is convenient to review the three schemes.

Definition 2 (The Digital Signature Scheme [10]). *It is the triple of algorithms* $\mathcal{S} = \langle \text{GEN}, \text{VERDS}, \text{SIGNDS} \rangle$, *such that*

- $\text{GEN}(1^\lambda) \rightarrow:$ *The generation procedure, given the security parameter* λ, *and outputs the key pair, i.e., verification and secret keys, respectively* vk *and* sk;
- $\text{SIGNDS}(\text{sk}, m) \rightarrow \sigma:$ *The sign procedure takes as input the secret key* sk *and the message* m *to output the signature* σ;
- $\text{VERDS}(\text{vk}, m, \sigma) \rightarrow \{0, 1\}:$ *The verification procedure takes the verification key* vk, *the message* m *and the signature* σ *to output* 1 *if the signature is valid, or* 0 *otherwise.*

*Moreover, the scheme is said to be resistant to Existential Unforgeable under Adaptive Chosen Message Attacks (**EUF-CMA**) if, with respect to the security parameter* λ, *for any PPT algorithm* $\mathcal{A}_{forger}$, *which can query the signature oracle* $\text{SIGNDS}(\text{sk}, \cdot)$ *for signatures on a polynomial number of messages* m_i, *it holds* $\Pr[(\text{vk}, \text{sk}) \leftarrow \text{GEN}(1^\lambda) : (m, \sigma) \leftarrow \mathcal{A}_{forger}^{\text{SIGNDS}(\text{sk}, \cdot)} \wedge m \neq m_i] < negl(\lambda)$, *where all the probabilities are computed over the random coins of the adversary and the signature algorithms. Furthermore,* $\Pr[(\text{vk}, \text{sk}) \leftarrow \text{GEN}(1^\lambda) : \text{VERDS}(\text{SIGNDS}(\text{sk}, m), \text{vk}, m) = 1] = 1$ *for every* m.

Definition 3 (Identity Based Signature (IBS) [22,26]). *The IBS scheme is a 5-algorithm tuple* IBS = $\langle \text{GEN}, \text{KEYDER}, \text{PUBKEYDER}, \text{SIGNIBS},$
$\text{VERIFYIBS} \rangle$, *which is an augmented version used in [16] of the originals proposed in [10]. Each algorithm is used as follows:*

- $\text{GEN}(1^\lambda) \rightarrow (\text{mvk}, \text{msk}):$ *The setup algorithm takes the security parameter and outputs the master key pair;*
- $\text{KEYDER}(\text{mvk}, \text{msk}, \ell) \rightarrow (\text{vk}_\ell, \text{sk}_\ell):$ *The regular signing key pair is derived with respect to the label* ℓ;
- $\text{PUBKEYDER}(\text{mvk}_\ell) \rightarrow \text{vk}_\ell:$ *It is possible derive only the verification key* PUBKEYDER *with only the label* ℓ *and the master verification key* mvk;
- $\text{SIGNIBS}(m, \text{sk}_\ell) \rightarrow \sigma:$ *This is the regular signing algorithm. That is, it requires only the message* m *and the secret key* sk;
- $\text{VERIFYIBS}(\sigma, m, \text{vk}_\ell) \rightarrow \{0, 1\}:$ *The verification[1] is performed, as usual, using the* vk, m *and* σ.

Given the space constraints and the loose connection with our proposed construction, we skip a full description of the security properties of the scheme. We refer the reader [16][Sect. 5] for a full description of them.

---

[1] Note that here, despite of being an Identity Based Signature, it requires vk_ℓ as input as it is defined in [16][Sect. 5].

Definition 4 (Combined Signature (CS) [16]). *The CS scheme is a 7-algorithm tuple* CS = ⟨MASTERKEYGEN, KEYSHAREGEN, COMBINEPUBKEY, COMBINEKEY, TESTKEY, SIGNCS, VERIFYCS⟩ *which was introduced informally in [24] and formally analized [16]. Each algorithm is used as follows:*

- MASTERKEYGEN(1^λ) → (mvk, msk): *The key generation algorithm takes the security parameter and outputs the master key pair;*
- KEYSHAREGEN(1^λ) → (vk, sk): *The key generation algorithm takes the security parameter and outputs a regular key pair;*
- COMBINEPUBKEY(mvk, vk) → cvk: *The combination algorithm combines both master and regular verification keys into a new verification key;*
- COMBINEKEY(mvk, msk, vk, sk) → (cvk, csk): *The combination algorithm receives both master and regular key pairs into a new combined key pair;*
- TESTKEY(vk, sk) → {0, 1}: *The test algorithm verifies if both keys are a regular key pair;*
- SIGNCS(m, csk) → σ: *It works as a regular signature generation algorithm which receives as input the message and the combined verification key;*
- VERIFYCS(σ, m, cvk) → {0, 1}: *The algorithm works as a regular verification signature algorithm which receives signature, message and the combined verification key.*

For similar reasons we refrain to describe the security properties of Definition 3, we also skip the the properties of Definition 4. Again, we refer the interested reader to [16][Sect. 9] for a full description of them. Later in Sect. 2.4, instances of these signature schemes are used in the payment-channel state and payment. Each participant of our protocol keeps one instance of the regular digital signature and three of the IBS (for payment, delay payment and HTLC) and one of the CS (for revocation of the old payment channel state).

2.3   The UTXO Model

Transactions in the Unspent Transactions Output (UTXO) Model, popularized by the Bitcoin Whitepaper [20], are composed by two parts: the set of *Inputs* $\mathcal{I}$, and the (ordered) list of *outputs* $\mathcal{O}$. A single output $o \in \mathcal{O}$ contains (1) the value of the output and (2) the condition to redeem that value, *e.g.*, [k : v, vk] for which k is the index number of the output the value v, and the witness for public key vk, meaning it requires the signature σ corresponding to vk. The condition could also include time constraints with respect the height of the latest block in the blockchain or the preimage of a hash value as in the HTLC. Furthermore, an input references existing output by pointing its index number in a transaction, that is Tx.$\mathcal{O}$[1] refers to the first output of transaction Tx. This mechanism of numbering the outputs is useful because $\mathcal{I}$ contains references of individual outputs in previous (settled) transactions. Settled transactions can be straightforwardly found in the distributed ledger, along with the witness (typically, a signature issued by the correct secret key) that allows a party to redeem the value of the original input.

Transaction Notation. Assume a participant A has the pair of public and secret key $(\mathsf{vk}, \mathsf{sk})$, if the pair controls a set of outputs $(o_1, o_2, o_3, \ldots)$, respectively in Tx_1, Tx_2 and Tx_3, then it is said that the state of A contains the mentioned outputs, i.e., $\Sigma_A = (o_1, o_2, o_3, \ldots)$. Thus, for example, a transaction $\mathsf{Tx}_{transfer}$ redeeming o_2, therefore transferring $\mathsf{v}/2$ to participant B and $\mathsf{v}/2$ to C is given by $\mathsf{Tx}_{transfer} \leftarrow \mathsf{Tx}\{\mathcal{I} : (\mathsf{Tx}_2.o_2); \mathcal{O} : [1 : \mathsf{v}/2, \mathsf{vk}_B], [2 : \mathsf{v}/2, \mathsf{vk}_C]\}$ and it requires, in order to be redeemed, the signature σ_A, as it contains $\mathsf{Tx}_2.o_2$ in its input set $\mathcal{I}$. Figure 1 illustrates this example.

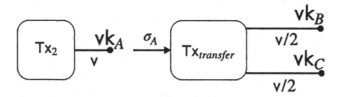

Fig. 1. In order to publish $\mathsf{Tx}_{transfer}$ and therefore redeem the output from Tx_2 and transfer values to B and C, A needs to provide a signature σ_A. In the multisig setting, it may also be possible that two signatures are necessary to redeem the output. Lightning Networks (later) relies on such a setting.

2.4   The Lightning Network

The Lightning Network (LN) [24] takes full advantage of the above model to move transactions outside of the ledger into the so-called Layer-2. Moreover LN was thoroughly described in [16], which shed light on some of the inner workings of the deployed protocol. In particular, it investigated the interplay between the different signature schemes and the HTLC hash value when funds are exchanged between more than two participants, i.e., a payment network. Briefly, in order to illustrate it, consider the existing channel between two players A and B. Without loss of generality, assume that only A has transferred some funds c_A to the channel AB. Assume also that another channel, say BC, exists between B and C, and similarly only B has funded it with c_B.

The main goal of the construction is to offer a way to transfer values from A to C without the creation of the channel AC. For that purpose, C picks a random value x and sends its hash value $y = H(x)$ directly to A. The protocol initiates by A triggering B in order to send the amount v to C, and the overall dynamics is inverted. That is, B, after being triggered by A, pays C the same amount to be transferred, i.e., v, and receives x in exchange. At this point, B is in deficit, because it did not received v yet. Then B exchanges x for v with A which can verify the equality $y = H(x)$.

Remark 1. In comparison to [16,24] our design for the channel has also two players: the Merchant and the Risk Buyer (as in [16,24]), however its use of the HTLC differs. The latter picks the HTLC pre-image x, keeps it secret while disclosing $y = H(x)$ to the Merchant. This design contrasts with [16,24] because in our case the provider of y, *i.e.*, Risk Buyer, is also the one receiving the payment. Later, in our construction, it is shown that the HTLC value x is used to both the delayed release of the payment, when Risk Buyer discloses x to the Merchant, and receiving the funds via the blockchain when publishing the transaction in the ledger.

Initial Setting. The above outlined protocol is a simplification, given that the actual implementation of a payment channel protocol is involved and requires a careful change of states between all the participants. In fact, the creation procedure of each pairwise channel, *e.g.*, between A and B, requires each participant to issue (1) a single *Funding* Transaction Tx_F and (2) a pair of *Commit* Transactions Tx_{commit}; one denoted *local* and the other *remote*. They differ for the signature used, A's or B's, to redeem the funding transactions.

Each participant keeps its key pairs: the regular signature key pair (vk, sk), the IBS key pairs $(\text{vk}_{dpay}, \text{sk}_{dpay})$, $(\text{vk}_{pay}, \text{sk}_{pay})$, and $(\text{vk}_{htlc}, \text{sk}_{htlc})$ for the HTLC, and the CS $(\text{vk}_{rev}, \text{sk}_{rev})$ as outlined in Sect. 2.2. It also keeps track of the counterpart's IBS verification keys vk_{dpay}, vk_{pay} and vk_{htlc}. Series of payments are performed as series of Commit Transaction exchanges between the two participants (with the first Commit Transaction pair being $n = 1$ for a n-long sequence). On every new payment, a new state of the channel is created. It is performed by generating a pair of new transactions, and their signatures, along with freshly derived key pairs are generated, and old committed transactions are revoked (by sharing the revocation keys with the counterpart). For a full specification of the mechanism we refer the reader to [16]. For now, it is enough to look into the two types of transaction pairs. They are

- Funding: The transaction Tx_F contains an output $o = [1 : c_A, \text{vk}_A]$, therefore $\text{Tx}_F.\mathcal{O}[1] = (c_A, \text{vk}_A \wedge \text{vk}_B)$, and it will be available on the ledger after the next transactions are signed;
- Commit: The first Commit Transaction redeems their outputs (if published), requiring only the signatures on their inputs as witness. However both transactions are kept locally when the channel is active. Concretely, A keeps the following transactions (analogously for B),

$$\text{Tx}^A_{local} \leftarrow \text{Tx}\{\mathcal{I} : (\text{Tx}_{F_A}.\mathcal{O}[1]); \mathcal{O} : [1 : c_A, \text{vk}^B_{rev,n=1} \vee (\text{vk}^A_{dpay,n=1}, \Delta_B)],$$
$$[2 : c_B, \text{vk}^B_{pay,n=1}]\}; \ and$$

$$\text{Tx}^A_{remote} \leftarrow \text{Tx}\{\mathcal{I} : (\text{Tx}_{F_B}.\mathcal{O}[1]); \mathcal{O} : [1 : c_A, \text{vk}^A_{pay,n=1}],$$
$$[2 : c_B, \text{vk}^A_{rev,n=1} \vee (\text{vk}^B_{dpay,n=1}, \Delta_A)]\},$$

along with signatures σ_A and σ_B with respect to vk_A and vk_B respectively.

Furthermore they also depend on the IBS keys, where $\text{vk}^B_{rev,n=1}$, $\text{vk}^B_{pay,n=1}$, $\text{vk}^B_{dpay,n=1}$ are the counterpart's verification keys, and $\text{vk}^A_{pay,n=1}$, $\text{vk}^A_{rev,n=1}$, $\text{vk}^A_{dpay,n=1}$ are the participant's own verification keys, along with the agreed delay

Δ_A and Δ_B which are arbitrarily chosen by each participant and exchanged prior to the creation of the Funding transactions.

Payment and State Revocation. Payments are performed by altering the balance, *i.e.*, c_A and c_B, via the exchange of new pairs of transactions from the initial state, *i.e.*, $\mathsf{Tx}_{remote,1}$ and $\mathsf{Tx}_{local,1}$. The initial state $n = 1$ progresses to the new state $n = 2$, *i.e.*, $\mathsf{Tx}_{remote,2}$ and $\mathsf{Tx}_{local,2}$ via exchange of signatures and new derived keys. Crucially, older states need to be "revoked" which is performed by the computation of the secret revocation key $\mathsf{sh}_{rev,n=1}$ of the old state. The main idea is that a participant is not financially incentivized to publish a transaction from an old state, because the counterpart can use its newly computed revocation key to redeem the funds. Briefly, if a participant publishes an old state, the counterpart can take all the funds of the channel. It is important to remark that the secret revocation key is only computed when the state is agreed to be "old", which prevents any party to misuse it.

During the HTLC, there is an intermediate state create by a pair of transaction $tx_{A,htlc}$ and $tx_{B,htlc}$, under locally derived HTLC keys ($\mathsf{vh}_{htlc}, \mathsf{vt}_{htlc}$), which redeems the outputs of the state transactions $\mathsf{Tx}_{remote,n}$ and $\mathsf{Tx}_{local,n}$ for the state n. A thorough discussion of revocation and the HTLC mechanism can be found in [16].

Time Analysis. The $n-$hop payment channel/network requires a careful setting between the (relative) time delay parameters $\Delta_1, \ldots, \Delta_{n-1}$, for the dispute of the payments, within each pairwise channel, in addition to the confirmation time of the consensus protocol, *i.e.*, $\Delta_{confirmation}$. This parameter is a theoretic value only, however, the security of deployed systems relies on timing values to be larger than $\Delta_{confirmation}$ such as the dispute time delay parameter Δ_{HTLC} when performing the HTLC procedure as well as Δ_A and Δ_B. While $\Delta_{confirmation}$ is unknown, values for Δ_{HTLC}, Δ_A and Δ_B are set by the implementation [19,23] in an attempt to capture the real delay of the protocol. The parameter Δ_{HTLC} can vary from 14 blocks [23] to a value between 14 and 144 blocks [19] whereas parameters Δ_A and Δ_B are set between 6 and 17 blocks[2]. In Maravedí, we remark that the dispute time delays are arbitrarily picked by each participant of the channel, say Δ_A and Δ_B, as it is defined in [16], and there is also the dispute time delay parameter Δ_{HTLC} when performing the HTLC procedure. In our construction we require that Δ_A, Δ_B, Δ_{HTLC} are greater than $\Delta_{confirmation}$, which, likewise [19,23], can be set by the concrete implementation. In Sect. 5, we only rely on Δ_A and Δ_B, for the Merchant and Risk Buyer, respectively, and Δ_{HTLC} for the intermediate state given it is a pairwise payment channel.

3 Desiderata

We overview the main requirements/characteristics, *i.e.*, desiderata for a protocol to trade risk, for each of the three classes of participants, namely *Customer*, *Merchant* and *Risk-Buyer*. We denote them respectively by C, M and R.

---

[2] https://github.com/lightningnetwork/lnd/blob/master/lnrpc/lightning.proto.

Let us start with the requirements/characteristics from C's point of view:

- **Instantaneous Finality:** The transaction performed between C and M should be instantaneous. That is, no confirmation time is required. Similarly to a physical transaction with physical goods;
- **Ad Hoc Availability:** The participant C should not be required to know M in advance. In the sense that any sort of interaction or preparation must not be required between M and C;
- **Background Availability:** The participant C may know R, and may interact with it via a direct communication channel prior to be in direct contact with M (it is the same for R later);
- **Trustless Trade:** There is no trust assumed between C and M.

From now we list the requirements/characteristics for M:

- **Instantaneous Settlement:** The merchant M should be in contact with R which allow instantaneous payment which can be created prior to any transaction between C and M;
- **Direct Interaction:** All transactions are exchanged via the direct (not necessarily secure) communication channel between C and M, and M and R;
- **Risk Trade Security:** For each accepted transaction, with an arbitrary value, M receives from R the same value minus a discount, via the already established payment channel (analogous[3] for R);
- **Trustless Risk Buyer:** There is no trust assumed between M and R (the same in the point of view of R).

Lastly we list the requirements/characteristics for R:

- **Allowed Pre-processing:** Prior to any performed transaction between C and M, a "pre-processing" phase is *allowed* (not necessarily related to a payment channel) to implement a instantaneous payment method between M and R with enough payment capacity;
- **Background Availability:** The participant R can potentially keep a list of (ledger) addresses for multiple customers C_i (for accessing the risk of buying C's risk, for example, and it is identical to C's case);
- **Risk Trade Security:** For every transaction accepted by M, R should receive the equal value (after the confirmation time) by publishing a regular transaction (*e.g.*, issued by C) in the ledger (analogous[4] for M).
- **Trustless Merchant:** There is no trust assumed between R and M (the same in the point of view of M).

We remark that C and R do not necessarily interact directly, unless they prior to the execution of the protocol. For example, in order to share "background" as in

---

[3] That is, the procedure of R and M are comparable in certain respects. In other words, they are not quite the same, because R does not receive anything. It, instead, pays the same value minus a discount to M, being its counterpart in the (single-hop) payment channel.

[4] In the sense of what already explained earlier.

the *Background Availability*. Therefore, we let it out of the desiderata. However, in the general case they do not necessarily trust each other.

For clarification, our protocol handles two types of transactions which we denote by *payment channel transaction* and *regular transaction*. Whereas the former is the transaction between M and R over the payment channel, the later is the one that relies on the blockchain confirmation time, and issued by C to be redeemed by R. Technically, there are only small differences between the two types which become clear later, however we highlight this terminology to avoid ambiguities and improve readability.

4   Outline of the Construction

The main phases of our protocol are *Protocol Set up*, *Issuing Transaction Proposal*, *Risk Buying*, and *Settlement* performed by M, C and R all with access to their respective states Σ_i for $i \in \{M, C, R\}$ via the ledger. Furthermore, we assume they have a pairwise direct communication channel. Their interaction happens through direct exchange of transactions: (1) Tx_C a regular transaction to be redeemed by R via ledger, and (2) the payment channel transaction Tx_R to be issued by R and assigned to M. Both transactions require the reveal of the HTLC preimage x picked by R. In addition to the value x, the payment channel transaction Tx_R requires signatures from R and M as it is standard in [24].

Our model starts with the instantiation of the payment channel in the beginning of a trading day as a "pre-processing" phase.

Protocol Set Up. Initially, each participant generates locally the verification and secret key pair (vk_i, sk_i) for $i \in \{M, C, R\}$. On the beginning of each trading day, R initiates a payment channel with M. Note that before accepting any transactions (from C), M and R are required to wait until the confirmation of the channel initialization as given by the consensus layer. This waiting time assures both players that the channel can be safely used.

Transaction Proposal. After the earlier described initial setting, assume a merchant M receives a transaction proposal $Tp = (v, vk_C)$ from C, for a value v. The Merchant M directly contacts R through a separated (and independent) communication channel, and offers Tp for trade.

Risk Buying. In the case R accepts Tp, then it hands back (d, vk_R, y) to M where y is the image for the HTLC, d is the discount of the value v, vk_R is its own public key where the payment should be directed, *i.e.,* regular transaction. At this point, M (1) signals C that the deal can continue by handing y to C, and (2) requests R the payment, which will be done via the payment channel. It follows that C generates (Tx_C, σ_C), where σ_C is the signature of Tx_C with respect to vk_C, and returns (Tx_C, σ_C) to M, while R and M perform the payment in the channel, *i.e.,* progress the channel from, say, state n to $n + 1$. At this point the intermediate state, for the HTLC, is created and both M and R revoke the previous ones.

Settlement. At this point, M has (Tx_C, σ_C) and submits it to R which receives in exchange of the HTLC pre-image x such that $y = h(x)$. Since M and R have both signatures for Tx_R and the value x for the HTLC hash value, the payment over the channel is performed for the value of $v - d$ to M, and R has (Tx_C, σ_C) which can be redeemed with its publication in the ledger. At this point, M already assured its payment in the channel, whereas R has to wait the confirmation time to settle its payment via the consensus protocol. As far as M is concerned the procedure is over therefore it can initiate another transaction with another customer any time. The properties of the channel assure M that its payment is guaranteed and available by the time of the closure of the channel. By the end of the trading day, both R and M jointly decide to close the channel, which frees the payments for M. This procedure is a regular one from any payment channel.

Remark 2. The overall actions rely on the procedures of a payment channel protocol like [16]. However our protocol uses the HTLC technique in a different way. That is, by adding the hash value into both Tx_C and Tx_R, by the time of the settlement of the transaction Tx_R on the chain the preimage is publicly disclosed, thus M can redeem the value received within the channel.

Remark 3. The early description briefly outlines the actions performed, however it is critical to note that the transaction via a payment channel is done by synchronized changes in the channel status of the participants. In particular, the preimage revealing is not performed by an exchange of Tx_R. In fact, the "transfer of Tx_R" is an interactive process that both players instantiate the new state and revoke the previous one (as it is standard in payment channels).

5   Our Protocol: Maravedí

Here we thoroughly describe our construction for the model in Sect. 4. We start by providing a general intuition of the protocol.

5.1   Intuition

Our protocol relies on the channel between M and R and it is an adaptation from LN as it is described in [16]. Here we skip the full specification of the payment channel, we refer the reader to [16] for a thorough description. For our purposes it suffices to describe the final configuration between the two parties by the end of the setup of the channel. Then we concretely describe our protocol and our adaptation to the use of the HTLC technique.

After exchanging of initial keys, the established requested delay time, *i.e.,* Δ_R and Δ_M, the participants perform the signing and publication of, respectively, the initial Commit Transactions, *i.e.,* Tx_{local} and Tx_{remote}, and the Funding Transaction Tx_{F_R}. Each payment received by the Merchant M from the Customer C is processed via the payment channel transaction (instantaneous payment) and a regular transaction (slow payment, performed in the ledger). Therefore the execution of the protocol starts from an initial set up, with $n = 1$ with the initial Commit Transaction. At a later moment, upon receiving a customer transaction, with the last signed Commit Transaction with index n, the protocol progresses to a new (intermediate) state for HTLC, *i.e.*, $n = n + 1$, and then to the final balance with (valid) state $n = n + 2$. Figure 2 illustrates the progress through the three states. Namely, it outlines the inclusion, and the removal, of the outputs into the locally kept pairs of Commit Transactions.

The closing of the channel works like a regular LN channel, *i.e.*, as described in [16]. Our protocol leverages on the original HTLC technique by atomically conditioning the payment channel transaction and the regular transaction, by adding the HTLC value to the latter and the former. With this setting, by the time R cashes in the payment via the ledger, it reveals the HTLC preimage allowing M to also redeem its own payment within the channel, even if R did not reveal the value previously. Note that, as in the regular payment channel, it is required that both participants are online.

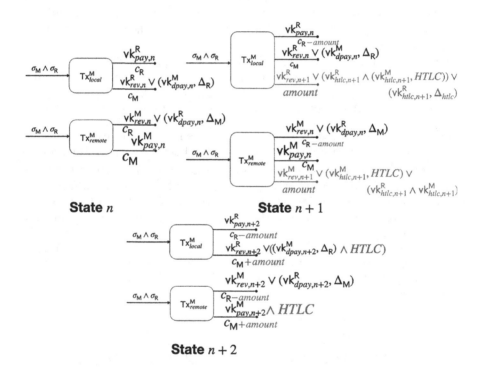

Fig. 2. This sequence of states illustrates the transferring of *amount*, and it depicts as the pairs of Commit Transactions kept locally by the merchant M. Note that in the intermediate state n + 1, in order to redeem the outputs, it is necessary to disclose the preimage of the HTLC value or wait for the delay Δ_{htlc}. Moreover the final state $n + 2$ the amount is transferred to the final outputs and conditioned to the revealing of the HTLC value. We highlight the update in the transactions in the intermediate state in blue, and the adaption of our protocol atomically payment between M and R in red. (Color figure online)

5.2 Concrete Construction

Maravedí progresses from the initial setting, the "pre-processing" phase, which is the creation of a regular LN channel. Thus it progresses as the phases outlined in Sect. 4. Hence we start from the initial state and by quickly reviewing the initial key generation. We remark that the initial phase is a regular creation of the LN channel, therefore we only briefly recall it. We refer the reader to a full discussion in [16].

Protocol Setup Up. As a regular LN channel construction, R and M generate private information and exchange cryptography keys. They are

- Randomnesses: seed^i for $i \in \{R, M\}$ which is used with the PRF in order to generate new randomness for the keys to be derived on each state of the channel;
- IBS Master keys: These keys, as pointed in [16], are necessary to optimize the exchange of keys. They are $\mathrm{GEN}(1^\lambda) \to (\mathsf{mvk}^i_{dpay}, \mathsf{msk}^i_{dpay}), (\mathsf{mvk}^i_{pay}, \mathsf{msk}^i_{pay})$, $(\mathsf{mvk}^i_{htlc}, \mathsf{msk}^i_{htlc}), (\mathsf{vk}^i_{com}, \mathsf{sk}^i_{com})$ for $i \in \{R, M\}$, and they are used to derive new keys for the each new state;
- CS Master keys: This key pair is also used to optimize the key exchange. Furthermore it is used to generate the revocation key which allows the participant to revoke an old state of the channel. The key pairs are given by setting $\mathrm{MASTERKEYGEN}(1^\lambda) \to (\mathsf{mvk}^i_{rev}, \mathsf{msk}^i_{rev})$ for $i \in \{R, M\}$.

These initial keys are used to generate and derive new keys for each state. Concretely, R has $\mathsf{vk_R}, \mathsf{sk_R}$ to create the channel, and starts by generating, for the first state, $(\mathsf{vk}^R_{com,1}, \mathsf{sk}^R_{com,1}), \mathsf{vk}^R_{pay,1}, \mathsf{vk}^R_{rev,1}, \mathsf{vk}^R_{dpay,1}, \mathsf{vk}^R_{htlc,2}$ (and its respective secret keys), and keeps track of $\mathsf{vk}^M_{rev,1}, \mathsf{vk}^M_{pay,1}, \mathsf{vk}^M_{dpay,1}, \mathsf{vk}^M_{htlc,2}$ which are M public keys. Vice-versa for M which also keeps track of R's verification keys. Note that both parties also have their respective keys regarding the Funding Transaction $\mathsf{vk_R}$ and $\mathsf{vk_M}$.

Later, R accesses its state Σ_R in the ledger to issue the Funding Transaction, and exchanges it (after the local Commit Transactions are securely signed and exchanged). In the end of the process, R keeps the following two Commit Transactions

$$\mathrm{Tx}^R_{local} \leftarrow \mathrm{Tx}\{\mathcal{I} : (\mathrm{Tx}_{F_R}.\mathcal{O}[1]); \mathcal{O} : [1 : c, \mathsf{vk}^M_{rev,1} \vee (\mathsf{vk}^R_{dpay,1}, \Delta_M)], [2 : 0, \mathsf{vk}^M_{pay,1}]\},$$

$$\mathrm{Tx}^R_{remote} \leftarrow \mathrm{Tx}\{\mathcal{I} : (\mathrm{Tx}_{F_R}.\mathcal{O}[1]); \mathcal{O} : [1 : c, \mathsf{vk}^R_{pay,1}], [2 : 0, \mathsf{vk}^R_{rev,1} \vee (\mathsf{vk}^M_{dpay,1}, \Delta_R)]\},$$

while M keeps

$$\mathrm{Tx}^M_{local} \leftarrow \mathrm{Tx}\{\mathcal{I} : (\mathrm{Tx}_{F_R}.\mathcal{O}[1]); \mathcal{O} : [1 : c, \mathsf{vk}^R_{pay,1}], [2 : 0, \mathsf{vk}^R_{rev,1} \vee (\mathsf{vk}^M_{dpay,1}, \Delta_R)]\},$$

$$\mathrm{Tx}^M_{remote} \leftarrow \mathrm{Tx}\{\mathcal{I} : (\mathrm{Tx}_{F_R}.\mathcal{O}[1]); \mathcal{O} : [1 : c, \mathsf{vk}^M_{rev,1} \vee (\mathsf{vk}^R_{dpay,1}, \Delta_M)], [1 : 0, \mathsf{vk}^M_{pay,1}]\},$$

with both participants having either the signature σ_R or σ_M for each of the locally kept transactions. Note that both transactions rely on the original funds

c provided by R in the Funding Transaction Tx_{F_R}. Although M can also add funds to the channel, as in a regular payment channel, in our construction, it just receives them from R, therefore a single source of funds suffices for us.

Each participant keeps track of the last n committed transactions, starting from $n = 1$, such that $\text{Tx}_{remote} = \text{Tx}_{remote,1}$ and $\text{Tx}_{local} = \text{Tx}_{local,1}$. Moreover, the channel is assigned with a flag Channel to monitor the channel with a pair of values $(id, note)$ initially set empty, i.e., Channel $\leftarrow \perp$, such that $note$ is a string which identifies the state of the channel, and id is an identifier for the payment to be performed.

Transaction Proposal. According to the early described model, C submits a transaction proposal $\text{Tp} = (\text{v}, \text{vk}_C)$, for an amount v and C's verification key, to M which performs the following

- Picks a uniformly random unique identifier $payid$
- Sets Channel$^M \leftarrow (payid, \cdot)$
- Checks if there is a payment channel with R with capacity greater than v
- Adds to the list pendingGetPay the tuple $(\text{vk}_C, \text{v}, payid, \cdot, \text{"Waiting update"})$
- Submits $(\text{vk}_C, \text{v}, payid)$ to R via a direct communication channel.

The lists pendingPay and pendingGetPay are used to keep track of the payments and their current status on either participants.

Risk Buying/Preparation. Given a hash function H, R picks the value of the HTLC preimage, and, jointly with M, prepares its pair of local transactions, i.e., Tx_{local} and Tx_{remote}. That is, R performs as follows upon receiving $(\text{vk}_C, \text{v}, payid)$:

- Verifies if $\nexists (\text{vk}_C, \alpha, \beta, \theta, \gamma, payid, \cdot)$ in pendingPay for any α, β, θ and γ. Otherwise, close the channel
- Picks a random value x in the domain of H
- Sets Channel$^R \leftarrow (payid, \cdot)$
- Sets $(\text{vk}_C, \text{vk}_M, H(x), x, \text{v}, payid, \text{"}Waiting update\text{"})$ to pendingPay
- Picks Δ_{htlc}, for delay period, and sends $(payid, H(x), \Delta_{htlc})$ to M

Upon receiving the message $(payid, y, \Delta_{htlc})$ from R, M prepares its local transactions accordingly, which concretely means to add new outputs into the local kept transactions Tx_{local} and Tx_{remote}. The new outputs are related to the value of the received hash value y. In other words, M proceeds to perform the following upon receiving $(payid, y, \Delta_{htlc})$:

- If $(\text{vk}_C, \text{v}, payid, \cdot, \text{"}Waiting update\text{"}) = \text{pendingGetPay}$, then
  - Removes "Waiting update" from the entry, and adds y to the entry, i.e., $(\text{vk}_C, \text{v}, payid, y, \cdot) \in \text{pendingGetPay}$
- Update its locally kept transactions by adding the third output (in blue) with respect to the HTLC state on each transaction:

$$\text{Tx}^M_{local} \leftarrow \text{Tx}\{\mathcal{I} : (\text{Tx}_{F_R}.\mathcal{O}[1]); \mathcal{O} : [1 : c_R - (\text{v} - \text{d}), \text{vk}^R_{pay,n}],$$
$$[2 : c_M, \text{vk}^R_{rev,n} \vee (\text{vk}^M_{dpay,n}, \Delta_R)],$$
$$[3 : \text{v} - \text{d}, \text{vk}^R_{rev,n+1} \vee (\text{vk}^R_{htlc,n+1} \wedge (\text{vk}^M_{htlc,n+1}, y)) \vee (\text{vk}^R_{htlc,n+1}, \Delta_{htlc})]\},$$

$$\mathsf{Tx}^{\mathsf{M}}_{remote} \leftarrow \mathsf{Tx}\{\mathcal{I} : (\mathsf{Tx}_{F_{\mathsf{R}}}.\mathcal{O}[1]); \mathcal{O} : [1 : c_{\mathsf{R}}-(\mathsf{v}-\mathsf{d}), \mathsf{vk}^{\mathsf{M}}_{rev,n} \vee (\mathsf{vk}^{\mathsf{R}}_{dpay,n}, \Delta_{\mathsf{M}})],$$

$$[2 : c_{\mathsf{M}}, \mathsf{vk}^{\mathsf{M}}_{pay,n}],$$

$$[3 : \mathsf{v}-\mathsf{d}, \mathsf{vk}^{\mathsf{M}}_{rev,n+1} \vee (\mathsf{vk}^{\mathsf{M}}_{htlc,n+1}, y) \vee (\mathsf{vk}^{\mathsf{M}}_{htlc,n+1} \wedge \mathsf{vk}^{\mathsf{R}}_{htlc,n+1})]\},$$

where c_{R} and c_{M} are the current balances, and the public keys derived from the initial state, in the channel for the $n-$th payment

- Forward $(\mathsf{v}, \mathsf{vk}_{\mathsf{R}}, y)$ to C, which replies with $(\mathsf{Tx}_{\mathsf{C}}, \sigma_{\mathsf{C}})$ such that $\mathsf{Tx}_{\mathsf{C}} \leftarrow \mathsf{Tx}\{\mathcal{I} : o \in \Sigma_{\mathsf{C}}; \mathcal{O} : [1 : \mathsf{v}, \mathsf{vk}_{\mathsf{R}} \wedge y]\}$ which pays directly to R (redeeming C's outputs in Σ_{C}) conditionally to the disclosure of the preimage of y. Hence M submits (UPDATEADDHTLC, $payid$) message to R, meaning R can update its locally kept transactions.

At this point, only M has prepared its internally kept transactions. Thus it is R's turn to set its transaction variables similarly.

- Verifies if $\exists(\mathsf{vk}_{\mathsf{C}}, \alpha, \beta, \theta, \gamma, payid, note)$ in pendingPay for any α, β, θ and γ, and $note = $ "$Waitingupdate$". Otherwise, close the channel
- Upon receiving the message (UPDATEADDHTLC,$payid$), R updates (in blue) its local transactions as follows:

$$\mathsf{Tx}^{\mathsf{R}}_{local} \leftarrow \mathsf{Tx}\{\mathcal{I} : (\mathsf{Tx}_{F_{\mathsf{R}}}.\mathcal{O}[1]); \mathcal{O} : [1 : c_{\mathsf{R}}-(\mathsf{v}-\mathsf{d}), \mathsf{vk}^{\mathsf{M}}_{rev,n} \vee (\mathsf{vk}^{\mathsf{R}}_{dpay,n}, \Delta_{\mathsf{M}})],$$

$$[2 : c_{\mathsf{M}}, \mathsf{vk}^{\mathsf{M}}_{pay,n}],$$

$$[3 : \mathsf{v}-\mathsf{d}, \mathsf{vk}^{\mathsf{M}}_{rev,n+1} \vee (\mathsf{vk}^{\mathsf{M}}_{htlc,n+1}, y) \vee (\mathsf{vk}^{\mathsf{M}}_{htlc,n+1} \wedge \mathsf{vk}^{\mathsf{R}}_{htlc,n+1})]\};$$

$$\mathsf{Tx}^{\mathsf{R}}_{remote} \leftarrow \mathsf{Tx}\{\mathcal{I} : (\mathsf{Tx}_{F_{\mathsf{R}}}.\mathcal{O}[1]); \mathcal{O} : [1 : c_{\mathsf{R}}-(\mathsf{v}-\mathsf{d}), \mathsf{vk}^{\mathsf{R}}_{pay,n}],$$

$$[2 : c_{\mathsf{M}}, \mathsf{vk}^{\mathsf{R}}_{rev,n} \vee (\mathsf{vk}^{\mathsf{M}}_{dpay,n}, \Delta_{\mathsf{R}})],$$

$$[3 : \mathsf{v}-\mathsf{d}, \mathsf{vk}^{\mathsf{R}}_{rev,n+1} \vee (\mathsf{vk}^{\mathsf{R}}_{htlc,n+1} \wedge (\mathsf{vk}^{\mathsf{M}}_{htlc,n+1}, y)) \vee (\mathsf{vk}^{\mathsf{R}}_{htlc,n+1}, \Delta_{htlc})]\}.$$

- R moves $(\mathsf{vk}_{\mathsf{C}}, \mathsf{vk}_{\mathsf{M}}, H(x), x, \mathsf{v}, payid, note)$ from pendingPay to paid, and sets pendingPay $= \bot$
- Sets $(payid, x) \rightarrow$ pendingFulfill

Risk Buying/Agreement-R *Side*. At this point, M and R proceed to create new HTLC Commitment transactions which relies on the previously updated transactions, respectively redeeming their HTLC outputs. First, R performs the following, assuming, as before, $\mathsf{Tx}^{\mathsf{R}}_{remote,n}$ is the last signed transaction:

- Verifies if $\mathsf{Tx}^{\mathsf{R}}_{remote} \neq \mathsf{Tx}^{\mathsf{R}}_{remote,n}$. Otherwise stop
- Verifies $(payid, note) = $ Channel^{R}, such that $note \neq$ "$waitingfor$ REVOKEANDACK"

- Sets $\text{Tx}_{remote,n+1}^{R} \leftarrow \text{Tx}_{remote}^{R}$
- Sets $\sigma_{remote,n+1,R} \leftarrow \text{SIGNDS}(\text{Tx}_{remote,n+1}^{R}, \text{sk}_R)$
- Issue an unsigned Remote HTLC transaction

$$\text{Tx}_{remHTLC,n+1}^{R} \leftarrow \text{Tx}\{\mathcal{I} : (\text{Tx}_{remote,n+1}^{R}.\mathcal{O}[3]);$$
$$\mathcal{O} : [1 : v - d, \text{vk}_{rev,n+1}^{R} \vee (\text{vk}_{dpay,n+1}^{M}, \Delta_R)]\}$$

- Set $\sigma_{htlc,n+1,M} \leftarrow \text{SIGNIBS}(\text{Tx}_{remHTLC,n+1}^{R}, \text{sk}_{htlc,n+1}^{R})$
- Set $note \leftarrow$ "$waiting for \text{REVOKEANDACK}$", and $\text{Channel}^R \leftarrow (payid, note)$
- Send M the tuple $(payid, \sigma_{remote,n+1,R}, \sigma_{htlc,n+1,R})$

At this point R creates a new status by sending the necessary signatures to M (and revoking the previous state), which verifies its secret key sh_R for the $(n + 1)$-th Commit Transaction, and transaction that redeems the newly added output (which sets the funds in a special state due to the HTLC technique). Therefore M performs the following upon receiving the signatures $(payid, ComSig, HTLCSig)$, respectively for the Commit and HTLC Transactions:

- Verifies $(payid, note)$ = Channel^M, such that $note \neq$ "$waiting for \text{REVOKEANDACK}$", otherwise stop
- Let $\text{Tx}_{local,n}^{M}$ be the last signed transaction, then it verifies if $\text{Tx}_{local}^{M} \neq \text{Tx}_{local,n}^{M}$. Otherwise stop
- If $\text{VERDS}(ComSig, \text{Tx}_{local}^{M}, \text{vk}_R) = 0$, then close the channel
- Sets

$$\text{Tx}_{localHTLC,n+1}^{M} \leftarrow \text{Tx}\{\mathcal{I} : \text{Tx}_{local}^{M}.\mathcal{O}[3];$$
$$\mathcal{O} : [1 : v - d, \text{vk}_{rev,n+1}^{R} \vee (\text{vk}_{dpay,n+1}^{M}, \Delta_R)]\}$$

- If $\text{VERIFYIBS}(HTLCSig, \text{Tx}_{localHTLC,n+1}^{M}, \text{vk}_{htlc,n+1}^{R}) = 0$, then close the channel
- Sets $note \leftarrow$ "$irrevocably committed$" and adds $(\text{Tx}_{local}^{M}, note)$ to the list pendingLocalCom^M
- Sets $\text{prand}_{n+2}^{M} \leftarrow \text{PRF}(\text{seed}^M, n + 2)$
- Sets $(\text{vk}_{com,n+2}^{M}, sk_{com,n+2}^{M}) \leftarrow \text{KEYSHAREGEN}(1^\lambda, \text{prand}_{n+2}^{M})$
- Send $(payid, \text{sk}_{com,n}^{M}, \text{vk}_{com,n+2}^{M})$ to R

We remark that disclosing the previous key $\text{sk}_{com,n}^{M}$ is part of the revocation process to invalidate the previous state of the channel. Such a mechanism allows R to combine the keys (property of the Combined Signature Scheme as outlined in Sect. 2), and to obtain the secret revocation key $\text{sk}_{rev,n}^{R}$.

From now, on R's side, it starts the final step of this phase: verifies whether the received keys from M are correct, derive new ones and update the flags. Concretely, upon receiving $(payid, \text{sk}_{com,n}^{M}, \text{vk}_{com,n+2}^{M})$, R proceeds as follows:

- Retrieve *note* from $\mathtt{Channel}^R$, and verify if *note* = *"waiting for* REVOKE ANDACK". Otherwise close the channel
- If TESTKEY$(\mathsf{vk}^M_{com,n}, \mathsf{sk}^M_{com,n}) = 0$, then close the channel
- Set *note* ← *"irrevocably committed"*, and add to the list $\mathtt{pendingRemoteCom}^R$ the tuple $(\mathsf{Tx}^R_{remote}, note)$
- Derive new keys by setting
  - $\mathsf{sk}^R_{rev,n} \leftarrow$ COMBINEKEY$(\mathsf{msk}^R_{rev}, \mathsf{msk}^R_{rev}, \mathsf{vk}^M_{com,n}, \mathsf{sk}^M_{com,n})$
  - $\mathsf{vk}^R_{rev,n+2} \leftarrow$ COMBINEPUBKEY$(\mathsf{msk}^R_{rev}, \mathsf{vk}^M_{com,n+2})$
  - $\mathsf{vk}^M_{rev,n+2} \leftarrow$ COMBINEPUBKEY$(\mathsf{msk}^R_{rev}, \mathsf{vk}^R_{com,n+2})$
  - $(\mathsf{vk}^R_{dpay,n+2}, \mathsf{sk}^R_{dpay,n+2}) \leftarrow$ KEYDER$(\mathsf{mvk}^R_{dpay}, \mathsf{msk}^R_{dpay}, \mathsf{vk}^R_{com,n+2})$
  - $\mathsf{vk}^M_{dpay,n+2} \leftarrow$ PUBKEYDER$(\mathsf{mvk}^M_{dpay}, \mathsf{vk}^M_{com,n+2})$
  - $(\mathsf{vk}^R_{pay,n+2}, \mathsf{sk}^R_{pay,n+2}) \leftarrow$ KEYDER$(\mathsf{mvk}^R_{pay}, \mathsf{msk}^R, \mathsf{vk}^R_{com,n+2})$
  - $\mathsf{vk}^M_{pay,n+2} \leftarrow$ PUBKEYDER$(\mathsf{mvk}^M_{pay}, \mathsf{vk}^M_{com,n+2})$
  - $(\mathsf{vk}^R_{htlc,n+2}, \mathsf{sk}^R_{htlc,n+2}) \leftarrow$ KEYDER$(\mathsf{mvk}^R_{htlc}, \mathsf{msk}^R_{htlc}, \mathsf{vk}^R_{com,n+2})$
  - $\mathsf{vk}^M_{htlc,n+2} \leftarrow$ PUBKEYDER$(\mathsf{mvk}^M_{htlc}, \mathsf{vk}^M_{com,n+2})$
- Set *note* ← " · ", and update $\mathtt{Channel}^R$

At this point R computed the $\mathsf{sk}^R_{rev,n}$ meaning that the n-th state is "irrevocably revoked" because if the counterpart M tries to publish this state R can use it to redeem all the contents of the channel via the second output of Tx^M_{local}. Furthermore, an intermediate state is partially created by Tx^R_{remote} where the funds $(v - d)$ are carried. In order to fully create the intermediate state, it is necessary that M performs its side of the procedure.

***Risk Buying/Agreement*-M *Side*.** The case is analogous to the R, which means that both states, for M and R, are committed. Briefly M generates the signature $\sigma_{remote,n+1,M} \leftarrow$ SIGNDS$(\mathsf{Tx}^M_{remote,n+1}, \mathsf{sk}_M)$, for $\mathsf{Tx}^M_{remote,n+1} \leftarrow \mathsf{Tx}^M_{remote}$, and issues a unsigned remote HTLC transaction

$$\mathsf{Tx}^M_{remHTLC,n+1} \leftarrow \mathsf{Tx}\{\mathcal{I} : (\mathsf{Tx}^M_{remote,n}.\mathcal{O}[3]);$$
$$\mathcal{O} : [1 : v - d, \mathsf{vk}^M_{rev,n+1} \vee (\mathsf{vk}^R_{dpay,n+1}, \Delta_M)]\},$$

and sets

$$\sigma_{htlc,n+1,M} \leftarrow \text{SIGNIBS}(\mathsf{Tx}^M_{remHTLC,n+1}, \mathsf{sk}^M_{htlc,n+1}),$$

and submits to R which verifies both $\sigma_{remote,n+1,M}$ and $\sigma_{htlc,n+1,M}$ (which R verifies with its locally kept $\mathsf{Tx}^R_{localHTLC,n+1}$). Moreover M derives the new keys, namely, $\mathsf{vk}^M_{rev,n+2}$, $\mathsf{vk}^R_{rev,n+2}$, $(\mathsf{vk}^M_{dpay,n+2}, \mathsf{sk}^M_{dpay,n+2})$, $\mathsf{vk}^R_{dpay,n+2}$, $(\mathsf{vk}^M_{pay,n+2}, \mathsf{sk}^M_{pay,n+2})$, $\mathsf{vk}^R_{pay,n+2}$, $(\mathsf{vk}^M_{htlc,n+2}, \mathsf{sk}^M_{htlc,n+2})$, $\mathsf{vk}^R_{htlc,n+2}$. In particular, M also computes the revocation key $\mathsf{sk}^M_{rev,n}$ (in a similar fashion as R did).

Crucially, the participants keep the states in two lists, namely, for $i \in \{M, R\}$, $\mathtt{pendingLocalCom}^i$ and $\mathtt{pendingRemoteCom}^i$, in order to keep track of the committed transactions. This design guarantees that the new state is revoked only when the next one is signed on both sides.

Settlement. Here, the previous state n is successfully revoked on both sides, however the funds are in the intermediated HTLC state $n+1$. For now it remains (1) to move to the final value to state $n + 2$ (when M receives the funds); (2) R to reveal the preimage x to M; and (3) M to submit $(\text{Tx}_{buy}, \sigma_{buy})$ to R. This final step allows R to cash the value later via the ledger when it publishes the transaction. However it is first necessary to finalize the payment within the channel, which means to revoke the state $n + 1$. Therefore R verifies whether M has not submitted its transaction to the ledger as follows

– Reads the ledger to update the outputs in the state $\Sigma_{\textsf{R}}$
– R checks if M has not submitted transaction to the ledger. That is, if the outputs $\text{Tx}^{\textsf{R}}_{remote}.\mathcal{O} \notin \Sigma_{\textsf{R}}$, then
  • Send message $(\textsc{Settlement}, payid)$ to M
  Otherwise
  • if $\exists(\alpha, \beta, \gamma, H(x), x, payid, note) = \texttt{paid}$, then remove the entry
  • Set

$$\text{Tx}^{\textsf{R}}_{pay} \leftarrow \text{Tx}\{\mathcal{I} : \text{Tx}^{\textsf{R}}_{remote,com}.\mathcal{O}[3]; \mathcal{O} : [1 : \textsf{v} - \textsf{d}, \textsf{vk}^{\textsf{R}}_{htlc,n}]\}$$

  • Set $\sigma_{pay} \leftarrow \textsc{SignIBS}(\text{Tx}_{pay}, \textsf{sk}^{\textsf{R}}_{htlc,n})$
  • Submit $(\text{Tx}_{pay}, \sigma_{pay})$ to ledger

In case M has not submitted the transaction to the ledger, then it receives $(\textsc{Settlement}, payid)$, and it performs

– Verifies $(payid, note) = \texttt{Channel}^{\textsf{M}}$, such that $note \neq$ "$waiting for$ $\textsc{RevokeAndAck}$", otherwise stop
– M removes the outputs (added in the preparation phase) of its locally kept remote and local transactions, and update the balance. That is, it sets

$$\text{Tx}^{\textsf{M}}_{local} \leftarrow \text{Tx}\{\mathcal{I} : (\text{Tx}_{F_{\textsf{R}}}.\mathcal{O}[1]); \mathcal{O} : [1 : c_{\textsf{R}}-(\textsf{v} - \textsf{d}), \textsf{vk}^{\textsf{R}}_{pay,n+2}],$$
$$[2 : c_{\textsf{M}}+(\textsf{v} - \textsf{d}), \textsf{vk}^{\textsf{R}}_{rev,n+2} \vee ((\textsf{vk}^{\textsf{M}}_{dpay,n+2}, \Delta_{\textsf{R}})\wedge y)]\},$$

and

$$\text{Tx}^{\textsf{M}}_{remote} \leftarrow \text{Tx}\{\mathcal{I} : (\text{Tx}_{F_{\textsf{R}}}.\mathcal{O}[1]);$$
$$\mathcal{O} : [1 : c_{\textsf{R}}-(\textsf{v} - \textsf{d}), \textsf{vk}^{\textsf{M}}_{rev,n+2} \vee (\textsf{vk}^{\textsf{R}}_{dpay,n+2}, \Delta_{\textsf{M}})],$$
$$[2 : c_{\textsf{M}}+(\textsf{v} - \textsf{d}), \textsf{vk}^{\textsf{M}}_{pay,n+2}\wedge y]\}.$$

– Sets $\sigma_{remote,n+2,\textsf{M}} \leftarrow \textsc{SignDS}(\text{Tx}^{\textsf{M}}_{remote}, \textsf{sk}_{\textsf{M}})$
– Sets $note \leftarrow$ "$waiting for \textsc{RevokeAndAck}$", and $\texttt{Channel}^{\textsf{M}} \leftarrow (payid, note)$
– Sends R the tuple $(payid, \sigma_{remote,n+2,\textsf{M}})$

Note that the preimage of y (in red) is necessary to redeem the output, and it will only be available after R discloses it, upon receiving the transaction issued by C.

From this point, in case R verifies M's signature on its local version of the transaction it can revoke its old state $n + 1$. Thus R starts by creating the locally kept Commit Transactions for state $n + 2$. Upon receiving $(payid, ComSig)$, R does as follows:

- Analogous to the procedure performed by M, R updates its new state by removing the HTLC outputs and adjusting the balance:

$$\mathrm{Tx}^{\mathsf{R}}_{local} \leftarrow \mathrm{Tx}\{\mathcal{I} : (\mathrm{Tx}_{F_{\mathsf{R}}}.\mathcal{O}[1]);$$
$$\mathcal{O} : [1 : c_{\mathsf{R}}-(v-\mathsf{d}), \mathsf{vk}^{\mathsf{M}}_{rev,n+2} \vee (\mathsf{vk}^{\mathsf{R}}_{dpay,n+2}, \Delta_{\mathsf{M}})],$$
$$[2 : c_{\mathsf{M}}+(v-\mathsf{d}), \mathsf{vk}^{\mathsf{M}}_{pay,n+2}\wedge y]\}; and$$

$$\mathrm{Tx}^{\mathsf{R}}_{remote} \leftarrow \mathrm{Tx}\{\mathcal{I} : (\mathrm{Tx}_{F_{\mathsf{R}}}.\mathcal{O}[1]); \mathcal{O} : [1 : c_{\mathsf{R}}-(v-\mathsf{d}), \mathsf{vk}^{\mathsf{R}}_{pay,n+2}],$$
$$[2 : c_{\mathsf{M}}+(v-\mathsf{d}), \mathsf{vk}^{\mathsf{R}}_{rev,n+2} \vee ((\mathsf{vk}^{\mathsf{M}}_{dpay,n+2}, \Delta_{\mathsf{R}})\wedge y)]\}.$$

- If $\mathrm{VERDS}(ComSig, \mathrm{Tx}^{\mathsf{R}}_{local}, \mathsf{vk_M}) = 0$, then close the channel
- Verifies $(payid, note)$ = $\mathtt{Channel}$, such that $note \neq$ "$waiting\,for\,\mathrm{REVOKEANDACK}$"
- Sets $note \leftarrow$ "$irrevocably\,committed$" and $\mathtt{pendingLocalCom}^{\mathsf{R}} \leftarrow (\mathrm{Tx}^{\mathsf{R}}_{local}, note)$
- Sets $\mathrm{prand}^{\mathsf{R}}_{n+3} \leftarrow \mathrm{PRF}(seed^{\mathsf{R}}, n+3)$
- Sets $(\mathsf{vk}^{\mathsf{R}}_{com,n+3}, sk^{\mathsf{R}}_{com,n+3}) \leftarrow \mathrm{KEYSHAREGEN}(1^{\lambda}, \mathrm{prand}^{\mathsf{R}}_{n+3})$
- Sends $(payid, \mathsf{sk}^{\mathsf{R}}_{com,n+1}, \mathsf{vk}^{\mathsf{R}}_{com,n+3})$ to M

As before, the disclosing of $\mathsf{sk}^{\mathsf{R}}_{com,n+1}$ allows M to compute the revocation key and therefore R has revoked the $n+1$ state of the channel on its side. From this point, M can also revoke its state, and derive a whole new set of keys for the next state. The derivation on M's side is similar as before

- $\mathsf{sk}^{\mathsf{M}}_{rev,n+1} \leftarrow \mathrm{COMBINEKEY}(\mathsf{msk}^{\mathsf{M}}_{rev}, \mathsf{msk}^{\mathsf{M}}_{rev}, \mathsf{vk}^{\mathsf{R}}_{com,n+1}, \mathsf{sk}^{\mathsf{R}}_{com,n+1})$
- $\mathsf{vk}^{\mathsf{M}}_{rev,n+3} \leftarrow \mathrm{COMBINEPUBKEY}(\mathsf{msk}^{\mathsf{M}}_{rev}, \mathsf{vk}^{\mathsf{R}}_{com,n+3})$
- $\mathsf{vk}^{\mathsf{R}}_{rev,n+3} \leftarrow \mathrm{COMBINEPUBKEY}(\mathsf{msk}^{\mathsf{M}}_{rev}, \mathsf{vk}^{\mathsf{R}}_{com,n+3})$
- $(\mathsf{vk}^{\mathsf{M}}_{dpay,n+3}, \mathsf{sk}^{\mathsf{M}}_{dpay,n+3}) \leftarrow \mathrm{KEYDER}(\mathsf{mvk}^{\mathsf{M}}_{dpay}, \mathsf{msk}^{\mathsf{M}}_{dpay}, \mathsf{vk}^{\mathsf{M}}_{com,n+3})$
- $\mathsf{vk}^{\mathsf{R}}_{dpay,n+3} \leftarrow \mathrm{PUBKEYDER}(\mathsf{mvk}^{\mathsf{R}}_{dpay}, \mathsf{vk}^{\mathsf{R}}_{com,n+3})$
- $(\mathsf{vk}^{\mathsf{M}}_{pay,n+3}, \mathsf{sk}^{\mathsf{M}}_{pay,n+3}) \leftarrow \mathrm{KEYDER}(\mathsf{mvk}^{\mathsf{M}}_{pay}, \mathsf{msk}^{\mathsf{M}}, \mathsf{vk}^{\mathsf{M}}_{com,n+3})$
- $\mathsf{vk}^{\mathsf{R}}_{pay,n+3} \leftarrow \mathrm{PUBKEYDER}(\mathsf{mvk}^{\mathsf{R}}_{pay}, \mathsf{vk}^{\mathsf{R}}_{com,n+3})$
- $(\mathsf{vk}^{\mathsf{M}}_{htlc,n+3}, \mathsf{sk}^{\mathsf{M}}_{htlc,n+3}) \leftarrow \mathrm{KEYDER}(\mathsf{mvk}^{\mathsf{M}}_{htlc}, \mathsf{msk}^{\mathsf{M}}_{htlc}, \mathsf{vk}^{\mathsf{M}}_{com,n+3})$
- $\mathsf{vk}^{\mathsf{R}}_{htlc,n+3} \leftarrow \mathrm{PUBKEYDER}(\mathsf{mvk}^{\mathsf{R}}_{htlc}, \mathsf{vk}^{\mathsf{R}}_{com,n+3})$
- Set $note \leftarrow$ "$\cdot$", and update $\mathtt{Channel}^{\mathsf{M}}$

Analogously, M revokes its state channel when verifying the signature of R with its locally kept transaction. Therefore R performs as follows

- Sets $\sigma_{remote,n+2,\mathsf{R}} \leftarrow \mathrm{SIGNDS}(\mathrm{Tx}^{\mathsf{R}}_{remote}, \mathsf{sk_R})$
- Sets $note \leftarrow$ "$waiting\,for\,\mathrm{REVOKEANDACK}$", and $\mathtt{Channel}^{\mathsf{R}} \leftarrow (payid, note)$
- Sends M the tuple $(payid, \sigma_{remote,n+2,\mathsf{R}})$

Upon receiving $(payid, Comsig)$, If $\mathrm{VERDS}(ComSig, \mathrm{Tx}^{\mathsf{M}}_{local}, \mathsf{vk_R}) = 0$, then close the channel. Otherwise M does the following:

- Verifies $(payid, note)$ $=$ $\mathtt{Channel}^M$, such that $note \neq \text{``}waiting\,for\,\text{REVOKEANDACK''}$
- Sets $note \leftarrow \text{``}irrevocably\,committed\text{''}$ and $\mathtt{pendingLocalCom}^M \leftarrow (\mathsf{Tx}^R_{local}, note)$
- Sets $\mathsf{prand}^M_{n+3} \leftarrow \mathrm{PRF}(\mathsf{seed}^M, n+3)$
- Sets $(\mathsf{vk}^M_{com,n+3}, \mathsf{sk}^M_{com,n+3}) \leftarrow \mathrm{KEYSHAREGEN}(1^\lambda, \mathsf{prand}^M_{n+3})$
- Sends $(payid, \mathsf{sk}^M_{com,n+1}, \mathsf{vk}^M_{com,n+3})$ to R

The secret key $\mathsf{sk}^M_{com,n+1}$ is disclosed by M, triggering the key derivation phase and, therefore, the revocation of the old state. As before, R derives the new set of keys. For completeness, the keys are $\mathsf{vk}^R_{rev,n+3}$, $\mathsf{vk}^M_{rev,n+3}$, $(\mathsf{vk}^R_{dpay,n+3}, \mathsf{sk}^R_{dpay,n+3})$, $\mathsf{vk}^M_{dpay,n+3}$, $(\mathsf{vk}^R_{pay,n+3}, \mathsf{sk}^R_{pay,n+3})$, $(\mathsf{vk}^R_{htlc,n+3}, \mathsf{sk}^R_{htlc,n+3})$, $\mathsf{vk}^M_{pay,n+3}$, $\mathsf{vk}^M_{htlc,n+3}$. In particular, R computes the revocation key $\mathsf{sk}^R_{rev,n+1}$.

At this point, the only valid (not revoked) state is $n+2$, and the balance for R is $c_R - (v-d)$, whereas for M, it is $c_M + (v-d)$ (and initial amounts of, respectively, c_R and c_M before the payment). Note that the last signed transaction requires the preimage of y. Therefore both participants perform as follows

- M submits to R the tuple $(\mathsf{Tx}_C, \sigma_C)$ received from C
- R removes $(payid, x)$ from $\mathtt{pendingFulfill}$, sets both $\mathtt{pendingFulfill}$ and $\mathtt{paid}$ to $\bot$, and submits x to M
- M sets $\mathtt{Channel}^M$ and $\mathtt{pendingGetPay}$ to $\bot$
- M delivers the purchased good to C
- R submits $(\mathsf{Tx}_C, \sigma_C, x)$ to ledger, and sets $\mathtt{Channel}^R \leftarrow \bot$

We remark that in order to cash in the whole amount (without the discount d), R publishes $(\mathsf{Tx}_C, \sigma_C, x)$ which allows that, even without communicating directly to M the value x, M to obtain the value from the ledger and therefore can redeem the payment within the channel.

Remark 4. We emphasize that closing the channel, cooperatively or not, in our construction is done with the same procedure of a regular LN channel. Thus, we refer the reader to [16] for a full discussion on the matter.

6   Security Analysis

Here we discuss two complementary security features of our construction: the (1) payment channel based security and its performance, and the (2) risk trade security. While the former is based on the security of LN and its financial punishment mechanism, the latter formally proves the novel property of our construction, *i.e.*, the guaranteed payment between the Merchant M and the Risk Buyer R. This is the main novel security result of this work. We later discuss its resistance against *collusion* attacks. Finally we review our construction in the light of the identified desiderata in Sect. 3.

We start by discussing the online security of our construction.

6.1   Online Security and Performance

The first key observation, and also a downside of our construction, is that both M and R need to be online during the execution of the protocol. That is a direct feature of the payment channel design we rely on for the instantaneous payment property. However, we remark that solutions like watchtowers [1,2] can be used along with our construction which minimizes the online time.

The online period is necessary because either one of the participants can maliciously claim an old state (possibly with higher balance) of the channel. In such an attack the claimer publishes an old (already revoked) Commit Transaction. A closer look at the locally kept transactions tells us that the outputs of such transactions require a delay period in order to be redeemed (which could be either Δ_M or Δ_R) as concretely described in Sect. 5. Given the design of the state (in particular the locally kept transactions), another output can be redeemed instead with the revocation public key during this period (which could be either $vk_{rev,n}^M$ or $vk_{rev,n}^R$). In conclusion, with such a transaction published, the revocation key can be used by the attacked participant to take the funds from the channel and punish the attacker.

We recall that the progression of the protocol, from state n and $n+1$ as shown in Sect. 5 (state $n+2$ is not revoked), follows the order that (1) first the participant receives from the counterpart the signature to the next state, then (2) it releases the necessary private information for the computation of the revocation secret key (again, it could be either $sk_{rev,n}^M$ or $sk_{rev,n}^R$, depending on who is performing the attack). This strict step order guarantees that both participants are always committed to a transaction, which can be used to financially disincentivize the early described old state attack.

Lastly, it is not hard to see, but we remark for completeness, that the direct communication channels between the participants can be plain, *i.e.*, not needed to be secure, since the transactions/messages are signed. In particular, we remark that the transaction which carries the payment to R will be widely known for the verification of its validity in the ledger.

Collusion Cases. We start by pointing out that C has a security advantage as it directly transacts with M (not within a channel). The basic observation is that as far as C is concerned, the transaction is completed when it hands its signed transaction (during the *Risk Buying/Preparation Phase*) to M and it receives the purchased good. In particular, if the transaction is for a physical item, then it makes the transaction completion even more easily verifiable on C's side. To conclude, a collusion between M and R do not have effect, since C can verify its own payment along with the received item.

Similarly with the case when C colludes with either M or R. Here again, once C delivers its signed transaction to M (via the direct communication channel, not the payment channel), the protocol is carried by M and R as it is a single hop channel. Consequently, trust between C and M is not needed since they transact directly. Furthermore, trust between M and R is also not needed because they interact via the payment channel which already assumes mistrusting parties.

Given the security guarantees provided by the payment channel, we can say with confidence that the only attack case is when the adversary, which can be either M or R, after receiving its payment, does not follow the protocol and, thus, does not pay its counterpart. Our novel use of the HTLC technique allows the payment to both parties to be *atomic*, meaning if one receives the payment, the other will necessarily receive it too. We denote this property *Risk Trade Security*, and prove that Maravedí has this property in Sect. 6.2.

Performance. We argue that the efficiency is equivalent to the [24] as described in [16], since the number of operations is the same. Our construction leverages on a single pairwise channel, *i.e.*, between M and R, as C does not interact in the channel, therefore it is not a multihop channel network. We highlight that the phases, namely, *Risk Buying/Agreement-R Side Phase* and *Risk Buying/Agreement-M Side Phase*, jointly are equivalent to a single state change of the LN channel (which R and M do sequentially). Similarly to the *Settlement Phase*. That is both sides jointly progress to the next state of the channel, by performing operations locally and sequentially.

- *Risk Buying/Agreement-R Side* + *Risk Buying/Agreement-M Side*: 4 signature generations, 6 key combinations and 12 key derivations;
- *Settlement Phase*: 4 signature generations, 6 key combinations and 12 key derivations.

These figures are based on the construction in [16]. The only adaption that we introduce are the y values (in red) as in Fig. 2. This small change makes us confident that in practice our construction is as efficient as LN implementations.

6.2   Risk Trade Security

Our design prevents that M, or R, receives the payment and prevents its respective counterpart to receive it too. Recall that our protocol deals with two types of transaction (1) regular transaction to be redeemed in the ledger (important to R), and (2) the payment transactions (important to M). The disclosing of the HTLC value x happens only in the final steps during the **Settlement** Phase which enforces the atomicity (in the sense of unlocking funds) of the transactions (1) and (2), despite of being in two different layers.

We concretely prove the early discussion in the following theorem.

Theorem 1. *Given that the protocol in Sect. 5.2 is jointly executed by C, M and R such that C issues* (Tx_C, σ_C), *if R redeems* Tx_C, *then M redeems the funds received from R.*

Proof. Note that up to the Settlement Phase, M has received (Tx_C, σ_C), however it has not handed it to R. Likewise, R has picked the HTLC value y, such that, $y = H(x)$ for the used hash function H. Furthermore, up to this phase the protocol has performed like a payment channel. In particular, it performs until the only valid (not revoked) state is $n + 2$.

Now assume, a malicious Risk Buyer R^* which receives (Tx_C, σ_C) from M, then aborts the protocol without disclosing x to M. Note that by aborting the protocol, M can also close the channel by signing the locally kept transaction

$$Tx_{local}^{R^*} \leftarrow Tx\{\mathcal{I} : (Tx_{F_{R^*}}.\mathcal{O}[1]);$$

$$\mathcal{O} : [1 : c_{R^*} - (v - d), vk_{rev,n+2}^{M} \vee (vk_{dpay,n+2}^{R^*}, \Delta_M)],$$

$$[2 : c_M + (v - d), vk_{pay,n+2}^{M} \wedge y]\};$$

and publishing $(Tx_{local}^{R^*}, \sigma_R, \sigma_M)$ for the priorly received σ_R from R (when the state was created). Note $Tx_{local}^{R^*}$ redeems the outputs from the Funding Transaction $Tx_{F_{R^*}}$ but cannot be further redeemed by M as it did not receive the HTLC preimage x.

Now assume that R^* redeems its received transaction Tx_C, such that $Tx_C \leftarrow Tx\{\mathcal{I} : o \in \Sigma_C; \mathcal{O} : [1 : v, vk_{R^*} \wedge y]\}$, meaning it has publicly disclosed σ_R and x, such that $y = H(x)$. Consequently, M can now issue a transaction, say Tx_{redeem}, such that $Tx_{redeem} \leftarrow Tx\{\mathcal{I} : (Tx_{local}^{R^*}.\mathcal{O}[1]); \mathcal{O} : [1 : c_M - (v - d), vk_M]\}$, signs it and publishes the tuple $(Tx_{redeem}, \sigma_M, x)$ in order to transfer $c_M - (v - d)$ to its known key vk_M, thereby giving the theorem.

Remark 5 (A Note on Collusion). Note that the earlier theorem is enough to show the security of our protocol even regarding collusion of any two of the participants as it was also discussed in Sect. 6.1. Briefly, since C only issues a regular transaction (for a physical or digital good) as it is not part of the pairwise channel, a meaningful collusion attack would pair C with either (1) M or (2) R. In both cases, it is covered by the security of the channel construction, *i.e.*, it is still a single hop channel but the colluding C is playing along with either of the sides of the channel. In case of (1), R cannot use the received (regular) transaction to transfer the funds, therefore it aborts the protocol without disclosing the HTLC value. Thus preventing any loss of funds since. On the other hand, in case of (2), all the funds to be used for payment would be in control of the colluding parties, *i.e.*, C and R, except for the payments already performed to M, which are protected by the past states of the channel. If R (and C) denies the payment to M in the channel, M and R funds will be locked in the channel and C does not receive the purchased goods (M does not hand it). Furthermore, R cannot receive its funds in the ledger (which would reveal the HTLC value). However, we showcase that R is financially incentivized to not abort the protocol, and, therefore, publish the transaction in the ledger, given the small profit on each transaction it receives.

6.3   Desiderata

We start by observing that our hybrid approach of relying on the LN protocol in order to "buy the risk" already provides us with the *Instantaneous Finality* and *Instantaneous Settlement* properties from Sect. 3. It also easily allows the requirement of *Direct Interaction*, since transactions are exchanged directly between the participants in such a protocol. Our design also puts forth a *Allowed Pre-processing* phase which in our case is the creation of the channel itself.

The creation of the LN channel does not require trust between the participants, therefore our construction also supports *Trustless Merchant* and *Trustless Risk Buyer*. Furthermore the interaction between the Customer and the Merchant does not require any trust, and can be readily available since it just requires the direct exchange of transactions. Therefore we also have *Ad Hoc Availability*.

In the case of *Trustless Trade*, our protocol does not address the situation of a malicious Merchant which may deny receiving the initial transaction. We highlight that although it may abort the protocol, it is not financially incentivized to do so, since it is expected to receive funds from the Risk Buyer.

It is important to notice that our protocol is generic enough to support *Background Availability* both for the Customer and the Risk Buyer, although we did not explore more this property in this work. One example is that the Customer, prior to the interaction of the Merchant, may have received a list of addresses of the Risk Buyer, therefore it only issues transactions to the addresses in the list, leaving no room for the Merchant to try to deviate the funds.

Finally, Sect. 6.2 showed a formal proof that our protocol provides *Risk Trade Security* for both the Merchant and the Risk Buyer in the sense that both are guaranteed to not lose funds.

7   Final Remarks

This work presented the Maravedí Protocol which introduces a novel technique to implement *instantaneous finality* for transactions. Instead of previous works, which focus on techniques to provide faster finality of blocks in a consensus protocol, our technique relaxes that criteria by addressing the finality for a single transaction for a single participant, the Merchant. The main intuition is that the receiver of the transaction relies on a third party which covers the risk of the transaction not be fulfilled in the consensus layer.

We investigated the early mentioned risk trade approach and discussed the main ideas for the "risk trade" in a 3-player model of Customer-Merchant-Risk Buyer, outlining its desiderata. We have emphasized that relying on TPS ration to discuss efficiency with decentralized ledger protocols, and in particular to compare it with credit card companies network, may be misleading. The main reason is that blockchain based systems rely on 2-party, *i.e.*, payer and payee, while ours allows the relaxation of the definition of *finality* and the risk trade.

As mentioned earlier, our protocol guarantees that the Merchant will receive the funds while performing a transaction. The guarantee is instantaneous, hence *instantaneous finality*. We devised a hybrid technique which uses a consensus based transaction (slow settlement) and a payment channel transaction (instantaneous settlement). The Maravedí Protocol is based on the Lightning Network, however we proposed an adaption to assure that both the Merchant and the Risk Buyer receive the funds correctly.

Our novel design allows the Risk Buyer to profit on every transaction. It may seem that the game theoretical dynamics of such design may inspire new businesses. It is important to observe that we did not investigate composability properties of our protocol, similarly to what was done in [16] by employing the UC Framework. We leave the study of these properties, both game theoretical dynamics and composability for future work.

Acknowledgements. We would like to thank the anonymous reviewers of Africacrypt Conference 2023 for the insightful and detailed comments on the initial submission. Their comments were gladly added to this manuscript.

References

1. Avarikioti, G., Thyfronitis Litos, O.S., Wattenhofer, R.: Cerberus channels: incentivizing watchtowers for bitcoin. Cryptology ePrint Archive, Report 2019/1092 (2019). https://eprint.iacr.org/2019/1092
2. Avarikioti, Z., Thyfronitis Litos, O.S., Wattenhofer, R.: CERBERUS channels: incentivizing watchtowers for bitcoin. In: Bonneau, J., Heninger, N. (eds.) FC 2020. LNCS, vol. 12059, pp. 346–366. Springer, Cham (2020). https://doi.org/10.1007/978-3-030-51280-4_19
3. Castro, M., Liskov, B.: Practical byzantine fault tolerance (1999)
4. David, B., Gaži, P., Kiayias, A., Russell, A.: Ouroboros Praos: an adaptively-secure, semi-synchronous proof-of-stake blockchain. In: Nielsen, J.B., Rijmen, V. (eds.) EUROCRYPT 2018. LNCS, vol. 10821, pp. 66–98. Springer, Cham (2018). https://doi.org/10.1007/978-3-319-78375-8_3
5. Dinsdale-Young, T., Magri, B., Matt, C., Nielsen, J.B., Tschudi, D.: Afgjort: a partially synchronous finality layer for blockchains. In: Galdi, C., Kolesnikov, V. (eds.) SCN 2020. LNCS, vol. 12238, pp. 24–44. Springer, Cham (2020). https://doi.org/10.1007/978-3-030-57990-6_2
6. Dziembowski, S., Eckey, L., Faust, S., Malinowski, D.: Perun: virtual payment hubs over cryptocurrencies. In: 2019 IEEE Symposium on Security and Privacy, 19–23 May 2019, pp. 106–123, San Francisco, CA, USA. IEEE Computer Society Press (2019)
7. Dziembowski, S., Faust, S., Hostáková, K.: General state channel networks. In: Lie, D., Mannan, M., Backes, M., Wang, X.F. (eds.) 25th Conference on Computer and Communications Security (ACM CCS 2018), 15–19 October 2018, pp. 949–966, Toronto, ON, Canada. ACM Press (2018)
8. Cardano Stack Exchange. Confusion about the time until true immutability (2022). https://cardano.stackexchange.com/questions/8943/confusion-about-the-time-until-true-immutability. Accessed 12 Sept 2022
9. Gilad, Y., Hemo, R., Micali, S., Vlachos, G., Zeldovich, N.: Algorand: scaling byzantine agreements for cryptocurrencies. In: Proceedings of the 26th Symposium on Operating Systems Principles (SOSP 2017), pp. 51–68, New York, NY, USA. ACM (2017)
10. Goldwasser, S., Micali, S., Rivest, R.L.: A "paradoxical" solution to the signature problem. In: Blakley, G.R., Chaum, D. (eds.) CRYPTO 1984. LNCS, vol. 196, p. 467. Springer, Heidelberg (1985). https://doi.org/10.1007/3-540-39568-7_37
11. Pay Hub: Payments hub. https://paymentshub.io. Accessed Feb 2023
12. Jourenko, M., Kurazumi, K., Larangeira, M., Tanaka, K.: SoK: a taxonomy for layer-2 scalability related protocols for cryptocurrencies. Cryptology ePrint Archive, Report 2019/352 (2019). https://eprint.iacr.org/2019/352

13. Jourenko, M., Larangeira, M., Tanaka, K.: Lightweight virtual payment channels. In: Krenn, S., Shulman, H., Vaudenay, S. (eds.) CANS 2020. LNCS, vol. 12579, pp. 365–384. Springer, Cham (2020). https://doi.org/10.1007/978-3-030-65411-5_18

14. Jourenko, M., Larangeira, M., Tanaka, K.: Payment trees: low collateral payments for payment channel networks. In: Borisov, N., Diaz, C. (eds.) FC 2021. LNCS, vol. 12675, pp. 189–208. Springer, Heidelberg (2021). https://doi.org/10.1007/978-3-662-64331-0_10

15. Khalil, R., Zamyatin, A., Felley, G., Moreno-Sanchez, P., Gervais, A.: Commitchains: secure, scalable off-chain payments. Cryptology ePrint Archive, Paper 2018/642 (2018). https://eprint.iacr.org/2018/642

16. Kiayias, A., Litos, O.S.T.: A composable security treatment of the lightning network. Cryptology ePrint Archive, Report 2019/778 (2019). https://eprint.iacr.org/2019/778

17. Malavolta, G., Moreno-Sanchez, P., Kate, A., Maffei, M., Ravi, S.: Concurrency and privacy with payment-channel networks. In: Thuraisingham, B.M., Evans, D., Malkin, T., Xu, D. (eds.) 24th Conference on Computer and Communications Security (ACM CCS 2017), 31 October–2 November 2017, pp. 455–471, Dallas, TX, USA. ACM Press (2017)

18. Miller, A., Bentov, I., Bakshi, S., Kumaresan, R., McCorry, P.: Sprites and state channels: payment networks that go faster than lightning. In: Goldberg, I., Moore, T. (eds.) FC 2019. LNCS, vol. 11598, pp. 508–526. Springer, Cham (2019). https://doi.org/10.1007/978-3-030-32101-7_30

19. Mizrahi, A., Zohar, A.: Congestion attacks in payment channel networks. In: Borisov, N., Diaz, C. (eds.) FC 2021. LNCS, vol. 12675, pp. 170–188. Springer, Heidelberg (2021). https://doi.org/10.1007/978-3-662-64331-0_9

20. Nakamoto, S.: Bitcoin: a peer-to-peer electronic cash system (2008)

21. Pass, R., Shi, E.: Thunderella: blockchains with optimistic instant confirmation. In: Nielsen, J.B., Rijmen, V. (eds.) EUROCRYPT 2018. LNCS, vol. 10821, pp. 3–33. Springer, Cham (2018). https://doi.org/10.1007/978-3-319-78375-8_1

22. Paterson, K.G., Schuldt, J.C.N.: Efficient identity-based signatures secure in the standard model. In: Batten, L.M., Safavi-Naini, R. (eds.) ACISP 2006. LNCS, vol. 4058, pp. 207–222. Springer, Heidelberg (2006). https://doi.org/10.1007/11780656_18

23. Pérez-Solà, C., Ranchal-Pedrosa, A., Herrera-Joancomartí, J., Navarro-Arribas, G., Garcia-Alfaro, J.: LockDown: balance availability attack against lightning network channels. In: Bonneau, J., Heninger, N. (eds.) FC 2020. LNCS, vol. 12059, pp. 245–263. Springer, Cham (2020). https://doi.org/10.1007/978-3-030-51280-4_14

24. Poon, J., Dryja, T.: The bitcoin lightning network: scalable off-chain instant payments (2016). https://lightning.network/lightning-network-paper.pdf

25. Sedgwick, K.: No, Visa doesn't handle 24,000 TPS and neither does your pet blockchain (2018). https://news.bitcoin.com/no-visa-doesnt-handle-24000-tps-and-neither-does-your-pet-blockchain/. Accessed 12 Sept 2022

26. Shamir, A.: Identity-based cryptosystems and signature schemes. In: Blakley, G.R., Chaum, D. (eds.) CRYPTO 1984. LNCS, vol. 196, pp. 47–53. Springer, Heidelberg (1985). https://doi.org/10.1007/3-540-39568-7_5

27. Wood, G.: Ethereum: a secure decentralised generalised transaction ledger. Ethereum Proj. Yellow Pap. **151**, 1–32 (2014)

Lattice-Based Cryptography

ComBo: A Novel Functional Bootstrapping Method for Efficient Evaluation of Nonlinear Functions in the Encrypted Domain

Pierre-Emmanuel Clet[✉], Aymen Boudguiga, Renaud Sirdey,
and Martin Zuber

Université Paris-Saclay, CEA LIST, 91120 Palaiseau, France
{pierre-emmanuel.clet,aymen.boudguiga,renaud.sirdey,martin.zuber}@cea.fr

Abstract. The application of Fully Homomorphic Encryption (FHE) to privacy issues arising in inference or training of neural networks has been actively researched over the last few years. Yet, although practical performances have been demonstrated on certain classes of neural networks, the inherent high computational cost of FHE operators has prevented the scaling capabilities of FHE-based encrypted domain inference to the large and deep networks used to deliver advanced classification functions such as image interpretation tasks. To achieve this goal, a new hope is coming from TFHE functional bootstrapping which, rather than being just used for refreshing ciphertexts (i.e., reducing their noise level), can be used to evaluate operators which are difficult to express as low complexity arithmetic circuits, at no additional cost. In this work, we first propose ComBo (Composition of Bootstrappings) a new full domain functional bootstrapping method with TFHE for evaluating any function of domain and codomain the real torus $\mathbb{T}$ by using a small number of bootstrappings. This result improves on previous approaches: like them, we allow for evaluating any functions, but with error rates reduced by a factor of up to 2^{80}. This claim is supported by a theoretical analysis of the error rate of other functional bootstrapping methods from the literature. The paper is concluded by extensive experimental results demonstrating that our method achieves better performances in terms of both time and precision, in particular for the Rectified Linear Unit (ReLU) function, a nonlinear activation function commonly used in neural networks. As such, this work provides a fundamental building-block towards scaling the homomorphic evaluation of neural networks over encrypted data.

Keywords: FHE · TFHE · functional bootstrapping · ReLU · ComBo

This work was supported by the France 2030 ANR Project ANR-22-PECY-003 Secure-Compute.

1   Introduction

Machine learning application to the analysis of private data, such as health or genomic data, has encouraged the use of homomorphic encryption for private inference or prediction with classification or regression algorithms where the ML models and/or their inputs are encrypted homomorphically [3,7,11,12,25,33,34]. Even training machine learning models with privacy guarantees on the training data has been investigated in the centralized [14,26,29,30] and collaborative [1,31] settings. In practice, machine learning algorithms and especially neural networks require the computation of non-linear activation functions such as the sign, ReLU or sigmoid functions. Still, computing non-linear functions homomorphically remains challenging. For levelled homomorphic schemes such as BFV [9,23] or CKKS [13], non-linear functions have to be approximated by polynomials. However, the precision of these approximations differs with respect to the considered plaintext space (i.e., input range), approximation polynomial degree and its coefficients size, and has a direct impact on the multiplicative depth and parameters of the cryptosystem. The more precise is the approximation, the larger are the cryptosystem parameters and the slower is the computation. On the other hand, homomorphic encryption schemes having an efficient bootstrapping, such as TFHE [15,18] or FHEW [22], can be tweaked to encode functions via look-up table (LUT) evaluations within their bootstrapping procedure. Hence, rather than being just used for refreshing ciphertexts (i.e., reducing their noise level), the bootstrapping becomes *functional* [8] or *programmable* [19] by allowing the evaluation of arbitrary functions as a bonus. These capabilities result in promising new approaches for improving the overall performances of homomorphic calculations, making the FHE "API" better suited to the evaluation of mathematical operators which are difficult to express as low complexity arithmetic circuits. It is also important to note that FHE cryptosystems can be hybridized, for example BFV ciphertexts can be efficiently (and homomorphically) turned into TFHE ones [5,33]. As such, the building blocks discussed in this paper are of relevance also in the setting where the desired encrypted-domain calculation can be split into a preprocessing step more efficiently done using BFV (e.g. several inner product or distance computations) followed by a nonlinear postprocessing step (such as an activation function or an argmin) which can then be more conveniently performed by exploiting TFHE functional bootstrapping. In this work, we thus systematize and further investigate the capabilities of TFHE functional bootstrapping.

Contributions – The main contribution of this paper is a novel functional bootstrapping algorithm[1]. It is a *full domain* functional bootstrapping algorithm in the sense that it does not require to add a bit of padding to the encoding of the messages (as described clearly in [19]). There are several other such methods in the literature. We show that ours is the best option to date for single-digit operations on the full torus (where a message is encoded into a single ciphertext).

---

[1] This paper is an updated version of the eprint [21].

There are several other contributions in this paper. We present them succinctly here:

- Our *novel functional bootstrapping algorithm* (ComBo) is built by composing several bootstrapping operations. It is based on the idea to separate any function in a even and odd part and then compute both in parallel. We present several versions to increase its efficiency and show that our method is the most accurate among state-of-the art full domain bootstrapping algorithms.
- We *implement and test* our algorithms by evaluating several functions homomorphically. Among them, the Rectified Linear Unit (ReLU) function is of particular interest for private neural network applications. This allows us to compare the computational overhead of our algorithm with other existing methods.
- In order to compare the error rate of the different existing methods (which this work aims to reduce), *we develop an error analysis methodology* and describe it in detail. This shows that *our algorithm improves on previous approaches*, most of the time by a significant margin. This methodology, we argue, is the most appropriate way to compare similar algorithms and can be reused for further research on the subject to improve comparability.
- As a bonus, in order to compare our algorithm fairly to other previous solutions from the community, *we introduce consistent notations for describing all existing solutions and their error probabilities in a unified way*. We also fully implemented and tested all of them. We consider that this strengthens the present paper and can be considered, in and of itself, a worthy contribution to the development of the field.

Related Works – In 2016, the TFHE paper made a breakthrough by proposing an efficient bootstrapping for homomorphic gate computation. Then, Bourse et al. [7] and Izabachene et al. [25] used the same bootstrapping algorithm for extracting the (encrypted) sign of an encrypted input. Boura et al. [6] showed later that TFHE bootstrapping could be extended to support a wider class of functionalities. Indeed, TFHE bootstrapping naturally allows to encode function evaluation via their representation as look-up tables (LUTs). Recently, different approaches have been investigated for functional bootstrapping improvement. In particular, Kluczniak and Schild [27], Liu et al. [28] and Yang et al. [32] proposed methods that take into consideration the negacyclicity of the cyclotomic polynomial used within the bootstrapping, for encoding look-up tables over the full real torus $\mathbb{T}$. Meanwhile, Guimarães et al. [24] extended the ideas in Bourse et al. [8] to support the evaluation of certain activation functions such as the sigmoid. One last method (WoP-PBS), presented in Chillotti et al. [20] achieves a functional bootstrapping over the full torus using a BFV type multiplication, which was designed for and only applicable to parameter sets much larger than standard TFHE parameters. Besides, since the probabilistic behavior of decryption also appears during the bootstrapping procedure, the error rate analysis of homomorphic computation are becoming of interest when using TFHE as shown in [2,24].

Paper Organization – The remainder of this paper is organized as follows. Section 2 reviews TFHE building blocks. Section 3 describes the functional bootstrapping idea coming from the TFHE gate bootstrapping. Section 4 presents our new functional bootstrapping method ComBo in full detail. It also describes, under a unified formalism, the other available methods for single digit functional bootstrapping. Finally, Sect. 6 provides experimental results for ComBo and compares it to the other methods which we also implemented. These results are provided for both generic LUT evaluations over encrypted data as well as the ReLU neural network activation function.

2   TFHE

2.1   Notations

In the upcoming sections, we denote vectors by bold letters and so, each vector $\boldsymbol{x}$ of n elements is described as: $\boldsymbol{x} = (x_1, \ldots, x_n)$. $\langle \boldsymbol{x}, \boldsymbol{y} \rangle$ is the inner product of two vectors $\boldsymbol{x}$ and $\boldsymbol{y}$. We denote matrices by capital letters, and the set of matrices with m rows and n columns with entries sampled in $\mathbb{K}$ by $\mathcal{M}_{m,n}(\mathbb{K})$.

We refer to the real torus $\mathbb{R}/\mathbb{Z}$ as $\mathbb{T}$. $\mathbb{T}_N[X]$ denotes the $\mathbb{Z}$-module $\mathbb{R}[X]/(X^N + 1) \mod [1]$ of torus polynomials, where N is a power of 2. $\mathcal{R}$ is the ring $\mathbb{Z}[X]/(X^N + 1)$ and its subring of polynomials with binary coefficients is $\mathbb{B}_N[X] = \mathbb{B}[X]/(X^N + 1)$ ($\mathbb{B} = \{0, 1\}$). Finally, we denote respectively by $[x]_\mathbb{T}$, $[x]_{\mathbb{T}_N[X]}$ and $[x]_\mathcal{R}$ the encryption of x over $\mathbb{T}$, $\mathbb{T}_N[X]$ or $\mathcal{R}$.

$x \xleftarrow{\$} \mathbb{K}$ denotes sampling x uniformly from $\mathbb{K}$, while $x \xleftarrow{\mathcal{N}(\mu, \sigma^2)} \mathbb{K}$ refers to sampling x from $\mathbb{K}$ following a Gaussian distribution of mean μ and variance σ^2. Given $x \xleftarrow{\mathcal{N}(\mu, \sigma^2)} \mathbb{R}$, the probability $P(a \leq x \leq b)$ is equal to $\frac{1}{2}(erf(\frac{b-\mu}{\sqrt{2}\sigma}) - erf(\frac{a-\mu}{\sqrt{2}\sigma}))$, where erf is Gauss error function; $erf(x) = \frac{2}{\sqrt{\pi}} \int_0^x e^{-t^2}$. If $\mu = 0$, we will denote $P(-a \leq x \leq a) = erf(\frac{a}{\sqrt{2}\sigma})$ by $\mathcal{P}(a, \sigma^2)$. The same result and notation apply for $x \xleftarrow{\mathcal{N}(0, \sigma^2)} \mathbb{T}$ as long as the distribution is concentrated as described in [18].

Given a function $f : \mathbb{T} \to \mathbb{T}$ and an integer k, we define $\text{LUT}_k(f)$ to be the Look-Up Table defined by the set of k pairs $(i, f(\frac{i}{k}))$ for $i \in [\![0, k-1]\!]$. We will write $\text{LUT}(f)$ when the value of k is tacit.

Given a function $f : \mathbb{T} \to \mathbb{T}$ and an integer $k \leq N$, we define a polynomial $P_{f,k} \in \mathbb{T}_N[X]$ of degree N as: $P_{f,k} = \sum_{i=0}^{N-1} f\left(\frac{\lfloor \frac{k \cdot i}{2N} \rfloor}{k}\right) \cdot X^i$. If k is a divisor of $2N$, $P_{f,k}$ can be written as $P_{f,k} = \sum_{i=0}^{\frac{k}{2}-1} \sum_{j=0}^{\frac{2N}{k}-1} f(\frac{i}{k}) \cdot X^{\frac{2N}{k} \cdot i + j}$. For simplicity sake, we will write P_f instead of $P_{f,k}$ when the value k is tacit.

2.2   TFHE Structures

The TFHE encryption scheme was proposed in 2016 [15]. It improves the FHEW cryptosystem [22] and introduces the TLWE problem as an adaptation of the LWE problem to $\mathbb{T}$. It was updated later in [16] and both works were recently unified in [18]. The TFHE scheme is implemented in the TFHE library [17]. TFHE relies on three structures to encrypt plaintexts defined over $\mathbb{T}$, $\mathbb{T}_N[X]$ or $\mathcal{R}$:

- **TLWE Sample:** $(\boldsymbol{a}, b)$ is a valid TLWE sample if $\boldsymbol{a} \xleftarrow{\$} \mathbb{T}^n$ and $b \in \mathbb{T}$ verifies $b = \langle \boldsymbol{a}, \boldsymbol{s} \rangle + e$, where $\boldsymbol{s} \xleftarrow{\$} \mathbb{B}^n$ is the secret key, and $e \xleftarrow{\mathcal{N}(0,\sigma^2)} \mathbb{T}$. Then, $(\boldsymbol{a}, b)$ is a fresh TLWE encryption of 0.
- **TRLWE Sample:** a pair $(\boldsymbol{a}, b) \in \mathbb{T}_N[X]^k \times \mathbb{T}_N[X]$ is a valid TRLWE sample if $\boldsymbol{a} \xleftarrow{\$} \mathbb{T}_N[X]^k$, and $b = \langle \boldsymbol{a}, \boldsymbol{s} \rangle + e$, where $\boldsymbol{s} \xleftarrow{\$} \mathbb{B}_N[X]^k$ is a TRLWE secret key and $e \xleftarrow{\mathcal{N}(0,\sigma^2)} \mathbb{T}_N[X]$ is a noise polynomial. In this case, $(\boldsymbol{a}, b)$ is a fresh TRLWE encryption of 0.

  The TRLWE decision problem consists of distinguishing TRLWE samples from random samples in $\mathbb{T}_N[X]^k \times \mathbb{T}_N[X]$. Meanwhile, the TRLWE search problem consists in finding the private polynomial $\boldsymbol{s}$ given arbitrarily many TRLWE samples. When $N = 1$ and k is large, the TRLWE decision and search problems become the TLWE decision and search problems, respectively.

  Let $\mathcal{M} \subset \mathbb{T}_N[X]$ (or $\mathcal{M} \subset \mathbb{T}$) be the discrete message space[2]. To encrypt a message $m \in \mathcal{M}$, we add $(\boldsymbol{0}, m) \in \{0\}^k \times \mathcal{M}$ to a TRLWE sample (or to a TLWE sample if $\mathcal{M} \subset \mathbb{T}$). In the following, we refer to an encryption of m with the secret key $\boldsymbol{s}$ as a T(R)LWE ciphertext noted $\boldsymbol{c} \in \text{T(R)LWE}_{\boldsymbol{s}}(m)$.

  To decrypt a ciphertext $\boldsymbol{c} \in \text{T(R)LWE}_{\boldsymbol{s}}(m)$, we compute its *phase* $\phi(\boldsymbol{c}) = b - \langle \boldsymbol{a}, \boldsymbol{s} \rangle = m + e$. Then, we round it to the nearest element of $\mathcal{M}$. Therefore, if the error e was chosen to be small enough (yet high enough to ensure security), the decryption will be accurate.
- **TRGSW Sample:** a valid TRGSW sample is a vector of TRLWE samples. To encrypt a message $m \in \mathcal{R}$, we add $m \cdot H$ to a TRGSW sample, where H is a gadget matrix[3] using an integer B_g as a base for its decomposition. Chilotti et al. [18] defines an external product between a TRGSW sample A encrypting $m_a \in \mathcal{R}$ and a TRLWE sample $\boldsymbol{b}$ encrypting $m_b \in \mathbb{T}_N[X]$. This external product consists in multiplying A by the approximate decomposition of $\boldsymbol{b}$ with respect to H (Definition 3.12 in [18]). It yields an encryption of $m_a \cdot m_b$ i.e., a TRLWE sample $\boldsymbol{c} \in \text{TRLWE}_{\boldsymbol{s}}(m_a \cdot m_b)$. Otherwise, the external product allows also to compute a controlled MUX gate (CMUX) where the selector is $C_b \in \text{TRGSW}_{\boldsymbol{s}}(b), b \in \{0, 1\}$, and the inputs are $\boldsymbol{c}_0 \in \text{TRLWE}_{\boldsymbol{s}}(m_0)$ and $\boldsymbol{c}_1 \in \text{TRLWE}_{\boldsymbol{s}}(m_1)$.

---

[2] In practice, we discretize the Torus with respect to our plaintext modulus. For example, the usual encryption of a message $m \in \mathbb{Z}_4 = \{0, 1, 2, 3\}$ would be one of the following value $\{0, 0.25, 0.5, 0.75\}$.

[3] Refer to Definition 3.6 and Lemma 3.7 in TFHE paper [18] for more information about the gadget matrix H.

2.3   TFHE Bootstrapping

TFHE bootstrapping relies mainly on three building blocks:

- **Blind Rotate:** rotates a plaintext polynomial encrypted as a TRLWE ciphertext by an encrypted position. It takes as inputs: a TRLWE ciphertext $c \in$ $\mathrm{TRLWE}_k(m)$, a vector $(a_1, \ldots, a_n, a_{n+1} = b)$ where $\forall i$, $a_i \in \mathbb{Z}_{2N}$, and n TRGSW ciphertexts encrypting $(s_1, \ldots, s_n)$ where $\forall i$, $s_i \in \mathbb{B}$. It returns a TRLWE ciphertext $c' \in \mathrm{TRLWE}_k(X^{\langle a,s \rangle - b} \cdot m)$. In this paper, we will refer to this algorithm as BlindRotate. With respect to independence heuristic[4] stated in [18], the variance $\mathcal{V}_{BR}$ of the resulting noise after a BlindRotate satisfies the formula:

$$\mathcal{V}_{BR} < V_c + n \left((k+1)\ell N \left(\frac{B_g}{2} \right)^2 \vartheta_{BK} + \frac{(1+kN)}{4 \cdot B_g^{2l}} \right)$$

where V_c is the variance of the noise of the input ciphertext c, and ϑ_{BK} is the variance of the error of the bootstrapping key. In the following, we define:

$$\mathcal{E}_{BR} = n \left((k+1)\ell N \left(\frac{B_g}{2} \right)^2 \vartheta_{BK} + \frac{(1+kN)}{4 \cdot B_g^{2l}} \right)$$

- **TLWE Sample Extract:** takes as inputs both a ciphertext $c \in$ $\mathrm{TRLWE}_k(m)$ and a position $p \in [\![0, N[\![$, and returns a TLWE ciphertext $c' \in \mathrm{TLWE}_k(m_p)$ where m_p is the pth coefficient of the polynomial m. In this paper, we will refer to this algorithm as SampleExtract. This algorithm does not add any noise to the ciphertext.
- **Public Functional Keyswitching:** transforms a set of p ciphertexts $c_i \in$ $\mathrm{TLWE}_k(m_i)$ into the resulting ciphertext $c' \in \mathrm{T(R)LWE}_s(f(m_1, \ldots, m_p))$, where $f()$ is a public linear morphism from $\mathbb{T}^p$ to $\mathbb{T}_{\overline{N}}[X]$. This algorithm uses 2 specific parameters, namely B_{KS} which is used as a base to decompose some coefficients, and t which gives the precision of the decomposition. Note that functional keyswitching serves at changing encryption keys and parameters. In this paper, we will refer to this algorithm as KeySwitch. As stated in [18,24], the variance $\mathcal{V}_{KS}$ of the resulting noise after KeySwitch follows the formula[5]:

$$\mathcal{V}_{KS} < R^2 \cdot V_c + n\overline{N} \left(t\vartheta_{KS} + \frac{B_{KS}^{-2t}}{4} \right)$$

where V_c is the variance of the noise of the input ciphertext c, R is the Lipschitz constant of f and ϑ_{KS} the variance of the error of the keyswitching key. Note that n is a parameter of the input ciphertext, while $\overline{N}$ is a parameter

---

[4] The independence heuristic ensures that all the coefficients of the errors of TLWE, TRLWE or TRGSW samples are independent and concentrated. More precisely, they are σ-subgaussian where σ is their standard deviation.

[5] Note that there is a discrepancy in the original TFHE papers [15,16,18] between the theorem and the proof.

of the output ciphertext. Thus, $\overline{N} = 1$ if the output is a TLWE ciphertext. In this paper and in most cases, $R = 1$. In the following, we define:

$$\mathcal{E}_{KS}^{n,\overline{N}} = n\overline{N}\left(\vartheta_{KS} + \frac{B_{KS}^{-2t}}{4}\right)$$

TFHE comes with two bootstrapping algorithms. The first one is the gate bootstrapping. It aims at reducing the noise level of a TLWE sample that encrypts the result of a boolean gate evaluation on two ciphertexts, each of them encrypting a binary input. The binary nature of inputs/outputs of this algorithm is not due to inherent limitations of the TFHE scheme but rather to the fact that the authors of the paper were building a bitwise set of operators for which this bootstrapping operation was perfectly fitted.

TFHE gate bootstrapping steps are summarized in Algorithm 1. Note that $\{0, 1\}$ is encoded as $\{0, \frac{1}{2}\}$. Step 1 consists in selecting a value $\mu \in \mathbb{T}$ which will serve later for setting the coefficients of the test polynomial $testv$ (in step 3). Step 2 rescales the components of the input ciphertext c as elements of $\mathbb{Z}_{2N}$. Step 3 defines the test polynomial $testv$. Note that for all $p \in [\![0, 2N[\![$, the constant term of $testv \cdot X^p$ is μ if $p \in]\!]\frac{N}{2}, \frac{3N}{2}]\!]$ and $-\mu$ otherwise. Step 4 returns an accumulator $ACC \in \text{TRLWE}_{s'}(testv \cdot X^{\langle \bar{a},s \rangle - \bar{b}})$. Indeed, the constant term of ACC is $-\mu$ if c encrypts 0, or μ if c encrypts $\frac{1}{2}$ as long as the noise of the ciphertext is small enough. Then, step 5 creates a new ciphertext $\overline{c}$ by extracting the constant term of ACC and adding to it $(\mathbf{0}, \mu)$. That is, $\overline{c}$ either encrypts 0 if c encrypts 0, or m if c encrypts $\frac{1}{2}$ (By choosing $m = \frac{1}{2}$, we get a fresh encryption of c). Since a bootstrapping operation can be summarized as a BlindRotate over a noiseless TRLWE followed by a KeySwitch, the bootstrapping noise ($\mathcal{V}_{BS}$) satisfies: $\mathcal{V}_{BS} < \mathcal{E}_{BR} + \mathcal{E}_{KS}^{N,1}$.

Algorithm 1. TFHE gate bootstrapping [18]

Input: a constant $m \in \mathbb{T}$, a TLWE sample $c = (\boldsymbol{a}, b) \in \text{TLWE}_s(x \cdot \frac{1}{2})$ with $x \in \mathbb{B}$, a bootstrapping key $BK_{s \to s'} = (BK_i \in \text{TRGSW}_{S'}(s_i))_{i \in [\![1,n]\!]}$ where S' is the TRLWE interpretation of a secret key $\boldsymbol{s}'$
Output: a TLWE sample $\overline{c} \in \text{TLWE}_s(x.m)$
1: Let $\mu = \frac{1}{2}m \in \mathbb{T}$ (pick one of the two possible values)
2: Let $\bar{b} = \lfloor 2Nb \rceil$ and $\bar{a}_i = \lfloor 2Na_i \rceil \in \mathbb{Z}, \forall i \in [\![1,n]\!]$
3: Let $testv := (1 + X + \cdots + X^{N-1}) \cdot X^{\frac{N}{2}} \cdot \mu \in \mathbb{T}_N[X]$
4: $ACC \leftarrow \text{BlindRotate}((\mathbf{0}, testv), (\bar{a}_1, \ldots, \bar{a}_n, \bar{b}), (BK_1, \ldots, BK_n))$
5: $\overline{c} = (\mathbf{0}, \mu) + \text{SampleExtract}(ACC)$
6: return $\text{KeySwitch}_{s' \to s}(\overline{c})$

TFHE specifies a second type of bootstrapping called *circuit bootstrapping*. It converts TLWE samples into TRGSW samples and serves mainly for TFHE used in a leveled manner. This additional type of bootstrapping will not be discussed further in this paper.

3 TFHE Functional Bootstrapping

3.1 Encoding and Decoding

Our goal is to build a homomorphic LUT for any function $f : \mathbb{Z}_p \to \mathbb{Z}_p$ for any integer p. As we are using TFHE, every message from $\mathbb{Z}_p$ has to be encoded in $\mathbb{T}$. To that end, we use the encoding function:

$$E_p : \begin{array}{c} \mathbb{Z}_p \to \mathbb{T} \\ k \mapsto \frac{k}{p} \end{array}$$

and its corresponding decoding function:

$$D_p : \begin{array}{c} \mathbb{T} \to \mathbb{Z}_p \\ x \mapsto \lfloor x \cdot p \rceil \end{array}$$

Finally, we specify a torus-to-torus function $f_\mathbb{T}$ to get $f = D_p \circ f_\mathbb{T} \circ E_p$.

$$
\begin{array}{ccc}
\mathbb{Z}_p & \xrightarrow{\ f=D_p \circ f_\mathbb{T} \circ E_p\ } & \mathbb{Z}_p \\
E_p \downarrow & & \uparrow D_p \\
\mathbb{T} & \xrightarrow{\ \ f_\mathbb{T}\ \ } & \mathbb{T}
\end{array}
$$

Since the function $f_\mathbb{T} = E_p \circ f \circ D_p$ makes the diagram commutative, we consider this function as the encoding of f over $\mathbb{T}$.

We use $m^{(p)}$ to refer to a message in $\mathbb{Z}_p$, and m to refer to $E_p(m^{(p)})$. That is, m is the representation of $m^{(p)}$ in $\mathbb{T}$ after discretization.

3.2 Functional Bootstrapping Idea

The original bootstrapping algorithm from [15] had already all the tools to implement a LUT of any negacyclic function[6]. In particular, TFHE is well-suited for $\frac{1}{2}$-antiperiodic function, as the plaintext space for TFHE is $\mathbb{T}$, where $[0, \frac{1}{2}[$ corresponds to positive values and $[\frac{1}{2}, 1[$ to negative ones, and the bootstrapping step 2 of the Algorithm 1 encodes elements from $\mathbb{T}$ into powers of X modulo $(X^N + 1)$, where $\forall \alpha \in [\![0, N[\![, \ X^{\alpha+N} \equiv -X^\alpha \bmod [X^N + 1]$.

Boura et al. [6] were the first to use the term *functional bootstrapping* for TFHE. They describe how TFHE bootstrapping computes a sign function. In addition, they use bootstrapping to build a Rectified Linear Unit (ReLU). However, they do not delve into the details of how to implement the ReLU in practice[7].

Algorithm 2 describes a sign computation with the TFHE bootstrapping. It returns μ if m is positive (i.e., $m \in [0, \frac{1}{2}[$), and $-\mu$ if m is negative.

When we look at the building blocks of Algorithm 2, we notice that we can build more complex functions just by changing the coefficients of the test

---

[6] Negacyclic functions are antiperiodic functions over $\mathbb{T}$ with period $\frac{1}{2}$, i.e., verifying $f(x) = -f(x + \frac{1}{2})$.

[7] They build the function $2 \times$ReLU from an absolute value function, but do not explain how to divide by two to get the ReLU result.

Algorithm 2. Sign extraction with bootstrapping

Input: a constant $\mu \in \mathbb{T}$, a TLWE sample $c = (a, b) \in \text{TLWE}_s(m)$ with $m \in \mathbb{T}$,
  a bootstrapping key $BK_{s \to s'} = (BK_i \in \text{TRGSW}_{S'}(s_i))_{i \in [\![1,n]\!]}$ where S' is the
  TRLWE interpretation of a secret key s'
Output: a TLWE sample $\bar{c} \in \text{TLWE}_s(\mu.sign(m))$
  1: Let $\bar{b} = \lfloor 2Nb \rceil$ and $\bar{a}_i = \lfloor 2Na_i \rceil \in \mathbb{Z}, \forall i \in [\![1, n]\!]$
  2: Let $testv := (1 + X + \cdots + X^{N-1}) \cdot \mu \in \mathbb{T}_N[X]$
  3: $ACC \leftarrow \text{BlindRotate}((0, testv), (\bar{a}_1, \ldots, \bar{a}_n, \bar{b}), (BK_1, \ldots, BK_n))$
  4: $\bar{c} = \text{SampleExtract}(ACC)$
  5: return $\text{KeySwitch}_{s' \to s}(\bar{c})$

---

polynomial $testv$. Indeed, if we consider $t = \sum_{i=0}^{N-1} t_i \cdot X^i$ where $t_i \in \mathbb{T}$ and $t^*(x)$ is the function:

$$t^* : \quad \begin{array}{ccc} [\![-N, N-1]\!] & \to & \mathbb{T} \\ i & \mapsto & \begin{cases} t_i & \text{if } i \in [\![0, N[\![} \\ -t_{i+N} & \text{if } i \in [\![-N, 0[\![} \end{cases} \end{array} ,$$

the output of the bootstrapping of a TLWE ciphertext $[x]_{\mathbb{T}} = (a, b)$ with the test polynomial $testv = t$ is $[t^*(\phi(\bar{a}, \bar{b}))]_{\mathbb{T}}$, where $(\bar{a}, \bar{b})$ is the rescaled version of (a, b) in $\mathbb{Z}_{2N}$ (line 1 of Algorithm 2).

Indeed, we first remind that for any positive integer i s.t. $0 \le i < N$, we have:

$$testv.X^{-i} = t_i + \cdots - t_0 X^{N-i} - \cdots - t_{i-1} X^{N-1} \bmod [X^N + 1] \quad (1)$$

Then, we notice that BlindRotate (line 3 of Algorithm 2) computes $testv \cdot X^{-\phi(\bar{a}, \bar{b})}$. Therefore, we get using Eq. (1) the following results:

– if $\phi(\bar{a}, \bar{b}) \in [\![0, N[\![}$, the constant term of $testv \cdot X^{-\phi(\bar{a}, \bar{b})}$ is $t_{\phi(\bar{a}, \bar{b})}$.
– if $\phi(\bar{a}, \bar{b}) \in [\![-N, 0[\![}$, we have:
  $testv \cdot X^{-\phi(\bar{a}, \bar{b})} = -testv \cdot X^{-\phi(\bar{a}, \bar{b})-N} \bmod [X^N + 1]$
  with $(\phi(\bar{a}, \bar{b}) + N) \in [\![0, N[\![}$. So, the constant term of $testv \cdot X^{-\phi(\bar{a}, \bar{b})}$ is $-t_{\phi(\bar{a}, \bar{b})+N}$.

All that remains for the bootstrapping algorithm is extracting the previous constant term (in line 4) and keyswitching (in line 5) to get the TLWE sample $[t^*(\phi(\bar{a}, \bar{b}))]_{\mathbb{T}}$.

Now, we can tweak the previous idea to evaluate discretized functions. Let $f : \mathbb{Z}_p \to \mathbb{Z}_p$ be any negacyclic function over $\mathbb{Z}_p$ and $f_{\mathbb{T}} = E_p \circ f \circ D_p$. We call $\tilde{f}$ the well-defined function $f_{\mathbb{T}} \circ E_{2N}$ that satisfies:

$$\tilde{f} : \quad \begin{array}{ccc} [\![-N, N-1]\!] & \to & \mathbb{T} \\ x & \mapsto & \begin{cases} f_{\mathbb{T}}(\frac{x}{2N}) & \text{if } x \in [\![0, N[\![} \\ -f_{\mathbb{T}}(\frac{x+N}{2N}) & \text{if } x \in [\![-N, 0[\![} \end{cases} \end{array} \quad (2)$$

Let P_f be the polynomial $P_f = \sum_{i=0}^{N-1} \tilde{f}(i) \cdot X^i$. Now, if we apply the bootstrapping Algorithm 2 to a TLWE ciphertext $[m]_{\mathbb{T}} = (\boldsymbol{a}, b)$ with $m^{(p)} \in \mathbb{Z}_p$ and $testv = P_f$, it outputs $[\tilde{f}(\phi(\bar{\boldsymbol{a}}, \bar{b}))]_{\mathbb{T}}$. That is, Algorithm 2 allows the encoding of the function f as long as $\frac{\phi(\bar{\boldsymbol{a}}, \bar{b})}{2N} = m + e'$, for some e' small enough. Further details on the variance of e' and the error probability of the bootstrapping are given in Sect. 5.

3.3 Example of Functional Bootstrapping in $\mathbb{Z}_4$

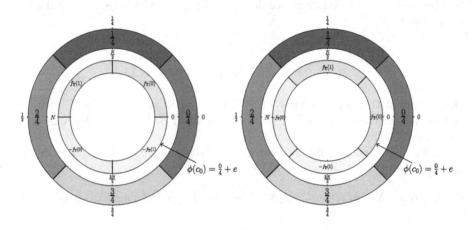

Fig. 1. Functional bootstrapping outputs with $\mathbb{Z}_4$ as plaintext space.

As an example, let us consider the plaintext space $\mathbb{Z}_4$ and a negacyclic function f. We represent $\mathbb{Z}_4$ in $\mathbb{T}$ by the set $\{\frac{0}{4}, \frac{1}{4}, \frac{2}{4}, \frac{3}{4}\}$. We denote by $f_{\mathbb{T}}$ a function over $\mathbb{T}$ that satisfies: $f_{\mathbb{T}}(\frac{i}{4}) = \frac{f(i)}{4}$ for all $i \in [\![0,3]\!]$. We consider a ciphertext c_0 encrypting the value 0. We present in Algorithm 3 the functional bootstrapping algorithm that computes $LUT(f)$. We use the notation $P_{f,k}$ from Sect. 2.1.

In step 2 of Algorithm 3, we set the test polynomial $testv = P_{f_{\mathbb{T}},4} \cdot X^{-\frac{N}{4}}$, where $P_{f_{\mathbb{T}},4}$ encodes a look up table corresponding to $f_{\mathbb{T}}$, and $X^{-\frac{N}{4}}$ is an offset term.

In Fig. 1, we describe the action of the offset $X^{-\frac{N}{4}}$ on $P_{f_{\mathbb{T}},4}$. We represent in the outer circle the possible phases associated to each entry from our plaintext space $\mathbb{Z}_4$. Meanwhile, we represent in the inner circle the returned coefficients after a bootstrapping. In the left part of Fig. 1, we consider the result of the bootstrapping algorithm without the offset. We note that the red part of the inner and outer circles do not overlap. So, whenever the error term e in the phase is negative (even for small values of e), the considered functional bootstrapping outputs an incorrect value. In our example, the bootstrapping returns $f_{\mathbb{T}}(\frac{3}{4}) =$

Algorithm 3. TFHE functional bootstrapping example

Input: a TLWE sample $c = (a, b) \in \text{TLWE}_s(m)$ with $x \in \{\frac{0}{4}, \frac{1}{4}, \frac{2}{4}, \frac{3}{4}\}$, a bootstrapping key $BK_{s \to s'} = (BK_i \in \text{TRGSW}_{S'}(s_i))_{i \in [\![1,n]\!]}$ where S' is the TRLWE interpretation of a secret key s'

Output: a TLWE sample $\overline{c} \in \text{TLWE}_s(f_{\mathbb{T}}(m))$

1: Let $\overline{b} = \lfloor 2Nb \rceil$ and $\overline{a}_i = \lfloor 2Na_i \rceil \in \mathbb{Z}, \forall i \in [\![1,n]\!]$
2: Let $testv := P_{f_{\mathbb{T}}, 4} \cdot X^{-\frac{N}{4}} \in \mathbb{T}_N[X]$
3: $ACC \leftarrow \text{BlindRotate}((\mathbf{0}, testv), (\overline{a}_1, \ldots, \overline{a}_n, \overline{b}), (BK_1, \ldots, BK_n))$
4: $\overline{c} = \text{SampleExtract}(ACC)$
5: return $\text{KeySwitch}_{s' \to s}(\overline{c})$

$-f_{\mathbb{T}}(\frac{1}{4})$ instead of $f_{\mathbb{T}}(0)$. Meanwhile, in the right part of the Fig. 1, we consider the bootstrapping algorithm with the offset. Now, the red part of the inner and outer circles overlap, and so, the functional bootstrapping returns the right value as long as the error term remains small enough.

For a given plaintext space $\mathbb{Z}_p$, the offset is $X^{-\lfloor \frac{N}{p} \rceil}$. We assume from now on that p divides N to ease notations and formulas.

3.4 Multi-value Functional Bootstrapping

Carpov et al. [10] introduced a nice method for evaluating multiple LUTs with one bootstrapping. They factor the test polynomial P_{f_i} associated to the function f_i into a product of two polynomials v_0 and v_i, where v_0 is a common factor to all P_{f_i}. Indeed, they notice that:

$$(1 + X + \cdots + X^{N-1}) \cdot (1 - X) = 2 \bmod [X^N + 1] \tag{3}$$

Let $P_{f_i} = \sum_{j=0}^{N-1} \alpha_{i,j} X^j$ with $\alpha_{i,j} \in \mathbb{T}$, and $q \in \mathbb{N}^*$ the smallest integer so that: $\forall i, q \cdot (1 - X) \cdot P_{f_i} \in \mathbb{Z}[X]$ (q is a divisor of p). We get using Eq. (3):

$$P_{f_i} = \frac{1}{2q} \cdot (1 + \cdots + X^{N-1}) \cdot (q \cdot (1 - X) \cdot P_{f_i}) \bmod [X^N + 1]$$

$$= v_0 \cdot v_i \bmod [X^N + 1]$$

where:

$$v_0 = \frac{1}{2q} \cdot (1 + \cdots + X^{N-1})$$

$$v_i = q \cdot (\alpha_{i,0} + \alpha_{i,N-1} + \sum_{j=1}^{N-1} (\alpha_{i,j} - \alpha_{i,j-1}) \cdot X^j)$$

Thanks to this factorization, it becomes possible to compute many LUTs with one bootstrapping. Indeed, we just have to set the initial test polynomial to $testv = v_0$ during the bootstrapping. Then, after the BlindRotate, we multiply the obtained ACC by each v_i corresponding to LUT(f_i) to obtain ACC_i.

Algorithm 4. Multi-value bootstrapping

Input: a TLWE sample $c = (a, b) \in \text{TLWE}_s(m)$ with $m \in \mathbb{T}$, a bootstrapping key $BK_{s \to s'} = (BK_i \in \text{TRGSW}_{S'}(s_i))_{i \in [\![1,n]\!]}$ where S' is the TRLWE interpretation of a secret key s', k LUTs s.t. $\text{LUT}(f_i) = v_0.v_i, \forall i \in [\![1, k]\!]$

Output: a list of k TLWE ciphertexts $\overline{c}_i \in \text{TLWE}_s(f_i(\frac{\phi(\overline{a}, \overline{b})}{2N}))$

1: Let $\overline{b} = \lfloor 2Nb \rceil$ and $\overline{a}_i = \lfloor 2Na_i \rceil \in \mathbb{Z}, \forall i \in [\![1, n]\!]$
2: Let $testv := v_0$
3: $\text{ACC} \leftarrow \text{BlindRotate}((0, testv), (\overline{a}_1, \dots, \overline{a}_n, \overline{b}), (BK_1, \dots, BK_n))$
4: **for** $i \leftarrow 1$ to k **do**
5:      $\text{ACC}_i := \text{ACC} \cdot v_i$
6:      $\overline{c}_i = \text{SampleExtract}(\text{ACC}_i)$
7:      **return** $\text{KeySwitch}_{s' \to s}(\overline{c}_i)$

---

4   Look-Up-Tables over a Single Ciphertext

In Sect. 3.2, we demonstrated that functional bootstrapping can serve to compute $\text{LUT}(f)$ for any negacyclic function f. In this section, we describe 4 different ways to specify homomorphic LUTs for *any* function (i.e., not necessarily negacyclic ones). We present 3 solutions from the state of the art [19, 27, 32] in Sects. 4.1, 4.2 and 4.3, and our novel method ComBo in Sect. 4.4. In addition, we discuss a solution to reduce the noise of the functional bootstrapping from [27] in Sect. 4.2.

As in Sect. 3.1, we call $f_{\mathbb{T}} : \mathbb{T} \to \mathbb{T}$ the function that specifies our homomorphic LUT, and $f : \mathbb{Z}_p \to \mathbb{Z}_p$ its corresponding function over the input and output space $\mathbb{Z}_p$.

4.1   Partial Domain Functional Bootstrapping – Half-Torus

The Half-Torus method gets around the negacyclic restriction of functional bootstrapping by encoding values only on $[0, \frac{1}{2}[$ (i.e., half of the torus). Let's consider the test polynomial P_h for a given negacyclic function h. Recall Eq. 2 that defines the output of the bootstrapping operation as:

$$
\tilde{h} : \begin{array}{c} [\![-N, N-1]\!] \to \\ x \end{array} \begin{array}{c} \mathbb{T} \\ \mapsto \left\{ \begin{array}{ll} h(\frac{x}{2N}) & \text{if } x \in [\![0, N[\![\\ -h(\frac{x+N}{2N}) & \text{if } x \in [\![-N, 0[\![\end{array} \right. \end{array}
$$

As we restrict the encoding space to $[0, \frac{1}{2}[$, we also restrict $\tilde{h}$ domain to $[\![0, N[\![$, where h has no negacyclic property. That is, we get a method to evaluate a LUT with a *single* bootstrapping.

4.2   Full Domain Functional Bootstrapping – FDFB

Kluczniak and Schild [27] specified FDFB to evaluate encrypted LUTs of domain the full torus $\mathbb{T}$. Let's consider a TLWE ciphertext $[m]_{\mathbb{T}}$ given a message $m^{(p)} \in$

$\mathbb{Z}_p$. We denote by g the function:

$$g: \begin{array}{l} \mathbb{T} \to \quad \mathbb{T} \\ x \mapsto -f_{\mathbb{T}}(x + \tfrac{1}{2}) \end{array}$$

We denote by $q \in \mathbb{N}^*$ the smallest integer such that $q \cdot (P_f - P_g)$ is a polynomial with coefficients in $\mathbb{Z}$. Then, we define $P_1 = q \cdot P_f$ and $P_2 = q \cdot P_g$. We note that the coefficients of $P_f - P_g$ are multiples of $\frac{1}{p}$ in $\mathbb{T}$, where $\mathbb{T}$ corresponds to $[-\frac{1}{2}, \frac{1}{2}[$. We note that q is a divisor of p and $P_2 - P_1$ has coefficients of norm lower or equal to $\frac{q}{2}$.

We define the Heaviside function H as:

$$H : x \mapsto \begin{cases} 1 & \text{if } x \geq 0 \\ 0 & \text{if } x < 0 \end{cases}$$

We can express H by using the sign function as follows: $H(x) = \frac{\text{sign}(x)+1}{2}$.

In order to evaluate a LUT, we first compute $[E_q(H(m))]_{\mathbb{T}}$ with one bootstrapping (using Algorithm 2) and deduce $[E_q((1 - H)(m))]_{\mathbb{T}} = (0, \frac{1}{q}) - [E_q(H(m))]_{\mathbb{T}}$. Then, we make a keyswitch to transform the TLWE sample $[E_q((1 - H)(m))]_{\mathbb{T}}$ into a TRLWE sample $[E_q((1 - H)(m))]_{\mathbb{T}_N[X]}$. Finally, we define:

$$c_{\text{LUT}} = (P_2 - P_1) \cdot [E_q((1 - H)(m))]_{\mathbb{T}_N[X]} + (0, P_f)$$

such that:

$$c_{\text{LUT}} = \begin{cases} [P_f]_{\mathbb{T}_N[X]} & \text{if } m \geq 0 \\ [P_g]_{\mathbb{T}_N[X]} & \text{if } m < 0 \end{cases}$$

We note that depending on the sign of m, c_{LUT} is a TRLWE encryption of P_f or P_g, the test polynomials of f or g, respectively. As such, we obtain $[f_{\mathbb{T}}(m)]_{\mathbb{T}}$ after a second bootstrapping with $[m]_{\mathbb{T}}$ as input and c_{LUT} as a test polynomial.

We can reduce the noise of c_{LUT} by applying to P_f and P_g the factorization described in Sect. 3.4. First, we replace the polynomials P_f and P_g by $v_f = (1 - X) \cdot P_f$ and $v_g = (1 - X) \cdot P_g$, respectively. Thanks to the redundancy of the coefficients of P_f and P_g, v_f and v_g have at most $\frac{p}{2}$ non null coefficients. We denote by $q' \in \mathbb{N}^*$ the smallest integer such that $q' \cdot (v_f - v_g)$ is a polynomial with coefficients in $\mathbb{Z}$. We ensure that $q' \leq q$ as $q \cdot (1 - X) \cdot (P_f - P_g) = (1 - X) \cdot (q \cdot (P_f - P_g))$ has coefficients in $\mathbb{Z}$. Then, we define $v_1 = q' \cdot v_f$ and $v_2 = q' \cdot v_g$. We get that $v_2 - v_1$ has coefficients in $\mathbb{Z}$ of norm lower or equal to q'. Finally, we compute a TRLWE encryption of $\sum_{i=0}^{N-1} X^i \cdot E_{2 \cdot q'}((1 - H)(m))$ from the TLWE sample $[E_{2 \cdot q'}((1 - H)(m))]_{\mathbb{T}}$, by applying a KeySwitch. We get:

$$c_{\text{LUT}} = (v_2 - v_1) \cdot [\sum_{i=0}^{N-1} X^i \cdot E_{2 \cdot q'}((1 - H)(m))]_{\mathbb{T}_N[X]} + (0, P_f)$$

such that:

$$c_{\text{LUT}} = \begin{cases} [P_f]_{\mathbb{T}_N[X]} & \text{if } m \geq 0 \\ [P_g]_{\mathbb{T}_N[X]} & \text{if } m < 0 \end{cases}$$

4.3   Full Domain Functional Bootstrapping – TOTA

Both Liu et al. [28] and Yan et al. [32] independently proposed the same app-roach[8] to evaluate arbitrary functions over the torus using a functional boot-strapping. As such, we refer to both methods in this paper with the name TOTA (as proposed by Yan et al.). Let's consider a ciphertext $[m_1]_\mathbb{T} = (\boldsymbol{a}, b = \langle \boldsymbol{a}, \boldsymbol{s} \rangle + m_1 + e)$. Then, by dividing each coefficient of this ciphertext by 2, we get a ciphertext $[m_2]_\mathbb{T} = (\frac{\boldsymbol{a}}{2}, \langle \frac{\boldsymbol{a}}{2}, \boldsymbol{s} \rangle + m_2 + \frac{e}{2})$ where $m_2 = \frac{m_1}{2} + \frac{k}{2}$ with $k \in \{0, 1\}$ and $\frac{m_1}{2} \in [0, \frac{1}{2}[$. Using the original bootstrapping algorithm, we compute $[\frac{\text{sign}(m_2)}{4}]_\mathbb{T}$ an encryption of $\frac{\text{sign}(m_2)}{4} = \begin{cases} \frac{1}{4} & \text{if } k = 0 \\ -\frac{1}{4} & \text{if } k = 1 \end{cases}$. Then, we get an encryption of $\frac{m_1}{2}$ by computing: $[m_2]_\mathbb{T} - [\frac{\text{sign}(m_2)}{4}]_\mathbb{T} + (\boldsymbol{0}, \frac{1}{4})$.

For any function $f_\mathbb{T}$, let's define $f_{(2)}$ such that $f_{(2)}(x) = f_\mathbb{T}(2x)$. Since $\frac{m_1}{2} \in [0, \frac{1}{2}[$, we can compute $f_{(2)}(\frac{m_1}{2})$ with a single bootstrapping using the partial domain approach from 4.1, and $f_{(2)}(\frac{m_1}{2}) = f_\mathbb{T}(m_1)$.

4.4   Full Domain Functional Bootstrapping with Composition - ComBo

In this section, we present ComBo, a novel method to compute any function using the full (discretized) torus as plaintext space. We will assume that p is even and fixed[9].

Pseudo Odd Functions: We call pseudo odd function a function f that satisfies: $\forall x \in \mathbb{Z}_p,\ f(-x - 1) = -f(x)$.

Let f be a pseudo odd function over $\mathbb{Z}_p$. We define the following negacyclic functions:

$$f_{\text{neg}} : \begin{array}{c} [\![0, p - 1]\!] \to \\ x \end{array} \quad \begin{array}{c} \mathbb{Z}_p \\ \mapsto \begin{cases} f(x) & \text{if } x \in [\![0, \frac{p}{2} - 1]\!] \\ -f(x - \frac{p}{2}) & \text{if } x \in [\![\frac{p}{2}, p - 1]\!] \end{cases} \end{array}$$

and

$$\text{Id}_{\text{neg}} : \begin{array}{c} [\![0, p - 1]\!] \to \\ x \end{array} \quad \begin{array}{c} \mathbb{R}_p \\ \mapsto \begin{cases} x + \frac{1}{2} & \text{if } x \in [\![0, \frac{p}{2} - 1]\!] \\ \frac{p}{2} - x - \frac{1}{2} & \text{if } x \in [\![\frac{p}{2}, p - 1]\!] \end{cases} \end{array}$$

Since these 2 functions are negacyclic, they can be computed with the usual negacyclic functional bootstrapping (presented in Sect. 3.2).

Note that $(\text{Id}_{\text{neg}} - \frac{1}{2})$ is a bijection of $\mathbb{Z}_p$ that satisfies the equality $(\text{Id}_{\text{neg}} - \frac{1}{2})(x) = x$, for all $x \in [\![0, \frac{p}{2} - 1]\!]$. Otherwise, for all $x \in [\![\frac{p}{2}, p - 1]\!]$, $(\text{Id}_{\text{neg}} - \frac{1}{2})(x) = \frac{p}{2} - x - 1$. In $\mathbb{Z}_p$, $\forall x \in [\![\frac{p}{2}, p - 1]\!]$, we have $(\frac{p}{2} - x - 1) \in [\![\frac{p}{2}, p - 1]\!]$.

Now, we compose it with f_{neg} to obtain: $f_{\text{neg}} \circ (\text{Id}_{\text{neg}} - \frac{1}{2})(x) = f_{\text{neg}}(x) = f(x)$ if $x \in [\![0, \frac{p}{2} - 1]\!]$. If $x \in [\![\frac{p}{2}, p - 1]\!]$, $f_{\text{neg}} \circ (\text{Id}_{\text{neg}} - \frac{1}{2})(x) = f_{\text{neg}}(\frac{p}{2} - x - 1) = -f(-x - 1)$. Since f is pseudo odd, we have: $-f(-x - 1) = f(x)$.

---

[8] Although both papers use different notations, both methods rescale the message space into the first half of the torus before applying a half torus functional boot-strapping. In both cases, a sign evaluation is performed to compute that rescaling.

[9] If p is odd, we set $p := p + 1$ to get back to the assumption that p is even.

Pseudo Even Functions: We call pseudo even function a function f that satisfies: $\forall x \in \mathbb{Z}_p$, $f(-x - 1) = f(x)$.

Let f be a pseudo even function over $\mathbb{Z}_p$. We define the following negacyclic functions:

$$f_{\text{neg}} : \begin{array}{ccc} [\![0, p-1]\!] & \to & \mathbb{Z}_p \\ x & \mapsto & \left\{ \begin{array}{ll} f(x) & \text{if } x \in [\![0, \frac{p}{2}-1]\!] \\ -f(x - \frac{p}{2}) & \text{if } x \in [\![\frac{p}{2}, p-1]\!] \end{array} \right. \end{array}$$

and

$$\text{abs}_{\text{neg}} : \begin{array}{ccc} [\![0, p-1]\!] & \to & \mathbb{R}_p \\ x & \mapsto & \left\{ \begin{array}{ll} x + \frac{p}{4} + \frac{1}{2} & \text{if } x \in [\![0, \frac{p}{2}-1]\!] \\ \frac{p}{4} - x - \frac{1}{2} & \text{if } x \in [\![\frac{p}{2}, p-1]\!] \end{array} \right. \end{array}$$

Since these 2 functions are also negacyclic, they can similarly be computed with the usual negacyclic functional bootstrapping (presented in Sect. 3.2).

Note that $(\text{abs}_{\text{neg}} - \frac{p}{4} - \frac{1}{2})$ satisfies the equality $(\text{abs}_{\text{neg}} - \frac{p}{4} - \frac{1}{2})(x) = x$ for all $x \in [\![0, \frac{p}{2}-1]\!]$. However, if $x \in [\![\frac{p}{2}, p-1]\!]$, $(\text{abs}_{\text{neg}} - \frac{p}{4} - \frac{1}{2})(x) = -x-1 \in [\![0, \frac{p}{2}-1]\!]$. As such, we ensure that the function $(\text{abs}_{\text{neg}} - \frac{p}{4} - \frac{1}{2})$ behaves similarly to the absolute value function.

It follows that $f_{\text{neg}} \circ (\text{abs}_{\text{neg}} - \frac{p}{4} - \frac{1}{2})(x) = f_{\text{neg}}(x) = f(x)$ if $x \in [\![0, \frac{p}{2}-1]\!]$. If $x \in [\![\frac{p}{2}, p-1]\!]$, $f_{\text{neg}} \circ (\text{abs}_{\text{neg}} - \frac{p}{4} - \frac{1}{2})(x) = f_{\text{neg}}(-x - 1) = f(-x - 1)$. Since f is pseudo even, we have $f(-x - 1) = f(x)$.

Any Function: We write any function $f \in \mathbb{Z}_p$ as a sum of a pseudo even function and a pseudo odd function: $f(x) = f_{\text{even}}(x) + f_{\text{odd}}(x)$, where $f_{\text{even}}(x) = \frac{f(x)+f(-x-1)}{2}$ and $f_{\text{odd}}(x) = \frac{f(x)-f(-x-1)}{2}$. Besides, we build any pseudo odd or pseudo even function with at most 2 bootstrappings. So, we can build any function with at most 4 bootstrappings.

We describe in Algorithm 5 the overall algorithm for running ComBo. We denote by $\text{FB}[f]((\boldsymbol{a}, b))$ the application of the negacyclic functional bootstrapping procedure using the test vector $P_{\frac{f}{p}}$ (as defined in Sect. 2.1) and applied to a ciphertext $(\boldsymbol{a}, b)$ given a function $f : \mathbb{Z}_p \to \mathbb{R}_p$.

Correctness: If we assume that the negacyclic functional bootstrapping (FB) is correct, we obtain by Algorithm 5 a ciphertext $[\frac{f(m)}{p}]_{\mathbb{T}}$ where $m \in \mathbb{Z}_p$ is the input of the algorithm and $f : \mathbb{Z}_p \to \mathbb{Z}_p$ is the target function. Indeed, Step 1 computes an encryption of $\frac{\text{Id}_{\text{neg}}(m)}{p}$ since Id_{neg} is a negacyclic function. Step 2 computes an encryption of $\frac{\text{Id}_{\text{neg}}(m) - \frac{1}{2}}{p} = \frac{(\text{Id}_{\text{neg}} - \frac{1}{2})(m)}{p}$. Let us refer by f_{neg} to the negacyclic function corresponding to f_{odd} over $[\![0, \frac{p}{2}-1]\!]$. Then Step 3 computes an encryption of $\frac{f_{\text{neg}} \circ (\text{Id}_{\text{neg}} - \frac{1}{2})(m)}{p}$: the encoding of $f_{\text{odd}}(m)$ over $\mathbb{T}$ (as discussed in the paragraph about pseudo odd functions in Sect. 4.4). Similarly, Steps 4 to 6 compute an encryption of the encoding of $f_{\text{even}}(m)$ over $\mathbb{T}$. Finally, Step 7 computes the sum of the pseudo odd and pseudo even outputs which results in an encryption of $\frac{f(m)}{p}$: the encoding of $f(m)$ over $\mathbb{T}$.

In practice, we can reduce the (single-shot) computation time by using parallelism (e.g. multithreading or SIMD) for evaluating the pseudo odd and pseudo even functions simultaneously. So, we end-up with a computation time of 2

Algorithm 5. ComBo

Input: a TLWE sample $[\frac{m}{p}]_T \in \text{TLWE}_s(\frac{m}{p})$ with $m \in \mathbb{Z}_p$, a bootstrapping key
$BK_{s \to s'} = (BK_i \in \text{TRGSW}_{S'}(s_i))_{i \in [\![1,n]\!]}$ where S' is the TRLWE interpretation of a secret key s', a target function $f : \mathbb{Z}_p \to \mathbb{Z}_p$, and the two functions
$f_{\text{odd}} : \begin{matrix} \mathbb{Z}_p \to \\ x \mapsto \end{matrix} \begin{matrix} \mathbb{R}_p \\ \frac{f(x)-f(-x-1)}{2} \end{matrix}$ and $f_{\text{even}} : \begin{matrix} \mathbb{Z}_p \to \\ x \mapsto \end{matrix} \begin{matrix} \mathbb{R}_p \\ \frac{f(x)+f(-x-1)}{2} \end{matrix}$

Output: a TLWE ciphertext $(a',b') = [\frac{f(m)}{p}]_T \in \text{TLWE}_s(\frac{f(m)}{p})$

1: $(a,b) = \text{FB}[\text{Id}_{\text{neg}}]([\frac{m}{p}]_T)$ ▷ Start of pseudo odd computation
2: $(a,b) = (a, b - \frac{1}{2p})$
3: $(a_{\text{odd}}, b_{\text{odd}}) = \text{FB}[f_{\text{odd}}]((a,b))$ ▷ End of pseudo odd computation
4: $(a,b) = \text{FB}[\text{abs}_{\text{neg}}]([\frac{m}{p}]_T)$ ▷ Start of pseudo even computation
5: $(a,b) = (a, b - \frac{1}{2p} - \frac{1}{4})$
6: $(a_{\text{even}}, b_{\text{even}}) = \text{FB}[f_{\text{even}}]((a,b))$ ▷ End of pseudo even computation
7: $(a',b') = (a_{\text{odd}}, b_{\text{odd}}) + (a_{\text{even}}, b_{\text{even}})$

bootstrappings. We can alternatively reduce the number of bootstrappings to 3 thanks to the multi-value functional bootstrapping (see Sect. 3.4).

From now on, we call ComBoMV the ComBo method when used with the multi-value bootstrapping, and ComboP with parallelism.

Examples: We describe how to build the functions Id, and ReLU with ComBo.

For Id, the decomposition in pseudo even and pseudo odd functions gives $\text{Id}(x) = (-\frac{1}{2}) + (x + \frac{1}{2})$. The pseudo even function $\text{Id}_{\text{even}} = -\frac{1}{2}$ is a constant and does not require any bootstrapping. We only have to compute the pseudo odd function $\text{Id}_{\text{odd}} = x + \frac{1}{2}$. In this case, we have no need for multithreading or multi-value bootstrapping.

For ReLU, the decomposition gives $\text{ReLU}(x) = \text{ReLU}_{\text{even}}(x) + \text{ReLU}_{\text{odd}}(x)$ where:

$$\text{ReLU}_{\text{even}} : x \mapsto \begin{cases} \frac{x}{2} & \text{if } x \in [\![0, \frac{p}{2} - 1]\!] \\ -\frac{x}{2} - \frac{1}{2} & \text{otherwise} \end{cases}$$

$$\text{ReLU}_{\text{odd}} : x \mapsto \begin{cases} \frac{x}{2} & \text{if } x \in [\![0, \frac{p}{2} - 1]\!] \\ \frac{x}{2} + \frac{1}{2} & \text{otherwise} \end{cases}$$

Applying ComBo naively results in 4 bootstrappings. However, we can actually compute $\text{ReLU}_{\text{even}}$ with only 1 bootstrapping as for abs_{neg}. This specific improvement is useful for ComBo, as it reduces the number of consecutive bootstrappings to 3.

5   Error Rate and Noise Variance

In this section, we analyze the noise variance and error rate for the aforementioned functional bootstrapping methods. We refer to each bootstrapping method by its acronym as defined in Sect. 4.

5.1   Noise Variance

The noise variance of a bootstrapped ciphertext depends on the operations applied to the input ciphertext during the bootstrapping. Table 1 gives the theoretical variance of each of these operations. These formulas are taken from [18].

Table 1. Obtained noise variances when applying basic operations to independent inputs: c_i is a TLWE ciphertext of variance V_i, C_i is a TRLWE ciphertext of variance V_i, P is a plaintext polynomial and $v \in \mathbb{Z}_{2N}^{n+1}$.

Operation	Variance
$c_i + c_j$	$V_i + V_j$
$C_i + C_j$	$V_i + V_j$
$P \cdot C_i$	$\|P\|_2^2 \cdot V_i$
Keyswitch(c_i)	$V_i + \mathcal{E}_{KS}^{n,\overline{N}}$
BlindRotate(C_i, v)	$V_i + \mathcal{E}_{BR}$
Bootstrap(c_i)	$\mathcal{E}_{BR} + \mathcal{E}_{KS}^{N,1}$

Each of the bootstrapping methods of Sect. 4 relies on a composition of the operations from Table 1. So, we compute their resulting variances in Table 2 by simply composing the formulas from Table 1.

Table 2. Output noise variance of the aforementioned functional bootstrapping methods

Bootstrapping	Variance
Half-Torus	$\mathcal{E}_{BR} + \mathcal{E}_{KS}^{N,1}$
FDFB	$\|v_2 - v_1\|_2^2 \cdot (\mathcal{E}_{BR} + \mathcal{E}_{KS}^{N,1} + \mathcal{E}_{KS}^{n,N}) + \mathcal{E}_{BR} + \mathcal{E}_{KS}^{N,1}$
TOTA	$\mathcal{E}_{BR} + \mathcal{E}_{KS}^{N,1}$
ComBo & ComBoP	$2 \cdot (\mathcal{E}_{BR} + \mathcal{E}_{KS}^{N,1})$
ComBoMV	$(\|v_1\|_2^2 + \|v_2\|_2^2) \cdot \mathcal{E}_{BR} + 2 \cdot \mathcal{E}_{KS}^{N,1}$

We identify in Table 2 two kinds of functional bootstrapping algorithms. On the one hand, we have functional bootstrapping algorithms that do not use any intermediary polynomial multiplication and end-up with a similar noise growth to a gate bootstrapping. On the other hand, we have functional bootstrapping algorithms that have a quadratic growth of the output noise variance with respect to the norm of the used test polynomial. For this second category, we can reduce the output noise by using the factorization technique described in Sect. 3.4.

5.2 Probability of Error

We discuss in this section the probabilities of error of all the functional boot-strapping methods from Sect. 4. Similar approaches to compute the probability of error of functional bootstrapping can be found in [2,24].

We first consider a single BlindRotate operation given a message $m^{(p)} \in \mathbb{Z}_p$, a TLWE ciphertext (a, b) where $b = (\langle a, s \rangle + m + e)$, and a TRLWE ciphertext $(0, t)$, where t is the test polynomial. Following the notation from Sect. 3.1, we have $m = E_p(m^{(p)})$.

As mentioned in Sect. 3.2, applying a BlindRotate and extracting the first coefficient outputs $[t^*(\phi(\bar{a}, \bar{b}))]_\mathbb{T}$. Hence, we need the equality $[t^*(\phi(\bar{a}, \bar{b}))] = [f(m)]$ to hold true for any message $m^{(p)}$ in order to compute $\mathrm{LUT}_p(f)$ for a given negacyclic function f. To that end, we consider $t = P_{f,p} \cdot X^{-\frac{N}{p}}$ assuming that p divides N (we motivated this choice in Fig. 1 and Sect. 3.3). Note that $\phi(\bar{a}, \bar{b}) = 2N \cdot (m + e + r) \bmod [2N]$ where r is an error introduced when scaling and rounding the coefficients of (a, b) from $\mathbb{T}$ to $\mathbb{Z}_{2N}$. Thus, we have:

$$[t^*(\phi(\bar{a}, \bar{b}))] = \left[f \left(\frac{\left\lfloor \frac{p \cdot (\phi(\bar{a}, \bar{b}) + \frac{N}{p})}{2N} \right\rfloor}{p} \right) \right] = \left[f \left(\frac{\lfloor p \cdot (m + e + r) + \frac{1}{2} \rfloor}{p} \right) \right]$$

It follows that $[t^*(\phi(\bar{a}, \bar{b}))] = [f(m)]$ as long as $|e + r| < \frac{1}{2p}$. The error r follows a translated Irwin-Hall distribution with variance $\frac{n+1}{48 \cdot N^2}$ that, as is well known, can be closely approximated by a centered Gaussian distribution. With the assumptions that e and r are independent random variables, the probability that $|e + r| < \frac{1}{2p}$ is $\mathcal{P}(\frac{1}{2p}, V_c + V_r)$, where V_c and V_r are respectively the variances of the ciphertext and r, and $\mathcal{P}$ is the notation introduced in Sect. 2.1. The probability of error is then $1 - \mathcal{P}(\frac{1}{2p}, V_c + V_r)$.

When multiple BlindRotate operations occur during a functional bootstrap-ping, each of them must succeed to ensure a correct computation. We can use the well known formulas of probabilities for independent or correlated events to find the overall probability of error of a functional bootstrapping method.

The probabilities of success of the functional bootstrapping methods from Sect. 4 are summarized in Table 3. We denote by:

$$V = \mathcal{E}_{BR} + \mathcal{E}_{KS}^{N,1}$$

the variance of a simple gate bootstrapping, and by:

$$V_i = ||v_i||_2^2 \cdot \mathcal{E}_{BR} + \mathcal{E}_{KS}^{N,1}$$

the variance of a bootstrapping using an intermediary polynomial multiplication.

The variances and the value of p given as inputs to the formulas of Table 3 have a high impact on the error rate. Indeed, $1 - \mathcal{P}(a, V)$ gets exponentially closer to 0 when a increases or when V decreases. For example, for a given p and V, the error rate of the Half-Torus method (i.e., $(1 - \mathcal{P}(\frac{1}{4p}, V))$) is higher than the probability of error of FDFB $(1 - \mathcal{P}(\frac{1}{2p}, V))$.

Table 3. Probability of success for each functional bootstrapping method with plaintext size p

Bootstrapping	Probability of success
Half-Torus	$\mathcal{P}(\dfrac{1}{4 \cdot p}, V_c + V_r)$
FDFB	$\mathcal{P}(\dfrac{1}{2 \cdot p}, V_c + V_r)$
TOTA	$\mathcal{P}(\dfrac{1}{4}, V_c + V_r) \cdot \mathcal{P}(\dfrac{1}{4 \cdot p}, \dfrac{V_c}{4} + V_r + V)$
ComBo & ComBoP	$\mathcal{P}(\dfrac{1}{2 \cdot p}, V_c + V_r) \cdot \mathcal{P}(\dfrac{1}{2 \cdot p}, V + V_r)^2$
ComBoMV	$\mathcal{P}(\dfrac{1}{2 \cdot p}, V_c + V_r) \cdot \displaystyle\prod_{i=0}^{1} \mathcal{P}(\dfrac{1}{2 \cdot p}, V_i + V_r)$

6 Experimental Results

In this section, we compare the computation time and the error rate for the functional bootstrapping methods of Sect. 4. We wrap up this section with a time-error trade-off analysis. All experiments[10] were implemented on an Intel Core i5-8250U CPU @ 1.60 GHz by building on the TFHE open source library[11].

6.1 Parameters

We present in Table 4 the parameter sets used for our tests. We generate these parameters by following the guidelines below:

- We fix the security level λ to 128 bits, which is the lowest security level considered as secure by present day standard.
- For efficiency, we want N to be a small power of 2. We notice that for $N = 512$, the noise level required for ensuring security is too large to compute properly a functional bootstrapping. Thus, we choose $N = 1024$, which is the default value for the degree of the cyclotomic polynomial with TFHE.
- We note $\sigma_{\mathbb{T}_N[X]}$ the standard deviation used for the noise of the bootstrapping key and the keyswitch key from TLWE to TRLWE. We use the lattice-estimator [4] to set $\sigma_{\mathbb{T}_N[X]}$ as low as possible with respect to the security level λ. Thus, $\sigma_{\mathbb{T}_N[X]} = 5.6 \cdot 10^{-8}$.
- For efficiency, we choose values of n lower than N. As such, we generate sets of parameters for all n between 700 and 1024 by step of 100.
- We note $\sigma_{\mathbb{T}}$ the standard deviation used for the noise of the keyswitch key from TLWE to TLWE and fresh ciphertexts. For each n, we use the lattice-estimator to set $\sigma_{\mathbb{T}}$ as low as possible with respect to the security level λ.

---

[10] Code available at: https://github.com/CEA-LIST/Cingulata/experiments/tfhe-funcbootstrap-experiments.zip.
[11] https://github.com/tfhe/tfhe.

The remaining parameters, present in Table 4, are unrelated to the security level of the cryptosystem. We choose them using the following guidelines:

- We consider the Half-Torus method as the baseline for the error rate of each method. As such, we tailor sets of parameters to reach an error rate close to 2^{-30} using the Half-Torus method for a plaintext space of $p = 8$.
- For faster bootstrapping operations, we need to have l as low as possible. We still need to select l high enough to reach the target error rate.
- For given l, n, N, and $\sigma_{\mathbb{T}_N[X]}$, we choose B_g to minimize the noise of the BlindRotate.
- For lower noise, we need B_{KS} to be as high as possible. Since the size of the keys grows with the basis, we set it to 1024 to avoid memory issues.
- For faster keyswitching operations, we need to have t as low as possible. We still need to select t high enough to reach the target error rate. Given the choice of B_{KS}, we find that $t = 2$ is the optimal choice.

Table 4. Selected parameter sets with $p = 8$, $N = 1024$, $B_{KS} = 1024$, $t = 2$, and $\lambda = 128$, following the guidelines of Sect. 6.1

Set	n	l	B_g	$\sigma_\mathbb{T}$	$\sigma_{\mathbb{T}_N[X]}$
1	1024	5	16	$5.6e^{-08}$	$5.6e^{-08}$
2	1024	4	32	$5.6e^{-08}$	$5.6e^{-08}$
3	900	4	32	$5.1e^{-07}$	$5.6e^{-08}$
4	900	3	64	$5.1e^{-07}$	$5.6e^{-08}$
5	800	4	32	$3.1e^{-06}$	$5.6e^{-08}$
6	800	3	64	$3.1e^{-06}$	$5.6e^{-08}$
7	700	4	32	$1.9e^{-05}$	$5.6e^{-08}$
8	700	3	64	$1.9e^{-05}$	$5.6e^{-08}$

6.2 Error Rate

In this section, we compute the probability of error for the functional bootstrapping methods of Sect. 4 with respect to every set of parameters described in Table 4.

In order to have a fair evaluation of the ability to consecutively bootstrap with the same method, we assume that the input to each method immediately follows a bootstrapping with the same method. We present in Table 5 the obtained error rates with respect to each method.

We note that the error rate of each method does not depend on the function computed during the bootstrapping except for FDFB and ComBoMV. Thus, we define a dedicated analysis methodology for these methods:

- For FDFB, we evaluate the error rate for the functions Id and ReLU as well as the worst case that maximizes the output noise. Since we use the multi-value bootstrapping factorization (described in Sect. 3.4), the worst case test polynomial $v_2 - v_1$ has $\frac{p}{2}$ non-zero values each equal to p. If we apply the FDFB error variance formula from Table 2, we obtain the worst case noise bound for the output ciphertext: $\frac{p^3}{2} \cdot (\mathcal{E}_{BR} + \mathcal{E}_{KS}^{N,1} + \mathcal{E}_{KS}^{n,N}) + \mathcal{E}_{BR} + \mathcal{E}_{KS}^{N,1}$.
- For ComBoMV, we follow the decomposition $f_{odd,neg} \circ Id_{neg} + f_{even,neg} \circ abs_{neg}$ given in Sect. 4.4, and use a multi-value bootstrapping to compute Id_{neg} and abs_{neg} at the same time. As such, the error rate becomes independent from the computed function.

Table 5. $-\log_2$ of error rate for $p = 8$

Set		1	2	3	4	5	6	7	8
Half-Torus		34	28	32	20	36	23	39	25
TOTA		33	27	30	18	34	20	36	22
FDFB	Worst	7	3	3	1	3	1	3	1
	Id	55	27	31	11	34	13	35	14
	ReLU	55	27	31	11	34	13	35	14
ComBo		116	85	97	50	108	56	116	61
ComBoP		116	85	97	50	108	56	116	61
ComBoMV		46	21	23	8	26	9	29	10

In Table 5, we show that for any given set of parameters, the probability of error is almost identical between TOTA and Half-Torus, or slightly in favor of the latter. Meanwhile, ComBo and ComBoP outperform the other methods in every case by at least 30 orders of magnitude.

We notice that FDFB and ComBoMV do not behave in the same fashion as the other methods with respect to changes in parameters:

- They favorably compare to the others when the noise of the input ciphertext is small compared to V_r, as in set 1 where ComBoMV reaches an error rate of 2^{-46} while the Half-Torus method reaches an error rate of 2^{-34}. In these cases, the overhead of the noise created by the intermediary polynomial multiplication is absorbed by V_r.
- They unfavorably compare to the other methods when V_r is small compared to the noise of the input ciphertext, as in set 8 where ComBoMV reaches an error rate of 2^{-10} while the Half-Torus method reaches an error rate of 2^{-25}.

In addition, for FDFB, the specific values of the polynomial ($P_2 - P_1$ from Sect. 4.2) also have to be taken into account when trying to gauge whether the parameters are favorable or not towards FDFB use. Indeed, in simple cases such as the ReLU and Id functions, we can see a huge improvement (from 2^{-7} to 2^{-55} for the set 1) compared to the worst case approximation for FDFB.

6.3   Time Performance

The Half-Torus method is the fastest as it requires one BlindRotate. Then, TOTA is slightly faster than FDFB as it requires less KeySwitch operations. It is also on par with ComBoP as the parallelism overhead is negligible. As far as the ComBo method is concerned, the number of BlindRotate depends on the evaluated function. For a simple function such as the absolute value, its speed is identical to the Half-Torus method. Meanwhile, more complex functions need up to 4 bootstrappings. So, a sequential execution of ComBo becomes twice slower than TOTA and FDFB. Note however that these latter methods are intrinsically sequential. As such, they cannot outperform ComBoP.

As a bonus, we obtain a rule of thumb to get the computation time of each functional bootstrapping method. Indeed, multiplying the computation time of one bootstrapping with the number of consecutive BlindRotate gives accurate estimations of the result from Table 6. We remind that the computation time of one bootstrapping is almost equal to the time required to run to 1 BlindRotate plus 1 KeySwitch.

Table 6. Computation time in ms

Set		1	2	3	4	5	6	7	8
Half-Torus		135.0	126.1	101.4	94.6	97.4	84.5	85.5	72.0
TOTA		274.7	252.4	209.3	189.3	194.9	169.1	174.3	147.9
FDFB		287.0	268.1	220.5	203.2	207.4	181.2	182.8	157.8
ComBo	abs	136.5	126.0	104.9	94.6	97.5	84.5	87.0	74.2
	generic	551.5	503.6	417.7	378.0	389.6	337.5	341.4	296.5
ComBoP		273.6	258.8	211.1	200.1	205.3	182.1	183.3	153.5
ComBoMV		419.0	386.2	319.7	290.9	299.0	260.1	262.0	224.6

Another way of showing ComBoP advantages is to compute the time performance of each method given their *own* optimized parameter set with respect to the same target error rate and plaintext space of size p. When doing so, we get the following example results with a target error rate of 2^{-32}:

- **p = 4:** We achieve a speed up of x1.04 versus TOTA, x1.1 versus FDFB (ReLU) and x2 versus FDFB (worst case).
- **p = 8:** We achieve a speed up of x1.09 versus TOTA, x1.12 versus FDFB (ReLU) and x4 versus FDFB (worst case).
- **p = 16:** We achieve a speed up of x1.12 versus TOTA, x1.4 versus FDFB (ReLU) and x2 versus FDFB (worst case).

Besides, ComBo, ComBoP and ComBoMV are the only method allowing for parameters using $N = 1024$ when $p = 16$. This lead to ciphertexts twice smaller in this specific case, which is another important metric for FHE computations.

6.4   Wrapping-Up: Time-Error Trade-Offs

We summarize the trade-offs between the computation time and the error rate for each method in Fig. 2 and Fig. 3. We separate the sets defined in Table 4 in order to have better readability of the figures.

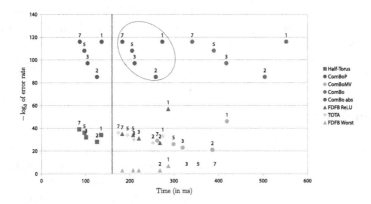

Fig. 2. Time-Error trade-off for parameters $1, 2, 3, 5$ and 7

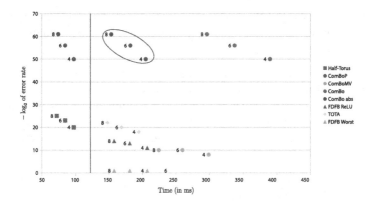

Fig. 3. Time-Error trade-off for parameters $4, 6$ and 8

For FDFB, we represent both the worst case and the ReLU, which is the best case among the functions we considered. For ComBo, ComBoMV and ComBoP methods, the best case is represented with the absolute value function and noted ComBo abs. The ComBo, ComBoMV and ComBoP points are all relative to a generic function following the pseudo even and pseudo odd decomposition from Sect. 4.4.

Fast operations will result in having points closer to the left. Meanwhile, a low error rate corresponds to points close to the upper parts of the graphs from Figs. 2 and 3. With those two considerations in mind, we notice that the only methods on the left of the red line are the Half-Torus method and ComBo in the best case scenario. In this specific scenario, the ComBo method is the best in all regards. For functions requiring more bootstrappings, a compromise between speed and error rate must be made. In the red circle lies the points relative to the ComBoP method. We can clearly see that it is both more accurate and faster than all the other methods except for the Half-Torus one. Thus, it is the best alternative to the Half-Torus method among the suggested functional bootstrapping.

7   Conclusion

Through the use of several bootstrappings and, most of the time, additional operations, every full domain method adds some output noise when compared to the partial domain method (Sect. 4.1). So the bottom line is: does a larger initial plaintext space make up for the added noise and computation time?

Table 5 and Table 6 confirm that the Yan et al. [32] (TOTA) method is both less accurate and twice as time-consuming than the partial domain method. Both Kluczniak and Schild's [27] (FDFB) and ComBoP methods provide a better accuracy than the partial domain method for well chosen parameters with varying additional computational costs.

Among the above full-domain methods, ComBoP achieves the best performance and accuracy. Furthermore, it outperforms the partial domain method in the following cases:

- The parameters of the cryptosystem are limited due to application constraints and the error rate of the Half-Torus is too large.
- Intermediate operations such as additions and multiplications push messages out of the Half-Torus space.
- Modular arithmetic is needed (which is impossible with the partial domain method).

When none of the above applies, however, the Half-Torus bootstrapping method still achieves better performances. This illustrates the fact, that there is no universal best method for functional bootstrapping and that one should carefully choose the most appropriate one depending on his or her application constraints. This paper's methodology and unified analysis gives a complete set of tools for making these choices.

ComBo (Sect. 4.4) has a smaller error rate than any other method available in the literature. In addition, as it allows to perform two bootstrappings in parallel, it may come without additional computational cost compared to the other full domain methods which are intrinsically serial. As such, ComBoP appears especially well adapted to benefit from the SIMD instruction sets available in modern processors. Furthermore, ComBo is particularly suited to homomorphic evaluation of functions such as ReLU, one of the key building-blocks for enabling advanced deep learning functions over encrypted data at larger scale.

References

1. Madi, A., et al.: A secure federated learning framework using homomorphic encryption and verifiable computing. In: 2021 Reconciling Data Analytics, Automation, Privacy, and Security: A Big Data Challenge (RDAAPS), pp. 1–8. IEEE (2021). https://doi.org/10.1109/RDAAPS48126.2021.9452005
2. Bergerat, L., et al.: Parameter optimization and larger precision for (T)FHE. J. Cryptol. **36**, 28 (2023). https://doi.org/10.1007/s00145-023-09463-5
3. Xie, P., et al.: Crypto-nets: neural networks over encrypted data. arXiv preprint arXiv:1412.6181 (2014)
4. Albrecht, M.R., Player, R., Scott, S.: On the concrete hardness of learning with errors. J. Math. Cryptol. **9**(3), 169–203 (2015)
5. Boura, C., Gama, N., Georgieva, M., Jetchev, D.: CHIMERA: combining ring-LWE-based fully homomorphic encryption schemes. J. Math. Cryptol. **14**(1), 316–338 (2020). https://doi.org/10.1515/jmc-2019-0026
6. Boura, C., Gama, N., Georgieva, M., Jetchev, D.: Simulating homomorphic evaluation of deep learning predictions. In: Dolev, S., Hendler, D., Lodha, S., Yung, M. (eds.) CSCML 2019. LNCS, vol. 11527, pp. 212–230. Springer, Cham (2019). https://doi.org/10.1007/978-3-030-20951-3_20
7. Bourse, F., Minelli, M., Minihold, M., Paillier, P.: Fast homomorphic evaluation of deep discretized neural networks. In: Shacham, H., Boldyreva, A. (eds.) CRYPTO 2018. LNCS, vol. 10993, pp. 483–512. Springer, Cham (2018). https://doi.org/10.1007/978-3-319-96878-0_17
8. Bourse, F., Sanders, O., Traoré, J.: Improved secure integer comparison via homomorphic encryption. In: Jarecki, S. (ed.) CT-RSA 2020. LNCS, vol. 12006, pp. 391–416. Springer, Cham (2020). https://doi.org/10.1007/978-3-030-40186-3_17
9. Brakerski, Z.: Fully homomorphic encryption without modulus switching from classical GapSVP. In: Safavi-Naini, R., Canetti, R. (eds.) CRYPTO 2012. LNCS, vol. 7417, pp. 868–886. Springer, Heidelberg (2012). https://doi.org/10.1007/978-3-642-32009-5_50
10. Carpov, S., Izabachène, M., Mollimard, V.: New techniques for multi-value input homomorphic evaluation and applications. In: Matsui, M. (ed.) CT-RSA 2019. LNCS, vol. 11405, pp. 106–126. Springer, Cham (2019). https://doi.org/10.1007/978-3-030-12612-4_6
11. Chabanne, H., Lescuyer, R., Milgram, J., Morel, C., Prouff, E.: Recognition over encrypted faces. In: Renault, É., Boumerdassi, S., Bouzefrane, S. (eds.) Mobile, Secure, and Programmable Networking (MSPN 2018). LNCS, vol. 11005, pp. 174–191. Springer, Cham (2019). https://doi.org/10.1007/978-3-030-03101-5_16
12. Chabanne, H., De Wargny, A., Milgram, J., Morel, C., Prouff, E.: Privacy-preserving classification on deep neural network. Cryptology ePrint Archive, Report 2017/035. 2017 (2017)
13. Cheon, J.H., Kim, A., Kim, M., Song, Y.: Homomorphic encryption for arithmetic of approximate numbers. In: Takagi, T., Peyrin, T. (eds.) ASIACRYPT 2017. LNCS, vol. 10624, pp. 409–437. Springer, Cham (2017). https://doi.org/10.1007/978-3-319-70694-8_15

14. Cheon, J.H., Kim, D., Park, J.H.: Towards a practical clustering analysis over encrypted data. IACR Cryptol. ePrint Arch. **2019**, 465 (2019)
15. Chillotti, I., Gama, N., Georgieva, M., Izabachène, M.: Faster fully homomorphic encryption: bootstrapping in less than 0.1 seconds. In: Cheon, J.H., Takagi, T. (eds.) ASIACRYPT 2016. LNCS, vol. 10031, pp. 3–33. Springer, Heidelberg (2016). https://doi.org/10.1007/978-3-662-53887-6_1
16. Chillotti, I., Gama, N., Georgieva, M., Izabachène, M.: Faster packed homomorphic operations and efficient circuit bootstrapping for TFHE. In: Takagi, T., Peyrin, T. (eds.) ASIACRYPT 2017. LNCS, vol. 10624, pp. 377–408. Springer, Cham (2017). https://doi.org/10.1007/978-3-319-70694-8_14
17. Chillotti, I., Gama, N., Georgieva, M., Izabachène, M.: TFHE: fast fully homomorphic encryption library
18. Chillotti, I., Gama, N., Georgieva, M., Izabachène, M.: TFHE: fast fully homomorphic encryption over the torus. J. Cryptol. **33**(1), 34–91 (2019). https://doi.org/10.1007/s00145-019-09319-x
19. Chillotti, I., Joye, M., Paillier, P.: Programmable bootstrapping enables efficient homomorphic inference of deep neural networks. In: Dolev, S., Margalit, O., Pinkas, B., Schwarzmann, A. (eds.) CSCML 2021. LNCS, vol. 12716, pp. 1–19. Springer, Cham (2021). https://doi.org/10.1007/978-3-030-78086-9_1
20. Chillotti, I., Ligier, D., Orfila, J.-B., Tap, S.: Improved programmable bootstrapping with larger precision and efficient arithmetic circuits for TFHE. In: Tibouchi, M., Wang, H. (eds.) ASIACRYPT 2021. LNCS, vol. 13092, pp. 670–699. Springer, Cham (2021). https://doi.org/10.1007/978-3-030-92078-4_23
21. Pierre-Emmanuel Clet, Martin Zuber, Aymen Boudguiga, Renaud Sirdey, and Cédric Gouy-Pailler. Putting up the swiss army knife of homomorphic calculations by means of TFHE functional bootstrapping. Cryptology ePrint Archive, Paper 2022/149. https://eprint.iacr.org/2022/149. 2022
22. Ducas, L., Micciancio, D.: FHEW: bootstrapping homomorphic encryption in less than a second. In: Oswald, E., Fischlin, M. (eds.) EUROCRYPT 2015. LNCS, vol. 9056, pp. 617–640. Springer, Heidelberg (2015). https://doi.org/10.1007/978-3-662-46800-5_24
23. Fan, J., Vercauteren, F.: Somewhat practical fully homomorphic encryption. Cryptology ePrint Archive (2012). https://ia.cr/2012/144
24. Guimarães, A., Borin, E., Aranha, D.F.: Revisiting the functional bootstrap in TFHE. IACR Trans. Cryptogr. Hardw. Embed. Syst. **2021**, 229–253 (2021)
25. Izabachène, M., Sirdey, R., Zuber, M.: Practical fully homomorphic encryption for fully masked neural networks. In: Mu, Y., Deng, R.H., Huang, X. (eds.) CANS 2019. LNCS, vol. 11829, pp. 24–36. Springer, Cham (2019). https://doi.org/10.1007/978-3-030-31578-8_2
26. Jäschke, A., Armknecht, F.: Unsupervised machine learning on encrypted data. In: Cid, C., Jacobson Jr., M. (eds.) Selected Areas in Cryptography (SAC 2018). LNCS, vol. 11349, pp. 453–478. Springer, Cham (2019). https://doi.org/10.1007/978-3-030-10970-7_21
27. Kluczniak, K., Schild, L.: FDFB: full domain functional bootstrapping towards practical fully homomorphic encryption. arXiv preprint arXiv:2109.02731 (2021)
28. Liu, Z., Micciancio, D., Polyakov, Y.: Large-precision homomorphic sign evaluation using FHEW/TFHE bootstrapping. In: Agrawal, S., Lin, D. (eds.) Advances in Cryptology (ASIACRYPT 2022). LNCS, vol. 13792, pp. 130–160. Springer, Cham (2022). https://doi.org/10.1007/978-3-031-22966-4_5

29. Lou, Q., Feng, B., Charles Fox, G., Jiang, L.: Glyph: fast and accurately training deep neural networks on encrypted data. Adv. Neural. Inf. Process. Syst. **33**, 9193–9202 (2020)
30. Nandakumar, K., Ratha, N., Pankanti, S., Halevi, S.: Towards deep neural network training on encrypted data. In: 2019 IEEE/CVF Conference on Computer Vision and Pattern Recognition Workshops (CVPRW), pp. 40–48 (2019). https://doi.org/10.1109/CVPRW.2019.00011
31. Grivet Sébert, A., Pinot, R., Zuber, M., Gouy-Pailler, C., Sirdey, R.: SPEED: secure, PrivatE, and efficient deep learning. Mach. Learn. **110**, 675–694 (2021). https://doi.org/10.1007/s10994-021-05970-3
32. Yang, Z., Xie, X., Shen, H., Chen, S., Zhou, J.: TOTA: fully homomorphic encryption with smaller parameters and stronger security. Cryptology ePrint Archive, Report 2021/1347 (2021). https://ia.cr/2021/1347
33. Zuber, M., Carpov, S., Sirdey, R.: Towards real-time hidden speaker recognition by means of fully homomorphic encryption. In: Meng, W., Gollmann, D., Jensen, C.D., Zhou, J. (eds.) ICICS 2020. LNCS, vol. 12282, pp. 403–421. Springer, Cham (2020). https://doi.org/10.1007/978-3-030-61078-4_23
34. Zuber, M., Sirdey, R.: Efficient homomorphic evaluation of k-NN classifiers. Proc. Priv. Enh. Technol. **2021**(2), 111–129 (2021). https://doi.org/10.2478/popets-2021-0020

Concrete Security from Worst-Case to Average-Case Lattice Reductions

Joel Gärtner$^{(\boxtimes)}$ (iD)

KTH Royal Institute of Technology, Stockholm, Sweden
jgartner@kth.se

Abstract. A famous reduction by Regev shows that random instances of the Learning With Errors (LWE) problem are asymptotically at least as hard as a worst-case lattice problem. As such, by assuming that standard lattice problems are hard to solve, the asymptotic security of cryptosystems based on the LWE problem is guaranteed. However, it has not been clear to which extent, if any, this reduction provides support for the security of present concrete parametrizations.

In this work we therefore use Regev's reduction to parametrize a cryptosystem, providing a reference as to what parameters are required to actually claim security from this reduction. This requires us to account for the concrete performance of this reduction, allowing the first parametrization of a cryptosystem that is provably secure based only on a conservative hardness estimate for a standard lattice problem. Even though we attempt to optimize the reduction, our system still requires significantly larger parameters than typical LWE-based cryptosystems, highlighting the significant gap between parameters that are used in practice and those for which worst-case reductions actually are applicable.

Keywords: Post-quantum cryptography · Lattice-based cryptography · Learning With Errors · Provable security · Public Key Cryptography

1 Introduction

With the conclusion of the third round of the NIST post-quantum standardization process, lattice-based cryptography is one step closer to see widespread adoption. As a result of this third round, NIST have selected the lattice-based Key Encapsulation Mechanism (KEM) Kyber [23] for standardization.

Kyber is a cryptosystem with security based on the assumed hardness of a structured version of the Learning With Errors (LWE) problem. LWE is a relatively new problem that was first introduced by Regev in 2005 [18]. In the same paper, Regev showed that it is asymptotically at least as hard to solve random instances of the LWE problem as it is to solve a worst-case instance of a standard lattice problem on a quantum computer. As lattice problems are believed to be hard to solve, Regev could reasonably claim that LWE is a hard problem, even though no one had analyzed this problem before.

N. El Mrabet et al. (Eds.): AFRICACRYPT 2023, LNCS 14064, pp. 344–369, 2023.
https://doi.org/10.1007/978-3-031-37679-5_15

The hardness of structured versions of LWE, such as the module-LWE problem that Kyber is based on, are also supported by this type of reduction from worst-case lattice problems [11,13]. These reductions provide an argument for using these problems for cryptography but are typically not used to argue for the concrete security of cryptosystems. Instead cryptosystems typically base their security directly on an estimate for the concrete hardness of the relevant version of the LWE problem.

When estimating the hardness of LWE, one typically considers the primal and dual lattice attacks. These attacks are based upon transforming an LWE instance into a lattice problem, which is solved by using standard lattice algorithms. As such, the concrete hardness of the LWE problem is extrapolated based on the performance of lattice algorithms [1].

It may further be argued that the worst-case to average-case reductions serve as a qualitative argument for the security of LWE-based cryptosystems with Micciancio and Regev [15] meaning that it "assures us that there are no fundamental flaws in the design of our cryptographic construction". This may serve as a reason to prefer LWE-based schemes over other lattice-based schemes, such as NTRU. Furthermore, as the hardness of the LWE problem is guaranteed if lattice problems are hard, it may have resulted in less focus on non-lattice based algorithms to solve LWE, since we in some sense are guaranteed that these can not perform better than lattice algorithms.

However, although these types of arguments may be reasonable in an asymptotic sense, it has not previously been clear if they, at least to some extent, are applicable to parameters used in practice. While Micciancio and Regev also mention that using the reductions to set parameters seems to be overly conservative, there has not really been any investigation to how large such parameters actually would have to be.

If parameters supported by the reductions have similar size to the ones used in practice they would still serve as a lower bound on how much the security could drop in a cryptosystem. This reasoning has for example been used by Peikert when arguing for the importance of worst-case reductions in lattice-based security [17]. However, if the reductions only support schemes with significantly larger parameters than typical cryptosystems, even at relatively low security levels, then the support these worst-case reductions provide to typical schemes is questionable.

In order to investigate to which extent such reductions provide any security lower bounds or other qualitative support for typical LWE-based cryptosystems, we investigate a cryptosystem with security that is actually based on such a worst-case to average-case reduction. This cryptosystem is parametrized to take into account the concrete performance of used reductions and is based on a reasonable estimate on the concrete hardness of the underlying problem. This guarantees that the system remains secure as long as there are no significant improvements in the efficiency of lattice algorithms.

The concrete performance of Regev's reduction has been analyzed in some previous works [4,7,21]. Furthermore, a cryptosystem parametrized through the reduction was also proposed in [7], with parameter sizes comparable to a typical LWE-based cryptosystem. However, this parametrization mainly focused on the efficiency of the reduction and was not based on a realistic estimate for the hardness of the underlying problem. Therefore, there has not previously been any good reference for which parameters are required by a cryptosystem to have its concrete security supported by Regev's reduction.

Worth noting is that the specification of FrodoKEM [16], another LWE-based cryptosystem very similar to ours, also includes a reduction from a worst-case lattice problem. However, for FrodoKEM, this reduction is mainly as a qualitative argument for the security of the system and there is no analysis of which concrete parameters are supported by the reduction. The reduction essentially corresponds to a single classical step of Regev's full quantum reduction, resulting in the reduction solving a less standard lattice problem but with less requirements on the cryptosystem. We do not expect this approach to support the security of cryptosystems that use significantly smaller parameters than the ones we propose in this paper and we therefore consider Regev's full reduction from a more standard lattice problem.

1.1   Our Contributions

In this work we construct a cryptosystem that is parametrized based on a version of Regev's original quantum reduction from worst-case lattice problems to average case LWE [19]. As such, the security of this cryptosystem is actually guaranteed by the concrete hardness of a well studied standard lattice problem. This provides a reference to what parameters are required for similar reductions to say something meaningful about the concrete security of a cryptosystem.

Using this reduction to parametrize our cryptosystem requires that we keep track of its concrete performance, both in terms of running time and approximation factor for which it solves the underlying lattice problem. To allow our cryptosystem to use smaller parameters, we modify Regev's original reduction in order to improve its concrete efficiency. Even with these modifications, both the running time and the approximation factor of the reduction are relatively large and our cryptosystem requires significantly larger parameters than typical LWE-based cryptosystems.

Currently proposed LWE based cryptosystems are typically parametrized with a dimension n that is approximately 1000 when targeting 256 bits of security. Meanwhile, our cryptosystem that targets 128 bits of OW-CPA post-quantum security requires using a dimension $n \approx 39300$. We also consider an alternative version of the LWE problem which allows a more efficient version of Regev's reduction. Using this version of the LWE problem for our cryptosystem therefore allows a more efficient parametrization, with this version having the same security guarantees while using $n \approx 32800$.

Even if we completely ignore the running time of the reduction, our cryptosystem requires a dimension $n \approx 9400$ when targeting 128-bits of OW-CPA security. It thus seems like significantly larger parameters than those used by typical LWE-based cryptosystems are required in order for these types of worst-case to average-case reductions to say anything meaningful about the systems security. While this does not indicate that currently proposed LWE-based cryptosystems are insecure, it does mean that the security of these schemes is far from supported by arguments that rely on these types of reductions.

As such, we do not consider it reasonable to use these reductions as an argument for a lower bound on the security of LWE-based cryptosystems used in practice. Furthermore, we do not deem similar worst-case to average-case reductions to be a strong argument in favour of typical LWE-based cryptosystems over other lattice-based systems, such as NTRU.

1.2 Overview

Cryptosystem. The cryptosystem we construct in this paper is based on the Lindner-Peikert scheme [12], in a similar way to FrodoKEM [16]. To parametrize our cryptosystem, we use a reduction from an approximate version of the Shortest Independent Vector Problem (SIVP). This allows us to guarantee the claimed security of our cryptosystem unless algorithms that solve this problem improve significantly.

We also consider a slight modification of traditional LWE-based cryptosystems by letting the system use a variable error distribution. As this version of the cryptosystem allows a more efficient reduction, it can be parametrized with smaller parameters while arguing for the same security.

Considerations for Parametrization. In order to use Regev's reduction to parametrize our cryptosystem, we must analyze it in detail. While the efficiency of a reduction is often considered in an asymptotic sense, this is not sufficient for a concrete parametrization of a cryptosystem. Instead, we must know the concrete time the reduction requires to solve the underlying problem when using an adversary against our cryptosystem. This allows us to guarantee that any adversary against the claimed security of our cryptosystem implies an algorithm that is more efficient than what our conservative hardness estimate for the underlying lattice problem predict to be possible.

To account for the efficiency of a reduction, we must consider its run time T_R and success probability p_R. These depend both on the run time T_O of the oracle used by the reduction as well as its success probability p_O. A combined measure for a reductions efficiency is given by its tightness gap $(T_R p_O)/(p_R T_O)$ as defined in [4]. The tightness gap of Regev's original reduction has been analyzed in previous works [4,7,21], but these works did not attempt to optimize the reduction for better concrete efficiency. Because of this, we provide our own analysis of the efficiency of a somewhat optimized version of Regev's reduction.

As defined, the tightness gap of a reduction relates to the efficiency of running the reduction. It does however not take into account the concrete hardness of the underlying problem, something which is arguably more important if using the reduction to parametrize a cryptosystem. This aspect of the reduction was not considered in any detail in any of the previous works that analyzed the tightness gap in Regev's reduction.

Our more realistic hardness estimate for approximate SIVP is the primary reason why our parametrizations use significantly larger parameters than the ones proposed in the master thesis of Gates [7], which also accounted for the concrete efficiency of Regev's reduction. Instead of considering the hardness of approximate SIVP, Gates's parametrization was based on the assumption that this problem is as hard as an exact lattice problem. For the relatively large approximation factor for which the reduction solves approximate SIVP, this significantly overestimates the hardness of the underlying problem.

Security Proof and Its Efficiency. We argue for the security of our cryptosystem through a series of reductions, all detailed in Sect. 4. Here we present an outline of the different steps and their efficiency. For readability, we omit some constants in this overview, a luxury we naturally can not afford in the full proof.

For the proof, we assume that there is an adversary against our cryptosystem that requires time T to achieve advantage ε_a. Furthermore, we consider versions of our cryptosystem that are parametrized with a dimension n and with elements in $\mathbb{Z}_q$.

The first step in our security proof is to show that we can use this adversary against the OW-CPA security of our cryptosystem to solve a Decision-LWE (DLWE) problem, which is accomplished through a standard hybrid argument. This is detailed in Theorem 2 which, with $k = n$, results in an algorithm that solves a DLWE instance with negligible failure probability in time $\mathcal{O}(n \cdot T/\varepsilon_a)$.

While not having a large tightness gap, this step still has a significant impact on the efficiency of the full reduction. This is due it determining how many samples that are required by the constructed DLWE oracle in order to decide if these samples are from an LWE distribution. As we are required to amplify the initially small success probability of the adversary to essentially 1, we require $N = \mathcal{O}(n^2/\varepsilon_a)$ LWE samples. Since the performance of later steps of the reduction depends on this relatively large N, this greatly affects the efficiency of the full reduction.

Next, we use this DLWE oracle in order to solve the search-LWE problem that appears in Regev's reduction. Part of this is accomplished by a search to decision reduction that requires using an DLWE oracle nq times to solve a search-LWE problem with the same error distribution, as detailed in Lemma 4.

The search-LWE problem that must be solved in Regev's reduction is actually stated in terms of an unknown error distribution. To handle this unknown error distribution we may use the same approach as Regev used in [19], with somewhat improved analysis. This results in having to use the DLWE oracle a total of $10N \cdot n^2 q$ times with $M = nN$ LWE samples in order to solve this search-LWE problem, as detailed in Lemma 7. As N is large, this step has a significant impact on the running time of the reduction.

We can also solve this search-LWE problem more efficiently by considering an DLWE oracle constructed from an adversary against our modified cryptosystem with variable error distribution. This approach, given by Lemma 8, only requires using the DLWE oracle nq times to solve the search-LWE problem, while also only requiring $M = N$ different LWE samples. This step of the reduction is thus significantly more efficient when using our modified cryptosystem, which is the reason why it can be parametrized with smaller parameters.

Finally, Regev's quantum reduction allows us to use our ability to solve search LWE in order to solve an arbitrary approximate SIVP instance. By not considering an intermediate reduction from discrete Gaussian sampling, we somewhat improve the efficiency of this step. This allows us to solve the target approximate SIVP instance by using $3n^2 M$ calls to an LWE oracle that handles unknown error distribution, as detailed in Theorem 3.

In conclusion, an adversary against the cryptosystem with fixed error distribution can be used to solve approximate SIVP in time

$$\mathcal{O}(qn^6 N^2 \cdot T/\varepsilon_a) = \mathcal{O}(qn^{10} \cdot T/\varepsilon_a^3)$$

with constants given in Theorem 4 with $k = n$. Using the above mentioned improvements, an adversary against our cryptosystem with variable error distribution can be used to solve approximate SIVP in time

$$\mathcal{O}(qn^4 N \cdot T/\varepsilon_a) = \mathcal{O}(qn^6 \cdot T/\varepsilon_a^2)$$

with constants given in Theorem 5.

An adversary against the claimed 128 bits of security of our cryptosystems will have $T/\varepsilon_a \leq 2^{128}$. By itself, this bound is not sufficient to calculate the running time of the reduction. Instead, we consider the worst-case, where $T = 1$ and $\varepsilon_a = 2^{-128}$. This results in the dependence on ε_a to be one of the most significant reasons for the long run time of the reduction.

As such, one of the largest contributor to the inefficiency of the reduction is the fact that the LWE oracle constructed from an adversary against our cryptosystem requires a large number of LWE samples. Previous analyses of the tightness gap of Regev's reduction have not accounted for this and instead assumed that the provided LWE oracle only requires as many LWE samples as exposed in a single instance of a cryptosystem.[1] However, thanks to our optimizations compared to previous works, our final reduction is still approximately as efficient as the claimed efficiency in these previous works.

Hardness Estimate. In order to provide any concrete security guarantees from a reduction, we require that an adversary against the cryptosystem could be used with the reduction in order to solve some concrete problem more efficiently than we believe to be possible. As such, to parametrize our cryptosystem we need an estimate for the difficulty of solving the underlying lattice problem.

---

[1] That the LWE oracle provided to Regev's reduction will require many LWE samples was also noticed in a paper by Koblitz et al. [10] that analyzed a similar reduction for ring-LWE.

With our security reduction, an adversary against our cryptosystem can be used to solve a worst-case instance of approximate SIVP. This worst-case instance is obviously at least as hard as a random instance of this problem. As nothing indicates that SIVP on random lattices is an easier problem than SIVP on other lattices, assuming that worst-case SIVP is as hard as SIVP on random lattices should not significantly underestimate the hardness of the problem. As such, the hardness of SIVP on random lattices serves as a reasonable hardness estimate for worst-case SIVP.

For our hardness estimate on random lattices, we relate the hardness of SIVP with a well studied approximate version of the shortest vector problem (SVP), namely Hermite-SVP. This is in fact the same problem that is typically considered when estimating the hardness of LWE, allowing much of the previous research into the concrete hardness of LWE to be directly relevant for our parametrization as well.

It is however important to note that the security of our cryptosystem is dependent on the hardness Hermite-SVP in a completely different way compared to a typical LWE-based cryptosystem. For a typical LWE-based cryptosystem, algorithms that solve Hermite-SVP more efficiently would be sufficient to break the cryptosystem. However, these cryptosystems could potentially be vulnerable to other types of attacks, even without lattice algorithms improving.

In contrast to this, our proposed cryptosystem is provably secure as long as lattice algorithms do not improve significantly. As such, while concrete attacks against our cryptosystem could improve, they will be unable to break the claimed 128 bits of OW-CPA security unless Hermite-SVP is a significantly easier problem than we currently believe it is.

2   Background

2.1   Notation

Matrices are written with bold upper case letters A and vectors bold lower case letters s. Sampling a value x from a distribution $\mathcal{X}$ is expressed as $x \leftarrow \mathcal{X}$ and the result of a randomized function f with input x is similarly denoted $y \leftarrow f(x)$. Distributions are expressed with calligraphic letters $\mathcal{X}$ and $\mathcal{U}(X)$ corresponds to the uniform distribution over the set X. The size of a set X is denoted by $|X|$. Concatenation of bitstrings b_0, b_1 is denoted $b_0\|b_1$, while for matrices and vectors $A\|v$ corresponds to the matrix generated by the columns of the concatenated matrices and vectors.

2.2   Gaussian Distributions

We define Ψ_β for any $\beta \in \mathbb{R}^+$ to be a distribution corresponding to sampling from a mean 0 normal distribution with standard deviation $\beta/\sqrt{2\pi}$ and reducing the result modulo 1. In order to calculate statistical distance between Ψ_α and Ψ_β, the following lemma will be used.

Lemma 1 (Claim 2.2 from [19]). *For any $0 < \alpha < \beta \le 2\alpha$,*

$$\Delta(\Psi_\alpha, \Psi_\beta) \le 9\left(\frac{\beta}{\alpha} - 1\right)$$

The sum of samples from two different mean 0 normal distributions with standard deviation α and β respectively is a mean 0 normal distribution with standard deviation $\sqrt{\alpha^2 + \beta^2}$. This also implies that the sum of a sample from Ψ_α and a sample from Ψ_β is distributed as a sample from $\Psi_{\sqrt{\alpha^2 + \beta^2}}$.

We define $\overline{\mathcal{X}}$ for an arbitrary distribution $\mathcal{X}$ over $[0, 1)$ to be the rounded distribution over $\mathbb{Z}_q$ given by $\lfloor qx \rceil \mod q$ with $x \leftarrow \mathcal{X}$ for some implicit q. In particular, we will use the rounded Gaussian distribution $\overline{\Psi}_\alpha$.

2.3   Lattices

A full rank integer lattice L can be described by an invertible basis $\boldsymbol{B} \in \mathbb{Z}^{n \times n}$, which we denote as $L = L(\boldsymbol{B})$. The lattice consists of all points $\boldsymbol{v} = \boldsymbol{B}\boldsymbol{x}$ where $\boldsymbol{x}$ is some vector in $\mathbb{Z}^n$. The dual of a lattice is defined as

$$L^* = \{\boldsymbol{v} \in \mathbb{R}^n : \boldsymbol{v} \cdot \boldsymbol{w} \in \mathbb{Z} \; \forall \boldsymbol{w} \in L\}$$

and a basis for the dual of a full rank lattice is given by $\boldsymbol{B}^* = (\boldsymbol{B}^{-1})^T$. The determinant $\det(L)$ of a full rank lattice L is equal to the absolute value of the determinant of any basis for the lattice. The determinant of the dual lattice is the inverse of the determinant of the primal lattice.

The length of the shortest non-zero vector in a lattice L is denoted by $\lambda_1(L)$, which is equivalent to the radius of the smallest ball around the origin that contains a non-zero lattice vector. Similarly, $\lambda_n(L)$ is the radius of the smallest ball that contains n linearly independent lattice vectors. The following transference theorem by Banaszczyk relates these values on the lattice and its dual.

Lemma 2 (Theorem 2.1 from [2]). *For any n-dimensional lattice L,*

$$1 \le \lambda_1(L) \cdot \lambda_n(L^*) \le n \ .$$

We denote a discrete Gaussian distribution with width r over a lattice L by $D_{L,r}$. This is the distribution with support on L and where the probability of $\boldsymbol{v} \in L$ is proportional to $\exp(-\pi \|\boldsymbol{v}/r\|^2)$.

Several lattice problems are known to be NP-hard to solve. The quantum reduction from [19] is not directly related to such a NP-hard problem but instead to SIVP$_\gamma$, an approximate version of the Shortest Independent Vector Problem (SIVP) which is not believed to be NP-hard for the relevant approximation factor γ. The definition of SIVP$_\gamma$ follows, with the exact problem corresponding to $\gamma = 1$.

Definition 1 (SIVP$_\gamma$). *An instance of SIVP$_\gamma$ is given by an n dimensional lattice L. The goal is to output n linearly independent vectors in L that all are shorter than $\gamma(n) \cdot \lambda_n(L)$.*

Two other lattice problems used in this paper are the Bounded Distance Decoding (BDD) problem and an approximate version of the Shortest Vector Problem (SVP) called Hermite-SVP. The definitions of these problems follow

Definition 2 (BDD). *An instance of the BDD problem is given by a distance bound d, a lattice L and a point x that is guaranteed to be at most a distance d from L. The solution to the problem is a vector $v \in L$ such that $\|v - x\| \leq d$.*

Definition 3 (γ-Hermite-SVP). *An instance of γ-Hermite-SVP is given by an n dimensional lattice L. The goal is to output a non-zero lattice vector with length at most $\gamma \cdot \det(L)^{1/n}$.*

In general we can not predict the length of the shortest vector in a lattice based on its determinant. In a random lattice we can however estimate its length by using the Gaussian heuristic. This predicts that the expected value of $\lambda_1(L)$ is $\sqrt{\frac{n}{2\pi e}} \cdot \det(L)^{1/n}$. Asymptotically it is proven that the Gaussian heuristic correctly predicts the expected length of the shortest vector in a random lattice [5,20,24].

In Regev's reduction the so called smoothing parameter $\eta_\varepsilon(L)$ is used extensively. We bound the value of this parameter by using the following bound, corresponding to Lemma 3.2 from [14] with the addition of the second inequality directly following from Lemma 2.

Lemma 3. *For any n-dimensional lattice L,*

$$\eta_{\varepsilon(n)}(L) \leq \sqrt{n}/\lambda_1(L^*) \leq \sqrt{n} \cdot \lambda_n(L)$$

where $\varepsilon(n) = 2^{-n}$

2.4 Learning with Errors

The Learning With Errors (LWE) problem was first introduced by Regev in [19] and is parametrized by a dimension n, an integer modulus q and an error distribution $\mathcal{X}$. Regev showed a quantum reduction from SIVP$_\gamma$ for a polynomially sized γ to the LWE problem with q a polynomially bounded prime and $\mathcal{X}$ a Gaussian distribution. In the reduction from SIVP$_\gamma$, the following definition of an LWE distribution is used.

Definition 4 (LWE distribution). *Let n, q be positive integers, and let ϕ be a distribution over $[0, 1)$. For $s \in \mathbb{Z}^n$, the LWE distribution $A_{s,\phi}$ is the distribution over $\mathbb{Z}_q^n \times [0, 1)$ obtained by choosing $a \in \mathbb{Z}_q^n$ uniformly at random and an error $e \in [0, 1)$ from ϕ and outputting the pair*

$$\left(a, b = \frac{\langle a, s \rangle}{q} + e \mod 1 \right) \in \mathbb{Z}_q^n \times [0, 1)$$

It is usually preferable to only work with integers when using the LWE problem in applications. Therefore, we also use the following discrete version of an LWE distribution.

Definition 5 (Discrete LWE distribution). *Let n, q be positive integers, and let $\mathcal{X}$ be a distribution over $\mathbb{Z}_q$. For $\boldsymbol{s} \in \mathbb{Z}^n$ the LWE distribution $A_{\boldsymbol{s},\mathcal{X}}$ is the distribution over $\mathbb{Z}_q^n \times \mathbb{Z}_q$ obtained by choosing $\boldsymbol{a} \in \mathbb{Z}_q^n$ uniformly at random and an integer error $e \in \mathbb{Z}_q$ from $\mathcal{X}$ and outputting the pair*

$$(\boldsymbol{a}, b = \langle \boldsymbol{a}, \boldsymbol{s} \rangle + e \mod q) \in \mathbb{Z}_q^n \times \mathbb{Z}_q$$

In this work, both types of LWE distributions are considered and can be distinguished by the sample space of its error distribution. It is easily seen that we can transform samples from a continuous LWE distribution into samples from a discrete LWE distribution with a rounded error distribution. This is for example detailed in Lemma 4.3 of [19].

There is both a search and a decision version of the LWE problem which we define next.

Definition 6 (Search-LWE problem). *The $LWE(\mathcal{X}, m)$ problem is to recover any secret $\boldsymbol{s} \in \mathbb{Z}_q^n$ when given m samples from $A_{\boldsymbol{s},\mathcal{X}}$.*

Definition 7 (Decision-LWE problem). *Let $\mathcal{D}$ be some unknown distribution that is either uniformly random or $A_{\boldsymbol{s},\mathcal{X}}$ for some $\boldsymbol{s} \in \mathbb{Z}_q^n$. The $DLWE(\mathcal{X}, m)$ problem is to determine if $\mathcal{D}$ is an LWE distribution or not when given m samples from $\mathcal{D}$.*

The following lemma shows that decision- and search-LWE are more or less equivalent problems. This is the same statement as in Lemma 4.2 from [19] except for also including the number of calls and the probability of success, which follow easily from Regev's proof. Worth noting is that we can ensure that W' only requires N samples from $A_{\boldsymbol{s},\mathcal{X}}$ by reusing the same LWE samples every time W is used.

Lemma 4. *Let q be a prime, n, N integers and $\mathcal{X}$ be some distribution on $\mathbb{Z}_q$. Assume that we have access to an oracle W that solves a $DLWE(\mathcal{X}, N)$ problem with a failure probability of at most ε. Then there exists an algorithm W' that solves the $LWE(\mathcal{X}, N)$ problem except for with probability at most $nq\varepsilon$.*

In normal-form LWE, elements of the secret vector are sampled from the error distribution. This following lemma shows that instances of the LWE problem with their secret sampled in this way are essentially as hard as a worst case instance of LWE.

Lemma 5 (Theorem 5.10 from [16]). *Let $q = p^e$ be a prime power and $\mathcal{X}$ be some distribution over $\mathbb{Z}_q$. There is a deterministic polynomial time transformation that, for arbitrary $\boldsymbol{s} \in \mathbb{Z}_q^n$, maps $A_{\boldsymbol{s},\mathcal{X}}$ to $A_{\boldsymbol{x},\mathcal{X}}$ where $\boldsymbol{x} \leftarrow \mathcal{X}^n$, and maps $\mathcal{U}(\mathbb{Z}_q^n \times \mathbb{Z}_q)$ to itself. The process fails with probability at most 2^{-k} for arbitrary k by using an initial $n + k$ samples from $A_{\boldsymbol{s},\mathcal{X}}$. After these initial samples, samples from $A_{\boldsymbol{s},\mathcal{X}}$ are directly transformed into samples from $A_{\boldsymbol{x},\mathcal{X}}$.*

3   Cryptosystem

3.1   OW-CPA Secure Public Key Encryption

In this paper we construct Public Key Encryption (PKE) scheme which we parametrize to target 128 bits of OW-CPA security. The cryptosystem is essentially constructed as the Lindner-Peikert scheme [12], in a similar way to FrodoKEM [16]. Our cryptosystem also supports using a variable error distribution, as this allows it to be supported by a more efficient security reduction.

The algorithms for key generation, encryption and decryption in our cryptosystem are described in Fig. 1. Parameters for the cryptosystem are positive integers $n, \overline{n}$ and B, a prime q and a set $I \subset (0,1)$ which determines which error distributions the cryptosystem uses. The resulting cryptosystem encrypts $\ell = B \cdot \overline{n}^2$ bits per encryption and has a decryption failure probability that depends on the parametrization, as detailed in Sect. 3.2.

The specific error distributions used by the cryptosystem are determined by the set I, with the squared standard deviation of the error distribution determined by a sample from $\mathcal{U}(I)$ every time that a new LWE distribution is required. An ordinary LWE-based cryptosystem is recovered by using a set with a single element $I = \{\alpha^2\}$ while our other parametrization uses a larger set with $I = [\alpha^2, 3\alpha^2/2]$.

We parametrize all our cryptosystems with $B = 4$ and with $\overline{n}$ either 8 or 12. Remaining parameters are selected such that $\alpha q \approx 2\sqrt{n}$ and so that the decryption failure probability is sufficiently small. This leads to us selecting $q = \mathcal{O}(n^{3/2})$ and $\alpha = \mathcal{O}(n^{-1})$, meaning that all other parameters are determined by the choice of dimension n, allowing us to find the optimal n that achieves our targeted security. More details regarding the chosen parameters are presented in Sect. 6.

The LWE sampling algorithm in Fig. 1 returns $(\boldsymbol{b}_i = \boldsymbol{A}\boldsymbol{s}_i + \boldsymbol{e}_i, \boldsymbol{s}_i)$ for a given $\boldsymbol{A}$ and is repeated $\overline{n}$ times in both key generation and encryption. From these sampled columns, we construct matrices $\boldsymbol{B} = \boldsymbol{b}_1\| \dots \|\boldsymbol{b}_{\overline{n}}$ and $\boldsymbol{S} = \boldsymbol{s}_1\| \dots \|\boldsymbol{s}_{\overline{n}}$, which is denoted as $(\boldsymbol{B}, \boldsymbol{S}) = \text{LWEGen}_I(.)^{\overline{n}}$ in the algorithm descriptions.

For encryption, $\boldsymbol{A}$ and $\boldsymbol{B}$ are concatenated and transposed, which is used to generate

$$\boldsymbol{C} = (\boldsymbol{A}\|\boldsymbol{B})^T \boldsymbol{S}' + \boldsymbol{E}' .$$

The next step thus splits this matrix to $\boldsymbol{C}_1 \approx (\boldsymbol{S}')^T \boldsymbol{A}$ and $\boldsymbol{V} \approx (\boldsymbol{S}')^T \boldsymbol{B}$ with their respective parts of the error matrix $\boldsymbol{E}'$.

3.2   Correctness of Decryption

Our PKE is constructed in such a way that there is a probability of incorrect decryption. While we can not remove this decryption failure probability completely, by using the following lemma, we can limit it to such an extent that it does not affect the usefulness of our PKE.

PKE.Gen()
$A \leftarrow \mathcal{U}(\mathbb{Z}_q^{n \times n})$
$(B, S) \leftarrow \text{LWEGen}_I(A)^{\overline{n}}$
return $(pk = (A, B), sk = S)$

PKE.Enc(pk, m)
$(A, B) = pk$
$(C, S') = \text{LWEGen}_I((A \| B)^T)^{\overline{n}}$
Split $C \in \mathbb{Z}_q^{(n+\overline{n}) \times \overline{n}}$ into $C_1 \in \mathbb{Z}_q^{\overline{n} \times n}$
and $V \in \mathbb{Z}_q^{\overline{n} \times \overline{n}}$ with $C = C_1^T \| V^T$
$M \in \mathbb{Z}_q^{\overline{n} \times \overline{n}} = \text{encode}(m)$
$C_2 = V + M \mod q$
return $ct = (C_1, C_2)$

PKE.Dec($S = sk, ct$)
$(C_1, C_2) = ct$
$m = \text{decode}(C_2 - C_1 S \mod q)$
return m

LWEGen$_J(A \in \mathbb{Z}_q^{m \times k})$
$\alpha^2 \leftarrow \mathcal{U}(J)$
$s \leftarrow \overline{\Psi}_\alpha^k; e \leftarrow \overline{\Psi}_\alpha^m$
$b = As + e \mod q$
return (b, s)

Encoding encode(m) with $|m| = \ell = B \cdot \overline{n}^2$
Split m into B-bit substrings and interpret as numbers b_i, for integers $0 \le i < \overline{n}^2$
Let M be a $\overline{n} \times \overline{n}$ matrix
On position x, y in M let it have the value $b_{x+\overline{n} \cdot y} \cdot \lfloor q/2^B \rfloor$
return M

Decoding decode(M) with $M \in \mathbb{Z}_q^{\overline{n} \times \overline{n}}$
For integers $0 \le x < \overline{n}$ and $0 \le y < \overline{n}$ let $M_{x,y}$ be the element on position x, y in M
Let $b_{x+y \cdot \overline{n}} = \lfloor M_{x,y} \cdot 2^B/q \rceil \mod 2^B$
return $m = b_0 \| b_1 \ldots \| b_{\overline{n}^2 - 1}$, bitstring combined from all b_i

Fig. 1. Algorithms for the cryptosystem with PKE.Gen() for key-generation, PKE.Enc(pk, m) for encryption and PKE.Dec(sk, ct) for decryption with the other algorithms used as subroutines.

Lemma 6. *Let $\delta > 2^{-n}$ be a real number, ζ^2 be the maximal value in I and assume that $\zeta q > 2\sqrt{n}$ and $\zeta < n^{-1/2}2^{-(B+4)}$. Then, the decryption error probability per symbol is bounded from above by δ if*

$$(\zeta q)^2 \le \frac{q\sqrt{\pi}}{2^{B+2}\sqrt{2n \ln(1/\delta)}} \ .$$

This is essentially the same statement as in Lemma 3.1 of [12], but using a rounded Gaussian distribution instead of a discrete Gaussian distribution. Besides also including trivial handling of a variable error distribution, it is otherwise essentially the same proof as in [12] and we therefore do not include it here.

3.3 QROM IND-CCA Secure KEM

Besides parametrizations of an OW-CPA secure PKE, we also provide parametrizations of a related IND-CCA secure Key Encapsulation Mechanism (KEM). This KEM is constructed with the FO$^{\not\perp}$ transform [6,8] and its security is guaranteed by a non-tight reduction in the quantum random oracle model.

While many of the NIST candidates for post-quantum secure KEMs use some version of the FO$^{\not\perp}$ transform, these schemes do not account for the non-tightness of its security proof. We account for this non-tightness in our parametrization, allowing us to actually guarantee the claimed security of our KEM. The actual provable security given by the transform is detailed in the following theorem from [9], where KEM-I is the FO$^{\not\perp}$ transform of PKE.

We do not describe the details of this theorem and instead instead refer to [9] for these. We do however note that M is the message space of the PKE and that the PKE is δ-correct means that

$$\mathbb{E}\left(\max_{m \in M} \Pr\left[\text{PKE.Dec}(sk, c) \neq m : c \leftarrow \text{PKE.Enc}(pk, m)\right]\right) \leq \delta$$

where expectation is taken over $(pk, sk) \leftarrow \text{PKE.Gen}()$.

Theorem 1 (Theorem 1 from [9]). *If* PKE *is* δ-correct, for any IND-CCA $\mathcal{B}$ *against* KEM-I, *issuing at most* q_D *queries to the decapsulation oracle* DECAPS, *at most* q_G *queries to the random oracle* G *and at most* q_H *queries to the random oracle* H, *there exists a* OW-CPA *adversary* $\mathcal{A}$ *against* PKE *such that*

$$\text{ADV}_{\text{KEM-I}}^{\text{IND-CCA}}(\mathcal{B}) \leq \frac{2q_H}{\sqrt{|M|}} + 4q_G\sqrt{\delta} + 2(q_G + q_H) \cdot \sqrt{\text{ADV}_{\text{PKE}}^{\text{OW-CPA}}(\mathcal{A})}$$

and the running time of $\mathcal{A}$ *is about that of* $\mathcal{B}$.

4   Proof of Security

In this section we detail the reductions which prove that the security of our cryptosystem is guaranteed by the assumed concrete hardness of SIVP$_{\gamma_R}$. To show this, we begin in Subsect. 4.1 by detailing how an adversary against our cryptosystem can be used to solve a DLWE instance.

In order to solve an SIVP$_{\gamma_R}$ instance, we consider a version of Regev's quantum reduction from [19] which we detail in Subsect. 4.3. Our version of this reduction requires an LWE oracle that, with overwhelming probability, solves LWE(Ψ_β) for some unknown $\beta \in [\alpha/\sqrt{2}, \alpha]$ with α a known parameter. This LWE oracle is constructed in different ways depending on if we consider a parametrization with fixed or variable error distribution. The different ways we construct this LWE oracle are described in Subsect. 4.2.

Finally, in Subsect. 4.4 we combine all the parts of the proof into Theorems 4 and 5 that directly relate the concrete security of parametrizations of our cryptosystem with the hardness of SIVP$_{\gamma_R}$.

4.1   Solving DLWE with the Help of an Adversary

In this subsection we detail how an adversary against our cryptosystem can be used to solve a DLWE instance. For the cryptosystem with fixed error distribution this follows easily from a standard hybrid argument. A similar hybrid argument could be applied to show that an adversary against the cryptosystem with variable error distribution also allows solving a version of DLWE with the same variable error distribution.

However, Theorem 2 actually claims something stronger, namely that we can use an adversary against our cryptosystem parametrized with some set I in order to solve a DLWE problem with error distributions that depend on a different set I'. To formalize this, we first introduce a version of LWE with variable error distribution. We define this as a distribution over LWE distributions such that all sampled LWE distributions share the same secret. The different LWE distributions do however not necessarily share the same error distribution.

Definition 8 (LWE with variable error distribution). *Let n, q be positive integers, $J \subset [0, 1)$ be a set and $s \in \mathbb{Z}_q^n$. We define $A_{s,J}$ to be a distribution where a sample consists of the distribution A_{s,Ψ_ζ} where $\zeta^2 \leftarrow \mathcal{U}(J)$.*

We also define a decision LWE problem related to these distributions of distributions. This $DLWE(J, m)$ problem is a more general version of the ordinary $DLWE(\Psi_\alpha, m)$ problem, which is recovered by simply letting $J = \{\alpha^2\}$.

Definition 9. *Let $J \subset [0, 1)$ be a set and n, q, m be positive integers. Let $\mathcal{D}$ either be $A_{s,J}$ or a distribution of distributions that always returns $\mathcal{U}(\mathbb{Z}_q^{n+1})$. The $DLWE(J, m)$ problem is to determine which is the case when given a total of at most m samples in $\mathbb{Z}_q^{n+1}$ from distributions given by $\mathcal{D}$.*

With these definitions, we now state the theorem that relates the security of our cryptosystem with the hardness of this DLWE problem. This theorem is applicable to both parametrizations with a fixed error distribution as well as the ones with a variable error distribution. Note that our cryptosystem is parametrized with the set I and with a message space size of $2^\ell = 2^{B\overline{n}^2}$.

Theorem 2. *Let $I' \subseteq (0, 1)$ be some unknown set that contains I such that $|I| / |I'| = \kappa \leq 1$ and let $k > 0$ be an integer. Furthermore, assume that $\mathcal{A}$ is an algorithm with advantage ε_a against the OW-CPA security of our PKE and that $\varepsilon_a \kappa^{2\overline{n}}/2 \geq 2^{-\ell}$. Then, we can solve a $DLWE(I', N)$ instance where $N = 3n \cdot 2^{14} \frac{\overline{n}^2 k}{\varepsilon_a \kappa^{4\overline{n}}}$ by using $\mathcal{A}$ no more than $2^{15} \frac{\overline{n}^3 k}{\varepsilon_a \kappa^{4\overline{n}}}$ times. The resulting DLWE algorithm has a failure probability of at most*

$$2^{\overline{n}+14-n} \frac{\overline{n}^2 k}{\varepsilon_a \kappa^{4\overline{n}}} + (2\overline{n} + 1)2^{-k} .$$

As the DLWE problem solved by the reduction may be defined in terms of $I' \neq I$, we can not directly prove the theorem via an ordinary hybrid argument. Instead, we use that $I \subseteq I'$ and $|I| / |I'| = \kappa$, giving that with probability κ, an element sampled from $\mathcal{U}(I')$ is also an element of I. Furthermore, if $\zeta \leftarrow \mathcal{U}(I')$ is in I, then it is distributed as if sampled from $\mathcal{U}(I)$. As such, altering our cryptosystem by replacing one sample from $\mathcal{U}(I)$ with a sample from $\mathcal{U}(I')$ can at most decrease an adversaries success probability by a factor κ. This corresponds exactly to replacing one of the LWE distributions in the cryptosystem with a rounded normal-form version of a distribution from $A_{s,I'}$.

For the proof, we consider a series of $4\bar{n} + 1$ hybrid versions of our cryptosystem. The first version of the system is exactly the original cryptosystem. The $2i$:th version of the system is the same as the previous version but with i:th LWE distribution given by $\text{LWEGen}_{I'}(\cdot)$ instead of $\text{LWEGen}_I(\cdot)$. In hybrid version $2i + 1$, this distribution is instead replaced with a uniform distribution. Using the input distribution from an $\text{DLWE}(I', N)$ instance for the i:th distribution thus results in messages encrypted with either hybrid version $2i$ or $2i+1$, depending on if the input distribution is an LWE distribution or a uniform distribution.

The adversaries success probability against the original cryptosystem is at least ε_a. Using the adversary against hybrid versions of the cryptosystems, we are guaranteed that its success probability against versions $2i - 1$ and $2i$ can differ by at most a factor κ. Furthermore, the success probability of the adversary against version $4\bar{n} + 1$, where all distributions is uniformly random, is $2^{-\ell}$. As such, if $\varepsilon_a \kappa^{2\bar{n}}/2 \geq 2^{-\ell}$, there must be some i such that the there is a noticeable difference in the adversaries success probability against hybrid versions $2i$ and $2i + 1$.

For this choice of i, we use the input distribution in an $\text{DLWE}(I', N)$ instance to encrypt random messages with hybrid version either $2i$ or $2i+1$ of our cryptosystem. This results in a noticeable difference in the adversaries success probability depending on what the distribution actually is. Detecting this difference in success probability provides the solution to the $\text{DLWE}(I', N)$ instance. The specific bounds in Theorem 2 follows from using the Chernoff-Hoeffding theorem to actually distinguish between the distributions. Due to space constraints, we omit the proof of the specifics of this theorem and instead include the proof in an extended version.

4.2   Solving LWE with a DLWE Oracle

Using Lemma 4 we can transform an oracle that can distinguish between A_{s,Ψ_α} and $\mathcal{U}(\mathbb{Z}_q^n \times [0,1))$ into an oracle that can recover s from A_{s,Ψ_α}. This is not sufficient for the main reduction of [19] as it requires an LWE oracle that can recover s from A_{s,Ψ_β} for some unknown $\beta \in [\alpha/\sqrt{2}, \alpha]$.

This version of the LWE problem is solved in two separate ways depending on which type of DLWE oracle an adversary against the specific parametrization of our cryptosystem provides. For parametrizations with $I = \{\alpha^2\}$ we use the same approach as in [19]. For the parametrizations with $I = [\alpha^2, 3\alpha^2/2]$ we have an alternative, more efficient way, to construct the required LWE oracle.

We first consider our parametrizations that use a fixed error distribution with $I = \{\alpha^2\}$. In this case, using Theorem 2 allows using an adversary against our cryptosystem to solve $\text{DLWE}(\Psi_\alpha, N)$. Using Lemma 4, this allows us to also solve $\text{LWE}(\Psi_\alpha, N)$. Finally, we use Lemma 7 in order to actually solve $\text{LWE}(\Psi_\beta, nN)$ for unknown $\beta \in [\alpha/\sqrt{2}, \alpha]$.

Compared to previous analysis of the efficiency of this lemma, our version requires a factor $N/10$ less LWE oracle calls, which is significant as N is large. This is accomplished by choosing the set Z more carefully compared to the original proof in [19].

Lemma 7 (Variant of Lemma 3.7 from [19]). *Let n, q be positive integers and W be an algorithm that solves $LWE(\Psi_\alpha, N)$, with a failure probability of at most $1/20$. Then there is an algorithm W' that, by using W at most $10nN$ times, solves $LWE(\Psi_\beta, nN)$ for arbitrary $\beta \in [\alpha/\sqrt{2}, \alpha]$, except for with negligible probability.*

Proof. We define a set Z to be all integer multiples of $\alpha^2/(20N)$ between $\alpha^2/2$ and α^2. For each of the elements $\zeta \in Z$, we add a sample from $\Psi_{\sqrt{\zeta}}$ to each of the nN samples provided from A_{s,Ψ_β}. This results in nN samples from $A_{s,\Psi_{\sqrt{\beta^2+\zeta}}}$ for each $\zeta \in Z$. This guarantees that there is some $\zeta \in Z$ such that

$$\alpha^2 \leq \beta^2 + \zeta \leq \left(1 + \frac{1}{20N}\right)\alpha^2$$

and Lemma 1 gives us that, for this ζ, the statistical distance between $\Psi_{\sqrt{\beta^2+\zeta}}$ and Ψ_α is at most $9/(20N)$. As such, the statistical distance between N samples from A_{s,Ψ_α} and N samples from $A_{s,\Psi_{\sqrt{\beta^2+\zeta}}}$ is at most $9/20$ for this choice of ζ.

As the LWE oracle has a failure probability of at most $1/20$, this guarantees that the oracle succeeds in recovering s with success probability at least $1/2$ when given N samples from $A_{s,\Psi_{\sqrt{\beta^2+\zeta}}}$ instead of N samples from A_{s,Ψ_α}. Repeating this same procedure n times, with independent samples, thus ensures that, except for with probability at most 2^{-n}, we will produce the correct solution at least once.

As we perform this procedure for every $\zeta \in Z$, we are thus guaranteed that, except for with probability at most 2^{-n}, the correct s is found at least once. Using Lemma 3.6 from [19] allows us to verify whether or not a candidate solution s' is the actual solution s, meaning that it is sufficient that the correct s is found once. This lemma was analyzed in [21] where they show that with a minor change to the procedure described in [19], it can be ensured that its failure probability is insignificant for parameters that are relevant in this work. As only N samples from $A_{s,\sqrt{\beta^2+\zeta}}$ are used for finding the candidate s', we can use the remaining $(n-1)N$ independent samples for this verification. $\qquad\square$

For our alternative parametrization, where $I = [\alpha^2, 3\alpha^2/2]$, Theorem 2 allows an adversary to be used to solve an $DLWE(I', N)$ instance for some I' that contains I. With $\beta \in [\alpha/\sqrt{2}, \alpha]$ we are guaranteed that $I' = [\beta^2, \beta^2 + \alpha^2]$ contains I and that $|I'|/|I| = 2$. This motivates the following lemma which allows to solve $DLWE(\Psi_\beta, N)$, even though β is unknown. Using Lemma 4 this also allows us to solve the corresponding search-LWE problem.

Lemma 8. *Let α, β be two positive numbers and let $I' = [\beta^2, \beta^2 + \alpha^2]$. Then, an instance of the $DLWE(\Psi_\beta, N)$ problem can be transformed into an instance of the $DLWE(I', N)$ problem without knowing β.*

Proof. For each new distribution requested in the DLWE(I', N) instance, sample a new ζ uniformly at random from $[0, \alpha^2]$. Samples from this new distribution are produced by sampling $(\boldsymbol{a}, b)$ from the DLWE(Ψ_β, N) instance and returning $(\boldsymbol{a}, b + e \mod 1)$ where e is sampled from $\Psi_{\sqrt{\zeta}}$.

If the input distribution was uniformly random, then so is the output distribution. If instead $b = \langle \boldsymbol{a}, \boldsymbol{s} \rangle + e'$ for some $\boldsymbol{s}$ and with $e' \leftarrow \Psi_\beta$, we see that the sum $e + e' \mod 1$ is distributed as $\Psi_{\sqrt{\beta^2 + \zeta}}$. Therefore, the resulting distribution is $A_{\boldsymbol{s}, \Psi_{\sqrt{\beta^2 + \zeta}}}$. As $\zeta \leftarrow \mathcal{U}([0, \alpha^2])$, this corresponds exactly to $A_{\boldsymbol{s}, \Psi_{\sqrt{\zeta'}}}$ with $\zeta' \leftarrow \mathcal{U}([\beta^2, \beta^2 + \alpha^2])$ which is the expected distribution for an DLWE(I', N) instance. □

4.3 Solving SIVP with the Help of an LWE Oracle

By using a version of Regev's quantum reduction from [19], we are able to solve SIVP with the help of an LWE oracle. The efficiency of Regev's reduction has already been investigated in previous works [4,7,21] with the most recent result concluding that $2n^3 \cdot 3n^3 N^3$ LWE oracle calls are required when using an LWE oracle that requires N LWE samples. We are able to achieve the same result with fewer LWE oracle calls and therefore present our version of this reduction.

For simplicity, this work will not consider the success probability of the reduction in greater detail and we are instead satisfied with an exponentially small failure probability. In an extended version of this work, we do however keep track of the success probability of the reduction, allowing a trade-off between the success probability and efficiency of the reduction. This more thorough analysis of the reduction is able to support the security of more efficient parametrizations of our cryptosystem. For reference, these parametrizations are included in Appendix A.

Our version of the main theorem from [19] together with information about the number of LWE oracle calls it requires is given by Theorem 3. Besides keeping track of the number of calls to the provided LWE oracle, the proof is essentially that of Regev. Because of this, we will not go through the details of the proof, instead only describing the reduction at a high level while keeping track of the number of required oracle calls.

In order to improve the efficiency of the reduction, our version of this theorem solves SIVP$_{\gamma_R}$ directly. The original reduction instead solves the target SIVP$_{\gamma_R}$ instance by solving multiple discrete Gaussian sampling problems, as detailed in Lemma 3.17 of [19]. Instead, we use that the solution to the discrete Gaussian sampling problem already samples from many intermediate discrete Gaussian distributions. By using these samples, we are able to directly solve SIVP$_{\gamma_R}$ directly, saving a factor $2n^3$ in the number of required oracle calls compared to using Lemma 3.17 from [19].

Theorem 3 (Version of Theorem 3.1 in [19]). *Let L be an arbitrary lattice, n, q, M be positive integers, $\alpha < 1$ some positive number such that $\alpha q > 2\sqrt{n}$ and let $\varepsilon = \varepsilon(n)$ be some negligible function. Furthermore, let W be an oracle* *that solves $LWE(\Psi_\beta, M)$ for arbitrary $\beta \in [\alpha/\sqrt{2}, \alpha]$. Then there is a quantum algorithm that, by using W at most $3n^2M$ times, solves $SIVP_{\sqrt{2}nq}$ except for with negligible probability.*

Proof. The reduction consists of a quantum algorithm that produces samples from a discrete Gaussian distribution over the lattice. To accomplish this, the reduction uses the LWE oracle in order to solve BDD instances on the dual lattice. To use the LWE oracle, a BDD instance is combined with samples from a discrete Gaussian distribution over the lattice, transforming it into samples from an LWE distribution.

The reduction thus requires samples from a discrete Gaussian distribution over the lattice in order to produce samples from same type of distribution. If the provided LWE oracle is sufficiently strong, the output discrete Gaussian distribution has a smaller width than the input distribution, allowing it to make progress and function as an iterative step.

For the number of oracle calls required by this reduction, we first note that the quantum algorithm produces a discrete Gaussian sample by only using a quantum accessible BDD oracle once. As such, the number of LWE oracle calls required by this quantum algorithm is the same as the number required to solve a single BDD instance.

To solve a BDD instance, we use M samples from a discrete Gaussian distribution in order to transform the BDD instance into M samples from A_{s, Ψ_β} where $\beta \in [\alpha/\sqrt{2}, \alpha]$ is unknown. Thus, the provided LWE oracle can recover s, which provides partial information about the solution to the BDD instance. With this information, the input BDD instance can be transformed into another BDD instance with a smaller distance bound. By repeating this process n times, we decrease the distance bound enough for us to be able to efficiently solve the BDD instance. Each repetition can reuse the same M discrete Gaussian samples and we thus solve the initial BDD instance with these samples while using the LWE oracle n times.

With the quantum algorithm, this allows us to produce a single sample from another discrete Gaussian distribution. Reusing the same M samples from the input discrete Gaussian distribution allows us to produce more independent output samples. As such, repeating this process M times produces sufficiently many samples for them to be used as input to the next iterative step.

To start the process, we find a r_0 such that $2^{-n} \cdot \lambda_n(L) < r_0 < \lambda_n(L)$ and define intermediate widths $r_i = (\alpha q/\sqrt{n})^i r_0$. This ensures that we can efficiently sample from $D_{L, r_{3n}}$ as $r_{3n} = (\alpha q/\sqrt{n})^{3n} > 2^{2n}\lambda_n(L)$ is large enough. Furthermore, if the iterative step is given input from D_{L, r_i}, the output samples are from $D_{L, r_i\sqrt{n}/(\alpha q)} = D_{L, r_{i-1}}$. As such, by starting the iterative process with width r_{3n} we are able to produce samples from D_{L, r_j} for $j < 3n$.

The quantum algorithm is only guaranteed to work if the input is samples from $D_{L, r}$ with $r > \sqrt{2}q\eta_\varepsilon(L)$. As we can not calculate $\eta_\varepsilon(L)$ efficiently, we do not necessarily know what discrete Gaussian distributions we actually can produce samples from. Furthermore, the process might not fail in an obvious way, meaning that we do not necessarily know when to stop it. Therefore we consider all produced samples and take the subset of these consisting of n linearly independent vectors that are as short as possible.

We will correctly produce samples from D_{L,r_j} for some $r_j \leq \sqrt{2}q\eta_\varepsilon(L)$. This is the case as $r_0 < \lambda_n(L) < \sqrt{2}q\eta_\varepsilon(L)$, and if we are able to produce samples for $r_i > \sqrt{2}q\eta_\varepsilon(L)$ these samples can be used as input to the next quantum algorithm to produce samples from $D_{L,r_{i-1}}$.

Thus, we are guaranteed that the chosen vectors are at least as short as the ones correctly produced from D_{L,r_j} for some $r_j \leq \sqrt{2}q\eta_\varepsilon(L)$. By the same argument as for Lemma 3.17 in [19], we see that the $M > n^2$ vectors produced from this discrete Gaussian distribution will contain n linearly independent vectors shorter than $\sqrt{2n}q\eta_\varepsilon(L)$ except for with negligible probability.

Finally, as we do not analyze the failure probability of the reduction in greater detail here, we use $\varepsilon = 2^{-n}$ to ensure its impact on the reduction failure probability is negligible. As such, Lemma 3 shows that the length of these vectors is at most $\sqrt{2}nq \cdot \lambda_n$ and the produced vectors thus solve SIVP$_{\sqrt{2}nq}$.

In total, we thus require M discrete Gaussian samples for each of the $3n$ different widths r_j. As such, we must run the quantum algorithm at most $3nM$ times. Furthermore, each iteration of the quantum algorithm requires using the LWE oracle n times and we must thus use the LWE oracle a total of $3n^2M$ times. $\qquad\square$

4.4   Security Based on Hardness of SIVP$_{\gamma_R}$

The following theorem combines the relevant statements from previous subsections in order to directly guarantee the concrete security of our cryptosystem with fixed error distribution based only on the hardness of worst-case SIVP$_{\sqrt{2}nq}$.

Theorem 4. *Let our PKE be parametrized with $I = \{\alpha^2\}$ such that $\alpha q > 2\sqrt{n}$ and let k be an integer larger than $\log(40nq(\overline{n}+1))$. Furthermore, let $\mathcal{A}$ be an adversary that achieves an advantage of 2^{-d} against the OW-CPA security of this parametrization by running in time at most T and assume that $\ell = B\overline{n}^2 \geq d+1$. Then, there exists a quantum algorithm that solves worst-case SIVP$_{\sqrt{2}nq}$ in time*

$$270k^3 n^7 \overline{n}^7 q \cdot 2^{3d+43} \cdot T$$

with negligible failure probability.

Proof. We begin by using the adversary with Theorem 2 to solve the DLWE(I', N) problem with $I' = I = \{\alpha^2\}$. Next, using Lemma 4 the corresponding search problem is solved, while Lemma 7 allows the search problem with unknown error distribution to be solved. Finally, using Theorem 3 allows solving the target SIVP$_{\sqrt{2}nq}$ instance.

The number of required calls to the adversary is at most

$$3n^2 Nn \cdot 10nN \cdot 2^{d+15}k\overline{n}^3 \cdot nq = 270k^3 n^7 \overline{n}^7 q \cdot 2^{3d+43}$$

where $N = 3n\overline{n}^2 k \cdot 2^{d+14}$ is given by Theorem 2.

Using Lemma 7 requires that our LWE oracle has a failure probability of at most $1/20$. As our LWE oracle is created by combining Theorem 2 and Lemma 4, it has an error probability of at most

$$2^{\overline{n}+14-n}\frac{\overline{n}^2 k}{\varepsilon_a \kappa^{4\overline{n}}} + (2\overline{n}+1)2^{-k} \leq 2nq(\overline{n}+1)2^{-k} \ .$$

and we therefore require $k > \log(40nq(\overline{n}+1))$. $\qquad\qquad\qquad\qquad\qquad\square$

For the cryptosystem with variable error distribution we are able to use the following, more efficient, version of Theorem 4.

Theorem 5 (Alternative version of Theorem 4). *Let our PKE be parametrized with $I = [\alpha^2, 3\alpha^2/2)$ such that $\alpha q > 2\sqrt{n}$ and let k be an arbitrary integer. Furthermore, let $\mathcal{A}$ be an adversary that achieves an advantage of 2^{-d} against the OW-CPA security of this parametrization by running in time at most T and assume that $\ell = B\overline{n}^2 \geq d + 2\overline{n} + 1$. Then, there exists a quantum algorithm that solves worst-case $SIVP_{\sqrt{2}nq}$ in time*

$$9n^6\overline{n}^5 q \cdot 2^{2d+29+4\overline{n}} \cdot T$$

with a negligible failure probability.

Proof. We begin by using the adversary with Theorem 2 in order to solve the DLWE(I', N) problem with $I' = [\beta^2, \beta^2 + \alpha^2]$ for some unknown $\beta \in [\alpha/\sqrt{2}, \alpha]$. Next, we use Lemma 8 to solve the DLWE(Ψ_β, N) problem and by using Lemma 4 we solve the corresponding search problem. Finally, using Theorem 3 the target SIVP$_{\sqrt{2}nq}$ instance is solved.

As we known that $\alpha/\sqrt{2} \leq \beta \leq \alpha$, I' is a set that contains I and where $|I|/|I'| = 1/2$. Thus, Theorem 2 with $\kappa = 1/2$ can be used to solve the DLWE(I', N) problem, even though β, and therefore I', is unknown. This gives the number of required calls to $\mathcal{A}$ for every use of Theorem 2 as $\overline{n}^3 n \cdot 2^{d+15+4\overline{n}}$.

The total number of required calls is thus

$$3Nn^2 \cdot n\overline{n}^3 \cdot 2^{d+15+4\overline{n}} \cdot nq = 9n^6\overline{n}^5 q \cdot 2^{2d+29+8\overline{n}}$$

where $N = 3n^2\overline{n}^2 \cdot 2^{d+14+4\overline{n}}$ is given by Theorem 2 with $k = n$. $\qquad\square$

5   Hardness Estimate

In this section we detail the concrete hardness estimate for SIVP$_\gamma$ on which the security of our cryptosystem is based. While the reduction actually solves a worst-case SIVP$_\gamma$ instance, we instead conservatively consider the concrete hardness of SIVP$_\gamma$ on random lattices. As there does not seem to be anything indicating that there are SIVP instances that are significantly harder than instances on random lattices, this should serve as a reasonable hardness estimate for the worst-case problem, without significantly underestimating its concrete hardness.

To estimate the hardness of SIVP$_\gamma$ on random lattices, we relate this problem to γ_H-Hermite-SVP on the same lattice but for another approximation factor γ_H. In general, a solution to SIVP$_\gamma$ may be arbitrarily far from a solution to a γ_H-Hermite-SVP instance, but this is not the expected behaviour on random lattices, as detailed in the following lemma.

Lemma 9. *Let L be a lattice such that the Gaussian heuristic holds on L^*. Then $\lambda_n(L) \leq \sqrt{2n\pi e} \cdot \det(L)^{1/n}$.*

Proof. The lemma is directly given by combining the bound $\lambda_1^* \lambda_n \leq n$ from Lemma 2 with the Gaussian heuristic for the length of the first minima on the dual lattice.   □

With Lemma 9, we see that an algorithm that solves SIVP$_\gamma$ on random lattices asymptotically also solves ($\sqrt{2n\pi e} \cdot \gamma$)-Hermite-SVP on random lattices. As such, estimating the hardness for ($\sqrt{2n\pi e} \cdot \gamma$)-Hermite-SVP on random lattices also leads to a hardness estimate for SIVP$_\gamma$.

There has been significant research into the concrete hardness of Hermite-SVP due to its relevance when parametrizing LWE-based cryptosystems. This allows our hardness estimate for this problem to be based on assuming that current algorithms that solve this problem are optimal. Our hardness estimate is therefore based on the performance of the BKZ lattice reduction algorithm [22], as in practice this is the most efficient algorithm that solves Hermite-SVP.

The BKZ algorithm is parametrized with a blocksize β and works by solving exact SVP in sublattices of dimension β. Based on assuming that the Gaussian heuristic holds in all relevant sublattices, it can be shown [5] that the algorithm asymptotically finds vectors of length

$$\left(\frac{\beta}{2\pi e} \cdot (\pi\beta)^{\frac{1}{\beta}} \right)^{\frac{n}{2(\beta-1)}} \det(L)^{1/n} . \tag{1}$$

Our hardness estimate assumes that this describes the concrete performance of BKZ for the relevant dimensions, as also done in for example [1].

We conservatively estimate that running BKZ takes no longer than solving a single exact SVP instance in dimension β. The asymptotically most efficient algorithms that solve exact SVP are sieving algorithms and, as we target post-quantum security and use a quantum reduction, we consider the performance of the most efficient quantum sieving algorithm. This algorithm runs in time $2^{0.2570\beta+o(\beta)}$ [3] and ignoring the subexponential factors in its running time should serve as a conservative estimate on its performance. We therefore assume that SVP in dimension β require at least time $2^{0.2570\beta}$ to solve.

We thus assume that we can achieve the approximation factor in (1) in time T with $\beta = \log(T)/0.2570$. We also assume that this is the most efficient algorithm that solves Hermite-SVP on random lattices. Combined with with Lemma 9 this leads to a hardness estimate for SIVP$_\gamma$, as detailed in the following conjecture.

Conjecture 1 (Concrete hardness of approximate SIVP). There is no quantum algorithm that solves worst-case SIVP_γ in time T_C with approximation factor smaller than

$$\gamma_C = \left((\pi\beta)^{1/\beta} \frac{\beta}{2\pi e} \right)^{\frac{n}{2(\beta-1)}} \cdot \frac{1}{\sqrt{2n\pi e}}$$

where $\beta = \log(T_C)/0.2570$.

6 Parametrization

We parametrize our cryptosystem so that, assuming Conjecture 1 holds, the parametrizations are provably secure based on either Theorem 4 or Theorem 5. All the systems use $B = 4$ and the OW-CPA secure PKEs use $\bar{n} = 8$ while the IND-CCA secure KEMs use $\bar{n} = 12$. Thus, the message space has size $2^\ell = 2^{256}$ for the OW-CPA secure systems and $2^\ell = 2^{576}$ for the IND-CCA secure systems. The ordinary LWE based systems are parametrized with $I = \{\alpha\}$ while the systems with a variable error distribution use $I = [\alpha^2, 3\alpha^2/2]$.

Our parametrizations target a per symbol decryption failure probability of 2^{-32} for OW-CPA secure schemes and 2^{-526} for IND-CCA secure KEMs. The following Theorem shows that, assuming Conjecture 1 holds, our systems parametrized like this, with n, α and q detailed in Table 1, provably have the claimed security.

Theorem 6. *Assuming that Conjecture 1 holds, there is no adversary against 128-bits of OW-CPA (IND-CCA) security of our PKE (KEM) with the parametrizations specified in Table 1.*

Proof. An adversary against the 128-bit security of our cryptosystems parametrized as in Table 1 would imply a quantum algorithm that contradicts Conjecture 1. This algorithm is given by either Theorem 4 or Theorem 5 and would solve $\text{SIVP}_{\sqrt{2}nq}$ in time $T(n)$ given by the relevant theorem.

An adversary with running time T_a and advantage ε_a will contradict the claimed 128 bits of OW-CPA security of our parametrizations if $T_a/\varepsilon_a < 2^{128}$. When calculating the reduction running time for our parametrizations, we consider the worst-case where $T_a = 1$ and $\varepsilon_a = 2^{-128}$. This reduction running time is presented in row $\lceil \log(T(n)) \rceil$ of Table 1.

From Conjecture 1, we have that running in time $T(n)$, the reduction should not be able to solve SIVP_γ for $\gamma < \gamma_C$ where

$$\gamma_C = \left((\pi\beta)^{1/\beta} \frac{\beta}{2\pi e} \right)^{\frac{n}{2(\beta-1)}} \cdot \frac{1}{\sqrt{2n\pi e}} \tag{2}$$

with $\beta = \log(T(n))/0.2570$. This is contradicted by an adversary against the claimed security of the parametrizations presented in Table 1, as the reduction solves SIVP_{γ_R} with $\gamma_R = \sqrt{2}nq < \gamma_C$ when both use time $T(n)$. As such, the claimed security of these parametrizations is guaranteed by only assuming that Conjecture 1 is correct.

The IND-CCA secure KEMs are instead based on a PKE that targets 518 bits of OW-CPA security. From this, Theorem 1 gives that an adversaries advantage against the IND-CCA security of the KEM is limited by $(q_G + q_H)2^{-256}$. As such, by limiting the adversary to 2^{128} QROM queries, the KEM is guaranteed the claimed 128 bits of IND-CCA security.

Our parameters are selected such that $\alpha q > 2\sqrt{n}$, q is a prime and the decryption failure probability, as given by Lemma 6, is sufficiently small. In order to minimize $\gamma_R = \sqrt{2}nq$, we select q to be the smallest prime that satisfies all inequalities, giving a unique $q = \mathcal{O}(n^{3/2})$ for any given n.

This allows us, for any given n, to select α and q and calculate γ_R and $T(n)$, which also gives us γ_C. Comparing γ_C and γ_R allows us to determine if the parametrization is provably secure under Conjecture 1. The parameters presented in Table 1 are found through a search script to have the minimal n such that $\gamma_R < \gamma_C$ when α and q are selected as described.   □

Table 1. Values for n and $\lceil\log(q)\rceil$ for different parameterizations that target 128 bits of the type of security specified in "Security" row with type of system given by the "Error distribution" row. The $\lceil\log(T(n))\rceil$ and $\lceil\log(\gamma_R)\rceil$ rows indicates the reduction running time and its approximation factor respectively. Finally, the β row shows which block-size β the reductions performance is compared against.

Security	OW-CPA	OW-CPA	IND-CCA	IND-CCA
Error distribution	Fixed	Variable	Fixed	Variable
n	39333	32817	104109	79537
$\lceil\log(q)\rceil$	34	34	37	37
$\lceil\log(T(n))\rceil$	614	491	1802	1317
$\lceil\log(\gamma_R)\rceil$	50	50	55	54
β	2389	1910	7011	5124

7   Conclusion

The parameters we use for our cryptosystem are significantly larger than what is typically used for LWE-based cryptosystems. A large reason for this is the inefficiency of Regev's quantum reduction and further improving its efficiency could potentially allow it to support the security of cryptosystems that use smaller parameters. However, only optimizing the run time of the reduction is insufficient for it to support the security of typical LWE-based cryptosystems.

To see this, we consider a parametrization where we completely disregard the run time of the reduction and thus assume that an adversary against the cryptosystem implies a solution to $\mathrm{SIVP}_{\sqrt{2}nq}$ in time 2^{128}. This approach still results in a parametrization using a dimension $n \approx 9400$ to argue for 128 bits of OW-CPA security. Thus, the large approximation factors for which the reduction solves SIVP_γ is an arguably bigger reason for the large parameters required in our cryptosystem.

It thus seems like it would be hard to improve this reduction to such an extent that it actually supports parametrizations close to those of typical LWE-based schemes. Any such improvement would not only have to significantly improve the reductions efficiency, but also solve a harder lattice problem.

This does not directly indicate that typical LWE-based cryptosystems are insecure. It does however mean that attacks against these systems could improve significantly, without necessarily implying any progress in algorithms for general lattice problems. As such, arguments about the concrete security of typical lattice-based cryptosystems can not reasonably be considered to be supported by similar worst-case to average-case reductions.

In contrast to this, our parametrizations are provably secure based on the assumed hardness of standard lattice problems. Thus, unless lattice algorithms improve significantly, these parametrizations are guaranteed to be secure. While far too inefficient for most use-cases, our parametrizations actually provide the first concrete systems with provable security based only on the hardness of standard lattice problems.

Acknowledgments. This research has been supported in part by the Swedish Armed Forces and was conducted at KTH Center for Cyber Defense and Information Security (CDIS). The author would like to thank Johan Håstad for his helpful input.

A   More Parametrizations

In Table 2 we include some additional, more efficient, parametrizations of our cryptosystem that are supported by a more detailed analysis of the same reductions used for the parametrizations in Table 1. This more detailed analysis is included in an extended version of this work and keeps track of the reduction failure probability. As we can accept a small but noticeable reduction failure probability, this allows more efficient parametrizations. This is mainly thanks to letting us consider the smoothing parameter $\eta_\varepsilon(L)$ for $\varepsilon > 2^{-n}$, allowing us to solve SIVP_{γ_R} with an approximation factor γ_R that is smaller than $\sqrt{2}nq$.

Table 2. Equivalent parametrizations as in Table 1 but based on versions of Theorem 4 and Theorem 5 that more carefully consider the failure probability of the reduction.

Security	OW-CPA	OW-CPA	IND-CCA	IND-CCA
Error distribution	Fixed	Variable	Fixed	Variable
n	35696	29848	96580	73948
$\lceil\log(q)\rceil$	34	34	37	37
$\lceil\log(T(n))\rceil$	600	479	1789	1305
$\lceil\log(\gamma_R)\rceil$	45	45	50	50
β	2335	1862	6959	5077

References

1. Albrecht, M.R., et al.: Estimate all the LWE, NTRU schemes! In: Catalano, D., De Prisco, R. (eds.) SCN 2018. LNCS, vol. 11035, pp. 351–367. Springer, Cham (2018). https://doi.org/10.1007/978-3-319-98113-0_19
2. Banaszczyk, W.: New bounds in some transference theorems in the geometry of numbers. Math. Ann. **296**(1), 625–635 (1993). https://doi.org/10.1007/BF01445125
3. Chailloux, A., Loyer, J.: Lattice sieving via quantum random walks. In: Tibouchi, M., Wang, H. (eds.) ASIACRYPT 2021. LNCS, vol. 13093, pp. 63–91. Springer, Cham (2021). https://doi.org/10.1007/978-3-030-92068-5_3
4. Chatterjee, S., Koblitz, N., Menezes, A., Sarkar, P.: Another look at tightness II: practical issues in cryptography. In: Phan, R.C.-W., Yung, M. (eds.) Mycrypt 2016. LNCS, vol. 10311, pp. 21–55. Springer, Cham (2017). https://doi.org/10.1007/978-3-319-61273-7_3
5. Chen, Y.: Réduction de réseau et sécurité concrète du chiffrement complètement homomorphe. Ph.D. thesis, Université Paris Diderot (2013). http://www.theses.fr/2013PA077242. 2013PA077242
6. Fujisaki, E., Okamoto, T.: Secure integration of asymmetric and symmetric encryption schemes. J. Cryptol. **26**(1), 80–101 (2011). https://doi.org/10.1007/s00145-011-9114-1
7. Gates, F.: Reduction-Respecting Parameters for Lattice-Based Cryptosystems. Master's thesis, McMaster University (2018)
8. Hofheinz, D., Hövelmanns, K., Kiltz, E.: A modular analysis of the Fujisaki-Okamoto transformation. In: Kalai, Y., Reyzin, L. (eds.) TCC 2017. LNCS, vol. 10677, pp. 341–371. Springer, Cham (2017). https://doi.org/10.1007/978-3-319-70500-2_12
9. Jiang, H., Zhang, Z., Chen, L., Wang, H., Ma, Z.: IND-CCA-secure key encapsulation mechanism in the quantum random oracle model, revisited. In: Shacham, H., Boldyreva, A. (eds.) CRYPTO 2018. LNCS, vol. 10993, pp. 96–125. Springer, Cham (2018). https://doi.org/10.1007/978-3-319-96878-0_4
10. Koblitz, N., Samajder, S., Sarkar, P., Singha, S.: Concrete analysis of approximate ideal-SIVP to decision ring-LWE reduction. Adv. Math. Commun. (2022). https://doi.org/10.3934/amc.2022082
11. Langlois, A., Stehlé, D.: Worst-case to average-case reductions for module lattices. Des. Codes Crypt. **75**(3), 565–599 (2014). https://doi.org/10.1007/s10623-014-9938-4
12. Lindner, R., Peikert, C.: Better key sizes (and attacks) for LWE-based encryption. In: Kiayias, A. (ed.) CT-RSA 2011. LNCS, vol. 6558, pp. 319–339. Springer, Heidelberg (2011). https://doi.org/10.1007/978-3-642-19074-2_21
13. Lyubashevsky, V., Peikert, C., Regev, O.: On ideal lattices and learning with errors over rings. In: Gilbert, H. (ed.) EUROCRYPT 2010. LNCS, vol. 6110, pp. 1–23. Springer, Heidelberg (2010). https://doi.org/10.1007/978-3-642-13190-5_1
14. Micciancio, D., Regev, O.: Worst-case to average-case reductions based on Gaussian measures. In: 45th Annual Symposium on Foundations of Computer Science, pp. 372–381. IEEE Computer Society Press, Rome (2004). https://doi.org/10.1109/FOCS.2004.72
15. Micciancio, D., Regev, O.: Lattice-based Cryptography. In: Bernstein, D.J., Buchmann, J., Dahmen, E. (eds.) Post-Quantum Cryptography, pp. 147–191. Springer, Heidelberg (2009). https://doi.org/10.1007/978-3-540-88702-7_5

16. Naehrig, M., et al.: FrodoKEM. Technical report, National Institute of Standards and Technology (2020). https://csrc.nist.gov/projects/post-quantum-cryptography/post-quantum-cryptography-standardization/round-3-submissions
17. Pekert, C.: What does GCHQ'S "cautionary tale" mean for lattice cryptography?. https://web.eecs.umich.edu/~cpeikert/soliloquy.html
18. Regev, O.: On lattices, learning with errors, random linear codes, and cryptography. In: Proceedings of the Thirty-Seventh Annual ACM Symposium on Theory of Computing, pp. 84–93. STOC 2005, Association for Computing Machinery, New York (2005). https://doi.org/10.1145/1060590.1060603
19. Regev, O.: On lattices, learning with errors, random linear codes, and cryptography. J. ACM **56**(6), 1–40 (2009). https://doi.org/10.1145/1568318.1568324
20. Rogers, C.A.: The number of lattice points in a set. In: Proceedings of the London Mathematical Society, vol. s3–6(2), pp. 305–320 (1956). https://doi.org/10.1112/plms/s3-6.2.305
21. Sarkar, P., Singha, S.: Verifying solutions to LWE with implications for concrete security. Adv. Math. Commun. **15**(2), 257–266 (2021). https://doi.org/10.3934/amc.2020057
22. Schnorr, C., Euchner, M.: Lattice basis reduction: improved practical algorithms and solving subset sum problems. Math. Program. **66**, 181–199 (1994). https://doi.org/10.1007/BF01581144
23. Schwabe, P., et al.: CRYSTALS-KYBER. Technical report, National Institute of Standards and Technology (2022). https://csrc.nist.gov/Projects/post-quantum-cryptography/selected-algorithms-2022
24. Södergren, A.: On the Poisson distribution of lengths of lattice vectors in a random lattice. Math. Z. **269**(3–4), 945–954 (2011). https://doi.org/10.1007/s00209-010-0772-8

Finding and Evaluating Parameters
for BGV

Johannes Mono[1(✉)], Chiara Marcolla[2], Georg Land[1,3], Tim Güneysu[1,3],
and Najwa Aaraj[2]

[1] Ruhr University Bochum, Horst Görtz Institute for IT Security, Bochum, Germany
{johannes.mono,georg.land,tim.gueneysu}@rub.de
[2] Technology Innovation Institute, Abu Dhabi, United Arab Emirates
{chiara.marcolla,najwa.aaraj}@tii.ae
[3] DFKI GmbH, Cyber-Physical Systems, Bremen, Germany

Abstract. Fully Homomorphic Encryption (FHE) is a groundbreaking technology that allows for arbitrary computations to be performed on encrypted data. State-of-the-art schemes such as Brakerski Gentry Vaikuntanathan (BGV) are based on the Learning with Errors over rings (RLWE) assumption where each ciphertext has an associated error that grows with each homomorphic operation. For correctness, the error needs to stay below a certain threshold, requiring a trade-off between security and error margin for computations in the parameters. Choosing the parameters accordingly, for example, the polynomial degree or the ciphertext modulus, is challenging and requires expert knowledge specific to each scheme.

In this work, we improve the parameter generation across all steps of its process. We provide a comprehensive analysis for BGV in the Double Chinese Remainder Theorem (DCRT) representation providing more accurate and better bounds than previous work on the DCRT, and empirically derive a closed formula linking the security level, the polynomial degree, and the ciphertext modulus. Additionally, we introduce new circuit models and combine our theoretical work in an easy-to-use parameter generator for researchers and practitioners interested in using BGV for secure computation.

Our formula results in better security estimates than previous closed formulas while our DCRT analysis results in reduced prime sizes of up to 42% compared to previous work.

Keywords: Fully Homomorphic Encryption · BGV Scheme ·
Parameter Generation · RLWE Security · DCRT Representation

1 Introduction

Since Gentry's seminal work in 2009 [18], fully homomorphic encryption (fully homomorphic encryption (FHE)) has attracted much attention from the cryptographic research community [1,26,27]. FHE enables arbitrary computations on encrypted data and thus opens up new possibilities in data processing. As

N. El Mrabet et al. (Eds.): AFRICACRYPT 2023, LNCS 14064, pp. 370–394, 2023.
https://doi.org/10.1007/978-3-031-37679-5_16

an example, hospitals analyzing health information can work only on encrypted data and provide clients with an encrypted result, thus not risking leaking any sensitive data.

The BGV scheme [9] is currently considered one of the state-of-the-art FHE schemes. BGV is based on the Learning with Errors (LWE) problem and its ring variant RLWE [25,30]. RLWE-based FHE schemes, including BGV, need to keep the error associated with each ciphertext below a certain threshold, as decryption would fail otherwise. This requires a trade-off between security (small ciphertext modulus), and error margin (large ciphertext modulus) [26].

In general, choosing parameters for FHE schemes such as the polynomial degree d or the ciphertext modulus q is challenging and requires expert knowledge specific to each scheme. Multiple parameters must be considered, and users and developers alike need to take many deliberate choices when using state-of-the-art software libraries. A real-world example is the programming interface of PALISADE [29], an open-source FHE library that also implements BGV. A user needs to choose a polynomial implementation as well as seven additional parameters that all influence the polynomial degree as well as the ciphertext modulus (Listing 1.1).

```
auto ctx = CryptoContext<DCRTPoly>::BGVrns(
    2,                      // cyclic order
    65537,                  // plaintext modulus
    HEStd_128_classic,      // security level
    3.2,                    // error standard deviation
    2,                      // multiplicative depth
    OPTIMIZED,              // secret distribution
    BV);                    // key switching method
```

Listing 1.1. BGV setup routine in PALISADE

This flexibility can be valuable for researchers familiar with FHE. For other users, however, this burden of choice increases the difficulty of generating a reasonable and secure FHE instance.

There are several challenges within the parameter selection process that need to be addressed in order to choose correct and secure parameters. Given a FHE scheme, we first adjust the error growth analysis depending on implementation choices as well as use-case-specific requirements and then compute error bounds for each individual operation. Using these bounds, we model the homomorphic circuit and determine a lower bound on the ciphertext modulus. Finally, we need to select the polynomial degree sufficiently large enough to provide a secure scheme instantiation for the desired security level. In the following, we will highlight the current state-of-the-art for each step in this process.

Related Work. For BGV, there currently are two main approaches to analyzing the error growth: the canonical norm [11,13,22] and the infinity norm [23]. While the canonical norm is known to result in better parameters, the only work analyzing BGV operations in the Double Chinese Remainder Theorem (DCRT) representation is the latter using the less optimal infinity norm. Since current state-of-the-art libraries all use the DCRT for efficient implementation, correctly modeling it in the bound computation is essential. Costache et al. [12] present an *average-case noise* analysis approach for BGV which is tailored to the dynamic noise estimation in HElib [21]. However, while there are case studies with specific parameter sets [10], the more general circuit models for static parameter generation have remained simple, excluding for example operations such as rotations [19] or the constant multiplication [23].

One challenge in standardizing FHE schemes in general is determining the optimal parameter sets for various cryptographic schemes. To address this challenge, several efforts have been made. For instance, Bergerat *et al.* [7] proposed a framework for parameter selection in TFHE-like schemes, whereas Biasioli *et al.* [8] extended this work, developing an interactive parameter generator for the FV scheme [16] that supports an arbitrary circuit model. The Homomorphic Encryption Standard [3] provides parameter sets based on the Lattice Estimator [5], a software tool to determine the security level of RLWE instances. More specifically, the standard gives upper limits on the size of the ciphertext modulus for certain security levels λ and polynomial degrees d in the form of lookup tables. Libraries such as PALISADE then use these lookup tables for fast security estimation during parameter generation. However, as FHE parameters depend on the specific use case, the trade-off is non-optimized parameter sets leading to larger parameters than necessary. This can adversely affect the runtime, memory usage, and overall performance of FHE implementations.

Contribution. The main idea of our work is to improve the current state-of-the-art of parameter selection process in all three steps of the process. Moreover, we aim to improve the usability of the BGV scheme. To achieve this goal, our work provides the following contributions:

- We provide a comprehensive analysis of noise growth in BGV using the canonical embedding norm for the DCRT representation, the current state-of-the-art for implementing RLWE-based schemes. To the best of our knowledge, these bounds are currently the best theoretical bounds for the BGV scheme with the DCRT representation.
- We empirically derive a closed formula computing the security for a given ciphertext modulus and polynomial degree. This enables the fast evaluation of a security estimate in the last step of the parameter selection process (Sect. 3.6).
- We provide new circuit models considering additional cases such as rotations or constant multiplications resulting in closer matching noise estimates for different use cases (Sect. 3).
- Using our theoretical and empirical formulas, we provide an interactive parameter generator for the leveled BGV scheme (Sect. 3.7). Additionally, the generator outputs easy-to-use code snippets for the generated parameters for multiple state-of-the-art libraries.

2   Preliminaries and Mathematical Background

We start with general notations that we will use in the remainder of this work. For a positive integer m, we denote by $\mathbb{Z}_m$ the ring of integers modulo m and by $\mathbb{Z}_m^* = \{x \in \mathbb{Z}_m \mid (x, m) = 1\}$ the multiplicative group of units. We denote by $R = \mathbb{Z}[x]/\langle \Phi_m(x) \rangle$ and by $R_p = \mathbb{Z}_p[x]/\langle \Phi_m(x) \rangle$, where p is an integer and $\Phi_m(x)$ is the cyclotomic polynomial (see Sect. 2.1).

With t and q we denote the plaintext and the ciphertext modulus, respectively, and with $\mathcal{R}_t$ and $\mathcal{R}_q$ the plaintext and ciphertext space, respectively. Moreover, we set $t \equiv 1 \mod m$ and q as a chain of primes, such that $q = q_{L-1} = \prod_{j=0}^{L-1} p_j$ where the p_i are roughly the same size and $p_i \equiv 1 \mod m$. The multiplicative depth M of the circuit determines the number of primes $L = M + 1$. Thus, for any level ℓ, we have $q_\ell = \prod_{j=0}^{\ell} p_j$.

Polynomials are denoted by lower letters such as a, and vectors of polynomials are denoted in bold as $\mathbf{a}$. Polynomial multiplication is denoted as $a \cdot b$ while multiplication with a scalar t is denoted as ta. Let $x \in \mathbb{R}$, we write $[x]_m \in [-m/2, m/2)$ for the centered representative of $x \mod m$.

We denoted by χ_e the RLWE error distribution, typically a discrete Gaussian with standard deviation $\sigma = 3.19$ [3] and variance $V_e = \sigma^2$, and by χ_s the secret key distribution with variance V_s. In general, if χ is a probabilistic distribution and $a \in R$ is a random polynomial, we write $a \leftarrow \chi$ sampling each coefficient independently from χ.

2.1   Cyclotomic Polynomials

Let $\mathbb{F}$ be a field and m be a positive integer. A m-th *root of unity* is a number $\zeta \in \mathbb{F}$ satisfying the equation $\zeta^m = 1$. It is called *primitive* if m is the smallest positive integer for which $\zeta^m = 1$. The m-th *cyclotomic polynomial* is defined as $\Phi_m(x) = \prod_{(j,m)=1}(x - \zeta^j)$. The degree of Φ_m is $\phi(m) = m \prod_{p|m} (1 - 1/p) = |\mathbb{Z}_m^*|$, Euler's totient function.

2.2   Canonical Embedding and Norm

Let $a \in R$ be a polynomial. We recall that the *infinity norm* of a is defined as $\|a\|_\infty = \max\{|a_i| : 0 \le i \le \phi(m) - 1\}$. If we consider two polynomials $a, b \in R$, the infinity norm of their product is bounded by $\|ab\|_\infty \le \delta_R \|a\|_\infty \|b\|_\infty$, where δ_R is the *expansion factor*. The *canonical embedding* of a is the vector obtained by evaluating a at all primitive m-th roots of unity. The *canonical embedding norm* of $a \in R$ is defined as $\|a\|^{can} = \max_{j \in \mathbb{Z}_m^*} |a(\zeta^j)|$. For a vector of polynomials $\mathbf{a} = (a_0, \ldots, a_{n-1}) \in R^n$, the canonical embedding norm is defined as $\|\mathbf{a}\|^{can} = \max_i \|a_i\|^{can}$. For any polynomial $a, b \in R$ and the *ring expansion factor* c_m, the following properties hold:

$$\|a\|^{can} \le \phi(m)\|a\|_\infty, \quad \|ab\|^{can} \le \|a\|^{can}\|b\|^{can}, \text{ and } \|a\|_\infty \le c_m\|a\|^{can}.$$

Note that $c_m = 1$ if $\Phi_m(x)$ is a power-of-two [14].

Let us consider a random $a \in R$ where each coefficient is sampled independently from one of the following zero-mean distributions:

- the discrete Gaussian distribution $\mathcal{DG}_q(\sigma^2)$ over $[-q/2, q/2)$;
- the discrete Binomial distribution $\mathcal{DB}_q(\sigma^2)$ over $[-q/2, q/2)$;
- the uniform distribution $\mathcal{U}_q$ over $\mathbb{Z}_q$;
- the uniform distribution $\mathcal{U}_3$ over $\{-1, 0, 1\}$;
- the distribution $\mathcal{ZO}(\rho)$ over $\{-1, 0, 1\}$ with probability $\rho/2$ for -1 and 1 and probability $1 - \rho$ for 0.

The random variable $a(\zeta)$ has variance $V = \phi(m)V_a$, where V_a is the variance of each coefficient a_i of a. More specifically,

$$a_i \in \mathcal{U}_q \quad \Rightarrow V_a \approx q^2/12, \qquad a_i \in \mathcal{U}_3 \quad \Rightarrow V_a = 2/3,$$
$$a_i \in \mathcal{DG}_q(\sigma^2) \Rightarrow V_a = \sigma^2, \qquad a_i \in \mathcal{ZO}(\rho) \Rightarrow V_a = \rho. \tag{1}$$

Then, the canonical norm is bounded by $\|a\|^{can} \leq D\sqrt{\phi(m)V_a}$ for some D. The probability that the variable a exceeds its standard deviation by more than a factor of D is rough $\mathrm{erfc}(D)$ for the complementary error function $\mathrm{erfc}(\cdot)$. Commonly used values are $\mathrm{erfc}(6) \approx 2^{-55}$ and $\mathrm{erfc}(5) \approx 2^{-40}$ [13].

For $a, b \in R$ chosen independently randomly, and a constant γ, it holds that

$$V_{a+b} = V_a + V_b, \quad V_{\gamma a} = \gamma^2 V_a, \text{ and } V_{ab} = \phi(m)V_a V_b.$$

We assume that messages behave as if selected uniformly at random from $\mathcal{U}_t$, that is, $\|m\|^{can} \leq Dt\sqrt{\phi(m)/12}$.

2.3   Lattices and Hermite Factor

Let $B = (\mathbf{b}_1, \ldots, \mathbf{b}_k)$ be linearly independent vectors in $\mathcal{R}^n$, then the *lattice* $\mathcal{L}(B)$ generated by the *base* B is defined by $\mathcal{L} = \mathcal{L}(B) = \{\sum_{i=1}^{k} \gamma_i \mathbf{b}_i : \gamma_i \in \mathbb{Z}, \mathbf{b}_i \in B\}$. The dimension k of a lattice $\mathcal{L} \subset \mathcal{R}^n$ is called *rank*. The *volume* or *determinant* of $\mathcal{L}$ is defined as $\mathsf{Vol}(\mathcal{L}) = \sqrt{\det(B^t B)}$. If $\mathcal{L}$ is a full rank lattice, that is when $k = n$, we have $\mathsf{Vol}(\mathcal{L}) = |\det(B)|$. Finally, we can define the *Hermite factor* δ_0^k as

$$\delta_0^k = \frac{\|\mathbf{b}_1\|}{\mathsf{Vol}(\mathcal{L})^{1/k}} \tag{2}$$

where $\mathbf{b}_1$ is the shortest vector in the reduced base B of the lattice $\mathcal{L}$. The factor δ_0 is called the *root Hermite factor*.

2.4   Security of RLWE-Based Schemes

The LWE problem is to find the secret vector $\mathbf{s} \in \mathbb{Z}_q^n$ given $\mathbf{b} \in \mathbb{Z}_q^m$ and $A \in (\mathbb{Z}_q)^{m \times n}$ with $A\mathbf{s} + \mathbf{e} = \mathbf{b} \bmod q$, $\mathbf{e} \in \mathbb{Z}_q^m$ is sampled from the error distribution χ_e. The security of LWE-based schemes depends on the intractability of this problem, and attacks on these schemes are based on finding efficient algorithms to solve them [26]. In [5], the authors presented three different methodologies to solve the LWE problem, and the central part of two of them is based on lattice reduction. Namely, starting from a bad (i. e. long) lattice basis, find a better (i. e. reduced and more orthogonal) basis.

The most well-known lattice reduction algorithm used in practice is Block Korkin-Zolotarev (BKZ) due to Schnorr and Euchner [31]. In these algorithms, the time complexity and the outcome quality are characterized by the Hermite factor [17]. Specifically, the run time of the BKZ algorithm is higher when the root Hermite factor δ_0 is smaller [31]. This result is also supported by a realistic estimation [5] where the authors show that the log of the time complexity to get a root Hermite factor δ_0 using BKZ with block size β is

$$\log(t_{BKZ})(\delta_0) = \Omega\left(-\frac{\log(\log \delta_0)}{\log \delta_0}\right). \tag{3}$$

For RLWE-based schemes, the same considerations apply. If we correctly choose the error distribution, then there are no better attacks on RLWE than on LWE [3]. This is because the best-known attacks do not leverage any property of the ring structure [26].

2.5   The BGV Scheme

The BGV scheme is a state-of-the-art FHE scheme based on the RLWE assumption. As is typical with RLWE-based schemes, implementations of BGV use the DCRT representation for polynomials. The DCRT leverages two separate Chinese Remainder Theorem (CRT) decompositions: the residue number system (RNS) and the Number Theoretic Transform (NTT). The RNS decomposes each coefficient of a polynomial with respect to each prime p_i. Additionally, the NTT decomposes each polynomial into linear terms modulo $(x - \zeta^j)$ for all m-th roots of unity ζ^j. Usually, the BGV scheme is used for leveled circuits, that is, circuits with a somewhat low multiplicative depth, as bootstrapping is very expensive [19]. Hence, this work will focus on the leveled version of the BGV scheme.

In the following, we recall the definitions and noise analysis for encryption and the scheme's arithmetic operations [11,22]. For modulus switching and key switching, we will provide only the definitions and noise bounds, including the RNS variants, and provide a thorough noise analysis later in Sect. 3.

KeyGen(λ)

Define parameters and distributions with respect to λ. Sample $s \leftarrow \chi_s$, $a \leftarrow \mathcal{U}_{q_L}$ and $e \leftarrow \chi_e$. Output

$$\mathsf{sk} = s \text{ and } \mathsf{pk} = (b, a) \equiv (-a \cdot s + te, a) \pmod{q_L}.$$

$\text{Enc}_{\text{pk}}(m)$

Receive plaintext $m \in \mathcal{R}_t$ for $\text{pk} = (b, a)$. Sample $u \leftarrow \chi_s$ and $e_0, e_1 \leftarrow \chi_e$. Output $\mathfrak{c} = (\mathbf{c}, L, \nu_{\text{clean}})$ with

$$\mathbf{c} = (c_0, c_1) \equiv (b \cdot u + te_0 + m, a \cdot u + te_1) \quad (\text{mod } q_L).$$

$\text{Dec}_{\text{sk}}(\mathfrak{c})$

Receive extended ciphertext $\mathfrak{c} = (\mathbf{c}, \ell, \nu)$ for $\text{sk} = s$. Decrypt with

$$c_0 + c_1 \cdot s \equiv m + te \quad (\text{mod } q_\ell)$$

and output $m \equiv m + te \bmod t$.

$\text{Add}(\mathfrak{c}, \mathfrak{c}')$

Receive extended ciphertexts $\mathfrak{c} = (\mathbf{c}, \ell, \nu)$ and $\mathfrak{c}' = (\mathbf{c}', \ell, \nu')$. Output $(\mathbf{c} + \mathbf{c}', \ell, \nu_{\text{add}})$.

$\text{Mul}(\mathfrak{c}, \mathfrak{c}')$

Receive extended ciphertexts $\mathfrak{c} = (\mathbf{c}, \ell, \nu)$ and $\mathfrak{c}' = (\mathbf{c}', \ell, \nu')$. Output $((c_0 \cdot c_0', c_0 \cdot c_1' + c_1 \cdot c_0', c_1 \cdot c_1'), \ell, \nu_{\text{mul}})$.

$\text{MulConst}(\alpha, \mathfrak{c})$

Receive constant polynomial $\alpha \in \mathcal{R}_t$ and extended ciphertext $\mathfrak{c} = (\mathbf{c}, \ell, \nu)$. Output $(\alpha \cdot \mathbf{c}, \ell, \nu_{\text{const}})$.

Let $\mathfrak{c} = (\mathbf{c}, \ell, \nu)$ be the *extended ciphertext*, where $\mathbf{c}$ is a ciphertext, ℓ denotes the level and ν the *critical quantity* of $\mathbf{c}$. The critical quantity is defined as the polynomial $\nu = [c_0 + c_1 \cdot s]_{q_\ell}$ for the associated level ℓ [13]. Note that the decryption is correct as long as the error does not wrap around the modulus q_ℓ, that is, $\|\nu\|_\infty \leq c_m \|\nu\|^{can} < q_\ell/2$. For encryption operation, we have

$$\|[c_0 + c_1 \cdot s]_{q_\ell}\|^{can} \leq \mathsf{B}_{\text{clean}} = Dt\sqrt{\phi(m)\left(\frac{1}{12} + 2\phi(m)V_eV_s + V_e\right)}. \quad (4)$$

For the arithmetic operation, correctness follows as long as the bound on each critical quantity stays below the decryption threshold with

$$\nu_{\text{add}} = \nu + \nu' = [c_0 + c_1 \cdot s]_{q_\ell} + [c_0' + c_1' \cdot s]_{q_\ell} \equiv m + m' \bmod t$$
$$\Rightarrow \|\nu_{\text{add}}\|^{can} \leq \|\nu\|^{can} + \|\nu'\|^{can}$$
$$\nu_{\text{mul}} = \nu \cdot \nu' = [c_0 + c_1 \cdot s]_{q_\ell} \cdot [c_0' + c_1' \cdot s]_{q_\ell} \equiv m \cdot m' \bmod t$$
$$\Rightarrow \|\nu_{\text{mul}}\|^{can} \leq \|\nu\|^{can}\|\nu'\|^{can}$$
$$\nu_{\text{const}} = \alpha \cdot \nu = \alpha \cdot [c_0 + c_1 \cdot s]_{q_\ell} \equiv \alpha \cdot m \bmod t$$
$$\Rightarrow \|\nu_{\text{const}}\|^{can} \leq D\sqrt{\phi(m)^2 V_\alpha V_\nu} \leq t\sqrt{\phi(m)/12} \|\nu\|^{can} = \mathsf{B}_{\text{const}}\|\nu\|^{can}. \quad (5)$$

Here, we consider the constant α to be uniformly distributed in $\mathcal{R}_t$, where the bound on ν_{const} is established in [15]. The output of the multiplication is a ciphertext in $\mathcal{R}_q \times \mathcal{R}_q \times \mathcal{R}_q$ and can be transformed back to a ciphertext in $\mathcal{R}_q \times \mathcal{R}_q$ encrypting the same message via key switching.

Modulus Switching. Modulus switching reduces the associated level and the critical quantity for a ciphertext, enabling leveled homomorphic computations. The idea is to switch from a ciphertext modulus q_ℓ to a ciphertext modulus $q_{\ell'} = q_{\ell-k}$ for some $k \in \mathbb{Z}$. We thus multiply the ciphertext by $\frac{q_{\ell'}}{q_\ell}$, roughly reducing the error by the same factor.

ModSwitch$(\mathfrak{c}, \ell')$

Receive extended ciphertext $\mathfrak{c} = (\mathbf{c}, \ell, \nu)$ and target level $\ell' = \ell - k$.
Set $\boldsymbol{\delta} = t[-\mathbf{c}t^{-1}]_{q_\ell/q_{\ell'}}$ and

$$\mathbf{c}' = \frac{q_{\ell'}}{q_\ell}(\mathbf{c} + \boldsymbol{\delta}) \pmod{q_{\ell'}}.$$

Output $(\mathbf{c}', \ell', \nu_{\mathsf{ms}})$.

For $k = 1$, $\frac{q_{\ell'}}{q_\ell} = \frac{1}{p_\ell}$ and the bound on the error is $\|\nu_{\mathsf{ms}}\|^{can} = \frac{1}{p_\ell}\|\nu\|^{can} + \mathsf{B}_{\mathsf{scale}}$ with

$$\mathsf{B}_{\mathsf{scale}} = Dt\sqrt{\frac{\phi(m)}{12}}(1 + \phi(m)V_s) \quad [11]. \tag{6}$$

Note that decryption is correct as long as $\|\nu\|^{can} < \frac{q_\ell}{2c_m} - p_\ell\mathsf{B}_{\mathsf{scale}}$.

For $k > 1$ in the DCRT representation, we apply a *fast base extension* from $q_\ell/q_{\ell'}$ to $q_{\ell'}$ for $\boldsymbol{\delta}$. For two RNS bases $q = \prod_{i=1}^{\kappa} q_i$ and $q' = \prod_{j=1}^{\kappa'} q_j'$ and a polynomial α, it is defined as

$$\mathsf{BaseExt}(\alpha, q, q') = \sum_{i=1}^{\kappa}\left[\alpha\frac{q_i}{q}\right]_{q_i}\frac{q}{q_i} \pmod{q_j'} \quad \forall j \in \{1, ..., \kappa'\}. \tag{7}$$

This outputs $\alpha + qu$ in the RNS base q'. We analyze the impact of the error in Sect. 3.

Key Switching. Key switching is used for (i) reducing the degree of a ciphertext polynomial, usually the output of a multiplication, or (ii) changing the key after a rotation. For multiplication, we convert the ciphertext term $c_2 \cdot s^2$ to a polynomial $c_0^{\mathsf{ks}} + c_1^{\mathsf{ks}} \cdot s$, and for a rotation, we convert the ciphertext term $c_1 \cdot \mathsf{rot}(s)$ to a polynomial $c_0^{\mathsf{ks}} + c_1^{\mathsf{ks}} \cdot s$. In the following, we will only analyze multiplication, and more specifically, we will output $\mathbf{c}' = (c_0 + c_0^{\mathsf{ks}}, c_1 + c_1^{\mathsf{ks}})$ and denote the ciphertext term we want to remove by c_2. This also covers rotations as one only has to consider the term we want to remove as c_1 and an output of $(c_0 + c_0^{\mathsf{ks}}, c_1^{\mathsf{ks}})$.

Unfortunately, the error after a naïve application of key switching grows quickly, and thus several variants exist to reduce its growth. This work considers the three main variants: the Brakerski Vaikuntanathan (BV) variant, the Gentry Halevi Smart (GHS) variant, and the Hybrid variant.

BV Variant. The BV variant decomposes c_2 with respect to a base β to reduce the error growth [9]. For polynomials a and b and $l = \lfloor \log_\beta q_\ell \rceil + 1$, we define

$$\mathcal{D}_\beta(a) = ([a]_\beta, [\lfloor a/\beta \rfloor]_\beta, \ldots, [\lfloor a/\beta^{l-1} \rfloor]_\beta)$$
$$\mathcal{P}_\beta(b) = ([b]_{q_\ell}, [b\beta]_{q_\ell}, \ldots, [b\beta^{l-1}]_{q_\ell}).$$

KeySwitchGen$^{\mathsf{BV}}(s, s^2)$

Receive secret key s' and secret key target s.
Sample $\mathbf{a} \leftarrow \mathcal{U}_{q_L}^l$, $\mathbf{e} \leftarrow \chi_e^l$ and output key switching key

$$\mathsf{ks}^{\mathsf{BV}} = (\mathbf{ks}_0^{\mathsf{BV}}, \mathbf{ks}_1^{\mathsf{BV}}) = (-\mathbf{a} \cdot s + t\mathbf{e} + \mathcal{P}_\beta(s^2), \mathbf{a}) \pmod{q_L}.$$

KeySwitch$^{\mathsf{BV}}(\mathbf{ks}^{\mathsf{BV}}, \mathfrak{c})$

Receive extended ciphertext $\mathfrak{c} = (\mathbf{c}, \ell, \nu)$ and key switching key $\mathsf{ks}^{\mathsf{BV}}$.
Switch key for $c_0 + c_1 \cdot s + c_2 \cdot s^2$ with

$$\mathbf{c}' = (c_0 + \langle \mathcal{D}_\beta(c_2), \mathbf{ks}_0^{\mathsf{BV}} \rangle, c_1 + \langle \mathcal{D}_\beta(c_2), \mathbf{ks}_1^{\mathsf{BV}} \rangle) \pmod{q_\ell}$$

and output $(\mathbf{c}', \ell, \nu_{\mathsf{ks}}^{\mathsf{BV}})$.

The error after the BV key switching is $\|\nu_{\mathsf{ks}}^{\mathsf{BV}}\|^{can} \leq \|\nu\|^{can} + \beta\sqrt{\log_\beta(q_\ell)}\mathsf{B}_{\mathsf{ks}}$ with

$$\mathsf{B}_{\mathsf{ks}} = Dt\phi(m)\sqrt{V_e/12} \quad [11]. \tag{8}$$

BV-RNS Variant. For the BV-RNS variant, we additionally define $\mathcal{D}_{p_i}$ and $\mathcal{P}_{p_i}$ not with respect to some digit decomposition β, but to the already existing RNS decomposition which we hence can apply for free during the key switching process.

$$\mathcal{D}_{p_i}(a) = \left(\left[a \left(\frac{q_\ell}{p_0} \right)^{-1} \right]_{p_0}, \ldots, \left[a \left(\frac{q_\ell}{p_\ell} \right)^{-1} \right]_{p_\ell} \right)$$
$$\mathcal{P}_{p_i}(b) = \left(\left[b\frac{q_\ell}{p_0} \right]_{q_\ell}, \ldots, \left[b\frac{q_\ell}{p_\ell} \right]_{q_\ell} \right).$$

Since this itself does not reduce the error enough, we apply both decompositions at the same time with $\langle \mathcal{D}_\beta(\mathcal{D}_{p_i}(a)), \mathcal{P}_{p_i}(\mathcal{P}_\beta(b)) \rangle = a \cdot b \bmod q_\ell$. We analyze the noise growth in Sect. 3.

GHS Variant. The GHS variant [19] switches to a larger ciphertext modulus $Q_\ell = q_\ell P$ with P and q coprime. Then, key switching takes place in $\mathcal{R}_{Q_\ell}$ and, by modulus switching back down to q_ℓ, the error is reduced again. As a tradeoff, we have to make sure that our RLWE instances are secure with respect to Q_ℓ.

KeySwitchGen$^{\text{GHS}}(s, s^2)$ ─────────────────────

Receive secret key s^2 and secret key target s.
Sample $a \leftarrow \mathcal{U}_{Q_L}$, $e \leftarrow \chi_e$ and output key switching key

$$\text{ks}^{\text{GHS}} = (\text{ks}_0^{\text{GHS}}, \text{ks}_1^{\text{GHS}}) \equiv (-a \cdot s + te + Ps^2, a) \pmod{Q_L}.$$

KeySwitch$^{\text{GHS}}(\mathbf{ks}, \mathfrak{c})$ ─────────────────────

Receive extended ciphertext $\mathfrak{c} = (\mathbf{c}, \ell, \nu)$ and key switching key ks^{GHS}.
For $c_0 + c_1 \cdot s + c_2 \cdot s^2$, switch key with

$$\mathbf{c}' \equiv (Pc_0 + c_2 \cdot \text{ks}_0^{\text{GHS}}, Pc_1 + c_2 \cdot \text{ks}_1^{\text{GHS}}) \bmod Q_\ell.$$

Set $\boldsymbol{\delta} = t[-\mathbf{c}'t^{-1}]_P$, modulus switch back with

$$\mathbf{c}'' = \frac{1}{P}(\mathbf{c}' + \boldsymbol{\delta}) \pmod{q_\ell}.$$

Output $(\mathbf{c}'', \ell, \nu_{\text{ks}}^{\text{GHS}})$.

The error after the GHS key switching is $\|\nu_{\text{ks}}^{\text{GHS}}\|^{can} \leq \|\nu\|^{can} + \frac{q_\ell}{P}\mathsf{B}_{\text{ks}} + \mathsf{B}_{\text{scale}}$, where B_{ks} and $\mathsf{B}_{\text{scale}}$ are as in Eqs. (8) and (6), respectively [19]. Decryption, and thus key switching, is correct as long as $\|\nu\|^{can} < \frac{q_\ell}{2c_m} - \frac{q_\ell}{P}\mathsf{B}_{\text{ks}} + \mathsf{B}_{\text{scale}}$.

GHS-RNS Variant. For the RNS variant of GHS, we set $P = \prod_{j=1}^{k} P_j$ such that $P_i \equiv 1 \mod m$ and extend $\boldsymbol{\delta}$ from P to q_ℓ (see also modulus switching in Sect. 2.5). Additionally, we extend c_2 from q_ℓ to Q_ℓ. We analyze the noise growth in Sect. 3.

Hybrid Variant. The Hybrid variant combines the BV and GHS variants.

KeySwitchGen$^{\text{Hybrid}}(s, s^2)$ ─────────────────────

Receive secret key s^2 and secret key target s.
Sample $\mathbf{a} \leftarrow \mathcal{U}_{q_L}^l$, $\mathbf{e} \leftarrow \chi_e^l$ and output key switching key

$$\text{ks}^{\text{Hybrid}} = (\text{ks}_0^{\text{Hybrid}}, \text{ks}_1^{\text{Hybrid}}) \equiv (-\mathbf{a} \cdot s + t\mathbf{e} + P\mathcal{P}_\beta(s^2), \mathbf{a}) \pmod{Q_L}.$$

KeySwitch$^{\text{Hybrid}}(\mathbf{ks}^{\text{Hybrid}}, \mathfrak{c})$ ─────────────────────

Receive extended ciphertext $\mathfrak{c} = (\mathbf{c}, \ell, \nu)$ and key switching key $\text{ks}^{\text{Hybrid}}$.
For $c_0 + c_1 \cdot s + c_2 \cdot s^2$, switch key with

$$\mathbf{c}' \equiv (Pc_0 + \langle \mathcal{D}_\beta(c_2), \text{ks}_0^{\text{Hybrid}} \rangle, Pc_1 + \langle \mathcal{D}_\beta(c_2), \text{ks}_1^{\text{Hybrid}} \rangle) \bmod Q_\ell.$$

Set $\boldsymbol{\delta} = t[-\mathbf{c}'t^{-1}]_P$, modulus switch back with $\mathbf{c}'' = \frac{1}{P}(\mathbf{c}' + \boldsymbol{\delta}) \pmod{q_\ell}$ and output $(\mathbf{c}'', \ell, \nu_{\text{ks}}^{\text{Hybrid}})$.

Correctness follows by combining the proofs of each variant. The bounds also follow similarly, since before scaling down we have $\nu' = \nu P + \beta\sqrt{\log_\beta q_\ell}B_{ks}$. Thus, the error after the modulus switching procedure is thus bounded by

$$\|\nu_{ks}^{\text{Hybrid}}\|^{can} \leq \frac{q_\ell}{Q_\ell}\|\nu'\|^{can} + B_{scale}$$

$$\leq \|\nu\|^{can} + \frac{\beta\sqrt{\log_\beta q_\ell}}{P}B_{ks} + B_{scale}.$$

Hybrid-RNS Variant. The Hybrid-RNS variant combines the RNS adaptations of each variant. However, instead of decomposing with respect to each single RNS prime, we group the primes into ω chunks of (at most) size $l = \lceil\frac{L}{\omega}\rceil$ and do not apply the decomposition to the base β. Hence, we set $\tilde{q}_i = \prod_{j=il}^{il+l-1} p_j$ and define $\mathcal{D}_{\tilde{q}_i}$ and $\mathcal{P}_{\tilde{q}_i}$ as

$$\mathcal{D}_{\tilde{q}_i}(\alpha) = \left(\left[\alpha\left(\frac{q_\ell}{\tilde{q}_0}\right)^{-1}\right]_{\tilde{q}_0}, \ldots, \left[\alpha\left(\frac{q_\ell}{\tilde{q}_{l-1}}\right)^{-1}\right]_{\tilde{q}_{l-1}}\right)$$

$$\mathcal{P}_{\tilde{q}_i}(\beta) = \left(\left[\beta\frac{q_\ell}{\tilde{q}_0}\right]_{q_\ell}, \ldots, \left[\beta\frac{q_\ell}{\tilde{q}_{l-1}}\right]_{q_\ell}\right).$$

We now have to extend c_2 from each $\tilde{q}_i$ to Q_ℓ instead. We analyze the noise growth in Sect. 3.

3   Improving the Parameter Generation Process

In this section, we provide our improvements to the parameter generation process. First, we offer new bounds for modulus switching and key switching in the DCRT representation. These bounds enable correct analysis for essential BGV operations, such as rotations supporting different methods for key switching. Afterward, we suggest an improvement to circuit models in general and define new circuit models. We analyze these models with our newly improved bounds and provide closed formulas to compute the individual primes. Finally, we introduce the empirically derived, closed security formula for our parameter generator and shortly describe the generator itself.

3.1   New DCRT Bounds for Modulus Switching

For modulus switching, we can either scale by a single modulus or by multiple moduli. When scaling by a single modulus, the bound B_{scale} is as in Eq. (6).

When scaling by $\jmath > 1$ moduli, however, we have to adjust our bound due to the base extension of $t[-ct^{-1}]_{q_\ell/q_{\ell'}}$ from $q_\ell/q_{\ell'}$ to $q_{\ell'}$ with $\ell' = \ell - \jmath$. Considering Eq. (7), we extend each δ_i as

$$\delta_i = t\,\text{BaseExt}(-c_i t^{-1}, \frac{q_\ell}{q_{\ell'}}, q_{\ell'}) = t\sum_{i=\ell'+1}^{\ell}\left[-c_i t^{-1}\frac{p_i}{q_\ell/q_{\ell'}}\right]_{p_i}\frac{q_\ell/q_{\ell'}}{p_i} \pmod{q_{\ell'}}$$

Then, the variance V_{δ_i} follows as

$$V_{\delta_i} = t^2 {}_{j} V_{p_i} \frac{(q_\ell/q_{\ell'})^2}{p_i^2} = t^2 {}_{j} \frac{(q_\ell/q_{\ell'})^2}{12}.$$

Thus, we introduce a factor of j compared to the non-extended variance of δ_i and the correct bound follows as $\|\nu_{\mathsf{ms}}\|^{can} \le \frac{q_{\ell'}}{q_\ell} \|\nu\|^{can} + \sqrt{j} \mathsf{B}_{\mathsf{scale}}$.

3.2 New DCRT Bounds for Key Switching

For the BV-RNS variant, $\mathcal{D}_{p_i}$ decomposes to each individual modulus and the key switching is bound by

$$\|\nu_{\mathsf{ks}}^{\mathsf{BV-RNS}}\|^{can} \le \|\nu\|^{can} + \|t\langle \mathcal{D}_{p_i}(c_2), \mathbf{e}\rangle\|^{can}$$
$$\le \|\nu\|^{can} + \sqrt{\ell+1}\max(p_i)\mathsf{B}_{\mathsf{ks}}.$$

Assuming $p_i < p_j$ for $i < j$, this simplifies to

$$\|\nu_{\mathsf{ks}}^{\mathsf{BV-RNS}}\|^{can} \le \|\nu\|^{can} + \sqrt{\ell+1}p_\ell \mathsf{B}_{\mathsf{ks}}.$$

Applying the additional decomposition $\mathcal{D}_\beta$ results in our final bound

$$\|\nu_{\mathsf{ks}}^{\mathsf{BV-RNS}}\|^{can} \le \|\nu\|^{can} + \sqrt{l+1}\beta\sqrt{\log_\beta p_\ell}\mathsf{B}_{\mathsf{ks}}.$$

For the GHS-RNS variant, we have two additional errors from the base extension: once for extending c_2 from q_ℓ to Q_ℓ and once for extending δ from P to Q_ℓ. When extending c_2 and multiplying with the key switching key, this results in

$$c_0' + c_1's \equiv Pc_0 + (c_2 + q_\ell u) \cdot \mathsf{ks}_0 + (Pc_1 + (c_2 + q_\ell u) \cdot \mathsf{ks}_1)s \quad (\bmod\ Q_\ell)$$
$$\equiv P[c_0 + c_1 s + c_2 s^2]_{q_\ell} + t(c_2 + q_\ell u)e \quad (\bmod\ Q_\ell)$$

increasing the noise to $\|\nu'\|^{can} \le P\|\nu\|^{can} + \sqrt{\ell+1}q_\ell \mathsf{B}_{\mathsf{ks}}$. When extending δ, the additional noise behaves as equivalent to our modulus switching analysis. Thus, for $P = \prod_{j=1}^{k} P_j$, we get a factor of $\sqrt{k}$ and overall

$$\|\nu_{\mathsf{ks}}^{\mathsf{GHS-RNS}}\|^{can} \le \|\nu\|^{can} + \sqrt{\ell+1}\frac{q_\ell}{P}\mathsf{B}_{\mathsf{ks}} + \sqrt{k}\mathsf{B}_{\mathsf{scale}}.$$

For the Hybrid-RNS variant, we can combine our previous analyses. However, we again have to adjust because we decompose the ciphertext modulus into ω products $\tilde{q}$ and not necessarily to each individual RNS prime. The fast base extension takes place before the dot product, for an upper bound we now consider $\max \tilde{q}_i$ instead of $\max q_i$ leading to

$$\|\nu_{\mathsf{ks}}^{\mathsf{Hybrid-RNS}}\|^{can} \le \|\nu\|^{can} + \sqrt{\omega(\ell+1)}\frac{\max(\tilde{q}_i)}{P}\mathsf{B}_{\mathsf{ks}} + \sqrt{k}\mathsf{B}_{\mathsf{scale}}.$$

If we again assume $p_i < p_j$ for $i < j$, this simplifies to

$$\|\nu_{\mathsf{ks}}^{\mathsf{Hybrid-RNS}}\|^{can} \le \|\nu\|^{can} + \sqrt{\omega(\ell+1)}\frac{p_\ell^{\lceil \ell/\omega \rceil}}{P}\mathsf{B}_{\mathsf{ks}} + \sqrt{k}\mathsf{B}_{\mathsf{scale}}.$$

3.3   Modeling the Homomorphic Circuit

We generally split the homomorphic circuit into levels and reduce the ciphertext noise to a base level B using modulus switching. The multiplicative depth M determines the modulus count $L = M + 1$, which can be split into three types: top, middle, and bottom modulus.

- The top modulus p_{L-1} is the first modulus in the prime chain. Before any operation, we reduce the fresh encryption noise B_{clean} down to the base noise B using modulus switching. We continue in level $L-2$ with the middle modulus.
- The middle modulus p_ℓ at level $1 \le \ell \le L-2$ reduces the noise back to B after the arithmetic operations as defined by the model (see below) using the modulus switching procedure. This reduces the modulus from q_ℓ to $q_{\ell-1}$ until the last modulus $q_0 = p_0$.
- For the bottom modulus p_0, we can still perform all arithmetic operations within our model. However, we do not scale down to B. Instead, this modulus is large enough to perform decryption correctly. Instead of performing a key switching including modulus switching for the final multiplication, we decrypt right after this multiplication using sk and sk^2, reducing the overall amount of operations that are performed.

This work studies the circuit models depicted in Fig. 1.

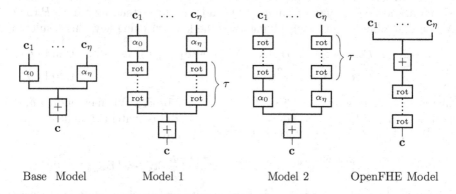

Fig. 1. Our analysis models are depicted as circuits.

After the initial modulus switching, we operate on η ciphertexts c_i in parallel. In our Model 1, we perform one constant multiplication followed by τ rotations. Finally, the ciphertexts are accumulated and used as input to one multiplication before modulus switching is applied. In Model 2, we switch the rotations and constant multiplications, corresponding to the worst possible noise growth. For $\tau = 0$, we refer to the model as Base Model and provide separate formulas as it simplifies analysis and thus also reduces the ciphertext modulus size. For comparison with previous work, we also define the model as used in the

OpenFHE library [6,23]. For the OpenFHE model, the multiplication is before the circuit with an input noise of B^2 for each c_i. Note that within our models, all parameters can be chosen as required by the use case.

3.4   Determining Modulus Sizes

In the following, we determine the modulus size by computing bounds for the individual primes in the modulus chain. Based on our models, we assume that after each level, we apply modulus switching to go down to a certain noise level B. Given the top modulus, we scale down to B right after the encryption. With the middle modulus, we scale down the level noise back to B after each level. Finally, with the bottom modulus, we perform our leveled computation followed by the decryption.

Middle Modulus. We describe our approach by first analyzing the middle modulus p_ℓ in the base model: considering η ciphertexts c_i with a starting noise of B, we apply a constant multiplication, thus the noise increments to $\mathsf{B}_{\mathsf{const}}B$, and add up all the ciphertexts, increasing the noise to $\eta\mathsf{B}_{\mathsf{const}}B$. When multiplying two ciphertexts within this model, the noise after the multiplication grows to $(\eta\mathsf{B}_{\mathsf{const}}B)^2$.

We conclude the level by applying a key switching for the multiplication, increasing the noise by ν_{ks}, as well as a modulus switching which scales the noise back down. This results in the inequality

$$\frac{(\eta\mathsf{B}_{\mathsf{const}}B)^2 + \nu_{\mathsf{ks}}}{p_\ell} + \mathsf{B}_{\mathsf{scale}} < B \tag{9}$$

where the key switching noise ν_{ks} depends on the key switching method with

$$\nu_{\mathsf{ks}} = f_0\mathsf{B}_{\mathsf{ks}} + \sqrt{f_1}\mathsf{B}_{\mathsf{scale}} \tag{10}$$

and

$$f_0 = \begin{cases} \beta\sqrt{\log_\beta q_\ell} & \text{for BV} \\ \sqrt{\ell+1}\beta\sqrt{\log_\beta p_\ell} & \text{for BV-RNS} \\ q_\ell/P & \text{for GHS} \\ \sqrt{\ell+1}q_\ell/P & \text{for GHS-RNS} \\ \beta\sqrt{\log_\beta q_\ell}/P & \text{for Hybrid} \\ \sqrt{\omega(\ell+1)}p_\ell^{\lceil L/\omega\rceil}/P & \text{for Hybrid-RNS} \end{cases} \quad \text{and } f_1 = \begin{cases} 0 & \text{for BV} \\ 0 & \text{for BV-RNS} \\ 1 & \text{for GHS} \\ k & \text{for GHS-RNS} \\ 1 & \text{for Hybrid} \\ k & \text{for Hybrid-RNS} \end{cases}.$$

We similarly model the noise growth in the other models, resulting in the inequalities

$$\frac{\eta^2(\mathsf{B}_{\mathsf{const}}B + \tau\nu_{\mathsf{ks}})^2 + \nu_{\mathsf{ks}}}{p_\ell} + \mathsf{B}_{\mathsf{scale}} < B \qquad \text{for our model 1,}$$

$$\frac{\eta^2\mathsf{B}_{\mathsf{const}}^2(B + \tau\nu_{\mathsf{ks}})^2 + \nu_{\mathsf{ks}}}{p_\ell} + \mathsf{B}_{\mathsf{scale}} < B \qquad \text{for our model 2,} \qquad (11)$$

$$\frac{\eta B^2 + (\tau + 1)\nu_{\mathsf{ks}}}{p_\ell} + \mathsf{B}_{\mathsf{scale}} < B \qquad \text{for the OpenFHE model.}$$

Solving these inequalities then determines a value for B and the sizes of our middle moduli p_ℓ. In the following, we use $\varepsilon = \eta\mathsf{B}_{\mathsf{const}}$ and $\xi = \varepsilon^2$ to simplify notation. If constant multiplications are not required, we set $\mathsf{B}_{\mathsf{const}} = 1$.

Top Modulus. For the top modulus, we simply want to reduce the encryption noise to B using the modulus switching, hence we set

$$\frac{\mathsf{B}_{\mathsf{clean}}}{p_{L-1}} + \mathsf{B}_{\mathsf{scale}} < B \iff p_{L-1} > \frac{\mathsf{B}_{\mathsf{clean}}}{B - \mathsf{B}_{\mathsf{scale}}}. \qquad (12)$$

Bottom Modulus. For the bottom modulus $p_0 = q_0$, we do not apply the key switching for the multiplication or the modulus switching afterward while still allowing the computations as defined in the respective circuit models. To ensure correct decryption, we require that $\|\nu\|_\infty \le c_m\|\nu\|^{can} < q_\ell/2$. For our models, this results in the following bounds for the bottom modulus:

$$p_0 > 2c_m(\eta\mathsf{B}_{\mathsf{const}}B)^2 \qquad \text{for our base model,}$$

$$p_0 > 2c_m\eta^2(\mathsf{B}_{\mathsf{const}}B + \tau\nu_{\mathsf{ks}})^2 \qquad \text{for our model 1,}$$

$$p_0 > 2c_m\eta^2\mathsf{B}_{\mathsf{const}}^2(B + \tau\nu_{\mathsf{ks}})^2 \qquad \text{for our model 2,} \qquad (13)$$

$$p_0 > 2c_m\eta B^2 + \tau\nu_{\mathsf{ks}} \qquad \text{for the OpenFHE model.}$$

Thus, we simply choose each bottom modulus larger than the corresponding bound in the respective model.

3.5 Computing the Noise Bound B

In the following, considering the different key-switching procedures, we determine the bound B required to select the size of our individual moduli in the modulus chain. We apply our method exemplary to Model 2 with the worst-case noise growth. The same techniques can, however, be applied to simpler models as well.

Note that for GHS and Hybrid key switching as well as its RNS variants, we can merge the key switching with the modulus switching and directly switch down to a smaller modulus, that is, from Q_ℓ to $q_{\ell-1}$ decreasing the noise by $q_{\ell-1}/Q_\ell = 1/(Pp_\ell)$. Including this optimization, in the specific case of GHS and Hybrid key switching, we have to adjust Eq. (11) for Model 2 to

$$\frac{\eta^2 \mathsf{B}_{\mathsf{const}}^2 (B + \tau \nu_{\mathsf{ks}})^2 + f_0 \mathsf{B}_{\mathsf{scale}}}{p_\ell} + \sqrt{f_1'} \mathsf{B}_{\mathsf{scale}} < B \qquad (14)$$

where

$$f_1' = \begin{cases} 1 & \text{for GHS, and Hybrid} \\ k+1 & \text{for GHS-RNS, and Hybrid-RNS.} \end{cases}$$

BV Key-Switching. To compute the noise bound B we have to consider the Eq. (11). Note that, since the p_ℓ's have roughly the same size, $f_0^{\mathsf{BV}} \sim f_0^{\mathsf{BV-RNS}}$. Indeed, $f_0^{\mathsf{BV}} = \beta\sqrt{\log_\beta q_\ell} \sim \beta\sqrt{(\ell+1)\log_\beta(p_\ell)}$. Since $\log_\beta(p_\ell) \leq \log_2(p_\ell)$, we can set $f_0 = f_0^{\mathsf{BV}} = f_0^{\mathsf{BV-RNS}} = \beta\sqrt{(\ell+1)\log_2(p_\ell)}$. Moreover, for p_ℓ big enough, we have that $f_0 \mathsf{B}_{\mathsf{ks}}/p_\ell \sim 0$. Then, Eq. (11) becomes

$$\frac{\xi B^2}{p_\ell} + \left(\frac{2\xi\tau f_0 \mathsf{B}_{\mathsf{ks}}}{p_\ell} - 1\right) B + \frac{(\varepsilon\tau f_0 \mathsf{B}_{\mathsf{ks}})^2}{p_\ell} + \mathsf{B}_{\mathsf{scale}} < 0.$$

Because of the previous inequality, in the indeterminate B, must have a positive discriminant, we have

$$1 - \frac{4\xi\tau f_0 \mathsf{B}_{\mathsf{ks}}}{p_\ell} - \frac{4\xi\mathsf{B}_{\mathsf{scale}}}{p_\ell} \geq 0 \iff p_\ell > 4\xi(\tau f_0 \mathsf{B}_{\mathsf{ks}} + \mathsf{B}_{\mathsf{scale}}). \qquad (15)$$

Thus we can set

$$p_1 \sim \ldots \sim p_{L-2} \sim 4\xi(3\tau\beta\sqrt{(L-1)\log_2(t\phi(m))}\mathsf{B}_{\mathsf{ks}} + \mathsf{B}_{\mathsf{scale}}), \qquad (16)$$

Indeed, considering p_ℓ as in Eq. (16), the Eq. (15) holds. Moreover, since the discriminant ~ 0, we have

$$B \sim \frac{1}{2\xi/p_\ell} \sim 2(3\tau\beta\sqrt{(L-1)\log_2(t\phi(m))}\mathsf{B}_{\mathsf{ks}} + \mathsf{B}_{\mathsf{scale}}). \qquad (17)$$

where $\beta \geq 2$.

We can now compute the bottom modulus p_0 starting from Eq. (13). This equation becomes $z > \varepsilon B + \varepsilon\tau\omega\mathsf{B}_{\mathsf{ks}}\sqrt{\log_\omega(2c_m z^2)}$ where $z = \sqrt{q_0/2c_m}$, i.e., $q_0 = 2c_m z^2$. Since $\sqrt{\log_\omega(2c_m)} + \sqrt{2\log_\omega z} > \sqrt{\log_\omega(2c_m z^2)}$, it is enough to prove that

$$z > \varepsilon B + \varepsilon\tau\omega\mathsf{B}_{\mathsf{ks}}\left(\sqrt{\log_\omega(2c_m)} + \sqrt{2\log_\omega z}\right) \qquad (18)$$

We claim that this inequality holds for $z = 2\varepsilon B$. Indeed, Eq. (18) becomes

$$\frac{\varepsilon B}{\varepsilon\tau\omega\mathsf{B}_{\mathsf{ks}}} - \sqrt{\log_\omega(2c_m)} > \sqrt{2\log_\omega(2\varepsilon B)}.$$

Since B is as in Eq. (17), then $2\varepsilon B < \mathsf{B}_{\mathsf{ks}}^3$, so the previous inequality holds since $2\sqrt{L-1}\log_\omega(\mathsf{B}_{\mathsf{ks}}) + \frac{2\mathsf{B}_{\mathsf{scale}}}{\tau\omega\mathsf{B}_{\mathsf{ks}}} > \sqrt{6\log_\omega(\mathsf{B}_{\mathsf{ks}})} > \sqrt{2\log_\omega(2\varepsilon B)}$. Namely, $p_0 > 8c_m\xi B^2$.

Base Model. When $\tau = 0$, Eq. (11) becomes

$$\xi B^2 / p_\ell + \beta \sqrt{(\ell + 1) \log_2(p_\ell)} \mathsf{B}_{\mathsf{ks}} / p_\ell + \mathsf{B}_{\mathsf{scale}} < B.$$

Following the same argument as before, we must have a positive discriminant and thus we have $p_1 \sim \ldots \sim p_{L-2} \sim 4\xi\mathsf{B}_{\mathsf{scale}}$, $B \sim \frac{p_\ell}{2\xi} \sim 2\mathsf{B}_{\mathsf{scale}}$ and $p_0 > 2c_m\xi B^2 = 8c_m\xi\mathsf{B}_{\mathsf{scale}}^2$.

GHS and Hybrid Key-Switching. Equation (14) becomes

$$\frac{\xi B^2}{p_\ell} + \frac{2\xi\tau}{p_\ell}\left(f_0\mathsf{B}_{\mathsf{ks}} + \sqrt{f_1}\mathsf{B}_{\mathsf{scale}}\right)B + \frac{\xi\tau^2}{p_\ell}\left(f_0\mathsf{B}_{\mathsf{ks}} + \sqrt{f_1}\mathsf{B}_{\mathsf{scale}}\right)^2 + \frac{f_0}{p_\ell}\mathsf{B}_{\mathsf{ks}} + \sqrt{f_1'}\mathsf{B}_{\mathsf{scale}} < B. \tag{19}$$

To solve this inequality in B, we follow the idea of Gentry *et al.* [19]. Let

$$R_\ell = \frac{\xi\tau^2}{p_\ell}\left(f_0\mathsf{B}_{\mathsf{ks}} + \sqrt{f_1}\mathsf{B}_{\mathsf{scale}}\right)^2 + \frac{f_0}{p_\ell}\mathsf{B}_{\mathsf{ks}} + \sqrt{f_1'}\mathsf{B}_{\mathsf{scale}}$$

Since R_ℓ increases with larger ℓ's, we have to satisfy this inequality for the largest modulus $\ell = L - 2$. Moreover, $R_{L-2} > f_1\mathsf{B}_{\mathsf{scale}}$. Since we want that this term is as close to $\mathsf{B}_{\mathsf{scale}}$ as possible, we have to set $f_0 \sim \mathsf{B}_{\mathsf{scale}}/K\mathsf{B}_{\mathsf{ks}}$, for a *large enough* constant $K \in \mathbb{N}$ (i.e., we can take $K \sim 100$). Namely,

$$P \sim \begin{cases} Kq_{L-2}\mathsf{B}_{\mathsf{ks}}/\mathsf{B}_{\mathsf{scale}} & \text{for GHS} \\ K\sqrt{L-1}q_{L-2}\mathsf{B}_{\mathsf{ks}}/\mathsf{B}_{\mathsf{scale}} & \text{for GHS-RNS} \\ K\beta\sqrt{\log_\beta(q_{L-2})}\mathsf{B}_{\mathsf{ks}}/\mathsf{B}_{\mathsf{scale}} & \text{for Hybrid} \\ K\sqrt{\omega(L-1)}p_{L-2}^{L/\omega}\mathsf{B}_{\mathsf{ks}}/\mathsf{B}_{\mathsf{scale}} & \text{for Hybrid-RNS.} \end{cases} \tag{20}$$

Equation (19) becomes $\frac{\xi B^2}{p_\ell} + (\frac{2\xi\tau\sqrt{f_1}}{p_\ell}\mathsf{B}_{\mathsf{scale}} - 1)B + \frac{\xi\tau^2 f_1}{p_\ell}\mathsf{B}_{\mathsf{scale}}^2 + \sqrt{f_1'}\mathsf{B}_{\mathsf{scale}} < 0$. Thus, to satisfy this equation (in B), we again must have a positive discriminant, that is, $1 - 4\xi(\sqrt{f_1'} + \tau\sqrt{f_1})\mathsf{B}_{\mathsf{scale}}/p_\ell \geq 0$. We then have

$$p_1 \sim \ldots \sim p_{L-2} \sim 4\xi(\sqrt{f_1'} + \tau\sqrt{f_1})\mathsf{B}_{\mathsf{scale}}. \tag{21}$$

Finally, if we set p_ℓ as in (21), we have the discriminate equal to zero and we can find B with

$$B \sim (2\sqrt{f_1'} + \tau\sqrt{f_1})\mathsf{B}_{\mathsf{scale}}. \tag{22}$$

Now we can compute, the bottom modulus p_0, which is the last modulus in the prime chain, starting from Eq. (13). Since P is as in Eq. (20), $\tau\nu_{\mathsf{ks}} = \tau(f_0\mathsf{B}_{\mathsf{ks}}/P + \sqrt{f_1}\mathsf{B}_{\mathsf{scale}}) \sim \tau\sqrt{f_1}\mathsf{B}_{\mathsf{scale}}$ and thanks to Eq. (22), we have

$$p_0 > 2c_m\xi(B + \tau\nu_{\mathsf{ks}})^2 \sim 8c_m\xi((\sqrt{f_1'} + \tau\sqrt{f_1})\mathsf{B}_{\mathsf{scale}})^2. \tag{23}$$

Base Model. For the base model with $\tau = 0$, Eq. (21) to (23) are as before, instead P as in Eq. 20 can be decrease to either $Kq_{L-3}B_{ks}/B_{scale}$ in the GHS case or $Kq_{L-3}\sqrt{L-2}B_{ks}/B_{scale}$ for GHS-RNS. Indeed, R_ℓ changes to either $\frac{q_{\ell-1}}{P}B_{ks} + f_1^{ks}B_{scale}$ (GHS) or $\frac{q_{\ell-1}\sqrt{L-2}}{P}B_{ks} + f_1^{ks}B_{scale}$ (GHS-RNS) (see also [19] for the specific case when $\tau = 0$ and $B_{clean} = 1$).

Modulus Size for Power-of-Two Cyclotomics. In Tables 1 and 2, we summarize the moduli size considering $\Phi_m(x) = x^n + 1$ and $n = 2^\kappa$ (and so $m = 2n$ and $\phi(m) = n$) in the case of Model 2 and Base Model depicted in Fig. 1, respectively. We denoted by G/H, the GHS, and the Hybrid key-switching variant without RNS, respectively. It is worth noting that in the case of G/H-RNS, we approximate $\tau\sqrt{k} + 2\sqrt{k+1} - 1 \sim \sqrt{k}(\tau + 2)$.

Table 1. Modului size for power-of-two polynomial in the case of Model 2.

p_0	$32\eta^2 B_{const}^2 \left(3\tau\beta\sqrt{(L-1)\log_2(t\phi(m))}B_{ks} + B_{scale}\right)^2$	BV
	$8\left(\eta(\tau+1)B_{const}B_{scale}\right)^2$	G/H
	$8k\left(\eta(\tau+1)B_{const}B_{scale}\right)^2$	G/H-RNS
p_ℓ	$4\eta^2 B_{const}^2 \left(3\tau\beta\sqrt{(L-1)\log_2(t\phi(m))}B_{ks} + B_{scale}\right)$	BV
	$4\eta^2(\tau+1)B_{const}^2 B_{scale}$	G/H
	$4\eta^2\sqrt{k}(\tau+1)B_{const}^2 B_{scale}$	G/H-RNS
p_{L-1}	$B_{clean}/\left(6\tau\beta\sqrt{(L-1)\log_2(t\phi(m))}B_{ks} + B_{scale}\right)$	BV
	$B_{clean}/(\tau+1)B_{scale}$	G/H
	$B_{clean}/\sqrt{k}(\tau+2)B_{scale}$	G/H-RNS

Table 2. Base Model, namely, case with $\tau = 0$.

p_0	p_ℓ	p_{L-1}	
$8k\xi B_{scale}^2$	$4\sqrt{k}\xi B_{scale}$	$B_{clean}/(2\sqrt{k}-1)B_{scale}$	G/H-RNS
$8\xi B_{scale}^2$	$4\xi B_{scale}$	B_{clean}/B_{scale}	else

3.6 Security Analysis

In previous works, Costache and Smart [13], following Gentry *et al.* [19] analysis, used the security formula by Lindner-Peikert [24], that is $\log t_{BKZ}(\delta_0) = 1.8/\log\delta_0 - 110$. Lindner and Peikert's estimation has a few inaccuracies [2] and turns out to be too optimistic. Thus, Costache *et al.* [11] propose parameters according to the Homomorphic Encryption Standard [4] for a uniformly distributed ternary secret and $\lambda = 128$.

To enable a more flexible and faster parameter selection, we propose an empirically derived formula linking the security level λ with the dimension n for a given ciphertext modulus size $(\log q)$. This enables a fast security estimate for parameter generation. Let us consider a full-rank lattice $\mathcal{L}$. We know that the shortest vector of $\mathcal{L}$ has norm $||\mathbf{b_1}|| = \delta_0^k q^{n/k}$ (see Eq. (2)). To perform lattice reduction on $\mathcal{L}$, the LWE attacker has to choose the number of samples M, namely the subdimension, such that $||\mathbf{b_1}|| = \delta_0^M q^{n/M}$ is minimized.

Micciancio and Regev [28] showed that this minimum is obtained when $M = \sqrt{n \log q / \log \delta_0}$. We can suppose that we should reduce the basis enough so that $||\mathbf{b_1}|| = q$. This implies that $\log q = \log(\delta_0^M q^{n/M}) = 2\sqrt{n \log q \log \delta_0}$, that is

$$n = \log q / (4 \log \delta_0). \tag{24}$$

Substituting Eq. (24) in Eq. (3), we have a bound linking λ, n. Then, we do the following:

1. We run the Lattice Estimator [5] for the dimensions $n = 2^k$ as well as the secret distribution $\chi_s = \mathcal{U}_3$ and $\chi_s = \chi_e$. We choose $k \in \{10, \dots, 15\}$ following the Homomorphic Encryption Standard [3]. Generating this necessary data, especially for higher degrees, is computationally intensive. For $\log q = 600$ and $n = 2^{15}$ for example, it takes roughly 2.5 h to evaluate the security for three attacks.
2. Starting from the theoretical bound linking λ, n, and q, we find a parameterized function that follows the data points generated with the lattice estimator.
3. Finally, we model the resulting formula with coupled optimization to find the best constants. To ensure that our model provides accurate estimations of security levels, we place constraints on the selection of constants. Specifically, we instructed the model to choose constants such that the resulting output slightly underestimates the security level rather than overestimating it. This ensures that we maintain a high degree of confidence in the estimated model (see Table 4) while avoiding potential false assurances that could have resulted from overestimation.

Using this process, the resulting function is

$$\lambda \approx -\log\left(\frac{A \log q}{n}\right) \frac{Bn}{\log q} + C \left(\frac{\log q}{n}\right)^D \log\left(\frac{n}{\log q}\right) \tag{25}$$

with constants

$$A = 0.05 \quad B = 0.33 \quad C = 17.88 \quad D = 0.65 \quad \text{if } \chi_s = \mathcal{U}_3 \text{ and}$$
$$A = 3.87 \quad B = 0.74 \quad C = 12.72 \quad D = 0.17 \quad \text{if } \chi_s = \chi_e.$$

3.7   A Parameter Generator for BGV

The parameter generator for BGV provides an accessible way to our theoretical work. Most importantly, developers can use the generator and receive a simple code example for state-of-the-art libraries. The generator itself is written in Python and will be publicly available. On request, we can also disclose the code to the reviewers.

Supporting Arbitrary Circuit Models. Although we only theoretically analyze some circuit models in our work, the generator itself is easily extendable to arbitrary circuit models that an advanced user can compose by themself. This, however, requires a simplification of the key switching bound for each variant, as we otherwise have circular dependencies on the size of the moduli in the prime chain.

We take a straightforward and practical-oriented approach: We assume a bound on $p_\ell \leq 2^b$, per default $2^b = 2^{128}$, and extrapolate the bound to q_ℓ as $L2^b$. For the BV, BV-RNS, and Hybrid variants, we fix β and ω, per default as $\beta = 2^{10}$ and $\omega = 3$. For the extension modulus P, we choose a constant K, per default $K = 100$. Then, we set $P = KL2^b$ for the GHS and GHS-RNS variants, $P = K\beta\sqrt{\log_\beta L2^b}$ for the Hybrid variant and $P = K\sqrt{\omega L}(2^b)^{\lceil L/\omega \rceil}$ for the Hybrid-RNS variant. We can now easily compose different circuit models using these constant bounds and solve the inequalities for B programmatically by finding the local minimum in the interval $[0, 2^b]$.

Using the Parameter Generator. An interactive mode prompts the user with several questions for required and optional inputs. We list the required inputs in the first part and optional inputs in the second part of Table 3. After providing all the required information, the user receives the output in text form and, if the library option is chosen, the generated code. The output for the ciphertext modulus contains the bound on the ciphertext modulus itself as well as the bounds for the bottom, middle and top modulus, respectively. The generated code is a setup routine for the chosen library and provides references to further code examples within the respective library.

Table 3. Required and optional inputs to the parameter generator

Model	'Base', 'Model1', 'Model2', 'OpenFHE'
t or $\log t$	any integer ≥ 2
λ or m	any integer ≥ 40 or ≥ 4, respectively
M, η	any integer > 0
τ	any integer ≥ 0
Library	'None', 'OpenFHE', 'PALISADE', 'SEAL'
Full Batching	full batching with t, 'True' or 'False'
Secret Distribution	'Ternary', 'Error'
Key Switching	'Hybrid', 'BV', 'GHS'
β	any integer ≥ 2
ω	any integer ≥ 1

Limitations. Due to the internal workings of the libraries, we cannot guarantee that all parameter sets work. For example, OpenFHE supports only a plaintext modulus of up to 60 bits. Thus, choosing a larger plaintext modulus will result in non-working code. However, we are happy to work with the community to integrate checks on these constraints as users encounter them.

4   Results

In the following, we compare our security formula as well as our bounds theoretically and practically to previous work.

4.1   Security Parameter Evaluation

In Table 4, we compare the security levels provided by our formula with the Lattice Estimator and the LP model. For the LP model, we use $\lambda \leq 7.2n/\log q - 78.9$, substituting Eq. (24) in the LP formula, where the runtime is expressed in units of computation rather than seconds. Our formula yields estimations very close to those computed using the Lattice Estimator, whereas those computed using the LP method tend to overestimate the security level in almost every case.

Table 4. Comparison between the security level provided by our formula, the Lattice estimator, and the LP model with secret distribution $\mathcal{U}_3$.

$n = 2^{10}$				$n = 2^{15}$			
$\log q$	Estimator	Our Work	LP	$\log q$	Estimator	Our Work	LP
16	221	222	382	400	303	291	511
18	195	195	331	460	258	250	434
19	184	184	244	586	196	192	324
25	137	137	216	598	192	188	317
26	132	132	216	850	131	129	199
27	127	127	216	859	129	128	196
30	114	114	167	870	128	126	192
35	97	97	132	871	127	126	192
42	80	81	97	1300	86	84	103
43	79	79	93	1400	80	78	89

It is worth noting, however, that as shown in Table 4, the accuracy of our estimation decreases slightly as n increases. Nevertheless, for almost all values of $\log q$, our estimation provides the correct security level, with underestimation occurring only in rare corner cases. In Fig. 2, we provide a visualization of the formula together with the original data points by the Lattice Estimator for the secret distribution $\mathcal{U}_3$. Note that for the GHS and Hybrid key switching variants, we have to consider the bigger modulus size $\log Q = \log qP$ to evaluate security.

4.2   Parameter Generation

We now compare our bounds theoretically with Kim *et al.* [23], who use the infinity norm, and practically with the implementation of their theoretical work in OpenFHE [6].

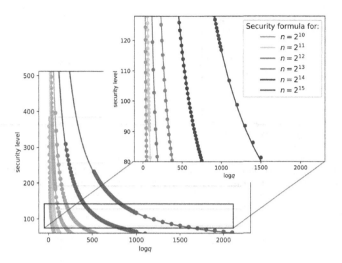

Fig. 2. The security formula with data points of the Lattice Estimator for $\chi_s = \mathcal{U}_3$.

Comparing our bounds theoretically, we use the ring expansion factor $\delta_{\mathcal{R}} = \phi(m)$ for the infinity norm. Here, our results are up to 20% better for the bottom modulus and up to 42% better for the middle modulus (see also Fig. 3), reducing the size of the full ciphertext modulus significantly. Our better results for the top modulus on the other hand do not have any effect in practice as for NTT compatibility, we have to choose each modulus $p > m$ anyway.

For an actual application of the bounds, Kim *et al.* [23] suggest using the expansion factor $\delta_{\mathcal{R}} = 2\sqrt{\phi(m)}$ instead of $\delta_{\mathcal{R}} = \phi(m)$ as the probability of the latter is exponentially low and the former is closer to observations in practice [20]. The parameter generation in OpenFHE also uses this heuristic expansion factor. Interestingly enough, this generates moduli sizes that are very similar compared to our bounds based on the purely theoretical approach with the canonical embedding norm. However, in the middle moduli, which for increasing multiplicative depth is dominating the overall modulus size, we still perform better than the heuristic bound with the infinity norm.

For the security level $\lambda = 128$, the plaintext modulus $t = 2^{16} + 1$, secret key distribution $\chi_s = \mathcal{U}_3$, and $D = 6$, we map our results in the OpenFHE model without any rotations, that is $\tau = 0$, and compare them with the results of OpenFHE theoretically in Fig. 3, that is with $\delta_{\mathcal{R}} = d$, and practically in Fig. 4, that is for $\delta_{\mathcal{R}} = 2\sqrt{d}$. For a fair comparison of p_0, we used $p_0 p_1$ for OpenFHE as their model does not allow any operations in the last level compared to our bottom modulus.

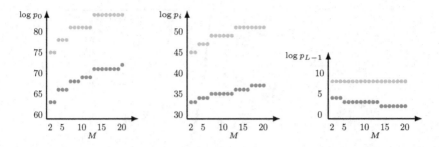

Fig. 3. Comparison of theoretical prime sizes across multiplicative depths M with $\lambda = 128$ and $t = 2^{16} + 1$ for OpenFHE ◉ and our ● parameter generation.

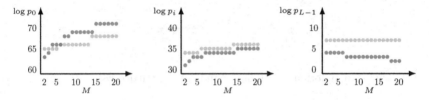

Fig. 4. Comparison of practical prime sizes across multiplicative depths M with $\lambda = 128$ and $t = 2^{16} + 1$ for OpenFHE ◉ and our ● parameter generation (● is matching).

5   Conclusion

Choosing parameters such as the polynomial degree or the ciphertext modulus is challenging for BGV and requires an in-depth analysis of the noise growth for each operation. Use-case-specific aspects, such as the order of operations, impact noise growth, further increasing the challenge with parameter generation. Additionally, the generated parameter sets have to be secure with respect to the underlying RLWE assumption, requiring good lower bounds on the ciphertext modulus.

In this work, we improve the parameter generation across all steps of its process. First, we extend previous analyses bringing together the DCRT representation and the canonical embedding norm and improving upon the existing state-of-the-art. Using these bounds, we proposed new circuit models, including essential BGV operations such as constant multiplication or rotations. Additionally, we provide an empirically derived, closed formula to estimate the security for a given parameter set based on coupled optimization for different secret key distributions. Finally, we combine our theoretical research and implement our results in an interactive parameter generator for BGV, which outputs easy-to-use code snippets for the state-of-the-art libraries OpenFHE, PALISADE, and SEAL.

Acknowledgement. The work described in this paper has been supported by the Deutsche Forschungsgemeinschaft (DFG, German Research Foundation) under Germany's Excellence Strategy - EXC 2092 CASA - 390781972. We also would like to thank Anna Hambitzer for her helpful comments on coupled optimization.

References

1. Acar, A., Aksu, H., Uluagac, A.S., Conti, M.: A survey on homomorphic encryption schemes: theory and implementation. ACM Comput. Surv. (CSUR) **51**(4), 1–35 (2018)
2. Albrecht, M.R.: On dual lattice attacks against small-secret LWE and parameter choices in HElib and SEAL. In: Coron, J.-S., Nielsen, J.B. (eds.) EUROCRYPT 2017. LNCS, vol. 10211, pp. 103–129. Springer, Cham (2017). https://doi.org/10.1007/978-3-319-56614-6_4
3. Albrecht, M.R., et al.: Homomorphic encryption security standard. Technical report. Toronto, Canada (2018). https://HomomorphicEncryption.org
4. Albrecht, M.R., Cid, C., Faugere, J.C., Fitzpatrick, R., Perret, L.: On the complexity of the BKW algorithm on LWE. Des. Codes Crypt. **74**(2), 325–354 (2015)
5. Albrecht, M.R., Player, R., Scott, S.: On the concrete hardness of learning with errors. J. Math. Crypt. **9**(3), 169–203 (2015)
6. Badawi, A.A., et al.: OpenFHE: open-source fully homomorphic encryption library. Cryptology ePrint Archive, Paper 2022/915 (2022). https://eprint.iacr.org/2022/915
7. Bergerat, L., et al.: Parameter Optimization & Larger Precision for (T) FHE. Cryptology ePrint Archive (2022)
8. Biasioli, B., Marcolla, C., Calderini, M., Mono, J.: Improving and Automating BFV Parameters Selection: An Average-Case Approach. Cryptology ePrint Archive (2023)
9. Brakerski, Z., Vaikuntanathan, V.: Fully homomorphic encryption from ring-LWE and security for key dependent messages. In: Rogaway, P. (ed.) CRYPTO 2011. LNCS, vol. 6841, pp. 505–524. Springer, Heidelberg (2011). https://doi.org/10.1007/978-3-642-22792-9_29
10. Chen, H., Kim, M., Razenshteyn, I., Rotaru, D., Song, Y., Wagh, S.: Maliciously secure matrix multiplication with applications to private deep learning. In: Moriai, S., Wang, H. (eds.) ASIACRYPT 2020. LNCS, vol. 12493, pp. 31–59. Springer, Cham (2020). https://doi.org/10.1007/978-3-030-64840-4_2
11. Costache, A., Laine, K., Player, R.: Evaluating the effectiveness of heuristic worst-case noise analysis in FHE. In: Chen, L., Li, N., Liang, K., Schneider, S. (eds.) ESORICS 2020. LNCS, vol. 12309, pp. 546–565. Springer, Cham (2020). https://doi.org/10.1007/978-3-030-59013-0_27
12. Costache, A., Nürnberger, L., Player, R.: Optimizations and trade-offs for helib. Cryptology ePrint Archive (2023)
13. Costache, A., Smart, N.P.: Which ring based somewhat homomorphic encryption scheme is best? In: Sako, K. (ed.) CT-RSA 2016. LNCS, vol. 9610, pp. 325–340. Springer, Cham (2016). https://doi.org/10.1007/978-3-319-29485-8_19
14. Damgård, I., Pastro, V., Smart, N., Zakarias, S.: Multiparty computation from somewhat homomorphic encryption. In: Safavi-Naini, R., Canetti, R. (eds.) CRYPTO 2012. LNCS, vol. 7417, pp. 643–662. Springer, Heidelberg (2012). https://doi.org/10.1007/978-3-642-32009-5_38
15. Di Giusto, A., Marcolla, C.: Breaking the power-of-two barrier: noise estimation for BGV in NTT-friendly rings. Cryptology ePrint Archive, Paper 2023/783 (2023)
16. Fan, J., Vercauteren, F.: Somewhat practical fully homomorphic encryption. IACR Cryptology ePrint Archive (2012)
17. Gama, N., Nguyen, P.Q.: Predicting lattice reduction. In: Smart, N. (ed.) EUROCRYPT 2008. LNCS, vol. 4965, pp. 31–51. Springer, Heidelberg (2008). https://doi.org/10.1007/978-3-540-78967-3_3

18. Gentry, C.: A Fully Homomorphic Encryption Scheme, vol. 20. Stanford university, Stanford (2009)
19. Gentry, C., Halevi, S., Smart, N.P.: Homomorphic evaluation of the AES circuit. In: Safavi-Naini, R., Canetti, R. (eds.) CRYPTO 2012. LNCS, vol. 7417, pp. 850–867. Springer, Heidelberg (2012). https://doi.org/10.1007/978-3-642-32009-5_49
20. Halevi, S., Polyakov, Y., Shoup, V.: An improved RNS variant of the BFV homomorphic encryption scheme. In: Matsui, M. (ed.) CT-RSA 2019. LNCS, vol. 11405, pp. 83–105. Springer, Cham (2019). https://doi.org/10.1007/978-3-030-12612-4_5
21. Halevi, S., Shoup, V.: Design and implementation of HElib: a homomorphic encryption library. Cryptology ePrint Archive (2020)
22. Iliashenko, I.: Optimisations of fully homomorphic encryption (2019)
23. Kim, A., Polyakov, Y., Zucca, V.: Revisiting homomorphic encryption schemes for finite fields. In: Tibouchi, M., Wang, H. (eds.) ASIACRYPT 2021. LNCS, vol. 13092, pp. 608–639. Springer, Cham (2021). https://doi.org/10.1007/978-3-030-92078-4_21
24. Lindner, R., Peikert, C.: Better key sizes (and attacks) for LWE-based encryption. In: Kiayias, A. (ed.) CT-RSA 2011. LNCS, vol. 6558, pp. 319–339. Springer, Heidelberg (2011). https://doi.org/10.1007/978-3-642-19074-2_21
25. Lyubashevsky, V., Peikert, C., Regev, O.: On ideal lattices and learning with errors over rings. In: Gilbert, H. (ed.) EUROCRYPT 2010. LNCS, vol. 6110, pp. 1–23. Springer, Heidelberg (2010). https://doi.org/10.1007/978-3-642-13190-5_1
26. Marcolla, C., Sucasas, V., Manzano, M., Bassoli, R., Fitzek, F.H., Aaraj, N.: Survey on fully homomorphic encryption, theory, and applications. Proc. IEEE 110(10), 1572–1609 (2022)
27. Martins, P., Sousa, L., Mariano, A.: A survey on fully homomorphic encryption: an engineering perspective. ACM Comput. Surv. (CSUR) 50(6), 1–33 (2017)
28. Micciancio, D., Regev, O.: Lattice-based cryptography. In: Bernstein, D.J., Buchmann, J., Dahmen, E. (eds.) Post-Quantum Cryptography, pp. 147–191. Springer, Heidelberg (2009). https://doi.org/10.1007/978-3-540-88702-7_5 ISBN 978-3-540-88702-7
29. PALISADE (2022). https://palisade-crypto.org
30. Regev, O.: On lattices, learning with errors, random linear codes, and cryptography. In: Proceedings of the Thirty-seventh Annual ACM Symposium on Theory of Computing, pp. 84–93 (2005)
31. Schnorr, C.P., Euchner, M.: Lattice basis reduction: improved practical algorithms and solving subset sum problems. Math. Program. 66(1–3), 181–199 (1994)

Quantum Search-to-Decision Reduction for the LWE Problem

Kyohei Sudo[1], Masayuki Tezuka[2]([✉]), Keisuke Hara[3,4]([✉]),
and Yusuke Yoshida[2]([✉])

[1] Osaka University, Osaka, Japan
u358338c@ecs.osaka-u.ac.jp
[2] Tokyo Institute of Technology, Tokyo, Japan
tezuka.m@tsuruoka-nct.ac.jp, yoshida.y.aw@m.titech.ac.jp
[3] National Institute of Advanced Industrial Science and Technology (AIST),
Tokyo, Japan
hara-keisuke@aist.go.jp
[4] Yokohama National University, Yokohama, Japan

Abstract. The learning with errors (LWE) problem is one of the fundamental problems in cryptography and it has many applications in post-quantum cryptography. There are two variants of the problem, the decisional-LWE problem, and the search-LWE problem. LWE search-to-decision reduction shows that the hardness of the search-LWE problem can be reduced to the hardness of the decisional-LWE problem. The efficiency of the reduction can be regarded as the gap in difficulty between the problems.

We initiate a study of quantum search-to-decision reduction for the LWE problem and propose a reduction that satisfies sample-preserving. In sample-preserving reduction, it preserves all parameters even the number of instances. Especially, our quantum reduction invokes the distinguisher only 2 times to solve the search-LWE problem, while classical reductions require a polynomial number of invocations. Furthermore, we give a way to amplify the success probability of the reduction algorithm. Our amplified reduction works with fewer LWE samples compared to the classical reduction that has a high success probability. Our reduction algorithm supports a wide class of error distributions and also provides a search-to-decision reduction for the learning parity with noise problem.

In the process of constructing the search-to-decision reduction, we give a quantum Goldreich-Levin theorem over $\mathbb{Z}_q$ where q is prime. In short, this theorem states that, if a hardcore predicate $a \cdot s \pmod q$ can be predicted with probability distinctly greater than $1/q$ with respect to a uniformly random $a \in \mathbb{Z}_q^n$, then it is possible to determine $s \in \mathbb{Z}_q^n$.

Keywords: Learning with errors · Learning parity with noise · Search-to-decision reduction · Goldreich-Levin theorem · Quantum reduction · Query complexity · Sample complexity

A part of this work is supported by JST CREST JP-MJCR2113 and MIC JPJ000254.

N. El Mrabet et al. (Eds.): AFRICACRYPT 2023, LNCS 14064, pp. 395–413, 2023.
https://doi.org/10.1007/978-3-031-37679-5_17

1   Introduction

Quantum algorithms run on a quantum computer and they have the potential to solve some problems faster than classical computation, for example, Shor's algorithm has been shown to solve factorization efficiently. In the same way, we can investigate a quantum reduction algorithm that could be more efficient than the known classical reduction algorithms. Reduction algorithms play an important role in cryptography to transform one problem into another problem. Intuitively, problem A is reducible to problem B, if an algorithm for solving problem B could also be used as a subroutine to solve problem A. In this sense, search-to-decision reduction for the learning with errors (LWE) problem is to show the decisional-LWE problem is as hard as the search-LWE problem.

The LWE problem introduced by Regev [25] is one of the fundamental computational problems in cryptography. The LWE samples consist of a pair (A, y) of a uniformly random matrix $A \in \mathbb{Z}_q^{m \times n}$ together with $y = A \cdot s + e$ for randomly chosen error term $e \leftarrow \chi^m$ (small Gaussian noise is commonly used) where m is the number of samples. LWE has two main variations: The search-LWE problem asks to find a secret string $s \in \mathbb{Z}_q^n$, given a system of noisy linear equations (A, y), while the decisional-LWE problem asks to distinguish between the distribution of the LWE samples $\{(A, y) | s \xleftarrow{\$} \mathbb{Z}_q^n, A \xleftarrow{\$} \mathbb{Z}_q^{m \times n}, e \leftarrow \chi^m, y := A \cdot s + e\}$ and uniformly random distribution $\{(A, r) | A \xleftarrow{\$} \mathbb{Z}_q^{m \times n}, r \xleftarrow{\$} \mathbb{Z}_q^m\}$.

There are two standard facts in LWE hardness. The first is more trivial, which says that there is a reduction from the decisional-LWE to the search-LWE: Whenever the pair (A, b) is randomly chosen $A \xleftarrow{\$} \mathbb{Z}_q^{m \times n}, b \xleftarrow{\$} \mathbb{Z}_q^m$, then with overwhelming probability the vector b is going to be far away from the lattice, thus there does not exist a coordinates vector s such that $A \cdot s$ is close to b, thus if we can break search-LWE and find s, we can check whether b is close to $A \cdot s$ or not, which constitutes an algorithm that breaks decisional-LWE. The second known fact is less trivial and says that the search-LWE can be reduced to the decisional-LWE. These previously known reductions use a distinguisher for the decisional-LWE to extract the secret string s and break the search-LWE. More delicately, the way that these reductions work is that the search-LWE adversary uses classical oracle access to the distinguisher.

There exist hardness proofs based on reductions from worst-case lattice problems (BDD/gapSVP), which are considered to be hard not only for classical computers but also for quantum computers. As a consequence, the hardness of the decisional-LWE problem serves as the security source of many post-quantum cryptographic primitives, such as oblivious transfer [24], identity-based encryption [3,12,15], fully homomorphic encryption [10], etc.

Prior Works. There are various incomparable search-to-decision reductions for the LWE problem [6,9,20,21,23,25]. Regev [25] who introduced the LWE problem showed search-to-decision reduction in [25]. It imposes constraints that modulus q must be prime and bounded by $poly(n)$. Research on search-to-decision reduction has been conducted in the direction of loosening the restriction on modulus q, but they incur some loss in the LWE parameters. Peikert [23] extends Regev's reduction for the case where q can be expressed as a product of distinct prime numbers in $poly(n)$, but it requires the error distribution to be Gaussian. Applebaum, Cash, Peikert, and Sahai [6] give a reduction for the case where the modulus can be a prime power $q = p^e$. The above algorithms have the property that the run-time scales linearly with q in common. It could make the reductions meaningless for large q. Micciancio and Peikert [21] give a reduction that runs in $poly(\log q)$. Micciancio and Mol [20] give a search-to-decision reduction in another direction. They show a sample-preserving reduction, which shows that if the pseudorandomness of the LWE problem holds, the LWE problem with the same number of samples is invertible. The state-of-the-art results constitute an adversary that makes polynomially many such classical queries to the distinguisher in order to break search-LWE, and the extra computations that the search-LWE adversary makes on the side (between its queries to the decisional-LWE adversary) are also classical. What this work aims to do is to use quantum computations and quantum queries to the decisional-LWE adversary in order to speed up the reduction - use fewer queries and less computation time.

Practical Importance of Quantum Search-to-Decision Reduction. The LWE challenge [1] is the foundation for ensuring the difficulty of the LWE problem. In practice, the LWE challenge is intended to solve *search* LWE problems. Based on the results of the LWE challenge, the parameter size n is selected, at which we can trust that the search-LWE problem is hard enough.

Suppose that there is a cryptographic scheme whose security is reduced to the hardness of the decisional-LWE problem. Intuitively, if the security of the scheme is to be ensured based on the LWE challenge of size n, the size of the scheme should be $loss_{s2d}(n)$ plus the security loss of the scheme itself, where $loss_{s2d}(\cdot)$ is the reduction loss in a search-to-decision reduction.

When a quantum computer arises, a quantum version of the LWE challenge will be held and the parameter n_Q ($\geq n$) will be determined for the LWE problem to be hard for the quantum computer. Then, should the size of the scheme be selected based on $loss_{s2d}(n_Q)$? If we know the efficiency $loss_{Qs2d}(\cdot)$ of quantum search-to-decision reduction, we know that we can actually implement the scheme with a size based on $loss_{Qs2d}(n_Q)$, which is expected to partially mitigate the effect of the increase of n_Q over n.

1.1   Our Contribution

Quantum Search-to-Decision Reduction. In this work, we investigate a quantum search-to-decision reduction for the LWE problem and we discuss the efficiency of our algorithm and classical ones. We compare the efficiency of our reduction and the classical ones by three aspects, success probability, query complexity, and sample complexity. We treat the distinguisher as a blackbox and the query complexity of an algorithm is measured by the number of queries to the distinguisher in the algorithm while it finds the secret string s of the search-LWE problem. The sample complexity of an algorithm is measured by the number of LWE instances that it takes. In this paper, we propose three variations of the reduction algorithms.

- The first one is an algorithm that also serves as the basis for the other two. It finds s with probability at least $\frac{4\epsilon^3}{27q(q-1)^2}$ using distinguisher 2 times. And it is also a sample-preserve reduction, i.e., it needs m sample of LWE instances to find s where m is the number of instances required by the distinguisher to solve the decisional-LWE problem.
- The second algorithm is an evolution of the sample-preserve one. It amplifies the probability of success of the first algorithm instead of increasing the complexities. It finds s with probability $\Omega(\frac{\epsilon}{q})$ using distinguisher $\mathcal{O}(\frac{q}{\epsilon})$ times.
- The third algorithm is a version of a higher probability of success through further iterations. It finds s with probability $1 - o(1)$ using distinguisher $\mathcal{O}(\frac{q^2 \log n}{\epsilon^2})$ times.

We remark that our reductions have some constraints on parameters. Our reductions require q to be prime. The second and third require that we can verify from the instances of the LWE problem whether it is the correct answer for the LWE problem given some input $s' \in \mathbb{Z}_q^n$. We believe that this condition does not impose a strong limitation on the use of LWE as a basis for cryptographic primitives. The existence of more efficient or less restrictive classical/quantum search-to-decision reduction is an open problem.

Table 1. Comparison of the algorithms performance. n is a size of the LWE problem, m is the number of instances required by the distinguisher to solve the decisional LWE problem, ϵ is the advantage of the distinguisher.

	Success probability	Query complexity	Sample complexity	Classical/Quantum
Reg05* [25]	$1 - o(1)$	$\tilde{\mathcal{O}}(\frac{nq}{\epsilon^2})$	$\tilde{\mathcal{O}}(\frac{mnq}{\epsilon^2})$	Classical
MM11** [20]	$\frac{1}{poly(n)}$	$poly(n)$	m	Classical
Theorem 2	$\frac{4\epsilon^3}{27q(q-1)^2}$	2	m	Quantum
Theorem 3	$\Omega(\frac{\epsilon}{q})$	$\mathcal{O}(\frac{q}{\epsilon})$	$m + \mathcal{O}(n)$	Quantum
Corollary 1	$1 - o(1)$	$\mathcal{O}(\frac{q^2 \log n}{\epsilon^2})$	$\tilde{\mathcal{O}}(\frac{mq}{\epsilon})$	Quantum

* The numbers in this line are from a simplified version of the reduction by Regev. The specific construction of the algorithm is described in Appendix B.
** The success probability and the query complexity of this algorithm are very complex. The specific values are given in Appendix B.

Extension of Quantum Goldreich-Levin Theorem. The Goldreich-Levin Theorem [16] is a cornerstone theorem in computer science and has been studied from various aspects [2,16,17,19,22]. This theorem states that any (strong) one-way function f can be easily transformed into a function of the required form $g(x,r) := (f(x),r)$ where $x, r \in \mathbb{Z}_2^n$ and it has a hard-core predicate $x \cdot r$ (mod 2). Roughly speaking, a (strong) one-way function is a function that can be efficiently computed but is hard to compute in the reverse direction, and a hard-core predicate of a function is a bit that can be efficiently computed from the input to the function and no efficient algorithm can guess it from the output of the function with probability distinctly higher than one-half. Adcock and Cleve investigate a quantum Goldreich-Levin theorem [2]. Roughly, they show that the reduction from quantum one-way functions to quantum hard-core predicates is quantitatively more efficient than the classical version.

In the process of constructing the quantum search-to-decision reduction, we give a further generalized theorem of the quantum Goldreich-Levin theorem by Adcock and Cleve. Namely, we show that if there exists a predictor that predicts $a \cdot s \pmod{q}$ where $a, s \in \mathbb{Z}_q^n$ and q to be prime with probability $\frac{1}{q} + \delta$ over the choice of $a \leftarrow \mathbb{Z}_q^n$, then we can find s with probability at least $(\frac{q\delta}{q-1})^2$ while accessing the predictor 2 times.

Concurrent Work of Quantum Goldreich-Levin Theorem. Recently, Ananth et al. [5] independently investigated a quantum Goldreich-Levin theorem for the field $\mathbb{Z}_q$. They obtain this result by converting the classical Goldreich-Levin theorem for the field $\mathbb{Z}_q$ by Dodis et al. [13] into quantum reduction, by using the recent work of Bitansky et al. [8]. Specifically, they show that a distinguisher D that, given auxiliary input Aux, can distinguish between $(a, a \cdot s)$ and (a, r) where s is randomly chosen from $H \subset \mathbb{Z}_q^n$ can be converted into a quantum extractor that can extract s given Aux.

While their quantum algorithm relies on the classical Goldreich-Levin theorem for the field $\mathbb{Z}_q$ by Dodis et al. [13], in which the distinguisher with advantage ϵ is used $poly(n, |H|, \frac{1}{\epsilon})$ times to extract s and its success probability is $\frac{\epsilon^3}{512 \cdot n \cdot q^2}$. On the other hand, our quantum algorithm can find s by accessing the distinguisher 2 times with probability $(\frac{\epsilon}{q-1})^2$, given that the distinguisher with advantage ϵ implies the predictor with advantage $\frac{\epsilon}{q}$ (by the similar reasoning as in Sect. 3. Lemma 1.). Furthermore, There is no need to make the subset from which s is chosen small.

1.2 Technical Overview

We describe our techniques for proving our results on quantum search-to-decision reduction for the LWE problem. Our construction of the search-to-decision reduction consists of two parts. For the first part, we construct a predictor from the distinguisher of the decisional-LWE problem, and for the second part, we construct an algorithm that finds s using the predictor. This reduction strategy can be interpreted as making a prediction-to-decision reduction and a search-to-prediction reduction. We note that the idea of the search-to-decision reduction via unpredictability is the same as that of classical reduction by Micciancio and Mol [20], Applebaum, Ishai, and Kushilevitz [7]. We found a quantum speed-up in the second part of the reduction and we call it as generalized quantum Goldreich-Levin theorem. Then we provide an overview of this theorem.

Quantum Goldreich-Levin Theorem. We first review the quantum Goldreich-Levin theorem by Adcock and Cleve [2]. We call an unitary operation U_P is a quantum (s, q, ϵ)-predictor, if the last register of $U_P |a\rangle |0^l\rangle |0\rangle$ is measured in computational basis, yielding the value $P(a)$, then $\Pr[P(a) = a \cdot s \pmod{q}] > \frac{1}{q} + \epsilon$ holds where $a, s \in \mathbb{Z}_q^n$ and the probability depends on over choice of $a \xleftarrow{\$} \mathbb{Z}_q^n$.

We denote

$$U_P \ket{a} \ket{0^l} \ket{0} = \alpha_{a,0} \ket{\phi_{a,0}} \ket{a \cdot s} + \alpha_{a,1} \ket{\phi_{a,1}} \ket{a \cdot s + 1}$$

where U_P is a $(s, 2, \epsilon)$-predictor, $\alpha_{a,0}$ and $\alpha_{a,1}$ are complex number. Since for a random uniformly distributed $a \xleftarrow{\$} \{0,1\}^n$, measuring the last register of $U_P \ket{a} \ket{0^l} \ket{0}$ yields $a \cdot s \pmod 2$ with probability at least $\frac{1}{2} + \epsilon$, it follows that

$$\frac{1}{2^n} \sum_{a \in \{0,1\}^n} |\alpha_{a,0}|^2 \geq \frac{1}{2} + \epsilon \tag{1}$$

and

$$\frac{1}{2^n} \sum_{a \in \{0,1\}^n} |\alpha_{a,1}|^2 < \frac{1}{2} + \epsilon. \tag{2}$$

We explain their quantum reduction algorithm step by step. First, pass the superposition states $\frac{1}{\sqrt{2^n}} \sum_{a \in \{0,1\}^n} \ket{a} \ket{0^l} \ket{0}$ through the $(s, 2, \epsilon)$-predictor U_P, multiply the phase by $(-1)^y$ according to the value of the last register y, pass the states through conjugate transpose of the predictor $U_P^\dagger$ and we get the states $\frac{1}{\sqrt{2^n}} \sum_{a \in \{0,1\}^n} \left(\sum_{b \in \{0,1\}} (-1)^{a \cdot s + b} |\alpha_{a,b}|^2 \right) \ket{a} \ket{0^l} \ket{0}$. By measuring the first register in Fourier basis, we could obtain s. The probability of yielding s when the first register is measured in the Fourier basis, is the square of the inner product of this state and $QFT^{\otimes n} \ket{s} = \frac{1}{\sqrt{2^n}} \sum_{a \in \{0,1\}^n} (-1)^{a \cdot s} \ket{a}$, which is $|\frac{1}{2^n} \sum_{a \in \{0,1\}^n} (|\alpha_{a,0}|^2 - |\alpha_{a,1}|^2)|^2$. Using the fact of (1) and (2), we can find s with probability at least $\left| \left(\frac{1}{2} + \epsilon \right) - \left(\frac{1}{2} - \epsilon \right) \right|^2 = 4\epsilon^2$.

Difficulty. Next, we show that naive expansion of the quantum Goldreich-Levin results in a (s, q, ϵ)-predictor where $q \neq 2$ does not work. As in the quantum Goldreich-Levin algorithm, pass the superposition states $\frac{1}{\sqrt{q^n}} \sum_{a \in \mathbb{Z}_q^n} \ket{a} \ket{0^l} \ket{0}$ through the predictor U_P, multiply the phase by ω_q^y according to the value of the last register y, pass the states through conjugate transpose of the predictor $U_P^\dagger$ and we get the states $\frac{1}{\sqrt{q^n}} \sum_{a \in \mathbb{Z}_q^n} \left(\sum_{j \in \mathbb{Z}_q} \omega_q^{a \cdot s + j} |\alpha_{a,j}|^2 \right) \ket{a} \ket{0^l} \ket{0}$. If we measure the first register in the Fourier basis, the probability of yielding s is the square of the inner product of this state and $QFT^{\otimes n} \ket{s} = \frac{1}{\sqrt{q^n}} \sum_{a \in \mathbb{Z}_q^n} \omega_q^{a \cdot s} \ket{a}$, which is $|\frac{1}{q^n} \sum_{a \in \mathbb{Z}_q^n} \sum_{j \in \mathbb{Z}_q} \omega_q^j |\alpha_{a,j}|^2|^2$. Define $\Pr(j) := \Pr[P(a) = a \cdot s + j \pmod q]$ as a probability of the gap between the predictor's prediction and inner product is j, then this probability can be written as $|\sum_{j \in \mathbb{Z}_q} \omega_q^j \Pr(j)|^2$. This value cannot be guaranteed some lower bound unless the advantage is very high such that $\epsilon \geq \frac{1}{2} - \frac{1}{q} + \delta$.

Solution. To get around this obstacle, our key idea is to use the property of cyclic group $\mathbb{Z}_q^*$. For all element $j \in \mathbb{Z}_q^*$, j determines a bijection $r \mapsto rj$ on $\mathbb{Z}_q$ and it maps 0 to 0. Using this property, we can say that

$$\frac{1}{q-1} \sum_{r \in \mathbb{Z}_q^*} \omega_q^{rj} \Pr(j) = \begin{cases} \Pr(0) & \text{if } j = 0 \\ \frac{-1}{q-1} \Pr(j) & \text{if } j \neq 0. \end{cases} \tag{3}$$

We will use this property to improve the algorithm. First, prepare the superposition states $\frac{1}{\sqrt{q^n(q-1)}} \sum_{a \in \mathbb{Z}_q^n} \sum_{r \in \mathbb{Z}_q^*} |r\rangle |a\rangle |0^l\rangle |0\rangle$ through the predictor U_P (apply the second to the last register), multiply the last register by the first register r, multiply the phase by ω_q^y according to the value of the last register y, divide the last register by the first register r(multiply r^{-1}), pass the states through conjugate transpose of the predictor $\mathsf{U}_P^\dagger$ (apply the second to the last register), multiply the second register by the first register r and we get the states $\frac{1}{\sqrt{q^n(q-1)}} \sum_{a,r,j} \omega_q^{r(a\cdot s+j)} |\alpha_{a,j}|^2 |r\rangle |ra\rangle |0^l\rangle |0\rangle$. If we measure the second register in Fourier basis, the probability of yielding s is the square of the inner product of this state and $(I \otimes QFT^{\otimes n})(\frac{1}{\sqrt{q-1}} \sum_{r \in \mathbb{Z}_q^*} |r\rangle) |s\rangle = \frac{1}{\sqrt{q^n(q-1)}} \sum_{b \in \mathbb{Z}_q^n} \sum_{r \in \mathbb{Z}_q^*} \omega_q^{b\cdot s} |r\rangle |b\rangle = \frac{1}{\sqrt{q^n(q-1)}} \sum_{a,r} \omega_q^{r(a\cdot s)} |r\rangle |ra\rangle |0^l\rangle |0\rangle$. Finally, we get

$$\Pr[s \text{ is measured}] = \left| \frac{1}{q^n(q-1)} \sum_{a,r,j} \omega_q^{rj} |\alpha_{a,j}|^2 \right|^2$$

$$= \left| \Pr(0) - \frac{1}{q-1} \sum_{j \neq 0} P(j) \right|^2$$

$$\geq \left(\frac{q\epsilon}{q-1} \right)^2.$$

This result is consistent with quantum Goldreich-Levin results and is a successful generalization.

2 Preliminaries

2.1 Notation and Definitions

In this paper, we use the following notations and definitions. For a finite set S, $s \xleftarrow{\$} S$ denotes choosing an element s from S uniformly at random. For a distribution D, $d \leftarrow D$ denotes sampling an element d according to distribution D. We use standard asymptotic notations $\mathcal{O}(\cdot)$, $o(\cdot)$, $\Omega(\cdot)$, $\Theta(\cdot)$, etc. We use $\tilde{\mathcal{O}}$ (resp. $\tilde{\Theta}$) notation which overlooks quantities poly-logarithmic in appearing arguments, that is, $\tilde{\mathcal{O}}(x) := \mathcal{O}(x(\log x)^{\Theta(1)})$ (resp. $\tilde{\Theta}(x) := \Theta(x(\log x)^{\Theta(1)})$). We denote by ω_n the complex root of unity of order n: $\omega_n := e^{\frac{2\pi i}{n}}$.

2.2 Quantum Computing

Let I be the identity operator. We denote $U^\dagger$ as the Hermitian conjugate of a unitary operation U. For operations that use auxiliary inputs $|0^l\rangle$, we often omit them for simplicity. Quantum Fourier transformation QFT over $\mathbb{Z}_q$ is a map $|x\rangle \mapsto \sum_{y \in \mathbb{Z}_q} \omega_q^{xy} |y\rangle$. We use the fact $QFT^{\otimes n} |x\rangle = \sum_{y \in \mathbb{Z}_q^n} \omega_q^{x \cdot y} |y\rangle$ where $x \in \mathbb{Z}_q^n$. We use the fact that there is a phase kickback algorithm and it maps $|x\rangle |0^l\rangle \mapsto \omega_q^x |x\rangle |0^l\rangle$. This algorithm can be achieved by controlled-U where unitary U has eigenvalue ω_q.

3   Search-to-Decision Reduction for the Learning with Errors Problem

The learning with errors (LWE) problem has two main variants, the search-LWE problem and the decisional-LWE problem. The search $\mathsf{LWE}_{n,m,q,\chi}$ problem asks to find s chosen uniformly random from $\mathbb{Z}_q^n$ given m LWE samples $\mathcal{LWE}_{n,m,s,q,\chi} := \{(A,y) | A \xleftarrow{\$} \mathbb{Z}_q^{m \times n}, e \leftarrow \chi^m, y := A \cdot s + e\}$. The decisional $\mathsf{LWE}_{n,m,q,\chi}$ problem asks to distinguish between $\mathcal{LWE}_{n,m,s,q,\chi}$ and a uniformly random distribution $\{(A,r) | A \xleftarrow{\$} \mathbb{Z}_q^{m \times n}, r \xleftarrow{\$} \mathbb{Z}_q^m\}$.

The learning parity with noise (LPN) problem is the special case of $\mathsf{LWE}_{n,m,q,\chi}$ problem for $q = 2$ and $\chi = \mathsf{Ber}_\mu$.

In this section, we show a search-to-decision reduction using quantum computing. Our construction of the search-to-decision reduction consists of two parts. For the first part, we construct a predictor from the distinguisher of the decisional-LWE problem, and for the second part, we construct an algorithm that finds s using a predictor. This reduction strategy can be interpreted as making a search-to-prediction reduction and a prediction-to-decision reduction. We note that the idea of the search-to-decision reduction via prediction is the same as that of classical reduction by Micciancio and Mol [20], Applebaum, Ishai, and Kushilevitz [7] and Dottling [14].

We define a quantum distinguisher for the decisional-LWE problem.

Definition 1. *A quantum ϵ-distinguisher for the decisional* $\mathsf{LWE}_{n,m,q,\chi}$ *problem is unitary operation* U_D *such that, the last register of* $U_D |A,y\rangle |0^l\rangle |0\rangle$ *is measured in computational basis, yielding the value* $D(A,y) \in \{0,1\}$, *then* $\Pr[D(A,y) = 0 | s \xleftarrow{\$} \mathbb{Z}_q^n, (A,y) \leftarrow \mathcal{LWE}_{n,m,s,q,\chi}\}] - \Pr[D(A,r) = 0 | A \xleftarrow{\$} \mathbb{Z}_q^{m \times n}, r \xleftarrow{\$} \mathbb{Z}_q^m] > \epsilon$ *holds.*

As in the definition, the last register of $U_D |A,y\rangle |0^l\rangle |0\rangle$ is measured in the computational basis, in this paper, we denote this as $D(A,y)$.

Next, we define a quantum predictor for the LWE problem.

Definition 2. *A quantum (s, ϵ)-predictor is unitary operation* U_P *such that, the last register of* $U_P |x\rangle |0^l\rangle |0\rangle$ *is measured in computational basis, yielding the value* $P(x)$, *then* $\Pr[P(x) = x \cdot s \pmod q] > \frac{1}{q} + \epsilon$ *holds.*

As in the definition, the last register of $U_P |x\rangle |0^l\rangle |0\rangle$ is measured in the computational basis, in this paper, we denote this as $P(x)$.

3.1 Sample-Preserve Reduction

In this section, we propose a quantum sample-preserve reduction between the search-LWE and the decisional-LWE.

The following Lemma states that there is a prediction-to-decision reduction for the LWE problem.

Lemma 1 (Prediction-to-decision reduction). *If there is a quantum ϵ-distinguisher for the decisional* $\mathsf{LWE}_{n,m,q,\chi}$ *problem* U_D, *then we can construct a quantum $(s, \frac{2\epsilon}{3q})$-predictor with probability at least $\frac{\epsilon}{3q}$ over choice of $s \xleftarrow{\$} \mathbb{Z}_q^n$, $(A, y) \leftarrow \mathcal{LWE}_{n,m,s,q,\chi}$ and random coins. It invokes U_D once.*

Proof of Lemma 1. Let $s \xleftarrow{\$} \mathbb{Z}_q^n$, $(A, y) \leftarrow \mathcal{LWE}_{n,m,s,q,\chi}$, $t \xleftarrow{\$} \mathbb{Z}_q^m$, $x \xleftarrow{\$} \mathbb{Z}_q^n$. Defining $A' = A + t \cdot x^T$, the following equality holds[1]

$$
\begin{aligned}
&\Pr[D(A', y) = x \cdot s] \\
&= \Pr[x \cdot s = 0] \Pr[D(A', y) = x \cdot s | x \cdot s = 0] \\
&\quad + \Pr[x \cdot s = 1] \Pr[D(A', y) = x \cdot s | x \cdot s = 1] \\
&= \frac{1}{q} \Pr[D(A', A' \cdot s + e) = 0] + \frac{1}{q} \Pr[D(A', A' \cdot s + e - t) = 1] \\
&= \frac{1}{q} (\Pr[D(A', A' \cdot s + e) = 0] + (1 - \Pr[D(A', A' \cdot s + e - t) = 0])) \\
&> \frac{1}{q} + \frac{\epsilon}{q}.
\end{aligned}
$$

Next we show that, when fixing variables except x, the following inequality (4) holds with probability $\frac{\epsilon}{3q}$ over choice of $s \xleftarrow{\$} \mathbb{Z}_q^n$, $(A, y) \leftarrow \mathcal{LWE}_{n,m,s,q,\chi}$ and $t \xleftarrow{\$} \mathbb{Z}_q^m$

$$
\Pr_{x \xleftarrow{\$} \mathbb{Z}_q^n} [D(A', y) = x \cdot s] > \frac{1}{q} + \frac{2\epsilon}{3q}. \tag{4}
$$

---

[1] We derived our results by considering $(A', A's + e - t)$ as a uniform random sample, similar to [7,14]. However, we became aware of the possibility that this randomness may not be uniform, based on a comment from one of the reviewers. To address this concern, we will provide a detailed proof or an alternative prediction-to-decision reduction in the full version of the paper.

Define a set $G = \{(s, A, y, t)|$ Inequality (4) holds $\}$. By the definition of G, when $s \xleftarrow{\$} \mathbb{Z}_q^n$, $(A, y) \leftarrow \mathcal{LWE}_{n,m,s,q,\chi}$ and $t \xleftarrow{\$} \mathbb{Z}_q^m$, then

$$\Pr[D(A', y) = x \cdot s]$$
$$= \Pr[D(A', y) = x \cdot s \wedge (s, A, y, t) \in G] + \Pr[D(A', y) = x \cdot s \wedge (s, A, y, t) \notin G]$$
$$< \Pr[(s, A, y, t) \in G] + \frac{1}{q} + \frac{2\epsilon}{3q}$$

holds. Hence $\Pr[(s, A, y, t) \in G] > \frac{\epsilon}{3q}$ holds. This means that, when fixing variables except x, the following Inequality (4) holds with probability $\frac{\epsilon}{3q}$ over choice of $s \xleftarrow{\$} \mathbb{Z}_q^n$, $(A, y) \leftarrow \mathcal{LWE}_{n,m,s,q,\chi}$ and $t \xleftarrow{\$} \mathbb{Z}_q^m$. From the above discussion, the lemma can be satisfied by constructing a quantum predictor U_P as follows. Given $|x\rangle |0^{l'}\rangle |0\rangle$ compute $|x\rangle |A', y\rangle |0^l\rangle |0\rangle$ and apply U_D and get $(I \otimes \mathsf{U}_D) |r\rangle |A', y\rangle |0^l\rangle |0\rangle$. Then measure the last register of this state, yielding $D(A', y)$ and inequality (4) holds with probability at least $\frac{\epsilon}{3q}$ over choice of $s \xleftarrow{\$} \mathbb{Z}_q^n$, $(A, y) \leftarrow \mathcal{LWE}_{n,m,s,q,\chi}$ and random coins. Therefore This algorithm U_P is a quantum $(s, \frac{2\epsilon}{3q})$-predictor with probability at least $\frac{\epsilon}{3q}$ over choice of $s \xleftarrow{\$} \mathbb{Z}_q^n$, $(A, y) \leftarrow \mathcal{LWE}_{n,m,s,q,\chi}$ and random coins.   □

We next show a prediction-to-decision reduction, that is, the expansion version of the quantum Goldreich-Levin theorem.

Theorem 1 (Expansion version of quantum Goldreich-Levin theorem). *Let q be a prime. If there is a quantum (s, δ)-predictor U_P, then there is a quantum algorithm that finds s with probability at least $(\frac{q\delta}{q-1})^2$. It invokes U_P and $\mathsf{U}_P^\dagger$ once each.*

Proof of Theorem 1. We construct a quantum algorithm that finds s using a quantum (s, δ)-predictor U_P.

First, prepare the superposition states $\frac{1}{\sqrt{q^n(q-1)}} \sum_{a \in \mathbb{Z}_q^n} \sum_{r \in \mathbb{Z}_q^*} |r\rangle |a\rangle |0^l\rangle |0\rangle$ through the predictor U_P(apply the second to the last register), multiply the last register by the first register r, multiply the phase by ω_q^y according to the value of the last register y, divide the last register by the first register r(multiply r^{-1}), pass the states through conjugate transpose of the predictor $\mathsf{U}_P^\dagger$(apply the second to the last register), multiply the second register by the first register r and we get the states $|\phi\rangle := \frac{1}{\sqrt{q^n(q-1)}} \sum_{a,r,j} \omega_q^{r(a \cdot s + j)} |\alpha_{a,j}|^2 |r\rangle |ra\rangle |0^l\rangle |0\rangle$. If we measure the second register in Fourier basis, the probability of yielding s is the square of the inner product of this state and $(I \otimes QFT^{\otimes n})(\frac{1}{\sqrt{q-1}} \sum_{r \in \mathbb{Z}_q^*} |r\rangle) |s\rangle = \frac{1}{\sqrt{q^n(q-1)}} \sum_{b \in \mathbb{Z}_q^n} \sum_{r \in \mathbb{Z}_q^*} \omega_q^{b \cdot s} |r\rangle |b\rangle = \frac{1}{\sqrt{q^n(q-1)}} \sum_{a,r} \omega_q^{r(a \cdot s)} |r\rangle |ra\rangle |0^l\rangle |0\rangle$. Finally, we get

$$\Pr[s \text{ is measured}] = \left| \frac{1}{q^n(q-1)} \sum_{a,r,j} \omega_q^{rj} |\alpha_{a,j}|^2 \right|^2$$

$$= \left| \frac{1}{q^n} |\alpha_{a,0}|^2 + \frac{1}{q^n(q-1)} \sum_{j \in \mathbb{Z}_q^*} (-|\alpha_{a,j}|^2) \right|^2$$

$$> \left| \left(\frac{1}{q} + \delta \right) - \frac{1}{q-1} \left(1 - \left(\frac{1}{q} + \delta \right) \right) \right|^2$$

$$= \left(\frac{q\delta}{q-1} \right)^2.$$

The second equality follows by the fact that for all elements $j \in \mathbb{Z}_q^*$, j determines a bijection $r \mapsto rj$ on $\mathbb{Z}_q$ and it maps 0 to 0. This result is consistent with the quantum Goldreich-Levin result where $q = 2$ and is a successful generalization.

$\square$

Theorem 2. *Let q be a prime. If there is a quantum ϵ-distinguisher U_D for the decisional* $\mathsf{LWE}_{n,m,q,\chi}$ *problem, then there is a quantum algorithm that solves the search* $\mathsf{LWE}_{n,m,q,\chi}$ *problem with probability at least $\frac{4\epsilon^3}{27q(q-1)^2}$ using U_D and $\mathsf{U}_D^\dagger$ once each.*

Proof of Theorem 2. This theorem follows immediately from Lemma 1. and Theorem 1. $\square$

We stress that Theorem 1 gives a quantum sample-preserving search-to-decision reduction for the LWE problem, i.e., we can find s with some polynomial probability with sample complexity m, where m is the number of instances required by the distinguisher to solve the decisional-LWE problem. Next, we consider the complexity of obtaining s with high probability using this algorithm in the following section. We use this algorithm as a basic building block of the amplified reduction algorithms.

3.2   Amplify the Success Probability

We show how to amplify the success probability of the reduction algorithm given in Sect. 3.1. However, this process increases query complexity and sample complexity.

We propose an algorithm, Verify, that tests a candidate solution for the LWE problem. We first sample $(a_i, y_i)_{i \in [\mathcal{O}(n)]} \leftarrow \mathcal{LWE}_{n,\mathcal{O}(n),s,q,\chi}$ and construct Verify to test a candidate s' by simply checking that $a_i \cdot s \approx y_i$. We believe that we can determine whether the input is a solution of the LWE problem by checking that $a_i \cdot s \approx y_i$ with high frequency, even when the error distribution is the Gaussian distribution. Here, we present only the case where the error distribution is over $\{-\lfloor \frac{q}{4} \rfloor, -\lfloor \frac{q}{4} \rfloor + 1, \ldots, \lfloor \frac{q}{4} \rfloor - 1, \lfloor \frac{q}{4} \rfloor\}$ for readability and to provide intuition for how the algorithm works.

Lemma 2. *Let χ to be a probability distribution over $\{-\lfloor\frac{q}{4}\rfloor, -\lfloor\frac{q}{4}\rfloor+1, \ldots, \lfloor\frac{q}{4}\rfloor-1, \lfloor\frac{q}{4}\rfloor\}$, we can construct an algorithm Verify using $\mathcal{O}(n)$ samples, and it satisfies the following functionality (5) with probability $1 - o(1)$*

$$\mathsf{Verify}(s') = \begin{cases} 1 & \text{if } s' = s \\ 0 & \text{if } s' \neq s. \end{cases} \tag{5}$$

The description of the algorithm Verify that satisfies the conditions of (5) can be given as follows:
Initially, sample $(a_i, y_i)_{i \in [cn]} \leftarrow \mathcal{LWE}_{n,cn,s,q,\chi}$. Upon receiving input $s' \in \mathbb{Z}_q^n$, Verify works as follows.

$\mathsf{Verify}(s')$:

$\quad for\ i \in \{1, 2, ..., cn\}$
$\quad\quad if\ |(a_i \cdot s' - y_i)| > \lceil\frac{q}{4}\rceil\ output\ 0$
$\quad output\ 1$

Proof of Lemma 2. Let us analyze the probability that the Verify satisfies the condition (5).

$$\Pr[\mathsf{Verify} \text{ satisfies } (5)] = \Pr[\mathsf{Verify}(s) = 1 \wedge \forall s' \neq s, \mathsf{Verify}(s') = 0]$$
$$\geq \Pr[\mathsf{Verify}(s) = 1] \cdot \Pr[\forall s' \neq s, \mathsf{Verify}(s') = 0]$$
$$\geq \Pr[\mathsf{Verify}(s) = 1] \cdot \left(1 - \sum_{s' \neq s} \Pr[\mathsf{Verify}(s') = 1]\right)$$
$$\geq 1 \cdot \left(1 - (q^n - 1)\left(\frac{2\lfloor\frac{q}{4}\rfloor + 1}{q}\right)^{cn}\right)$$
$$\geq 1 - \left(\frac{(\lfloor\frac{q}{2}\rfloor + 1)^c}{q^{(c-1)}}\right)^n$$

If we take c large enough, Verify satisfies (5) with probability $1 - o(1)$.   □

We can use this Verify to amplify the success probability of the sample-preserving reduction algorithm. However, the success probability of our reduction can be increased more efficiently by the quantum-specific repetition technique "amplitude amplification [11]" than by simply judging the answer each time. We define a quantum version of the verification algorithm $\mathsf{U_{Verify}}$ as follows.

Definition 3. *A quantum verification algorithm is a unitary operation $\mathsf{U_{Verify}}$ such that the following functionality (6)*

$$\mathsf{U_{Verify}}\,|s'\rangle = \begin{cases} -|s'\rangle & \text{if } s' = s \\ |s'\rangle & \text{if } s' \neq s \end{cases} \tag{6}$$

holds.

Lemma 3. *We can construct a quantum algorithm* $\mathsf{U}_{\mathsf{Verify}}$ *from* Verify *that satisfies the condition (5).*

Proof of Lemma 3. This lemma can be achieved by phase kickback. From Lemma 2 there exists a verification algorithm satisfying (5), then there exist an unitary operation such that

$$\mathsf{U}_{\mathsf{Verify}} |s'\rangle |0\rangle = \begin{cases} |s'\rangle |1\rangle & \text{if } s' = s \\ |s'\rangle |0\rangle & \text{if } s' \neq s \end{cases} \tag{7}$$

holds.

Consider the following quantum operation. When given $|s'\rangle |0\rangle$, apply $\mathsf{U}_{\mathsf{Verify}}$, multiply the phase by $(-1)^y$ according to the value of the second register y and apply $\mathsf{U}_{\mathsf{Verify}}^\dagger$. We get $-|s'\rangle |0\rangle$ when $s' = s$ otherwise we get $|s'\rangle |0\rangle$.

□

Theorem 3. *Let* q *be a prime and* χ *be a probability distribution over* $\{-\lfloor \frac{q}{4} \rfloor, -\lfloor \frac{q}{4} \rfloor + 1, \ldots, \lfloor \frac{q}{4} \rfloor - 1, \lfloor \frac{q}{4} \rfloor\}$. *If there is a quantum* ϵ-*distinguisher* U_D *for the decisional* $\mathsf{LWE}_{n,m,q,\chi}$ *problem, then there is a quantum algorithm that solves the search* $\mathsf{LWE}_{n,m',q,\chi}$ *problem with probability* $\Omega(\frac{\epsilon}{q})$ *using* U_D *and* $\mathsf{U}_D^\dagger$ $\mathcal{O}(\frac{q}{\epsilon})$ *times, where* $m' = m + \mathcal{O}(n)$.

Proof of Theorem 3. Initially, s is chosen uniform random from $\mathbb{Z}_q^n$, we get $(A, y) \leftarrow \mathcal{LWE}_{n,m,s,q,\chi}$ and samples random coins. From Lemma 1 and Theorem 2 we can construct a quantum algorithm U_S using U_D and $\mathsf{U}_D^\dagger$ once each, and that satisfies

$$|\langle s| \mathsf{U}_S |0^n\rangle|^2 > \frac{4\epsilon^2}{9(q-1)^2} \tag{8}$$

with probability $\frac{\epsilon}{3q}$ over choice of $s \xleftarrow{\$} \mathbb{Z}_q^n$, $(A, y) \leftarrow \mathcal{LWE}_{n,m,s,q,\chi}$ and random coins. From Lemma 2 and Lemma 3 we can construct a verification algorithm Verify (resp. a quantum algorithm $\mathsf{U}_{\mathsf{Verify}}$) that satisfies (5) (resp. (6)) with constant probability using $\mathcal{O}(n)$ samples of $\mathcal{LWE}_{n,m,s,q,\chi}$.

Assuming that U_S satisfies (8), Verify satisfies (5), and $\mathsf{U}_{\mathsf{Verify}}$ satisfies (6), consider the following procedure. The procedure is to compute

$$\left(-\mathsf{U}_S(\mathsf{I} - |0^n\rangle \langle 0^n|)\mathsf{U}_S^\dagger \mathsf{U}_{\mathsf{Verify}}\right)^k \mathsf{U}_S |0^n\rangle,$$

measures states in the computational basis, test it by Verify. As shown in [11], if this is carried out for a suitably generated sequence of values of k, we can find s with the expected total number of executions of U_S and $\mathsf{U}_S^\dagger$ until a successful verification occurs is $\mathcal{O}(\frac{q}{\epsilon})$. From the construction of U_S, we get the following conclusions. We can find s with probability $\Omega(\frac{\epsilon}{q})$ using U_D and $\mathsf{U}_D^\dagger$ $\mathcal{O}(\frac{q}{\epsilon})$ times, and with sample complexity $m + \mathcal{O}(n)$.

□

We remark that our reduction holds for a variety of other error distributions. It simply requires that we can verify from the samples whether it is the correct answer or not given some input $s' \in \mathbb{Z}_q^n$. For example, the verification algorithm for the case where $q = 2$ and the error distributed from the Bernoulli distribution is given in Appendix A.

Next, we consider how we can raise the success probability of our reduction algorithm to $1 - o(1)$. Simply repeating the algorithm does not efficiently increase the success probability. There are two reasons why we cannot simply repeat the algorithm given in Sect. 3.1.

- Whether the predictor U_P has desired property depends on the choice of $s \xleftarrow{\$} \mathbb{Z}_q^n$ (see Lemma 1).
- And the amplitude amplification algorithm would keep running until it finds s in time inversely proportional to the advantage of U_P.

We can overcome the first problem by re-randomize the secret s. By sampling $s^* \xleftarrow{\$} \mathbb{Z}_q^n$ and using $(A, y') := (A, y + A \cdot s^*)$, easily follows that, the distribution $\{(A, y')\}$ is equal to $\mathcal{LWE}_{n,m,s,q,\chi}$. The second problem can be overcome by parallel computing. For example, if we produce $\lceil \frac{3q \log n}{\epsilon} \rceil$ of predictors then there exist a predictor $U_{P,i}$ that has advantage $\frac{2\epsilon}{3q}$ with probability at least $1 - \frac{1}{n}$. If any part of the parallel computation has an output that passes the verification algorithm, it is the answer. Hence we can find s with probability $1 - o(1)$ by computing in parallel. This algorithm is described below.

Reduction Algorithm with high success probability

Choose $\tilde{\mathcal{O}}(n)$ samples from $\mathcal{LWE}_{n,m,s,q,\chi}$, and construct Verify

for $i = 1, \ldots, \lceil \frac{3q \log n}{\epsilon} \rceil$:

    Choose m samples of LWE instances (A_i, y_i)

    Sample a random vector $s_i^* \leftarrow \mathbb{Z}_q^n$, set $(A_i, y_i') := (A_i, y_i + A_i \cdot s_i^*)$, and construct $U_{P,i}$

    Construct $\text{Verify}_i(x) := \text{Verify}(x - s_i^*)$ and $U_{Verify,i}$

Run the second reduction algorithm in parallel

If there is a s_j that passes the j-th verification test Verify_j, then output $s = s_j - s_j^*$

From Lemma 2, we can construct a verification algorithm Verify that satisfies (5) with probability $1 - o(1)$ using $\tilde{\mathcal{O}}(n)$ samples of $\mathcal{LWE}_{n,m,s,q,\chi}$. Hence, The above algorithm has success probability $1 - o(1)$, invokes U_D $\mathcal{O}(\frac{q^2 \log n}{\epsilon^2})$ times, and using $\tilde{\mathcal{O}}(\frac{mq}{\epsilon}) = \mathcal{O}(\frac{mq \log n}{\epsilon}) + \mathcal{O}(n)$ samples of $\mathcal{LWE}_{n,m,s,q,\chi}$. We get the following corollary.

Corollary 1. *Let q be a prime and χ be a probability distribution over $\{-\lfloor \frac{q}{4} \rfloor, -\lfloor \frac{q}{4} \rfloor + 1, \ldots, \lfloor \frac{q}{4} \rfloor - 1, \lfloor \frac{q}{4} \rfloor\}$. If there is a quantum ϵ-distinguisher U_D for the decisional $\mathsf{LWE}_{n,m,q,\chi}$ problem, then there is a quantum algorithm that solves the search $\mathsf{LWE}_{n,m',q,\chi}$ problem with probability $1 - o(1)$ using U_D and $U_D^\dagger$ $\mathcal{O}(\frac{q^2 \log n}{\epsilon^2})$ times, where $m' = \tilde{\mathcal{O}}(\frac{mq}{\epsilon})$.*

4   Conclusion

In this section, we display the efficiency of our reduction algorithms. We also give the comparisons listed in Table 1. The sample-preserve one shows that we can find s with a probability at least $\frac{4\epsilon^3}{27q(q-1)^2}$ and query complexity 2. Compared to the previous sample-preserve reduction by [20], it dramatically reduces query complexity. The second algorithm give by Theorem 3 performs amplitude amplification and has $\mathcal{O}(\frac{q^2}{\epsilon^2})$ times higher success probability than the sample-preserve one, but the query complexity is $\mathcal{O}(\frac{q}{\epsilon})$ times higher and the sample complexity increases by $\mathcal{O}(n)$. We stress that this trade-off is specific to quantum computation. Additionally, we get the reduction algorithm that has success probability $1 - o(1)$ with query complexity $\mathcal{O}(\frac{q^2 \log n}{\epsilon^2})$ and sample complexity $\tilde{\mathcal{O}}(\frac{mq}{\epsilon})$. It is characterized by a lower sample complexity than the classical one, which also has a high success probability. It is interesting to note that, while our quantum reduction shows an advantage in query complexity in the comparison of sample preserve reductions, it has an advantage in sample complexity in the comparison of reductions with a high probability of success.

A   Search-to-Decision Reduction for the LPN problem

We show that there is a quantum search-to-decision reduction for the learning parity with noise problem. First, from Theorem 2 we immediately obtain the following corollary.

Corollary 2. *If there is a quantum ϵ-distinguisher U_D for the decisional* $\mathsf{LWE}_{n,m,2,\mathsf{Ber}_\mu}$ *problem, then there is a quantum algorithm that solves the search* $\mathsf{LWE}_{n,m,2,\mathsf{Ber}_\mu}$ *problem with probability at least $\frac{2\epsilon^3}{27}$ using U_D and $\mathsf{U}_D^\dagger$ once each.*

As in the case of the LWE problem, we can amplify the success probability by constructing an algorithm Verify that judges the solution.

Lemma 4. *We can construct an algorithm* Verify_{LPN}, *and it satisfies the following functionality (9) with desired probability $0 < c < \frac{2^n - 1}{2^n}$.*
For all $x \in \{0,1\}^n$,

$$\mathsf{Verify}_{LPN}(x) = \begin{cases} 1 & if\ x = s \\ 0 & if\ x \neq s. \end{cases} \tag{9}$$

Proof of Lemma 4. Initially, sample $(A, y) \leftarrow \mathcal{LPN}_{s,\mu}^l$, where $A \in \{0,1\}^{l \times n}$ is a random Boolean matrix, $l = \left\lceil -\left(\frac{6}{(\frac{1}{2}-\mu)^2} \log_e(\frac{1}{2}(\frac{1}{2^n} - \frac{c}{2^n-1}))\right)\right\rceil = \mathcal{O}(n)$ and $y = A \cdot s \oplus e$ is a noisy inner products, note that $e \in \{0,1\}^l$ is errors distributed from Ber_μ^l. Upon receiving input $x \in \{0,1\}^n$, Verify_{LPN} works as follows.

$$\text{Verify}_{LPN}(x):$$
$$\text{if } |weight(A \cdot x \oplus y) - \mu l| < \tfrac{1}{2}(\tfrac{1}{2} - \mu)l$$
$$\text{then output } 1$$
$$\text{else output } 0$$

Note that the function $weight(\cdot)$ outputs the Hamming distance. If $x = s$, since $A \cdot x \oplus e = y$, $A \cdot x \oplus y = e$. Since e is distributed from the Bernoulli distribution Ber_μ^l, $\mathbb{E}(weight(A \cdot x \oplus y)) = \mathbb{E}(weight(e)) = \mu l$. If $x \neq s$, $A \cdot x \oplus y$ is uniformly random, since A is sampled uniformly random. Therefore $\mathbb{E}(weight(A \cdot x \oplus y)) = \tfrac{1}{2}l$. Let us analyze the probability that the Verify_{LPN} satisfies the condition (9).

$$
\begin{aligned}
\Pr[\text{Verify}_{LPN} \text{ satisfies } (9)] &= \Pr[\text{Verify}_{LPN}(s) = 1 \wedge \forall s' \neq s, \text{Verify}_{LPN}(s') = 0] \\
&\geq \Pr[\text{Verify}_{LPN}(s) = 1] \cdot \Pr[\forall s' \neq s, \text{Verify}_{LPN}(s') = 0] \\
&\geq \Pr[\text{Verify}_{LPN}(s) = 1] \cdot \left(1 - \sum_{s' \neq s} \Pr[\text{Verify}_{LPN}(s') = 1]\right) \\
&\geq \left(1 - 2e^{-\frac{l}{12\mu}(\frac{1}{2} - \mu)^2}\right)\left(1 - (2^n - 1)\left(2e^{-\frac{l}{6}(\frac{1}{2} - \mu)^2}\right)\right) \\
&\geq \left(1 - \left(\frac{1}{2^n} - \frac{c}{2^n - 1}\right)^{\frac{1}{2\mu}}\right)\left(1 - (2^n - 1)\left(\frac{1}{2^n} - \frac{c}{2^n - 1}\right)\right) \\
&\geq \left(1 - \left(\frac{1}{2^n} - \frac{c}{2^n - 1}\right)\right)\left(1 - 2^n\left(\frac{1}{2^n} - \frac{c}{2^n - 1}\right)\right) \\
&\geq \left(1 - \frac{1}{2^n}\right)\frac{2^n c}{2^n - 1} \\
&= c
\end{aligned}
$$

The second inequality follows from union bound, and the third inequality follows from Chernoff bound. □

Corollary 3. *If there is a quantum ϵ-distinguisher U_D for the decisional $\mathsf{LWE}_{n,m,2,\text{Ber}_\mu}$ problem, then there is a quantum algorithm that solves the search $\mathsf{LWE}_{n,m',2,\text{Ber}_\mu}$ problem with probability $\Omega(\epsilon)$ using U_D and $\mathsf{U}_D^\dagger$ $\mathcal{O}(1/\epsilon)$ times, where $m' = m + \mathcal{O}(n)$.*

The proof of this corollary is given in the same way as in Theorem 3. We give the comparisons listed in Table 2.

Table 2. Comparison of the algorithms performance. n is a size of the LPN problem, m is the number of instances required by the distinguisher to solve the decisional LPN problem, ϵ is the advantage of the distinguisher.

	Success probability (at least)	Query complexity	Sample complexity	Classical/Quantum
KS06 [18]	$\frac{\epsilon}{4}$	$\mathcal{O}(\frac{n \log n}{\epsilon^2})$	$\mathcal{O}(\frac{mn \log n}{\epsilon^2})$	Classical
AIK07 [7]	$\Omega(\frac{\epsilon^3}{n})$	$\mathcal{O}(\frac{n^2}{\epsilon^2})$	m	Classical
Corollary 2	$\frac{2\epsilon^3}{27}$	2	m	Quantum
Corollary 3	$\Omega(\epsilon)$	$\mathcal{O}(\frac{1}{\epsilon})$	$m + \mathcal{O}(n)$	Quantum

B   Classical Search-to-Decision Reduction for the LWE

B.1   A Simple Reduction

In this section we give a simple classical search-to-decision reduction by [26]. It is based on the reduction given by Regev [25] and is useful for comparing efficiency.

Definition 4. *A (classical) algorithm D said to be a ϵ-distinguisher for the decisional* $\mathsf{LWE}_{n,m,q,\chi}$ *problem if* $|\Pr[D(A,y) = 1|s \xleftarrow{\$} \{0,1\}^n, (A,y) \leftarrow \mathcal{LWE}_{n,m,s,q,\chi}^m] - \Pr[D(A,r) = 1|A \xleftarrow{\$} \mathbb{Z}_q^{m\times n}, r \xleftarrow{\$} \mathbb{Z}_q^m]| > \epsilon$ *holds.*

The algorithm below solves the search $\mathsf{LWE}_{n,m',q,\chi}$ problem with probability $1-o(1)$ using D $\tilde{O}(\frac{nq}{\epsilon^2})$ times where $m' = \tilde{O}(\frac{nmq}{\epsilon^2})$. For a detailed analysis, please refer to [26].

B.2   Complexity of MM11 [20]

In this section, we give a brief analysis of the search-to-decision reduction by Micciancio and Mol [20]. Their search-to-decision reduction for LWE is shown via search-to-decision reduction for the knapsack functions. This induces a negligible fraction of loss in the success probability. Let δ be an advantage of the distinguisher. From ([20], Proposition3.9 and Lemma3.4) the success probability of the search-to-decision reduction for the knapsack functions is $\frac{\epsilon}{3}$ where $\epsilon \geq \left(\frac{d^{*3}\tilde{\delta}}{d^3(d^*-1)}\right)(2 - \frac{\pi^2}{6})$ and $\tilde{\delta}$ is some noticeable such that $\tilde{\delta} \leq \delta$. Using the fact that $d^* \geq s$ and $\tilde{d} \leq 2ms^2$, we have $\frac{\epsilon}{3} = \Omega(\frac{\tilde{\delta}}{m^3 s^4})$. Substituting q for s, we get the success probability of their search-to-decision reduction for LWE $\Omega(\frac{\tilde{\delta}}{m^3 q^4}) - \mathsf{negl}(n)$.

Classical reduction algorithm

---

for $i = 1, \ldots, n$:
    for $j = 0, \ldots, q - 1$:
        for $l = 1, \ldots, L = \tilde{O}(\frac{1}{\epsilon^2})$:
            Choose a fresh block of LWE instances (A_l, y_l)
            Sample a random vector $c_l \leftarrow \mathbb{Z}_q^m$, and let $C_l \in \mathbb{Z}_q^{m\times n}$ be the matrix whose
            i-th row is c_l, and whose other entries are all zero
            Let $A_l' := A_l + C_l$, and $y_l' := y_l + j \cdot c_l$
            Run the distinguisher $D(A_l', b_l')$ and let the output be called d_l
            If $maj(d_1, ..., d_L) = 1$ (meaning that the distinguisher guesses LWE) then set $s_i = j$
            Else, continue to the next iteration of the loop
Output $s = s_1 \ldots s_n$

In ([20], Lemma 3.4), they use Significant Fourier Transform [4] with $\tau = \frac{\epsilon^2}{4}$, $N = |\mathbb{Z}_{d^*}^l|$ and $\|f\|_2 = \|f\|_\infty = 1$. The running time of Significant Fourier Transform is at most $\tilde{\Theta}(\log N(\frac{\|f\|_2^2}{\tau})^{1.5}(\frac{\|f\|_\infty^2}{\eta^2})^2 \lg \frac{1}{\mu})$ for $\eta = \Theta(min\{\tau, \sqrt{\tau}, \frac{\tau}{\|f\|_\infty}\})$ and

$\mu = 1/\mathcal{O}((\frac{\|f\|_\infty^2}{\tau})^{1.5}\log N)$. Substituting $\tau = \frac{\epsilon^2}{4}$, $N = d^*m$ and $\|f\|_2 = \|f\|_\infty = 1$, we get $\tilde{\Theta}(\log N (\frac{\|f\|_2^2}{\tau})^{1.5}(\frac{\|f\|_\infty^2}{\eta})^2 \lg \frac{1}{\mu}) = \tilde{\mathcal{O}}(\frac{\log(d^*l)}{\epsilon^{11}})$. Hence From ([20], Proposition 3.9 and Lemma 3.4), the query complexity of the search-to-decision reduction for LWE is $\tilde{\Theta}(\frac{\log(d^*m)}{\epsilon^{11}})\mathcal{O}(1) = \tilde{\mathcal{O}}(\frac{\log(d^*m)}{\epsilon^{11}})$ where d^* is some polynomial such that $d^* \geq q$.

References

1. LWE challenge website. https://www.latticechallenge.org/lwe_challenge/challenge.php
2. Adcock, M., Cleve, R.: A quantum Goldreich-Levin Theorem with cryptographic applications. In: Alt, H., Ferreira, A. (eds.) STACS 2002. LNCS, vol. 2285, pp. 323–334. Springer, Heidelberg (2002). https://doi.org/10.1007/3-540-45841-7_26
3. Agrawal, S., Boneh, D., Boyen, X.: Efficient lattice (H)IBE in the standard model. In: Gilbert, H. (ed.) EUROCRYPT 2010. LNCS, vol. 6110, pp. 553–572. Springer, Heidelberg (2010). https://doi.org/10.1007/978-3-642-13190-5_28
4. Akavia, A.: Learning noisy characters, MPC, and cryptographic hardcore predicates. PhD thesis, Massachusetts Institute of Technology, Cambridge, MA, USA (2008)
5. Ananth, P., Poremba, A., Vaikuntanathan, V.: Revocable cryptography from learning with errors. Cryptology ePrint Archive, Paper 2023/325 (2023). https://eprint.iacr.org/2023/325
6. Applebaum, B., Cash, D., Peikert, C., Sahai, A.: Fast cryptographic primitives and circular-secure encryption based on hard learning problems. In: Halevi, S. (ed.) CRYPTO 2009. LNCS, vol. 5677, pp. 595–618. Springer, Heidelberg (2009). https://doi.org/10.1007/978-3-642-03356-8_35
7. Applebaum, B., Ishai, Y., Kushilevitz, E.: Cryptography with constant input locality. In: Menezes, A. (ed.) CRYPTO 2007. LNCS, vol. 4622, pp. 92–110. Springer, Heidelberg (2007). https://doi.org/10.1007/978-3-540-74143-5_6
8. Bitansky, N., Brakerski, Z., Kalai, Y.T.: Constructive post-quantum reductions. In: Dodis, Y., Shrimpton, T. (eds.) CRYPTO 2022. LNCS, vol. 13509, pp. 654–683. Springer, Cham (2022). https://doi.org/10.1007/978-3-031-15982-4_22
9. Brakerski, Z., Langlois, A., Peikert, C., Regev, O., Stehlé, D.: Classical hardness of learning with errors. In: Boneh, D., Roughgarden, T., Feigenbaum, J (eds.) Symposium on Theory of Computing Conference, STOC 2013, Palo Alto, CA, USA, 1–4 June 1–4 2013, pp. 575–584. ACM (2013)
10. Brakerski, Z., Vaikuntanathan, V.: Efficient fully homomorphic encryption from (standard) LWE. In: Ostrovsky, R (ed.) IEEE 52nd Annual Symposium on Foundations of Computer Science, FOCS 2011, Palm Springs, CA, USA, 22–25 October 22–25 2011, pp. 97–106. IEEE Computer Society (2011)
11. Brassard, G., Hoyer, P., Mosca, M., Tapp, A.: Quantum Amplitude Amplification and Estimation (2002)
12. Cash, D., Hofheinz, D., Kiltz, E., Peikert, C.: Bonsai trees, or how to delegate a lattice basis. In: Gilbert, H. (ed.) EUROCRYPT 2010. LNCS, vol. 6110, pp. 523–552. Springer, Heidelberg (2010). https://doi.org/10.1007/978-3-642-13190-5_27
13. Dodis, Y., Goldwasser, S., Tauman Kalai, Y., Peikert, C., Vaikuntanathan, V.: Public-key encryption schemes with auxiliary inputs. In: Micciancio, D. (ed.) TCC 2010. LNCS, vol. 5978, pp. 361–381. Springer, Heidelberg (2010). https://doi.org/10.1007/978-3-642-11799-2_22

14. Döttling, N.: Low noise LPN: KDM secure public key encryption and sample amplification. In: Katz, J. (ed.) PKC 2015. LNCS, vol. 9020, pp. 604–626. Springer, Heidelberg (2015). https://doi.org/10.1007/978-3-662-46447-2_27

15. Gentry, C., Peikert, C., Vaikuntanathan, V.: Trapdoors for hard lattices and new cryptographic constructions. In: Dwork, C (ed.) Proceedings of the 40th Annual ACM Symposium on Theory of Computing, Victoria, British Columbia, Canada, 17–20 May 17–20 2008, pp. 197–206. ACM (2008)

16. Goldreich, O., Levin, L.A.: A hard-core predicate for all one-way functions. In: Johnson, D.S (ed.), Proceedings of the 21st Annual ACM Symposium on Theory of Computing, 14–17 May 14–17 1989, Seattle, Washington, USA, pp. 25–32. ACM (1989)

17. Grigorescu, E., Kopparty, S., Sudan, M.: Local decoding and testing for homomorphisms. In: Díaz, J., Jansen, K., Rolim, J.D.P., Zwick, U. (eds.) APPROX/RANDOM -2006. LNCS, vol. 4110, pp. 375–385. Springer, Heidelberg (2006). https://doi.org/10.1007/11830924_35

18. Katz, J., Shin, J.S.: Parallel and concurrent security of the HB and HB$^+$ protocols. In: Vaudenay, S. (ed.) EUROCRYPT 2006. LNCS, vol. 4004, pp. 73–87. Springer, Heidelberg (2006). https://doi.org/10.1007/11761679_6

19. Li, H.: Quantum algorithms for the Goldreich-Levin learning problem. Quantum Inf. Process. **19**(10), 395 (2020)

20. Micciancio, D., Mol, P.: Pseudorandom knapsacks and the sample complexity of LWE search-to-decision reductions. In: Rogaway, P. (ed.) CRYPTO 2011. LNCS, vol. 6841, pp. 465–484. Springer, Heidelberg (2011). https://doi.org/10.1007/978-3-642-22792-9_26

21. Micciancio, D., Peikert, C.: Trapdoors for lattices: simpler, tighter, faster, smaller. In: Pointcheval, D., Johansson, T. (eds.) EUROCRYPT 2012. LNCS, vol. 7237, pp. 700–718. Springer, Heidelberg (2012). https://doi.org/10.1007/978-3-642-29011-4_41

22. Newton, P.: Novel Linearity Tests with Applications to Lattices and Learning Problems. PhD thesis, UC Riverside (2022)

23. Peikert, C.: Public-key cryptosystems from the worst-case shortest vector problem: extended abstract. In: Mitzenmacher, M (Ed.) Proceedings of the 41st Annual ACM Symposium on Theory of Computing, STOC 2009, Bethesda, MD, USA, May 31–June 2 2009, pp. 333–342. ACM (2009)

24. Peikert, C., Vaikuntanathan, V., Waters, B.: A framework for efficient and composable oblivious transfer. In: Wagner, D. (ed.) CRYPTO 2008. LNCS, vol. 5157, pp. 554–571. Springer, Heidelberg (2008). https://doi.org/10.1007/978-3-540-85174-5_31

25. Regev, O.: On lattices, learning with errors, random linear codes, and cryptography. In: Gabow, H.N., Fagin, R (ed.) Proceedings of the 37th Annual ACM Symposium on Theory of Computing, Baltimore, MD, USA, 22–24 May 22–24 2005, pp. 84–93. ACM (2005)

26. Vaikuntanathan, V.: Lattices, learning with errors and post-quantum cryptography. https://people.csail.mit.edu/vinodv/CS294/lecturenotes.pdf

Implementations

Fast Falcon Signature Generation and Verification Using ARMv8 NEON Instructions

Duc Tri Nguyen[(✉)][iD] and Kris Gaj[iD]

George Mason University, Fairfax, VA 22030, USA
{dnguye69,kgaj}@gmu.edu

Abstract. We present our speed records for Falcon signature generation and verification on ARMv8-A architecture. Our implementations are benchmarked on Apple M1 'Firestorm', Raspberry Pi 4 Cortex-A72, and Jetson AGX Xavier. Our optimized signature generation is 2× slower, but signature verification is 3–3.9× faster than the state-of-the-art CRYSTALS-Dilithium implementation on the same platforms. Faster signature verification may be particularly useful for the client side on constrained devices. Our Falcon implementation outperforms the previous work targeting Jetson AGX Xavier by the factors 1.48× for signing in `falcon512` and `falcon1024`, 1.52× for verifying in `falcon512`, and 1.70× for verifying in `falcon1024`. We achieve improvement in Falcon signature generation by supporting a larger subset of possible parameter values for FFT-related functions and applying our compressed twiddle-factor table to reduce memory usage. We also demonstrate that the recently proposed signature scheme Hawk, sharing optimized functionality with Falcon, has 3.3× faster signature generation and 1.6–1.9× slower signature verification when implemented on the same ARMv8 processors as Falcon.

Keywords: Number Theoretic Transform · Fast Fourier Transform · Post-Quantum Cryptography · Falcon · Hawk · ARMv8 · NEON

1 Introduction

When large quantum computers arrive, Shor's algorithm [39] will break almost all currently deployed public-key cryptography in polynomial time [16] due to its capability to obliterate two cryptographic bastions: the integer factorization and discrete logarithm problems. While there is no known quantum computer capable of running Shor's algorithm with parameters required to break current public-key standards, selecting, standardizing, and deploying their replacements have already started.

In 2016, NIST announced the Post-Quantum Cryptography (PQC) standardization process aimed at developing new public-key standards resistant to quantum computers. In July 2022, NIST announced the choice of three digital signature algorithms [2]: CRYSTALS-Dilithium [5], Falcon [23], and SPHINCS+ [11] for a likely standardization within the next two years. Additionally, NIST has already standardized two stateful signature schemes, XMSS [26] and LMS [34].

© The Author(s), under exclusive license to Springer Nature Switzerland AG 2023
N. El Mrabet et al. (Eds.): AFRICACRYPT 2023, LNCS 14064, pp. 417–441, 2023.
https://doi.org/10.1007/978-3-031-37679-5_18

Compared to Elliptic Curve Cryptography and RSA, PQC digital signatures have imposed additional implementation constraints, such as bigger key and signature sizes, higher memory usage, support for floating-point operations, etc. In many common applications, such as the distribution of software updates and the use of digital certificates, a signature is generated once by the server but verified over and over again by clients forming the network.

In this paper, we examine the PQC digital signatures' speed on ARMv8-A platforms. NEON is an alternative name for Advanced Single Instruction Multiple Data (ASIMD) extension, available since ARMv7. NEON includes additional instructions that can perform arithmetic operations in parallel on multiple data streams. It also provides a developer with 32 128-bit vector registers. Each register can store two 64-bit, four 32-bit, eight 16-bit, or sixteen 8-bit integer data elements. NEON instructions can perform the same arithmetic operation simultaneously on the corresponding elements of two 128-bit registers and store the results in the respective fields of a third register. Thus, an ideal speed-up vs. traditional single-instruction single-data (SISD) ARM instructions varies between 2 (for 64-bit operands) and 16 (for 8-bit operands).

In this work, we developed an optimized implementation of Falcon targeting ARMv8 cores. We then reused a significant portion of our Falcon code to implement Hawk – a new lattice-based signature scheme proposed in Sept. 2022 [21]. Although this scheme is not a candidate in the NIST PQC standardization process yet, it may be potentially still submitted for consideration in response to the new NIST call, with the deadline in June 2023.

We then benchmarked our implementation and existing implementations of Falcon, Hawk, CRYSTALS-Dilithium, SPHINCS+, and XMSS using the 'Firestorm' core of Apple M1 (being a part of MacBook Air) and the Cortex-A72 core (being a part of Raspberry Pi 4), as these platforms are widely available for benchmarking. However, we expect that similar rankings of candidates can be achieved using other ARMv8 cores (a.k.a. microarchitectures of ARMv8).

Contributions. In this paper, we overcome the high complexity of the Falcon implementation and present a speed record for its **S**ignature generation and **V**erification on two different ARMv8 processors.

In a signature generation, we constructed vectorized scalable FFT implementation that can be applied to any FFT level greater than five. We compressed the twiddle factor table in our FFT implementation using a method inspired by the complex *conjugate* root of FFT. In particular, we reduced the size of this table from *16 Kilobytes* in the reference implementation down to *4 Kilobytes* in our new `ref` and `neon` implementations. The modified FFT implementation with 4× smaller twiddle factor table is not specific to any processor. Thus, it can be used on any platform, including constrained devices with limited storage or memory.

In the **V**erify operation, we applied the best-known Number Theoretic Transform (NTT) implementation techniques to speed up its operation for Falcon-specific parameters. Additionally, we present the exhaustive search bound analysis applied to twiddle factors per NTT level aimed at minimizing the number of Barrett reductions in Forward and Inverse NTT.

We also optimized the performance of hash-based signatures, and comprehensively compare three stateless and one stateful digital signature schemes selected by NIST for standardization – Falcon, CRYSTALS-Dilithium, SPHINCS$^+$, and XMSS – and one recently-proposed lattice-based scheme Hawk. We rank them according to signature size, public-key size, and Sign and Verify operations' performance using the best implementations available to date.

Our code is publicly available at https://github.com/GMUCERG/Falcon_ NEON

2   Previous Work

The paper by Streit et al. [40] was the first work about a NEON-based ARMv8 implementation of the lattice-based public-key encryption scheme New Hope Simple. Other works implement Kyber [41], SIKE [28], and FrodoKEM [32] on ARMv8. The most recent works on the lattice-based finalists NTRU, Saber, and CRYSTALS-Kyber are reported by Nguyen et al. [35,36]. The paper improved polynomial multiplication and compared the performance of vectorized Toom-Cook and NTT implementations. Notably, the work by Becker et al. [6] showed a vectorized NEON NTT implementation superior to Toom-Cook, introduced fast Barrett multiplication, and special use of multiply-return-high-only sq[r]dmulh instructions. The SIMD implementation of Falcon was reported by Pornin [37] and Kim et al. [31]. On the application side, Falcon is the only viable option in hybrid, partial, and pure PQC V2V design described in the work of Bindel et al. [12]

In the area of low-power implementations, most previous works targeted the ARM Cortex-M4 [29]. In particular, Botros et al. [14], and Alkim et al. [3] developed Cortex-M4 implementations of Kyber. Karmakar et al. [30] reported results for Saber. Chung et al. [17] on Saber and NTRU, and later work by Becker et al. [8] improved Saber by a large margin on Cortex-M4/M55. The latest work by Abdulrahman et al. [1] improved Kyber and Dilithium performance on Cortex-M4.

The most comprehensive Fast Fourier Transform (FFT) work is by Becoulet et al. [9][1]. The publications by Frigo et al. [24] and Blake et al. [13] describe the SIMD FFT implementations.

3   Background

Table 1 summarizes values of parameters n and q for various signature schemes and NIST security levels. n is a parameter in the cyclotomic polynomial $\phi = (x^n + 1)$, and q is a prime defining a ring $\mathbb{Z}_q[x]/(\phi)$. The sizes of the public key

---

[1] https://github.com/diaxen/fft-garden.

Table 1. Parameter sets, key sizes, and signature sizes for FALCON, HAWK, DILITHIUM, XMSS, and SPHINCS$^+$. The last column shows the signature size ratio in comparison to FALCON512, DILITHIUM3, or FALCON1024, depending on the security level.

	NIST level	n	q	$|pk|$	$|sig|$	$|pk + sig|$	$|sig|$ ratio
FALCON512	I	512	12,289	897	<u>652</u>	1,549	<u>1.00</u>
HAWK512			65,537	1,006	542	1,548	0.83
DILITHIUM2	II	256	8,380,417	1,312	2,420	3,732	3.71
XMSS^{16}-SHA256		-	-	64	2,692	2,756	4.12
SPHINCS$^+$128s	I	-	-	32	7,856	7,888	12.05
SPHINCS$^+$128f		-	-	32	17,088	17,120	26.21
DILITHIUM3		256	8,380,417	1,952	3,293	5,245	<u>1.00</u>
SPHINCS$^+$192s	III	-	-	48	16,224	16,272	4.93
SPHINCS$^+$192f		-	-	48	35,664	35,712	10.83
FALCON1024		1024	12,289	1,793	<u>1,261</u>	3,054	<u>1.00</u>
HAWK1024			65,537	2,329	1,195	3,524	0.95
DILITHIUM5	V	256	8,380,417	2,592	4,595	7,187	3.64
SPHINCS$^+$256s		-	-	64	29,792	29,856	23.62
SPHINCS$^+$256f		-	-	64	49,856	49,920	39.53

and signature in bytes (**B**) are denoted with $|pk|$ and $|sig|$. The signature ratio $|sig|$ ratio is the result of dividing the signature size of other schemes by the signature size of FALCON512, DILITHIUM3, and FALCON1024.

3.1 Falcon

Falcon is a lattice-based signature scheme utilizing the 'hash-and-sign' paradigm. The security of Falcon is based on the hardness of the Short Integer Solution problem over NTRU lattices, and the security proofs are given in the random oracle model with tight reduction. Falcon is difficult to implement, requiring tree data structures, extensive floating-point operations, and random sampling from several discrete Gaussian distributions. The upsides of Falcon are its small public keys and signatures as compared to Dilithium. As shown in Table 1, the signature size of Falcon at the highest NIST security level is still smaller than that of the lowest security level of Dilithium, XMSS, and SPHINCS$^+$. Key generation in Falcon is expensive. However, a key can be generated once and reused later.

The signature generation (Algorithm 1) of Falcon first computes hash value c from message m and salt r. Then, it uses (f, g, F, G) from the secret key components to compute two short values s_1, s_2 such that $s_1 + s_2 h = c \bmod (\phi, q)$. Falcon relies extensively on floating-point computations during signature generation, used in Fast Fourier Transform (FFT) over the ring $\mathbb{Q}[x]/(\phi)$, and Gaussian and Fast Fourier Sampling (ffSampling) for Falcon tree T.

The signature verification (Algorithm 2) checks if two short values (s_1, s_2) are in acceptance bound $\lfloor \beta^2 \rfloor$ using the knowledge from public key pk, and signature

---

Algorithm 1: Falcon Sign

Input: A message m, a secret key sk, a bound $\lceil \beta^2 \rceil$
Output: $sig = (r, s)$

1   $r \leftarrow \{0, 1\}^{320}$ uniformly $c \leftarrow \texttt{HashToPoint}(r\|m, q, n)$

2   $t \leftarrow \left(-\frac{1}{q} \text{FFT}(c) \odot \text{FFT}(F), \frac{1}{q} \text{FFT}(c) \odot \text{FFT}(f) \right)$ $\triangleright$ $t \in \mathbb{Q}[x]/(\phi)$

3   **do**

4   **do**

5       $z \leftarrow \texttt{ffSampling}_n(t, T)$

6       $s = (t - z)\hat{B}$ $\triangleright$ $s \in$ Gaussian distribution: $s \sim D_{(c,0)+\Lambda(B),\sigma,0}$

7   **while** $\|s^2\| > \lfloor \beta^2 \rfloor$;

8     $(s_1, s_2) \leftarrow \text{invFFT}(s)$ $\triangleright$ $s_1 + s_2 h = c \bmod (\phi, q)$

9     $s \leftarrow \texttt{Compress}(s_2, 8 \cdot sbytelen - 328)$

10   **while** $(s = \perp)$;

11   return $sig = (r, s)$

Algorithm 2: Falcon Verify

Input: A message m, $sig = (r, s)$, $pk = h \in \mathbb{Z}_q[x]/(\phi)$, a bound $\lfloor \beta^2 \rfloor$
Output: Accept or reject

1   $c \leftarrow \texttt{HashToPoint}(r\|m, q, n)$ $s_2 \leftarrow \texttt{Decompress}(s, 8 \cdot \text{sbytelen} - 328)$

2   **if** $(s_2 = \perp)$ **then**

3   reject

4   $s_1 \leftarrow c - s_2 h \bmod (\phi, q)$ $\triangleright$ $|s_1| < \frac{q}{2}$ and $s_1 \in \mathbb{Z}_q[x]/(\phi)$

5   **if** $\|(s_1, s_2)\|^2 \leq \lfloor \beta^2 \rfloor$ **then**

6   accept ;

7   **else**

8   reject

(r, s). If the condition at line 5 is satisfied, then the signature is valid; otherwise, it is rejected. As opposed to signature generation, Falcon Verify operates only over integers.

Falcon supports only NIST security levels 1 and 5. A more detailed description of the underlying operations can be found in the Falcon specification [23].

3.2 Dilithium

Dilithium is a member of the Cryptographic Suite for Algebraic Lattices (CRYS-TALS) along with the key encapsulation mechanism (KEM) Kyber. The core operations of Dilithium are the arithmetic of polynomial matrices and vectors. Unlike 'hash-and-sign' used in Falcon, Dilithium applies the Fiat-Shamir with Aborts [20,33] style signature scheme and bases its security upon the Module Learning with Errors (M-LWE) and Module Short Integer Solution (M-SIS) problems.

Compared with Falcon, Dilithium only operates over the integer ring $\mathbb{Z}_q[x]/(\phi)$ with $\phi = (x^n + 1)$. Thus, it is easier to deploy in environments lacking floating-point units. Dilithium supports three NIST security levels: 2, 3, and 5, and its parameters are shown in Table 1. More details can be found in the Dilithium specification [5].

3.3 XMSS

XMSS [26] (eXtended Merkle Signature Scheme) is a stateful hash-based signature scheme based on Winternitz One-Time Signature Plus (WOTS+) [27]. XMSS requires state tracking because the private key is updated every time a signature is generated. Hence, the key management of XMSS is considered difficult. Consequently, XMSS should only be used in highly controlled environments [19]. The advantages of XMSS over SPHINCS+ are smaller signature sizes and better performance. XMSS is a single-tree scheme, with a multi-tree variant XMSS^{MT} also included in the specification. The security of XMSS relies on the complexity of the collision search of an underlying hashing algorithm.

Single-tree XMSS has faster signature generation and verification than the multi-tree XMSS^{MT} and comes with three tree heights: $h = [10, 16, 20]$, which can produce up to 2^h signatures. We select a single-tree variant of XMSS with a reasonable number of signatures, 2^{16}, and choose optimized SHA256 as underlying hash functions. This variant is denoted as XMSS^{16}-SHA256 in Table 1.

3.4 SPHINCS+

SPHINCS+ [11] is a stateless hash-based signature scheme that avoids the complexities of state management associated with using stateful hash-based signatures. SPHINCS+ security also relies on hash algorithms. The algorithm is considered a conservative choice, preventing any future attacks on lattice-based signatures. SPHINCS+ provides 'simple' and 'robust' construction. The 'robust' construction affects the security proof and runtime. In addition, small ('s') and fast parameters ('f') influence execution time. These parameter set variants are over 128, 192, and 256 quantum security bits.

Based on the performance provided in the specification of SPHINCS+, we select the 'simple' construction, and both 's' and 'f' parameters for NIST security levels 1, 3, and 5, as shown in Table 1. Unlike in XMSS, we select optimized SHAKE as the underlying hash function.

3.5 Hawk

Hawk is a recent signature algorithm proposed by Ducas et al. [21] based on the Lattice Isomorphism Problem (LIP). Hawk avoids the complexities of the floating-point discrete Gaussian sampling, which is a bottleneck in our optimized Falcon implementation. Hawk chooses to sample in a simple lattice $\mathbb{Z}^n$ [10, 22] with a hidden rotation.

An AVX2 implementation of HAWK1024 is faster than the equivalent implementation of FALCON1024 by 3.9× and 2.2×. With our optimized neon implementation of Falcon, we decided to port our optimized Falcon code to Hawk and investigate if such performance gaps between Hawk and Falcon still hold. In this work, we select HAWK512 and HAWK1024 at NIST security levels 1 and 5.

4 Number Theoretic Transform Implementation

The Number Theoretic Transform (NTT) is a transformation used as a basis for a polynomial multiplication algorithm with the time complexity of $O(n \log n)$ [18]. In Falcon, the NTT algorithm is used for polynomial multiplication over the ring $\mathbf{R}_q = \mathbb{Z}_q[x]/(x^n + 1)$, where degree $n = [512, 1024]$ and $q = 12289 = 2^{13} + 2^{12} + 1$ with $q = 1 \bmod 2n$.

Complete NTT is similar to traditional FFT (Fast Fourier Transform) but uses the root of unity in the discrete field rather than in a set of real numbers. NTT and NTT^{-1} are forward and inverse operations, where $NTT^{-1}(NTT(f)) = f$ for all $f \in \mathbf{R}_q$.

$NTT(A) * NTT(B)$ denotes pointwise multiplication. Polynomial multiplication using NTT is shown in Eq. 1.

$$C(x) = A(x) \times B(x) = NTT^{-1}(NTT(A) * NTT(B)) \qquad (1)$$

4.1 Barrett Multiplication

In our Falcon implementation, Barrett multiplication is used extensively when one factor is known [6]. As shown in Algorithm 3, b must be a known constant, and $b' = [(b \cdot R/q)/2]$, where [ ] represent truncation. In fact, b and b' in NTT are from the precomputed table ω_i and ω'_i.

Algorithm 3: Signed Barrett multiplication with a constant [6]

Input: Any $|a| < R = 2^w$, constant $|b| < q$ and $b' = [(b \cdot R/q)/2]$

Output: $c = \texttt{barrett\_mul}(a, b, b') = a \cdot b \bmod q$, and $|c| < \frac{3q}{2} < \frac{R}{2}$

1 $t \leftarrow \texttt{sqrdmulh}(a, b')$ ▷ $\texttt{hi(round}((2 \cdot a \cdot b'))$

2 $c \leftarrow \texttt{mul}(a, b)$ ▷ $\texttt{lo}(a \cdot b)$

3 $c \leftarrow \texttt{mls}(c, t, q)$ ▷ $\texttt{lo}(c - t \cdot q)$

4.2   Montgomery Multiplication

First, Falcon Verify computes only one polynomial multiplication (as in line 4 of Algorithm 2). Two polynomials (s_2, h) are converted to NTT domain. Then, we perform pointwise multiplication between two polynomials in NTT domain. To efficiently compute modular reduction for two unknown factors during pointwise multiplication, the conventional way is to convert one polynomial to the Montgomery domain and perform Montgomery multiplication. Eventually, the multiplication with a constant factor n^{-1} is applied at the end of Inverse NTT. We apply a small tweak by embedding n^{-1} into Montgomery conversion during pointwise multiplication ($a_i b_i n^{-1}$ instead of $a_i b_i$ for $i \in [0, \ldots, n-1]$) to avoid multiplications with n^{-1} in Inverse NTT.

The Montgomery n^{-1} conversion uses Barrett multiplication with a known factor $a_{mont} = \texttt{barrett\_mul}(a, b, b')$, with $b = R \cdot n^{-1} \bmod q$. Furthermore, it is beneficial at the instruction level to embed n^{-1} when n is a power of 2 in Montgomery conversion. In particular, when $(R, n) = (2^{16}, 2^{10})$ then $b = R \cdot n^{-1} = 2^{16} \cdot 2^{-10} = 2^6 \bmod q$. Hence, multiply instruction at line 2 of Algorithm 3 can be replaced by a cheaper shift left (\texttt{shl}) instruction.

Secondly, we apply Montgomery multiplication *with rounding* for pointwise multiplication (Sect. 3 in Becker et al. [6]).

4.3   Minimizing the Number of Barrett Reductions

In Barrett multiplication (Algorithm 3), the theoretical bound of output c is in $-\frac{3q}{2} \leq c < \frac{3q}{2}$. Details of the proof can be found in Becker et al. [6]. Given that $q = 12289, R = 2^{16}$, the maximum bound of signed arithmetic centered around 0 is $2.6q \approx \frac{R}{2}$ instead of $5.3q \approx R$ in unsigned arithmetic.

During Forward and Inverse NTT, we carefully control the bound of each coefficient by applying our strict Barrett multiplication bound analysis. The naive $2.6q$ bound assumption will lead to performing Barrett reduction after every NTT level. To minimize the number of Barrett reductions, we validate the range of $c = \texttt{barrett\_mul}(b, \omega, \omega')$ for all unknown values of $|b| < \frac{R}{2}$ and $\omega \in \omega_i$ and $\omega' \in \omega'_i$ table according to each NTT level by exhaustive search (aka. brute-force all possible values in space $R = 2^{16}$). The bound output c of \texttt{barrett_mul} is increasing if $|b| < q$ and <u>decreasing</u> if $|b| \geq q$. For example, if $\frac{b}{q} \approx (\underline{0.5}, 1.0, 2.0, 2.5)$, then after Barrett multiplication, the obtained bounds are $\frac{c}{q} \approx (\underline{0.69}, 0.87, 1.25, 1.44)$.

As a result, we were able to minimize the number of reduction points in the Forward and Inverse NTT from after every one NTT level to every two NTT levels. In our case, an exhaustive search works in an acceptable time for the 16-bit space. A formal, strict bound analysis instead of an exhaustive search approach is considered as future work.

Algorithm 4: Signed Barrett reduction [6] for prime $q = 12289$

Input: Any $|a| < R = 2^w$, constants $(q, w, v, i) = (12289, 16, 5461, 11)$

Output: $c = \texttt{barrett\_mod}(a, q) \equiv a \bmod q$, and $-\frac{q}{2} \leq c < \frac{q}{2}$

1   $t \leftarrow \texttt{sqdmulh}(a, v)$ ▷ $\texttt{hi}(2 \cdot a \cdot v)$

2   $t \leftarrow \texttt{srshr}(t, i)$ ▷ $\texttt{round}(t \gg i)$

3   $c \leftarrow \texttt{mls}(a, t, q)$ ▷ $\texttt{lo}(a - t \cdot q)$

4.4   Forward and Inverse NTT Implementation

Falcon uses NTT to compute polynomial multiplication in the Verify operation. To avoid a bit-reversal overhead, Cooley-Tukey (CT) and Gentleman-Sande (GS) butterflies are used for Forward and Inverse NTT, respectively.

Instead of vectorizing the original reference Falcon NTT implementation, we rewrite the NTT implementation to exploit cache temporal and spatial locality. Our NTT implementation is centered around 0 to use signed arithmetic instructions instead of the unsigned arithmetic approach used by default in Falcon. This choice of implementation significantly improved our work compared to Kim et al. [31] due to special $\texttt{sq[r]dmulh}$ instructions, which only work in signed arithmetic. We recommend utilizing multiply-return-high-only instruction for NTT implementation on any platform that supports it.

In Forward and Inverse NTT operations, $\texttt{barrett\_mul}$ is used extensively due to its compactness, thus yielding optimal performance, eliminating dependency chains by using only 3 instructions [6] rather than 9 instructions from Nguyen et al. [35,36]. At the instruction level, based on the Becker et al. [6] micro-architecture pipeline trick, we gather the addition and subtraction from multiple butterflies in a group and arrange multiple $\texttt{barret\_mul}$ together. Note that this behavior also appeared in modern compiler optimization. Since our implementation uses intrinsic instructions instead of assembly instructions, we confirmed that the output assembly code showed similar order of instructions as in intrinsic implementation. On the low-end Cortex-A72 ARMv8 processor, we achieved 10% performance improvement by grouping instructions compared with ungrouping multiply instructions. However, this improvement is negligible in the high-end Apple M1 processor.

In terms of storage, the Barrett multiplication requires twiddle factor table ω and additional storage for the precomputed table ω': $\omega_i' = [(\omega_i \cdot R/q)/2]$, where $\omega_i = \omega^i \bmod q$. We prepared the twiddle factor tables ω_i and ω_i' so that every read from such tables is in the forward direction, and each entry is loaded only once during the entire operation.

Our Forward and Inverse NTT consist of two loops with the constant-stride (cache-friendly) load and store into memory and the permutation following steps in Nguyen et al. [35,36]. Our Forward and Inverse NTT implementations are constructed by two loops, seven NTT levels are combined into the first loop, and the remaining two (resp. three) NTT levels are in the second loop for $n = 512$

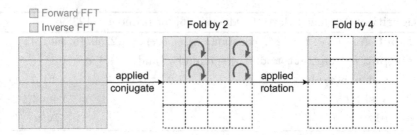

Fig. 1. Deriving full twiddle factor table by applying complex conjugate and rotation.

(resp. 1024). Each coefficient is loaded and stored once in each loop. With two loops, our implementation can reach up to $n = 2048, R = 2^{16}$ or $n = 1024, R = 2^{32}$ with a minimal number of load and store instructions.

5   Fast Fourier Transform Implementation

The Fast Fourier Transform (FFT) is a fast algorithm that computes a Discrete Fourier Transform from the time domain to the frequency domain and vice versa.

$$X_k = \sum_{n=0}^{N-1} x_n e^{-i2\pi kn/N} \text{ with } k \in [0, N-1] \tag{2}$$

The discrete Fourier transform in Eq. 2 has time complexity of $O(n^2)$. FFT improves the transformation with the time complexity of $O(n \log n)$ [18].

The advantage of FFT over NTT for polynomial multiplication is that the root of unity $e^{i2\pi/N}$ always exists for arbitrary N. Additionally, FFT suffers precision loss caused by rounding in the floating-point-number computations, while polynomial multiplication using NTT guarantees correctness due to NTT operating in the integer domain.

5.1   Compressed Twiddle Factor Table

In Falcon, each complex point utilizes 128 bits of storage. Reducing the required storage amount improves cache locality and minimizes memory requirements. Both improvements are especially important in constrained devices. When analyzing the twiddle factor table, we realized that the real and imaginary parts of complex points are repeated multiple times because of the complex number negation, conjugation, and rotation. For example, complex roots of $x^8 + 1$ can be derived from a single complex root $a = (a_{re}, a_{im})$ to $[a, -a, -ia, ia]$ as the first half of the roots, and $[\hat{a}, -\hat{a}, -i\hat{a}, i\hat{a}]$ as the second half of the roots. It is notable that the second half is the *complex conjugate* of the first half, where $\hat{a} = conjugate(a) = (a_{re}, -a_{im})$. As a result, we only need to store $a = (a_{re}, a_{im})$

and use the add and subtract instructions to perform negation, conjugation, and rotation.

In summary, we fold the twiddle factor table by a factor of 2 by applying the *complex conjugate* to derive the second half from the first half. Furthermore, we use addition, subtraction, and rotation to derive the variants of complex roots within the first half, thus saving another factor of 2, as shown in Fig. 1. However, the FFT implementation in the reference implementation of Falcon no longer works with our new twiddle factor table (tw). As a result, we rewrite our FFT implementation in C to adopt our newly compressed twiddle factor table.

In general, we can compress complex roots from n down to $\frac{n}{4}$. In particular, when $n = 512, 1024$, the default twiddle factor table size is $16n$ bytes. With compressed twiddle factors, we only need to store $128, 256$ complex roots, and the table size becomes $4n$ bytes. A special case in $x^4 + 1$, when $a = (a_{re}, a_{im}) = (\sqrt{2}, \sqrt{2})$, thus we exploit the fact that $a_{re} = a_{im}$ to save multiply instructions by writing a separate loop at the beginning and end of Forward and Inverse FFT, respectively.

In Forward FFT, only the first half of the roots is used, while in Inverse FFT, only the second half is used.

Our Iterative SIMD FFT. Many FFT implementations prefer a recursive approach for high degree $N \geq 2^{13}$ [13,24], as it is more memory cache-friendly than the iterative approach. First, we decided to avoid using a vendor-specific library to maintain high portability. Secondly, we gave preference to an iterative approach to avoid function call overheads (since Falcon's $N \leq 1024$) and scheduling overheads for irregular butterfly patterns. Thirdly, we must support our compressed twiddle factor since the cost of deriving complex roots is minimal. Lastly, we focused on simplicity, so our code could be deployed and implemented on constrained devices and used as a starting point for hardware accelerator development.

In our literature search, we could not find either an FFT implementation or detailed algorithms fitting our needs. Hence, we wrote our own iterative FFT in C, then we vectorized our C FFT implementation. We are not aware of any published FFT implementation similar to our work.

5.2   Improved Forward FFT Implementation

Similar to NTT, we use Cooley-Tukey butterflies in Algorithms 5 and 6 to exploit the first half of the roots in Forward FFT. We rewrote the Forward FFT implementation, so each twiddle factor is always loaded once, and the program can take advantage of the cache spatial and temporal locality with constant access patterns when load and store instructions are executed. All the butterflies in Algorithm 9 are computed in place. Note that the two for loops from line 10 to 17 can be executed in parallel, which may be of interest when developing a hardware accelerator.

In a signature generation, at line 5 in Algorithm 1, Fast Fourier sampling (ffSampling) builds an FFT tree by traveling from the top level, $l = \log_2(N)$,

Algorithm 5: CT_BF	**Algorithm 6: CT_BF_90**
Input: a, b, ω	**Input:** a, b, ω
Output: $(a, b) = (a + \omega b, a - \omega b)$	**Output:** $(a, b) = (a + i\omega b, a - i\omega b)$
1 $t \leftarrow b * \omega$	1 $t \leftarrow b * (i\omega)$
2 $b \leftarrow a - t$	2 $b \leftarrow a - t$
3 $a \leftarrow a + t$	3 $a \leftarrow a + t$

Algorithm 7: GS_BF	**Algorithm 8: GS_BF_270**
Input: a, b, ω	**Input:** a, b, ω
Output: $(a, b) = (a + b, (a - b)\hat{\omega})$	**Output:** $(a, b) = (a + b, (a - b)i\hat{\omega})$
1 $t \leftarrow a - b$	1 $t \leftarrow b - a$ ▷ avoid negation
2 $a \leftarrow a + b$	2 $a \leftarrow a + b$
3 $b \leftarrow t * conjugate(\omega)$	3 $b \leftarrow t * conjugate(-i\omega)$

to the lower level $l-1, l-2, \ldots 1$, where N is a total number of real and imaginary points. Hence, FFT implementation must support all FFT levels from $\log_2(N)$ to 1.

Our C FFT implementation supports all levels of Forward and Inverse FFT trivially. However, our vectorized FFT must be tailored to support all FFT levels. Instead of vectorizing $l-1$ FFT implementations, first, we determined the maximum number of coefficients that can be computed using 32 vector registers. Then, we select $l = 5$ as the baseline to compute FFT that only uses one load and store per coefficient. To scale up to $l - 1$ FFT levels, we apply #FFT levels $= 5 + 2 \cdot x + 1 \cdot y$ where $2 \cdot x$ supports multiple of 2 FFT levels with x load and store per coefficient, and $1 \cdot y$ supports a single FFT level, we aim to minimize y to minimize load and store, thus $y \in \{0, 1\}$. In case $l < 5$, we unroll the FFT loop completely, and save instructions overhead. When $l \geq 5$, we use the base loop with $l = 5$ with 32 64-bit coefficients and implement two additional FFT loops. The second loop computes two FFT levels per iteration to save load and store instructions. The third loop is an unrolled version of a single FFT level per iteration. For example, when $N = 2^l = 2^{10}$, applied the formula above, $l = 5 \cdot \underline{1} + 2 \cdot \underline{2} + 1 \cdot \underline{1}$, in total, each coefficient is loaded and stored $4 = \underline{1} + \underline{2} + \underline{1}$ times.

In short, using three FFT loops, we can construct arbitrary FFT level $l \geq 5$ by using the base loop with 5 levels, then a multiple of two FFT levels by the second loop. Finally, the remaining FFT levels are handled by the third loop.

5.3   Improved Inverse FFT Implementation

The butterflies in Inverse FFT in Algorithm 7 and Algorithm 8 exploit complex *conjugate* by using add and subtract instructions. A tweak at no cost in line 1 of Algorithm 8 to avoid floating-point negation instruction **fneg** in line 3. Similar to Forward FFT, two loops from line 6 to 13 in Algorithm 10 can be

---

Algorithm 9: In-place cache-friendly Forward FFT (`split` storage)

Input: Polynomial $f \in \mathbb{Q}[x]/(x^{N/2} + 1)$, twiddle factor table `tw`
Output: $f = \text{FFT}(f)$

1   $\omega \leftarrow \text{tw}[0][0]$
2   **for** $j = 0$ **to** $N/4 - 1$ **do**
3     $\text{CT\_BF}(f[j], f[j + N/4], \omega)$ $\triangleright$ exploit $\omega_{re} = \omega_{im}$
4     $j \leftarrow j + 1$
5   $level \leftarrow 1$
6   **for** $len = N/8$ **to** 1 **do**
7     $k \leftarrow 0$ $\triangleright$ reset k at new $level$
8   **for** $s = 0$ **to** $N/2 - 1$ **do**
9       $\omega \leftarrow \text{tw}[level][k]$ $\triangleright$ ω is shared between two loops
10   **for** $j = s$ **to** $s + len - 1$ **do**
11         $\text{CT\_BF}(f[j], f[j + len], \omega)$
12         $j \leftarrow j + 1$
13       $s \leftarrow s + (len \ll 1)$ **for** $j = s$ **to** $s + len - 1$ **do**
14         $\text{CT\_BF\_90}(f[j], f[j + len], \omega)$
15         $j \leftarrow j + 1$
16       $s \leftarrow s + (len \ll 1)$
17       $k \leftarrow k + 1$ $\triangleright$ increase by *one* point
18     $level \leftarrow level + 1$ $\triangleright$ increase $level$
19     $len \leftarrow len \gg 1$ $\triangleright$ half distance

---

Algorithm 10: In-place cache-friendly Inverse FFT (`split` storage)

Input: Polynomial $f \in \mathbb{Q}[x]/(x^{N/2} + 1)$, twiddle factor table `tw`
Output: $f = \text{invFFT}(f)$

1   $level \leftarrow \log_2(N) - 2$ $\triangleright$ `tw` index starts at 0, and N/2 *re, im* points
2   **for** $len = 1$ **to** $N/8$ **do**
3     $k \leftarrow 0$ $\triangleright$ reset k at new $level$
4   **for** $s = 0$ **to** $N/2 - 1$ **do**
5       $\omega \leftarrow \text{tw}[level][k]$ $\triangleright$ ω is shared between two loops
6   **for** $j = s$ **to** $s + len - 1$ **do**
7         $\text{GS\_BF}(f[j], f[j + len], \omega)$
8         $j \leftarrow j + 1$
9       $s \leftarrow s + (len \ll 1)$
10   **for** $j = s$ **to** $s + len - 1$ **do**
11         $\text{GS\_BF\_270}(f[j], f[j + len], \omega)$
12         $j \leftarrow j + 1$
13       $s \leftarrow s + (len \ll 1)$
14       $k \leftarrow k + 1$ $\triangleright$ increase by *one* point
15     $level \leftarrow level - 1$ $\triangleright$ decrease $level$
16     $len \leftarrow len \ll 1$ $\triangleright$ double distance
17   $\omega \leftarrow \text{tw}[0][0] \cdot \frac{2}{N}$
18   **for** $j = 0$ **to** $N/4 - 1$ **do**
19     $\text{GS\_BF}(f[j], f[j + N/4], \omega)$ $\triangleright$ exploit $\omega_{re} = \omega_{im}$
20     $f[j] \leftarrow f[j] \cdot \frac{2}{N}$
21     $j \leftarrow j + 1$

executed in parallel and share the same twiddle factor ω. The last loop from line 17 to 21 multiplies $\frac{2}{N}$ by all coefficients of FFT, and exploits the special case of twiddle factor $\omega_{re} = \omega_{im}$. We also employ three FFT loop settings as described in Forward FFT to implement vectorized multi-level l of Inverse FFT to maximize vector registers usage, hence improving execution time. Note that butterflies in Algorithm 10 are computed in place.

5.4   Floating-Point Complex Instructions and Data Storage

ARMv8.3 supports two floating-point complex instructions: `fcadd` and `fcmla`. The floating-point complex `fcadd` instruction offers addition and counterclockwise rotation by 90 and 270°: $(a + ib)$ and $(a - ib)$. The combination of `fmul` and `fcmla` instructions can perform complex point multiplication $(a * b), (a * \hat{b})$, as shown in lines 1 and 3 of Algorithms 5 and 7 by applying counterclockwise rotation by 90 and 270°, respectively. Note that `fcmla` has the same cycle count as `fmla, fmls`.

The floating-point complex instructions offer a convenient way to compute *single pair* complex multiplications. Conversely, the `fmla, fmls` instructions require at least *two pairs* for complex multiplication. The only difference between floating-point complex instructions and traditional multiplication instructions is the data storage of real and imaginary values during the multiplication.

Our first approach is to use floating-point complex `fmul, fcmla, fcadd` instructions, where real and imaginary values are stored adjacent in memory (`adj` storage). This data storage setting is also seen in other FFT libraries, such as FFTW [24], and FFTS [13]. Complex multiplications using such instructions are demonstrated in Fig. 2. The second approach uses default data storage in Falcon: real and imaginary values are split into two locations (`split` storage). The complex multiplication using `fmul, fmla, and fmls` instructions is shown at Fig. 3. in Appendix A.

To find the highest performance gain, we implemented vectorized versions of the first and second approaches mentioned above. The former approach offers better cache locality for small $l \leq 4$. However, it introduces a vector permutation overhead to compute complex multiplication in lines 1 and 3 of Algorithms 6 and 8 using aforementioned floating-point complex instructions. Another disadvantage of the first approach is preventing the deployment of Falcon to devices that do not support ARMv8.3, such as Cortex-A53/A72 on Raspberry Pi 3/4, respectively. The latter approach can run on any ARMv8 platform. However, the second approach computes at least two complex point multiplications instead of one, and the pure C implementation is slightly faster compared to the original reference FFT implementation of Falcon. On the other hand, the pure C implementation of the first approach is slightly better than `split` storage in our experiment. We recommend using the first approach (`adj` storage) for non-vectorized implementation.

Eventually, we chose the second approach as our best-vectorized implementation and kept the reference implementation of the first approach in our code base for community interest. For $l \leq 2$, we unroll the loop, so the multiplication is done by scalar multiplication. By rearranging vector registers appropriately using LD2, LD4, ST2, ST4 instructions, when $l \geq 3$, the latter approach is slightly faster than the first approach when benchmarked on the high-end Apple M1 CPU.

5.5   Floating-Point to Integer Conversion

Notably, both GCC and Clang can generate native floating-point to integer conversion instructions during compilation. These instructions include fpr_floor, fpr_trunc using rounding toward zero instruction fcvtzs except for fpr_rint function. As described in the 64-bit floating-point to 64-bit signed integer fpr_rint implementation (a constant time conversion written in C), the obtained assembly language code generated by Clang and GCC, respectively, is not consistent and does not address constant-time concerns described in Howe et al. [25]. In our implementation on an aarch64 ARMv8, we use the rounding to the nearest with ties to even instruction fcvtns to convert a 64-bit floating-point to a 64-bit signed integer[2]. This single instruction, used to replace the whole fpr_rint implementation, costs 3 cycles on Cortex-A72/A78.

5.6   Rounding Concern in Floating-Point Fused Multiply-Add

Another concern while implementing vectorized code is floating-point rounding [4]. In ref implementation, when using the independent multiply (fmul) and add (fadd, fsub) instructions, the floating-point rounding occurs after multiplication and after addition. In the neon implementation, when we use Fused Multiply-Add instruction (fmla, fmls), the rounding is applied only after addition.

When we repeat our experiment with fpr_expm_p63 function used in Gaussian sampling to observe the rounding of fmla and (fmul, fadd), the differences between them grow. In our experiment, we sample random values as input to fpr_expm_p63 function on both Apple M1 and Cortex-A72, the differences are consistent in both CPUs[3], about 7,000 out of 100,000 output values of fpr_expm_63 function with fmla are different from (fmul, fadd).

We have carefully tested our implementation according to the test vectors and KATs (Known-Answer-Tests) provided by Falcon submitters. Although all tests passed, the security of the floating-point rounding differences in ARMv8 is unknown. Therefore, by default, our code uses the independent multiply (fmul) and add (fadd, fsub) instructions. We chose to optionally enable fmla instructions for benchmarking purposes only and observed negligible differences $3 \rightarrow 4\%$ between the two approaches in terms of the total execution time for the Sign operation, as shown in Table 2.

---

[2] https://godbolt.org/z/esP78P33b.
[3] https://godbolt.org/z/613vvzh3Y.

Table 2. Performance of Signature generation with Fused Multiply-Add instructions *enabled* (`fmla`), and *disabled* (`fmul`, `fadd`). Results are in *kc - kilocycles*.

CPU	neon Sign	(fmul, fadd)	fmla	fmla/(fmul, fadd)
Cortex-A72	falcon512	1,038.14	1,000.31	0.964
	falcon1024	2,132.08	2,046.53	0.960
Apple M1	falcon512	459.19	445.91	0.971
	falcon1024	914.91	885.63	0.968

6   Results

ARMv8 Intrinsics. are used for ease of implementation and to take advantage of the compiler optimizers. The optimizers know how intrinsics behave and tune performance toward the processor features such as aligning buffers, scheduling pipeline operations, and instruction ordering[4]. In our implementation, we always keep vector register usage under 32 and examine assembly language code obtained during our development process. We acknowledge that the compiler occasionally spills data from registers to memory and hides load/store latency through the instructions supporting pipelining.

Falcon, Hawk, and Dilithium. The reference implementation of Hawk[5] uses a fixed-point data type by default. Since our choice of processors supports floating-point arithmetic, we convert all fixed-point arithmetic to floating-point arithmetic and achieve a significant performance boost in reference implementation as compared to the default setting. Notably, this choice disables NTT implementation in Hawk Sign and Verify, while Falcon Verify explicitly uses integer arithmetic for NTT implementation by default. Although it is possible to vectorize NTT implementation in Hawk Verify, we consider this as future work. In both implementations, we measure the Sign operations in the dynamic signing - the secret key is expanded before signing, and we do not use floating-point emulation options. For Dilithium, we select the state-of-the-art ARMv8 implementation from Becker et al. [6].

XMSS, SPHINCS⁺. To construct a comprehensive digital signature comparison, we select the XMSS implementation[6] with the forward security by Buchmann et al. [15], which limited the way one-time signature keys are computed to enhance security. We accelerate SHA-256 by applying the OpenSSL SHA2-NI instruction set extensions in our **neon** implementation. For SPHINCS⁺, we select *s*, *f*-variant and 'simple' instantiation to compare with lattice-based signatures. Recent work by Becker et al. [7] proposed multiple settings to accelerate

---

[4] https://godbolt.org/z/zPr94YjYr.

[5] https://github.com/ludopulles/hawk-sign/.

[6] https://github.com/GMUCERG/xmssfs.

Keccak-f1600, combine with scalar, neon and SHA3 instructions. To make sure our hash-based signature is up-to-date, we measure and apply the best settings on Apple M1 to yield our best result for a hash-based signature.

The optimized implementation of SPHINCS[+7] already included high-speed Keccak-F1600×2 neon implementation. For both, the ref implementation is a pure C hash implementation.

Constant-Time Treatment. For operations that use floating-point arithmetic extensively, we use vectorized division instruction as in the reference implementation [37]. In Falcon **Verify**, there is only integer arithmetic. Thus, the division is replaced by modular multiplication. In both operations, secret data is not used in branch conditions or memory access patterns.

Benchmarking Setup. Our benchmarking setup for ARMv8 implementations included MacBook Air with Apple M1 @ 3.2 GHz, Jetson AGX Xavier @ 1.9 Ghz, and Raspberry Pi 4 with Cortex-A72 @ 1.8 GHz. For AVX2 implementations, we used a PC based on Intel 11th gen i7-1165G7 @ 2.8 GHz with Spectre and Meltdown mitigations disabled via a kernel parameter[8].

For cycle count on Cortex-A72, we used the pqax[9] framework . In Apple M1, we rewrote the work from Dougall Johnson[10] to perform cycle count[11]. On both platforms, we use Clang 13 with -O3, we let the compiler to do its best to vectorize pure C implementations, denoted as ref to fairly compare them with our neon implementations. Thus, we did not employ -fno-tree-vectorize option. We acknowledge that compiler automatically enables Fuse Multiply-Add to improve performance. Explicitly on Jetson AGX Xavier, we use Clang 6.0 and count cycle using similar method in the work of Seo et al. [38].

We report the average cycle count of 1,000 and 10,000 executions for hash-based and lattice-based signatures, respectively. Benchmarking is conducted using a single core and a single thread to fairly compare results with those obtained for lattice-based signatures, even though hash-based signatures can execute multiple hash operations in parallel.

Results for FFT and NTT. are summarized in Table 3 with FMA *enabled*. When $N \leq 4$, we realized that our vectorized code runs slower than the C implementation due to the FFT vectorized code being too short. Therefore, we use unroll ref implementation when $N \leq 4$, and neon for $N \geq 8$. In Table 3, when $N \geq 128$, our vectorized FFT achieved speed-up $1.9\times \rightarrow 2.3\times$ and $2.1\times \rightarrow 2.4\times$ compared to the ref implementation of the Forward and Inverse FFT on

---

[7] https://github.com/sphincs/sphincsplus.

[8] mitigations=off https://make-linux-fast-again.com/.

[9] https://github.com/mupq/pqax/tree/main/enable_ccr.

[10] https://github.com/dougallj.

[11] https://github.com/GMUCERG/PQC_NEON/blob/main/neon/kyber/m1cycles.c.

Table 3. Cycle counts for the implementation of FFT (with FMA *enabled*) and NTT with the size of N coefficients on Apple M1 and Cortex-A72 - neon vs. ref.

Apple M1	Forward FFT(*cycles*)			Inverse FFT(*cycles*)		
N	ref	neon	ref/neon	ref	neon	ref/neon
128	759	404	1.88	847	401	2.11
256	1,633	789	2.07	1,810	794	2.28
512	3,640	1,577	2.31	3,930	1,609	2.44
1024	7,998	3,489	2.29	8,541	3,547	2.41
	Forward NTT(*cycles*)			Inverse NTT(*cycles*)		
512	6,607	840	7.87	6,449	811^n	7.95
1024	13,783	1,693	8.14	13,335	$1,702^n$	7.83
Cortex-A72	Forward FFT(*cycles*)			Inverse FFT(*cycles*)		
N	ref	neon	ref/neon	ref	neon	ref/neon
128	2,529	1,155	2.19	2,799	1,216	2.30
256	5,474	2,770	1.98	6,037	2,913	2.07
512	11,807	5,951	1.98	13,136	6,135	2.14
1024	27,366	14,060	1.95	28,151	14,705	1.91
	Forward NTT(*cycles*)			Inverse NTT(*cycles*)		
512	22,582	3,561	6.34	22,251	$3,563^n$	6.25
1024	48,097	7,688	6.26	47,196	$7,872^n$	6.00
Intel i7-1165G7	Forward FFT(*cycles*)			Inverse FFT(*cycles*)		
N	REF	AVX2	REF/AVX2	REF	AVX2	REF/AVX2
128	787	481	1.64	873	499	1.75
256	1,640	966	1.70	1,798	1,024	1.76
512	3,486	2,040	1.71	3,790	2,138	1.77
1024	7,341	4,370	1.68	7,961	4,572	1.74

^{n} no multiplication with n^{-1} at the end of Inverse NTT

Apple M1, and $2.2\times \rightarrow 1.9\times$ in Forward and $2.3\times \rightarrow 1.9\times$ in Inverse FFT on Cortex-A72. These speed-ups are due to our unrolled vectorized implementation of FFT, which supports multiple FFT levels and twiddle-factor sharing.

In Falcon Verify, our benchmark of Inverse NTT is without multiplication by n^{-1} because we already embed this multiplication during Montgomery conversion. We achieve speed-up by $6.0\times$ and $7.8\times$ for NTT operations on Cortex-A72 and Apple M1, respectively. For both FFT and NTT, our neon implementation in both Cortex-A72 and Apple M1 achieve better speed-up ratio than the AVX2 implementation, as shown in Table 3. There is no AVX2 optimized implementation of Falcon Verify, it is the same as pure REF implementation. Overall, our neon NTT implementation is greatly improved compared to ref implementation, which determines the overall speed-up in Falcon Verify.

Comparison with Previous Work. As shown in Table 4, on the same platform, Jetson AGX Xavier, our NEON-based implementation of Falcon is consistently faster than the the implementation by Kim et al. [31]. The achieved

Table 4. Comparison with previous work by Kim et al. [31] on Jetson AGX Xavier. Additional results for Apple M1 and Raspberry Pi 4. Notation: *kc*-kilocycles.

| | Jetson AGX Xavier | | | | | |
| | ref(kc) | | neon(kc) | | ref/neon | |
	S	V	S	V	S	V
falcon512 [31]	580.7	48.0	498.6	29.0	1.16	1.65
falcon512 (Ours)	582.3	44.1	336.6	19.1	_1.73_	_2.31_
falcon1024 [31]	1,159.6	106.0	990.5	62.5	1.17	1.69
falcon1024 (Ours)	1,151.2	93.2	671.2	36.7	_1.72_	_2.54_
	Apple M1					
falcon512 (Ours)	654.0	43.5	442.0	22.7	1.48	1.92
falcon1024 (Ours)	1,310.8	89.3	882.1	42.9	1.49	2.08
	Raspberry Pi 4					
falcon512 (Ours)	1,490.7	126.3	1,001.9	58.8	1.49	2.15
falcon1024 (Ours)	3,084.8	274.3	2,048.9	130.4	1.51	2.10

speed-up vs. [31] is 1.48× for signing in `falcon512` and `falcon1024`, 1.52× for verifying in `falcon512`, and 1.70× for verifying in `falcon1024`.

In a signature generation, as compared to the Kim et al. [31] approach, we decided against replacing macro functions `FPC_MUL`, `FPC_DIV`, etc. Our manual work of unrolled versions of the Forward and Inverse FFT, as well as `splitfft`, `mergefft`, `mulfft`, etc. contribute to greatly improving the performance of Falcon. We also modify the code logic to reduce calling `memcpy` functions during operation and sharing twiddle factors, which greatly reduces memory load and store overhead. In signature verification, our NTT speed-up is 6.2× and 6.0× with respect to `ref` implementation for Forward and Inverse NTT, as shown in Table 3, while Kim et al. [31] only achieve less than 3× speed-up. The significant speed-up is accomplished due to our signed-integer implementation of NTT, with values centered around 0, while previous work used unsigned integer NTT.

Falcon and Dilithium. In Table 5, we rank our implementations with respect to the state-of-the-art CRYSTALS-Dilithium implementation from Becker et al. [6] across all security levels. Please note that in the top rows, only DILITHIUM2, XMSS[16]-SHA256 have security level 2, while the rest algorithms have security level 1. For all security levels of Falcon and Dilithium, when executed over messages of the size of 59 bytes, for **S**ignature generation, Falcon is comparable with Dilithium in `ref` implementations. However, the landscape drastically changes in the optimized `neon` implementations. Dilithium has an execution time 2× smaller than Falcon at the lowest and highest security levels.

Table 5. Signature generation and **V**erification speed comparison (with FMA *disabled*) over three security levels, for a 59-byte message. **ref** and **neon** results for Apple M1. *kc*-kilocycles.

Apple-M1 3.2 GHz	NIST level	ref(*kc*)		neon(*kc*)		ref/neon	
		S	V	S	V	S	V
FALCON512	I, II	654.0	43.5	459.2	22.7	1.42	1.92
HAWK512		138.6	34.6	117.7	27.1	1.18	1.27
DILITHIUM2^b		741.1	199.6	224.1	69.8	3.31	2.86
XMSS^{16}-SHA256^x		26,044.3	2,879.4	4,804.2	531.0	5.42	5.42
SPHINCS$^+$128s^s		1,950,265.0	1,982.4	549,130.7	658.6	3.55	3.01
SPHINCS$^+$128f^s		93,853.9	5,483.8	26,505.3	1,731.2	3.54	3.16
DILITHIUM3^b		1,218.0	329.2	365.2	104.8	3.33	3.14
SPHINCS$^+$192s^s	III	3,367,415.5	2,753.1	950,869.9	893.2	3.54	3.08
SPHINCS$^+$192f^s		151,245.2	8,191.5	42,815.1	2,515.8	3.53	3.25
FALCON1024	V	1,310.8	89.3	915.0	42.9	1.43	2.08
HAWK1024		279.7	73.7	236.9	58.5	1.18	1.26
DILITHIUM5^b		1,531.1	557.7	426.6	167.5	3.59	3.33
SPHINCS$^+$256s^s		2,938,702.4	3,929.3	840,259.4	1,317.5	3.50	2.98
SPHINCS$^+$256f^s		311,034.3	8,242.5	88,498.9	2,593.8	3.51	3.17

^{b} the work from Becker et al. [6]
^{s} our benchmark SPHINCS$^+$ *'simple'* variants using Keccak-f1600
^{x} our benchmark XMSS^{16}-SHA256 using SHA2 Crypto instruction

The speed-up ratio of Dilithium in ARMv8 is 3.3× as compared to **ref** implementation. This result is due to the size of operands in the vectorized implementation. Dilithium uses 32-bit integers and parallel hashing SHAKE128/256. This leads to a higher speed-up ratio as compared to 64-bit floating-point operations, serial hashing using SHAKE256, and serial sampling in Falcon. Additionally, the computation cost of floating-point operations is higher than for integers. Hence, we only achieve 1.42× speed-up (with FMA *disable*) compared to the **ref** implementation for the signature generation operation in Falcon. Although there are no floating-point computations in Falcon **V**erify, our speed-up is smaller than for Dilithium due to the serial hashing using SHAKE256. We believe that if Falcon adopts parallel hashing and parallel sampling algorithms, its performance could be further improved.

In **V**erification across all security levels, Falcon is consistently faster than Dilithium by 3.0× to 3.9× in both **ref** and **neon** implementations.

Hawk vs. Falcon and Dilithium. At security levels 1 and 5, Hawk outperforms both Falcon and Dilithium in **ref** and **neon** implementations. The exception is the **neon** implementation of Falcon Verify due to two polynomial multiplications in Hawk instead of one in Falcon. An optimized **neon** implementation of Hawk Verify is unlikely to be faster than Falcon Verify, even if Hawk has optimized **neon** NTT implementation in its signature verification. The performance of Hawk versus Falcon and Dilithium in Sign are 3.9× and 1.9× faster, and in Verify are 0.8× and 2.5× faster for the **neon** implementation at security level 1. Our `neon` implementation of Hawk achieves a similar speed-up ratio as in the case of AVX2 implementations reported in Ducas et al. [21] (Table 1).

Lattice-Based Signatures vs. Hash-Based Signatures. Notably, in Table 5, the execution times of Falcon, Dilithium, and Hawk lattice-based signatures are shorter than for XMSS and SPHINCS$^+$ hash-based signatures by orders of magnitude in both `ref` and `neon` implementations. In Verification alone, Falcon is faster than XMSS and SPHINCS$^+$ by 23.4 to 28.8×. Similarly, the Dilithium verification is faster than for XMSS and SPHINCS$^+$ by 7.6 to 9.4×. The speed-up of hash-based signatures is higher than for lattice-based signatures, and it can be even greater if parallelism is fully exploited, e.g., through multithreading in CPUs or GPUs. These improvements are left for future work.

Lattice-Based Signature in Constrained Devices. In Table 6, we rank the Verfication performance of Falcon, Dilithium, and Hawk. Notably, our Hawk Verify uses floating-point arithmetic, while the signature Verifications of Falcon and Dilithium only require integer operations. We exclude hash-based signatures from this comparison due to their low performance already shown for high-speed processors in Table 5. Falcon Verify at security level 5 is faster than Dilithium at security levels 1 and 5 by 2.2× and 6.1×. Hawk outperforms Dilithium and is only slower than Falcon in Verify operation by 1.6× and 1.9× at the same security level. In combination with Table 1, it is obvious that Falcon is more efficient than Dilithium in terms of both bandwidth and workload.

Table 6. Signature generation and Verification speed comparison (with FMA *disabled*) over three security levels, signing a 59-byte message. Ranking over the Verification speed ratio. `ref` and `neon` results for Cortex-A72. *kc*-kilocycles.

Cortex-A72 1.8 GHz	NIST Level	ref (kc)		neon (kc)		ref/neon		
		S	V	S	V	S	V	V ratio
FALCON512	I, II	1,553.4	127.8	1,044.6	<u>59.9</u>	1.49	2.09	<u>1.0</u>
HAWK512		400.3	127.1	315.9	94.8	1.26	1.34	1.6
DILITHIUM2^b		1,353.8	449.6	649.2	272.8	2.09	1.65	4.5
DILITHIUM3^b	III	2,308.6	728.9	1,089.4	447.5	2.12	1.63	-
FALCON1024	V	3,193.0	272.1	2,137.0	<u>125.2</u>	1.49	2.17	<u>1.0</u>
HAWK1024		822.1	300.0	655.2	236.9	1.25	1.27	1.9
DILITHIUM5^b		2,903.6	1,198.7	1,437.0	764.9	2.02	1.57	6.1

^{b} the work from Becker et al. [6]

7   Conclusions

Falcon is the only PQC digital signature scheme selected by NIST for standardization using floating-point operations. Unless significant changes are introduced to Falcon, floating-point instructions required in Key generation and Sign operations will continue to be a key limitation of Falcon deployment. Additionally, the complexity of serial sampling and serial hashing significantly reduces the performance of Falcon Key and Signature generation. We demonstrate that Hawk outperforms Dilithium and has a faster Signature than Falcon. Its performance and bandwidth may be interesting to the community.

In summary, we report the new speed record for Falcon Sign and Verify operations using NEON-based instruction on Cortex-A72 and Apple M1 ARMv8 devices. We present a comprehensive comparison in terms of performance and bandwidth for Falcon, CRYSTALS-Dilithium, XMSS, and SPHINCS$^+$ on both aforementioned devices. We believe that in some constrained protocol scenarios, where bandwidth and verification performance matter, Falcon is the better option than Dilithium, and lattice-based signatures are a far better choice than hash-based signatures in terms of key size and efficiency.

Lastly, we present a 7% mismatch between the Fuse Multiply-Add instructions on ARMv8 platforms. We recommend disabling the Fuse Multiply-Add instruction to guarantee implementation correctness. Further security analysis of this behavior is needed.

Acknowledgments. This work has been partially supported by the National Science Foundation under Grant No.: CNS-1801512 and by the US Department of Commerce (NIST) under Grant No.: 70NANB18H218.

A   Visualizing Complex Point Multiplication

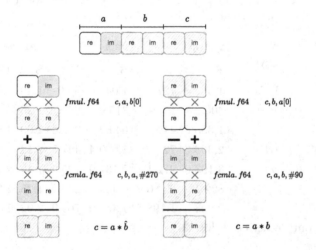

Fig. 2. Single pair complex multiplication using `fmul`, `fcmla`. Real and imagine points are stored adjacently.

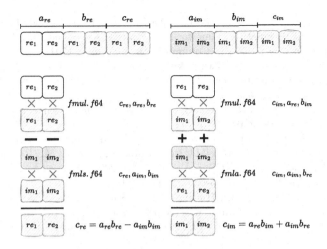

Fig. 3. Two pairs complex multiplication using `fmul`, `fmls`, `fmla`. Real and imagine points are stored separately.

References

1. Abdulrahman, A., Hwang, V., Kannwischer, M.J., Sprenkels, D.: Faster kyber and dilithium on the Cortex-M4. In: Ateniese, G., Venturi, D. (eds.) Applied Cryptography and Network Security, ACNS 2022. Lecture Notes in Computer Science, vol. 13269, pp. 853–871. Springer, Cham (2022). https://doi.org/10.1007/978-3-031-09234-3_42

2. Alagic, G., et al.: Status report on the third round of the NIST post-quantum cryptography standardization process (2022)

3. Alkim, E., Bilgin, Y.A., Cenk, M., Gérard, F.: Cortex-M4 optimizations for R, MLWE schemes. IACR TCHES **2020**(3), 336–357 (2020)

4. Andrysco, M., Nötzli, A., Brown, F., Jhala, R., Stefan, D.: Towards verified, constant-time floating point operations. In: ACM CCS 2018, pp. 1369–1382 (2018)

5. Bai, S., et al.: CRYSTALS-Dilithium: Algorithm Specifications and Supporting Documentation (Version 3.1) (2021)

6. Becker, H., Hwang, V., Kannwischer, M.J., Yang, B.Y., Yang, S.Y.: Neon NTT: faster dilithium, kyber, and saber on cortex-A72 and apple M1. IACR TCHES **1**, 221–244 (2022)

7. Becker, H., Kannwischer, M.J.: Hybrid scalar/vector implementations of Keccak and SPHINCS+ on AArch64. Cryptology ePrint Archive, Report 2022/1243

8. Becker, H., Mera, J.M.B., Karmakar, A., Yiu, J., Verbauwhede, I.: Polynomial multiplication on embedded vector architectures. IACR TCHES **2022**(1), 482–505 (2022)

9. Becoulet, A., Verguet, A.: A depth-first iterative algorithm for the conjugate pair fast Fourier transform. IEEE Trans. Sig. Process. **69**, 1537–1547 (2021). https://doi.org/10.1109/TSP.2021.3060279

10. Bennett, H., Ganju, A., Peetathawatchai, P., Stephens-Davidowitz, N.: Just how hard are rotations of $\mathbb{Z}^n$? Algorithms and cryptography with the simplest lattice. Cryptology ePrint Archive, Report 2021/1548 (2021)

11. Bernstein, D.J., Hülsing, A., Kölbl, S., Niederhagen, R., Rijneveld, J., Schwabe, P.: The SPHINCS+ signature framework. In: Proceedings of the 2019 ACM SIGSAC Conference on Computer and Communications Security (2019)
12. Bindel, N., McCarthy, S., Twardokus, G., Rahbari, H.: Drive (Quantum) safe! - towards post-quantum security for V2V communications. Cryptology ePrint Archive, Paper 2022/483 (2022)
13. Blake, A.M., Witten, I.H., Cree, M.J.: The fastest Fourier transform in the south. IEEE Trans. Sig. Proc. **61**, 4707–4716 (2013)
14. Botros, L., Kannwischer, M.J., Schwabe, P.: Memory-efficient high-speed implementation of Kyber on Cortex-M4. In: Buchmann, J., Nitaj, A., Rachidi, T. (eds.) AFRICACRYPT 2019. LNCS, vol. 11627, pp. 209–228. Springer, Cham (2019). https://doi.org/10.1007/978-3-030-23696-0_11
15. Buchmann, J., Dahmen, E., Hülsing, A.: XMSS - a practical forward secure signature scheme based on minimal security assumptions. In: Yang, B.-Y. (ed.) PQCrypto 2011. LNCS, vol. 7071, pp. 117–129. Springer, Heidelberg (2011). https://doi.org/10.1007/978-3-642-25405-5_8
16. Chen, L., et al.: Report on post-quantum cryptography. Technical Report. NIST IR 8105, National Institute of Standards and Technology (2016)
17. Chung, C.M.M., Hwang, V., Kannwischer, M.J., Seiler, G., Shih, C.J., Yang, B.Y.: NTT multiplication for NTT-unfriendly rings: new speed records for saber and NTRU on Cortex-M4 and AVX2. IACR Trans. Cryptographic Hardw. Embed. Syst. **2021**(2), 159–188 (2021)
18. Cooley, J.W., Tukey, J.W.: An algorithm for the machine calculation of complex Fourier series. Math. Comput. **19**, 297–301 (1965)
19. Cooper, D.A., et al.: Recommendation for stateful hash-based signature schemes. NIST Spec. Publ. SP **800**, 208 (2020)
20. Dagdelen, Ö., Fischlin, M., Gagliardoni, T.: The Fiat–Shamir transformation in a quantum world. In: Sako, K., Sarkar, P. (eds.) ASIACRYPT 2013. LNCS, vol. 8270, pp. 62–81. Springer, Heidelberg (2013). https://doi.org/10.1007/978-3-642-42045-0_4
21. Ducas, L., Postlethwaite, E.W., Pulles, L.N., van Woerden, W.: Hawk: module LIP makes lattice signatures fast, compact and simple. Cryptology ePrint Archive, Report 2022/1155 (2022). https://eprint.iacr.org/2022/1155
22. Ducas, L., van Woerden, W.P.J.: On the lattice isomorphism problem, quadratic forms, remarkable lattices, and cryptography. In: Dunkelman, O., Dziembowski, S. (eds.) EUROCRYPT 2022, Part III. Lecture Notes in Computer Science, vol. 13277, pp. 643–673. Springer, Cham (2022). https://doi.org/10.1007/978-3-031-07082-2_23
23. Fouque, P.A., et al.: Falcon: Fast-Fourier Lattice-based Compact Signatures over NTRU: Specifications v1.2 (2020)
24. Frigo, M., Johnson, S.G.: FFTW: fastest Fourier transform in the west. Astrophysics Source Code Library, pp. ascl-1201 (2012)
25. Howe, J., Westerbaan, B.: Benchmarking and Analysing the NIST PQC Finalist Lattice-Based Signature Schemes on the ARM Cortex M7. Cryptology ePrint Archive, Paper 2022/405 (2022)
26. Huelsing, A., Butin, D., Gazdag, S.L., Rijneveld, J., Mohaisen, A.: XMSS: eXtended Merkle Signature Scheme. RFC 8391 (2018). https://www.rfc-editor.org/info/rfc8391

27. Hülsing, A.: W-OTS+ – shorter signatures for hash-based signature schemes. In: Youssef, A., Nitaj, A., Hassanien, A.E. (eds.) AFRICACRYPT 2013. LNCS, vol. 7918, pp. 173–188. Springer, Heidelberg (2013). https://doi.org/10.1007/978-3-642-38553-7_10

28. Jalali, A., Azarderakhsh, R., Mozaffari Kermani, M., Campagna, M., Jao, D.: ARMv8 SIKE: optimized supersingular isogeny key encapsulation on ARMv8 processors. IEEE Trans. Circ. Syst. I: Regul. Pap. **66**, 4209–4218 (2019)

29. Kannwischer, M.J., Petri, R., Rijneveld, J., Schwabe, P., Stoffelen, K.: PQM4: post-quantum crypto library for the ARM Cortex-M4. https://github.com/mupq/pqm4

30. Karmakar, A., Bermudo Mera, J.M., Sinha Roy, S., Verbauwhede, I.: Saber on ARM. IACR Trans. Cryptographic Hardw. Embed. Syst. **2018**(3), 243–266 (2018)

31. Kim, Y., Song, J., Seo, S.C.: Accelerating falcon on ARMv8. IEEE Access **10**, 44446–44460 (2022). https://doi.org/10.1109/ACCESS.2022.3169784

32. Kwon, H., et al.: ARMed Frodo. In: Kim, H. (ed.) WISA 2021. LNCS, vol. 13009, pp. 206–217. Springer, Cham (2021). https://doi.org/10.1007/978-3-030-89432-0_17

33. Lyubashevsky, V.: Fiat-Shamir with aborts: applications to lattice and factoring-based signatures. In: Matsui, M. (ed.) ASIACRYPT 2009. LNCS, vol. 5912, pp. 598–616. Springer, Heidelberg (2009). https://doi.org/10.1007/978-3-642-10366-7_35

34. McGrew, D., Curcio, M., Fluhrer, S.: RFC 8554: Leighton-Micali hash-based signatures (2019). https://www.rfc-editor.org/rfc/rfc8554

35. Nguyen, D.T., Gaj, K.: Fast NEON-based multiplication for lattice-based NIST post-quantum cryptography finalists. In: Cheon, J.H., Tillich, J.-P. (eds.) PQCrypto 2021 2021. LNCS, vol. 12841, pp. 234–254. Springer, Cham (2021). https://doi.org/10.1007/978-3-030-81293-5_13

36. Nguyen, D.T., Gaj, K.: Optimized software implementations of CRYSTALS-Kyber, NTRU, and Saber using NEON-based special instructions of ARMv8. In: Proceedings of the NIST 3rd PQC Standardization Conference (NIST PQC 2021) (2021)

37. Pornin, T.: New Efficient, Constant-Time Implementations of Falcon. Cryptology ePrint Archive, Report 2019/893 (2019). https://eprint.iacr.org/2019/893

38. Seo, H., Sanal, P., Jalali, A., Azarderakhsh, R.: Optimized implementation of SIKE round 2 on 64-bit ARM Cortex-A processors. IEEE Trans. Circuits Syst. I Regul. Pap. **67**(8), 2659–2671 (2020)

39. Shor, P.: Algorithms for quantum computation: discrete logarithms and factoring. In: Proceedings 35th Annual Symposium on Foundations of Computer Science, pp. 124–134. IEEE Computer Society Press, Santa Fe, NM, USA (1994)

40. Streit, S., De Santis, F.: Post-quantum key exchange on ARMv8-A: a new hope for NEON made simple. IEEE Trans. Comput. **11**, 1651–1662 (2018)

41. Zhao, L., Zhang, J., Huang, J., Liu, Z., Hancke, G.: Efficient Implementation of kyber on Mobile devices. In: 2021 IEEE 27th International Conference on Parallel and Distributed Systems (ICPADS), pp. 506–513

Benchmarking and Analysing the NIST PQC Lattice-Based Signature Schemes Standards on the ARM Cortex M7

James Howe[1]([✉])[iD] and Bas Westerbaan[2][iD]

[1] SandboxAQ, Palo Alto, USA
james.howe@sandboxaq.com
[2] Cloudflare, Amsterdam, The Netherlands
bas@westerbaan.name

Abstract. This paper presents an analysis of the two lattice-based digital signature schemes, Dilithium and Falcon, which have been chosen by NIST for standardisation, on the ARM Cortex M7 using the STM32F767ZI NUCLEO-144 development board. This research is motivated by the ARM Cortex M7 device being the only processor in the Cortex-M family to offer a double precision (i.e., 64-bit) floating-point unit, making Falcon's implementations, requiring 53 bits of double precision, able to fully run native floating-point operations without any emulation. When benchmarking natively, Falcon shows significant speed-ups between 6.2–8.3x in clock cycles, 6.2–11.8x in runtime, and Dilithium does not show much improvement other than those gained by the slightly faster processor. We then present profiling results of the two schemes on the ARM Cortex M7 to show their respective bottlenecks and operations where the improvements are and can be made. This demonstrates, for example, that some operations in Falcon's procedures observe speed-ups by an order of magnitude. Finally, since Falcon's use of floating points is so rare in cryptography, we test the native FPU instructions on 4 different STM32 development boards with the ARM Cortex M7 and also a Raspberry Pi 3 which is used in some of Falcon's official benchmarking results. We find constant-time irregularities in all of these devices, which makes Falcon insecure on these devices for applications where signature generation can be timed by an attacker.

1 Introduction

Since NIST began their Post-Quantum Cryptography (PQC) Standardization Project [NIST15] there have been a number of instances where they have called for benchmarking and evaluations of the candidates on differing hardware platforms [NIST16, AAAS+19, AASA+20]. This prompted research into implementing these schemes on a variety of platforms in software, for example see PQClean [PQClean], SUPERCOP [SupCop], liboqs [liboqs], and pqm4

B. Westerbaan–The research in this paper was carried out while employed at PQShield.

N. El Mrabet et al. (Eds.): AFRICACRYPT 2023, LNCS 14064, pp. 442–462, 2023.
https://doi.org/10.1007/978-3-031-37679-5_19

[pqm4], and also in hardware [RBG20, HOK+18, HMO+21, BUC19, BUC19, XL21, BUC19, RMJ+21, Mar20, KRR+20, RB20].

In July 2022, NIST announced in their Round 3 status report [AAC+22] that their first set of PQC standards; one Key Encapsulation Mechanism (KEM) called CRYSTALS-Kyber [SAB+20], and three digital signature schemes called CRYSTALS-Dilithium [LDK+20], Falcon [PFH+20], and SPHINCS+ [HBD+20], with three of the four of these being from the family of lattice-based cryptography.

In their Round 2 status report, NIST [AASA+20] encouraged "more scrutiny of Falcon's implementation to determine whether the use of floating-point arithmetic makes implementation errors more likely than other schemes or provides an avenue for side-channel attacks". In this paper we look to bridge this gap by adding benchmarking, profiling, and analysing Falcon and Dilithium on the ARM Cortex M7. We choose this specific microcontroller for two reasons. Firstly, as it is very similar to the ARM Cortex M4, which was chosen by NIST as the preferred benchmarking target to enable fair comparisons. Secondly, the ARM Cortex M7 is the only processor in the Cortex-M family to offer sufficient double floating-point instructions, via a 64-bit floating-point unit (FPU), useful to Falcon's key generation and signing procedures. This adds another important evaluation criteria to comparisons between the two lattice-based signature schemes, especially when considering Falcon using a FPU, and investigating whether or not it is safe to use this for constant run-time. We use publicly available[1] code from the Falcon submission package and we take the Dilithium implementation from pqm4.

Falcon's round 3 code, similar to the round 2 version [Por19], provides support for embedded targets (i.e., the ARM Cortex M4) which can use either custom emulated floating-point operations (`FALCON_FPEMU`) or native floating-point operations (`FALCON_FPNATIVE`). For Dilithium, we use the code available on the pqm4 repository (which performed better than the code on PQClean). Code designed for the Cortex M3 and Cortex M4 processors is compatible with the Cortex M7 processor as long as it does not rely on bit-banding [ARM18].

1.1 Contributions

In Sect. 3, we benchmark Dilithium and Falcon on the ARM Cortex M7 using the STM32F767ZI NUCLEO-144 development board, using 1,000 executions per scheme and providing minimum, average, and maximum clock cycles, standard deviation and standard error, and average runtime (in milliseconds). For Falcon, we provide benchmarks for key generation, sign dynamic, sign tree, verify, and expand private key operations. We provide these results for both native (double precision) and emulated floating-point operations and proving comparisons between these and those results publicly available on the ARM Cortex M4. We also provide results for Falcon-1024 sign tree, which does not fit on the Cortex M4.

---

[1] See https://falcon-sign.info/.

For Dilithium, we benchmark the code from the pqm4 repository and in the same manner provide comparative results of Cortex M4 vs M7 performances. We also provide results for Dilithium's highest parameter set, which does not fit on the Cortex M4.

In Sect. 4, we profile Dilithium and Falcon to find their performance bottlenecks on the ARM Cortex M7, providing averages using 1,000 executions of each scheme. Specifically for Falcon, we provide what operations and functions benefit from using the board's 64-bit FPU the most. Indeed, we compare the profiling results using the Cortex M7's FPU against the profiling results on the same board where floating-point operations are emulated (as it does on the ARM Cortex M4). For Dilithium, we cannot compare this way (since it does not require floating points) and so we provide plain profiling results.

The link to code used in this paper has been removed to maintain anonymity. The code will be made publicly available after publication.

2   Background

Dilithium and Falcon are the two lattice-based signature schemes selected by NIST as PQC standards, and two of the three overall signatures selected for standardization.

Dilithium is the primary signature scheme and is based on the Fiat–Shamir with aborts paradigm, with its hardness relying on the decisional module-LWE and module-SIS problems. Algorithm 1 in Appendix A shows Dilithium's key generation, sign, and verify algorithms. In the third round, Dilithium offered three parameter sets satisfying the NIST security levels 2, 3, and 5 for being at least as hard to break as SHA-256, AES-192, and AES-256, respectively. Dilithium benefits from using the same polynomial ring $(\mathbb{Z}_q[X]/(X^n + 1))$ with a fixed degree ($n = 256$) and modulus ($q = 8380417$) and only requires sampling from the uniform distribution, making its implementation significantly simpler than for Falcon. Dilithium's performance profile offers balance for the core operations (key generation, signing, and verifying) and also key and signature sizes. Furthermore, Dilithium can be implemented with a relatively small amount of RAM [GKS20].

Falcon is based on the hash-then-sign paradigm over lattices, with its hardness relying on the NTRU assumption. Algorithm 2 in Appendix B shows Falcon's key generation, sign, and verify algorithms. In the third round, Falcon offered two parameter sets (for degree $n = 512$ and 1024) satisfying the NIST security levels 1 and 5 for being as hard to break as AES-128 and AES-256. Compared with Dilithium, Falcon is significantly more complex; relying on sampling over non-uniform distributions, with floating-point operations, and using tree data structures. However, Falcon benefits from having much smaller public key and signature sizes, while having similar signing and verification times. For more information on the details of these schemes, the reader is pointed to the specifications of Dilithium [LDK+20] and Falcon [PFH+20].

We benchmark Dilithium and Falcon on a 32-bit ARM Cortex M7 to mainly observe how much faster these signature schemes are on this device, compared to the ARM Cortex M4, and more specifically, to see the performances of Falcon using the ARM Cortex M7's 64-bit FPU. NIST decided on the ARM Cortex M4[2] as the preferred microcontroller target in order to make comparisons between each candidate easier. The ARM Cortex M4 and M7 are fairly similar cores; the M7 has all the ISA features available in the M4. However, the M7 offers additional support for double-precision floating point, a six stage (vs. three stage on the M4) instruction pipeline, and memory features like cache and tightly coupled memory (TCM). More specific differences are that the M7 will have faster branch predicting, plus it has two units for reading data from memory making it twice that of the M4.

The evaluation board we used for the benchmarking and profiling in this paper is the STM32 Nucleo-144 development board with STM32F767ZI MCU[3] which implements the ARMv7E-M instruction set. This is the extension of ARMv7-M that supports DSP type instructions (e.g., SIMD). The development board has a maximum clock frequency of 216 MHz, 2 MB of flash memory, 512 KB of SRAM. On the Cortex M7, the floating point architecture is based on FPv5, rather than FPv4 in Cortex-M4, so it has a few additional floating point instructions. We later utilize three more STM32 development boards (STM32H743ZI, STM32H723ZG, and STM32F769I-DISCO) and a Raspberry Pi 3 in order to check the constant runtime of Falcon more thoroughly.

All results reported in this paper used the GNU ARM embedded toolchain 10-2020-q4-major, i.e. GCC version 10.2.1 20201103, using optimization flags `-O2 -mcpu=cortex-m7 -march= -march=armv7e-m+fpv5+fp.dp`. All clock cycle results were obtained using the integrated clock cycle counter (`DWT->CYCCNT`).

3   Benchmarking on ARM Cortex M7

This section presents the results of benchmarking Dilithium (Table 1) and Falcon (Table 2) on the ARM Cortex M7 using the STM32F767ZI NUCLEO-144 development board. The values presented in the following tables are iterated over 1,000 runs of the operation. As noted previously, we provide results that are not available on the Cortex M4; Falcon-1024 sign tree and Dilithium for parameter set five.

The tables report minimum, average, and maximum clock cycles, as well as the standard deviation and standard error of the clock cycles, and the overall runtime in milliseconds clocked at 216 MHz. We run these benchmarks for each scheme's operation (e.g., verify) and for all parameter sets. Below each benchmarking row is a metric comparing the results on the Cortex M4 via pqm4

---

[2] See the NIST PQC forum: https://groups.google.com/a/list.nist.gov/g/pqc-forum/ c/cJxMq0_90gU/m/qbGEs3TXGwAJ.

[3] https://www.st.com/en/evaluation-tools/nucleo-f767zi.html.

(where available). Specific in the Falcon benchmarking however is another comparison metric to illustrate the performance gains of its operations using the Cortex M7's native 64-bit FPU.

We summarize clock cycle benchmarks of Dilithium and Falcon on the ARM Cortex M4 in Fig. 1 and on the ARM Cortex M7 in Fig. 2. The former figure copies Fig. 7 in the NIST third round report, showing that signing and verifying times for Dilithium require significantly less clock cycles than Falcon's tree signing and verify. When we replicate this figure for the ARM Cortex M7 we see a different story; Falcon requires *less* clock cycles than Dilithium where floating points are run natively, although emulated floats are still much slower.

The remaining details provide stack usage (Tables 3 and 5) and RAM usage (Tables 4 and 6) of the two signature schemes.

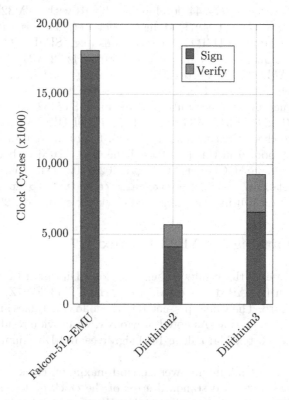

Fig. 1. Signature benchmarks of Dilithium and Falcon (tree) on ARM Cortex M4, results taken from Fig. 7 in [AAC+22].

James Howe and Bas Westerbaan

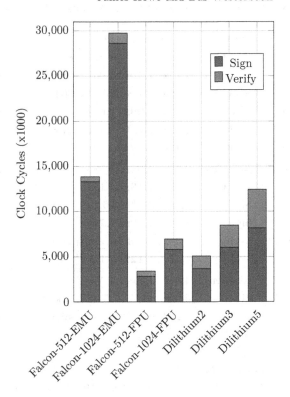

Fig. 2. Signature benchmarks of Dilithium and Falcon (tree) on the ARM Cortex M7, replicating Fig. 7 in [AAC+22].

3.1 Stack Usage and RAM Size

Tables 3 and 5 show stack usage of Dilithium and Falcon and Tables 4 and 6 show the RAM usage of Dilithium and Falcon on ARM Cortex M7. We calculate the stack usage by using the `avstack.pl`[4] tool, adapted to the ARM toolchain, and RAM was calculated using `meminfo`. Note that the implementations we benchmarked weren't optimized for low memory usage. Dilithium, for one, can be used in much more memory constrained environments than these numbers here suggest [GKS20].

4 Profiling on ARM Cortex M7

This section presents the profiling results of Dilithium and Falcon on the ARM Cortex M7 using the STM32F767ZI NUCLEO-144 development board. Firstly,

---

[4] https://dlbeer.co.nz/oss/avstack.html.

Table 1. Benchmarking results of Dilithium on the ARM Cortex M7 using the STM32F767ZI NUCLEO-144 development board. Results in KCycles.

Parameter Set	Operation	Min	Avg	Max	SDev/ SErr	Avg (ms)
Dilithium-2	Key Gen	1,390	1,437	1,479	81/3	6.7
M7 vs M4	Key Gen	1.13x	**1.10x**	1.06x	-/-	**1.40x**
Dilithium-2	Sign	1,835	3,658	16,440	604/17	16.9
M7 vs M4	Sign	1.19x	**1.09x**	0.64x	-/-	**1.40x**
Dilithium-2	Verify	1,428	1,429	1,432	27.8/0.9	6.6
M7 vs M4	Verify	1.12x	**1.12x**	1.12x	-/-	**1.42x**
Dilithium-3	Key Gen	2,563	2,566	2,569	37.6/1.2	11.9
M7 vs M4	Key Gen	1.12x	**1.13x**	1.12x	-/-	**1.44x**
Dilithium-3	Sign	2,981	6,009	26,208	65/9	20.7
M7 vs M4	Sign	1.12x	**1.19x**	0.78x	-/-	**2.06x**
Dilithium-3	Verify	2,452	2,453	2,456	26.5/0.8	11.4
M7 vs M4	Verify	1.12x	**1.12x**	1.11x	-/-	**1.43x**
Dilithium-5	KeyGen	4,312	4,368	4,436	54.4/1.7	20.2
Dilithium-5	Sign	5,020	8,157	35,653	99k/3k	37.8
Dilithium-5	Verify	4,282	4,287	4,292	46.5/1.5	19.8

we provide Figs. 3 and 4 profiling the acceptance rates of Dilithium's sign and Falcon's key generation procedures. Next, we profile the inner workings of Dilithium (Table 7) and Falcon (Table 8).

4.1   Rate of Acceptance in Dilithium and Falcon

The following figures illustrate the effective rejection rates of Dilithium's signing (Fig. 3) and Falcon's key generation (Fig. 4) procedures. Restart or rejection rates are shown in the figures' x-axis, with probabilities of acceptance shown in the y-axis.

4.2   Profiling Results of Dilithium and Falcon

The values presented in the following tables are iterated over 1,000 runs of the main operation (e.g., verify). As noted previously, for comparison, we provide profiling results for Falcon both with and without use of the FPU, and also provide the improvements over the results on the Cortex M4 provided in pqm4. For Dilithium, we only provide comparisons with pqm4 as it does not benefit at all from the FPU. Some lines of the tables will appear incomplete due to the fact that either that operation did not fit on the Cortex M4 (i.e., Falcon-1024 sign tree) or those results were not reported by pqm4 (i.e., Falcon's expand private key).

Table 2. Benchmarking results of Falcon on the ARM Cortex M7 using the STM32F767ZI NUCLEO-144 development board. Results in KCycles.

Parameter Set	Operation	Min	Avg	Max	SDev/ SErr	Avg (ms)
Falcon-512-FPU	Key Gen	44,196	77,475	256,115	226k/7k	358.7
Falcon-512-EMU	Key Gen	76,809	128,960	407,855	303k/9k	597.0
FPU vs EMU	Key Gen	1.74x	**1.66x**	1.59x	-/-	**1.66x**
Falcon-1024-FPU	Key Gen	127,602	193,707	807,321	921k/29k	896.8
Falcon-1024-EMU	Key Gen	202,216	342,533	1,669,083	2.4m/76k	1585.8
FPU vs EMU	Key Gen	1.58x	**1.76x**	2.07x	-/-	**1.77x**
Falcon-512-FPU	Sign Dyn	4,705	4,778	4,863	149/4	22.1
Falcon-512-EMU	Sign Dyn	29,278	29,447	29,640	188/6	136.3
FPU vs EMU	Sign Dyn	6.22x	**6.16x**	6.10x	-/-	**6.17x**
Falcon-1024-FPU	Sign Dyn	10,144	10,243	10,361	1408/44	47.4
Falcon-1024-EMU	Sign Dyn	64,445	64,681	64,957	3k/101	299.5
FPU vs EMU	Sign Dyn	6.35x	**6.31x**	6.27x	-/-	**6.32x**
Falcon-512-FPU	Sign Tree	2,756	2,836	2,927	6/.2	13.1
Falcon-512-EMU	Sign Tree	13,122	13,298	13,506	126/4	61.6
FPU vs EMU	Sign Tree	4.76x	**4.69x**	4.61x	-/-	**4.70x**
Falcon-1024-FPU	Sign Tree	5,707	5,812	5,919	1422/45	26.9
Falcon-1024-EMU	Sign Tree	28,384	28,621	28,877	3k/115	132.5
FPU vs EMU	Sign Tree	4.97x	**4.92x**	4.88x	-/-	**4.93x**
Falcon-512-FPU	Exp SK	1,406	1,407	1,410	8.6/0.3	6.5
Falcon-512-EMU	Exp SK	11,779	11,781	11,788	7/0.2	54.5
FPU vs EMU	Exp SK	8.38x	**8.37x**	8.36x	-/-	**8.38x**
Falcon-1024-FPU	Exp SK	3,071	3,075	3,080	39/1.3	14.2
Falcon-1024-EMU	Exp SK	26,095	26,101	26,120	109/3.5	120.8
FPU vs EMU	Exp SK	8.50x	**8.49x**	8.48x	-/-	**8.51x**

Table 3. Dilithium stack usage in bytes.

Parameter Set	Key Gen	Sign	Verify
Dilithium-2	38,444	52,052	36,332
Dilithium-3	60,972	79,728	57,836
Dilithium-5	97,836	122,708	92,908

Table 4. Dilithium RAM usage in bytes.

Parameter Set	Key Gen	Sign	Verify	Overall
Dilithium-2	9,627	13,035	9,107	13,035
Dilithium-3	15,259	19,947	14,483	19,947
Dilithium-5	24,475	30,699	23,251	30,699

Table 5. Falcon stack usage in bytes.

Parameter Set	Key Gen	Sign Dyn	Sign Tree	Verify
Falcon-512-FPU	1,156	1,920	1,872	556
Falcon-1024-FPU	1,156	1,920	1,872	556
Falcon-512-EMU	1,068	1,880	1,824	556
Falcon-1024-EMU	1,068	1,880	1,872	556

Table 6. Falcon RAM usage in bytes.

Parameter Set	Key Gen	Sign Dyn	Sign Tree	Verify	Overall (Dyn)	Overall (Tree)
Falcon-512-FPU	18,512	42,488	85,512	6,256	63,384	133,048
Falcon-1024-FPU	36,304	84,216	178,440	12,016	125,976	273,464
Falcon-512-EMU	18,512	42,488	85,512	6,256	63,384	133,048
Falcon-1024-EMU	36,304	84,216	178,440	12,016	125,976	273,464

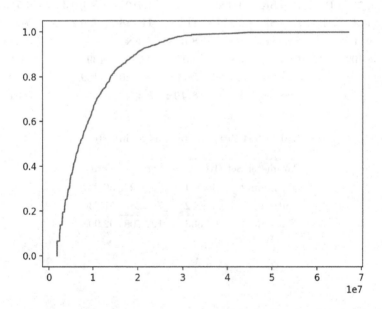

Fig. 3. The rejection rate in Dilithium's signing procedure.

As expected, a significant amount of time is spent on the generation of uniform randomness in both scheme's key generation and signing procedures. In Dilithium, we see this in the `expand matrix` and in `sample vector` type operations, slightly increasing, as expected, as the parameter sets increase.

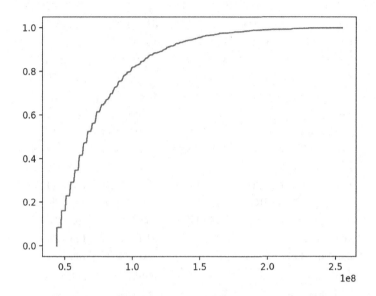

Fig. 4. The rejection rate in Falcon's key generation procedure.

For Falcon, the `poly small mkgauss` and `ffsampling` similarly consume significant amounts of clock cycles for generating randomness. However, for `ffsampling` we see significant improvements using the FPU as this operation intensively uses floating-points for Gaussian sampling [HPR+20] used for randomization. The FPU also enables significant speedups in the FFT multiplier used in key generation and signing.

We discuss these results in more detail in Sect. 6.

Table 7. Profiling Dilithium on the ARM Cortex M7 using the STM32F767ZI NUCLEO-144 development board. All values reported are in KCycles.

Key Generation	param2	param3	param5
get randomness	13 (0.9%)	13 (0.5%)	13 (0.30%)
expand matrix	971 (68%)	1,826 (71%)	3,417 (78%)
sample vector	182 (13%)	317 (12%)	343 (8%)
matrix/vector mult	124 (9%)	190 (7%)	300 (7%)
add error	45 (0.34%)	7 (0.28%)	10 (0.23%)
expand/write pub key	16 (1%)	25 (1%)	33 (0.76%)
get h/comp priv key	125 (9%)	188 (7%)	247 (6%)
Signing	param2	param3	param5
compute crh	13 (0.39%)	13 (0.24%)	14 (0.17%)
exp mat/transf vecs	1,092 (32%)	1,993 (35%)	3,656 (47%)
sample y vector	1,001 (29%)	1,538 (27%)	1,688 (22%)
matrix/vector mult	516 (15%)	946 (17%)	1,178 (15%)
decomp w/ call RO	547 (16%)	710 (13%)	693 (9%)
compute z	137 (4%)	233 (4%)	269 (3%)
check cs2	62 (2%)	91 (2%)	123 (2%)
compute hint	70 (2%)	110 (2%)	149 (2%)
Verifying	param2	param3	param5
compute crh	124 (9%)	181 (8%)	235 (6%)
matrix/vector mult	1,174 (84%)	2,119 (88%)	3,859 (91%)
reconstruct w1	24 (2%)	28 (1%)	38 (0.90%)
call ro verify chall	78 (6%)	78 (3%)	100 (2%)

Table 8. Profiling Falcon on the ARM Cortex M7 using the STM32F767ZI NUCLEO-144 development board. All values reported are in KCycles.

Key Generation	512-FPU	512-EMU	Vs.	1024-FPU	1024-EMU	Vs.
total ntru gen	77,095 (99%)	127,828 (100%)	**1.66x**	186,120 (100%)	332,876 (100%)	**1.79x**
—poly small mkgauss	34,733 (45%)	34,805 (27%)	1.00x	56,509 (30%)	57,033 (17%)	1.00x
—poly small sqnorm	28 (0.04%)	29 (0.02%)	1.04x	94 (0.05%)	94 (0.03%)	1.00x
—poly small to fp	40 (0.05%)	306 (0.24%)	**7.65x**	132 (0.07%)	989 (0.30%)	**7.50x**
—fft multiply	609 (0.80%)	10,496 (8%)	**17.2x**	2,277 (1%)	38,681 (12%)	**17.00x**
—poly invnorm2 fft	110 (0.14%)	1,446 (1%)	**13.2x**	421 (0.22%)	4,777 (1%)	**11.00x**
—poly adj fft	23 (0.03%)	12 (0.01%)	0.52x	70 (0.04%)	43 (0.01%)	0.60x
—poly mulconst	69 (0.09%)	354 (0.28%)	**5.13x**	218 (0.12%)	1,168 (0.35%)	**5.36x**
—poly mul autoadj fft	63 (0.08%)	383 (0.30%)	**6.08x**	237 (0.13%)	1272 (0.38%)	**5.37x**
—ifft multiply	683 (0.90%)	10,666 (8%)	**15.6x**	2,544 (1.36%)	39,071 (12%)	**15.4x**
—bnorm/fpr add	14 (0.02%)	184 (0.14%)	**13.1x**	35 (0.02%)	424 (0.13%)	**12.1x**
—compute public key	383 (0.49%)	383 (0.30%)	1.00x	887 (0.50%)	887 (0.27%)	1.00x
—solve ntru:	40,337 (52%)	68,764 (54%)	**1.70x**	122,696 (66%)	188,438 (56%)	**1.54x**
encode priv key	26 (0.03%)	26 (0.02%)	1.00x	52 (0.03%)	52 (0.02%)	1.00x
recomp sk and encode	384 (0.50%)	385 (0.3%)	1.00x	815 (0.44%)	815 (0.24%)	1.00x
Signing Dynamic	**512-FPU**	**512-EMU**	**Vs.**	**1024-FPU**	**1024-EMU**	**Vs.**
sign start	4 (0.08%)	4 (0.01%)	1.00x	4 (0.04%)	4 (0.01%)	1.00x
decode/comp priv key	488 (11%)	489 (1.69%)	1.00x	1,040 (11%)	1,040 (2%)	1.00x
hash mess to point	<1 (0.01%)	<1 (0.00%)	0.10x	<1 (0.00%)	<1 (0.00%)	1.00x
signature encode	11 (0.26%)	11 (0.04%)	1.00x	22 (0.24%)	22 (0.03%)	1.00x
convert basis to fft	241 (6%)	3,885 (13%)	**16.1x**	549 (6%)	8,751 (14%)	**15.9x**
comp gram matrix	67 (2%)	628 (2%)	**9.37x**	167 (2%)	1,290 (2%)	**7.72x**
apply lattice basis	89 (2%)	1,250 (4%)	**14.0x**	207 (2%)	2,756 (4%)	**13.3x**
ffsampling	2,814 (66%)	16,190 (56%)	**5.75x**	6,009 (65%)	35,324 (56%)	**5.88x**
recomp matrix basis	258 (6%)	3,900 (14%)	**15.1x**	586 (6%)	8,787 (14%)	**15.0x**
get lattice point	314 (7%)	2,527 (9%)	**8.05x**	706 (8%)	5,564 (8%)	**7.88x**
Signing Tree	**512-FPU**	**512-EMU**	**Vs.**	**1024-FPU**	**1024-EMU**	**Vs.**
sign start	4 (0.08%)	4 (0.03%)	1.00x	4 (0.07%)	4 (0.07%)	1.0x
get deg/check params	<1 (0.00%)	<1 (0.00%)	1.00x	<1 (0.00%)	<1 (0.00%)	1.0x
hash mess to point	<1 (0.01%)	<1 (0.00%)	1.00x	<1 (0.00%)	<1 (0.00%)	1.0x
sig encode	11 (0.46%)	11 (0.09%)	1.00x	22 (0.44%)	22 (0.08%)	1.00x
apply lattice basis	89 (3.70%)	1,255 (10%)	**14.1x**	194 (4%)	2,746 (9.87%)	**14.1x**
apply ff sampling	1,975 (82%)	9,081 (70%)	**4.60x**	406 (82%)	4,094 (82%)	**10.1x**
get lattice point	314 (13%)	2,527 (20%)	**8.05x**	706 (14%)	5,564 (14%)	**7.88x**
compute signature	135 (6%)	23 (0.18%)	0.17x	272 (5%)	46 (0.17%)	0.17x
Verifying	**512-FPU**	**512-EMU**	**Vs.**	**1024-FPU**	**1024-EMU**	**Vs.**
verf start	<1 (0.06%)	<1 (0.06%)	1.00x	<1 (0.03%)	<1 (0.00%)	1.00x
get degree via pk	<1 (0.01%)	<1 (0.01%)	1.00x	<1 (0.00%)	<1 (0.00%)	1.00x
decode pub key	9 (1.6%)	9 (2%)	1.00x	18 (2%)	18 (2%)	1.00x
decode sign	12 (2%)	12 (2%)	1.00x	24 (2%)	24 (2%)	1.00x
hash mess to point	312 (55%)	311 (55%)	1.00x	595 (52%)	595 (52%)	1.00x
verify sign	231 (41%)	231 (41%)	1.00x	501 (44%)	501 (44%)	1.00x
Expand Private Key	**512-FPU**	**512-EMU**	**Vs.**	**1024-FPU**	**1024-EMU**	**Vs.**
get priv deg	<1 (0.00%)	<1 (0.00%)	1.00x	<1 (0.00%)	<1 (0.00%)	1.00x
decode priv	494 (35%)	494 (4%)	1.00x	1,040 (34%)	1,040 (34%)	1.00x
expand priv key	905 (65%)	11,281 (96%)	**12.5x**	2,018 (66%)	25,010 (96%)	**12.3x**

5   Constant-Time Validation of Falcon's Floating-Point Operations

This section presents the constant runtime analysis of Falcon on the ARM Cortex M7. Technical manuals for ARM development boards often report cycle counts for FPU instructions[5], however ARM does not appear to make this information public for the Cortex M7 core.

We are specifically interested in Falcon's use of double precision floating points and how it exploits the devices' 64-bit floating point unit (FPU). This has not been investigated before since the primary evaluation target used for post-quantum schemes, the ARM Cortex M4, only has a 32-bit FPU, which is not sufficient for the 53-bit floating-point precision required by Falcon.

The double precision FPU on the ARM Cortex M7 is compliant with the IEEE-754 standard as thus supports the binary64 type. The IEEE-754 standard defines all aspects of floating-point numbers (i.e., their sign, exponent, and mantissa) so that hardware/software interoperability can be ensured. Thus, most if not all modern CPUs offer compliance with this standard within their dedicated FPUs used to speed-up floating-point operations.

We investigate the timings on the device used in the previous sections, the STM32F767ZI NUCLEO-144 development board, and due to the issues found we extended this to three other STM32 development boards (the STM32H743ZI, STM32H723ZG, and STM32F769I-DISCO) in order to see if this issue affected other development boards. We found the same issues occurred in all four development boards. We are aware of a similar experiment being run on the STM32H730[6]. We also further investigate timing issues on the Raspberry Pi 3, due to its use in evaluating the constant-time code of Falcon [Por19].

5.1   STM32 Development Boards

The issue discovered with the STM32 development boards was that the FPU operations were not fully constant time. We did not pursue ways to exploit this into an attack, but we felt this was worth reporting nonetheless. The code for testing this constant run-time is available on repository already provided.

For each floating-point instruction (e.g., vmul.f64), we wrote inline assembly of ten consecutive operations, given two random inputs, which we then averaged to find the required clock cycles. We used inline assembly to minimize the unwanted optimizations from the compiler, and clobbered registers where necessary. Using this approach minimizes the effect of surrounding instructions on the operations of interest, which for example would occur using C, and ensures that all execution is from cache. An example of this is shown in Listing 1.1 for the 64-bit floating point multiplication operation vmul.f64.

---

[5] For example, see the ARM Cortex-M4 Technical Reference Manual https://developer.arm.com/documentation/ddi0439/b/BEHJADED.

[6] https://www.quinapalus.com/cm7cycles.html.

The FPUs on the development boards typically provide two functions for each floating-point function; a 32-bit version (e.g., `vadd.f32`) and a 64-bit version (e.g., `vadd.f64`). Since we are concerned with Falcon which requires 53 bits of floating-point precision, we focus on the 64-bit (double-precision) floating-point functions. The IEEE 754 standard for floating-point binary representation is shown in Table 9 for `float` and `double` types. The double-precision binary floating-point format (binary64) expresses floating point numbers using a 1-bit sign value in the most significant position, 11 bits for the exponent in positions 62-to-52, and 52 bits for the significand in positions 51-to-0.

```
 1  asm volatile (
 2    "vldr d5, %2\n"
 3    "vldr d6, %3\n"
 4    "dmb\n"
 5    "isb\n"
 6    "ldr r1, %1\n"
 7      "vmul.f64 d4, d5, d6\n"
 8      "vmul.f64 d4, d5, d6\n"
 9      "vmul.f64 d4, d5, d6\n"
10      "vmul.f64 d4, d5, d6\n"
11      "vmul.f64 d4, d5, d6\n"
12      "vmul.f64 d4, d5, d6\n"
13      "vmul.f64 d4, d5, d6\n"
14      "vmul.f64 d4, d5, d6\n"
15      "vmul.f64 d4, d5, d6\n"
16      "vmul.f64 d4, d5, d6\n"
17    "ldr r2, %1\n"
18    "subs %0, r2, r1\n"
19    : "=r"(cycles) : "m"(DWT->CYCCNT),
20    "m"(r1), "m"(r2) : "r1", "r2",
21    "d4", "d5", "d6");
```

Listing 1.1. Code snippet of the testing framework we used to test the constant timeness of the double precision FPU on the STM32 development boards.

Table 9. IEEE 754 standard format for single (32-bit) and double precision (64-bit).

Type/ Precision	Sign	Exponent	Significand
float (32 bits)	31 (1 bit)	30:23 (8 bits)	22:0 (23 bits)
double (64 bits)	63 (1 bit)	62:52 (11 bits)	51:0 (52 bits)

We discovered variable timing behaviour in *all* double-precision floating-point functions on *all* the development boards we used in the experiments. We now focus on the double-precision floating-point addition (`vadd.f64`) function to illustrate and explain lower level timing irregularities.

The non-constant run-time was clearly observed when generating two random double-precision values for addition, with an average run-time of 16 clock cycles and standard deviation of 4.1. However, when we generated random values in the same range such they had the same exponents, the run-times were constant and consistent at 10 clock cycles. Moreover, when we mixed randomness from two fixed exponent ranges we observed constant and consistent run-times of 19 clock cycles.

5.2   Raspberry Pi 3

We also discovered a subtle issue with constant run-time on the Raspberry Pi 3, which itself has an ARM Cortex A53 core. This issue involves type casting, specifically, when casting a `double` to an `int64_t`, the operation rounds towards zero. There is no native instruction to do such a truncation on ARMv7. Thus instead, the compiler calls the runtime symbol `__fixdfi`, that is, `__aeabi_d2lz`. This may or may not be implemented in constant time. In LLVM it is not[7] and importantly it *leaks the sign*. This is the case for the Raspberry Pi 3 which they targeted in [Por19]. We reported this issue to the Falcon team and moreover proposed a constant time fix, which we show in Listing 1.2.

```
1  int64_t cast(double a) {
2      union {
3          double d;
4          uint64_t u;
5          int64_t i;
6      } x;
7      uint64_t mask;
8      uint32_t high, low;
9
10     x.d = a;
11
12     mask =  x.i >> 63;
13     x.u &= 0x7fffffffffffffffL;
14
15     // a / 0x1p32f;
16     high = x.d / 4294967296.f;
17
18     // high * 0x1p32f;
19     low = x.d - (double)high * 4294967296.f;
20     x.u = ((int64_t)high << 32) | low;
21
22     return (x.u & ((uint64_t)-1 - mask))
23       | ((-x.u) & mask);
24 }
```

Listing 1.2. The proposed fix for casting a `double` to an `int64_t` in LLVM.

---

[7] see for example https://github.com/llvm-mirror/compiler-rt/blob/69445f095c22aa
c2388f939bedebf224a6efcdaf/lib/builtins/fixdfdi.c#L18.

6   Results and Discussions

In Sect. 3, we observe from the benchmarking of Dilithium in Table 1 that all procedures show a slight improvement, but not many of significance in comparison to those reported on the ARM Cortex M4 in the pqm4 repository. The performance improvements seen range from 1.09–1.19x which essentially accounts for the slightly better performance of the Cortex M7 vs the Cortex M4 in general.

For Falcon, however, we see a lot of significant improvements from the benchmarking in Table 2, in particular we see that:

- Key generation does somewhat benefit from the FPU, showing a 1.66–1.76x improvement in comparison to emulated floating points. We also see similar results compared to the Cortex M4, with improvements between 2.21–2.56x.
- Sign dynamic has a significant improvement using the FPU; showing an increase between 6.16–6.31x between the emulated code and between 8.16–8.31x compared to the Cortex M4.
- Sign tree also has a significant improvement using the FPU; showing an increase between 4.69–4.92x between the emulated code and 6.23x compared to the Cortex M4 for Falcon-512 parameters. As already stated, Falcon-1024 sign tree cannot fit on the Cortex M4, but has been implemented in this research on the Cortex M7.
- Expanding the private key also has a significant improvement using the FPU; showing an increase between 8.37–8.49x between the emulated code.
- Verify shows little to know changes by using the FPU, due to it not requiring floating-point operations, and the slight decrease is probably due to the larger instruction pipeline on the M7.

In Sect. 3.1 we provided stack and RAM usage for Dilithium and Falcon. The most notable results are for Falcon which has a small increase (at most, 88 Bytes) in stack usage when the FPU is used.

In Sect. 4, we provide profiling results of the two signature schemes, which can point to areas in which these schemes could be optimised in the future. The profiling results of Dilithium in Table 7 perhaps offer little novel insights into the bottlenecks of its implementation on the Cortex M7. Dilithium has a much simpler implementation complexity in comparison to Falcon and this can be observed by the much more compact table of results. However, we can observe the elegance of its design and performance when comparing the results across parameter sets; seeing that some values change a little, and some increase proportional to the added computations required by the small change in each parameter set, afforded by fixing the polynomial ring and modulus.

We observe from the profiling of Falcon in Table 8 that the FPU improves, in comparison to emulation, floating-point operations in *key generation* by an order of magnitude, specifically in the following operations.

- Converting a small vector to floating point (poly_small_to_fp) improves by 7.5–7.65x, multiplying polynomials by a constant (poly_mulconst) and an adjoint (poly_mul_autoadj_fft) improves by 5.13–5.36x and 5.37–6.08x, respectively.

- Polynomial inversion to FFT format (`poly_invnorm2_fft`) saves between 11–13.2x.
- The normalisation step alongside `FPR` addition saves between 12.1–13.1x.
- FFT and iFFT operations improve by 15.4–17.2x, making this the biggest improvement of all operations in Falcon.

The FPU improves upon emulating floating-point operations in *sign dynamic* by an order of magnitude, specifically in the following operations.

- ffSampling improves by 5.75–5.88x, get lattice point and computing the Gram matrix (G) improves by 7.88–8.05x and 7.72–9.37x, respectively.
- Applying the lattice basis, recomputing the matrix basis, and converting the basis to FFT format save 13.3–14x, 15–15.1x, and 15.9–16.1x, respectively.
- Similar savings are noted for *sign tree* for applying the lattice basis, applying ffSampling, and getting the lattice point.
- Expanding the private key saves between 12.3–12.5x.

The FPU does not have any effect on Falcon's verification operation, this is essentially because it does not require floating-point operations and is a relatively computationally light procedure.

In Sect. 5, we find constant time issues with Falcon on four different STM32 development boards using the ARM Cortex M7 and the Raspberry Pi 3 using the ARM Cortex A53. The issues we found on the STM32 development boards were where the devices' dedicated floating-point unit was used (which can significantly speed-up Falcon), specifically the double-precision functions, were all shown to be non-constant-time. Specifically analysing the double-precision addition, we discovered the size of the significand influenced the runtime of this function.

We further investigated constant timeness on the Raspberry Pi 3, which uses the ARM Cortex A53, where we also found timing issues when casting from a `double` to an `int64_t`, and when implemented in LLVM, it is not constant time and leaks the sign of the value.

We reported these issues and our proposed fix to the Falcon team, but we did not investigate how to exploit this for a timing attack.

Overall, this research shows that when implementing Falcon the platform and/or situation it is used in should play a major consideration. At the very least, the processor should be checked for constant timeness *if* the FPU is being used. A recent Cloudflare blog[8] took note of our results and is currently only considering uses for Falcon in an offline manner, as they "feel it's too early to deploy Falcon where the timing of signature minting can be measured".

A   The Dilithium Signature Scheme

The Dilithium signature scheme is provided in Algorithm 1. The algorithms inside these procedures have been omitted for space, but the reader can refer to the specifications for more details [LDK+20].

---

[8] https://blog.cloudflare.com/nist-post-quantum-surprise/.

Algorithm 1: The CRYSTALS-Dilithium signature scheme [LDK+20].

---

1 **Procedure** KeyGen()
2 $\quad \zeta \leftarrow \{0,1\}^{256}$
3 $\quad (\rho, \rho', K) \leftarrow \{0,1\}^{256} \times \{0,1\}^{512} \times \{0,1\}^{256} := H(\zeta)$
4 $\quad \mathbf{A} \in R_q^{k \times \ell} = \mathsf{ExpandA}(\rho')$
5 $\quad \mathbf{t} = \mathbf{A} \cdot \mathbf{s}_1 + \mathbf{s}_2$
6 $\quad (\mathbf{t}_1, \mathbf{t}_0) = \mathsf{Power2Round}_q(\mathbf{t}, d)$
7 $\quad tr \in \{0,1\}^{256} := H(\rho \| \mathbf{t}_1)$
8 $\quad \mathbf{return} \ pk = (\rho, \mathbf{t}_1), sk = (\rho, K, tr, \mathbf{s}_1, \mathbf{s}_2, \mathbf{t}_0)$
9

---

1 **Procedure** Sign(sk, M)
2 $\quad \mathbf{A} \in R_q^{k \times \ell} := \mathsf{ExpandA}(\rho)$
3 $\quad \mu \in \{0,1\}^{512} := H(tr \| M)$
4 $\quad \kappa := 0, (\mathbf{z}, \mathbf{h}) = \bot$
5 $\quad \mathbf{while} \ (\mathbf{z}, \mathbf{h}) = \bot \ \mathbf{do}$
6 $\quad\quad \mathbf{y} \in S_{\gamma_1}^{\ell} := \mathsf{ExpandMask}(\rho', \kappa)$
7 $\quad\quad \mathbf{w} := \mathbf{A}\mathbf{y}$
8 $\quad\quad \mathbf{w}_1 := \mathsf{HighBits}_q(\mathbf{w}, 2\gamma_2)$
9 $\quad\quad \widetilde{c} \in \{0,1\}^{256} := H(\mu \| \mathbf{w}_1)$
10 $\quad\quad c \in B_\tau := \mathsf{SampleInBall}(\widetilde{c})$
11 $\quad\quad \mathbf{z} := \mathbf{y} + c\mathbf{s}_1$
12 $\quad\quad \mathbf{r}_0 := \mathsf{LowBits}_q(\mathbf{w} - c \cdot \mathbf{s}_2, 2\gamma_2)$
13 $\quad\quad \mathbf{if} \ \|\mathbf{z}\|_\infty \geq \gamma_1 - \beta \ \mathbf{or} \ \|\mathbf{r}_0\|_\infty \geq \gamma_2 - \beta \ \mathbf{then}$
14 $\quad\quad\quad (\mathbf{z}, \mathbf{h}) := \bot$
15 $\quad\quad \mathbf{else}$
16 $\quad\quad\quad \mathbf{h} := \mathsf{MakeHint}_q(-c\mathbf{t}_0, \mathbf{w} - c \cdot \mathbf{s}_2 + c \cdot \mathbf{t}_0, 2\gamma_2)$
17 $\quad\quad\quad \mathbf{if} \ \|c\mathbf{t}_0\|_\infty \geq \gamma_2 \ \mathbf{or} \ \mathsf{wt}(\mathbf{h}) > \omega \ \mathbf{then}$
18 $\quad\quad\quad\quad (\mathbf{z}, \mathbf{h}) = \bot$
19 $\quad\quad \mathbf{end}$
20 $\quad\quad \kappa = \kappa + \ell$
21 $\quad \mathbf{end}$
22 $\quad \mathbf{return} \ \sigma = (\widetilde{c}, \mathbf{z}, \mathbf{h})$
23

---

1 **Procedure** Verify(pk, $M, \sigma = (\widetilde{c}, \mathbf{z}, \mathbf{h})$))
2 $\quad \mathbf{A} \in R_q^{k \times \ell} := \mathsf{ExpandA}(\rho)$
3 $\quad \mu \in \{0,1\}^{512} := H(H(\rho \| \mathbf{t}_1) \| M)$
4 $\quad c \in B_\tau := \mathsf{SampleInBall}(\widetilde{c})$
5 $\quad \mathbf{w}_1 := \mathsf{UseHint}_q(\mathbf{h}, \mathbf{A} \cdot \mathbf{z} - c\mathbf{t}_1 \cdot 2^d, 2\gamma_2)$
6 $\quad \mathbf{return} \ [\![\|\mathbf{z}\|_\infty < \gamma_1 - \beta]\!] \ \mathrm{and} \ [\![\widetilde{c} = H(\mu \| \mathbf{w}_1')]\!] \ \mathrm{and} \ [\![\mathsf{wt}(\mathbf{h}) \leq \omega]\!]$

B   The Falcon Signature Scheme

The Falcon signature scheme is provided in Algorithm 2. The algorithms inside these procedures have been omitted for space, but the reader can refer to the specifications for more details [PFH+20].

Algorithm 2: The Falcon signature scheme [PFH+20].

---

1 **Procedure** KeyGen(ϕ,q)
2 $\quad$ $f, g, F, G \leftarrow$ NTRUGen(ϕ, q)
3 $\quad$ $\mathbf{B} \leftarrow \left[\begin{smallmatrix} g & -f \\ G & -F \end{smallmatrix}\right]$
4 $\quad$ $\hat{\mathbf{B}} \leftarrow$ FFT($\mathbf{B}$)
5 $\quad$ $\mathbf{G} \leftarrow \hat{\mathbf{B}} \times \hat{\mathbf{B}}^*$
6 $\quad$ $\mathsf{T} \leftarrow$ ffLDL*($\mathbf{G}$)
7 $\quad$ **for each leaf** *of* $\mathbf{T}$ **do**
8 $\quad\quad$ $|$ leaf.value $\leftarrow \sigma/\sqrt{\text{leaf.value}}$
9 $\quad$ **end**
10 $\quad$ $sk \leftarrow (\hat{\mathbf{B}}, \mathsf{T})$
11 $\quad$ $h \leftarrow gf^{-1} \mod q$
12 $\quad$ $pk \leftarrow h$
13 $\quad$ **return** (sk, pk)
14

---

1 **Procedure** Sign($m, sk, \lfloor \beta^2 \rfloor$)
2 $\quad$ $\mathbf{r} \leftarrow \{0,1\}^{320}$ uniformly
3 $\quad$ $c \leftarrow$ HashToPoint($\mathbf{r}\|\mathbf{m}, q, n$)
4 $\quad$ $\mathbf{t} \leftarrow (-\frac{1}{q}$FFT($c$) $\odot$ FFT(F), $-\frac{1}{q}$FFT(c) $\odot$ FFT(f))
5 $\quad$ **do**
6 $\quad\quad$ **do**
7 $\quad\quad\quad$ $|$ $\mathbf{z} \leftarrow$ ffSampling$_n(\mathbf{t}, \mathsf{T})$
8 $\quad\quad\quad$ $|$ $\mathbf{s} = (\mathbf{t} - \mathbf{z})\hat{\mathbf{B}}$
9 $\quad\quad$ **while** $\|\mathbf{s}\|^2 > \lfloor \beta^2 \rfloor$
10 $\quad\quad$ $(s_1, s_2) \leftarrow$ invFFT($\mathbf{s}$)
11 $\quad\quad$ $s \leftarrow$ Compress($s_2, 8 \cdot$ sbytelen $- 328$)
12 $\quad$ **while** $s = \bot$
13 $\quad$ **return** sig $= (r, s)$
14

---

1 **Procedure** Verify($m, $ sig$, pk, \lfloor \beta^2 \rfloor$))
2 $\quad$ $c \leftarrow$ HashToPoint($\mathbf{r}\|\mathbf{m}, q, n$)
3 $\quad$ $s_2 \leftarrow$ Decompress($s, 8 \cdot$ sbytelen $- 328$)
4 $\quad$ **if** $(s_2 = \bot)$ **then**
5 $\quad\quad$ $|$ Reject
6 $\quad$ $s_1 \leftarrow c - s_2 h \mod q$
7 $\quad$ **if** $\|(s_1, s_2)\|^2 \leq \lfloor \beta^2 \rfloor$ **then**
8 $\quad\quad$ $|$ Accept
9 $\quad$ **else**
10 $\quad\quad$ $|$ Reject

References

[AAAS+19] Alagic, G., et al.: Status report on the first round of the NIST post-quantum cryptography standardization process. US Department of Commerce, National Institute of Standards and Technology (2019)

[AAC+22] Alagic, G., et al.: Status report on the third round of the NIST post-quantum cryptography standardization process. Technical report, National Institute of Standards and Technology Gaithersburg, MD (2022)

[AASA+20] Alagic, G., et al.: status report on the second round of the NIST post-quantum cryptography standardization process. In: NIST, Technical report (2020)

[ARM18] ARM. Arm cortex-m7 processor: Technical reference manual. Revision r1p2 (2018). https://developer.arm.com/documentation/ddi0489/f/programmers-model/instruction-set-summary/binary-compatibility-with-other-cortex-processors

[BUC19] Banerjee, U., Ukyab, T.S., Chandrakasan, A.P.: Sapphire: a configurable crypto-processor for post-quantum lattice-based protocols. IACR TCHES, **2019**(4), 17–61, (2019). ISSN: 2569-2925. https://tches.iacr.org/index.php/TCHES/article/view/8344, https://doi.org/10.13154/tches.v2019.i4.17-61

[GKS20] Greconici, D.O.C., Kannwischer, M.J., Sprenkels, A.: Compact dilithium implementations on cortex-M3 and cortex-M4. Cryptology ePrint Archive, Report 2020/1278 (2020). https://eprint.iacr.org/2020/1278

[HBD+20] Hulsing, H., et al.: SPHINCS+. Technical report. National Institute of Standards and Technology (2020). https://csrc.nist.gov/projects/post-quantum-cryptography/round-3-submissions

[HMO+21] Howe, J., et al.: Exploring parallelism to improve the performance of FrodoKEM in hardware. J. Cryptographic Eng. **11**(4), 317–327 (2021). https://doi.org/10.1007/s13389-021-00258-7

[HOK+18] Howe, J., et al.: Standard lattice-based key encapsulation on embedded devices. IACR TCHES **2018**(3), 372–393 (2018). https://tches.iacr.org/index.php/TCHES/article/view/7279

[HPR+20] Paquin, C., Stebila, D., Tamvada, G.: Benchmarking post-quantum cryptography in TLS. In: Ding, J., Tillich, J.-P. (eds.) PQCrypto 2020. LNCS, vol. 12100, pp. 72–91. Springer, Cham (2020). https://doi.org/10.1007/978-3-030-44223-1_5

[KRR+20] Kales, D., Ramacher, S., Rechberger, C., Walch, R., Werner, M.: Efficient FPGA implementations of LowMC and picnic. In: Jarecki, S. (ed.) CT-RSA 2020. LNCS, vol. 12006, pp. 417–441. Springer, Cham (2020). https://doi.org/10.1007/978-3-030-40186-3_18

[LDK+20] Lyubashevsky, V., et al.: CRYSTALS-DILITHIUM. Technical report. National Institute of Standards and Technology (2020). https://csrc.nist.gov/projects/post-quantum-cryptography/round-3-submissions

[liboqs] Liboqs: C library for prototyping and experimenting with quantum-resistant cryptography. https://github.com/open-quantum-safe/liboqs

[Mar20] Marotzke, A.: A constant time full hardware implementation of streamlined NTRU prime. In: Liardet, P.-Y., Mentens, N. (eds.) CARDIS 2020. LNCS, vol. 12609, pp. 3–17. Springer, Cham (2021). https://doi.org/10.1007/978-3-030-68487-7_1

[NIST15] NIST. Post-quantum cryptography (2015). https://csrc.nist.gov/projects/post-quantum-cryptography. Accessed 26 June 2023

[NIST16] NIST. Submission requirements and evaluation criteria for the post-quantum cryptography standardization process (2016). https://csrc.nist.gov/CSRC/media/Projects/Post-Quantum-Cryptography/documents/call-for-proposals-final-dec-2016.pdf

[PFH+20] Prest, T., et al.: FALCON. Technical report. National Institute of Standards and Technology (2020). https://csrc.nist.gov/projects/post-quantum-cryptography/round-3-submissions

[Por19] Pornin, T.: New efficient, constant-time implementations of Falcon. Cryptology ePrint Archive, Report 2019/893, 2019. https://eprint.iacr.org/2019/893 (2019)

[PQClean] PQClean: clean, portable, tested implementations of post-quantum cryptography. https://github.com/PQClean/PQClean

[pqm4] PQM4: Post-quantum crypto library for the ARM Cortex-M4. https://github.com/mupq/pqm4

[RB20] Roy, S.S., Basso, A.: High-speed instruction-set coprocessor for lattice-based key encapsulation mechanism: saber in hardware. In: IACR TCHES **2020**(4), 443–466 (2020). ISSN: 2569-2925, https://tches.iacr.org/index.php/TCHES/article/view/8690

[RBG20] Jan Richter-Brockmann and Tim Güneysu. Folding BIKE: Scalable Hardware Implementation for Reconfigurable Devices. Cryptology ePrint Archive, Report 2020/897. https://eprint.iacr.org/2020/897 (2020)

[RMJ+21] Ricci, S., et al.: Implementing crystals-dilithium signature scheme on fpgas. Cryptology ePrint Archive, Report 2021/108 (2021)

[SAB+20] Schwabe, P., et al.: CRYSTALS-KYBER. Technical report. National Institute of Standards and Technology (2020). https://csrc.nist.gov/projects/post-quantum-cryptography/round-3-submissions

[SupCop] SUPERCOP: system for unified performance evaluation related to cryptographic operations and primitives. https://bench.cr.yp.to/supercop.html

[XL21] Xing, Y., Li, S.: A compact hardware implementation of CCA-secure key exchange mechanism CRYSTALS-KYBER on FPGA. IACR Trans. Cryptographic Hardw. Embed. Syst. **2021**(2), 328–356 (2021)

Theory

Impossibilities in Succinct Arguments: Black-Box Extraction and More

Matteo Campanelli[1], Chaya Ganesh[2], Hamidreza Khoshakhlagh[3(✉)], and Janno Siim[4]

[1] Protocol Labs, San Francisco, USA
matteo@protocol.ai
[2] Indian Institute of Science, Bengaluru, India
chaya@iisc.ac.in
[3] Concordium, Aarhus, Denmark
hk@concordium.com
[4] Simula UiB, Bergen, Norway
janno@simula.no

Abstract. The celebrated result by Gentry and Wichs established a theoretical barrier for succinct non-interactive arguments (SNARGs), showing that for (expressive enough) hard-on-average languages, we must assume non-falsifiable assumptions. We further investigate those barriers by showing new negative and positive results related to the proof size.

1. We start by formalizing a folklore lower bound for the proof size of black-box extractable arguments based on the hardness of the language. This separates knowledge-sound SNARGs (SNARKs) in the random oracle model (that can have black-box extraction) and those in the standard model.
2. We find a positive result in the non-adaptive setting. Under the existence of non-adaptively sound SNARGs (without extractability) and from standard assumptions, it is possible to build SNARKs with black-box extractability for a non-trivial subset of **NP**.
3. On the other hand, we show that (under some mild assumptions) all **NP** languages cannot have SNARKs with black-box extractability even in the non-adaptive setting.
4. The Gentry-Wichs result does not account for the preprocessing model, under which fall several efficient constructions. We show that also, in the preprocessing model, it is impossible to construct SNARGs that rely on falsifiable assumptions in a black-box way.

Along the way, we identify a class of non-trivial languages, which we dub "trapdoor languages", that can bypass these impossibility results.

1 Introduction

Proof systems have been studied extensively both in cryptography and in the theory of computation [21,26], and are a fundamental building block in various cryptographic constructions, including delegating computation [8,9] and

© The Author(s), under exclusive license to Springer Nature Switzerland AG 2023
N. El Mrabet et al. (Eds.): AFRICACRYPT 2023, LNCS 14064, pp. 465–489, 2023.
https://doi.org/10.1007/978-3-031-37679-5_20

privacy-preserving cryptocurrencies [7]. In a *succinct* proof, it is required that the communication be sublinear (ideally polylogarithmic) in the size of the non-deterministic witness used to verify the relation (*proof* succinctness). This requirement is often extended to verification complexity (*verification* succinctness).

Statistically-sound proofs are unlikely to allow for significant improvements in proof size [25, 47]. For **NP**, statistical soundness requires the prover to communicate, roughly, as much information as the size of the witness. In *argument systems* [11] where soundness is *computational*, proofs can potentially be shorter than the length of the witness.

Succinct Arguments. Succinct arguments were first studied by Kilian [34], who gave an interactive construction based on probabilistically checkable proofs (PCP) and collision-resistant hash functions. Kilian's construction was turned into a non-interactive argument in the random oracle model using the Fiat-Shamir heuristic [20] by Micali [40]. In the standard model (i.e., without idealized primitives), non-interactivity is achieved by a trusted party generating a Common Reference String (CRS) during a setup phase. The notion of *adaptive soundness* requires soundness to hold even when a malicious prover can choose the statement after receiving CRS. Otherwise, we call soundness non-adaptive.

In this work, we are concerned with the theoretical limitations for building succinct non-interactive arguments in the standard model[1]. One of the best-known impossibility results on SNARGs is that of Gentry and Wichs [24] (GW), which shows that in the standard model, adaptively-sound SNARGs for (hard enough) **NP** languages cannot be proven secure via a black-box (BB) reduction to a falsifiable assumption [41]. A falsifiable assumption is an assumption where the challenger can efficiently confirm that the challenge was broken[2].

A folklore way to interpret GW has been *"we cannot escape non-falsifiable assumptions to build SNARGs for **NP**"*. While essentially true, there are several caveats to this interpretation (which we discuss later in Sect. 6). We formally explore the boundaries of this simplifying interpretation, especially motivated by the focus on (composable) extractability [6, 36] and the popular model of "preprocessing SNARGs" in recent works [28]. We strive to provide a *modern* view of these topics, e.g., by adopting the language of indexed relations from [16].

(Black-Box) Knowledge Soundness. Knowledge soundness property requires that, whenever an efficient prover convinces the verifier, not only can we conclude that $x \in \mathcal{L}$, but also an **NP** witness w can be efficiently extracted. This helpful property is satisfied by many proof systems and is necessary for a lot of applications of succinct arguments. A Succinct Non-interactive ARgument of Knowledge (SNARK) is a SNARG with the knowledge soundness property.

Constructions of SNARKs for **NP** in the standard model all rely on non-falsifiable assumptions that are *knowledge-type* assumptions, guaranteeing the

---

[1] There exist efficient SNARKs (SNARGs of knowledge) in idealized models like ROM (random oracle model) [12] and GGM (generic group model) [28].

[2] For example, DLOG is a falsifiable assumption since the challenger can efficiently test if the adversary has found the correct discrete logarithm.

existence of an extractor that can output a discrete log "from" a specific adversary. These assumptions are non-falsifiable since they are *non-black-box*. They require knowledge of the internal state of the concrete adversarial algorithm. This contrasts with the milder *black-box* extraction, namely the ability to extract a witness from a malicious prover only using its input/output interface.

Whether we can build SNARKs with black-box extraction in the standard model is an elusive problem. In addition to being a theoretical curiosity, if answered positively, it would allow to construct more robust cryptographic protocols. Black-box extraction is required in composition security, e.g., in universal composability (or UC-security [14]) where the "ideal-world" simulator must extract a witness without knowledge of the environment's algorithm. If answered negatively, it would confirm the seeming incompatibility of SNARKs and UC. In this work, we then ask the question:

Is non-black-box extraction inherent to SNARKs?

Addressing this question is even more pressing because prior works [5,6,36] have noted that succinctness *must* be sacrificed for black-box extraction (see also Sect. 1.2). To the best of our knowledge, there was no formal treatment for this question prior to our work.

OUR FIRST CONTRIBUTION: We prove the folklore belief that black-box extraction is impossible for adaptive knowledge soundness in the standard model with proof-succinctness. This result separates the standard model and other idealized models in terms of what is possible for black-box extraction (for example, in the ROM there exist black-box extractable SNARKs [12]).

OUR SECOND CONTRIBUTION: We explore if the impossibility extends to the non-adaptive case. We find out that non-adaptive black-box extractability is possible for a non-trivial subset of **NP**—which encompasses hard problems such as knowledge of a discrete logarithm—by assuming the existence of a non-adaptively sound SNARG and some standard assumptions (FHE and CRHF). In particular, we show that a SNARG can be lifted to a SNARK with the features above for the class of languages **FewP** (roughly, **NP** with polynomial many witnesses). If the initial SNARG (non-adaptively sound) is based on falsifiable assumptions and in the standard model then so is the resulting SNARK. SNARGs exist that plausibly satisfy this requirement, specifically the NIZK construction based on iO in [45]. The latter is a *proof-succinct* NIZK since the proof consists only of the output of a PRF. This can be instantiated (for example) with the iO construction of [31], which requires sub-exponentially secure, but otherwise falsifiable assumptions[3]. Our transformation preserves ZK of the initial SNARG.

OUR THIRD CONTRIBUTION: A natural question is if the above SNARG for **FewP** can be extended to **NP**. The answer is no, under some mild assumptions.

---

[3] It is an open problem to obtain non-adaptively secure SNARGs from polynomial-time secure falsifiable assumptions. The SNARG in [39], was shown to be flawed [46].

We show that if the relation is $y = f(w)$ where f is an L-continuous leakage-resilient one-way function (CLR-OWF, a OWF where L bits may leak many times given that preimage w is updated), the proof size must be more than L bits. There exists a CLR-OWF under the discrete logarithm assumption [1] where L is linear in the size of w. Thus, the proof cannot be succinct.

Preprocessing and the GW Impossibility. In many applications we want to look beyond proof-succinctness and keep the verifier as efficient as possible. Ideally, we would like verification to run sublinearly in the size/time of the computation. It may seem counterintuitive that this is even possible: naturally, in circuit-based arguments for general computations the verifier should *at least* read the statement being proven. The latter includes both the description of the computation (i.e., the circuit) and its input (i.e., the deterministic input for an **NP** statement). There exists, however, a (commonly used) way around this problem: a *preprocessing* phase. In a preprocessing SNARG, the CRS depends on a specific circuit C, which is constructed once and for all and can later be used to prove/verify an unbounded number of proofs. This CRS is structured as the prover's CRS and the verifier's CRS, used by respective parties. The verifier's CRS is morally a digest of C. If the verifier's CRS is "short enough", the verification can be fast, requiring to read only the SNARG proof and a *partial* input description (the deterministic input to the C, without C itself); thus the verifier can run in time sublinear in $|C|$ (and in the witness size).

This preprocessing model encompasses a rich line of efficient SNARGs [27,28, 38,42]. The fact that it is a practically interesting model, as it achieves verifier-succinct SNARGs, further motivates a deeper theoretical understanding of it. A fundamental question is:

Can we construct preprocessing SNARGs based on falsifiable assumptions?

We argue this question has not been settled. First, none of the known preprocessing constructions rely on falsifiable assumptions. Also, known impossibility results do not inform us on the matter either. The Gentry-Wichs impossibility— which separates SNARGs and falsifiable assumptions—has long served as a justification to SNARGs for **NP** on non-falsifiable assumptions, *but it fails to shed light on the preprocessing setting*. The reason is that the GW result presumes a SNARG with a CRS with a specific pattern (we mean "prover's CRS" when we just say CRS from now on): their CRS cannot grow with the size of the instance, but should instead be bounded by a polynomial in the security parameter. In principle the question is then still open, more so because all existing preprocessing constructions, do have a CRS with the opposite pattern: it is usually as long as the instance[4].

Besides GW, other existing works also fail to provide an answer. For example, the work of [10] shows how to "bootstrap" a preprocessing SNARK into one without preprocessing to obtain a *complexity-preserving* SNARK, i.e., one

---

[4] For example, in pairing-based constructions such as [23] it consists of at least one group element per wire in the circuit to be proven.

without expensive preprocessing. The transformation can be applied to known SNARKs with expensive preprocessing to obtain a SNARK without the costly preprocessing. This complexity-preserving compilation, informally, establishes that preprocessing does not give any additional power; if preprocessing SNARKs were possible from falsifiable assumptions, one could apply the bootstrapping transformation and obtain short CRS SNARKs from falsifiable assumptions. Thus, any impossibility for SNARKs holds even for SNARKs that rely on expensive preprocessing. However, this bootstrapping crucially requires the *knowledge soundness* property and, therefore, only applies to SNARKs. The question of whether allowing a preprocessing phase allows constructing *SNARGs* based on falsifiable assumptions remains.

OUR FOURTH CONTRIBUTION: We fill the gap left by the GW result and show that even preprocessing SNARGs with a loosely-bounded CRS cannot be constructed from falsifiable assumptions in the standard model.

The Landscape of Impossibilities for Non-interactive Arguments. For our work to be as self-contained as possible, we complement the results above with an overarching view of impossibilities on non-interactive arguments (Sect. 6). This discussion strives to give a complete picture of existing impossibility results, related key properties of positive results, and gaps between positive and negative results. Motivated by the observation that preprocessing SNARGs do not come under the GW impossibility, we articulate the assumptions behind the impossibilities, and identify settings that would bypass them. Along the way, we formalize a class of languages that does not come under the Gentry-Wichs impossibility result. We dub them *trapdoor languages* (where there exists a "trapdoor" that makes the problem feasible) and exemplify several application settings that fall under the same category. Trapdoor languages can be thought of as a generalization of witness-sampleable (algebraic) languages in the work of [18].

1.1   Technical Overview

BB Extraction is Impossible for Any Hard Language (Adaptive Case). We show the impossibility of black-box extraction for non-interactive succinct arguments following the intuition that if an argument is too "small", it cannot contain information about a "long" witness. This makes extraction impossible since the extractor does not have any additional power, like access to the prover's randomness (as in non-black-box extractors for popular SNARKs) or the ability to rewind the prover (as in interactive arguments, such as Kilian's protocol).

Our result gives a precise characterization between the hardness of guessing the witness and the size of the proof. We show that if an efficient adversary can guess the witness at most with probability $\varepsilon(\lambda)$ and the knowledge soundness error of the argument system is $\varepsilon_{ks}(\lambda)$, then the proof size is at least $-\log(\varepsilon(\lambda) + \varepsilon_{ks}(\lambda))$ bits. For example, if we consider for simplicity that $\varepsilon_{ks}(\lambda) = 0$ and

$\varepsilon(\lambda) = 1/2^{\delta|w(\lambda)|}$ for some $\delta > 0$ and the witness size is $|w(\lambda)|$, then the proof size will be at least $\delta|w(\lambda)|$. In the full version of the paper, we show how to obtain a similar result based on the hardness of leakage-resilient OWFs.

BB Extraction is Possible for FewP (Non-adaptive Case). We then ask if the impossibility holds if we weaken the knowledge soundness requirement to be *non-adaptive*. Indeed, the non-adaptive case escapes the GW impossibility for SNARGs as we discuss in Sect. 6.1, and it is natural to hope for a positive result for extraction as well. In the non-adaptive knowledge soundness definition, the adversary chooses the statement before seeing the CRS, and then outputs a proof for the chosen statement. Intuitively, an extractor for such an adversary *does have* additional power – the extractor can rewind the prover to the point after the statement is chosen, sample different CRS'es and obtain multiple proofs for the same statement. Thus, non-adaptivity makes the prover stateful allowing for rewinding to be useful for an extractor[5]. We give a positive result in the non-adaptive case by showing a SNARK with black-box non-adaptive extraction (for a subset of **NP**). In the construction, we take advantage of our observation that the extractor can obtain more information by seeing multiple proofs corresponding to cleverly crafted CRS'es. At a high level, we ask the prover to encrypt a bit of the witness as part of the proof, in addition to proving the underlying relation. Given the secret key of the encryption scheme as the CRS trapdoor, the extractor can recover this witness bit. Now, the crafted CRS'es are such that they ask for different bits of the witness to be encrypted so that with every rewinding, the extractor learns a new bit until it can completely recover the witness.

While this works for valid statements with a *unique* witness, there are some subtleties that we need to address in order to show extraction for languages that have polynomially many witnesses, that is, class **FewP**. Here, the problem is that the adversary can choose to use a different witness each time, and there is no guarantee that the extractor can collect enough bits for any one witness. We now provide an overview of our construction. Let $\mathcal{R}$ be the relation for the language. We start with an existing SNARG for $\mathcal{R}$ and lift it to a SNARK. We use a Fully Homomorphic Encryption (FHE) scheme in order to hide the index of the bit the prover is asked to encrypt. Intuitively this is to hide the index so that the prover cannot adversarially choose a different witness for different indices. We augment the relation the SNARG proves to include a hash of the witness. Now the extractor keeps track of which witness it is extracting by using the hash to fingerprint. The extractor still needs to collect all bits of one witness. Here, we rely on the semantic security of the FHE scheme to show that the prover cannot consistently use witness w_1 for index i, and witness w_2, for index j. Since there are only polynomially many witnesses, assuming collision resistance of the hash function, the extractor succeeds in recovering all bits of some witness.

We also show that if the hash is encrypted and the initial SNARG has computational zero-knowledge, the resulting SNARK will also have computational zero-knowledge.

---

[5] Contrast this with the adaptive case, where the prover is stateless and rewinding is not useful.

BB Extraction is Impossible for All NP (Non-adaptive Case). The previous result, however, cannot be extended to all **NP** languages. We show this by relating an extractor's existence to breaking the relation's leakage resilience. A SNARK proof can be thought of as leakage on the witness. When this leakage is small, no extractor can succeed if the **NP** relation is leakage resilient. This impossibility due to leakage resilience is easy to see in the adaptive case. In non-adaptive extraction, an extractor can potentially rewind the adversary and obtain multiple proofs; akin to a leakage resilience adversary obtaining leakage multiple times. We formalize this connection using *continuous* leakage resilience. In L-leakage-resilient OWF (LR-OWF), one-wayness holds even if L bits of the preimage are leaked. In L-continuous LR-OWF (CLR-OWF), L bits can be leaked multiple times with the caveat that the preimage has to be updated before each leakage. Moreover, if for an OWF f we have $y = f(w)$ and w is updated to w', then also $y = f(w')$.

We connect this primitive to the impossibility of non-adaptive black-box knowledge soundness of SNARKs. Suppose we have a SNARK for the relation $y = f(w)$ where f, y are public, and w is the witness. We view the proof as leakage on the witness given to the adversary. If the proof is at most L bits long, then the extractor can learn at most L bits of information about the witness with each rewinding. Now if the adversary also updates its witness w between queries, L-CLR of f implies that the extractor cannot recover the witness. Thus, the SNARK proof is at least L bits long.

We can instantiate this result with $(1 - \frac{2}{n})|w|$-CLR-OWF from [1] which is based on the discrete logarithm assumption. The witness size $|w| = n \log q$, where q is the size of the discrete logarithm group and n is an input size parameter. Thus, the proof size will be asymptotically linear in $|w|$.

Extending GW to Preprocessing SNARGs. The central idea in the GW proof is to show that every SNARG for an **NP** language has a *simulatable* adversary. An unbounded adversarial prover that breaks soundness comes with an efficient simulator such that no efficient machine can tell whether it is interacting with the prover or the simulator. A black-box reduction is an efficient oracle-access machine that breaks some falsifiable assumption when given access to a successful adversary. Suppose the reduction given oracle access to the prover breaks the assumption. In that case, the efficient machine with oracle access to the efficient simulator also breaks it since the efficient challenger of the falsifiable assumption cannot distinguish the prover from the simulator. Thus, assuming a simulatable adversary, the theorem follows.

Our proof extending the GW impossibility to preprocessing SNARGs follows the GW template. We observe that the GW proof needs the CRS to be short in constructing a simulatable adversary: the reduction that has oracle access to either the computationally unbounded prover or the efficient simulator can query the oracle with 1^m where m is different from the security parameter n. If m is small enough compared to the actual security parameter n, then the reduction can distinguish the adversary from the simulator. Therefore, the proof modifies the simulator to behave differently in answering queries with a sufficiently small

m; this is done by hardcoding a table of responses as non-uniform advice. The table has hardcoded entries (x, π) for every m and every CRS. Therefore, the CRS size is bounded by a polynomial in the security parameter and cannot grow with the size of the instance.

When considering security-parameter preserving reductions, the reduction queries its oracle with the same security parameter. Therefore, a hardcoded table is unnecessary, and we show how the proof goes through when the size of the CRS depends on the instance, as in indexed relations. We leave the case with non-parameter-preserving reductions as an open problem.

1.2   Related Work

Succinctness vs Black-Box Extraction. Here we discuss works that trade succinctness for black-box extraction. C∅C∅ [36] and Tiramisu [6] aim at compiling a SNARK into a UC-secure scheme. However, this transformation results in NIZK arguments whose proof size and verification time are (quasi-)linear in the witness size. This degradation in succinctness is claimed to be unavoidable if one demands black-box extraction. In [5], Baghery et al. add black-box extraction to [28] SNARK. Although the proof size is again asymptotically linear in the witness size, the authors' goal is to strive for concrete efficiency. In [15], Chase et al. construct controlled malleable proofs that crucially require the stronger black-box version of extractability. Even though their starting point is a SNARG, to obtain black-box extraction of the controlled malleable proof, they give up succinctness and achieve controlled malleable NIZKs.

What is common in all the works above as an idea is to perform verifiable encryption by encrypting the witness and then proving knowledge of the value inside the ciphertext in addition to the original relation. The black-box extractor works by decrypting. This is why the black-box extractor comes at the cost of succinctness: the proof includes a ciphertext and a proof of correct encryption.

Other Works. The work in [33] proposes an alternative composability model to the UC model, which can (at least to some extent) use non-black-box extractability and knowledge-type assumptions. In this case, one can still obtain succinct UC SNARKs (under some restrictions) without needing black-box extraction.

2   Preliminaries

PPT stands for probabilistic polynomial time. We use λ to denote the security parameter. We write $x \leftarrow_{\$} X$ to denote that x is sampled from a distribution X. If X is a set, then $x \leftarrow_{\$} X$ denotes uniform sampling. We write $f(\lambda) = \mathsf{negl}(\lambda)$ when f is negligible in λ and $f(\lambda) = \mathsf{poly}(\lambda)$ when f is polynomial in λ. For an integer $N \geq 1$, we define $[N] := \{1, \ldots, N\}$.

Indistinguishability. We say that two distributions X_1 and X_2 are $(s(\lambda), \epsilon(\lambda))$-indistinguishable if for any circuit $\mathcal{D}$ of size $s(\lambda)$, we have $|\Pr[\mathcal{D}(X_1) = 1] - \Pr[\mathcal{D}(X_2) = 1]| \leq \epsilon(\lambda)$.

Hard-on-Average Problems. We define a language $\mathcal{L} \in \mathbf{NP}$ to be a hard-on-average problem if

- It has an efficient instance sampler $\mathsf{Samp}_{\mathcal{L}}(1^\lambda)$ that outputs $\mathsf{x} \in \mathcal{L}$ together with an **NP** witness w.
- There is an efficient sampler $\mathsf{Samp}_{\bar{\mathcal{L}}}(1^\lambda)$ that with an overwhelming probability outputs $\mathsf{x} \notin \mathcal{L}$.
- It is computationally hard to distinguish outputs of $\mathsf{Samp}_{\mathcal{L}}(1^\lambda)$ and $\mathsf{Samp}_{\bar{\mathcal{L}}}(1^\lambda)$.

Language $\mathcal{L}$ is $(s(\lambda), \epsilon(\lambda))$-hard if distributions of x from $\mathsf{Samp}_{\mathcal{L}}(1^\lambda)$ and $\mathsf{Samp}_{\bar{\mathcal{L}}}(1^\lambda)$ are $(s(\lambda), \epsilon(\lambda))$-indistinguishable. It is sub-exponentially hard if there exits some constant $\delta > 0$ such that previous distributions are $(s(\lambda), \epsilon(\lambda))$-indistinguishable for $s(\lambda) = 2^{\Omega(\lambda^\delta)}$ and $\epsilon(\lambda) = 1/2^{\Omega(\lambda^\delta)}$. Lastly, $\mathcal{L}$ is exponentially hard if the above holds and moreover $|\mathsf{x}| + |\mathsf{w}| = O(\lambda^\delta)$ for $(\mathsf{x}, \mathsf{w}) \leftarrow_{\$} \mathsf{Samp}_{\mathcal{L}}(1^\lambda)$.

Simple example is the DDH language where $\mathsf{Samp}_{\mathcal{L}}$ outputs group elements g^a, g^b, g^{ab}, where a, b are chosen uniformly at random and g is a group generator, and $\mathsf{Samp}_{\bar{\mathcal{L}}}$ outputs 3 random group elements g^a, g^b, g^c. More generally, hard-on-average problem is implied by the existence of one-way-functions since it is possible to construct a PRG from a one-way function [30].

Falsifiable Assumptions. Below we recall the notion of falsifiable assumptions.

Definition 1 ([24]). *A falsifiable cryptographic assumption $(\mathcal{C}, c)$ consists of a PPT challenger $\mathcal{C}$ and a constant $c \in [0, 1)$. We say that $\mathcal{A}$ wins $(\mathcal{C}, c)$ if $\mathcal{A}(1^\lambda)$ and $\mathcal{C}(1^\lambda)$ interact and finally $\mathcal{C}$ outputs 1. The assumption $(\mathcal{C}, c)$ holds if for all non-uniform PPT $\mathcal{A}$, $\Pr[\mathcal{A}$ wins $(\mathcal{C}, c)] \leq c + \mathsf{negl}(\lambda)$. Otherwise we say that $(\mathcal{C}, c)$ is false.*

Definition 1 captures most cryptographic assumptions from the literature. In the case of *search* assumptions (e.g., discrete logarithm problem and shortest vector problem), we set $c = 0$. In the case of *decisional* assumptions (e.g., decisional Diffie-Hellman, decisional Learning with Errors), we set $c = 1/2$ since the adversary can win with probability $1/2$ by random guessing. Knowledge assumptions [19,29] are seemingly non-falsifiable.

2.1 Continuous Leakage-Resilient OWFs

A leakage-resilient OWF (LR-OWF) f is a function that is one-way even when the adversary is allowed to learn arbitrary functions of $f(x)$'s preimage as long as this leakage is restricted to L bits. Continuous LR-OWF (CLR-OWF) in the floppy model [1,3] is a generalization of this where leakages can happen multiple times. In short, it assumes a master secret key which is kept in a leakage-free server (e.g., on a floppy disk) and then can be used to securely update the preimage x. L bits of leakage on the preimage can occur after each update.

Importantly however, updates have to preserve the output of the OWF, that is $f(x) = f(x')$ when x' is an update of x.

More formally, a CLR-OWF consists of the following probabilistic polynomial time (PPT) algorithms: (1) $\mathsf{KGen}(1^\lambda)$ that outputs a public parameter pp and an update key uk. (2) $\mathsf{Sample}(\mathsf{pp})$ takes as input the parameter pp and outputs a random OWF input x. (3) $\mathsf{Eval}(\mathsf{pp}, x)$ is a deterministic algorithm that produces the OWF output y. (4) $\mathsf{Update}(\mathsf{uk}, x)$ takes in the update key uk and x, and outputs an updated OWF input x'.

We assume that a CLR-OWF satisfies the following properties.

Correctness. For any $(\mathsf{pp}, \mathsf{uk}) \in \mathsf{KGen}(1^\lambda)$ and $x \in \{0, 1\}^*$, we have that $\mathsf{Eval}(\mathsf{pp}, \mathsf{Update}(\mathsf{uk}, x)) = \mathsf{Eval}(\mathsf{pp}, x)$.

L-Continuous leakage-resilience. Let $L = L(\lambda)$. For any PPT $\mathcal{A}$,

$$\Pr\left[\begin{array}{c} (\mathsf{pp}, \mathsf{uk}) \leftarrow \mathsf{KGen}(1^\lambda), x \leftarrow \mathsf{Sample}(\mathsf{pp}), \\ y \leftarrow \mathsf{Eval}(\mathsf{pp}, x), x' \leftarrow \mathcal{A}^{\mathsf{O}_L(\cdot)}(\mathsf{pp}, y) \end{array} : y = \mathsf{Eval}(\mathsf{pp}, x')\right] = \mathsf{negl}(\lambda),$$

where $\mathsf{O}_L(\cdot)$ is an oracle that takes as an input a leakage function $h : \{0, 1\}^* \rightarrow \{0, 1\}^L$, on which $\mathsf{O}_L(h)$ sets $x \leftarrow \mathsf{Update}(\mathsf{uk}, x)$ and then returns $h(x)$.

There exists CLR-OWFs [1], which can leak almost the full key.

2.2 Argument System

We recall the notion of non-interactive argument systems.

Definition 2 (Indexed relation [16]). *An indexed relation $\mathcal{R}$ is a set of triples $(\mathsf{i}, \mathsf{x}, \mathsf{w})$ where i is the index, x is the instance, and w is the **NP**-witness; the corresponding indexed language $\mathcal{L}(\mathcal{R})$ is the set of pairs (i, x) for which there exists a witness w such that $(\mathsf{i}, \mathsf{x}, \mathsf{w}) \in \mathcal{R}$. Indexed relation is associated with an efficient index sampling algorithm $\mathcal{I}$ that outputs an index i on input 1^λ.*

For example, i can be an arithmetic circuit and x and w public and private inputs to the circuit such that the circuit outputs 1. We say that an indexed language is a hard-on-average problem if it is defined like in Sect. 2, but additionally $\mathsf{Samp}_{\mathcal{L}}$ and $\mathsf{Samp}_{\bar{\mathcal{L}}}$ take $\mathsf{i} \leftarrow \mathcal{I}(1^\lambda)$ as an input.

A non-interactive argument system for an indexed relation $\mathcal{R}$ is a tuple of PPT algorithms $\Pi = (\mathsf{Setup}, \mathsf{P}, \mathsf{V})$. The setup algorithm $\mathsf{Setup}(1^\lambda, \mathsf{i})$ produces a common reference string crs and a trapdoor td. The prover algorithm $\mathsf{P}(\mathsf{crs}, \mathsf{x}, \mathsf{w})$ produces a proof π for the statement $(\mathsf{i}, \mathsf{x}) \in \mathcal{L}$. The verifier algorithm $\mathsf{V}(\mathsf{crs}, \mathsf{x}, \pi)$ decides if π is a valid proof for a statement (i, x) by outputting either 0 or 1. Notice that P and V are not directly given i as an input and instead get a crs which depends on i. This allows to potentially compress the index description by preprocessing.

We require that Π satisfies the following two properties.

Completeness. For all $(\mathsf{i}, \mathsf{x}, \mathsf{w}) \in \mathcal{R}$, $\Pr[(\mathsf{crs}, \mathsf{td}) \leftarrow \mathsf{Setup}(1^\lambda, \mathsf{i}), \pi \leftarrow \mathsf{P}(\mathsf{crs}, \mathsf{x}, \mathsf{w}) : \mathsf{V}(\mathsf{crs}, \mathsf{x}, \pi) = 1] = 1$.

Soundness. For all non-uniform PPT adversaries $\mathcal{A}$,

$$\Pr\left[\begin{array}{cc} i \leftarrow \mathcal{I}(1^\lambda), (\mathsf{crs}, \mathsf{td}) \leftarrow \mathsf{Setup}(1^\lambda, i) & \mathsf{V}(\mathsf{crs}, \mathsf{x}, \pi) = 1 \wedge \\ (\mathsf{x}, \pi) \leftarrow \mathcal{A}(1^\lambda, i, \mathsf{crs}) & (i, \mathsf{x}) \notin \mathcal{L} \end{array} : \right] = \mathsf{negl}(\lambda) \ .$$

In some parts of the paper (where it does not matter), we drop i and $\mathcal{I}(1^\lambda)$ from the definitions for simplicity. However, index plays a crucial role in Sect. 5.

We call an argument system a SNARG (succinct non-interactive argument) if additionally the following holds.

Proof succinctness. [24] Exists a constant $c < 1$ such that the length of the proof π is bounded by $\mathsf{suc}_c(\lambda, |\mathsf{x}|, |\mathsf{w}|) := \mathsf{poly}(\lambda) \cdot (|\mathsf{x}| + |\mathsf{w}|)^c$.

Various other succinctness definitions can be found from the literature. We occasionally discuss two other forms of succinctness.

Verifier succinctness. Exists a constant $c < 1$ such that the verifier's running time is bounded by $\mathsf{poly}(|\mathsf{x}| + \mathsf{suc}_c(\lambda, |\mathsf{x}|, |\mathsf{w}|))$.
CRS succinctness. CRS size is $\mathsf{poly}(\lambda)$. Importantly, CRS size is independent of $|i|$.

3   On Adaptively-Secure Black-Box Extraction

A folklore understanding is that if an argument has black-box knowledge soundness (i.e., there is an efficient algorithm Ext that can recover a witness from a proof by using a trapdoor and Ext is independent of adversary's code), then the proof has to be "as long as the witness". It is easy to see that such a statement is only partially accurate. Consider an argument system for some relation $\mathcal{R}_\mathcal{L}$ where $\mathcal{L}$ is an **NP**-language. The same argument system works for a modified relation $\mathcal{R}'_\mathcal{L} = \{(\mathsf{x}, \mathsf{w} \| 0^k) : (\mathsf{x}, \mathsf{w}) \in \mathcal{R}_\mathcal{L}\}$ where the witness is padded with k zeroes for an arbitrary number k. An extractor Ext for $\mathcal{R}'_\mathcal{L}$ needs to append 0^k to the witness it extracts for $\mathcal{R}_\mathcal{L}$. Notably, the proof length for $\mathcal{R}'_\mathcal{L}$ remains the same as for $\mathcal{R}_\mathcal{L}$ independently of witness padding length. This section correctly formalizes the folklore result about the proof size and witness length by associating the hardness of finding the witness with the size of the argument.

We begin by recalling the definition of black-box knowledge soundness.

Black-Box Knowledge Soundness. An argument system is black-box $\varepsilon_{ks}(\lambda)$-knowledge sound for a relation $\mathcal{R}$ if there exists a PPT extractor Ext, such that for any PPT adversary $\mathcal{A}$,

$$\Pr\left[\begin{array}{cc} (\mathsf{crs}, \mathsf{td}) \leftarrow \mathsf{Setup}(1^\lambda), (\mathsf{x}, \pi) \leftarrow \mathcal{A}(\mathsf{crs}) & \mathsf{V}(\mathsf{crs}, \mathsf{x}, \pi) = 1 \wedge \\ \mathsf{w} \leftarrow \mathsf{Ext}(\mathsf{crs}, \mathsf{td}, \mathsf{x}, \pi) & (\mathsf{x}, \mathsf{w}) \notin \mathcal{R} \end{array} : \right] \leq \varepsilon_{ks}(\lambda) \ .$$

We say the argument system is black-box knowledge sound if $\varepsilon_{ks}(\lambda) = \mathsf{negl}(\lambda)$.

We prove that if the witness of the language cannot be guessed, except for probability ε, then the proof size must be at least $-\log(\varepsilon + \varepsilon_{ks})$ bits long. We start by formalizing the witness guessing probability.

Definition 3. *Let $\mathcal{L}$ be an **NP** language and $\mathcal{R}_\mathcal{L}$ a corresponding relation. We say that an efficiently sampleable distribution $\mathcal{D}_\mathcal{L}$ over $\mathcal{L}$ is $\varepsilon(\lambda)$-witness-hard for a relation $\mathcal{R}_\mathcal{L}$ if for any PPT guesser $\mathcal{M}$, and any security parameter $\lambda \in \mathbb{N}$,*

$$\Pr[x \leftarrow \mathcal{D}(1^\lambda), w \leftarrow \mathcal{M}(1^\lambda, x) : (x, w) \in \mathcal{R}_\mathcal{L}] \leq \varepsilon(1^\lambda) .$$

Theorem 1. *Suppose an efficiently sampleable distribution $\mathcal{D}_\mathcal{L}$ over some **NP** language $\mathcal{L}$ is $\varepsilon(\lambda)$-witness-hard for a relation $\mathcal{R}_\mathcal{L}$. Let Π be an argument system that has (perfect) completeness and black-box $\varepsilon_{ks}(\lambda)$-knowledge soundness. Then the argument size of Π is at least $-\log(\varepsilon(\lambda) + \varepsilon_{ks}(\lambda))$ bits.*

Proof. Suppose that Π is an argument system with black-box extractor Ext and the argument size is bounded by $p(\lambda)$ bits. We construct a witness-guesser $\mathcal{M}^*$ (see Fig. 1), which picks a crs and an extraction key td and guesses uniformly randomly a proof π of size $p(\lambda)$ bits. It then returns the output of the black-box witness extractor Ext(crs, td, x, π).

Let us analyze the success probability $\varepsilon_{\mathcal{M}^*}$ of $\mathcal{M}^*$ in the witness-hardness game against $\mathcal{D}_\mathcal{L}$. Let $\mathcal{E}$ be the distribution (x, w, crs, π) obtained by running $x \leftarrow \mathcal{D}(1^\lambda)$ and $w \leftarrow \mathcal{M}^*(1^\lambda, x)$ (crs and π are generated inside $\mathcal{M}^*$). Then,

$$\begin{aligned}
\varepsilon_{\mathcal{M}^*} &= \Pr\left[(x, w, crs, \pi) \leftarrow \mathcal{E}(1^\lambda) : (x, w) \in \mathcal{R}_\mathcal{L}\right] \\
&\geq \Pr\left[(x, w, crs, \pi) \leftarrow \mathcal{E}(1^\lambda) : (x, w) \in \mathcal{R}_\mathcal{L} \wedge V(crs, x, \pi) = 1\right] \\
&= \Pr\left[(x, w, crs, \pi) \leftarrow \mathcal{E}(1^\lambda) : (x, w) \in \mathcal{R}_\mathcal{L} \mid V(crs, x, \pi) = 1\right] \\
&\quad \cdot \Pr\left[(x, w, crs, \pi) \leftarrow \mathcal{E}(1^\lambda) : V(crs, x, \pi) = 1\right] .
\end{aligned}$$

Let us analyze $\varepsilon_1 := \Pr\left[(x, w, crs, \pi) \leftarrow \mathcal{E}(1^\lambda) : V(crs, x, \pi) = 1\right]$ and $\varepsilon_2 := \Pr\left[(x, w, crs, \pi) \leftarrow \mathcal{E} : (x, w) \in \mathcal{R}_\mathcal{L} \mid V(crs, x, \pi) = 1\right]$ separately. Starting with ε_1, since $x \in \mathcal{L}$, by perfect completeness there exists at least one proof of size at most $p(\lambda)$ bits that is accepted by the verifier. Thus, $\varepsilon_1 \geq 1/2^{p(\lambda)}$. In order to lower bound ε_2, we construct an adversary $\mathcal{B}$ against black-box knowledge soundness. The adversary $\mathcal{B}$, described in Fig. 1, outputs $x \leftarrow \mathcal{D}_\mathcal{L}$ and a randomly sampled proof $\pi \leftarrow \{0, 1\}^{p(\lambda)}$. By inlining $\mathcal{B}$ into the black-box knowledge soundness game, we get $\Pr[(x, w, crs, \pi) \leftarrow \mathcal{E}(1^\lambda) : V(crs, x, \pi) = 1 \wedge (x, w) \notin \mathcal{R}_\mathcal{L}] \leq \varepsilon_{ks}(\lambda)$. That is

$$\begin{aligned}
&\Pr[(x, w, crs, \pi) \leftarrow \mathcal{E}(1^\lambda) : V(crs, x, \pi) = 1 \wedge (x, w) \notin \mathcal{R}_\mathcal{L}] \\
&= \Pr[(x, w, crs, \pi) \leftarrow \mathcal{E}(1^\lambda) : (x, w) \notin \mathcal{R}_\mathcal{L} \mid V(crs, x, \pi) = 1] \\
&\quad \cdot \Pr[(x, w, crs, \pi) \leftarrow \mathcal{E}(1^\lambda) : V(crs, x, \pi) = 1] \\
&\geq \Pr[(x, w, crs, \pi) \leftarrow \mathcal{E}(1^\lambda) : (x, w) \notin \mathcal{R}_\mathcal{L} \mid V(crs, x, \pi) = 1] \cdot \tfrac{1}{2^{p(\lambda)}} .
\end{aligned}$$

Thus, $\Pr[(x, w, crs, \pi) \leftarrow \mathcal{E}(1^\lambda) : (x, w) \notin \mathcal{R}_\mathcal{L} \mid V(crs, x, \pi) = 1] \leq \varepsilon_{ks}(\lambda) \cdot 2^{p(\lambda)}$, which means that $\varepsilon_2 > 1 - \varepsilon_{ks}(\lambda) \cdot 2^{p(\lambda)}$.

By combining those results, we get that $\varepsilon(\lambda) \geq \varepsilon_{\mathcal{M}^*} > \tfrac{1}{2^{p(\lambda)}} \cdot (1 - \varepsilon_{ks}(\lambda) \cdot 2^{p(\lambda)}) = \tfrac{1}{2^{p(\lambda)}} - \varepsilon_{ks}(\lambda)$. It follows that $\varepsilon(\lambda) + \varepsilon_{ks}(\lambda) > \tfrac{1}{2^{p(\lambda)}}$, which we can rewrite as $p(\lambda) > -\log(\varepsilon(\lambda) + \varepsilon_{ks}(\lambda))$. $\qquad\square$

$\mathcal{M}^*(1^\lambda, \mathsf{x})$	$\mathcal{B}(\mathsf{crs})$
$(\mathsf{crs}, \mathsf{td}) \leftarrow \mathsf{Setup}(1^\lambda); \pi \leftarrow\!\!\$\ \{0,1\}^{p(\lambda)}$	$\mathsf{x} \leftarrow \mathcal{D}(1^\lambda); \pi \leftarrow\!\!\$\ \{0,1\}^{p(\lambda)}$
$\mathbf{return}\ \mathsf{w} \leftarrow \mathsf{Ext}(\mathsf{crs}, \mathsf{td}, \mathsf{x}, \pi)$	$\mathbf{return}\ (\mathsf{x}, \pi)$

Fig. 1. $\mathcal{M}^*$ guesses a witness for $\mathcal{R}_\mathcal{L}$; $\mathcal{B}$: adversary for knowledge soundness.

To understand this claim better, let us consider for simplicity that $\varepsilon_{ks}(\lambda) = 0$. Then if $\varepsilon = \frac{1}{2^{k(\lambda)}}$, we obtain the lower bound $p(\lambda) \geq -\log(\frac{1}{2^{k(\lambda)}} + 0) = k(\lambda)$. In one extreme case, we can imagine that the best PPT witness guesser is no better than an algorithm that guesses the witness at random, i.e., $\varepsilon(\lambda) = 1/|\mathsf{w}|$. Then we would get the folklore result that $p(\lambda) = |\pi| \geq |\mathsf{w}|$. In the other extreme, suppose that the language is in P, in which case $\varepsilon(\lambda) = 1$. Then we get that $-\log(\varepsilon) = 0$, which fits the intuition that there is no need to communicate a proof for languages in P. However, in a typical situation (where we have some hard language), the lower bound falls somewhere between those extremes.

A closely related but somewhat less precise result can be directly concluded from leakage-resilient OWFs by viewing a proof as leakage on the witness. We explore this direction further in the full version of the paper.

4 Non-adaptive Black-Box Knowledge Soundness

This section defines non-adaptive black-box knowledge soundness and shows our positive result for **FewP** and a negative result for **NP**.

Below we define non-adaptive black-box *knowledge-soundness*. To the best of our knowledge it has not appeared in prior literature.

Definition 4 (Non-adaptive Black-box Knowledge Soundness.). *An argument system is non-adaptive black-box $\varepsilon_{ks}(\lambda)$-knowledge sound for a relation $\mathcal{R}$ if there exists a non-uniform PPT extractor Ext, such that for any non-uniform PPT adversary $\mathcal{A} = (\mathcal{A}_{inp}, \mathcal{A}_{prf})$,*

$$\Pr\left[\begin{array}{c} (\mathsf{x}, \mathsf{st}) \leftarrow \mathcal{A}_{inp}(1^\lambda), (\mathsf{crs}, \mathsf{td}) \leftarrow \mathsf{Setup}(1^\lambda) \\ \pi \leftarrow \mathcal{A}_{prf}(\mathsf{st}, \mathsf{crs}), \mathsf{w} \leftarrow \mathsf{Ext}^{\mathcal{A}_{prf}(\mathsf{st}, \cdot)}(\mathsf{crs}, \mathsf{td}, \mathsf{x}, \pi) \end{array} : \begin{array}{c} \mathsf{V}(\mathsf{crs}, \mathsf{x}, \pi) = 1 \\ \wedge (\mathsf{x}, \mathsf{w}) \notin \mathcal{R} \end{array}\right] \leq \varepsilon_{ks}(\lambda) \ .$$

We say that the argument system is (non-adaptively) black-box knowledge sound if $\varepsilon_{ks}(\lambda) = \mathsf{negl}(\lambda)$.

Remark 1. The adversary in Definition 4 is stateful only between the input-challenge stage and the proof-challenge stage (through st), but not otherwise. We also assume that on each query $\mathcal{A}_{prf}(\mathsf{st}, \cdot)$ gets fresh random coins.

4.1 A Construction for FewP

In this section, we show that, under the existence of fully homomorphic encryption, collision-resistant hash functions and SNARGs (not necessarily of knowledge) for a specific complexity class K, there exists a non-adaptively secure

SNARK with black-box extraction for K^6. We can obtain non-adaptive black-box knowledge soundness for a non-trivial subset of **NP** called **FewP**. The class **FewP** can be described as the class of languages admitting at most a polynomial number of witnesses. We remark that if one-way permutations exist, then $\mathbf{P} \neq \mathbf{FewP}^7$. One example of a natural application of a SNARK for **FewP** is proving knowledge of w such that $\mathcal{R}(\mathsf{w})$ is satisfied (for arbitrary relation $\mathcal{R}$) and w opens a perfectly binding commitment.

Further preliminaries for this section can be found in the full version of the paper, where we define the non-adaptive soundness of SNARG (which simply adapts Definition 4 to the non-extractable case) and the standard definitions of fully homomorphic encryption (FHE) and collision-resistant hash functions (CRHF) which will be tools in our construction.

We present our extractable construction in Fig. 2^8. As discussed in the introduction, its main intuition is that the prover provides a (ciphertext containing a) bit of the witness together with the proof. The index for which it is providing such a bit must be somehow hidden. This intuitively prevents the adversary from acting differently for different bits (e.g., using different valid witnesses). This allows us to extract by repeatedly asking the prover for a proof referring to a different index. To achieve the latter, we use an FHE scheme (see also Remark 2). When extracting, we will need to keep track of what witness we are extracting (since there could be several). We do this by using a fingerprint through a collision-resistant hash function. We encrypt the hash with some (not necessarily homomorphic) cryptosystem to obtain zero-knowledge (ZK). In fact, our soundness proof requires that the prover encrypts the hash with a different public key than the witness bit.

We denote FHE encryptions of a message x (with an implicit public-key that should be clear from the context) through double brackets $[\![x]\!]$.

THE EXTRACTOR FOR **FewP**. The extractor is presented in Fig. 3. It works by collecting different bits of the witness by decrypting ct_b (the ciphertext returned by the prover) and storing it in some table indexed by the corresponding hash. The crucial point is that there is only a polynomial number of witnesses and thus the extractor can (in the worst-case) "fingerprint" them all. Hashing the witness (through a collision-resistant hash function) keeps the proof succinct.

Theorem 2. *If $\Pi_\exists$ is a non-adaptively sound SNARG scheme for **NP**, FHE is a semantically secure FHE scheme, PKE is a sematically secure cryptosystem and H is a family of CRHFs, then the construction in Fig. 2 is a non-adaptive SNARK for **FewP** satisfying Definition 4. If $\Pi_\exists$ has additionally computational ZK, then so does the resulting SNARK.*

Proof (Sketch). Due to space limitations, we only give a high-level overview of the security proof. Detailed proofs are available in the full version of the paper.

---

[6] This class should include FHE encryption and CRHF and should be closed under conjunction. In our theorem statement, we simply require a SNARG for **NP**.

[7] More generally, if poly-to-one one-way functions exist then $\mathbf{P} \neq \mathbf{FewP}$ [2].

[8] A slightly simpler construction for the case of **UP** (**NP** statements with a unique witness) can be seen in the full version.

$\text{Setup}(1^\lambda)$

$(\hat{\text{crs}}, \hat{\text{td}}) \leftarrow \Pi_\exists.\text{Setup}(1^\lambda); i^* \leftarrow\$ [N_w]; (\text{pk}_{\text{FHE}}, \text{sk}_{\text{FHE}}) \leftarrow \text{FHE.KG}(1^\lambda)$

$\text{ct}_{i^*} \leftarrow \text{FHE.Enc}(\text{pk}_{\text{FHE}}, i^*); \text{hk} \leftarrow\$ \mathcal{K}_{\text{CRHF}}; (\text{pk}, \text{sk}) \leftarrow \text{PKE.KG}(1^\lambda)$

$\textbf{return } \left(\text{crs} := (\hat{\text{crs}}, \text{ct}_{i^*}, \text{hk}, \text{pk}_{\text{FHE}}, \text{pk}), \text{td} := (\text{sk}_{\text{FHE}}, \hat{\text{td}}, \text{sk})\right)$

$\text{P}(\text{crs}, \mathcal{R}, \text{x}, \text{w})$

$h \leftarrow H_{\text{hk}}(\text{w}); r \leftarrow\$ \text{PKE.Rnd}; \text{ct}_h \leftarrow \text{PKE.Enc}(\text{pk}, h; r)$

$\text{ct}_{\text{bit}} \leftarrow \text{FHE.Eval}(\text{pk}_{\text{FHE}}, f_{\text{proj}}, \text{ct}_{i^*}, \text{w}), \text{ where } f_{\text{proj}}(i, \text{w}) := \text{w}_i$

$\pi \leftarrow \Pi_\exists.\text{P}(\hat{\text{crs}}, \mathcal{R}', (\text{x}, \text{hk}, \text{pk}_{\text{FHE}}, \text{pk}, \text{ct}_h, \text{ct}_{i^*}, \text{ct}_{\text{bit}}), (\text{w}, r))$

$\quad \text{where } \mathcal{R}'(\text{x}, \text{hk}, \text{pk}_{\text{FHE}}, \text{pk}, \text{ct}_h, \text{ct}_{i^*}, \text{ct}_{\text{bit}}; (\text{w}, r)) \iff$
$\quad\quad \mathcal{R}(\text{x}, \text{w}) \wedge \text{ct}_h = \text{PKE.Enc}(\text{pk}, H_{\text{hk}}(\text{w}); r) \wedge \text{ct}_{\text{bit}} = \text{FHE.Eval}(\text{pk}_{\text{FHE}}, f_{\text{proj}}, \text{ct}_{i^*}, \text{w})$

$\textbf{return } \pi^* := (\pi, \text{ct}_h, \text{ct}_{\text{bit}})$

$\text{V}(\text{crs}, \mathcal{R}, \text{x}, \pi^*)$

$\text{Parse } \pi^* \text{ as } (\pi, \text{ct}_h, \text{ct}_{\text{bit}}); \textbf{return } \Pi_\exists.\text{V}(\hat{\text{crs}}, \mathcal{R}', (\text{x}, \text{hk}, \text{pk}_{\text{FHE}}, \text{pk}, \text{ct}_h, \text{ct}_{i^*}, \text{ct}_{\text{bit}}))$

$\quad \text{where } \mathcal{R}' \text{ is defined like above}$

Fig. 2. Non-adaptively secure black-box extractable construction for **FewP**. N_w is a bound on the witness size. $\Pi_\exists$ is the SNARG scheme.

$\mathcal{E}(\text{crs}, \text{td}, \text{x}, \pi)$	$\text{QIdx}(\text{x}, j)$

$\mathcal{E}(\text{crs}, \text{td}, \text{x}, \pi)$

Initialize empty table W
Retrieve $(\hat{\text{crs}}, \text{pk}_{\text{FHE}}, \text{pk}, \text{sk}_{\text{FHE}}, \text{sk}, \text{hk})$ from crs, td
$\textbf{for } j^* = 1, \ldots, N_w$
$\quad \text{Run } \text{QIdx}(\text{x}, j^*)$
$\textbf{endfor}$
Let h^* s.t. $W[h^*][j] \neq \perp$ for all j
$\textbf{return } W[h^*][1] \ldots W[h^*][N_w]$

$\text{QIdx}(\text{x}, j)$

$[\![j]\!] \leftarrow \text{FHE.Enc}(\text{pk}_{\text{FHE}}, j)$
Let $\text{crs}_j := (\hat{\text{crs}}, [\![j]\!], \text{hk}, \text{pk}_{\text{FHE}}, \text{pk})$
$\textbf{for } k = 1, \ldots, N_q = \text{poly}(\lambda)$
$\quad \text{Query } \mathcal{A}_{\text{prf}} \text{ on } (\text{crs}_j, \text{x})$
$\quad\quad \text{obtaining } \pi^* = (\pi, \text{ct}_h, \text{ct}_{\text{bit}})$
$\quad \text{If proof } \pi \text{ accepts then}$
$\quad\quad b \leftarrow \text{FHE.Dec}(\text{sk}_{\text{FHE}}, \text{ct}_{\text{bit}})$
$\quad \text{else } b \leftarrow \perp$
$\quad h \leftarrow \text{PKE.Dec}(\text{sk}, \text{ct}_h)$
$\quad \text{Set } W[h][j] \leftarrow b$
$\textbf{endfor}$

Fig. 3. Extractor for the case for **FewP**

The ZK simulator encrypts any value (e.g., 0) in ct_h and ct_{bit} and simulates the proof π of $\Pi_\exists$. Now computational ZK follows straightforwardly from the semantic security of PKE and FHE and from the computational ZK of $\Pi_\exists$.

The proof of knowledge-soundness is more involved. We use the extractor in Fig. 3. The extractor can have embedded N_w, a bound on the length of witnesses, since it is non-uniform. We define $S(j)$, for index j, as the set of strings h for which $W[h][j] \neq \perp$ after running $\text{QIdx}(\text{x}, j)$. That is,

$$S(j) := \left\{ h : W[h][j] \neq \bot \text{ after running } \mathsf{QIdx}(\mathsf{x}, j) \right\} \ .$$

From non-adaptive soundness of $\Pi_\exists$ it follows that for any $h \in S(j)$ there exists (with an overwhelming probability) w such that $\mathsf{R}(\mathsf{x}, \mathsf{w}) \wedge \mathsf{H}(\mathsf{w}) = h$. Therefore, $h \in S(j)$ intuitively means "the extractor holds the j-th bit of a witness w such that $\mathsf{H}(\mathsf{w}) = h$".

In order to argue black-box knowledge soundness, we must successfully extract from an adversary that, with non-negligible probability, returns an accepting proof. We show that for this type of adversary, it holds with a non-negligible probability that $\exists h \in \bigcap_{j=1}^{N_w} S(j)$ (this is key for extraction; see last line in extractor definition). We argue this is the case by combining two facts:

- $S(j) = S(j')$ with overwhelming probability for all j, j'. Intuitively this follows from the fact that j is encrypted with a semantically secure FHE.
- If $\Pr[\text{adversary returns an accepting proof}]$ is non-negligible, then $\Pr[S(j) \neq \emptyset]$ is non-negligible for any j, which also follows from semantic security of FHE.

Once the adversary fixes x, it also fixes a polynomial number of valid witnesses. Since the hashing key hk is picked after the adversary picks x, with an overwhelming probability, there are no two witnesses that hash to the same value. Thus, if $\exists h \in \bigcap_{j=1}^{N_w} S(j)$, then the string returned by the extractor is a witness with an overwhelming probability because $W[h][j]$ is a bit of a witness with overwhelming probability and because (except with negligible probability) there exists a unique w such that $\mathsf{H}_{\mathsf{hk}}(\mathsf{w}) = h$. This concludes the proof. □

Remark 2 (On replacing FHE with PIR). While our construction is described with FHE, we observe that the assumption of FHE can easily be replaced by the milder existence of Private Information Retrieval (or PIR) [17].

4.2   Impossibility for All NP

We now show that the previous constructive result cannot be extended from **FewP** to **NP**. We mentioned at the end of Sect. 3 that we could view the proof as a leakage of the witness and use leakage resilient (LR) cryptography to prove the impossibility of succinct black-box adaptive knowledge soundness. For the non-adaptive case, we can no longer view the SNARK proof as a *one-time* leakage since the extractor (LR adversary) has the ability to rewind the prover and obtain multiple proofs (leakages). Using *continuous leakage resilience*, we extend the impossibility to non-adaptive extraction.

Consider a L-CLR-OWF $\Sigma = (\mathsf{KGen}, \mathsf{Sample}, \mathsf{Eval}, \mathsf{Update})$. We define a relation $\mathcal{R}_\Sigma = \{((\mathsf{pp}, y), w) : \mathsf{pp} \in \mathsf{KGen}(1^\lambda), w \in \mathsf{Sample}(\mathsf{pp}), \mathsf{Eval}(\mathsf{pp}, w) = y\}$. Suppose there is a non-adaptive black-box extractable SNARK for $\mathcal{R}_\Sigma$. Let us further assume that the proof size of this SNARK is less than L bits.

We construct the following adversary $\mathcal{A}$. First, $\mathcal{A}$ samples $(\mathsf{pp}, \mathsf{uk}) \leftarrow \mathsf{KGen}(1^\lambda)$, a random w, and outputs $((\mathsf{pp}, y = \mathsf{Eval}(\mathsf{pp}, w)), \mathsf{st} = (\mathsf{pp}, \mathsf{uk}, w))$. Next, the extractor can query $\mathcal{A}(\mathsf{st}, \cdot)$ with different CRS'es and get proofs for the statement $(\mathsf{pp}, y) \in \mathcal{L}_{\mathcal{R}_\Sigma}$. Here we define $\mathcal{A}$'s behavior as follows: on each query, $\mathcal{A}$ updates w, that is it computes $w' \leftarrow \mathsf{Update}(\mathsf{uk}, w)$. Then it creates a proof with w', $\pi \leftarrow \mathsf{P}(\mathsf{crs}, (\mathsf{pp}, y), w')$, and returns π. This proof is at most size L, thus at most L bits of information about w' gets leaked. By L-CLR property it is not possible to recover a witness for (pp, y) from this amount of information. Hence, the extractor cannot extract the witness and such a SNARK cannot exist. We show this formally.

Theorem 3. *Let* $\Sigma = (\mathsf{KGen}, \mathsf{Sample}, \mathsf{Eval}, \mathsf{Update})$ *be an* L-*CLR-OWF and let* Π *be a non-adaptive black-box* $\varepsilon_{ks}(\lambda)$-*knowledge sound argument for* $\mathcal{R}_\Sigma$ *as defined above. If the proof size is less than* $L(\lambda)$ *bits, then* L-*CLR-OWF can be broken with probability* $1 - \varepsilon_{ks}(\lambda)$.

We provide a detailed proof in the full version. By combining Theorem 3 with the $(1 - \frac{2}{n})|w|$-CLR-OWF from [1] which is based on the discrete logarithm assumption, we obtain the result below. Here $|w| = n \log q$, where q is the size of discrete logarithm group and n determines the length of the CLR-OWF input.

Theorem 4. *If the discrete logarithm assumption holds in some group, then there exists an* **NP**-*language* $\mathcal{L}$ *such that any non-adaptive BB knowledge sound argument system for* $\mathcal{R}_\mathcal{L}$ *has a proof size* $\Omega(|w|)$ *where* $|w|$ *is the witness size.*

5   GW Impossibility for Preprocessing SNARGs

Careful study of [24] reveals that the CRS generation algorithm of a SNARG in their definition depends only on the security parameter. In other words, the proof separating SNARGs from falsifiable assumptions assumes that the SNARG is CRS succinct and does not allow preprocessing. Many modern SNARGs have a relatively large CRS, which depends on the size of the index i (e.g., a circuit description) in some way [13,16,22,23,28,44]. This makes it questionable if the impossibility result of Gentry and Wichs extends to such SNARGs. We reprove the impossibility theorem for SNARGs that are not necessarily CRS-succinct.

Let us recall the leakage lemma from [24]. We say that a distribution A over tuples (x, π) is an augmented distribution of X if x is distributed according to X and π is some arbitrary information, possibly correlated to x. More formally, we may write A is the distribution over (x, π) such that $x \leftarrow_s X$ and $\pi \leftarrow f(x)$ where f is some (randomized and possibly inefficiently computable) function.

Lemma 1 (Leakage lemma [24]). *There exists a polynomial* p *for which the following holds. Let* X_λ *and* $\bar{X}_\lambda$ *be two distributions that are* $(s(\lambda), \varepsilon(\lambda))$-*indistinguishable. Let* A_λ *over* (x, π) *be an augmented distribution of* X_λ, *where* $|\pi| = \ell(\lambda)$. *Then there exist an augmented distribution* $\bar{A}_\lambda$ *of* $\bar{X}_\lambda$ *such that* A_λ *and* $\bar{A}_\lambda$ *are* $(s^*(\lambda), \varepsilon^*(\lambda))$-*indistinguishable where* $s^*(\lambda) = s(\lambda)p(\varepsilon(\lambda)/2^{\ell(\lambda)})$ *and* $\varepsilon^*(\lambda) = 2\varepsilon(\lambda)$.

We also present some definitions which help to prove the main result.

Definition 5 (Breaking Adaptive Soundness [43]). *We say that an algorithm* $\mathcal{A}$ *breaks adaptive soundness of a SNARG Π for a language $\mathcal{L}$ with probability $\varepsilon(\cdot)$ if there exists an index* $i \in \mathcal{I}$ *such that for every $\lambda \in \mathbb{N}$,*

$$\Pr[\mathsf{crs} \leftarrow \mathsf{Setup}(1^\lambda, i), (x, \pi) \leftarrow \mathcal{A}(1^\lambda, \mathsf{crs}) : (i, x) \notin \mathcal{L} \wedge \mathsf{Verify}(\mathsf{crs}, x, \pi) = 1] \geq \varepsilon(\lambda).$$

Note that if $\varepsilon(\lambda)$ is non-negligible, then adaptive soundness cannot be satisfied.

Definition 6 (Soundness Reduction [43]). *We say that a PPT machine R is a black-box reduction for adaptive soundness of an argument Π based on a falsifiable assumption $(\mathcal{C}, c)$ if there exists a polynomial $p(\cdot, \cdot)$ such that for every $\mathcal{A}$ that breaks adaptive soundness with probability $\varepsilon(\cdot)$, for every $\lambda \in \mathbb{N}$, $R^{\mathcal{A}}(1^\lambda)$ wins $(\mathcal{C}, c)$ with a probability at least $p(\varepsilon(\lambda), 1/\lambda)$.*

We say that $R^{\mathcal{A}}$ is *security-parameter preserving* if additionally there exist a polynomial q such that $R^{\mathcal{A}}(1^\lambda)$ queries $\mathcal{A}$ with inputs of the form $(1^\lambda, x \in \{0,1\}^*)$ and at most $q(\lambda)$ times.

We start by stating two technical lemmas, which we prove in the full version of the paper.

Lemma 2. *If an indexed languages $\mathcal{L} \in \mathbf{NP}$ has a sub-exponentially hard-on-average problem, then for any $d > 0$, $\mathcal{L}$ also has a hard-on-average problem with $(2^{\lambda^d}, 1/2^{\lambda^d})$-indistinguishability.*

Lemma 3. *Let X_λ and $\bar{X}_\lambda$ be $(2^{\lambda^d}, 1/2^{\lambda^d})$-indistinguishable distributions for some integer $d \geq 2$. Let A_λ over (x, π) be an augmented distribution of X_λ, where $|\pi| = \ell(\lambda) = o(\lambda^d)$. Then there exists an augmented distribution $\bar{A}_\lambda$ of $\bar{X}_\lambda$ such that A_λ and $\bar{A}_\lambda$ are $(\mathsf{poly}(\lambda), \mathsf{negl}(\lambda))$-indistinguishable.*

Remark 3. Note that $(s(\lambda), \varepsilon(\lambda)) = (\mathsf{poly}(\lambda), \mathsf{negl}(\lambda))$-indistinguishability is not enough in the previous lemma because. Suppose $|\pi| = \ell(\lambda) = \lambda^{d-1}$. Then, $s^*(\lambda) = s(\lambda)p(\varepsilon(\lambda)/2^{\ell(\lambda)}) = \mathsf{poly}(\lambda)p(\mathsf{negl}(\lambda)/2^{\lambda^{d-1}}) = \mathsf{poly}(\lambda)p(2^{-\omega(\lambda^{d-1})}) = 2^{-\omega(\mathsf{poly}(\lambda))}$ given that p is not a constant polynomial. Thus, A_λ and $\bar{A}_\lambda$ would be (provably) indistinguishable only for very small circuits.

Now we are ready to restate the Gentry-Wichs impossibility result with respect to preprocessing SNARGs from Sect. 2.2.

Theorem 5. *Assume that,*

- $\mathcal{L}$ *is an indexed language with a sub-exponentially hard-on-average problem (see Sect. 2).*
- Π *is a SNARG for $\mathcal{L}$, i.e., it is complete, sound, and proof-succinct (but not necessarily verifier-succinct or CRS-succinct).*

Then, for any falsifiable assumption $(\mathcal{C}, c)$ either:

- $(\mathcal{C}, c)$ *is false or,*
- *there is no security-parameter preserving black-box reduction for adaptive soundness of Π based on $(\mathcal{C}, c)$.*

$\mathcal{A}^*(1^\lambda, \mathsf{crs}, \mathsf{i})$	$\mathsf{Emul}(1^\lambda, \mathsf{crs}, \mathsf{i})$	$O_i(1^\lambda, \mathsf{crs}, \mathsf{i})//\text{Initially } j = 1$
if $\mathsf{i} \notin \mathcal{I}(1^\lambda)$	if $\mathsf{i} \notin \mathcal{I}(1^\lambda)$ then return $\bot$	if $j \leq i$ then $(\mathsf{x}, \pi) \leftarrow \mathsf{Emul}(1^\lambda, \mathsf{crs}, \mathsf{i})$
return $\bot$	$(\mathsf{x}, \mathsf{w}) \leftarrow \mathsf{Samp}_{\mathcal{L}}(1^\lambda, \mathsf{i})$	else $(\mathsf{x}, \pi) \leftarrow \mathcal{A}^*(1^\lambda, \mathsf{crs}, \mathsf{i})$
$(\bar{\mathsf{x}}, \bar{\pi}) \leftarrow \bar{A}_{\lambda, \mathsf{i}, \mathsf{crs}}$	$\pi \leftarrow \mathsf{P}(\mathsf{crs}, \mathsf{x}, \mathsf{w})$	$j \leftarrow j + 1$
return $(\bar{\mathsf{x}}, \bar{\pi})$	return (x, π)	return (x, π)

Fig. 4. Soundness adversary $\mathcal{A}^*$; efficient emulator Emul; hybrid adversaries O_i

Proof. Suppose there exists a security-parameter preserving black-box reduction R for adaptive soundness of Π based on a falsifiable assumption $(\mathcal{C}, c)$ and that R makes at most $q(\lambda)$ queries to its oracle, where q is some polynomial. The proof idea is to construct a computationally unbounded adversary $\mathcal{A}^*$ that is able to break adaptive soundness. Then we show using Lemma 1 that there is an efficient emulator Emul that gives outputs which are indistinguishable from outputs of $\mathcal{A}^*$. Thus, if $R^{\mathcal{A}^*}(1^\lambda)$ is able to break the assumption $(\mathcal{C}, c)$, then so is $R^{\mathsf{Emul}}(1^\lambda)$ and it follows that $(\mathcal{C}, c)$ must be false.

Since Π is proof-succinct there exists some n such that the proof size ℓ is bounded by $\lambda^n \cdot (|\mathsf{x}| + |\mathsf{w}|)^{o(1)}$. Moreover by Lemma 2, since we assume that some sub-exponentially hard-on-average problem exists for $\mathcal{L}$, there also exists a sub-exponentially hard-on-average problem with $(2^{\lambda^{n+2}}, 1/2^{\lambda^{n+2}})$-indistinguishability. Let it be defined by an index sampler $\mathcal{I}$ and instance samplers $\mathsf{Samp}_{\mathcal{L}}$ and $\mathsf{Samp}_{\bar{\mathcal{L}}}$. It is more convenient to start from describing the emulator Emul before we describe $\mathcal{A}^*$. The emulator (see also Fig. 4) on input $(1^\lambda, \mathsf{crs}, \mathsf{i})$ checks that i is well-formed, samples $(\mathsf{x}, \mathsf{w}) \leftarrow \mathsf{Samp}_{\mathcal{L}}(1^\lambda, \mathsf{i})$, creates a proof $\pi \leftarrow \mathsf{P}(\mathsf{crs}, \mathsf{x}, \mathsf{w})$ and returns (x, π).

Notice that since $\mathsf{Samp}_{\mathcal{L}}$ runs in polynomial time in λ, then $|\mathsf{x}| = \mathsf{poly}(\lambda)$ and $|\mathsf{w}| = \mathsf{poly}(\lambda)$. Therefore, the proof size is $\ell(\lambda) = \lambda^{o(n^{d+2})}$.

Fix an arbitrary oracle input $(1^\lambda, \mathsf{crs}, \mathsf{i})$. Let $X_{\lambda, \mathsf{i}}$ be the distribution of x from sampling $(\mathsf{x}, \mathsf{w}) \leftarrow \mathsf{Samp}_{\mathcal{L}}(1^\lambda, \mathsf{i})$ and $\bar{X}_{\lambda, \mathsf{i}}$ the distribution of $\bar{\mathsf{x}}$ we get by sampling $\bar{\mathsf{x}} \leftarrow \mathsf{Samp}_{\bar{\mathcal{L}}}(1^\lambda, \mathsf{i})$. As we established, these distributions are $(2^{\lambda^{n+2}}, 1/2^{\lambda^{n+2}})$-indistinguishable. Let $A_{\lambda, \mathsf{i}, \mathsf{crs}}$ be the augmented distribution of $X_{\lambda, \mathsf{i}}$ defined as $(\mathsf{x}, \pi) \leftarrow \mathsf{Emul}(1^\lambda, \mathsf{crs}, \mathsf{i})$. By Lemma 3, there exists an augmented distribution $\bar{A}_{\lambda, \mathsf{i}, \mathsf{crs}}$ of $\bar{X}_{\lambda, \mathsf{i}}$ such that $A_{\lambda, \mathsf{i}, \mathsf{crs}}$ and $\bar{A}_{\lambda, \mathsf{i}, \mathsf{crs}}$ are $(\mathsf{poly}(\lambda), \mathsf{negl}(\lambda))$-indistinguishable.

Now we can describe the adversary $\mathcal{A}^*$. On the query input $(1^\lambda, \mathsf{crs}, \mathsf{i})$ it simply returns $(\bar{\mathsf{x}}, \bar{\pi}) \leftarrow_\$ \bar{A}_{\lambda, \mathsf{i}, \mathsf{crs}}$. Since $\bar{A}_{\lambda, \mathsf{i}, \mathsf{crs}}$ is not necessarily efficiently sampleable, $\mathcal{A}^*$ may be inefficient.

Our goal is to show that the assumption $(\mathcal{C}, c)$ is false if R exists, i.e., $\Pr[R^{\mathsf{Emul}}(1^\lambda) \text{ wins } (\mathcal{C}, c)] > c + \mathsf{negl}(\lambda)$. We show this in two parts.

1) $R^{\mathcal{A}^*} \mathit{wins}(\mathcal{C}, c)$: First, let $\varepsilon_{\mathcal{A}^*}(\lambda)$ be the probability that $\mathcal{A}^*$ breaks adaptive soundness of Π,

$$\varepsilon_{\mathcal{A}^*}(\lambda) := \Pr\left[\begin{matrix} \mathsf{i} \leftarrow \mathcal{I}(1^\lambda), \mathsf{crs} \leftarrow \mathsf{Setup}(1^\lambda, \mathsf{i}) \\ (\mathsf{x}, \pi) \leftarrow \mathcal{A}^*(1^\lambda, \mathsf{crs}, \mathsf{i}) \end{matrix} : (\mathsf{i}, \mathsf{x}) \notin \mathcal{L} \wedge \mathsf{V}(\mathsf{crs}, \mathsf{x}, \pi) = 1\right].$$

Let us first only consider the probability of the verifier accepting a proof,

$$\varepsilon_{\mathsf{Vf}=1}(\lambda) := \Pr\left[\begin{matrix} \mathsf{i} \leftarrow \mathcal{I}(1^\lambda), \mathsf{crs} \leftarrow \mathsf{Setup}(1^\lambda, \mathsf{i}), \\ (\mathsf{x}, \pi) \leftarrow \mathcal{A}^*(1^\lambda, \mathsf{crs}, \mathsf{i}) \end{matrix} : \mathsf{V}(\mathsf{crs}, \mathsf{x}, \pi) = 1\right].$$

Due to completeness, we know that $\varepsilon_{\mathsf{Emul}}(\lambda) = 1$, where

$$\varepsilon_{\mathsf{Emul}}(\lambda) := \Pr\left[\begin{matrix} \mathsf{i} \leftarrow \mathcal{I}(1^\lambda), \mathsf{crs} \leftarrow \mathsf{Setup}(1^\lambda, \mathsf{i}), \\ (\mathsf{x}, \pi) \leftarrow \mathsf{Emul}(1^\lambda, \mathsf{crs}, \mathsf{i}) \end{matrix} : \mathsf{V}(\mathsf{crs}, \mathsf{x}, \pi)\right] = 1.$$

Since V can be seen as a polynomial-size distinguisher for $A_{\lambda,\mathsf{i},\mathsf{crs}}$ and $\bar{A}_{\lambda,\mathsf{i},\mathsf{crs}}$, we get from before that $|\varepsilon_{\mathsf{Emul}}(\lambda) - \varepsilon_{\mathsf{Vf}=1}(\lambda)| \leq \mathsf{negl}(\lambda)$. Therefore, $1 - \mathsf{negl}(\lambda) \leq \varepsilon_{\mathsf{Vf}=1}$. Since $\Pr[\mathsf{i} \leftarrow \mathcal{I}(1^\lambda), \mathsf{crs} \leftarrow \mathsf{Setup}(1^\lambda, \mathsf{i}), (\mathsf{x}, \pi) \leftarrow \mathcal{A}^*(\mathsf{crs}, \mathsf{i}) : (\mathsf{i}, \mathsf{x}) \notin \mathcal{L}] = 1$, $\varepsilon_{\mathcal{A}^*} = \varepsilon_{\mathsf{Vf}=1} \geq 1 - \mathsf{negl}(\lambda)$. Thus, $\mathcal{A}^*$ breaks adaptive soundness with an overwhelming probability. Since we assumed a black-box reduction R, there must exist a polynomial $p(\cdot, \cdot)$ such that $R^{\mathcal{A}^*}(1^\lambda)$ breaks $(\mathcal{C}, c)$ with probability at least $p(1 - \mathsf{negl}(\lambda), 1/\lambda)$.

2) $R^{\mathcal{A}^*}$ is indistinguishable from R^{Emul}: Suppose R makes $q(\lambda)$ oracle queries. Let O_i for $i \in \{0, \ldots, q(\lambda)\}$ denote a stateful algorithm that we describe in the following. The machine O_i for the first i queries responds as Emul and for the rest of the queries $(1^\lambda, \mathsf{crs}, \mathsf{i})$ responds as $\mathcal{A}^*$ (see Fig. 4). In particular $O_0 = \mathcal{A}^*$ and $O_{q(\lambda)} = \mathsf{Emul}$. We denote $\varepsilon_i := \Pr[R^{O_i}(1^\lambda) \text{ wins } (\mathcal{C}, c)]$. We can again use indistinguishability of $A_{\lambda,\mathsf{i},\mathsf{crs}}$ and $\bar{A}_{\lambda,\mathsf{i},\mathsf{crs}}$ to show that $|\varepsilon_i - \varepsilon_{i+1}| \leq \mathsf{negl}(\lambda)$. Therefore, by triangle inequality $|\varepsilon_0 - \varepsilon_{q(\lambda)}| \leq q(\lambda)\mathsf{negl}(\lambda) = \mathsf{negl}(\lambda)$.

Since $\varepsilon_0 = \varepsilon_{\mathcal{A}}$, we get that $\Pr[R^{\mathsf{Emul}}(1^\lambda) \text{ wins } (\mathcal{C}, c)] = \varepsilon_{q(\lambda)} \geq \epsilon_{\mathcal{A}} - \mathsf{negl}(\lambda) = p(1 - \mathsf{negl}(\lambda), 1/\lambda) - \mathsf{negl}(\lambda)$. Thus, $R^{\mathsf{Emul}}(1^\lambda)$ can break the assumption $(\mathcal{C}, c)$ with an overwhelming probability. $\square$

6   Understanding SNARG Impossibilities

In this section, we attempt to provide a complete overview of known impossibilities for non-interactive arguments. This illustrates the precise assumptions behind these impossibilities in order to identify avenues for further research. The following are some of the major impossibility results.

1. Gentry-Wichs [24]: Adaptive soundness of a SNARG cannot be proven via a black-box reduction to a falsifiable assumption.
2. Pass [43]: Adaptive soundness of a statistical NIZK argument cannot be proven via a black-box reduction to a falsifiable assumption.
3. Groth [28]: Any pairing-based SNARK obtained from a NILP (a non-interactive linear proof) must contain at least 2 group elements, one in each of the pairing source groups.

Since [28] is relevant only in a very specific setting, and [43] is about general NIZKs, we will not focus on it in the rest of the paper. The proof idea of [24] is quite similar to our extension of it. We recall the proof idea of [43] in the full version. In the following, we discuss the impossibility result of [24].

6.1 Impossibility of Gentry-Wichs

We recall the main result of [24].

Theorem 6. *Let $\mathcal{L}$ be a sub-exponentially hard* **NP** *language and let Π be a SNARG for $\mathcal{L}$, satisfying completeness and proof succinctness. Then, for any falsifiable assumption $(\mathcal{C}, c)$, either $(\mathcal{C}, c)$ is false, or there is no black-box reduction showing the (adaptive) soundness of Π based on $(\mathcal{C}, c)$.*

We take a closer look at GW impossibility and enumerate the scenarios to which it *does not* apply. While some of these are known results, they are all scattered in the literature.

- **Non-adaptive soundness**: The impossibility holds only for *adaptive soundness*. The proof technique used in GW to rule out a black-box reduction uses a stateless adversary that outputs an instance proof pair (x, π) on input a CRS. In particular, this does not rule out our reductions that can rewind the prover and obtain different proofs for the same x, which is possible in the case of non-adaptive soundness. Recent work attempted to show tightness from new albeit falsifiable assumptions, but the construction was shown to be faulty [46].
- **Low-space non-deterministic computation**: The high-level idea of the GW impossibility result is a "leakage lemma" that says the following: assuming the underlying NP language is 2^ℓ-hard, a reduction that breaks the assumption, cannot distinguish between pairs (x, π) generated by a (possibly inefficient) cheating prover, where $x \notin L$ and π is a proof of length ℓ, and a pair $(\tilde{x}, \tilde{\pi})$ where $\tilde{x} \in L$ and $\tilde{\pi}$ is an efficiently generated proof. Therefore, for computations recognizable in $\mathsf{poly}(\lambda)$ time and $S(\lambda)$ space with a non-deterministic Turing machine (the class $NTISP(\mathsf{poly}(\lambda), S(\lambda))$), the GW result does not rule out the possibility of a SNARG with proofs of length $\mathsf{poly}(\lambda)(S(\lambda))$, since a computation in $NTISP(\mathsf{poly}(\lambda), S(\lambda))$ is in $DTIME(\mathsf{poly}(\lambda) \cdot 2^{S(\lambda)})$ which is not $\mathsf{poly}(\lambda) \cdot 2^{O(S(\lambda))}$-hard. The work of [4] constructs a delegation scheme for non-deterministic computations with a proof length that grows only with the space of the computation.
- **Preprocessing SNARGs**: The GW separation result holds for SNARGs that have a "short" CRS. More precisely, the impossibility proof requires that the size of the CRS depends only on the security parameter, and does not grow with the size of the instance. This gap is now closed with the current work.
- **Trapdoor languages**: For some languages there are efficient proofs [32,37] in the quasi-adaptive setting (QA-NIZK). These proofs have a constant number group elements – regardless of the instance size. The construction of [35] for languages consisting of linear subspaces of a vector space, have constant-sized proofs, achieve adaptive soundness (based on a falsifiable assumption) and perfect ZK. This seemingly contradicts the GW impossibility result (as well as the impossibility on perfect ZK [43]).[9] The results in the quasi-adaptive

---

[9] The proof of [35] contains 1 group element and bypasses the [28] impossibility as well. This is not contradictory because the [28] impossibility only applies to pairing-based NIZKs that are compiled from NILPs.

setting do not contradict the GW impossibility because the CRS hides a trapdoor for deciding membership in the language. The proof of GW rules out reductions that *cannot* efficiently detect when the soundness property is broken. We formalize this notion of *trapdoor languages* below.

Bypassing GW: Trapdoor Languages. Intuitively, a trapdoor language allows verifying membership in the language if one knows a trapdoor. Towards formalizing such languages, we illustrate it by taking the linear subspace language as an example. Recall the language of linear subspaces from [35]. We have a distribution $\mathcal{D}$ that outputs a language parameter $\mathsf{lpar} = [M]_1 \in \mathbb{G}_1^{n \times m}$[10] for some matrix M and the respective linear subspace language is defined as $\mathcal{L}_{[M]_1} = \{[\vec{x}]_1 \in \mathbb{G}_1^n \mid \exists \vec{w} \in \mathbb{Z}_p^m : \vec{x} = M \cdot \vec{w}\}$.

In the proof of [24], the reduction algorithm R that picks the CRS, (and in the case of the linear subspace language, also picks the language parameter lpar), should not efficiently distinguish between elements $\mathsf{x} \in \mathcal{L}$ from $\bar{\mathsf{x}} \in \overline{\mathcal{L}}$. The latter condition does not hold for linear subspace languages.

Observe that given both M and $\vec{x}$ as integers, by Kronecker-Capelli theorem there exists $\vec{w} \in \mathbb{Z}_p^m$ such that $\vec{x} = M\vec{w}$ (i.e., $[\vec{x}]_1 \in \mathcal{L}_{[M]_1}$) if and only if $\mathsf{rank}(M) = \mathsf{rank}(M \mid \vec{x})$. This test can be done even when given only $[x]_1$ and M. We discuss the precise details in the full version of our paper.

The above is sufficient to avoid the [24] impossibility. We now generalize this observation by defining a trapdoor language.

Definition 7. *Let $\mathcal{D}(1^\lambda)$ be an efficiently sampleable distribution that outputs $(\mathsf{lpar}, \mathsf{td})$ and each lpar is associated with a language $\mathcal{L}_{\mathsf{lpar}}$. A family of languages $\{\mathcal{L}_{\mathsf{lpar}}\}_{(\mathsf{lpar},\mathsf{td}) \in \mathcal{D}(1^\lambda), \lambda \in \mathbb{N}}$ are trapdoor languages if there exists a PPT decider $\mathcal{M}$ such that for all $\lambda \in \mathbb{N}$ and all $(\mathsf{lpar}, \mathsf{td}) \in \mathcal{D}(1^\lambda)$, $\mathsf{x} \in \mathcal{L} \Leftrightarrow \mathcal{M}(1^\lambda, \mathsf{lpar}, \mathsf{td}, \mathsf{x}) = 1$.*

The security definitions from Sect. 2.2 for non-interactive arguments slightly change in that the Setup takes the language parameter instead of index as input and outputs a CRS. The soundness definition in general is not efficiently falsifiable because checking $\mathsf{x} \notin \mathcal{L}$ is usually not efficient. However, with trapdoor languages it is falsifiable since $\mathcal{M}$ is efficient. In particular, a tautological assumption "Π is sound" becomes a falsifiable assumption.

Examples of Useful Trapdoor Languages. We are interested in "hard" trapdoor languages, i.e., trapdoor languages that are hard to decide without knowledge of td. Many common cryptographic problems fall into this category: linear subspace languages, statements about encrypted values, shuffle arguments, and set membership arguments.

We note that trapdoor languages are interesting, arise frequently in practice and GW impossibility does not apply. Can we construct SNARGs from falsifiable assumptions for trapdoor languages? We leave resolving this as an interesting open question, and believe that our formalization is a first step in identifying the middle ground where GW does not apply but the language remains interesting.

---

[10] Here, $\mathbb{G}_1$ is an additive pairing group and $[x]_1$ denotes a group element with a discrete logarithm x.

Acknowledgement. We thank the reviewers of CRYPTO 2022 for constructive feedback, in particular, for pointing out the connection between black-box extractability and leakage-resilient cryptography. We thank Helger Lipmaa for comments on the paper.

References

1. Agrawal, S., Dodis, Y., Vaikuntanathan, V., Wichs, D.: On continual leakage of discrete log representations. In: Sako, K., Sarkar, P. (eds.) ASIACRYPT 2013. LNCS, vol. 8270, pp. 401–420. Springer, Heidelberg (2013). https://doi.org/10. 1007/978-3-642-42045-0_21
2. Allender, E.W.: The complexity of sparse sets in P. In: Selman, A.L. (ed.) Structure in Complexity Theory. LNCS, vol. 223, pp. 1–11. Springer, Heidelberg (1986). https://doi.org/10.1007/3-540-16486-3_85
3. Alwen, J., Dodis, Y., Wichs, D.: Leakage-resilient public-key cryptography in the bounded-retrieval model. In: Halevi, S. (ed.) CRYPTO 2009. LNCS, vol. 5677, pp. 36–54. Springer, Heidelberg (2009). https://doi.org/10.1007/978-3-642-03356-8_3
4. Badrinarayanan, S., Kalai, Y.T., Khurana, D., Sahai, A., Wichs, D.: Succinct delegation for low-space non-deterministic computation. In: 50th ACM STOC. ACM Press (2018)
5. Baghery, K., Kohlweiss, M., Siim, J., Volkhov, M.: Another look at extraction and randomization of Groth's zk-SNARK. In: Borisov, N., Diaz, C. (eds.) FC 2021. LNCS, vol. 12674, pp. 457–475. Springer, Heidelberg (2021). https://doi.org/10. 1007/978-3-662-64322-8_22
6. Baghery, K., Sedaghat, M.: TIRAMISU: Black-box simulation extractable NIZKs in the updatable CRS model. In: Conti, M., Stevens, M., Krenn, S. (eds.) CANS 2021. LNCS, vol. 13099, pp. 531–551. Springer, Cham (2021). https://doi.org/10. 1007/978-3-030-92548-2_28
7. Ben-Sasson, E., et al.: Zerocash: decentralized anonymous payments from bitcoin. In: 2014 IEEE Symposium on Security and Privacy. IEEE Computer Society Press (2014)
8. Ben-Sasson, E., Chiesa, A., Genkin, D., Tromer, E., Virza, M.: SNARKs for C: verifying program executions succinctly and in zero knowledge. In: Canetti, R., Garay, J.A. (eds.) CRYPTO 2013. LNCS, vol. 8043, pp. 90–108. Springer, Heidelberg (2013). https://doi.org/10.1007/978-3-642-40084-1_6
9. Ben-Sasson, E., Chiesa, A., Tromer, E., Virza, M.: Succinct non-interactive zero knowledge for a von neumann architecture. In: USENIX Security 2014. USENIX Association (2014)
10. Bitansky, N., Canetti, R., Chiesa, A., Tromer, E.: Recursive composition and bootstrapping for SNARKS and proof-carrying data. In: 45th ACM STOC. ACM Press (2013)
11. Brassard, G., Chaum, D., Crépeau, C.: Minimum disclosure proofs of knowledge. J. Comput. Syst. Sci. **37**(2), 156–189 (1988)
12. Bünz, B., Bootle, J., Boneh, D., Poelstra, A., Wuille, P., Maxwell, G.: Bulletproofs: short proofs for confidential transactions and more. In: 2018 IEEE Symposium on Security and Privacy. IEEE Computer Society Press (2018)
13. Campanelli, M., Faonio, A., Fiore, D., Querol, A., Rodríguez, H.: Lunar: a toolbox for more efficient universal and updatable zkSNARKs and commit-and-prove extensions. Cryptology ePrint Archive, Report 2020/1069 (2020)

14. Canetti, R.: Universally composable security: a new paradigm for cryptographic protocols. In: 42nd FOCS. IEEE Computer Society Press (2001)
15. Chase, M., Kohlweiss, M., Lysyanskaya, A., Meiklejohn, S.: Succinct malleable NIZKs and an application to compact shuffles. In: Sahai, A. (ed.) TCC 2013. LNCS, vol. 7785, pp. 100–119. Springer, Heidelberg (2013). https://doi.org/10.1007/978-3-642-36594-2_6
16. Chiesa, A., Hu, Y., Maller, M., Mishra, P., Vesely, N., Ward, N.: Marlin: preprocessing zkSNARKs with universal and updatable SRS. In: Canteaut, A., Ishai, Y. (eds.) EUROCRYPT 2020. LNCS, vol. 12105, pp. 738–768. Springer, Cham (2020). https://doi.org/10.1007/978-3-030-45721-1_26
17. Chor, B., Goldreich, O., Kushilevitz, E., Sudan, M.: Private information retrieval. In: 36th FOCS. IEEE Computer Society Press (1995)
18. Couteau, G., Hartmann, D.: Shorter non-interactive zero-knowledge arguments and ZAPs for algebraic languages. In: Micciancio, D., Ristenpart, T. (eds.) CRYPTO 2020. LNCS, vol. 12172, pp. 768–798. Springer, Cham (2020). https://doi.org/10.1007/978-3-030-56877-1_27
19. Damgård, I.: Towards practical public key systems secure against chosen ciphertext attacks. In: Feigenbaum, J. (ed.) CRYPTO 1991. LNCS, vol. 576, pp. 445–456. Springer, Heidelberg (1992). https://doi.org/10.1007/3-540-46766-1_36
20. Fiat, A., Shamir, A.: How to prove yourself: practical solutions to identification and signature problems. In: Odlyzko, A.M. (ed.) CRYPTO 1986. LNCS, vol. 263, pp. 186–194. Springer, Heidelberg (1987). https://doi.org/10.1007/3-540-47721-7_12
21. Fortnow, L.: The complexity of perfect zero-knowledge (extended abstract). In: 19th ACM STOC. ACM Press (1987)
22. Gabizon, A., Williamson, Z.J., Ciobotaru, O.: PLONK: permutations over lagrange-bases for oecumenical noninteractive arguments of knowledge. Cryptology ePrint Archive, Report 2019/953 (2019)
23. Gennaro, R., Gentry, C., Parno, B., Raykova, M.: Quadratic span programs and succinct NIZKs without PCPs. In: Johansson, T., Nguyen, P.Q. (eds.) EUROCRYPT 2013. LNCS, vol. 7881, pp. 626–645. Springer, Heidelberg (2013). https://doi.org/10.1007/978-3-642-38348-9_37
24. Gentry, C., Wichs, D.: Separating succinct non-interactive arguments from all falsifiable assumptions. In: 43rd ACM STOC. ACM Press (2011)
25. Goldreich, O., Håstad, J.: On the complexity of interactive proofs with bounded communication. Inf. Process. Lett. 67(4), 205–214 (1998)
26. Goldreich, O., Micali, S., Wigderson, A.: Proofs that yield nothing but their validity and a methodology of cryptographic protocol design (extended abstract). In: 27th FOCS. IEEE Computer Society Press (1986)
27. Groth, J.: Short pairing-based non-interactive zero-knowledge arguments. In: Abe, M. (ed.) ASIACRYPT 2010. LNCS, vol. 6477, pp. 321–340. Springer, Heidelberg (2010). https://doi.org/10.1007/978-3-642-17373-8_19
28. Groth, J.: On the size of pairing-based non-interactive arguments. In: Fischlin, M., Coron, J.-S. (eds.) EUROCRYPT 2016. LNCS, vol. 9666, pp. 305–326. Springer, Heidelberg (2016). https://doi.org/10.1007/978-3-662-49896-5_11
29. Hada, S., Tanaka, T.: On the existence of 3-round zero-knowledge protocols. In: Krawczyk, H. (ed.) CRYPTO 1998. LNCS, vol. 1462, pp. 408–423. Springer, Heidelberg (1998). https://doi.org/10.1007/BFb0055744
30. Håstad, J., Impagliazzo, R., Levin, L.A., Luby, M.: A pseudorandom generator from any one-way function. SIAM J. Comput. 28(4), 1364–1396 (1999). https://doi.org/10.1137/S0097539793244708

31. Jain, A., Lin, H., Sahai, A.: Indistinguishability obfuscation from well-founded assumptions. In: Proceedings of the 53rd Annual ACM SIGACT Symposium on Theory of Computing, pp. 60–73. STOC 2021, Association for Computing Machinery, New York (2021). https://doi.org/10.1145/3406325.3451093

32. Jutla, C.S., Roy, A.: Shorter quasi-adaptive NIZK proofs for linear subspaces. In: Sako, K., Sarkar, P. (eds.) ASIACRYPT 2013. LNCS, vol. 8269, pp. 1–20. Springer, Heidelberg (2013). https://doi.org/10.1007/978-3-642-42033-7_1

33. Kerber, T., Kiayias, A., Kohlweiss, M.: Composition with knowledge assumptions. In: Malkin, T., Peikert, C. (eds.) CRYPTO 2021. LNCS, vol. 12828, pp. 364–393. Springer, Cham (2021). https://doi.org/10.1007/978-3-030-84259-8_13

34. Kilian, J.: A note on efficient zero-knowledge proofs and arguments. In: Proceedings of the Twenty-Fourth Annual ACM Symposium on Theory of Computing, pp. 723–732 (1992)

35. Kiltz, E., Wee, H.: Quasi-adaptive NIZK for linear subspaces revisited. In: Oswald, E., Fischlin, M. (eds.) EUROCRYPT 2015. LNCS, vol. 9057, pp. 101–128. Springer, Heidelberg (2015). https://doi.org/10.1007/978-3-662-46803-6_4

36. Kosba, A., et al.: C0C0: a framework for building composable zero-knowledge proofs. Cryptology ePrint Archive, Report 2015/1093 (2015)

37. Libert, B., Peters, T., Joye, M., Yung, M.: Non-malleability from Malleability: simulation-sound quasi-adaptive NIZK proofs and CCA2-secure encryption from homomorphic signatures. In: Nguyen, P.Q., Oswald, E. (eds.) EUROCRYPT 2014. LNCS, vol. 8441, pp. 514–532. Springer, Heidelberg (2014). https://doi.org/10.1007/978-3-642-55220-5_29

38. Lipmaa, H.: Progression-free sets and sublinear pairing-based non-interactive zero-knowledge arguments. In: Cramer, R. (ed.) TCC 2012. LNCS, vol. 7194, pp. 169–189. Springer, Heidelberg (2012). https://doi.org/10.1007/978-3-642-28914-9_10

39. Lipmaa, H., Pavlyk, K.: Gentry-Wichs is tight: a falsifiable non-adaptively sound SNARG. In: Tibouchi, M., Wang, H. (eds.) ASIACRYPT 2021. LNCS, vol. 13092, pp. 34–64. Springer, Cham (2021). https://doi.org/10.1007/978-3-030-92078-4_2

40. Micali, S.: CS proofs. In: Proceedings 35th Annual Symposium on Foundations of Computer Science, pp. 436–453. IEEE (1994)

41. Naor, M.: On cryptographic assumptions and challenges. In: Boneh, D. (ed.) CRYPTO 2003. LNCS, vol. 2729, pp. 96–109. Springer, Heidelberg (2003). https://doi.org/10.1007/978-3-540-45146-4_6

42. Parno, B., Howell, J., Gentry, C., Raykova, M.: Pinocchio: nearly practical verifiable computation. In: 2013 IEEE Symposium on Security and Privacy. IEEE Computer Society Press (2013)

43. Pass, R.: Unprovable security of perfect NIZK and non-interactive non-malleable commitments. In: Sahai, A. (ed.) TCC 2013. LNCS, vol. 7785, pp. 334–354. Springer, Heidelberg (2013). https://doi.org/10.1007/978-3-642-36594-2_19

44. Ràfols, C., Zapico, A.: An algebraic framework for universal and updatable SNARKs. In: Malkin, T., Peikert, C. (eds.) CRYPTO 2021. LNCS, vol. 12825, pp. 774–804. Springer, Cham (2021). https://doi.org/10.1007/978-3-030-84242-0_27

45. Sahai, A., Waters, B.: How to use indistinguishability obfuscation: deniable encryption, and more. In: 46th ACM STOC. ACM Press (2014)

46. Waters, B., Wu, D.J.: Batch arguments for np and more from standard bilinear group assumptions. Cryptology ePrint Archive, Paper 2022/336 (2022)

47. Wee, H.: On round-efficient argument systems. In: Caires, L., Italiano, G.F., Monteiro, L., Palamidessi, C., Yung, M. (eds.) ICALP 2005. LNCS, vol. 3580, pp. 140–152. Springer, Heidelberg (2005). https://doi.org/10.1007/11523468_12

Applications of Timed-Release Encryption with Implicit Authentication

Angelique Loe[1]($\boxtimes$), Liam Medley[1]●, Christian O'Connell[2],
and Elizabeth A. Quaglia[1]●

[1] Royal Holloway, University of London, London, UK
{angelique.loe.2016,liam.medley.2018,elizabeth.quaglia}@rhul.ac.uk
[2] Independent, London, UK
co362@cantab.ac.uk

Abstract. A whistleblower is a person who leaks sensitive information on a prominent individual or organisation engaging in an unlawful or immoral activity. Whistleblowing has the potential to mitigate corruption and fraud by identifying the misuse of capital. In extreme cases whistleblowing can also raise awareness about unethical practices to individuals by highlighting dangerous working conditions. Obtaining and sharing the sensitive information associated with whistleblowing can carry great risk to the individual or party revealing the data. In this paper we extend the notion of timed-release encryption to include a new security property which we term *implicit authentication*, with the goal of making the practice of whistleblowing safer.

We formally define the new primitive of timed-release encryption with implicit authentication (TRE-IA), providing rigorous game-base definitions. We then build a practical TRE-IA construction that satisfies the security requirements of this primitive, using repeated squaring in an RSA group, and the RSA-OAEP encryption scheme. We formally prove our construction secure and provide a performance analysis of our implementation in Python along with recommendations for practical deployment and integration with an existing whistleblowing tool SecureDrop.

Keywords: time-lock puzzle · timed-release encryption · applied cryptography

1 Introduction

In 2013, Edward Snowden leaked highly classified information from the National Security Agency [37,38]. This information was leaked at great personal risk. Other recent cases of whistleblowing include the Panama papers [32], the Paradise papers [9], and the Pandora papers [27]. Leaking information subjected the whistleblowers to personal danger due to the power and influence of the organisations whose data was leaked. In the case of the Panama papers, the whistleblower claimed their 'life was in danger' [21].

© The Author(s), under exclusive license to Springer Nature Switzerland AG 2023
N. El Mrabet et al. (Eds.): AFRICACRYPT 2023, LNCS 14064, pp. 490–515, 2023.
https://doi.org/10.1007/978-3-031-37679-5_21

In this work we construct a cryptographic tool based on timed-release encryption [17], which can augment existing tools for whistleblowers, such as Secure-Drop [2]. Our goal is to provide an element of guaranteed delay in the release of sensitive information which has potential to make the practice of whistleblowing safer. We model our solution on the Edward Snowden case, in which all classified material was destroyed before arriving in Russia, in order 'To protect himself from Russian leverage' [1].

We propose a construction which offers the concept of delay-based encryption for whistleblowers, to allow them to rely on cryptographic assurances rather than the trust of a journalist or ombudsman. The technique we introduce allows sensitive information to be encrypted in such a way that a) there is a predictable delay between the *receipt of the ciphertext* encapsulating the leaked information and the *release* of the information, and b) there is no way an adversary can forge a chosen document to insert alongside the genuine documents. This delay will afford the whistleblower time to destroy all classified material after encapsulating the material, and hence ensure their safety. In the Snowden case, the delay would have allowed passage to a safe harbour country without the sensitive information being decrypted until a specified time.

The core idea of our approach is to have two separate keys, an encryption key and decryption key, the latter being encoded as the solution to the *challenge*. The delay starts once the challenge is distributed. The whistleblower keeps the encryption key, used to encrypt the leaked information, and encapsulates its corresponding decryption key with a time-delay, such that it takes at least t time to recover. We provide the whistleblower with the ability to encrypt and distribute ciphertexts under the encryption key, without 'starting the clock' on the time-delay. At a time of their choosing, the whistleblower can distribute the challenge, upon which a sequential computation taking time t will output the decryption key for the ciphertexts. Due to the asymmetric nature of the encryption key and decryption key, once the decryption key is recovered, the whistleblower will still hold the exclusive ability to encrypt more data at a later date.

We formalise this through the introduction of a security property which we term *implicit authentication*, in order to provide the journalist receiving the leaked information with assurance that an adversarial party cannot encrypt a document of their choosing under the encryption key.

Paper Structure and Contributions. In the remainder of this section we detail our methodology in approaching this problem, outlining the security goals we desire and providing an overview of our construction, before discussing relevant related work. In Sect. 2 we formally define the primitive *TRE with implicit authentication* (TRE-IA), giving game-based definitions of the required security properties. In Sect. 3 we present our construction for a TRE-IA scheme, which is based upon the BBS-random number generator and RSA-OAEP encryption. In Sect. 4 we prove our construction is secure under the definitions given in Sect. 2. In Sect. 5 we provide a Python implementation of our construction, along with a performance analysis to demonstrate its practicality. We also provide a practical example of how to use TRE-IA with SecureDrop [2] to show how our construction would integrate with existing whistleblower tools.

1.1 Technical Overview

The goal of this work is to explore how a time-delay can be used by vulnerable parties such as whistleblowers in order to make the distribution of sensitive material safer. In order to do so, we introduce a novel construction based upon a clear set of properties, which we can implement in practice and which may augment existing whistleblower tools. Therefore, we define the following security goals that we believe may be helpful to a whistleblower based on the real life cases of the Panama papers leak [21] and the Edward Snowden leak [37,38].

1. An *adjustable time delay*: this will allow the whistleblower to destroy all materials that can be used against them. It also allows the whistleblower to have a configurable amount of time to reach a place of safety.
2. *Maximum flexibility*: this will allow the whistleblower to determine when a) they can encrypt and distribute messages and b) they can 'start the clock' for evaluating the delay. This is achieved through the separation of the cipher-texts and the *challenge*. When the challenge is distributed this starts the clock.
3. *Implicit authentication*: this ensures that no other entity can generate a document of their choice to insert into the leak.

Property 1 can be useful for a whistleblower to protect themselves from the dangers associated with carrying sensitive material. Property 2 allows a whistleblower to gather various different pieces of evidence over time and encrypt and distribute this evidence to journalists. The whistleblower can also ensure that the journalists cannot yet leak the material until a time delay has passed, thus mitigating risks to the personal safety of the whistleblower. We believe it is crucial that the whistleblower remains in control of all aspects of the system, and by giving the whistleblower the freedom to distribute ciphertexts *without* 'starting the clock' on the time delay, we minimise the trust placed in journalists, and provide the whistleblower with fine-grained control of when the documents are leaked.

Property 3 ensures that once the decryption key has been derived, it cannot be used by third parties to obtain the encryption key to encrypt their own messages. Without this property, it is possible for a third party to choose and encrypt their own fake material, and claim it is from the whistleblower.

We now describe the methodology of how we designed our construction.

Building Our Construction. Our base property, 1, can be achieved using various primitives, most notably time-lock puzzles (TLPs) and timed-release encryption (TRE). We will start our discussion with TLPs.

A time-lock puzzle [36] encrypts a message to the future, in such a way that once a solver spends a predictable amount of time evaluating the encrypted message, they obtain the plaintext message. One could think of using the naive approach of simply encrypting each message as a TLP and passing it to a journalist. This achieves property 1, however it limits the whistleblower to the condition that they encrypt all materials at once, and allows adversarial parties to impersonate the whistleblower. As we wish for the whistleblower to have a finer control of the encryption process we see that the latter method has limitations. For example, the whistleblower may wish for multiple messages to be encrypted. This is a reasonable assumption as the Panama papers exposed over eleven million leaked documents [32] and the Paradise papers exposed over thirteen million leaked documents [9]. Using only a basic TLP results in the loss of property 2, that is, the whistleblower loses the element of maximum flexibility. A more appropriate approach is to use a symmetric key as the solution to a TLP, and then distribute ciphertexts separately. This gives us a solution which is close to ideal, as ciphertexts can be distributed to journalists, with guarantees both time delay and flexibility as to when the whistleblower starts the clock. In other words, we can achieve properties 1 and 2 using this approach, however we are missing the implicit authentication property described in 3.

Our approach to fixing this problem is to require that the encryption key and decryption key are different, and more importantly, that one *cannot derive the encryption key from the decryption key*. If this is the case, a whistleblower can encapsulate the decryption key of a public-key encryption scheme, whilst keeping the encryption key secret.

As a starting point, we use TRE as defined by Chvojka et al., who show that one can generically construct TRE from a TLP and a public encryption scheme [17]. However, Chvojka et al.'s approach to constructing TRE does not give us the desired property of a secret encryption key, nor does it necessarily imply that it is impossible to derive the encryption key from the decryption key.

Therefore, to achieve these goals simultaneously we propose a variant of timed-release encryption, which we term TRE with implicit authentication (TRE-IA) and instantiate this with a construction based upon the BBS-CSPRNG random number generator [11], and the RSA-OAEP encryption scheme [8].

1.2 Related Work

Time, Delay, and Encryption. There are several primitives in the literature that have considered the component of time and delay in the context of encryption. Time-lock puzzles (TLPs) and the associated Timed-Release Crypto schemes, first proposed by Rivest et al. in [36], encrypt a message to the future. TLPs create a puzzle π from which a message m can be decrypted after time t. Timed-Release Crypto is closely related to TRE-IA in that it achieves a very similar functionality. However, there are differences between the two primitives: In essence, TRE-IA uses distinct (asymmetric) keys for encryption and decryption, as opposed to one symmetric key. In both primitives decryption keys are recovered after the delay, in order to decrypt the ciphertext. However, in TRE-IA only the decryption key is recovered. This leads to a different functionality: the whistleblower has control over what information is leaked (i.e., encrypted) as the sole holder of the encryption key.

Previous literature also discusses timed-release encryption (TRE) in two main forms. The classical definition of a TRE scheme is to use a third-party time-server to release messages after a given amount of time [16,29]. The most recent paper by Chvojka et al. defines TRE as a combination of a time-lock puzzle and public-key encryption [17]. This is in order to introduce the notion of a *sequential* TRE scheme, with the goal of building a public sequential-squaring service which acts as the time server. This allows many parties to time-lock messages, whilst only one party performs the lengthy computation. Conceptually, the classical definition of timed-release encryption differs from the Chvojka et al. scheme because the former relies on a trusted time-server. For the remainder of this work, when we write TRE we will be referring to the method of Chvojka et al.

The main difference between TRE and TRE-IA is the former requires encryption to be public rather than only a prerogative of the whistleblower: In TRE-IA the encryption key cannot be derived by the solver even when the decryption key is recovered. In a TRE-IA scheme assurance is provided through the property of implicit authentication that only the whistleblower can encrypt to the classic notion of a *public key* in a standard PKE scheme.

In the delay-based cryptography literature there are also Verifiable Delay Functions (VDFs), first proposed by Boneh et al. [12] and a new, closely related primitive called Delay Encryption (DE) [14], derived from VDFs. VDFs require a prover to compute a slow sequential computation of length t, also known as a challenge, and then efficiently prove to a verifier that they have done so. VDFs do not generate a ciphertext, or indeed have any method for encrypting data, and so are clearly distinct from TRE.

In DE, the concept of a *session* is introduced. A session consists of a session ID, which any party may encrypt a message to, and an extraction key. Any party may extract the session key, which allows for decryption of all messages encrypted to the session ID, and this extraction takes t time to run. This primitive is distinct from TRE-IA, in that DE allows anyone to encrypt to the session ID, compared to just the whistleblower being in control of encryption in TRE-IA.

Signcryption. A cryptographic primitive offering a similar property to implicit authentication (IA) is Signcryption [41–43]. IA provides the receiving party with assurance that the encrypted documents were sent by the whistleblower. The IA property states that only the holder of the private encryption key can generate a legitimate ciphertext that can be correctly decrypted to a chosen message. In a similar fashion the concept of Signcryption was introduced to provide a single computation that would simultaneously provide the authenticity from a digital signature scheme (DSS), and the confidentiality from a public-key encryption (PKE) scheme. However, Signcryption does not consider the property of delay which is crucial to our TRE-IA scheme.

Tools for Whistleblowers. A variety of tools exist which can provide protection to whistleblowers. The Tor [4] browser can be used to navigate the Internet anonymously, PGP [44] keys and encrypted email services can support the secure communication between a whistleblower and the investigative journalist, as well as end-to-end encrypted messaging services such as Signal [3]. Closely aligned to our intended end-goal is the SecureDrop [2] submission system, which enables whistleblowers to securely deliver documents containing leaked information. The novelty of our proposed solution in this space is the introduction of a delay, which provides, when combined with encryption, a time 'bubble' within which the whistleblower can reach safety. Indeed, we see TRE-IA as an addition to a whistleblower's toolbox featuring the property of a time-lock delay. In this context, we recognise that no tool is perfect and solutions which guarantee the safety of the whistleblower should be grounded in reality. Our proposed scheme represents a first, technological step towards introducing delay as a form of protection to whistleblowers. Accordingly, to provide an example of integrating with existing whistleblowing tooling, in Sect. 5.2 we show how the TRE-IA construction can be augmented to work with the SecureDrop tool.

We conclude this section by noting that the whistleblower use case is an illustrative example of how and why TRE-IA could be useful. We envisage TRE-IA being useful in further applications where a delay and the ability to control the release of sensitive information could help users in at risk situations.

2 Timed-Release Encryption with Implicit Authentication

We now provide the definition and properties of TRE-IA, which can be seen as an extension of the TRE primitive as defined by Chovjka et al. [17]. We deviate from the security model of Chvojka et al. in the following way: (i) to fit in with our model of the encryptor alone knowing the encryption key, we require that the encryptor runs setup, (ii) we introduce the new notion of implicit authentication. We provide an intuition of this security property, along with a detailed description of the game in the following section.

In the definition and security games that follow, $\mathcal{E}$ is the encryptor, $\mathcal{D}$ is the decryptor, $\mathcal{A}$ is the PPT adversary, $\leftarrow_R$ represents a probabilistic algorithm, and $\leftarrow$ represents a deterministic algorithm.

Definition of TRE-IA. A TRE-IA scheme consists of the following algorithms: (TRE.Setup, TRE.Gen, TRE.Enc, TRE.Solve, TRE.Dec), defined as follows.

- $pp, td \leftarrow_R$ TRE.Setup(1^λ). TRE.Setup is an algorithm run by $\mathcal{E}$ that takes as input security parameter 1^λ and outputs the public parameter pp and trapdoor td. $\mathcal{E}$ must keep td private. The parameter pp can be given to $\mathcal{D}$ after TRE.Setup completes. TRE.Setup runs in time poly(λ).

- $e, d, C, t \leftarrow_R$ TRE.Gen(pp, td, t). TRE.Gen is an algorithm run by $\mathcal{E}$ that takes as input the public parameter pp, the trapdoor td, and time parameter t and computes an encryption key e, decryption key d, and a public challenge C. The term t indicates the number of sequential steps required to evaluate C to recover the decryption key d when the trapdoor td is not known. The parameter t can be given to $\mathcal{D}$ after TRE.Gen completes. However, care must be taken when the challenge C is given to the decryptor $\mathcal{D}$. $\mathcal{E}$ must only provide challenge C when they wish to 'start the clock' on recovering the decryption key d. TRE.Gen runs in time poly(λ).

- $c \leftarrow_R$ TRE.Enc(m, e, pp). TRE.Enc is an algorithm run by $\mathcal{E}$ that takes as input a message m, encryption key e, and public parameter pp and outputs ciphertext c. The ciphertext c can be given to $\mathcal{D}$ after TRE.Enc completes. TRE.Enc runs in time poly(λ).

- $d \leftarrow$ TRE.Solve(pp, C, t). TRE.Solve is an algorithm run by $\mathcal{D}$ that takes as input the parameters pp, C, t and outputs the decryption key d. TRE.Solve requires t sequential steps to recover d with a run time of $(t)\mathsf{poly}(\lambda)$.
- $\{m', \perp\} \leftarrow$ TRE.Dec(c, d, pp). TRE.Dec is an algorithm run by $\mathcal{D}$ that takes as input the ciphertext c, decryption key d, and public parameter pp and outputs plaintext m' or error $\perp$. TRE.Dec runs in time $\mathsf{poly}(\lambda)$.

A TRE-IA scheme must satisfy the properties of *correctness*, *security*, and *implicit authentication*.

Correctness. Intuitively, a TRE-IA scheme is *correct* if any encrypted message can be decrypted successfully to the original plaintext using the corresponding decryption key with overwhelming probability. Namely, in the context of TRE-IA, the legitimate decryption key when input into TRE.Dec will recover the original message input into TRE.Enc. This is made precise in the Correctness game.

Correctness Game

1 $\mathcal{E}$ outputs the public parameter and trapdoor: $pp, td \leftarrow_{\text{R}}$ TRE.Setup(1^λ).
2 $\mathcal{E}$ outputs an encryption key, decryption key, challenge, and time parameter: $e, d, C, t \leftarrow_{\text{R}}$ TRE.Gen(pp, td, t).
3 $\mathcal{E}$ computes the ciphertext on message m: $c \leftarrow_{\text{R}}$ TRE.Enc(m, e, pp).
4 $\mathcal{D}$ recovers the decryption key: $d \leftarrow$ TRE.Solve(pp, C, t).
5 $\mathcal{D}$ decrypts the ciphertext: $m' \leftarrow$ TRE.Dec(c, d, pp).
   A TRE-IA scheme is correct if $m = m'$ with probability $1 - \mathsf{negl}(\lambda)$.

Security. In TRE-IA, similarly to the TRE definition presented by Chvokja et al. [17], *security* is defined as an indistinguishability game as follows:

Security Game

1 $\mathcal{E}$ outputs the public parameter and trapdoor $pp, td \leftarrow_{\text{R}}$ TRE.Setup(1^λ).
2 $\mathcal{E}$ outputs an encryption key, decryption key, challenge, and time parameter: $e, d, C, t \leftarrow_{\text{R}}$ TRE.Gen(pp, td, t).
3 $\mathcal{A}$ selects two messages of the same length (m_0, m_1) for $\mathcal{E}$.
4 $\mathcal{E}$ uniformly selects $b \in \{0, 1\}$, and encrypts m_b as $c \leftarrow_{\text{R}}$ TRE.Enc(m_b, e, pp).
5 $\mathcal{A}$ runs a preprocessing algorithm $\mathcal{A}_0$ on the public parameter and the ciphertext, and stores $\mathsf{st} \leftarrow \mathcal{A}_0(pp, c)$.
6 $\mathcal{E}$ sends C, t to $\mathcal{A}$.
7 $\mathcal{A}$ runs a PPT algorithm $\mathcal{A}_1$ which outputs $b' \leftarrow \mathcal{A}_1(\mathsf{st}, C, t)$, where $\mathcal{A}_1$ must run in fewer than t sequential steps.
   A TRE-IA scheme is secure if $b = b'$ with probability $\frac{1}{2} + \mathsf{negl}(\lambda)$.

Let an adversary $\mathcal{A}$ chooses two messages of the same length m_0 and m_1. $\mathcal{E}$ chooses one of these messages at random, which it encrypts and sends to $\mathcal{A}$. $\mathcal{A}$ then gets polynomial time to preprocess upon this ciphertext before receiving the challenge C. $\mathcal{A}$ must then make a guess *before* t sequential steps are computed. The scheme is *secure* if no PPT adversary $\mathcal{A}$ can gain an advantage in guessing which message was chosen by $\mathcal{E}$. This is made precise in the Security game.

Implicit Authentication Game

---

1 $\mathcal{E}$ outputs a key pair e, d, the public parameters pp, a trapdoor td, and a challenge C: $pp, td \leftarrow_{\textrm{R}} \textsf{TRE.Setup}(1^{\lambda})$, $e, d, C, t \leftarrow_{\textrm{R}} \textsf{TRE.Gen}(pp, td, t)$.

2 $\mathcal{E}$ sends the public parameter pp to the adversary $\mathcal{A}$.

3 $\mathcal{A}$ returns a target message m^* to $\mathcal{E}$.

4 $\mathcal{E}$ sends $\mathcal{A}$ the challenge C, time parameter t, and the decryption key d.

5 $\mathcal{A}$ is also given access to the encryption oracle $\mathcal{O}^{\textsf{Enc}}$, which takes as input a message $m' \neq m^*$, and returns $c' \leftarrow \textsf{TRE.Enc}(m', e, pp)$ if the message is valid, and $\perp$ otherwise.

6 $\mathcal{A}$ returns a ciphertext c to $\mathcal{E}$.

7 $\mathcal{A}$ wins the game if $m^* \leftarrow \textsf{TRE.Dec}(c, d, pp)$.

A TRE-IA scheme has implicit authentication if $\mathcal{A}$ wins the game with probability no greater than $\textsf{negl}(\lambda)$.

Implicit authentication is the new property we introduce in TRE, which ensures that an adversary is unable to *forge* a ciphertext for a message of their choice, hence providing an implicit guarantee that ciphertexts are authentic. In the context of our application, this property ensures that a malicious party cannot insert a document of their choice into the leak provided by a genuine whistleblower.

The idea of modelling security against a ciphertext forgery is inspired by the notions of plaintext integrity and ciphertext integrity [7,10] in the symmetric encryption setting. More specifically, plaintext integrity states that it should be infeasible to produce a ciphertext decrypting to any message which the sender has not encrypted, and ciphertext integrity requires that it be infeasible to produce a ciphertext not previously produced by the sender, regardless of whether or not the underlying plaintext is 'new' [7].

However, these existing notions do not directly map to the asymmetric-key setting, and TRE in particular, since the adversary, after time t, has access to the secret decryption key. This represents a challenge because it allows the adversary to select elements from the ciphertext space with non-negligible probability, and decrypt them to obtain a plaintext, and present this as a forgery. Whilst any message obtained this way will be not necessarily be 'meaningful', this approach makes a simple analogue of either ciphertext authenticity or plaintext authenticity difficult.

To overcome this, we took the approach of modelling our implicit authentication game as an encryption analogue of *selective* forgery [26,30], a property used in digital signature schemes where an adversary first commits to a target message m^* and is later challenged to forge a signature for this target message. The key difference in our implicit authentication game is that the adversary is instead asked to output an encryption of the target message, rather than a digital signature.

At a high-level, the TRE-IA game proceeds as follows. The adversary is first asked to output a message m^* that they wish to encrypt. The adversary is then given the decryption key, and access to an encryption oracle. Finally, the adversary is asked to output a ciphertext c to the challenger. The adversary wins the game if c decrypts to the message m^*. We make this precise in the Implicit Authentication game.

3   Construction of a TRE-IA Scheme

In this section we provide the implementation details of a concrete TRE with implicit authentication. The TLP element of our TRE-IA is derived from the construction of the Blum Blum Shub CSPRNG [11], and as such we name it the BBS-TRE. Our TRE-IA construction also uses the RSA-OAEP PKE scheme.

Recall that implicit authentication states that without access to the encryption key an adversary should not be able to forge a ciphertext for a message of their choice. When RSA is used in practice it is standard procedure to use $e = 65537$ as the public encryption exponent [6]. This does not allow for implicit authentication, as an adversary can guess this. Using any 'standard' fixed encryption key, or a key from a fixed small set will allow an adversary to guess this key, and hence encrypt a message as a ciphertext with more than negligible probability. As such, we design our construction to choose e at random, to ensure that we obtain the implicit authentication property whilst still conforming to the NIST SP-800-56B standard for random public exponent key pair generation [6], Sect. 6.3.2. Using the BBS-CSPRNG provides an elegant solution to integrating random keys in a TRE-IA setup, as seen in [28].

Next, we provide the notation required for our BBS-TRE. In the pseudo code of our algorithms := indicates assignment, = indicates equality, $\neq$ indicates inequality, () indicates a tuple, and // denotes a comment. The function $\texttt{prime}(j)$ outputs a random j-bit Gaussian prime. The function $\mathcal{U}(a, b)$ uniformly selects an integer that is between $a, b \in \mathbb{Z}$, where $a < b$ and a, b are inclusive. Also, the symbol $\wedge$ indicates logical conjunction (and).

Algorithm 4: Square and Multiply Binary Fast Modular Exponentiation Algorithm [18].

---

    input : (a, b, N), // $a, b, n \in \mathbb{N}$, $a^b \bmod N$
1 $d := 1$
2 $B := \texttt{bin}(b)$ // b in binary
3 **for** $j \in B$ **do**
4 | $d := d^2 \bmod N$
5 | **if** $j = 1$ **then**
6 | | $d := da \bmod N$
7 | **end**
8 **end**
    output: d

A notable selection of delay-based cryptographic schemes such as time-lock puzzles, verifiable delay functions, delay encryption, and timed-release encryption rely on the Rivest Shamir Wagner (RSW) time-lock assumption [13,29,33,36,39]. Like other RSW-based delay-based cryptographic schemes our BBS-TRE also relies on the RSW time-lock assumption.

Definition 1. *RSW time-lock assumption:*
Let $N = pq$ be an RSA modulus and uniformly select $x_0 \in \mathbb{Z}_N^*$. If adversary $\mathcal{A}$ does not know the factorisation or group order of N then calculating $x_t \equiv x_0^{2^t} \bmod N$ is a non-parallelisable calculation that will require t sequential modular exponentiations calculated with Algorithm 4 Square and Multiply [36].

Our BBS-TRE is summarised as follows:

$$pp := (N, k_0, k_1, G, H), td := \phi(N) \quad \leftarrow_{\text{R}} \quad \textsf{TRE.Setup}(1^\lambda)$$
$$e := d^{-1} \bmod \phi(N), d := x_0^{2^{t-1} \bmod \phi(N)} \bmod N,$$
$$C := (x_0, x_t), t \quad \leftarrow_{\text{R}} \quad \textsf{TRE.Gen}(pp, td, t)$$
$$c \quad \leftarrow_{\text{R}} \quad \textsf{TRE.Enc}(m, e, pp)$$
$$d := \sqrt{x_t} \quad \leftarrow \quad \textsf{TRE.Solve}(pp, C, t)$$
$$\{m, \perp\} \quad \leftarrow \quad \textsf{TRE.Dec}(c, d, pp)$$

In our BBS-TRE TRE.Setup outputs the public parameters N, k_0, k_1, G, H. The first parameter is the RSA modulus N which is a Blum integer. A Blum integer is the product of two Gaussian primes i.e. $N = pq$, where $p \equiv q \equiv 3 \bmod 4$ [11]. The modulus being a Blum integer is key requirement for the correctness of our scheme. The parameters k_0, k_1, G, H are the RSA-OAEP parameters which can be seen in detail in Algorithm 7. TRE.Setup also outputs the trapdoor $\phi(N) := (p-1)(q-1)$ and keeps this parameter private.

Next, the TRE.Gen algorithm outputs the encryption and decryption keys, the challenge (x_0, x_t) and the time parameter t. In the challenge (x_0, x_t) the term x_0 is a randomly sampled quadratic residue of N, denoted $x_0 \in \mathcal{QR}_N$. The decryption key d is calculated with the trapdoor using Algorithm 4 with the parameters $(x_0, 2^{t-1} \bmod \phi(N), N)$. If $\gcd(d, \phi(N)) = 1$, then in the challenge (x_0, x_t), the term x_t is set to $d^2 \bmod N$ and the encryption key e is set to $d^{-1} \bmod \phi(N)$. Next the TRE.Enc algorithm inputs a message m and the encryption key e and the public encryption parameters pp to output the ciphertext c using the RSA-OEAP PKE scheme. This scheme deviates from a traditional RSA-OAEP PKE scheme as the encryption key e remains private to ensure the property of implicit authentication.

Next, the TRE.Solve algorithm sequentially calculates the decryption key d using Algorithm 4 with the parameters $(x_0, 2^{t-1}, N)$. The RSW time-lock assumption tells us that finding the term d will require $t-1$ sequential modular exponentiations to calculate if the trapdoor $\phi(N)$ is not known. Finally, the TRE.Dec algorithm takes as input the ciphertext c and the decryption key d and the public parameters pp, and outputs either the message m or an error $\perp$ using the RSA-OEAP PKE scheme. We now provide the full details of our BBS-TRE algorithms.

1) $\mathcal{V}$ runs $pp, td \leftarrow_R$ Setup(1^λ) to generate the public parameter and trapdoor, as seen on Algorithm 5. The function prime(j) on lines 4 and 5 randomly generates j bit primes $p \equiv q \equiv 3 \bmod 4$. That is, $p \leftarrow_R$ prime(j). This guarantees that N, which is calculated on line 7, is a Blum integer. Next, the trapdoor is set to $\phi(N) := (p-1)(q-1)$. Next it runs the function params(1^k) which outputs the parameters for the RSA-OAEP PKE scheme. The parameters k_0, k_1 are integers fixed by RSA-OEAP, and the parameters G, H are cryptographically secure hashing functions. The public parameter is set to $pp := (N, k_0, k_1, G, H)$. The public parameter can be released to $\mathcal{D}$ after TRE.Setup is run, but the trapdoor must remain private. TRE.Setup outputs pp, td.

Algorithm 5: $\mathcal{E}$ runs TRE.Setup on security parameter 1^λ to output public parameter pp and trapdoor td.

---

    input : 1^λ
1 $p := 0$
2 $q := 0$
3 **while** $p \neq q$ **do**
4 | $p := $ prime($\frac{\lambda}{2}$)
5 | $q := $ prime($\frac{\lambda}{2}$)
6 **end**
7 $N := pq$
8 $\phi(N) := (p-1)(q-1)$
9 $k_0, k_1, G, H \leftarrow$ params(1^λ)
    output: $pp := (N, k_0, k_1, G, H), td := \phi(N)$

---

2) $\mathcal{E}$ runs $e, d, C, t \leftarrow_R$ TRE.Gen(pp, td, t) to generate the encryption and decryption keys and the challenge, as seen on Algorithm 6. First, TRE.Gen sets the variable gcd to 0. Next, TRE.Gen enters a while loop to generate an appropriate encryption and decryption exponent e, d for RSA-OAEP. This is done by first uniformly selecting $x \in \mathbb{Z}_N^*$ and computing $x_0 \equiv x^2 \bmod N$. Then TRE.Gen evaluates $d \equiv x_0^{2^{t-1} \bmod \phi(N)} \bmod N$. The decryption key d is calculated using Algorithm 4 with the parameters $(x_0, 2^{t-1} \bmod \phi(N), N)$. Note that $\mathcal{E}$ is able to reduce the exponent $2^{t-1} \bmod \phi(N)$ using the trapdoor. The while loop runs until the decryption key d computed on line 6 is coprime to $\phi(N)$. That is, until gcd $:=$ gcd($d, \phi(N)$) $= 1$. Once this is found the while loop exits and the term $x_t := d^2 \bmod N$ is calculated and the encryption key e is calculated using the extended Euclidean Algorithm. In Theorem 1 we prove that the while loop will terminate. Furthermore, we prove that in expectation the number of iterations the while loop will require to generate a challenge such that gcd $:=$ gcd($d, \phi(N)$) $= 1$ is $\frac{\pi^2}{3} \approx 3.3$. This finding and the associated proof is a key contribution of our concrete TRE-IA construction. Finally, the challenge C is set to the tuple (x_0, x_t). TRE.Gen then outputs

the encryption and decryption keys e, d and the challenge and time parameter C, t. The challenge that $\mathcal{D}$ must solve to recover the decryption key is: for seed x_0, find d such that $d \equiv \sqrt{x_t} \bmod N$. The encryption key e must remain private, and C and t must only be released to $\mathcal{D}$ once $\mathcal{E}$ would like the decryption key d to be extracted under the RSW time-lock assumption by using the TRE.Solve algorithm.

Algorithm 6: $\mathcal{E}$ runs TRE.Gen on public parameter, trapdoor, and time parameter pp, td, t to create the encryption and decryption exponents and the challenge e, d, C, t.

---

    input : $pp, \phi(N), t$ // $t \in \mathbb{N}$

1 $\gcd := 0$

2 **while** $\gcd \neq 1$ **do**

3      $x := \mathcal{U}(2, 2^{\frac{\lambda}{2}})$ // $x \in \mathbb{Z}_N^*$

4      $x_0 := x^2 \bmod N$

5      $d := x_0^{2^{t-1} \bmod \phi(N)} \bmod N$

6      $\gcd := \gcd(d, \phi(N))$

7 **end**

8 $x_t := d^2 \bmod N$

9 $e := d^{-1} \bmod \phi(N)$ // EEA

10 $C := (x_0, x_t)$

    output: e, d, C, t

---

3) $\mathcal{E}$ runs $c \leftarrow_{\text{R}}$ TRE.Enc(m, e, pp) to output ciphertext c, as seen on Algorithm 7. TRE.Enc is the encryption algorithm of the RSA-OAEP PKE scheme. Each step of the algorithm is described on the comments of each line. The final step is to output the ciphertext c. In a TRE scheme the ciphertext c can be released to the decryptor independently of the challenge and time parameter output by TRE.Gen.

Algorithm 7: $\mathcal{E}$ runs TRE.Enc on (m, e, pp) to output ciphertext c.

---

    input : m, e, pp

    // $pp := (N, k_0, k_1, G, H)$

1 $m' := m \parallel 0^{k_1}$ // Zero pad to $n - k_0$ bits

2 $r := \text{rand}(k_0)$ // Random k_0 bit number

3 $X := m' \oplus G_{n-k_0}(r)$ // Hash r to length $n - k_0$

4 $Y := r \oplus H_{k_0}(X)$ // Hash X to length k_0

5 $m'' := X \parallel Y$ // Create message object

6 $c := m''^e \bmod N$ // RSA encrypt

    output: c

---

4) $\mathcal{D}$ runs $d \leftarrow$ TRE.Solve(pp, C, t) to evaluate the challenge and output the decryption key as seen on Algorithm 8. First TRE.Solve calculates the term $\sqrt{x_t}$ by entering the parameters $(x_0, 2^{t-1}, N)$ into Algorithm 4. By the RSW

time-lock assumption it will take $t - 1$ sequential steps to calculate d because the trapdoor is not known by the decryptor $\mathcal{D}$. Next, TRE.Solve checks if $\sqrt{x_t}^2 \bmod N = x_t$ is true. If the condition is true, then d is set to $\sqrt{x_t}$ and output and the algorithm terminates.

5) $\mathcal{D}$ runs $\{m, \perp\} \leftarrow$ TRE.Dec(c, d, pp) to output the plaintext message m or $\perp$, as seen on Algorithm 9. TRE.Dec is the decryption algorithm of the RSA-OEAP PKE scheme. Each step of the algorithm is described on the comments of each line. The final step is to output the message m or $\perp$. By the correctness of the RSA-OAEP PKE scheme, if the parameter d extracted by TRE.Solve under the RSW time-lock assumption has the property $ed \equiv 1 \bmod \phi(N)$ (line 9 of TRE.Gen), then the message m will be recovered. Else, TRE.Dec will output $\perp$.

Algorithm 8: $\mathcal{D}$ runs TRE.Solve to evaluate pp, C, t and output the decryption key d.

input : pp, C, t
 // $pp := (N, k_0, k_1, G, H)$, $C := (x_0, x_t)$
1 $\sqrt{x_t} := x_0^{2^{t-1}} \bmod N$
2 if $\sqrt{x_t}^2 \bmod N = x_t$ then
3 | $d := \sqrt{x_t}$
4 end
output: d

We have presented a concrete construction for a TRE-IA based on a RSW TLP and the RSA-OAEP PKE scheme. We have done this by setting up an RSA modulus which is a Blum integer, generating a TLP challenge and a PKE key-pair, then time-locking the decryption key using the TLP. We then integrated our encryption and decryption exponents (the PKE-style key pair) into the RSA-OAEP scheme for the encryption of a message and the decryption of the ciphertext respectively. In the next sections we review the formal security analysis of our scheme and then give a performance analysis of a real implementation of our scheme.

Algorithm 9: $\mathcal{D}$ runs TRE.Dec on (c, d, pp) to recover message m or output $\perp$.

input : c, d, pp
 // $pp := (N, k_0, k_1, G, H)$
1 $m'' := c^d \bmod N$
2 $X := \lfloor m'' 2^{-k_0} \rfloor$ // Extract X
3 $Y := m'' \bmod 2^{k_0}$ // Extract Y
4 $r := Y \oplus H_{k_0}(X)$ // Recover r
5 $m' := X \oplus G_{n-k_0}(r)$ // Recover padded message
6 $m := m' 2^{-k_1}$ // Remove padding
output: $\{m, \perp\}$

4   Security Analysis

In this section we provide the security analysis of our concrete BBS-TRE scheme. First we prove that our BBS-TRE is correct and secure. We then prove that our scheme holds the property of implicit authentication.

We first provide proof of the correctness of our scheme. The outline of our proof will be as follows: first we will prove that TRE.Gen will terminate and generate a suitable RSW time-lock puzzle challenge, second we will prove that TRE.Solve will correctly output the decryption key d, third we will prove that the decryption key d is unique because N is a Blum integer, and finally we will prove that the decryption key will correctly return the original message m when it is used to decrypt the ciphertext c generated with the encryption exponent e.

First we must prove that the while loop in TRE.Gen will terminate and generate a suitable challenge and decryption key.

Theorem 1. *The while loop in* TRE.Gen *will in expectation take* $\frac{\pi^2}{3}$ *trials to generate a suitable challenge and decryption key d.*

Proof. The probability of two randomly selected integers being coprime is $\frac{6}{\pi^2}$ [24], Theorem 33. The Blum integer $N = pq$ generated with TRE.Setup is randomly selected using the Miller Rabin Monte Carlo algorithm [31]. Next, the $\phi(N)$ is calculated as $(p-1)(q-1)$. Therefore, $\phi(N)$ is always even. Each iteration of the while loop in TRE.Gen is a Bernoulli trial. In our Bernoulli trial N and hence $\phi(N)$ are randomly selected and the integer d on line 5 of TRE.Gen is also randomly selected. We model d as a random integer as it is an output of the BBS CSPRNG. In each trial, if $\gcd(d, \phi(N)) = 1$ the outcome is a success, otherwise if $\gcd(d, \phi(N)) \neq 1$ then the outcome is a failure. Therefore, in each trial, the probability of selecting two random integers which are coprime when one integer is even is $\frac{6}{2\pi^2} = \frac{3}{\pi^2}$.

Finally, the probability distribution of the number of Bernoulli trials required until one success is achieved forms a Geometric distribution $G \sim \mathsf{Geo}(\frac{3}{\pi^2})$. Therefore, in expectation, the number of Bernoulli trials required until a suitable challenge and decryption key d is selected such that $\gcd(d, \phi(N)) = 1$ is $\mathbb{E}(G) = \frac{\pi^2}{3} \approx 3.3$ trials.[1]

Second we must prove that the TRE.Solve algorithm correctly calculates the decryption key d. To prove this we must show that the Square and Multiply algorithm correctly calculates any term correctly in a BBS sequence. We first provide a brief summary of the BBS CSPRNG and subsequently a security analysis of our BBS-TRE for each of the required properties. The BBS CSPRNG [11] starts by selecting $x \in \mathbb{Z}_N^*$ and calculates the seed value $x_0 \equiv x^2 \bmod N$. To produce a string of t bits, the least significant bit is extracted from each term $x_i \equiv x_{i-1}^2 \bmod N$ for $i \in (1, \ldots, t)$. The equivalent representation of the first t terms of the sequence can be seen in Table 1.

---

[1] Numerical analysis also indicated that over thousands of trials, independent of the size of $\phi(N)$, the average number of iterations the while loop must run until a suitable challenge was found was 3.3.

Table 1. The first t terms of the BBS CSPRNG. The first row identifies which $i \in (1, \ldots, t)$ is being calculated. The second, third, and fourth rows are equivalent representations of the same term, i.e. in the penultimate column, for $i := t - 1$, the terms x_{t-1}, x_{t-2}^2, and $x^{2^{t-1}}$ are equivalent.

i	0 seed	1	2	$\ldots$	$t-2$	$t-1$	t
x_i	x_0	x_1	x_2	$\ldots$	x_{t-2}	x_{t-1}	x_t
x_{i-1}^2	x_0	x_0^2	x_1^2	$\ldots$	x_{t-3}^2	x_{t-2}^2	x_{t-1}^2
$x_0^{2^i}$	x_0	$x_0^{2^1}$	$x_0^{2^2}$	$\ldots$	$x_0^{2^{t-2}}$	$x_0^{2^{t-1}}$	$x_0^{2^t}$

Theorem 2. *Algorithm 4 Square and Multiply correctly calculates the x_i term of the BBS CSPRNG.*

Proof. The input to calculate the term x_i of the BBS CSPRNG takes as input $(x_0, 2^i, N)$, where x_0 is the seed term, and N is a Blum integer. Consider the base case when $i := 1$. The algorithm proceeds as follows: d is set to 1 and the exponent $b := 2^1$ is set to the binary string $B = 10$. Next, the algorithm enters the for loop on the first iteration. On the first iteration j is the first digit of B, which is 1. Next $d := 1$ is squared to output 1. Then the first conditional if statement is met as $j = 1$, therefore $d := 1 \cdot x_0 = x_0 \bmod N$, and the first iteration of the loop is done. On the second iteration j is the second digit of B, which is 0. Next, as d was set to x_0 on the first iteration d is now set to $x_0^2 \bmod N$ on the second iteration. The first conditional if statement is not met, and the loop terminates as the final digit of B was processed. The algorithm then returns $d := x_1 \equiv x_0^2 \equiv x_0^{2^1} \bmod N$, as required. Therefore, the base case is true.

By the inductive hypothesis we claim that for any $i := k$, the loop invariant of Algorithm 4 returns the term $x_0^{2^k} \bmod N$ after k iterations. Therefore after k iterations, where b was set to 2^{k+1}, Algorithm 4 will have $d := x_0^{2^k} \bmod N$, and j will be the final digit of $B := 10 \ldots 0$. For any k, the variable B will be a binary string starting with the digit 1 followed by a trail of k digits equal to 0. This means after the first iteration of the for loop all remaining $j \in B$ will be 0. Thus, at the $k+1$ iteration of the for loop d will be set to $x_k^2 \bmod N$, and by definition $x_k^2 \equiv x_{k+1} \equiv x_0^{2^{k+1}} \bmod N$. Finally, Algorithm 4 will terminate at the $k+1$ iteration as the final digit of B was processed, and the algorithm will return $d := x_0^{2^{k+1}} \bmod N$.

Lemma 1. *The TRE.Solve algorithm in the BBS-TRE correctly outputs the decryption key $d := x_{t-1}$.*

Proof. Suppose encryptor $\mathcal{E}$ honestly generates a random public parameter, challenge and time parameter $pp := (N, k_0, k_1, G, H), (C := (x_0, x_t), t)$ and presents these to an honest $\mathcal{D}$. Next, suppose $\mathcal{D}$ selects the legitimate evaluation algorithm TRE.Solve to evaluate (C, t). The TRE.Solve algorithm will calculate the decryption key d by entering the following parameters $(x_0, 2^{t-1}, N)$ into the Algorithm

4, which will output $d := x_0^{2^{t-1}} = x_{t-1} \bmod N$. TRE.Solve will correctly output the BBS term x_{t-1} with overwhelming probability due to the correctness of Algorithm 4 noted in Theorem 2. Therefore, the TRE.Solve algorithm will correctly output $d := x_{t-1}$.

Next we must prove that the decryption key $d := x_{t-1} = \sqrt{x_t} \bmod N$ output by TRE.Solve is unique. First we must recall that d by definition of being a term in a BBS CSPRNG sequence is a quadratic residue of the modulus N and provide a brief definition.

Definition 2. Quadratic residues. *Let $N = pq$, where p, q are λ bit primes. If $r \equiv x^2 \bmod N$, for some $x \in \mathbb{Z}_N^*$, we say that r is a quadratic residue of N. This is denoted as $r \in \mathcal{QR}_N$.*

Therefore, we must prove that the solution d to the follow equation is unique:

$$d := \sqrt{x_t} \bmod N \tag{1}$$

This challenge arises because the Chinese Remainder Theorem isomorphism indicates that when $N = pq$, where p, q are distinct odd primes, that Eq. 1 has four distinct solutions [25]. That is, $\pm a \equiv \pm b \equiv \sqrt{x_t} \bmod N$, where $a \neq b$.

Theorem 3. *If $N = pq$ is a Blum integer, then the decryption key d in our BBS-TRE extracted by TRE.Solve is unique.*

Proof. If $N = pq$ is a Blum integer with $p \equiv q \equiv 3 \bmod 4$, then $N \equiv 1 \bmod 4$. By the Chinese Remainder Theorem isomorphism every $r \in \mathcal{QR}_N$ has four distinct square roots $\pm a$ and $\pm b$. As N is a Blum integer, by the law of quadratic reciprocity $\mathcal{J}_N(a) = \mathcal{J}_N(-a)$ and $\mathcal{J}_N(b) = \mathcal{J}_N(-b)$, where $\mathcal{J}_N$ is the Jacobi symbol. It must be the case that $a^2 \equiv b^2 \bmod N$, which implies $(a - b)(a + b) \equiv 0 \bmod N$, which implies $(a - b) \mid N$ and $(a + b) \mid N$. That is, without loss of generality $(a - b) = kp$ and $(a + b) = \ell q$, where $k, \ell \in \mathbb{N}$. Therefore, $\mathcal{J}_p(a) = \mathcal{J}_p(b)$ and $\mathcal{J}_q(a) = \mathcal{J}_q(-b)$. As $p \equiv 3 \bmod 4$, the law of quadratic reciprocity tells us $\mathcal{J}_p(-1) = -1$, we have $\mathcal{J}_q(a)\mathcal{J}_p(-1) = \mathcal{J}_q(-b)\mathcal{J}_p(-1)$. This implies that $\mathcal{J}_N(-a) = \mathcal{J}_N(b)$ or written another way $\mathcal{J}_N(a) \neq \mathcal{J}_N(b)$.
   Without loss of generality, eliminate the two roots with $\mathcal{J}_N$ equal to -1, say $\mathcal{J}_N(b) = \mathcal{J}_N(-b) = -1$. This leaves $\mathcal{J}_N(a) = \mathcal{J}_N(-a) = 1$. It is the case that only one of $-a$ or a has $\mathcal{J}_p = \mathcal{J}_q = 1$ as $p \equiv 3 \bmod 4$. Therefore, it is this one that is the only quadratic residue modulo N [11].
   Returning to our BBS-TRE, by Lemma 1 the term $d := x_{t-1} \bmod N$ is correctly calculated by TRE.Solve and by definition it is a term in a BBS sequence. Therefore, d is a quadratic residue of the modulus N. Therefore, d is the only one of the four distinct square roots of x_t that is a quadratic residue of N.

For the final element of the correctness proof of our BBS-TRE construction we must prove that the decryption key d will correctly recover the message in an RSA-OAEP scheme.

Corollary 1. *The BBS-TRE is correct.*

Proof. By Theorem 1 we know that TRE.Gen will terminate and output a suitable RSW TLP challenge (C, t). By Theorem 2 and Lemma 1 we know that the decryption key d will be recovered by TRE.Solve. By Theorem 3 we know that the decryption key d against the modulus N is unique. From the Fermat-Euler Theorem [22] we know that the decryption key d calculated on line 5 of TRE.Gen is the same as the decryption key recovered by TRE.Solve on line 1. From the correctness of the Extended Euclidean Algorithm [25] we know that e calculated on line 9 of TRE.Gen is the multiplicative inverse of d. Finally, from the correctness of the RSA-OEAP scheme [8] we know that TRE.Dec will correctly recover the message m using decryption key d from the ciphertext c output by TRE.Enc using encryption key e with overwhelming probability.

Next we prove the security of our scheme. To prove the security of our scheme a set of arguments will need to be addressed. The outline of our proof will be as follows: First we prove that finding a square root   mod N when N is an RSA modulus is equivalent to factoring N. Second we prove that given the public parameters and the RSW challenge an adversary cannot derive the decryption key d in less than t sequential steps. Finally we prove that if $\mathcal{E}$ selects one of two equal length messages to encrypt using TRE.Enc and outputs ciphertext c, then the only way an adversary can guess with greater than $\frac{1}{2} + \mathsf{negl}(\lambda)$ probability which message was encrypted is to honestly run TRE.Solve and recover the decryption key d.

Theorem 4. *Let $N = pq$, where p and q are λ bit primes. Then given any $r \in \mathcal{QR}_N$, finding x such that $x^2 \equiv r \bmod N$ is equivalent to factoring N.*

Proof. Proof can be found in the paper by Rabin [34].

The next part of our proof of the security property is to show that the adversary cannot recover the decryption key in less than t sequential steps. If the adversary can recover d in less than t sequential steps then they can output b' equal to b with probability greater than $\frac{1}{2} + \mathsf{negl}(\lambda)$ by decrypting the ciphertext. Our proof is split into two parts: i) when $\mathcal{A}$ attempts to compute d in less than t sequential steps, and ii) when $\mathcal{A}$ attempts to recover $\sqrt{x_t} \bmod N$ using a method that does not use C, t. Therefore, our next step is to prove that the only way d can be recovered without knowing the factors (or trapdoor) of N is to honestly evaluate the challenge in t sequential steps.

Theorem 5. *Our BBS-TRE requires t sequential steps to recover the decryption key d.*

Proof. Suppose $\mathcal{E}$ honestly generates a random public parameter pp and generates the encryption key, decryption key, challenge, and time parameter e, d, C, t. Next $\mathcal{A}$ selects two messages of the same length m_0 and m_1 for $\mathcal{E}$ to encrypt. $\mathcal{E}$ uniformly selects $b \in \{0, 1\}$ and encrypts m_b. $\mathcal{A}$ produces a PPT algorithm $\mathcal{A}_0$ which pre-processes pp and c and outputs a state $\mathsf{st} \leftarrow \mathcal{A}_0(pp, c)$. $\mathcal{E}$ sends the challenge and time parameter to $\mathcal{A}$. $\mathcal{A}$ produces a PPT algorithm $\mathcal{A}_1$ to output $b' \leftarrow \mathcal{A}_1(\mathsf{st}, C, t)$.

We start by proving part i), that computing d reduces to the RSW time-lock assumption. First we recall from Lemma 1 that TRE.Solve correctly outputs the decryption key d in t sequential steps, and we know from Theorem 3 that the decryption key d is unique. Next we note that the pre-processing is carried out before the $\mathcal{A}$ is given the challenge and time parameter C, t. Therefore, the probability that $\mathcal{A}$ can compute d in less than t steps is negligible. Specifically, if TRE.Solve is honestly run, then d is calculated using Algorithm 4 with input $(x_0, 2^{t-1}, N)$. Therefore, by the RSW time-lock assumption, calculating d with Algorithm 4 requires $t - 1$ sequential steps.

Next, suppose $\mathcal{A}$ selects PPT algorithm $\mathcal{A}_{<t}$ to evaluate d in less than $t - 1$ sequential steps. However, using such an algorithm $\mathcal{A}_{<t}$ contradicts the RSW time-lock assumption.

What remains is to show that giving $\mathcal{A}$ the challenge and time parameter $C := (x_0, x_t), t$ does not allow them to take square roots mod N faster than sequential squaring. To see this, note that by construction x_0 and x_t are the seed term and t^{th} term in a BBS CSPRNG sequence [11]. Under the Generalised BBS assumption [13], knowledge of these terms does not allow finding $d = \sqrt{x_t}$ faster than sequential squaring unless $x_0^{2^{\lambda(\lambda(N))}}$ mod N is calculated efficiently, where $\lambda(N)$ is the Carmichael function [15]. Finding $x_0^{2^{\lambda(\lambda(N))}}$ efficiently is an open problem given by Theorem 9 of Blum et al. [11, 19, 23].

Next, we prove part ii). Observe that finding $d = \sqrt{x_t}$ mod N i.e. taking square roots mod N without challenge and time parameter C, t reduces to the open problem of integer factorisation, Theorem 4. Therefore, as N is an RSA modulus we assume it cannot be factored by any PPT algorithm with more than negligible probability. Therefore, the only way a PPT algorithm could recover the unique decryption key d when the factorisation (or trapdoor) of N is not known is to honestly run TRE.Solve

Theorem 5 proves that the adversary cannot recover d in less than t sequential steps to win the Security game. Therefore, to conclude our proof of the security property we must demonstrate that the adversary cannot guess b in less than t sequential steps without knowledge of the decryption key.

Theorem 6. *Our BBS-TRE scheme is secure.*

Proof. We first assume for a contradiction that a PPT adversary $\mathcal{A}$ can win the Security game with a non-negligible advantage.

Let IND-CPA^{RSA} be the standard IND-CPA game for RSA-OAEP [8]. We now recall the well-known result that RSA with OAEP padding is IND-CPA secure under the RSA assumption [20]. We will show that any adversary who can break the Security game can also break the RSA assumption.

When choosing the two messages in the Security game the adversary $\mathcal{A}$ has the same available information as they do in the IND-CPA^{RSA} game. We now analyse the difference between the two games when $\mathcal{A}$ receives the challenge and makes a guess. In the Security game, $\mathcal{A}$ is provided with an additional piece of information, the challenge C, but $\mathcal{A}$ is bounded by computational time t.

If an adversary wins the Security game with a non-negligible advantage without evaluating the challenge using algorithm $\mathcal{A}_0$, then they can also break the IND-CPA^{RSA} game with the same algorithm, as C is not provided to $\mathcal{A}_0$.

Next, given the challenge C, t and the state st the sequentiality property of Theorem 5 proves that if an adversary gains a non-negligible advantage by evaluating the challenge in time less than t with $\mathcal{A}_1$ then they are contradicting the RSW-time lock assumption. Therefore, for the adversary to gain a non-negligible advantage in the Security game, they must break either the RSW time-lock assumption, or the IND-CPA^{RSA} security game, and hence the RSA assumption. The adversary will therefore guess the correct message with probability at most $\frac{1}{2} + \mathsf{negl}(\lambda)$, and hence our TRE-IA scheme is secure according to the Security Game presented in Sect. 2.

We now prove that our scheme has the property of implicit authentication

Theorem 7. *Our TRE scheme provides the implicit authentication property.*

Proof. Suppose that the encryptor runs the TRE.Setup and TRE.Gen algorithms. Let $\mathcal{A}$ receive the RSA modulus N and the OAEP parameters (k_0, k_1, G, H), and let m^* be the target message it outputs.

Now let $\mathcal{A}$ receive the challenge C, the time parameter t, the decryption key d and have access to the encryption oracle $\mathcal{O}^{\mathsf{enc}}$.

In our construction d is chosen at random on lines 3–5 of TRE.Gen. As we are working in $\mathbb{Z}_N^*$ there is only one multiplicative inverse of d, which is the encryption key e calculated on line 9 of TRE.Gen. To derive e from d requires knowledge of $\phi(N)$, as $e := d^{-1} \bmod \phi(N)$. In order to learn $\phi(N)$, the adversary would need to factor the RSA modulus N, which is a well-known hard problem [34,35]. Therefore, unless the adversary can factor N, they cannot guess e with more than negligible probability. Therefore with overwhelming probability the adversary will not learn the trapdoor $\phi(N)$, and hence will not be able to derive e from d.

Using the encryption oracle $\mathcal{O}^{\mathsf{enc}}$ $\mathcal{A}$ can obtain polynomially many ciphertexts.

Recall from [8] that RSA-OAEP has ciphertext indistinguishability under chosen-plaintext attack, which guarantees indistinguishability between encryptions of messages. This property guarantees in particular that the adversary has no advantage in identifying a ciphertext that will allow them to win the IA game.

The adversary can choose random elements from the ciphertext space, and decrypt them using the decryption key d. However, without knowledge of the encryption key, any such ciphertext will decrypt to a random element of the message space.

As the size of the ciphertext space is exponential (explicitly it is the magnitude of $\mathbb{Z}_N^*$), and the adversary runs a PPT algorithm, there is a negligible chance of correctly guessing a ciphertext which decrypts to the target message m^*. Therefore the adversary will not win the implicit authentication game with greater than negligible probability.

5   Performance and Integration with SecureDrop

In this section we present an evaluation of how our TRE-IA scheme performs and provide a sample of how it can integrate with SecureDrop. We evaluate the run times of the algorithms executed by the encryptor (who is the whistleblower) and those executed by the decryptor. Our analysis compares the dispersion of run times of TRE-IA algorithms in our construction when different parameters are used for the modulus size. Based on the results of our analysis we present a number of recommendations for TRE implementations.

5.1   Performance Analysis

Our test setup consists of a virtual machine running on an Intel i7-6700K 4 GHz CPU and 24 GB of RAM. The guest OS is Ubuntu 18.04 running Python 3.8.10. The Crypto library 2.6.1 is used to generate random Blum integers. The code can be found in https://github.com/nxd0main/TRE-IA.

Our performance analysis consists of running six different trials. Each trial tests how different parameters impact the encryptor and decryptor algorithms run times on our TRE-IA scheme implementation. Trial 1 is tested against a 2048 bit modulus, with the time parameter t set to 10 million. Trial 1 is run 200 times. Each time Trial 1 is executed we record the individual run times of the TRE.Setup, TRE.Gen, TRE.Enc, TRE.Solve, and TRE.Dec algorithms. Trial $2, 3, 4, 5$ and 6 are similar to Trial 1 except they are tested against a $2560, 3072$, $3584, 4096$, and 4608 bit modulus, respectively. Table 2 summarises the trial parameters and a number of key descriptive statistics based on our analysis.

Table 2. Performance analysis trial parameters and descriptive statistics for TRE scheme run time tests. $\mu_{\mathcal{E}}^{*}$, $\mu_{\mathcal{E}}$, $\sigma_{\mathcal{E}}$, and $c_{\mathcal{E}}$ are the aggregated encryptor algorithms run time mean without the TRE.Setup algorithm, run time mean with the TRE.Setup algorithm standard deviation, and coefficient of variance, respectively. $\mu_{\mathcal{D}}$, $\sigma_{\mathcal{D}}$, $c_{\mathcal{D}}$, and $\beta_{\mathcal{D}}$ are the aggregated decryptor algorithms run time mean, standard deviation, coefficient of variance, and excess kurtosis, respectively.

Trial	Modulus [b]	runs	t	ℓ	$\mu_{\mathcal{E}}^{*}$ [s]	$\mu_{\mathcal{E}}$ [s]	$\sigma_{\mathcal{E}}$ [s]	$c_{\mathcal{E}}$	$\mu_{\mathcal{D}}$ [s]	$\sigma_{\mathcal{D}}$ [s]	$c_{\mathcal{D}}$	$\beta_{\mathcal{D}}$
1	2048	200	110^7	50	1.14	1.33	0.13	0.095	121.08	2.01	0.017	-0.18
2	2560	200	110^7	50	2.13	4.74	1.71	0.360	166.37	2.27	0.014	0.12
3	3072	200	110^7	50	3.57	4.07	0.33	0.081	221.41	2.25	0.010	-0.36
4	3584	200	110^7	50	5.54	12.08	4.56	0.378	284.07	2.93	0.010	0.15
5	4096	200	110^7	50	8.13	9.41	0.85	0.090	354.77	3.41	0.010	1.33
6	4608	200	110^7	50	11.31	25.02	8.38	0.335	432.73	4.08	0.009	4.98

Encryptor Analysis. We first provide an analysis of the distribution of the aggregated run time of the algorithms run by the encryptor $\mathcal{E}$. For each of the 200 iterations of the six trials in Table 2, the aggregated mean run time of the encryptor algorithms is noted under column $\mu_{\mathcal{E}}$ [s]. This column is the sum of the individual run times for TRE.Setup, TRE.Gen, and TRE.Enc algorithms. In the column noted $\mu_{\mathcal{E}}^*$ [s], the aggregated mean run time of the encryptor algorithms without TRE.Setup is recorded to illustrate the overhead of this algorithm.

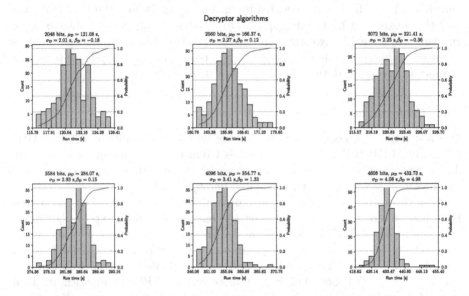

Fig. 1. Histogram with EDF for our BBS-TRE scheme Decryptor TRE.Solve and TRE.Dec algorithm run times. Heavy tailed distributions with high excess kurtosis can be seen on the 4096 bit and on the 4608 bit trial data. These trials show the probability of outliers is higher than a normal distribution. This can give a decryptor an inconsistent run time when extracting the decryption key and decrypting the ciphertext. If the selection of time parameter t is chosen to provide a specific time for the decryption of data for maximum impact, using parameters with a high probability of outlier run times is undesirable.

Table 2 also shows the standard deviation $\sigma_{\mathcal{E}}$ [s], and the coefficient of variance $c_{\mathcal{E}}$ for each trial. $c_{\mathcal{E}}$ allows us to normalise the dispersion of the run times around the mean for the different trials [5]. We see that the coefficient of variance is smaller for the 2048, 3072, and 4096 bit modulus indicating a tigher run time around the mean. Tigher dispersion is ideal to give a more consistent experience. As the encryptor may be under duress, knowledge of run times for operation would be essential.

Recommendations: Based on the analysis of encryptor algorithm performance, we recommend choosing the 2048 bit and 3072 bit modulus sizes to ensure fast and consistent run times demonstrated by their low mean run times and low coefficients of variance respectively.

Decryptor Analysis. Next, we provide analysis of the distribution of the aggregated run times of the algorithms run by the decryptor $\mathcal{D}$. The aggregated

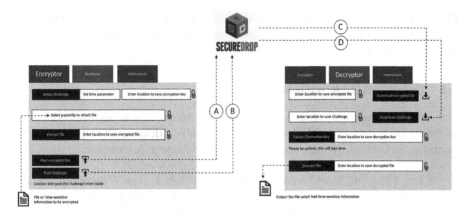

Fig. 2. SecureDrop integration with TRE-IA.

decryptor algorithm run time equals the sum of the TRE.Solve and TRE.Dec algorithms. The mean $\mu_\mathcal{D}$, standard deviation $\sigma_\mathcal{D}$, coefficient of variation $c_\mathcal{D}$, and excess kurtosis $\beta_\mathcal{D}$ for each trial can be seen in Table 2. The coefficient of variation remains consistently low between all trials in Table 2. This is ideal because having a low coefficient of variance for the decryptor algorithms indicates a tighter dispersion around the mean. By this measure, the decryptor algorithm run times appear to be consistent.

We also measure the dispersion properties of the decryptor run times using the excess kurtosis, denoted $\beta_\mathcal{D}$. Excess kurtosis provides information about the weight of the tails of a distribution [40]. Excess kurtosis also provides an indicator of the probability of outliers in the distribution. Therefore, lower excess kurtosis is ideal to provide assurance of consistent run times.

Figure 1 plots the histograms of the decryptor run times for each of the six trial types in Table 2. Each histogram also plots an empirical distribution function (EDF). Figure 1 shows us that the 2048 and 3072 bit BBS-TRE distributions show the lowest probability of outlier run times and that the 4096 bit and 4608 bit distributions show the highest probability of outlier run times.

The presence of heavy tailed distributions in our trials was unanticipated as the virtual machine resources and test parameters remained consistent. Having heavy tailed distributions with a high probability of outliers for decryptor algorithm run times when the same computational resource is provided is undesirable. For example, a decryptor extracting and decrypting the ciphertext on a 4608 bit construction would know from performance analysis that there is a 1 in 25 chance that they could take far longer than the expected mean time to extract the time-locked decryption key and decrypt the ciphertext.

Consider a concrete example extrapolated from the final histogram in Fig. 1 for the 4608 bit modulus. If $\mathcal{E}$ selected the parameter t such that the expected extraction and decryption time was 7 days (168 hours), then a decryptor may take 8 hours longer than the expected run time to recover the plaintext.

Recommendations: Based on the analysis of decryptor algorithm performance, we recommend using the 2048 and 3072 bit sizes which demonstrate the lowest probability of outlier run times.

5.2 Using TRE-IA with SecureDrop

Our TRE-IA construction could augment an existing whistleblowing tool known as SecureDrop by adding the property of guaranteed delay with implicit authentication. SecureDrop is 'an open source whistleblower submission system that can securely access documents from anonymous sources' [2].

In Fig. 2 the left hand box is the 'Encryptor' tab for the Whistleblower. The Setup Challenge button will run the TRE.Setup and TRE.Gen algorithms and allow the time parameter to be selected. Next there is dialogue box to securely save the encryption key e to maintain the property of IA. The dialogue box 'Encrypt file' will select the files that are required to be time-release encrypted by TRE.Enc. The whistleblower can then upload the public parameters and ciphertext at a time of their choosing, which is denoted by dashed-line A. The final button will upload the challenge to SecureDrop denoted by dashed-line B.

The right hand box is the 'Decryptor' tab for the receiving party. The decryptor can download and save the ciphertext as soon as it becomes available on SecureDrop denoted by dashed-line C. They will not be able to decrypt the ciphertext until the challenge becomes available and is downloaded, which is denoted by dashed-line D. Once the challenge is received the 'Extract Decryption Key' button will run TRE.Solve to recover d. Finally, the 'Decrypt file' will take the ciphertext, public parameters, and decryption key and run TRE.Dec to recover the original leaked file.

6 Conclusion

In this paper we introduced a variant of a delay-based primitive known as timed-release encryption with implicit authentication (TRE-IA). Implicit authentication is formally introduced with a game-based definition and we provide a concrete implementation with this property. Our implementation of a TRE-IA which we name the BBS-TRE uses the BBS CSPRNG and RSA-OAEP PKE as the building blocks. Our construction is implemented in Python and a performance evaluation against six common modulus sizes was provided. Our performance analysis allowed us to observe how the modulus size affected the run time consistency of the whistleblower and decryptor algorithms. Therefore, we were able to provide concrete recommendations for parameter selection for practical implementations of our TRE scheme. We also provided an example of how our TRE-IA scheme could be used in conjunction with the existing whistleblowing tool SecureDrop.

References

1. Edward Snowden's Motive Revealed: He Can 'Sleep at Night' (2014). https://www.nbcnews.com/feature/edward-snowden-interview/edward-snowdens-motive-revealed-he-can-sleep-night-n116851
2. SecureDrop Whistleblower Submission System (2021). https://securedrop.org
3. Signal Messaging (2021). https://signal.org/en
4. The Tor Project (2021). https://www.torproject.org
5. Abdi, H.: Coefficient of variation. In: Encyclopedia of Research Design (2010)
6. Barker, E., Chen, L., Roginsky, A., Vassilev, A., Davis, R., Simon, S.: SP 800-56b rev. 2, recommendation for pair-wise key-establishment using integer factorization cryptography. ITL Computer Security Resource Center (2019)
7. Bellare, M., Namprempre, C.: Authenticated encryption: relations among notions and analysis of the generic composition paradigm. In: Okamoto, T. (ed.) ASIACRYPT 2000. LNCS, vol. 1976, pp. 531–545. Springer, Heidelberg (2000). https://doi.org/10.1007/3-540-44448-3_41
8. Bellare, M., Rogaway, P.: Optimal asymmetric encryption. In: De Santis, A. (ed.) EUROCRYPT 1994. LNCS, vol. 950, pp. 92–111. Springer, Heidelberg (1995). https://doi.org/10.1007/BFb0053428
9. Berglez, P., Gearing, A.: The panama and paradise papers. The rise of a global fourth estate. Int. J. Commun. **12**, 20 (2018)
10. Berti, F., Koeune, F., Pereira, O., Peters, T., Standaert, F.: Ciphertext integrity with misuse and leakage: definition and efficient constructions with symmetric primitives. In: Proceedings of the 2018 on Asia Conference on Computer and Communications Security, pp. 37–50 (2018)
11. Blum, L., Blum, M., Shub, M.: A simple unpredictable pseudo-random number generator. J. Comput. **15**, 364–383 (1986)
12. Boneh, D., Bonneau, J., Bünz, B., Fisch, B.: Verifiable delay functions. In: Shacham, H., Boldyreva, A. (eds.) CRYPTO 2018. LNCS, vol. 10991, pp. 757–788. Springer, Cham (2018). https://doi.org/10.1007/978-3-319-96884-1_25
13. Boneh, D., Naor, M.: Timed commitments. In: Bellare, M. (ed.) CRYPTO 2000. LNCS, vol. 1880, pp. 236–254. Springer, Heidelberg (2000). https://doi.org/10.1007/3-540-44598-6_15
14. Burdges, J., De Feo, L.: Delay encryption. In: Canteaut, A., Standaert, F.-X. (eds.) EUROCRYPT 2021. LNCS, vol. 12696, pp. 302–326. Springer, Cham (2021). https://doi.org/10.1007/978-3-030-77870-5_11
15. Carmichael, R.: Note on a new number theory function. Bull. Am. Math. Soc. (1910)
16. Cathalo, J., Libert, B., Quisquater, J.-J.: Efficient and non-interactive timed-release encryption. In: Qing, S., Mao, W., López, J., Wang, G. (eds.) ICICS 2005. LNCS, vol. 3783, pp. 291–303. Springer, Heidelberg (2005). https://doi.org/10.1007/11602897_25
17. Chvojka, P., Jager, T., Slamanig, D., Striecks, C.: Versatile and sustainable timed-release encryption and sequential time-lock puzzles (extended abstract). In: Bertino, E., Shulman, H., Waidner, M. (eds.) ESORICS 2021. LNCS, vol. 12973, pp. 64–85. Springer, Cham (2021). https://doi.org/10.1007/978-3-030-88428-4_4
18. Cormen, T., Leiserson, C., Rivest, R., Stein, C.: Introduction to Algorithms. MIT Press, Cambridge (2009)
19. Friedlander, J., Pomerance, C., Shparlinski, I.: Period of the power generator and small values of Carmichael's function. Am. Math. Soc. Math. Comput. **70**, 1591–1605 (2000)

20. Fujisaki, E., Okamoto, T., Pointcheval, D., Stern, J.: RSA-OAEP is secure under the RSA assumption. In: Kilian, J. (ed.) CRYPTO 2001. LNCS, vol. 2139, pp. 260–274. Springer, Heidelberg (2001). https://doi.org/10.1007/3-540-44647-8_16
21. Garside, J.: Panama Papers: inside the Guardian's investigation into off-shore secrets (2016). https://www.theguardian.com/news/2016/apr/16/panama-papers-inside-the-guardians-investigation-into-offshore-secrets
22. Gauss, C.: Disquisitiones Arithmeticae. Yale University Press (2009)
23. Griffin, F., Shparlinski, I.: On the linear complexity profile of the power generator. IEEE Trans. Inf. Theory **46**, 2159–2162 (2000)
24. Hardy, G., Wright, E.: An Introduction to the Theory of Numbers. Oxford University Press, Oxford (1979)
25. Katz, J., Lindell, Y.: Introduction to Modern Cryptography, 2nd edn. CRC Press, Boca Raton (2014)
26. Lenstra, A.K., Shparlinski, I.E.: Selective forgery of RSA signatures with fixed-pattern padding. In: Naccache, D., Paillier, P. (eds.) PKC 2002. LNCS, vol. 2274, pp. 228–236. Springer, Heidelberg (2002). https://doi.org/10.1007/3-540-45664-3_16
27. Liedtke, M., Mattise, J.: Leaked "pandora papers" expose how billionaires and corrupt leaders hide wealth. Guardian (Sydney) (2021)
28. Loe, A., Medley, L., O'Connell, C., Quaglia, E.: TIDE: a novel approach to constructing timed-release encryption. In: Nguyen, K., Yang, G., Guo, F., Susilo, W. (eds.) ACISP 2022. LNCS, vol. 13494, pp. 244–264. Springer, Cham (2022). https://doi.org/10.1007/978-3-031-22301-3_13
29. Mao, W.: Timed-release cryptography. In: Vaudenay, S., Youssef, A.M. (eds.) SAC 2001. LNCS, vol. 2259, pp. 342–357. Springer, Heidelberg (2001). https://doi.org/10.1007/3-540-45537-X_27
30. Girault, M., Misarsky, J.-F.: Selective forgery of RSA signatures using redundancy. In: Fumy, W. (ed.) EUROCRYPT 1997. LNCS, vol. 1233, pp. 495–507. Springer, Heidelberg (1997). https://doi.org/10.1007/3-540-69053-0_34
31. Miller, G.: Riemann's hypothesis and tests for primality. J. Comput. Syst. Sci. **13**(3), 300–317 (1976)
32. O'Donovan, J., Wagner, H., Zeume, S.: The value of offshore secrets: evidence from the panama papers. Rev. Financ. Stud. **32**, 4117–4155 (2019)
33. Pietrzak, K.: Simple verifiable delay functions. In: 10th Innovations in Theoretical Computer Science Conference, ITCS 201 (2019)
34. Rabin, M.: Digitalized signatures and public-key functions as intractable as factorization. MIT/LCS/TR-212, MIT Laboratory for Computer Science (1979)
35. Rivest, R., Shamir, A., Adleman, L.: A method for obtaining digital signatures and public-key cryptosystems. Commun. ACM **21**, 120–126 (1983)
36. Rivest, R., Shamir, A., Wagner, D.: Time-lock puzzles and timed-release crypto. MIT/LCS/TR-684, MIT Laboratory for Computer Science (1996)
37. Scheuerman, W.: Whistleblowing as civil disobedience: the case of Edward Snowden. Philos. Soc. Criticism **40**, 609–628 (2014)
38. Verble, J.: The NSA and Edward Snowden: surveillance in the 21st century. ACM SIGCAS Comput. Soc. **44**, 14–20 (2014)
39. Wesolowski, B.: Efficient verifiable delay functions. In: Ishai, Y., Rijmen, V. (eds.) EUROCRYPT 2019. LNCS, vol. 11478, pp. 379–407. Springer, Cham (2019). https://doi.org/10.1007/978-3-030-17659-4_13
40. Westfall, P.: Kurtosis as Peakedness. Am. Stat. **68**, 91–195 (2014)

41. Zheng, Y.: Digital signcryption or how to achieve cost (signature & encryption) ≪ cost(signature) + cost(encryption). In: Kaliski, B.S. (ed.) CRYPTO 1997. LNCS, vol. 1294, pp. 165–179. Springer, Heidelberg (1997). https://doi.org/10. 1007/BFb0052234

42. Zheng, Y.: A new efficient signcryption scheme in the standard model. Secur. Commun. Netw. **8**(5), 703–878 (2015)

43. Zheng, Y., Imai, H.: How to construct efficient signcryption schemes on elliptic curves. In: Proceedings of IFIP SEC98, vol. 68, no. 5, pp. 227–233 (1998)

44. Zimmerman, P.: Why I Wrote PGP, Essays on PGP. Phil Zimmermann and Associates LLC (2013)

Author Index

N. El Mrabet et al. (Eds.): AFRICACRYPT 2023, LNCS 14064, pp. 517–518, 2023.
https://doi.org/10.1007/978-3-031-37679-5

Printed in the United States
by Baker & Taylor Publisher Services